Lincoln Christian College

P9-DEA-149

Gregorian Chant

GREGORIAN CHANT

by
WILLI APEL

INDIANA UNIVERSITY PRESS

BLOOMINGTON & LONDON

THIRD PRINTING 1966
ALL RIGHTS RESERVED
COPYRIGHT © 1958 BY INDIANA UNIVERSITY PRESS
LIBRARY OF CONGRESS CATALOG CARD NUMBER: 57-10729
MANUFACTURED IN THE UNITED STATES OF AMERICA

783.5
A p6

Alleluia Pascha nostrum, ℣. 2:
*Epulemur in azymis sinceritatis
et veritatis.*
(I Corinthians 5:8)

30541

Contents

Plates

following page 122

Text Figures are listed under subject entries in Index.

Preface and Acknowledgment

By way of general preface it will suffice to say that I have tried to put on the reader's table what the Apostle calls "the unleavened bread of sincerity and truth," cleansed from, or at least clearly separated from, the "sour dough" of conjecture and imagination. That the latter is an important ingredient of our spiritual and scientific nourishment, nobody will deny; but it is equally undeniable that it has often been added in greater quantity than is wholesome. At any rate, the reader is entitled to know what kind of food he is being given.

My first, and main acknowledgment is due Peter Wagner, the great scholar who, in his *Einführung in die Gregorianischen Melodien*, laid the foundation for so many studies of Gregorian chant, including the one presented here. Considering the fact that he called his three-volume publication an *Einführung*, I feel rather apologetic about the title, *Gregorian Chant*, chosen for this much smaller book. I wanted to avoid any such designation as "Introduction to Gregorian Chant," which would have put it on the same level with Wagner's standard work. Since I could not very well call it an "Introduction to the Introduction," I had to resign myself to giving it a name it hardly deserves.

In the second place, I wish to express my gratitude to Father Simeon Daly, librarian of the Archabbey of St. Meinrad, Indiana, who not only has very kindly welcomed me to his library but also, time and again, has sent me much-needed books and even brought them personally to my home.

Finally, I wish to acknowledge my indebtedness to Mr. Robert J. Snow who, because of his former association with St. Meinrad, was in a position to give me valuable help in matters primarily of a liturgical character. He has also been of great assistance in taking care of many of the hundreds of details that go into the preparation of a book.

The librarian of the Benedictine Abbey of Solesmes has sent me photographs for the plates included in this book. I wish to express my sincere thanks for his cooperation.

The publishing house of Desclée and Co., Printers to the Holy See and the Sacred Congregation of Rites, have kindly given the permission to take illustrations from their publications. For reasons which will become apparent to the reader, I have not reproduced the rhythmic signs which distinguish their books.

I am very glad to include in this book two chapters that are closely related to its main topic, and which put many of its aspects and problems into a new perspective: the chapter on Ambrosian chant contributed by Professor Roy H. Jesson, and that on Old-Roman chant written by Mr. Robert J. Snow, both of whom have studied at Indiana University. I hope that the results of their research will be as interesting to the readers as they were to me.

No true admirer of Gregorian chant can help looking with dismay at present trends toward providing organ accompaniments for the liturgical melodies. This practice, although ostensibly meant to promote the chant, is actually bound to destroy it. To what extent it has dulled the minds of "those that should hear" became clear to me during a conversation with a group of young seminarists, whom I met in a train several years ago. When I mentioned my interest in Gregorian chant, one of them said, his face radiant with delight, "Oh, Gregorian chant is so wonderful in our church; we have an organist who makes it sound like Debussy." I know that it does not always sound like that. In another church it may sound more like Vaughan Williams, and elsewhere like parallel organum. Invariably it will sound like "something" other than what it really is and what it should be. Moreover, the very variety of possibilities inherent in this practice is bound to weaken the catholicity of one of the most precious possessions of the Catholic Church. I have no right to voice an opinion in matters pertaining to the Church, but I am saddened to see a venerable tradition, which has been restored to new life after centuries of neglect and indifference, subjected once more to destructive practices.

WILLI APEL

Indiana University
January 1958

Bibliography

ABBREVIATION	TITLE
A	*Antiphonale Sacrosanctae Romanae Ecclesiae* . . . , Tournai, 1949 (Desclée, No. 820).
ACI	*Actes du Congrés International de Musique Sacrée, Rome, 1950* (also *Atti del Congresso* . . .), Tournai, 1952.
AM	*Antiphonale monasticum pro diurnis horis* . . . , Tournai, 1934 (Desclée, No. 818).
AMM	*Antiphonale missarum juxta ritum Sanctae Ecclesiae Mediolanensis*, Rome, 1935.
Anal. hymn.	*Analecta hymnica medii aevi,* ed. by G. M. Dreves and Clemens Blume, 55 vols., Leipzig, 1886-1922.
CS	Coussemaker, Charles Edmond Henri. *Scriptorum de musica medii aevi nova series,* 4 vols., Paris, 1864-76.
G	*Graduale Sacrosanctae Romanae Ecclesiae* . . . , Tournai, 1945 (Desclée, No. 696).
GS	Gerbert, Martin. *Scriptores ecclesiastici de musica,* 3 vols., St. Blasien, 1784. Facsimile edition, Milan, 1931.
HAM	Davison, A. T., and Willi Apel. *Historical Anthology of Music,* vol. I, Cambridge, 1946.
HDM	Apel, Willi. *Harvard Dictionary of Music,* Cambridge, 1945.
KJ	*Kirchenmusikalisches Jahrbuch,* Regensburg, 1885-1932; Cologne, 1950- .
L	*Liber usualis with Introduction and Rubrics in English,* Tournai, 1950 (Desclée, No. 801).
LR	*Liber responsorialis . . . juxta ritum monasticum,* Solesmes, 1895.
LVM	*Liber vesperalis juxta ritum Sanctae Ecclesiae Mediolanensis,* Rome, 1939.
MD	*Musica Disciplina,* Rome, 1948- .
MGG	*Musik in Geschichte und Gegenwart,* ed. by F. Blume, Kassel, 1949- .
Nombre	Mocquereau, Dom André. *Le Nombre musical grégorien,* 2 vols., Tournai, 1908, 1927.

Ott	Ott, C. *Offertoriale sive versus offertoriorum,* Tournai, 1935.
Pal. mus.	*Paléographie musicale,* 17 vols., Solesmes, 1889-1925.
	Migne, Jacques Paul. *Patrologiae cursus completus.*
Patr. gr.	*Series Graeca,* 166 vols., Paris, 1857-66.
Patr. lat.	*Series Latina,* 221 vols., Paris, 1844-55.
PM	*Processionale monasticum,* Solesmes, 1893.
Rass. Greg.	*Rassegna gregoriana,* Rome, 1902-14.
RCG	*Revue du chant grégorien,* Grenoble, 1892-1939.
RG	*Revue grégorienne,* Tournai, Rome, 1911- .
Sextuplex	Hesbert, Dom R.-J. *Antiphonale missarum sextuplex,* Paris, 1935.
TG	*Tribune de St. Gervais,* Paris, 1895-1929.
VP	*Variae preces ex liturgia . . . collectae,* Solesmes, 1901.
	Wagner, Peter, *Einführung in die gregorianischen Melodien,* 3 vols., Leipzig.
Wagner I	I: *Ursprung und Entwicklung der liturgischen Gesangsformen,* 1895; second edition, 1901; third edition, 1911. Translation of the second edition, *Origin and Development of the Forms of the Liturgical Chant,* London, 1907 (references are to the English edition).
Wagner II	II: *Neumenkunde,* 1905; second edition, 1912 (references are to the second edition).
Wagner III	III: *Gregorianische Formenlehre,* 1921.

OTHER BOOKS FREQUENTLY MENTIONED

Duchesne, L. M. O.	*Christian Worship, Its Origin and Evolution,* London, 1931.
Ferretti, Paolo.	*Esthétique grégorienne,* Tournai, 1938.
Gastoué, Amédée.	*Cours théorique et pratique de chant grégorien,* second edition, Paris, 1917.
———.	*Les Origines du chant romain,* Paris, 1907.

Gevaert, François Auguste. *La Mélopée antique dans le chant de l'église latine,* Paris, 1917.

Suñol, Dom Gregory. *Introduction à la paléographie musicale grégorienne,* Tournai, 1935.

For additional bibliography see Gustave Reese, *Music in the Middle Ages* (New York, 1940), pp. 431-45, and the article "Choral" in *MGG*.

NOTE: Page references without letter indication, e.g. [234], refer to the *Liber usualis* (see above, *L*).

1

The Liturgy
and Its
Development

CHAPTER ONE

Definition and Terminology

THE SUBJECT of this book is the traditional music of the Roman Catholic Church. Nowhere in music history is the term "traditional" more in place than in connection with this music which, rooted in the pre-Christian service of the Jews, adopted distinctive characteristics as early as the third and fourth centuries of the Christian era, was fully developed in the seventh century, expanded during the ensuing four hundred years, deteriorated in the sixteenth century, was restored in the late nineteenth century, and is used at present in essentially the same form it had about a thousand years ago.

While the first half of the two-thousand years' life of the chant was a period of continuous growth and all-embracing vitality, its existence during the second half was not without vicissitudes. From about 1000 on, polyphonic music, its own offspring, began to challenge the sovereignty of its parent and, beginning with the fifteenth century, organ music became a successful competitor. Even more detrimental were ideas, arising in the sixteenth century, which led to a revision of the old melodies, a revision actually amounting to a complete distortion of their essential qualities. In the seventeenth and eighteenth centuries what went under the name of "Gregorian chant" was only a shadow of its former self, and in the nineteenth century the whole tradition was threatened with extinction. Fortunately, rescue came from a group of scholars, mostly French, who devoted themselves to a study of the medieval manuscripts and immediately realized the supreme importance of their contents. One of the first in this group was L. Lambillotte, whose ideas were adopted and brought to final success by the monks of Solesmes. Owing to their endeavor—an endeavor which is no less a credit to musicology than the rediscovery of Bach, Palestrina, Schütz, or Monteverdi—the old tradition was brought to new life and, in 1903, was officially adopted by the Roman Church through a decree of Pope Pius X, a decree which may well be said to mark the beginning of the third millennium of Gregorian chant.

What is the meaning of this term? *Chant* is the generic designation for a body of traditional religious music, such as Hindu chant, Jewish chant, Byzantine chant, Russian chant, etc. Different though these various repertories are, they have one trait in common, that is, the purely melodic character of the music or, in other words, the absence of harmony, counterpoint or any other kind of accompaniment, especially instrumental. The performance is exclusively vocal, either by one singer or by several singing in unison. In this respect chant is similar to folksong, from which, however, it differs in the rhythmic aspect, since it usually lacks the principle of strict meter and measure commonly found in folksong.

The designation "Gregorian," generally used for the chant of the Roman Church, refers to Pope Gregory I, who ruled from 590 to 604, and who is generally believed to have played a decisive role in the final arrangement of the chants, each of which he (or rather, those to whom he had entrusted the task) assigned to a specific occasion of the liturgical year, according to a broadly conceived plan. True enough, the appropriateness of the term "Gregorian" can be (and has been) questioned. A first disadvantage of this term is that, strictly speaking, it excludes the early development leading up to the period of Gregory as well as the changes and additions that occurred later. Thus, some of the best-known items of the chant, the *Kyrie, Gloria, Credo, Sanctus,* and *Agnus Dei* of the Mass, are post-Gregorian. Moreover, Gregory's role in the development of the chant, as outlined above, is not certain beyond doubt and, in fact, has become highly questionable in the light of recent discoveries and investigations which make it probable that the repertory, as we know it today, was actually formed after Gregory. However, this does not necessarily mean that the "Gregorian legend" is entirely without foundation. It is possible that Gregory at least gave a decisive impetus and clear directions for a work that came to its fulfilment some time after him. Thus, even from the point of view of our present knowledge, the term "Gregorian chant" could be defended, and may well be retained, provided its ramifications are understood.

Some scholars, however, prefer to use the term "Roman chant," which has the advantage of implying nothing but the incontestable fact of the chant's intimate connection with the Church of Rome, thus distinguishing it from other bodies of Christian chant: e.g., Mozarabic, Milanese (Ambrosian), or Byzantine. Actually, this term is also open to criticism insofar as it carries the connotation not only of "Roman usage" but also of "Roman origin." Recent investigations have made it highly probable that the latter connotation is not correct. The repertory in question developed mainly in France and was not adopted in Rome until the thirteenth century, superseding an earlier repertory which could more properly be called "Roman" or even "Gregorian."[1]

Yet another term, documented as early as the tenth century and uni-

[1] For a fuller explanation of this question, see pp. 79ff.

versally employed in the later Middle Ages, is *cantus planus*,[2] surviving in the French *plain-chant* and in English plain song. German writers frequently use the term *Gregorianischer Choral.*

Gregorian (or Roman) chant is one of several branches of Christian chant that developed in the Western part of Europe, probably all out of one and the same archetype characterized, first of all, by the use of the Latin language. Originally, the official language of the Church, even in Rome, was Greek, and it was not until the third or fourth century that this was replaced by Latin in the Western part of the Christian world. Very likely the just-mentioned archetype reverts to this period. Out of it grew the four branches or, as they are often called, dialects of Western chant: the Gregorian in Rome, the Ambrosian in Milan, the Gallican in France, and the Mozarabic (or Visigothic) in Spain. Only scant remnants of the Gallican chant have come down to us, and the Mozarabic repertory is preserved only in early manuscripts, the musical notation of which cannot be accurately read.[3] The Ambrosian as well as the Gregorian repertory, on the other hand, are fully known to us, and both are in use to the present day, the former in Milan, the latter in all the other churches of the Roman Catholic denomination.

Recent scholarship has brought to light yet another dialect of Western chant, the so-called Old-Roman or City-Roman, a discovery which has shed new light on the early development of the chant and particularly on the long-disputed question as to the part that Pope Gregory had in its formation. This most interesting question will be discussed in a later chapter [see pp. 74ff].

[2] The original meaning of *cantus planus* was to distinguish a "low chant" (*planus,* i.e., plane, lying flat) from a *cantus acutus,* a "high chant." Thus, Oddo of Cluny (d. 942) employs the term *planus* synonymously with *gravis* or *humilis,* to indicate chants of the plagal modes: "sin autem planus fuerit cantus, plaga deuteri nominabitur" (*GS,* I, 259a). Similarly Guido distinguishes *graves et plani* from *acuti et alti* (*Micrologus,* ch. XII).

[3] Certain French Mss of Gregorian chant, e.g., the *Gradual* of St. Yrieix (*Pal. mus.,* XIII) include a number of melodies that are foreign to the Roman repertory and have therefore been claimed as Gallican. See A. Gastoué, *Le Chant gallican* (1939; also in *RCG,* XLI, XLII, XLIII). Of the Mozarabic repertory, only twenty-one pieces are preserved in a clearly readable notation. They are transcribed in C. Rojo and G. Prado, *El Canto Mozárabe* (1929), pp. 73ff.

CHAPTER TWO

The Structure of the Liturgy

I T GOES without saying that a knowledge of the Roman liturgy, at least of its basic aspects, is an indispensable prerequisite for any study of Gregorian chant, not only from the historical but also from stylistic and aesthetic points of view. It may be possible to examine or listen to a chant like the Gradual *Haec dies* and to admire its beauty without even knowing what a Gradual is nor to which feast this particular one belongs. A full understanding, however, of its form, its style, its musical values and significance cannot be gained without a knowledge of its liturgical function, and its relationship to other chants. To consider Gregorian chant as a "purely musical" discipline would involve the student in the same difficulties which, for a long time and occasionally even now, have beset philologists who considered the songs of the troubadours and Minnesingers as a "purely literary" affair, completely disregarding their intimate connection with music. It is therefore only natural that our study should begin with an explanation of liturgical matters, insofar as they have a bearing upon our main subject.

THE LITURGICAL YEAR

The calendar of the Roman Church includes a great number of feasts, and these fall into two main categories: the Feasts of the Lord and the Feasts of the Saints. We shall first consider the former category, known as Proper of the Time (*Proprium de Tempore, Temporale*), "Time" meaning the time of the Lord. It includes all the Sundays as well as the special feasts commemorating the events of His life, His birth, death, resurrection, etc.

The year of the Church starts, not with New Year, but with the First Sunday of Advent; that is, with the first of the four Sundays preceding Christmas (Nativity) which constitute a period in preparation for the arrival (L. *adventus*) of Christ. All the liturgical books, *Gradual, Antiphonal, Breviary, Liber usualis*, etc., open with the chants or prayers for the First Sunday of Advent.[1] Beginning with this day, the year can be divided into four periods: the first centering around the Nativity, the second leading up to Easter, the third leading up to Pentecost, and the fourth comprising the rest of the year.

The Christmas period continues with the Second, Third, and Fourth Sunday of Advent, the last being preceded by the Ember Week of Advent. In this week three days—Wednesday, Friday, and Saturday—are set apart for fasting and prayer. Altogether there are four such Ember Weeks [L. *Quatuor Temporum*], one in each of the four seasons of the calendar year. Only the Saturdays of these weeks are represented in the *Liber usualis,* the Wednesdays and Fridays being found in the *Gradual* and the *Antiphonal*.[2] After the Fourth Sunday of Advent comes the Nativity of Our Lord (Christmas) on December 25, which is followed, a week later, by the Circumcision of Our Lord on January 1 and, on January 6, by the Epiphany, which commemorates the adoration of the Magi (Three Holy Kings). The Sundays after Christmas are: Sunday within the Octave[3] of Christmas, Sunday between Circumcision and Epiphany, Sunday within the Octave of the Epiphany, and Second (Third, etc.) Sunday after the Epiphany. In the seventeenth century two feasts were introduced: that in honor of the Most Holy Name of Jesus, and the feast of the Holy Family. The first of these falls on the Sunday between the Circumcision and the Epiphany or, if no Sunday occurs between these two feasts, on January 2. The second falls on the Sunday within the Octave of the Epiphany. The traditional formulary for this Sunday is transferred to one of the following week days.

The second period starts with Septuagesima Sunday, that is, the ninth Sunday before Easter. Since Easter is a variable feast, whose date depends upon the moon,[4] the beginning of this period varies accordingly—from as early as January 18 to as late as February 21. As a consequence, the number of Sundays after Epiphany varies from a minimum of one to a maximum of six. Septuagesima Sunday is followed by Sexagesima, Quinquagesima, and Quadragesima Sunday.[5] The Wednesday before Quadragesima Sunday is

---

1 The earliest liturgical books, Sacramentaries and Lectionaries, start with the Nativity.

2 Except for the Ember Wednesday and Ember Friday after Pentecost. See the table on pp. 11f.

3 Octave means either the eighth day after a feast or the entire week, with daily commemorations.

4 Easter is the first Sunday after the full moon that falls on or next after the twenty-first of March.

5 Quadragesima [Lat., the fortieth] is the name for the forty-day period of Lent that starts with Ash Wednesday. Actually, this period consists of forty-six days (six weeks plus four days), but is reduced to forty because the six Sundays are excepted from the rule of fasting. Quadragesima Sunday is correctly named the First Sunday in Quadragesima, *Dominica prima Quadragesimae.* Quinquagesima (fiftieth), Sexagesima (sixtieth), and Septuagesima (seventieth) are designations formed in analogy to Quadragesima. These Sundays were gradually added, between *c.* 450 and 600, to the original period of forty

Ash Wednesday, the beginning of Lent, the long period of fasting before Easter. Quadragesima Sunday is therefore also called the First Sunday of Lent, and is followed by the Second, Third, and Fourth Sunday of Lent. The liturgical importance of the Lenten period is indicated by the fact that not only the Sundays but each week day has its individual liturgy and chants which, however, are found only in the complete books, the *Gradual* and the *Antiphonal*. Between the First and Second Sunday falls the Ember Week of Lent, represented in the *Liber usualis* by the Saturday only. After the Fourth Sunday of Lent the next two Sundays are Passion Sunday and Palm Sunday, the second of which opens the Holy Week leading to Easter. This is indeed the most solemn week of the entire liturgical year; each day is filled with a ritual of steadily increasing importance, elaboration, and impressiveness, especially Maundy Thursday, Good Friday, and Holy Saturday. The liturgy for these three days alone fills almost 150 pages in the *Liber usualis*. The crowning point is Easter Sunday, celebrating the Resurrection of Our Lord. Its miraculous event continues to be commemorated in daily celebrations during the ensuing week, called Easter Week (Easter Monday, Easter Tuesday, Wednesday in Easter Week, etc.).

The Saturday of this week marks the beginning of the third period, called Paschal Time. The next day is Low Sunday, also called Quasimodo Sunday, after the Introit *Quasimodo* which opens its Mass. This, being the first Sunday after Easter, is followed by a Second, Third, Fourth, and Fifth Sunday after Easter. The next Monday, Tuesday, and Wednesday are the Litanies or Rogation Days [L. *rogare,* to ask, to beg], days of special supplication which are followed, on Thursday, by the Ascension of Our Lord. The next Sunday is called Sunday within the Octave of the Ascension and precedes Whit Sunday (Whitsun Day) or the Feast of Pentecost, which commemorates the descent of the Holy Spirit on the Apostles. Similar to (and in imitation of) Easter Week, each day of the following week is celebrated in commemoration of Pentecost. The fact that this is also an Ember Week explains the varying designations for the single days: Whit Monday, Whit Tuesday, Ember Wednesday, Thursday in Whitsun Week, Ember Friday, and Ember Saturday. This is the end of Paschal Time.

The next day is Trinity Sunday, which marks the beginning of the final period of the year. The last major feast of the *Temporale,* Corpus Christi, falls on the Thursday thereafter, and is followed, on Friday of the next week, by the Feast of the Most Sacred Heart of Jesus. The Sundays of this season are simply numbered as Sundays after Pentecost, Trinity Sunday being the first in the series.[6] Since the date of Pentecost varies with

days. See Duchesne, *Christian Worship* (5th ed., 1931), p. 241; J. Froger, "Les Origines du temps de la septuagésime" (*RG,* XXVI, 17).

[6] According to an eleventh-century *Micrologus de ecclesiasticis observationibus* [*Patr. lat.* 151, p. 1019], the liturgy for the Feast of the Trinity was written by Albinus, i.e.,

that of Easter—it occurs exactly seven weeks after Easter, as is indicated by its name which is the Greek word for "the fiftieth" (day)—the number of these Sundays varies from a minimum of twenty-three to a maximum of twenty-eight, a fluctuation corresponding to that of the Sundays after Epiphany: the fewer Sundays after Epiphany, the more there are after Pentecost, and *vice versa*. In fact, the services for the additional Sundays after Pentecost are taken from those provided for the last Sundays after Epiphany [see *L* 1078]. The regular succession of Sundays in the final period is interrupted only by the Ember Week of September.

The following table gives the feasts just described in the form of a survey with page references to the *Liber usualis,* and also with the corresponding Latin names and page references to the *Graduale.* The latter is indispensable for a full study of Gregorian chant because it includes a number of Masses of great antiquity and importance that are not included in the *Liber,* particularly those for the weekdays of Lent. On the other hand, it has been deemed unnecessary to include the *Antiphonale* in our table, since the additional chants found in this book—mainly those for the Office Hours of the weekdays of Lent—are not of the same importance as are the Masses. Moreover, the student familiar with the *Graduale* will have no difficulty in finding the corresponding feasts in the *Antiphonale.* It should be noted that the Latin names for the days of the week, starting with Monday, are as follows: *Feria II, Feria III, Feria IV, Feria V, Feria VI, Sabbato,* and *Dominica. Feria* properly means feast day, and originally the term was indeed used for Sunday. Later it was employed for the subsequent days as well, Sunday being called *Feria I;* Monday, *Feria II;* Tuesday, *Feria III;* etc. Finally, the name *Feria I* was replaced by *Dominica* (Day of the Lord), while for Saturday the old name *Sabbato* was retained. (For an explanation of the letters a, b, c, d, e, given with a number of feasts, see pp. 58f.)

	L		G
First Sunday of Advent	317	Dominica I. Adventus	1
Second Sunday of Advent	327	Dominica II. Adventus	4
Third Sunday of Advent	334	Dominica III. Adventus	6
		Feria IV. Quatuor Temp. Adv.	9
		Feria VI. Quatuor Temp. Adv.	11
Saturday in Ember Week		Sabbato Quatuor Temp. Adv.	13
of Advent	343		

Alcuin (735-804), and provided with music by Stephanus of Liége, who has been tentatively identified with Stephen, bishop of Liége from 903 to 920. The author, like many others, opposed it as unnecessary since "all the Sundays abound with authentic Offices . . . in honor of the Holy Trinity." Not until the twelfth century was it officially adopted in the Roman liturgy, replacing the First Sunday of Pentecost, the Mass for which [G 310; not included in *L*] is shifted to the next free weekday.

[7] *In Albis* is short for *in albis depositis,* i.e., when the white [vestments worn by the newly baptized] were laid off.

As for the *Sanctorale,* a few general remarks will be sufficient. The numerous feasts for the Saints of the Roman Church are grouped under two categories, Common of Saints [1111-1302] and Proper of Saints [1303-1762]. The latter includes the feasts in honor of a specific Saint or, occasionally, two specific Saints, e.g., St. Andrew, St. Lawrence, SS. Peter and Paul, etc. In the early medieval books the feasts of the Lord as well as those of the Saints (then much fewer in number than now) were arranged together according to their succession during the year, and it was not until the thirteenth century that the groups were completely separated.[9] When this was done, some of the feasts of Saints were left in their original place, mainly those that occurred right after the Nativity, probably because their association with the Nativity was too close to be destroyed. To the present day the Proper of the Time includes five feasts of Saints: namely, St.

8 The Ember Week of September is fixed to follow after the Feast of the Exaltation of the Holy Cross, on September 14. It may fall as early as after the Thirteenth Sunday after Pentecost.

9 The normal arrangement in the early Mss is:
   (a) Advent to Septuagesima: *Temporale* and *Sanctorale* mixed;
   (b) Septuagesima to Fifth Sunday after Easter: *Temporale* only;
   (c) *Sanctorale* from April 14 (Tiburtius and Valerius) to November 30 (St. Andrew Apostle), also Ascension and Pentecost;
   (d) Trinity Sunday to last Sunday after Pentecost: *Temporale* only.
See the table of the liturgical year (from St. Gall *339*) in *Wagner I,* 280; also in Hesbert's *Antiphonale Missarum Sextuplex,* pp. 2-197.

Stephen on December 26 [414], St. John the Apostle on December 27 [421], Holy Innocents on December 28 [427], St. Thomas on December 29 [437], and St. Silvester on December 31 [440].

The Common of Saints gives the chants, prayers, etc., that are used for various Saints, these being grouped under categories such as Martyrs, Doctors, Virgins, Virgin Martyrs, etc. For instance, St. Jerome (*S. Hieronymus*) is a Doctor of the Church, and therefore the service for his feast is found in the Common of Doctors [1189], his name being inserted at the place marked *N.*, as in the Antiphon, the Prayer, and the Collect.[10]

The two corresponding sections in the *Graduale* are the *Proprium Sanctorum,* starting on p. 390 after the *Proprium de Tempore,* and the *Commune Sanctorum,* starting on p. [1]. In the *Antiphonale* the three main sections are found on pp. 210ff (*Proprium de Tempore*), 578ff (*Proprium Sanctorum*), and [1]ff (*Commune Sanctorum*).

THE LITURGICAL DAY

On any of the days of the liturgical calendar the service of divine worship is organized according to a definite and nearly invariable plan, which we shall now consider. It will be best to describe this service first in its fullest form, as held on high feasts in great churches or monasteries, outlining later the reductions that take place on other occasions and in other places.

Eight times during the day a service for the offering of prayer and worship is held. This is called the Divine Office (*Officium divinum*), Canonic Hours (*horae canonicae,* from *canon,* i.e., rule, law), or Office Hours. These are:

1. Matins (*matutinum*): before sunrise
2. Lauds (*laudes*): at sunrise
3. Prime (*ad primam horam*)
4. Terce (*ad tertiam horam*)
5. Sext (*ad sextam horam*)
6. None (*ad nonam horam*)
7. Vespers (*ad vesperam*): at sunset
8. Compline (*completorium*): before retiring

Prime, Terce, Sext, and None take their names from the old Roman calendar, in which the hours of the day were numbered from six in the morning (*prima hora*) to six in the afternoon (*duodecima hora*), so that mid-day was *sexta hora.* Naturally, the time when these Offices are held varies somewhat with the seasons of the year.

[10] Collect, i.e., the prayer offered by the priest at Mass, so-called because it represents the collected prayers of all present.

The hours from Prime to None are called Little or Lesser Hours, because of the greater simplicity of their services. Also the term Day Hours (*horae diurnae*) is used, properly, to denote all the Hours other than Matins, that is, from Lauds to Compline.

The Office Hours were not instituted together at a given date, but developed gradually during the first six centuries of the Christian era. The earliest was the Night Office, called Vigils (*vigiliae,* wakening), which had its origin in the custom of keeping watch the night before Easter, in expectation of the reappearance of Christ. Later this custom was observed weekly, before each Sunday, though no longer as a continuous gathering during the entire night. In the fourth century we find it divided into three separate Prayer Hours: one at sunset, when the lamps were lighted, and therefore called *lucernarium (lux,* light); one after midnight; and one at sunrise, called *laudes matutinae* (morning praise). Eventually these received the names Vespers, Matins (subdivided into three Nocturns), and Lauds. Terce, Sext, and None originally had the character of private Prayer Hours, held in the family or in small groups. The Rule of St. Benedict, dating from *c.* 530, is the earliest document containing the complete course of all the eight Office Hours.

In addition to the Office Hours, the daily ritual includes the Mass, which is of an entirely different character. The Office Hours are mainly occasions for prayer, similar to and, no doubt, partly derived from the prayer hours of the Jews. The Mass, on the other hand, is a service of distinctly Christian character, although it also incorporates elements of an ancient Jewish ritual.[1] It is essentially the commemoration of the Sacrifice of Christ on the Cross, taking on the form of a mystic repetition of the Last Supper. Like the Last Supper, the Mass took place originally in the evening, was later shifted to the morning hours, and is now generally celebrated in the forenoon, between Terce and Sext. Originally called *Eucharistia* (Eucharist; Greek for "good grace"), it was later called *Missa,* a term derived from the words of the closing benediction, "Ite, missa est" (Depart, this is the dismissal), and used as early as 400 (St. Ambrose).

As an example of a full service, that of Corpus Christi may be examined. It contains First Vespers [917], Compline [917], Matins [917], First Nocturn [922], Second Nocturn [928], Third Nocturn [934], Lauds [939], Prime [942], Terce [942], Mass [943] followed by the Procession [950], Sext [955], None [955], and Second Vespers [956]. Only a few other feasts, Nativity [364], Maundy Thursday [621], Good Friday [665], Holy Saturday [713], Easter [765], and Pentecost [862] have retained a service of similar completeness. All the others lack Matins, which, although one of the earliest and, together with the Mass, the most elaborate of the services, is now generally celebrated without music.

1 See pp. 23f.

THE LITURGICAL BOOKS

The division of the liturgy into Office and Mass is of fundamental importance in the structure of the chant, so much so that from the earliest time to the present day these two categories were assigned to different books. The chants for the Mass are contained in the *Gradual* (*Graduale*), those for the Office in the *Antiphonal* (*Antiphonale*). There are also two corresponding books containing the complete liturgical texts, of the musical items as well as of the prayers, lessons from Scriptures, psalms, etc. These are the *Missal* (*Missale*) for the Mass, and the *Breviary* (*Breviarium*) for the Office. This arrangement in four books has great advantages from the practical point of view, but it makes it difficult to gain a clear insight into the over-all structure of the liturgical day. For this reason the *Liber usualis* (book for general use) was published in 1896 (revised editions 1903, 1934). This volume combines the main contents of the four books, giving the various items in their proper order as they occur during the day and the year. It also takes care of certain practical needs resulting from the fact that present-day choirs and singers often do not have the thorough training customary in earlier centuries. Thus the method of singing the Vesper psalms is indicated more clearly and in greater detail than is the case in the *Antiphonal*.

It should be noticed, however, that the chants in the *Liber* do not tally in number with those of the *Gradual* and the *Antiphonal*. A brief glance at the indexes shows that in the *Liber* a considerable number of chants found in the other two books are omitted. Thus, the *Gradual* contains thirteen Tracts beginning with the letter A, the *Liber* only eight; the former fourteen Offertories beginning with the letter B, as against nine in the latter. The difference results from the omission, in the *Liber,* of a considerable number of services given in the *Gradual* and in the *Antiphonal*, mainly those for the *Feria* days of Lent and of the four Ember Weeks [see the table, pp. 9ff]. Particularly the Masses for these days are of great interest and importance because they belong to the oldest layer of the Gregorian repertory; they cannot be omitted in detailed studies such as appear later on in this book. Less consequential is the omission, in the *Liber,* of a number of Votive Masses, such as the *Missa Votiva de Sancta Cruce* (G [104]) and the one *contra paganos* (against the heathen; G [131]), and of most of the Masses *pro aliquibus locis* (for certain localities; G 1**– 115**).[1]

The *Antiphonal* gives the chants for all the Day Hours of the week, from Lauds of Sunday to Compline of Saturday (A 1-209), as well as for

[1] A Votive Mass is a Mass that may be celebrated on any day, usually upon the request of an individual; as for instance, in honor of his Patron Saint.

the Feasts of the Lord (*A* 210-576), of the Saints (*A* 578-931), and of the Common of Saints (*A* [2]–[192]). In the *Liber* the ordinary weekdays are represented only by the Psalms of Vespers and Compline [280-316], and the service of Lauds is given only for some of the highest feasts, such as the Nativity [395] and Good Friday [689].

On the other hand, the *Liber* includes some very important chants not found in the *Antiphonal*, that is, those for Matins of certain of the highest feasts [see p. 14] as well as those for the Office for the Dead [1779]. The service of Matins differs considerably from that of all the other Office Hours (Day Hours). It includes two types of chant not encountered elsewhere, that is, the Invitatories and the Great Responsories. The latter in particular are of the greatest importance in a study of Gregorian chant. The *Liber* includes a fair number of them, though not nearly enough to serve as a basis for a detailed investigation. For this one must turn to the medieval sources or, at least, to the *Liber Responsorialis* (*LR;* Solesmes, 1895), which contains the Night Service for a considerable number of feasts, according to the monastic rites. Yet another book containing additional chants of great interest is the *Processionale Monasticum* (*PM;* Solesmes, 1893), edited for the use of the French Benedictines who have preserved the medieval custom of solemn processions before the Masses for the greater Feasts of the Lord and of the Saints. Here again, the Responsories call for particular attention. Another special publication of great interest is C. Ott's *Offertoriale sive Versus Offertoriorum* (1935), which contains the Offertories with their verses such as were still in use in the twelfth and thirteenth centuries. Because of their many special traits these verses cannot be omitted from a study of Gregorian chant. Yet other Responsories can be found in a collection entitled *Variae Preces* (*VP;* Solesmes, 1901), which is also useful as a source for Hymns, Antiphons, and Sequences not included in the standard publications.

The rite of Rome has not been completely adopted by some of the monastic orders, such as the Benedictines, Cistercians, Dominicans, and Premonstratensians, who have retained their individual medieval tradition. The Office Hours especially, as observed by them, differ from the Roman usage in many particulars, liturgically as well as musically. The chants of the Cistercians, Dominicans, and Premonstratensians are of little interest from our point of view, since they represent late versions of the Roman chant, dating from the twelfth or thirteenth centuries.[2] Of no small importance, however, is the *Antiphonale monasticum . . . ordinis Sancti Benedicti* (*AM*), which was published in 1934 by the same Benedictine monks of Solesmes who prepared the books of the Roman usage. This often gives more authentic versions, particularly for the Hymns, and also

2 See, e.g., J. Borremans, *Le Chant liturgique traditionel des Prémontrés* (1914); D. Delalande, *Le Graduel des Prêcheurs* (1949).

contains a number of Antiphons and Hymns not found in the standard publications.[3]

The *Gradual* and the *Antiphonal* appeared in various editions which differ in many details:

1. *Liber Gradualis a Gregorio Magno olim ordinatus . . . in usum Congregationis Benedictinae . . . editus* (Tournai, 1883).
2. *Liber Gradualis juxta antiquorum codicum fidem restitutus . . . editio altera* (Solesmes, 1895).
3. *Graduale Sacrosanctae Romanae Ecclesiae de Tempore et de Sanctis SS. D. N. Pii X. . . . jussu restitutum et editum* (Vatican Press, Rome, 1908).
4. *Graduale* [etc., as under 3.] *et rhythmicis signis a Solesmensibus monachis diligenter ornatum* (Desclée et Cie., Tournai, 1908, 1924, 1945).
5. *Antiphonale Sacrosanctae Romanae Ecclesiae pro diurnis horis SS. D. N. Pii X. . . . jussu restitutum et editum* (Vatican Press, Rome, 1912).
6. *Antiphonale* [etc., as under 5.] *et rhythmicis signis a Solesmensibus monachis diligenter ornatum* (Desclée et Cie., Tournai, 1949).

Numbers 3 and 5 are known as the Vatican edition. Numbers 4 and 6 contain the "rhythmic signs" (*episema, ictus,* phrase marks, etc.) of Dom Mocquereau. All the other books were edited under the leadership of Dom Pothier.

ORDINARY AND PROPER

In our previous discussion of the liturgical day attention has been called to the division of the services into those of the Office Hours and those of the Mass. Another distinction, of almost equal importance, is that between Ordinary and Proper (*Ordinarium, Proprium*). This results from the fact that a great number of chants exist which can be, and are, used on many different occasions, and that there are also numerous others which are sung on only one specific occasion. Both types occur in the Office as well as in the Mass, so that there results a four-fold classification of the chants (and also, to a certain extent, of the spoken texts): Ordinary of the Office, Proper of the Office, Ordinary of the Mass, Proper of the Mass.

In the case of the Mass this distinction is well known and, indeed, of basic importance. Thus, the *Kyrie* belongs to the Ordinary of the Mass because it occurs in every Mass with the same text and with a limited number of melodies which vary only according to certain general categories of feasts. The Introit, on the other hand, is an item of the Proper of the Mass, because each Mass has its own Introit with individual text and mel-

[3] See J. Gajard, "Quelques précisions au sujet de l'Antiphonaire Monastique" (*RG,* XIX, 207); J. Jeanneteau, "L'Antiphonaire Monastique" (*RG,* XXXI, 209).

ody (aside from the possibility of an occasional transfer of an Introit melody from an older Mass to a more recent one).

In the Office we find essentially the same distinction, though less clearly indicated and much more varied in detail. For instance, the four Antiphons to the Blessed Virgin Mary belong strictly to the Ordinary; they are sung at Compline of Sundays and Feasts with an invariable text and melody, one during each of the four seasons of the year [273-276].[1] The Responsories, on the other hand, which are sung at Matins (e.g., Nativity [375ff] or Maundy Thursday [628ff]), usually three for each Nocturn, are strictly Proper.

Greater variation exists in the Hymns. Those for the Lesser Hours and for Compline are strictly Ordinary; *Jam lucis* for Prime, *Nunc Sancte* for Terce, *Rector potens* for Sext, *Rerum Deus* for None, and *Te lucis* for Compline [224, 235, etc.). Lauds and Vespers, however, not only have a different Hymn for each day of the week,[2] but also Proper ones for nearly all the feasts of the *Temporale* and the *Sanctorale*.

Many Office chants are partly Ordinary and partly Proper, in that the melodies are standard but the texts variable. An example of this kind are the Short Responsories (*responsoria brevia,* in distinction from the Great Responsories, *responsoria prolixa,* of Matins), which are sung at the Day Hours, from Prime to Compline. From the musical point of view these are Ordinary, there being mainly three melodies: one for Advent, one for Paschal Time, and one for the remaining part of the year, with different texts for Prime [229f], Terce [237f], etc. Many feasts, however, have their own Proper texts, particularly in the *Sanctorale* [e.g., 1174, 1175, 1244, 1403, etc.].

Even more complex is the picture presented by the five Psalms of Vespers. Basically, these are Ordinary, Psalms 109, 110, 111, 112, 113 being assigned to each Sunday [250ff], nos. 114, 115, 119, 120, 121 to each Monday [280ff], etc. However, on some feasts the plan is varied to a certain extent, as appears from the following examples:

Sunday, Holy Name [451]	Ps. 109, 110, 111, 112, 115
Sunday, Holy Family [467]	Ps. 109, 112, 121, 126, 147
Sunday, Holy Trinity [907]	Ps. 109, 110, 111, 112, 116
Nativity, First Vespers [364]	Ps. 109, 110, 111, 112, 116
Nativity, Second Vespers [411]	Ps. 109, 110, 111, 129, 131
Ascension [850]	Ps. 109, 110, 111, 112, 116

The last three examples show that the Psalms for Sunday (with 116 instead of 113) are also used on feasts such as the Nativity, which may fall on any day of the week, or Ascension, which always falls on a Thursday.

[1] These Antiphons are sung at the end of every Office Hour, unless this is immediately followed by another Hour.

[2] The hymns for the weekdays are given in the *Antiphonale*.

Even more important than these deviations is the element of variety introduced into the Psalms through the Antiphons with which they are connected. For instance, for Vespers of Sunday there are five Ordinary Antiphons "During the Year": *Dixit Dominus, Magna opera, Qui timet, Sit nomen,* and *Deus autem* [251ff]; these are used on most Sundays, an exception being, e.g., the four Sundays of Advent which have Proper Antiphons [323, 331, 338, 356]. Similarly, there are Ordinary Antiphons for all the days of the week, but many of the Feasts of Saints that occur throughout the year have their Proper Antiphons which replace the Ordinary ones.

In conclusion it may be remarked that the term "Proper" is used in two somewhat different meanings; one in opposition to Ordinary, the other in opposition to Common. The former is indicated when we speak of Proper of the Mass (or Office) as distinguished from Ordinary of the Mass (or Office), while the latter is indicated by the terms Proper of Saints and Common of Saints. Actually, all the chants of these two categories, as well as those of the Proper of the Lord, are "Proper" in the former meaning of the word. Were it not for the clumsiness of expression, one could designate them as "Proper of the Proper of the Lord," "Proper of the Proper of Saints," and "Proper of the Common of Saints"; or, to push the distinctions even further, one might speak of "Proper of the Mass for the Proper of Saints" (in the *Gradual*), "Proper of the Office for the Proper of the Lord" (in the *Antiphonal*), "Proper of the Mass and Office for the Common of Saints" (in the *Liber*), etc. All these are in opposition to "Ordinary of the Mass" and "Ordinary of the Office," categories in which, of course, no similar distinctions are possible.

THE OFFICE HOURS

In the earliest days of Christian worship the service consisted only of psalm-singing. The Book of Psalms became the most precious heritage which the Christians received from the Jews. In fact, it acquired a much greater importance in Christian worship than it had ever had before. Among the numerous reports telling us about psalm-singing among the early Christians, that of St. Chrysostom (347?-407) is particularly impressive:

When the faithful keep the vigil in the church during night, David is first, middle, and last. When hymns are sung at dawn, David is first, middle, and last. At the funeral processions and burials, David is first, middle, and last. In the holy monasteries, among the ranks of the heavenly hosts, David is first, middle, and last. In the monasteries of the virgins, imitators of St. Mary, David is first, middle, and last.[1]

Such was the enthusiasm for psalm-singing that some oriental monks sang thirty and more psalms during one night. When, in the fourth or fifth

[1] Gerbert, *De cantu et musica sacra* (2 vols., 1774), I, 64; *Wagner I,* 9.

centuries, the liturgy was regulated, Psalms were assigned to every Office Hour in numbers varying from as few as three to as many as eighteen.[2]

To the present day the Psalms form the nucleus of the Office Hours, there being nine for Matins, five for Vespers, four for Lauds, and three for each of the other Hours. Several of the longer Psalms, however, are subdivided into two, three, or more sections, each of which is counted as an individual Psalm. For instance, for Vespers of Saturday [307] only two Psalms, Ps. 143 and 144, are used, but the former is divided into two parts, 143.I, 143.II, the latter into three, 144.I, 144.II, 144.III, so that the total number is five, as required for Vespers. With rare exceptions, the Psalms are connected with an Antiphon, that is, a short text sung to an individual melody before and after each Psalm or, at the Lesser Hours and Compline, before and after the entire group of Psalms. A special place is reserved for Ps. 94, *Venite exsultemus Domino,* called Invitatory Psalm because it invites the faithful to "come and rejoice unto the Lord." It is sung at the beginning of Matins.

At an early time there were added to the Psalms a number of scriptural texts known as Canticles *(cantica),* which resemble the Psalms in their lyric and hymnic character. A distinction is made between the major Canticles, that is, those taken from the New Testament, and the lesser Canticles which are found in the Old Testament. The major Canticles are three, namely:

  I: Canticle of the Virgin Mary, *Magnificat anima mea Dominum* (My soul doth magnify the Lord; Luke 1:46-55); also called Canticle of the B. V. M. (Blessed Virgin Mary) or *Canticum B.M.V. (Beatae Mariae Virginis).*

 II: Canticle of Simeon, *Nunc dimittis servum tuum* (Lord, now lettest thou thy servant depart in peace; Luke 2:29-32).

III: Canticle of Zachary, *Benedictus Dominus Deus Israel* (Blessed be the Lord God of Israel; Luke 1:68-79).

Each of these is assigned to a specific Office Hour: the *Magnificat* to Vespers, the *Nunc dimittis* to Compline, and the *Benedictus Dominus* to Lauds. They stand at the close of the service, apart from the Psalms (which stand at its beginning), and are enframed by their own Antiphon.

The lesser Canticles are fourteen in number. They all belong to Lauds where, however, they occupy a different position from that of the major Canticles, being placed between the third and the fourth Psalm and thus bringing up the "Psalms" for Lauds to the same total number, five, as for Vespers. Two lesser Canticles are assigned to each day of the week, a

2 Gastoué, *Origines,* p. 207.

normal one used throughout the major part of the year, and a substitute employed mainly during Lent:[3]

Sunday:

I. Canticle of Daniel (Canticle of the Three Children, second part): *Benedicite omnia opera* (Daniel 3:56-58) [*A* 4].

Ia. Canticle of the Three Children, first part: *Benedictus es, Domine Deus patrum* (Daniel 3:52-57) [*A* 12].

Monday:

II. Canticle of David: *Benedictus es, Domine Deus Israel* (I Chronicles 29:10-13) [*A* 72].

IIa. Canticle of Isaiah: *Confitebor tibi Domine* (Isaiah 12:1-6) [*A* 76].

Tuesday:

III. Canticle of Tobias (Tobit): *Magnus es Domine* (Book of Tobit 13:1-10) [*A* 108].

IIIa. Canticle of Ezechias, *Ego dixi* (Isaiah 38:10-20) [*A* 112].

Wednesday:

IV. Canticle of Judith: *Hymnum cantemus Domino* (Book of Judith 16:15-21) [*A* 127].

IVa. Canticle of Anna: *Exsultavit cor meum* (I Samuel 2:1-10) [*A* 130].

Thursday:

V. Canticle of Jeremiah: *Audite verbum* (Jeremiah 31:10-14) [*A* 147].

Va. Canticle of Moses: *Cantemus Domino* (Exodus 15:1-19) [*A* 151].

Friday:

VI. Canticle of Isaiah: *Vere tu es* (Isaiah 45:15-26) [*A* 167].

VIa. Canticle of Habacuc: *Domine audivi* (Habakkuk 3:1-19) [A 171].

Saturday:

VII. Canticle of Ecclesiastes: *Miserere nostri* (Eccl. 36:1-16) [*A* 189].

VIIa. Canticle of Moses: *Audite coeli* (Deuteronomy 32:1-43) [*A* 192].

As mentioned previously, these Canticles are used at the beginning of Lauds between the third and fourth Psalms; in other words, as the fourth of the five Psalms. Thus, for Lauds of Friday we have: Ps. 98, Ps. 142, Ps. 84, Cant. VI, Ps. 147; and for the same during Lent: Ps. 50, Ps. 142, Ps. 84, Cant. VIa, Ps. 147.[4] In the *Liber,* which represents Lauds very incompletely, only four of the lesser Canticles appear; that of Sunday (I) for "Lauds of Feasts" [222], also for the Nativity [398] and the Burial of Very Young Children [1830]; that of Thursday in Lent (Va) for Maundy

[3] Since Lauds of ordinary Sundays and of weekdays are not represented in the *Liber,* reference is made to the *Antiphonale.*

[4] See *A* 164-168; 170-172.

Thursday [649]; that of Friday in Lent (VIa) for Good Friday [692]; and, deviating from the general scheme, that of Tuesday in Lent (IIIa) for Holy Saturday [736] and the Office of the Dead [1803]—the reason for the replacement being that this Canticle was considered as a prophetic description of the suffering of Christ.

To the Psalms and Canticles were added, perhaps as early as the third century, readings from the Scriptures, the so-called Lessons (*lectio*) and Chapters *(capitulum)*. These terms are somewhat confusing, since actually a Lesson is a lengthy section from Scripture, while a Chapter is no more than a single sentence. Lessons and Chapters are always followed by a chant, usually a Responsory *(responsorium)*; the former by a Great Responsory *(responsorium prolixum)*, a chant of considerable extension and elaboration; the latter, by a Short Responsory *(responsorium breve)*, a fairly short and simple type of chant.

Lessons followed by Great Responsories form the major part of the liturgy of Matins, which normally includes nine of them, three for each Nocturn [375ff; 626ff; 669ff; 715ff; 774ff; 873ff; 925ff; 1785ff].[5] In the other Office Hours reading from Scripture plays a much less prominent role, being limited to a single Chapter followed by a Short Responsory, except at Lauds and Vespers, where it is followed by a Hymn. Short Responsories as well as Hymns are concluded by a Versicle *(versiculum)*, a very short sentence with an answer. There is also a hymn in the four Lesser Hours and at Compline, but in a different position, that is, as the opening chant of the service.

Psalms and Canticles with Antiphons, Lessons and Chapters with Responsories, and Hymns constitute the nucleus of the Office Hours. In addition, there is an introduction consisting of prayers, *Pater noster, Ave Maria,* etc. [*L* xlix], followed by the Versicle *Deus in adjutorium* [250 and elsewhere]; and a conclusion including, among other items, the *Benedicamus Domino* [124], which was to play an important role in the early development of polyphonic music.[6] Disregarding these items as well as others such as the Commemoration of Saints at Vespers [262ff], the structure of the Office Hours of Sunday is shown in the following table, in which the musical items are italicized:[7]

[5] On feasts not falling in Lent the last Responsory was followed, and later replaced, by the *Te Deum* [Nativity, 392; Whit Sunday, 876; Corpus Christi, 939]. Easter Sunday and Whit Sunday have only one Nocturn. In early medieval practices the number of Responsories was often considerably greater. Thus, the ninth-century *Antiphonal* of Compiègne [see p. 53, no. 10] has seventeen Responsories for the Third Nocturn of the Nativity (*Patr. lat.* 78, p. 734). The monastic rites usually have four Responsories for each Nocturn, at least for feast days. See, e.g., the *Antiphonal* of Worcester, *Pal. mus.*, XII, Text, 14ff. Also the *Liber responsorialis* (*LR*).

[6] See Davison and Apel, *Historical Anthology of Music* (*HAM*), I, no. 28.

[7] The full Offices of all the weekdays are given in the *Antiphonale*.

MATINS   *Invitatory Ps. 94* with *Antiphon—Hymn.*

Nocturn I: 3 *Psalms* with 3 *Antiphons*—3 Lessons with 3 *Great Responsories.*

Nocturn II: same

Nocturn III: same

LAUDS   4 *Psalms* and 1 *Canticle* with 5 *Antiphons*—Chapter with *Hymn* and *Versicle—Canticle of Zachary* with *Antiphon.*

PRIME   *Hymn*—3 *Psalms* with 1 *Antiphon*—Chapter with *Short Responsory* and *Versicle.*

TERCE   Same as Prime

SEXT   Same as Prime

NONE   Same as Prime

VESPERS   5 *Psalms* with 5 *Antiphons*—Chapter with *Hymn* and *Versicle—Canticle B.V.M. (Magnificat)* with *Antiphon.*

COMPLINE   3 *Psalms* with 1 *Antiphon—Hymn*—Chapter with *Short Responsory—Canticle of Simeon* with *Antiphon—Antiphon B.V.M.*

The last item of this list, the Antiphons of the B.V.M., also called Marian Antiphons, are four chants of a relatively late date, probably not before the eleventh century. These are of great beauty and importance, and have played a particularly prominent role in the field of polyphonic composition. They are not Antiphons in the proper sense of the word, since they are not in any way connected with a Psalm or a Canticle. Rather they are independent chants of considerably greater extension and elaboration than the Antiphons proper, a characterization that also applies to the processional Antiphons sung during the Processions before Mass at such feasts as Palm Sunday or Purification [584, 1359]. Each of the four Antiphons of the B.V.M. is sung during one quarter of the year: the *Alma redemptoris mater* (Gracious Mother of the Redeemer) from Advent to February 1; *Ave regina caelorum* (Hail, Queen of the Heavens) from February 2 till Wednesday in Holy Week; *Regina caeli laetare* (Rejoice, Queen of the Heavens) from Holy Saturday till the week after Pentecost; and *Salve regina* (Hail, oh Queen), the most celebrated of all, from then till Advent [273-276; the "Simple Tones" given on pp. 277ff seem to be melodies of a fairly recent date].

THE MASS

The Mass has a considerably more complex, but also more fully integrated, structure than the Office Hours. In contrast to their seriate form, the Mass has a centric plan, organized around a text commemorating the Last Supper during which Christ referred to the bread and wine as eternal symbols of the flesh and blood of His body which was to be crucified on the next day. This is the so-called Canon of the Mass, beginning with the words: *Te igitur, clementissime Pater,* and culminating in the sentences: *Hoc est enim corpus meum* (For this is My Body) and *Hic est enim calix sanguinis mei, novi et aeterni testamenti: mysterium fidei: qui pro vobis et pro multis effundetur in remissionem peccatorum* (For this is the chalice of My blood, of the new and eternal testament: the mystery of faith; which shall be shed for you and for many unto the remission of sins). The Canon is preceded by the Preface, both of which constitute the Eucharistic Prayer (prayer of thanksgiving). They are separated by the *Sanctus,* which forms the conclusion of the Preface.

The Eucharistic Prayer (though not, of course, in its present-day form) is a very ancient part of the Mass. Perhaps even older are the items adopted from the Jewish rites, that is, congregational prayers and readings from Scripture. The former survive in the *oratio* or Collect (prayer of the collected faithful, offered by the priest), the latter in the *Lectio,* Epistle, and Gospel (*Evangelium*), that is, readings from the Old Testament, from the Epistles and from the four Gospels.[1] Normally the Mass has two readings, one from the Epistles and one from the Gospels, but on ferial days outside of Paschal Time the first reading is from the Old Testament [see, e.g., *L* 603]. Originally there were three readings, but this full scheme survives only on a few occasions: the Wednesdays of the four Ember Weeks, the Wednesday in the Fourth Week of Lent, and the Wednesday and Friday of Holy Week. From its inception the Mass included the Offering of bread and wine, the Eucharistic Prayer, and the Communion. The above items are very nearly those mentioned in the earliest description of the Mass by the Roman philosopher and martyr Justin,[2] which dates from the mid-second century.

At an undetermined time it became customary to sing Psalms between the three readings.[3] The first Lesson, from the Old Testament, was followed by a Psalm sung responsorially and later called *responsorium graduale* or simply Gradual.[4] Another Psalm, sung entirely by a soloist, was inserted between the second and the third reading, the Epistle and

1 The readings from the Gospels are called *Sequentia* (continuation), because originally they followed in a continuous order, of which, however, very little has remained.

2 See the List of Data, p. 39, no. 7.

3 According to Duchesne, *Christian Worship,* p. 168, the "practice of chanting psalms between the lections in the Mass is as old as these lections themselves, and both go back in direct line to the religious service of the Jewish Synagogue." However, no Psalms are mentioned by Justin.

4 The term *graduale* is usually explained as referring to the fact that this chant was sung from the steps (*gradus*) leading to the pulpit. Gastoué (*Origines,* p. 247) prefers to think that the original term, at least for the collection of Mass chants, was *Gradale, Liber gradalis,* derived from an adjective *gradalis* meaning "distinguished," "more beautiful." Cf. Oddo, *De Musica: in gradalibus* (*GS,* I, 276a) and the *Alia musica: antiphona gradalis* for the Introit (*GS,* I, 129b).

Gospel. This is the *cantus tractus* or Tract,[5] which, in the fifth or sixth century, was largely replaced by the Alleluia. When, during the fifth century, the reading from the Old Testament was suppressed, both the Gradual and the Tract (or the Alleluia) were placed, in immediate succession, between the Epistle and the Gospel.

In the course of time Psalms were also introduced to accompany the three main actions of the Mass—the entrance of the priest, the offering of bread and wine, and the distribution of bread and wine among the faithful. These are the Introit, the Offertory, and the Communion. Finally, there are a number of chants based on non-psalmodic texts, the *Kyrie, Gloria, Sanctus, Credo,* and *Agnus Dei,* which form the Ordinary of the Mass. Of these, the *Sanctus* is the only one which forms an integral part of the early Mass and, at the same time, the only one which has a text taken from the Old Testament (Isaiah 6:3). The *Credo,* on the other hand, is a very late accretion, dating approximately from the eleventh century.

In its late-medieval (11th/12th-century) and present-day form the Mass includes ten musical items; five of these are Ordinary, being common to all Masses, while the other five are Proper, i.e., varying from Mass to Mass. The Ordinary consists of the *Kyrie, Gloria, Credo, Sanctus,* and *Agnus Dei;* the Proper includes the Introit, Gradual, Alleluia (or Tract), Offertory, and Communion. Actually, there are two more Ordinary chants of the Mass, the *Asperges me* and the *Ite, missa est,* but these are usually not included among the Mass chants because they represent a prelude and postlude to the Mass rather than a part of it. The *Asperges me,* classified as an Antiphon, is sung during the aspersion of Holy Water, a ceremony preceding the Mass on Sunday. The *Ite, missa est* is a closing benediction, interesting mainly for the fact that its word *missa* (dismissal) has led to the term Mass, replacing the older name *Eucharistia.*

In addition to these ten musical items, the Mass includes others that, depending upon the solemnity and circumstances, are either said or sung to a recitation tone. Thus, there are "tones" for the Prayers [98], the Prophecy [102], the Epistle [104], the Gospel [106], and the Preface [109].

The full text of the Ordinary of the Mass is found in the *Liber,* pages 1 to 7. The items with variable texts such as the Introit, Gradual, etc., are mentioned in their respective places, except for the Communion, which comes after the second Ablution (before the rubric *"After the last Postcommunion").* The following table shows the items of the Mass arranged in four groups.

[5] According to *Wagner I,* 87, the term is the Latin translation of the Greek word *hirmos* which in Byzantine liturgy denotes a model melody. Late medieval writers (Durandus, 14th century) interpret it to mean "slow," "drawn-out" (from Lat. *trahere,* to draw). J. M. Tommasi (1649-1713; his *Opera omnia,* including *Gregori Magni opera omnia* re-edited, in 1747-53, by A. F. Vezzosi), interprets it as meaning *tractim,* continuously, i.e., without interruption by an antiphon or respond.

CHANTS		SPOKEN OR RECITED	
PROPER	ORDINARY	PROPER	ORDINARY
1. Introit			
	2. Kyrie		
	3. Gloria		
		4. Collect	
		5. Epistle	
6. Gradual			
7. Alleluia or Tract			
		8. Gospel	
	9. Credo		
10. Offertory			
			11. Offertory Prayers
		12. Secret	
		13. Preface	
	14. Sanctus		
			15. Canon
			16. Pater Noster
	17. Agnus Dei		
18. Communion			
			19. Postcommunion

Of the ten chants of the Mass the five making up the Proper are not only much older than the other five, but are also more important liturgically and more interesting musically. From the point of view of Gregorian chant, *Mass* plain and simple invariably means the Proper, in opposition to the prevailing terminology of the past five centuries according to which Mass means the Ordinary, as, for example, Bach's B-minor Mass or a Mass by Palestrina. The change of meaning occurred about 1300, when the items of the Ordinary were preferred for polyphonic composition, obviously because a polyphonic *Kyrie* or *Gloria* could be performed on practically every feast, while a polyphonic Gradual or Alleluia could be used only once a year.

The items of the Proper were in general use probably as early as 500, and by the time of Gregory this part of the Mass was fully standardized. Quite a different situation is presented by the Ordinary. The *Kyrie, Gloria,* and *Sanctus* were known in the earliest centuries of the Christian era but were used in the Office rather than in the Mass. The introduction of the *Gloria* into the Roman Mass is ascribed to Pope Symmachus (498-514); that of the *Kyrie,* to Pope Gregory I; while the *Sanctus* is said to have been instituted by Pope Sixtus I (*c.* 120). The *Agnus Dei* became a part of the Mass under the Greek Pope Sergius I (687-701); the *Credo,* although used at a much earlier time in the Mozarabic, Ambrosian, and Gallican rites, was not definitely introduced into the Roman Mass until the eleventh century, under Pope Benedict VIII (1012-24). Considering this situation, it is no wonder that the chants of the Ordinary are completely absent in the earliest manuscripts of Gregorian chant. They first appear sporadically in collections of tropes and sequences; later they form an appendix to the repertory of the Proper, and are usually given in separate divisions, one containing the *Kyries,* the next the *Glorias,* etc., a practice preserved to the present day for the *Credos.*

Most, if not all, of the items of the Ordinary originated in the Eastern Greek Church (Byzantium). Except for the *Gloria,* they were all originally sung by the congregation, a practice reflected in the simple style of the oldest melodies. Later, in the ninth century, they were taken over by the *schola* (church choir) and, in consequence, melodies of a somewhat more elaborate character appeared. The development and fixation of these chants remained largely an affair of individual churches or regional authorities, the Church of Rome being no longer interested in this matter or able to exercise control. As a result, during the later Middle Ages, there accrued a large repertory of chants for the Ordinary. An idea of its size can be formed from the fact that, according to recent research, there exist almost 300 different melodies for the *Agnus Dei.*[6] Throughout this period only sporadic efforts were made to combine specific melodies into a fixed cycle, in other words, to form definite Ordinaries assigned to certain categories of feasts [see p. 420]. The liturgical books of the present day contain eighteen such cycles; one for Paschal Time, one for Solemn Feasts, etc.; but most of these were not fixed until the issuance of the *Editio Vaticana,* in 1908. Thus Pope Pius X, who authorized the publication, may be said to have played a similar role for the Ordinary of the Mass as did Pope Gregory I for the Proper, thirteen hundred years earlier.

The present-day group of Ordinaries includes one for Paschal Time, two for Solemn Feasts, five for Double Feasts, two for Feasts of the Blessed Virgin, one for Sundays throughout the Year, two for Semi-doubles, one during Octaves, one for Simple Feasts, one for Ferias throughout the Year, one for the Sundays of Advent and Lent, and one for the Ferias throughout Advent and Lent, with six *Credos* being given separately [64, 90]. A note on p. 73 says expressly that "this Ordinary is not meant to be a matter of hard and fast rule" and that "in order to add greater solemnity, one or more of the following '*Chants ad libitum*' may be employed." The names, such as *Lux et origo, Kyrie fons bonitatis,* etc., given to most of these Ordinaries and to the *ad libitum* Kyries, refer to the fact that in the tenth and later centuries the *Kyrie* melodies were provided with additional words, such

[6] See the article "Agnus Dei" (Stäblein) in *MGG.*

as *Kyrie lux et origo eleison* (Lord, origin and light, . . .) or *Kyrie fons bonitatis eleison* (Lord, fountain of goodness . . .), the so-called tropes. Even after the tropes had been abolished the names survived.

EXCEPTIONAL MASSES

The statement that the Proper of the Mass consists of five items, Introit, Gradual, Alleluia, Offertory, and Communion, is not unreservedly correct. There exist exceptions in greater number and variety than is commonly thought to be the case. As was previously intimated, the chants of the Proper are of two types; those that follow a lesson and those that accompany an action. To the former category belong the Gradual and Alleluia; to the latter, the Introit, Offertory, and Communion. There is practically no variation in the action-chants. Introit, Offertory, and Communion form a part of every Mass, the only exceptions being those of Good Friday and Holy Saturday, which have none of them, and that of Whitsun Eve, which lacks the Introit.

Considerable variation, however, occurs in the field of the lesson-chants, mainly in connection with three liturgical periods of a special character, namely, the Season before Easter, Paschal Time, and the four Ember Weeks. In the pre-Easter Season the Alleluia is omitted (or, to express it correctly from the historical standpoint, was never introduced), in conformity with the somber character of the period leading up to the "darkest days" of the liturgical year, Good Friday and Holy Saturday. On the Sundays, Mondays, Wednesdays, and Fridays (*Dominica, Feria II, IV, VI*) of this period, that is, from Septuagesima Sunday till Wednesday in Holy Week, it is replaced by a Tract, but not on the other week days (*Feria III, V, Sabbato*), on which there remains only one lesson-chant, the Gradual. An exception to this organization occurs on the Wednesday before Passion Sunday (*Fer. IV. p. Dom. IV. Quad.; G* 145), which has two Graduals and a Tract. This is indeed a special day, the Day of the Great Scrutiny, that is, of examination of the catechumens for admission to baptism. The idea of replacing the Alleluia by a Tract was adopted for two special occasions of a somber character, the Feast of the Holy Innocents and the Mass for the Dead.

As if in recompense for the omission of the Alleluia in the pre-Easter Season, there follows shortly, from Saturday in Easter Week till Friday after Pentecost (Paschal Time), a period during which two Alleluias are sung, one of them in the place of the Gradual. The underlying principle of the Masses for Ember Days appears most clearly in those of Advent and September. In both these weeks the lesson-chants are: two Graduals for the Wednesday; one Gradual for the Friday; and four Graduals, a Hymn, and a Tract for the Saturday. In the Ember Week of Lent, which falls into the pre-Easter Season, the Wednesday and Friday each have a Gradual and a Tract, while in the Ember Week of Pentecost these two days have the two Alleluias customary in that period. Finally, the Saturday of this week of Pentecost has five Alleluias and a Tract. The following table shows the lesson-chants of these twelve days.

THE LESSON-CHANTS OF THE EMBER WEEKS

	FER. IV.	FER. VI.	SABBATO
Advent	2 Graduals	1 Gradual	4 Graduals, 1 Hymn, 1 Tract
Lent	1 Gradual, 1 Tract	1 Gradual, 1 Tract	4 Graduals, 1 Hymn, 1 Tract
Pentecost	2 Alleluias	2 Alleluias	5 Alleluias, 1 Tract
September	2 Graduals	1 Gradual	4 Graduals, 1 Hymn, 1 Tract

The use of a hymn in the Mass is, of course, quite contrary to expectation. Actually, the chant in question is the *Benedictus es Domine*, which is not a hymn at all, in the proper sense of the word, comparable to the hymns of the Office. While these have texts dating from the fourth century or later, written in strict verse, the *Benedictus es* is a scriptural text taken from the Book of Daniel, chapter 3, which (in an apocryphal section) tells the story of the three young Hebrews ("children") who were thrown into a fiery furnace because they refused to adore the statue of Nebuchadnezzar, and who were miraculously rescued by an angel, whereupon they sing an extended song of praise, known as the Song of the Three Children *(Cantus* or *Hymnus trium puerorum)*. Its first five verses (Daniel 3:52-56) form the basis for the Mass chant *Benedictus es Domine*, while the continuation (℣. 57-88) is used for the Canticle of Daniel, *Benedicite omnia opera* [see p. 21]. The use of the *Benedictus* in the above-mentioned three Masses is explained by the fact that their fifth Lesson relates the story of the three children, ending with the words *et benedicebant Deum in fornace, dicentes* (and they praised the Lord in the furnace, saying:), whereupon their song of praise follows in the form of a closing chant.[1]

Whatever type the lesson-chants may be, their number depends upon the number of readings, there being one chant between two readings. This, at least, was the original state of affairs when the Mass normally had three Lessons separated by two chants, an organization which is still preserved on the four Ember Wednesdays, e.g., that of Lent:

Lesson (Exodus)—Gradual—Epistle—Tract—Gospel

or in the Masses of Wednesday in Holy Week [613] and of Good Friday

[1] For special studies of the *Benedictus es* see: *Wagner III,* 361; Ferretti, p. 206; *Pal. mus.,* XIV, 222 (Gajard).

[694]. The connection between Lessons and chants is particularly evident in the Masses of the four Ember Saturdays, which have seven readings—five from the Old Testament, an Epistle, and a Gospel—with six chants between them. There are two other Masses with six chants, on Holy Saturday and on Whitsun Eve. The former has twelve Lessons (all "Prophecies" from the Old Testament), the latter eight. Originally, the four Ember Saturdays must also have had twelve Lessons, since in all the earliest manuscripts they are designated as *Sabbato in xii lectionibus*.[2]

The following table shows all the exceptional Masses, arranged according to number of lesson-chants.

	GRAD.	HYMN	ALL.	TRACT
A. MASSES WITH TWO LESSON-CHANTS				
(Normally)	(1	0	1	0)
1. Sundays from Septuagesima to Palm Sunday				
2. Mondays, Wednesdays; Fridays from Ash Wednesday to Wednesday in Holy Week	1	0	0	1
3. Holy Innocents[3]				
4. Mass of the Dead				
5. From Saturday after Easter to Friday after Pentecost (Paschal Time)	0	0	2	0
6. Feria IV. Quat. Temp. Adv., Sept.	2	0	0	0
7. Good Friday	0	0	0	2
B. MASSES WITH ONE LESSON-CHANT				
8. Feriae III., V., and Sabbato from Feria V. post Cineres to Maundy Thursday	1	0	0	0
9. Feria VI. Quat. Temp. Adv., Sept.				
10. Christmas Eve[3]				
11. Rogation Days	0	0	1	0
C. MASSES WITH THREE LESSON-CHANTS				
12. Feria IV. post Dom. IV. Quad.	2	0	0	1
D. MASSES WITH SIX LESSON-CHANTS				
13. Ember Saturdays of Advent. Lent, and September	4	1	0	1
14. Ember Saturday after Pentecost	0	0	5	1
15. Holy Saturday, Whitsun Eve[4]	0	0	1	5

Feasts given with their English names are found in the *Liber usualis;* those with Latin names, in the *Graduale.*

2 Hesbert *(Sextuplex,* p. xl) offers the explanation that the Ember Saturdays had six readings (no Gospel), each of which was read in Latin as well as in Greek.

3 The Masses of Holy Innocents and Christmas Eve have an Alleluia if they fall on a Sunday.

4 By a recent decree the Mass for Whitsun Eve has been changed to a normal Mass.

The two main variants in the structure of the Proper are those given in the above table under nos. 1, 2, and 5, the first two being valid for the period from Septuagesima to shortly before Easter, the third for the period of Paschal Time. Naturally these variants also apply to the Masses of the Common and Proper of Saints whenever they fall into these periods. Thus, for the Common of Holy Popes there is provided a Gradual, an Alleluia, a Tract, and a second Alleluia, with the remark that after Septuagesima the first Alleluia is to be replaced by the Tract, and in Paschal Time, the Gradual by the first Alleluia [1122² ff].

Yet another variation in the structure of the Proper of the Mass is the addition, on certain feasts, of a sequence. The present-day books contain five sequences, *Victimae paschali* for Easter and Easter Week, *Veni Sancte Spiritus* for Whit Sunday and Whitsun Week, *Lauda Sion* for Corpus Christi, *Stabat Mater* for the Feast of Seven Dolours, and *Dies irae* for the Mass of the Dead. These have not been included in the above tabulation. They are later additions which do not occur in the earliest manuscripts *(Sextuplex,* St. Gall *359, 339)*. On the other hand, in the heyday of the sequence (twelfth century and later) practically every Mass had one, so that, in this period, its presence was as normal a feature as was its absence before that time. Only after the Council of Trent (1545-63), which abolished nearly all the sequences, did the sequence become an exceptional component of certain Masses.

Regarding the Ordinary of the Mass, the only variants are the occasional omission of the *Gloria* and the *Credo*. The *Gloria* is omitted in Advent and Lent (except Maundy Thursday and Holy Saturday), on Holy Innocents, and certain other occasions; the *Credo,* on feasts of Martyrs, Virgins, Holy Women, among others. A few Masses, e.g., those of the Rogation Days and for the Dead, have neither *Gloria* nor *Credo*.

Entirely different from all the other Masses are those of Good Friday and Holy Saturday. The former is called Mass of the Presanctified, because the priest uses the Host consecrated on the previous day. It lacks all the action-chants as well as the chants of the Mass Ordinary. The Mass of Holy Saturday has none of the action-chants, and only the *Kyrie, Gloria,* and *Sanctus* of the Ordinary. With its numerous readings (twelve Prophecies), Prayers and special ceremonies of the Blessing of the Paschal Candle, Blessing of the Font, and Litany of Saints, the Mass of Holy Saturday is the most extended and elaborate of all.

Finally, mention may be made of special ceremonies celebrated before or after the Mass on certain feasts, such as the Blessing of the Ashes on Ash Wednesday [523], the Blessing of the Candles and the Procession on the Feast of Purification [1356], the Distribution of Palms and the Procession on Palm Sunday [583], the Adoration of the Cross on Good Friday

[704], and the Processions on Rogation Days [835] and Corpus Christi [950]. The chants sung during the ceremonies are mainly elaborate Antiphons (similar to the Antiphons to the B. V. M. in that they are not connected with a Psalm), Responsories, and Hymns, the latter especially during the Procession on Corpus Christi.

CHAPTER THREE

Origin and Development to *c.* 600

A DETAILED description of the development of Roman chant or of the related bodies of Christian chant lies outside the scope of this book, which is primarily devoted to investigations of style and form; nor would such a description be in line with the general principles of research on which our studies are based. Because of the scarcity of factual information regarding the development of chant, a large amount of conjecture and inductive reasoning is necessary in order to fill the wide areas about which we have no certain knowledge, and to answer, at least with a certain degree of probability, the numerous questions about which we have no documentary evidence. In fact, the various books that have been written on this subject consist to a considerable extent of such conjectural material. This in no way means that they are without validity or without value. One might single out for mention the first volume of P. Wagner's *Einführung in die Gregorianischen Melodien,* entitled *Ursprung und Entwicklung der liturgischen Gesangsformen* (2nd edition, 1901) which contains an excellent description of the historical development, combining the actual data with sound reasoning. The fact that this volume is available in an English translation[1] is one more reason for forgoing a presentation which, at best, would be nothing more than a rehash. The present chapter, then, is no more than a survey designed to provide the reader with the most necessary information about the evolutionary processes of which the Gregorian repertory is the final result. Short sketches dealing with the development of individual forms, such as the Responsories, Alleluias, etc., are included in the later chapters.

[1] *Introduction to the Gregorian Melodies* (1907). Also very useful, and extremely readable, is Duchesne's *Christian Worship,* which treats the development primarily from the liturgical point of view. More detailed, but also more controversial, are the explanations offered in Gastoué's *Les Origines du chant romain* (1907).

THE PRE-CHRISTIAN ROOTS

The Christian rite and its chant are rooted in the Jewish liturgy.[1] Different though the new message was from the teaching of the Synagogue, it was presented to the Jewish people in the forms to which they had been accustomed by a long tradition. Only a few of the many indications of this connection can be mentioned here. Thus, the Office Hours of the Church are modelled after the prayer hours of the Jews, which began with the evening prayer at sunset, the ancestor of Vespers in the Roman Office. Even the Mass, the main embodiment of the new faith, contains a Jewish element. It is the mystic repetition of the Last Supper which Christ celebrated with his disciples in imitation of the Jewish Passover. Perhaps the strongest and least varied bond exists in the Book of Psalms, which formed an important part of the Jewish service and was raised to even greater importance in the Christian liturgy. A number of Psalms actually retained their position, e.g., Ps. 94, *Venite exsultemus,* which served as an introductory Psalm for the evening service of the Jewish Sabbath, and which appears in the same function at the Night Service (Matins) of the Roman liturgy. It is hardly necessary to point out that the Amen and Alleluia are of Jewish origin, but less known is the fact that the *Sanctus* of the Mass, with its triple acclamation "Sanctus, Sanctus, Sanctus," is derived, together with the Greek-Byzantine *Trishagion* ("Hagios, hagios, hagios") from the Jewish *Kedusha,* "Kadosh, kadosh, kadosh."

In view of these numerous bonds between the two rituals, it is only natural to assume that there also existed a musical tradition leading from the Jewish to the earliest Christian chant. This surmise, formerly based only on inductive reasoning, has been scientifically established through the work of Idelsohn who, some thirty years ago, studied the religious chants of Jewish tribes in various parts of the East, mainly Yemen (South Arabia), Babylonia, Persia, and Syria.[2] An examination of these traditions revealed many striking similarities, clearly indicative of a common bond. Since it is impossible to assume that these tribes, living in the strictest isolation and in widely distant places, could have had any contacts sufficient to establish cultural relationships, the inevitable conclusion is that their musical tradition goes back to the time before they separated, that is, before the destruction of the second Temple of Jerusalem (70 B.C.) and the ensuing dispersion of the Jews. Thus we can form at least a

[1] See, e.g., A. Gastoué, "Les Origines hébraïques de liturgie et du chant chrétien" (*RCG,* XXXIV, XXXV); I. Schuster, "Delle origini e dello sviluppo del canto liturgico" (*Rass. Greg.,* XI, XII); C. Vivell, "Directe Entwicklung des römischen Kirchengesanges aus der vorchristlichen Musik" (*KJ,* XXIV); E. Werner, "The Common Ground in the Chant of Church and Synagogue" (*ACI,* p. 134).

[2] A. Z. Idelsohn, *Thesaurus of Hebrew Oriental Melodies,* 10 vols., 1914-32.

general idea of Jewish chant as it existed shortly before the rise of Christianity. The most important result from our point of view is the fact that there is a striking similarity of style between the ancient Jewish melodies and those of the Gregorian repertory, indicated by such basic traits as absence of regular meter, responsorial and antiphonal performance, prevailingly conjunct motion, psalmodic recitation, syllabic style mixed with melismas, and use of standard formulae. In the field of psalm recitation the principles and, occasionally, even the melodies themselves are practically identical. The basic elements of the Gregorian psalm tones, that is, unison recitation (*tenor*) for each half of the verse with initial and concluding formulae before and after each recitation (intonation, mediant, termination), are found particularly among the Jews of Yemen, who employ them not only for the Psalms but also for the Pentateuch and other books of Scripture. The Yemenite psalm melody shown in Fig. 1a[3] is practically identical with the first Gregorian psalm tone shown under b (termination on f; see *L* 113):

FIGURE 1

A- sar teno hode- ho   al hasso -   mo -jim.

Another remarkable example of parallelism exists in the Lamentations of Jeremiah, which are sung at Matins of the three days before Easter (Maundy Thursday, Good Friday, and Holy Saturday), the verses being numbered by the Hebrew letters, Aleph, Beth, Ghimel, etc. [626]. Manuscripts of the twelfth to fourteenth centuries give various recitation melodies for this text, and one of them (Fig. 2a), remarkable for its archaic flavor, is strikingly similar to a melody used by the Yemenite Jews for the same text (Fig. 2b).[4]

FIGURE 2

Several other Jewish parallels for Gregorian melodies have been pointed out by E. Werner:[5] for example, the *tonus peregrinus* which is employed

[3] Idelsohn, *Thesaurus*, I, 64. The text is Ps. 8, beginning of ℣. 2.

[4] Given in *Wagner III*, 239f, from (a) O. Fleischer, *Neumenstudien*, II (1897), 41; and (b) Idelsohn, *Thesaurus*, I, 88.

[5] See fn. 1.

for the Psalm *In exitu Israel* and which recurs almost identically in a psalm formula employed by the Yemenite Jews for the same text; or the archaic melodies for the *Te deum* [Simple Tone; *L* 1834] and the *Gloria XV* [57], both written in a pentatonic E-tonality which Clement of Alexandria (*c.* 150–*c.* 220) calls *tropos spondeiakos,* adding that it is in use in Jewish psalmody and recommending it as a model for Christian singers. Several other examples of this kind have been found. On the whole, however, the main argument rests not so much on individual examples as on the identity of the general premises of musical style.[6]

The validity of this argument becomes even more apparent if we turn to the examination of another question, that is, whether and to what extent elements of ancient Greek music entered into the formation of Christian chant. A Greek-Gregorian line of connection exists, without doubt, in the theoretical field of the scale systems, although to the present day scholars disagree as to whether the "Greek" end of this line is represented by pre-Christian Greek antiquity or by the Greek-Byzantine tradition of the sixth or seventh century after Christ. This fact has led to attempts to establish a similar relationship between the melodies of the ancient Greeks and those of the Gregorian repertory. Although only a few melodies of Greek antiquity have come down to us, they are sufficient to give a general impression of the stylistic principles of this tradition and, at the same time, show that these principles are almost diametrically opposed to those underlying the music of Christian worship. Not only are the ancient Greek melodies strictly metrical and almost completely syllabic but also indicative of an entirely different approach to melodic design. A typically Greek melody, such as the Delphic Hymn or the Hymn to the Sun,[7] is essentially a speech delivered in distinct musical pitches which are rather haphazardly selected and combined. The result is a musical line that is not (or only incidentally) subject to such general principles of melodic design as balance of rising and falling tendencies or reference to a tonal center, principles which are of basic importance in Gregorian chant. Passages like the beginning of the Hymn to the Sun (Fig. 3) are as un-Gregorian as possible, not only rhythmically but also melodically.

FIGURE 3

Chi·o·no· ble·pha·rou   pa·ter   A·ous,   rho·do·es·san hos an·ty·ga po·lon

Actually, the case made for the Greek-origin theory rests upon a single piece of evidence, that is, the melodic similarity between the Seikilos Song,

6 See pp. 180, 186, and 362f.
7 See *HAM*, nos. 7a, b.

Hoson zes, and the Antiphon *Hosanna filio David* from Palm Sunday.[8] However, in spite of a few striking details, the proof of identity is, on the whole, hardly more convincing than the attempt to derive the melody of *God save the King* from the Antiphon *Unxerunt Salomonem* [987].[9] At any rate, it goes without saying that such an isolated case proves nothing.

A somewhat better case can be made for the theory of a Graeco-Christian and, later on, Byzantine influence. An isolated example of a very early period is the Oxyrhynchos Hymn,[10] a Christian hymn in the Greek language, dating from the end of the third century: ". . . Let all the waves of the rushing rivers give praise to our Father and Son and Holy Spirit, let all powers sing with them: amen, amen. Power, praise [and glory unto God], the only Giver of all goods: amen, amen." On the whole, the music for this hymn (Fig. 4) is written in the ancient Greek style, with its strikingly "atomic" design resulting, as it were, from the mere addition of pitches. Formations such as the two descending fifths that occur in close succession on *hymnounton d'hemon* or the leap of a sixth on *pasai* are as foreign to Gregorian style as can be. Different trends, however, are notice-

FIGURE 4

hym-noun- ton d'he - mon pa - te- ra k'hyi -on   k'ha - gi - on   pneu - ma.   Pa -   sei

dy - na-meis . . . pan-   ton   a - ga -thon.   A -   men,   a - men.

able in the closing part of the hymn, particularly in the final cadence on "amen, amen," which shows an unmistakable similarity to a Gregorian cadence.

In a recent publication, *Eastern Elements in Western Chant* (1947), E. Wellesz has tried to demonstrate the existence of musical relationships between the Eastern (Byzantine) and Western (Ambrosian, Gregorian) repertory of chant, interpreting them as influence from the East to the West. His proofs are rarely conclusive and his claims of priority on behalf of the Eastern chant are often arbitrary. We do not mean to deny that Eastern and Western chant have something in common, but this common bond must be sought not so much in their finished repertories of the eighth or ninth century as in their primeval stages during the first four centuries of the Christian era. Thus we wholly agree with the following

[8] See *HAM*, no. 7c; *L* 578. Both melodies are shown simultaneously in G. Reese, *Music in the Middle Ages* (1940), p. 115.

[9] *Times* (London), Sept. 5, 1931.

[10] So called because it is contained in a group of papyri found near Oxyrhynchos in Middle Egypt. See the article "Oxyrhynchos Hymn" in *HDM*. Our version is taken from E. Wellesz, *A History of Byzantine Music and Hymnography* (1949), pp. 126f.

statement found in Wellesz' *A History of Byzantine Music and Hymnography* (1949): "It is obvious that the oldest versions of both Byzantine and Gregorian melodies go back to a common source, the music of the Churches of Antioch and Jerusalem, which in their turn derived from the music of the Jews" (p. 35).

HISTORICAL DATA FROM THE FIRST TO THE EIGHTH CENTURIES

We have previously alluded to the scarcity of documentary evidence concerning the early development of Christian chant.[1] What little there is, however, is all the more valuable and indispensable since it forms the basis for all inferences, conclusions, and hypotheses that can be, and have been, made in order to arrive at a more complete and coherent picture. Following is a succinct presentation of these data, in the form of a chronological list.[2]

LIST OF DOCUMENTARY DATA

FIRST CENTURY

1. *C.* 60: Philo of Alexandria (born *c.* 20), a Jewish chronicler, describes antiphonal singing, performed by men and women, among the *Therapeutae,* a Jewish sect whose faith was a mixture of Biblical and Platonic elements [*W* 14 (17); *R* 60]. See nos. 5, 17, 21, 30.
2. *C.* 90: Pope Clement I refers in a letter (written in Greek) to the use of the "Hagios, Hagios, Hagios" (*Trishagion*), the Greek form of the *Sanctus* [*R* 115]. See nos. 6, 44.
3. *C.* 90: In the same letter Pope Clement gives evidence of psalm-singing (in

1 Perhaps we should say: scarcity of *relevant* documentary evidence. Thousands of references to singing exist in the writings of the Church Fathers and of early chroniclers. In fact, Gerbert's *De cantu et musica sacra* (2 vols., 1774) is nothing but a gigantic compilation (still occasionally useful) of such references. Very little of this, however, is of actual importance from our point of view.

2 Compiled from a number of books which may be consulted for source indications and further details: *D*: Duchesne, *Christian Worship; G*: Gastoué, *Les Origines . . .; Gé*: Gérold, *Histoire de la musique* (1936); *Ger*: Gerbert, *De Cantu; L*: Lang, *Music in Western Civilization; M*: G. Morin, *Les véritables origines du chant grégorien* (1912); *R*: Reese, *Music in the Middle Ages; W*: Wagner, *Introduction to Gregorian Chant,* with page references to the German edition, *Einführung,* vol. I (1901), in parentheses.

The present writer assumes no responsibility for the accuracy of these data or of their interpretation. Some of them may well turn out to be unreliable. The most recent studies of the early development of Christian music are: H. Hucke, "Die Entwicklung des christlichen Kultgesangs zum Gregorianischen Gesang" (*Römische Quartalschrift für Christliche Altertumskunde und Kirchengeschichte,* XLVIII [1953], 147); and B. Stäblein, article "Frühchristliche Musik" (*MGG*).

Rome?) by warning the faithful not to sing the Psalms at the feasts of the pagans, lest they should appear similar to the music of the kithara players and minstrels [*G* 45].

4. The Apocryphal Acts of John the Evangelist (died *c.* 100) contain a reference to *aulos* playing and dancing in connection with the singing of hymns [*Gé* 135]. See no. 9.

SECOND CENTURY

5. *C.* 115: Pliny, the Younger, in a letter to the Roman emperor Trajan, mentions the Night Office (Vigils, Matins) and, possibly, antiphonal singing among the Christians of Bithynia [*W* 109 (127); *R* 60; *L* 43; *G* 45]. See nos. 11, 23, 27, 41.

6. *C.* 120: Pope Sixtus I is reported to have introduced the *Sanctus* into the Mass [*W* 99 (116)].

7. *C.* 150: Justin Martyr (d. 162) describes the Mass at Rome as consisting of readings from the Old and New Testament, a sermon, an offering of bread and wine, prayer of the faithful, the "kiss of peace," eucharistic (thanksgiving) prayer, and communion [*L* 45; *D* 50]. Notice the absence of psalm-singing (Introit, Gradual, etc.). See nos. 33, 34.

8. Early Latin translations of the Bible, now collectively referred to as the *Itala*. However, Greek remains the official language of the Church until the third century, even in Rome. See nos. 12, 31, 54.

9. Clement of Alexandria (*c.* 150–*c.* 220) forbids the use of instruments and of chromatic music in the churches [*W* 12, 13 (14, 16); *R* 61; *G* 45].

10. The Church Father Tertullian (*c.* 155–*c.* 222), active in Carthage, mentions responsorial psalmody (*cantus responsorius*), probably with reference to Rome [*W* 16 (19); *R* 62]. See nos. 15, 24, 53.

11. Tertullian mentions the three earliest Office Hours, Vigils, Lauds, and Vespers, in Carthage [*L* 44]; also Terce, Sext, and None as private prayer hours [*D* 447].

THIRD CENTURY

12. First indications of Latin liturgy in Rome [*W* 44 (51); *L* 49; *G* 46].

13. The Syrian Bardesanes (d. 223) and his son, Harmonios, write a Gnostic Psalter, i.e., hymn-like versions of the Psalms written from the point of view of Gnosticism (a combination of Christian doctrine with oriental and hellenistic elements) [*W* 38 (44); *R* 70]. See nos. 14, 20, 22, 25, 28.

14. 269: Council of Antioch. The great popularity of hymn-singing appears from the fact that the Council reproached the bishop Paul of Samosata for abolishing them in his church [*W* 37 (43)].

15. Athanasius (259-313), on the occasion of a persecution of Christians in Alexandria, orders the singing of a Psalm with the people responding: "quoniam in aeternum misericordia eius." [*W* 15f (19)].

16. Athanasius (according to St. Augustine) insisted that the Psalms should be sung with such moderate inflexion (*tam modico flexu vocis*) that it sounded like speech rather than singing [*W* 27 (31); *R* 62]. This has been considered as in-

direct evidence that fairly elaborate methods of singing existed at that time. See nos. 18, 32.

17. Eusebius (c. 260–c. 340), bishop of Caesarea in Palestine, mentions Philo's report (see no. 1) and says that the same practice exists among the Christians of his time [W 14 (17)].

18. Eusebius bears witness that the Psalms were sung "in melodious tone," i.e., not merely recited [R 62].

FOURTH CENTURY

19. 313: Edict of Constantinople, which raised the Christian faith to the status of an officially recognized religion, thus making an end to the persecutions and removing any obstacles to free development in liturgy or chant.

20. C. 340: St. Ephraim (306-73) of Syria writes the first Christian hymns (in Greek), in order to combat the heretical hymns of Bardesanes (see no. 13) [W 38 (45); R 69].

21. C. 350: Two monks, Flavianus and Diodorus, import antiphonal psalmody from the heretical Syrian Church into the Christian-orthodox Church of Antioch (Syria) [W 18 (22); R 68; L 46; G 50; D 114].

22. C. 350: Hilarius (d. 367), bishop of Poitiers (France) writes the first Latin hymns, after the model of St. Ephraim (see no. 20) [W 39 (46); L 48].

23. Hilarius mentions Vespers, Nocturns, and Lauds in France [W 111 (129)].

24. C. 375: St. Basil (c. 330-79), in a letter to the people of Caesarea, speaks of the singing of Psalms, both antiphonally and responsorially, in all parts of the Orient [W 21 (24f); R 63; Gé 137].

25. The Council of Laodicea (c. 360-81) forbids the singing of hymns [W 38 (44); L 47].

26. The Council of Laodicea established a *schola cantorum* [L 52]. See nos. 36, 49.

27. C. 385: The Spanish abbess Etheria (formerly called Sylvia or Egeria) makes a pilgrimage to Jerusalem and gives a detailed report about the liturgy there, mentioning a full Office (Vigils, Lauds, Terce, Sext, None, and Vespers) with Psalms, Antiphons, Hymns, Lessons, Responds, and Collects; also an incipient cycle of the year including Nativity, Lent, Palm Sunday, Holy Week, Easter, and Pentecost [R 65; L 44; D 541ff; Gé 138].

28. St. Ambrose (340-97) introduces antiphonal psalmody and hymns into Milan [W 22 (26); R 104; L 46, 48].

29. Pope Damasus I (366-84), advised by St. Jerome (330-420), undertakes the first organization of the liturgy and chant in Rome, after the model of the Church of Jerusalem [W 167 (191); R 119; G 51; M 79].

30. Damasus introduces antiphonal singing and the Alleluia into Rome [W 81 (95); R 63; L 46; see, however, pp. 376f]. See nos. 37, 45, 47.

31. C. 400: St. Jerome finishes the first complete Latin translation of the Bible, the *Vulgata* (Vulgate), which supersedes the *Itala*.

32. C. 400: Cassian gives evidence of ornate methods of singing in some monasteries of the Orient [W 29 (34); G 209], and mentions the *Gloria Patri* as a closing verse for antiphonal Psalms [Ger 43].

33. *C.* 400: Augustine (354-430), bishop of Hippo in North Africa, makes reference to various Mass chants: (a) the Gradual as a (complete) Psalm between the readings from Scripture and from the Gospels [*W* 72 (84)]; (b) the Alleluia as an extended vocalization, though without specific reference to the Mass [*W* 32 (38)]; and (c) the chants of the Offertory and the Communion which he introduced into Carthage [*W* 93, 103 (109, 120); *R* 64; *D* 173f].

FIFTH CENTURY

34. Celestine I (422-32) is said to have ordered the singing of antiphonal Psalms before the Offering. This has been interpreted as the earliest, though rather questionable, evidence of the Introit [*W* 57 (67); *R* 119; *G* 81; *M* 54].

35. Pope Leo I (440-61) is said to have been the first to institute an *annalis cantus,* i.e., a cycle of chants for the whole year [*W* 167 (191); *M* 79). Also ascribed to him is a Sacramentary, known as the Leonine Sacramentary [*D* 135ff]. See nos. 38, 39, 50, 55, 56.

36. Leo I founded a monastery for the training of singers, the earliest indication of a *schola cantorum* in Rome [*L* 53]. See no. 49.

37. The Greek church historian Sozomenos (*c.* 450) reports that the Alleluia was sung in Rome only once each year, on Easter Sunday [Migne, *Patrologia graeca* 67, p. 1475].

38. Pope Gelasius (492-96) is mentioned in connection with another *annalis cantus* [*W* 167 (192); *M* 79] and another Sacramentary, the Gelasian [*W* 167 (192); *D* 125ff].

SIXTH CENTURY

39. Popes Symmachus (498-514), Johannes (523-26), and Bonifacius (530-32) all are said to have worked on a *cantus annalis* (or *cantilena anni circuli*), a cycle of chants for the whole year [*W* 168 (192); *M* 79].

40. *C.* 510: Pope Symmachus extends the use of the *Gloria* of the Mass over the entire year, Sundays and Feasts of Martyrs [*W* 67 (80)].

41. *C.* 530: St. Benedict (died *c.* 543) establishes a complete liturgy for the Offices of the entire year (Benedictine Rule) with Matins, Lauds, Prime, Terce, Sext, None, Vespers and Compline [*W* 112 (131)].

42. St. Benedict mentions (introduces?) the *psalmus in directum* [*W* 23f (27f)].

43. 529: The Council of Vaison (France) introduces the *Kyrie eleison* into the Gallican Mass, in a statement which implies that it had been introduced some time before into the Roman Mass [*W* 64 (75); *D* 165]. See no. 48.

44. 529: The Council of Vaison orders the use of the *Sanctus* in all Masses [*W* 99f (117)].

45. Cassiodorus (*c.* 485-580) describes the Alleluia as a *jubilus,* i.e., an extended vocalization (without mentioning a verse) [*W* 33 (39)].

46. 589: The Council of Toledo (Spain) adopts the *Credo* of the Greek Church for use in the Mozarabic liturgy [*W* 89 (105)].

47. *C.* 600: Pope Gregory I (590-604) orders the use of the Alleluia for the entire year, except for the period of Lent [*W* 81 (95); *R* 180].

48. Gregory adds the *Christe eleison* to the *Kyrie* [*W* 65 (76)].

49. Gregory establishes (or reorganizes; see no. 36) the Roman *schola cantorum* [*W* 172 (197); *R* 121].

50. Gregory is said to have edited a *cantus anni circuli nobilis* (a famous cycle of chants for the year) [*W* 168 (192)].

51. Gregory is said to have written a *cento antiphonarius* (compilation [literally, patch-work] of chants) [*W* 172 (197)].

SEVENTH CENTURY

52. 608: Introduction of the Feast of the Dedication of a Church [*W* 182, fn. 3 (209)].

53. Isidore of Seville (*c.* 570-636) gives a clear description of responsorial psalmody [*W* 16 (20)].

54. Isidore says that the Vulgate (see no. 31) is now universally employed [*M* 45].

55. Pope Martinus (649-55) is said to have edited a *cantus annalis* [*W* 168 (192)].

56. *C.* 650: Three Roman abbots, Catolenus, Maurianus, and Virbonus, are each reported to have written a *cantus annalis nobilis* [*W* 168 (192); *M* 81].

57. The Greek Pope Sergius I (687-701; Council of Trullo, 692) introduces the Processions for three Feasts of the Virgin: Annunciation, Assumption, and Nativity [*W* 182 (209)].

58. Pope Sergius introduces the Feast of the Exaltation of the Cross [*W* 182 (209)].

59. Pope Sergius introduces the *Agnus Dei* into the Roman Mass [*W* 101 (119); *D* 186].

EIGHTH CENTURY

60. *C.* 725: Pope Gregory II (715-31) introduces the Masses for all the Thursdays of Lent [*W* 181 (207); *D* 246].

It is understood that these data should not be taken at their face value. They must be carefully evaluated both as to their reliability and as to their meaning before they can be used as the foundation material for a study of the development of chant, a study which also has to take into consideration many other things, such as facts of a purely liturgical character or internal evidence derived from an analysis of the melodies. Perhaps it is not superfluous to illustrate this situation by a few examples. A typical case of questionable reliability is no. 6 of the above list, according to which Pope Sixtus I introduced the *Sanctus* into the Mass. This information comes from a *Liber Pontificalis* (a book describing the deeds of the popes) which was compiled from *c.* 600 to *c.* 800, that is, nearly five hundred years after the event to which it refers. Even admitting the accuracy of the report, we have no evidence that the *Sanctus* was sung at this remote time or, if it was sung, that the melody had any connection with extant *Sanctus* melodies preserved in manuscripts of the tenth or eleventh centuries. Another fact worthy of note is that in the chronological list hymns appear centuries before any mention is made of, for instance, the Graduals (see nos. 14 and 33). They are indeed a considerably older item of the liturgy, at least in the East, but this statement implies nothing regarding the antiquity of their melodies as compared with those of the Graduals. The fact that hymns existed in the third century, Antiphons in the fourth (see no. 27), or the Introit in the fifth (see no. 34) is of interest and importance from the liturgical point of view, but is of little value for the investigation of the development of the musical repertory, for which we have to rely on entirely different criteria.

On the basis of historical data such as those given above and other considerations, scholars have been able to trace with a reasonable degree of certitude the development of liturgy and chant. For our purpose a summary description will suffice.

FROM THE FIRST CENTURY TO c. 380

The earliest development took place in the East, particularly in Jerusalem and Antioch. The most primitive service was the Night Office of Saturday (the Jewish Sabbath), held in the hours before dawn, between cock-crow and sun-rise. It was followed by the Mass, which therefore fell in the early hours of Sunday. Thus, Sunday became the Day of the Lord and assumed the function of the weekly feast day. The Night Service consisted of readings, prayers, and Psalms, the latter of which were probably sung by a soloist, with congregational responses. The Mass consisted mainly of readings from the Old and New Testaments, a sermon, offerings, and communion (see Data, no. 7), possibly without any singing. As early as the second century we find three Offices: Vespers at the beginning of the night, the Vigil (later called Nocturn or Matins) during the last hours of the night, and Lauds in the first hours of the morning. The Lesser Hours—Terce, Sext, and None—existed at an early time as hours for private prayers (as in a family), but later became an official institution.

We are very fortunate to possess a detailed account of the complete service as it was celebrated in Jerusalem about A. D. 385, at the very end of the period we are here concerned with. This information is contained in a unique document known as the *Peregrinatio Etheriae* (formerly, *Silviae*) which is the account of a pilgrimage to the holy places of the East undertaken by the nun Etheria, who wrote the report for the sisters of her nunnery, which was probably in north-west Spain. After detailed descriptions of her journey to various places (Mount Sinai, Mount Nebo, return to

Constantinople) she informs her sisters about the "operatio singulis diebus cotidie in locis sanctis," the order of the liturgy day by day in the Holy Places.[1] Here we find most interesting details about the Daily Offices at Matins, Sext, None, and Vespers; the Vigils and the Mass of Sunday; and the special celebrations for Epiphany (the section for Nativity is lost), the Feast of the Presentation of Christ in the Temple (not adopted into the Roman rite), the period of Lent with celebrations on all weekdays except the Thursdays [see Data, no. 60], Holy Week, Easter Sunday, Ascension, and Whit Sunday. For most of these services special places of worship are mentioned, such as the various churches in Jerusalem (*Anastasis,* Church of the Resurrection with the Holy Sepulchre; *Crux,* Church of the Holy Cross; *Martyrium,* the Great Basilica; *Sion,* the Church on Mount Sion); or outside, in Bethlehem, Bethany, Gethsemane, or on the Mount of Olives. Thus, at Epiphany the Vigils were celebrated in Bethlehem, the Mass in Jerusalem; on Palm Sunday the Vigils were held in the Anastasis and at the Cross, Mass was celebrated in the Martyrium, and there was an evening procession to the Mount of Olives; Maundy Thursday had a night service on the Mount of Olives and a morning service at Gethsemane; etc. These customs had a profound influence on the organization of the service in Rome, where the feasts were also assigned to different churches, known as Stations (*Statio ad Crucem, Statio ad Sanctam Mariam*), some of them built in direct imitation of those of Jerusalem. Finally, there was a special feast, celebrated with great solemnity, for the Dedication of Churches, in commemoration of the day when the churches of *Anastasis* and *Martyrium* had been consecrated (this, Etheria reports, was also the day when the Cross of the Lord had been found).

While most of the information given by Etheria is of a liturgical character, we also learn something about the music which accompanied the celebrations. Nearly every Office has the remark: "dicuntur ymni et antiphonae aptae diei ipsi" (Hymns and Antiphons proper for the day are said[2]) or a similar one to the same effect. Other remarks are: "dicuntur ymni et psalmi responduntur, similiter et antiphonae" (Hymns are said, and Psalms are sung with responses, and also Antiphons), or "dicuntur psalmi responsorii, vicibus antiphonae" (responsorial Psalms are said, in alternation with Antiphons). In connection with Vespers we hear that there was a memorial service during which a choir of boys always responded with *Kyrie eleison* after each name. No chanting is mentioned in connection with the Mass, except for hymns sung after Mass by the monks who

---

1 W. Heraeus, *Silviae vel potius Aetheriae peregrinatio ad loca sancta* (1921); John H. Bernard, *The Pilgrimage of Saint Silvia* (1891). The description of the liturgy in Jerusalem is reproduced in Duchesne's *Christian Worship,* pp. 492ff (Latin) and 541ff (English).

2 *Dicuntur* ("are said") does not mean that these items were spoken.

accompanied the bishop from the church of the Cross to the church of the *Anastasis*.

Exactly what these terms mean is, of course, to a certain extent open to doubt. Probably the only unequivocal one is *psalmus responsorius*, which means that the Psalm was sung with the congregation responding after each verse. As to the *ymni* so frequently mentioned, the natural assumption is that these mean hymns, but this is not shared by Duchesne who remarks[3] that *ymni*, far from being metrical hymns, are just another designation for Psalms or Canticles. It is true that the term does occur in this meaning, e.g., in a passage from Augustine: "ut hymni ad altare dicerentur de psalmorum libro" (that hymns should be said at the altar from the Book of Psalms). However, it may also have the meaning of hymns (though not necessarily metrical, as are those of St. Ambrose), and Etheria's remark: "dicuntur ymni et psalmi responduntur" would be without point if *ymni* meant the same as *psalmi*. The great popularity of hymns is well attested in the third and fourth centuries (see nos. 14, 20); it is perhaps significant that hardly fifty years before Etheria's pilgrimage St. Ephraim had written the first Christian hymns, which were so successful that a decade later hymns appeared in the western part of the Christian world (no. 22). It is true that at about the time of Etheria's journey the Council of Laodicea interdicted the use of hymns. It is reasonable, however, to assume that this decree had no immediate effect in Jerusalem, since it is well known that hymns continued to play a prominent role in the Greek liturgy (Byzantium), much in contrast to that of Rome, where the decree of Laodicea led to a complete suppression of hymns until they were reintroduced about the eleventh century. In sum, there is no reason to doubt that Etheria's *ymni* were hymns.

There is less certainty about the meaning of Etheria's frequently mentioned *antiphonae*. The question is whether *antiphona* means Antiphon in the later sense of the word, i.e., a short text and melody which is repeated, like a refrain, after each verse of a Psalm (today only at the beginning and at the end); or whether it stands for *psalmus antiphonus*, i.e., a Psalm sung antiphonally by two answering choruses. The former interpretation would, of course, indicate a more advanced stage in the evolution of antiphonal psalmody, and scholars usually consider the *Peregrinatio* as evidence that this stage had been reached near the end of the fourth century.[4] The situation would be clear if we found a reference such as *psalmus cum antiphona*, but this does not occur. We hear only about "psalmi responduntur, similiter et antiphonae" (Duchesne, p. 492), "psalmi lucernares sed et antiphonae" (p. 493), "psalmi responsorii, vicibus antiphonae"

[3] *Christian Worship*, p. 492.

[4] Cf. *Wagner I*, 23, fn. 2, referring to F. Cabrol's *Dictionnaire d'archéologie chrétienne et de liturgie* (1907-53), s.v. "Antiphone."

(p. 501), or "ymni et antiphonae" (p. 505, etc.); it is quite obvious that in most of these cases *antiphonae* means full Psalms sung antiphonally, not just the short Antiphons, which were never sung alone. Only the "psalmi lucernares sed et antiphonae" (Vesper Psalms but also Antiphons) could be interpreted as an indication that Antiphons in the proper sense of the word were sung in connection with the Vesper Psalms.

FROM DAMASUS TO GREGORY

With the beginning of the fifth century the center of attention shifts from the East to the West. The first general organization of liturgy and chant at Rome is usually assigned to the pontificate of Damasus I, who reigned from 366 to 384 [see no. 29]. Although this assignment is not confirmed by contemporary documents, it receives some support from what is known of ecclesiastical affairs of that time as well as from later documents. The clearest statement is contained in a report from the seventh or eighth century enumerating a number of popes who had contributed to the formation of Roman liturgy and chant. The list opens with Damasus who, we are told, "instituted and decreed the ecclesiastical order with the help of the priest St. Jerome who, with the permission of the pope himself, had transmitted it from Jerusalem."[1] Although this is a relatively late testi-

1 This list appears at the end of the earliest *Ordo Romanus,* usually called *Ordo Romanus Gerbert* [see List of Sources, p. 53, no. 4], and also at the end of a report of a Frankish monk who, about 800, visited monasteries in Rome and tells us mostly about the rituals at the meals of the Roman monks: *De prandio monachorum (Patr. lat.* 138, p. 1346). As for its documentary value, this list of "musical" popes represents one of the most striking cases of disagreement among liturgical scholars. P. Wagner considered it as a fairly trustworthy report of a Frankish monk *(Wagner I,* 166). In 1923, Silva-Tarouca ("Giovanni archicantor di S. Pietro a Roma e l'Ordo Romanus da lui composta" [*Atti della Pontificia Accademia di archeologia,* Serie III, Memorie, vol. I, parte 1, 1923, p. 159]) identified its author with the Roman archicantor Johannes who, about 680, was sent to England by Pope Agathon, and suggested that Johannes wrote the *Ordo* at that time as the result of his teaching activities at the monastery of Wearmouth. This theory was adopted by B. Stäblein, who considered the list as the "bedeutsamste und grundlegendste Dokument zur Frühgeschichte des liturgischen Gesanges in Rom" (*ACI,* p. 273), particularly in view of the fact that its alleged author was an archicantor (we would say, chapel master) at St. Peter's, a man who obviously was in a position to speak with authority about musical matters. Silva-Tarouca's theory was regarded as doubtful by J. Froger (*Les Chants de la messe aux VIIIe et IXe siècles* [1950], p. 6) and completely rejected by M. Andrieu ("Les Ordines Romani" [*Spicilegium sacrum Lovaniense,* fasc. 24, 1951]), who considers the list in question as a rather worthless eighth-century compilation of Frankish origin.

We have reported in some detail the "case history" of this document, because it is a rather typical example of a situation frequently encountered in connection with early liturgical sources. Whether Andrieu's opinion is going to be the final word in this question, I dare not predict. I consider the report as valid, although no more or less so than practically all the other documents concerning the early history of liturgical chant.

mony, there is no reason to doubt the correctness of this information. It tallies with the fact that in 382, near the end of Damasus' pontificate, a Council was held in Rome—one of the first to take place in the western part of the Christian world—which was attended by Greek and Syrian bishops. From this it is reasonably safe to conclude that under Damasus, and perhaps more specifically at the Council of Rome, the liturgy of Jerusalem was introduced into the Roman usage. The above-mentioned report makes no allusion to chant, as it does in connection with later popes, who are credited with having instituted an *annalis cantus*. That the transmission from the East to the West of an *ordo ecclesiasticus* also entailed to some extent the transfer of musical elements, can hardly be doubted; perhaps the very absence of an allusion to *cantus* in connection with Damasus can be considered as an indication that whatever chant was necessary was adopted from the Eastern rites. To a certain extent this surmise is confirmed in a famous letter of Gregory I, in which Pope Damasus is said to have adopted from the Church of Jerusalem a certain practice concerning the use of the Alleluia.[2] Another explicit reference to musical matters is found in the *Liber pontificalis,* a list of popes and their activities begun in the sixth century and continued, by a succession of chroniclers, into the eighth century. This work states that "He (Damasus) ordered that the psalms be sung day and night in all churches; this order was binding on all priests, bishops, and monasteries."[3]

We may then assume that about A. D. 400 there existed in Rome an ecclesiastical order which in its organization of both liturgy and chant was somewhat similar to that known to us from the *Peregrinatio Etheriae.* Judging from the later development it is safe to say that one major difference was the omission of hymns, due to the decree of the Council of Laodicaea.

While we are thus fairly well informed about the primitive stage of the Roman liturgy, we know very little about its development in the ensuing two or three centuries. Aside from details mentioned in our List of Data, such as the more extended use of the *Gloria* under Pope Symmachus (no. 40) and of the Alleluia under Gregory (no. 47), the only information comes once more from the previously mentioned report, which tells us that, after Damasus, a number of popes—Leo I (440-61), Gelasius (492-96), Symmachus (498-514), Johannes (523-26), Bonifacius (530-32), Gregory (590-604), and Martinus (649-53)—edited an *annalis cantus omnis,* a cycle of chants for the entire liturgical year. If we accept this testimony (and I see no reason why we should not) we may perhaps conclude that under Pope Leo I, about the middle of the fifth century, a first attempt was made to replace the "Eastern" chant by a new *cantus annalis,* probably of

[2] For more details see pp. 376f.

[3] *Liber pontificalis,* ed. by Duchesnes (2 vols., 1886, 1892), I, 213.

Western origin; and also that during the ensuing centuries several popes, of whom Gregory was one of the last, contributed to the further development and consolidation of this Roman cycle of chant.

This, of course, leads us right into the "Gregorian" problem, so often discussed with contradictory results. It is to Pope Gregory, and to him alone, that the organization of the Roman chant is assigned by a tradition, according to which Gregory was the author of a *liber antiphonarius,* i.e., a book containing the liturgical chants.[4] The earliest testimony to this effect dates from *c.* 750, when Egbert, Bishop of York, tells us in his *De institutione catholica* that certain English customs concerning Lent and Ember Weeks were ordered by Gregory "in suo antiphonario et missali" (in his book of chants and in his book of prayers) and were brought to England by his missionary, St. Augustine. Probably next in succession is a poem ascribed to Pope Hadrian I (772-95) which is found at the beginning of several early Antiphonaries (e.g. the *Gradual of Monza,* late 8th century; see List of Sources, no. 7 [pp. 53f]), which says that "hic libellus musicae artis" (this book of musical art) was composed by "Gregory, through deeds and name a worthy leader, who has ascended to the highest honor at the place where his ancestors lived." Amalarius of Metz (*c.* 780–*c.* 850) says: "Gregorius . . . ordinavit ordinem psallendi in psalterio et antiphonario" (he ordained the order of the psalmody in the Psalter and in the Antiphonary). Walafrid Strabo (*c.* 808-49), Abbot of Reichenau, mentions a tradition ("traditur . . .") according to which Gregory regulated not only the order of the Masses and Consecrations but also to a large extent the arrangement of the chants as it is now observed. Passing over some testimonies of lesser importance we finally come to the crown-witness, Gregory's biographer Johannes Diaconus, whose *Vita Sancti Gregorii,* written about 872, contains a chapter inscribed: *Antiphonarium centonizans cantorum constituit scholam* (He compiled an Antiphonary and founded a school of singers). The chapter begins with the sentence: "In the house of the Lord, like another wise Solomon, he compiled in the most diligent manner a collection called Antiphonary, which is of the greatest usefulness."

With John the Deacon's biography the tradition implied in the term "Gregorian chant" became so firmly established that it would be pointless to pursue it any further. It found an expression not only in such designations as *cantus Gregorianus* and *Antiphonarius S. Gregorii,* but also in pictorial representations showing Gregory sitting on the papal throne and dictating to a scribe the melodies that a heavenly dove, perched on his shoulder, is whispering into his ears.

Aside from abortive attempts to deny it made in the eighteenth cen-

[4] For more details, see, e.g., G. Morin, *Les véritables origines du chant grégorien* (1890, 1912).

tury,[5] this tradition remained unchallenged until 1890, when the Belgian musicologist Gevaert published a pamphlet, *Les Origines du chant liturgique de l'église latine,* in which he severely attacked the "Gregorian legend," maintaining that its chief witness, John the Deacon, is entirely untrustworthy, and that the role traditionally assigned to Gregory I was actually performed by a number of Greek and Syrian popes—Agathon, Leo II, Sergius I, Gregory II, and Gregory III—who reigned from 678 till 741. His ideas, however, were almost unanimously refuted by other scholars such as Morin, Cagin, Wagner, Frere, and Gastoué,[6] with the result that the old tradition was once more accepted as basically correct.

It is only recently that several liturgists have adopted a different attitude in this question; they either deny Gregory the role traditionally assigned to him[7] or qualify it in one way or another. It is an indisputable fact that, in all his voluminous writings and numerous letters, Gregory rarely makes any remark which could be interpreted as indicating an interest or activity in the field of liturgical chant. On the contrary, a rather hostile attitude is noticeable in one of his decrees, issued in 595, in which he speaks about the "reprehensible custom" of selecting deacons only because of their musical skill and beautiful voice, and in which he orders that all chants, except for the recitation of the Gospel, be sung by clerics of a lower rank.[8] As for the exact nature of Gregory's alleged role in the formation of the chant, the older notion that he had actually composed the melodies as found in the manuscripts of the ninth or tenth centuries had long been abandoned if only for the obvious reason that it would be impossible for one man to write the several thousands of chants that are required for the Office Hours and the Mass, even if he could devote all his life to this task. No less improbable is the notion that this feat was achieved by a number of men working under his direction. The analytical and comparative studies of chant that have been made during the past fifty years show beyond any doubt that the melodies of the Roman repertory were not written at one given period, but are the result of multiple evolutionary and cumulative processes which must have extended over several centuries.

There remains the possibility that Gregory took an active and decisive part, either personally or through directives given to his subordinates, in the final organization and codification of the chant, continuing and bring-

[5] Pierre Gussanville, in an edition of the works of Pope Gregory (1675), and Georg von Eckhart in *De rebus Franciae orientalis* (1729), I, 718.

[6] See, e.g., *Wagner I,* 169; Gastoué, *Origines,* pp. 85ff.

[7] Without, however, accepting Gevaert's theory regarding the later Gregorys or the Greek popes.

[8] Reprinted in Gastoué's *Les Origines,* Appendix A.

ing to a certain conclusion the work to which a number of earlier popes had already made some contribution. This theory would, at least, be in keeping with historical possibilities. It would mean that a considerable repertory of melodies had accrued during the centuries before Gregory, for whom it remained to collect the melodies, to assign them a definite position in the cycle of the year, and possibly to add some new ones for feasts that he introduced; all this, of course, with the *proviso* that these things were done under his direction rather than by himself in person.

This, indeed, seems to have been the view held by the aforementioned "Gregorianists" (Morin, Cagin, and others) who rose in opposition to the iconoclastic ideas proposed by Gevaert. Plausible and sensible though this view is, and in spite of the numerous "proofs" adduced in its support, it has been considerably shaken, if not definitely refuted, by recent investigations which make it highly probable that the melodies of the Roman chant, as we find them in the earliest manuscripts, are post-Gregorian, dating from a period at least fifty, if not a hundred or more, years after Gregory. We shall return to this interesting question at the end of the next chapter.

CHAPTER FOUR

The Development after 600

I<small>N THE</small> period after Gregory we find ourselves on more solid ground owing to the fact that from the seventh century on there exist sources in the proper sense of the word, that is, manuscripts that provide full information about the liturgy and the chant, rather than documents containing isolated historical data, as is largely the case in the first six centuries. These sources are important not only for the present purpose of outlining the development of liturgy and chant but also in connection with specific problems of form and style such as will come up in our analytical investigations. A brief description of the various types of sources and a list of the most important among them follows:

THE SOURCES

These can be divided roughly into five groups: (A) purely liturgical manuscripts; (B) collections of chants without musical notation; (C) tonaries; (D) theoretical writings; and (E) musical sources.

A. At the beginning stand certain documents which, although they contain neither the texts nor the music of the chants, are nevertheless important because they throw a clear light upon liturgical matters, mainly the order and number of feasts during the year. To this group belong the *Sacramentaries,* books written for the special use of the priest or the officiating bishop, and which contain only the texts spoken by him, such as the prayers and the variable Prefaces for the Canon of the Mass. These texts are given in their proper liturgical order, beginning with the Nativity and continuing through the year.[1] Thus, they furnish a clear picture of the liturgical calendar as it existed from the fifth century on. The *Sacramentaries* have been the subject of numerous studies on the part of liturgical scholars who have tried to strip off later accretions and to determine their original contents. They are usually, though not very properly, designated

---

[1] The early liturgical Mss start with the Nativity, except those containing the chants (*Graduals, Antiphonals*).

as the Leonine, Gelasian, and Gregorian *Sacramentaries,* referring to the Popes Leo I (440-61), Gelasius (492-96), and Gregory I (590-604).[2]

Another group of liturgical documents are the *Lectionaries* and *Evangeliaries,* which contain respectively the readings from Scripture (*Lectio libri Sapientiae, Lectio epistolae,* etc.) and from the Gospels (*Sequentia Evangelii*) for the Mass, arranged in the same manner as the *Sacramentaries.* The oldest of these is the *Comes* (companion, instruction book) of Würzburg, whose contents go back to the seventh century.

Of a different character are the books commonly referred to as *Ordo Romanus.* These contain detailed descriptions of the liturgy as celebrated by the pope, descriptions not only interesting in themselves but also important in our attempts to determine the early form of Mass chants, such as the Introits or Offertories with their verses.[3]

B. The second group of manuscripts is much more intimately connected with our subject. These are essentially *Graduals,* i.e., collections of the chants of the Mass, but without musical notation. Their value lies in the fact that they are considerably earlier than the *Graduals* provided with music. The oldest of these is the *Gradual of Monza,* written in the eighth century with gold and silver letters on purple parchment. Another, the *Gradual of Compiègne,* also includes an *Antiphonal,* the earliest known collection of chants (texts only) for the Office Hours.

C. Equally valuable for the study of the earlier phases of Roman chant are the Tonaries (*tonarius, tonale*) of the eighth, ninth, and tenth centuries. These are essentially catalogues in which a number of chants are listed according to their mode, and often with further distinctions within each modal category. They furnish important information about the Antiphons and Responsories of the Office, although some of them also include certain antiphonal Mass chants, that is, Introits and Communions.

D. This group comprises the theoretical writings of the Middle Ages, which are best known as a source of information regarding the development and establishment of the system of the eight church modes. Not a few of them, however, contain interesting and remarkably astute stylistic analyses of individual chants. In fact, it is here that for the first time we encounter efforts in the direction of style criticism, not dissimilar in essence to those of Glareanus or of modern musicologists.

E. The last and, of course, by far the most important group is formed by the musical manuscripts, the *Graduals* and *Antiphonals* with musical notation. Aside from a few eighth-century fragments, the earliest of these

2 For a summary of the *Sacramentaries* and the problems presented by them, see Duchesne, *Worship,* pp. 120ff, and particularly J. A. Jungmann, *Missarum Solemnia* (2 vols., 1948), I, 77ff [English edition, *The Mass of the Roman Rite,* I, 60ff].

3 The definite edition of the *Ordines* is M. Andrieu, *Les Ordines romani du haut moyen âge* (3 vols., 1931-35). See also J. Froger, *Les Chants de la messe,* pp. 5ff.

is the *Codex 359* of St. Gall, dating from *c.* 900. This, as well as those from the tenth century, is written in staffless neumes which represent only the general melodic motion, low-to-high, high-to-low, high-to-low-to-high, etc., but without indication of the pitches or intervals involved. It is only in the sources of the eleventh century that the neumes become diastematic, so that the melodies can be accurately read.

The following list of sources indicates the most important representatives of the five categories just described.

LIST OF SOURCES

A. Liturgical Sources

1. *Leonine Sacramentary.* This is an extensive and rather disorganized collection of prayers preserved in a single seventh-century manuscript. It is thought to represent the state of affairs at about A. D. 450 and later. Reproduced in Migne, *Patrologia latina* 55, pp. 21-156.

2. *Gelasian Sacramentary.* This is a well organized book of Mass texts, preserved in an early eighth-century manuscript. Its earliest contents go back to the time of Pope Gelasius (492-96). Reproduced in *Patr. lat.* 74, pp. 1055-1244.

3. *Gregorian Sacramentary.* This is essentially a collection of prayers, etc., that was sent in 785 by Pope Hadrian I (772-95) to Charlemagne upon his request for a *Sacramentary* by Gregory. Formerly it was thought to represent a period considerably later than Gregory, but today liturgists are inclined to accept it as written by him or in his time. It is also referred to as the *Sacramentary of Hadrian.*

4. *Ordo Romanus Gerbert* (*c.* 700?), so called because it was first published by Gerbert in his *Monumenta veteris liturgiae alemanniae* (1779).[4]

5. *Ordo Romanus primus* (*c.* 775).

6. *Ordo of St. Amand* (9th century).

B. Graduals and Antiphonaries without Musical Notation

7. *Gradual of Monza* (near Milan; late 8th century).

8. *Gradual of Rheinau* (abbey in Zurich; 9th century).[5]

9. *Gradual of Mont-Blandin* (abbey near Ghent; *c.* 800).

10. *Gradual and Antiphonary of Compiègne* (north of Paris; *c.* 870), also known as the *Antiphonary of Charles the Bald* (d. 877).

11. *Gradual of Corbie* (near Amiens; *c.* 900).

12. *Gradual of Senlis* (north of Paris; late 9th century).

The six manuscripts of this group form the basis of an extremely important publication by Dom R.-J. Hesbert, entitled *Antiphonale Missarum Sextuplex* (1935), in which their contents are shown in comparative tabu-

---

[4] Concerning this *Ordo* and the list of popes appended to it, see p. 46, fn. 1.

[5] According to Hesbert (*Sextuplex,* p. xii) the *Gradual* of Rheinau was written for the abbey of Nivelles in Belgium (south of Brussels).

lations. Aside from the *Gradual of Monza* (which is often designated as a *Cantatorium,* because it includes only the solo chants—Graduals, Alleluias, and Tracts) the manuscripts are called, somewhat misleadingly, *Antiphonals.* This is an abbreviation of *Antiphonale missarum,* the old name for the books containing the chants of the Mass, in distinction from *Antiphonale Officii,* the present-day *Antiphonal.* The Codex of Compiègne (no. 10) contains, in addition to the *Gradual* section, a full *Antiphonal* which has been published under the very confusing title of *Liber responsalis sive Antiphonarius S. Gregorii Magni.*[6]

C. Tonaries

We include here only extensive catalogues of chants. Rudimentary tonaries occur also in some of the treatises under D (nos. 21, 22).[7]

13. *Tonarius of Regino* (abbot of Prüm in West-Germany, near Luxembourg; d. 915). Published in *CS,* II, 1ff, in facsimile and reprint). Because of its comprehensiveness and early date, this is the most important of all the tonaries.

14. *Intonarium of Oddo* (either the abbot of Cluny who died in 942, or, more probably, a ninth-century abbot of St. Maur-des-Fossés, in Paris). Published in *CS,* II, 117ff, after an eleventh-century copy with staff notation. A short *Tonarius* also in *GS,* I, 248.

15. *De modorum formulis* (by Guido of Arezzo?). *CS,* II, 81.

16. *Tonarius of Berno* (Augiensis, i.e., from Reichenau near Constance; d. 1048). *GS,* II, 79. *Prologus ad tonarium, GS,* II, 62.

D. Theoretical Writings

The following list includes only treatises dealing with some aspect of chant, not those concerned only with the old Greek modes.

17. Alcuin (753-814): *Musica. GS,* I, 26f. A short report including the earliest mention of the eight church modes.

18. Amalarius of Metz (*c.* 780-850), author of two extensive and very important works on liturgical matters: *De ecclesiasticis officiis* and *De ordine antiphonarii.* Published in *Patr. lat.* 105, pp. 985ff and 1243ff; also in J. M. Hanssens, *Amalarii episcopi opera omnia liturgica* (1948), vol. II (under the title *Liber officialis*) and vol. III.

19. Aurelianus of Réomé (mid-ninth century): *Musica disciplina. GS,* I, 27. An extended treatise containing, after a discussion of the Greek modes, a full explanation of the church modes with numerous examples (pp. 39-59), as well as a final chapter (*Caput XX*) about the liturgical position of the various chants.

20. Hucbald of St. Amand (near Valenciennes; *c.* 840-930): *De harmonica institutione. GS,* I, 104. Deals with the various intervals, citing examples from Introits, Responsories, etc.

6 *Patr. lat.* 78, pp. 726ff.

7 Recently a considerably earlier tonary, dating from *c.* 800, has been found. See M. Huglo, "Un Tonaire du Graduel de la fin du VIIIe siècle" (*RG,* XXXI, 224).

21. *Musica enchiriadis* (*c.* 900; formerly ascribed to Hucbald). *GS,* I, 152. This treatise, famous as the earliest source for polyphonic music, also contains important information pertinent to Gregorian chant, e.g., chromatic tones. The few melodies which it includes (in daseian notation) are the earliest that can be read.

22. *Alia musica* (formerly ascribed to Hucbald; *c.* 900). *GS,* I, 125ff; see W. Mühlmann, *Die Alia Musica,* 1914. This very confused treatise, often quoted in connection with the problem of the transition from the Greek scales to the church modes, also contains a more realistic description of the individual modes with examples from Gregorian chant, as well as a commentator's *Nova expositio* of the same matter. German translation of these two portions in Mühlmann, pp. 62-69 and 71-74.

23. *Commemoratio brevis de tonis et psalmis modulendis* (formerly ascribed to Hucbald; *c.* 900). *GS,* I, 213. Contains valuable information about the early stage of the psalm tones as well as a tonary which, though limited in scope, is important because the melodies, which are given with clearly readable musical notation (in daseian symbols), date from almost two hundred years before the earliest manuscripts with clearly readable neumes.

24. Regino [see no. 13]: *De harmonica institutione. GS,* I, 230. Contains an initial paragraph important for its references to *anomaliae modorum,* that is, Antiphons that do not fit within the modal system.

25. Oddo of Cluny [see no. 14]: *Dialogus de musica* (perhaps written by a pupil of Oddo). *GS,* I, 252. This treatise is important because it contains the earliest use of the modern scale letters (Oddonic letters), additional examples of anomalous chants, and detailed explanations of the ambitus of the various modes. German translation, by P. Bohn, in *Monatshefte für Musikgeschichte,* XII (1880), 24, 39.

E. Musical Manuscripts

The following list includes only those that have been published, for the most part, in the *Paléographie musicale (PM).*[8]

I. Graduals (*Antiphonale missarum*):

26. *Cod. 359 of St. Gall* (9th-10th century). *PM,* Second Series, vol. II; also P. Lambillotte, *Antiphonaire de S. Grégoire* (1851). This is a *Cantatorium,* containing only the solo chants of the Mass, the others (Introits, Offertories, Communions) being indicated only by their incipits.

27. *Cod. 239 of Laon* (10th century). *PM,* X.

28. *Cod. 339 of St. Gall* (10th century). *PM,* I.

29. *Cod. 47 of Chartres* (10th century). *PM,* XI.

30. *Cod. 121 of Einsiedeln* (10th century). *PM,* IV.

31. *Gradual of St. Yrieix* (*Cod. lat. 903* of the Bibl. nat., Paris; 11th century). *PM,* XIII.

[8] For fuller lists see, e.g., Gastoué, *Origines,* pp. 250ff; *Wagner II,* xiff; G. Suñol, *Introduction à la paléographie musicale grégorienne* (1935), pp. 640ff.

32. *Cod. H 159 of Montpellier* (11th century). *PM*, VIII. This is unique because it contains the chants of the Mass arranged according to modes
(hence the name *Antiphonarium tonale missarum*), and because the
melodies are notated in two ways; by means of staffless neumes and of
letters, each written in a separate row above the text (hence the name
bilingual *Gradual*).

33. *Beneventan Gradual* (*Cod. 10673* of the Vatican Library; early 11th
century). *PM*, XIV.

34. *Codex VI. 34 of Benevento* (11th-12th century). *PM*, XV.

35. *Ambrosian Gradual* (*Cod. 34209* of the British Museum; 12th century).
PM, V (facsimile) and VI (transcriptions). This is the earliest among the
few sources for Ambrosian chant.

36. *Gradual of Salisbury* (13th century). Ed. by W. H. Frere, *Graduale
Sarisburiense* (1894).

II. Antiphonals:

37. *Codex Hartker* (*Cod. 390-91* of St. Gall, 10th century). *PM*, Second Series,
vol. I. Named after the monk Hartker of St. Gall, who wrote this famous
manuscript.

38. *Cod. 601 of Lucca* (11th-12th century). *PM*, IX.

39. *Cod. f. 160 of Worcester* (13th century). *PM*, XII.

40. *Antiphonal of Salisbury* (13th century). Ed. by W. H. Frere, *Antiphonale
Sarisburiense* (1901-25).

THE CYCLE OF FEASTS

While in the pre-Gregorian era our knowledge is limited to a succession
of widely separated and often unrelated facts—small luminous points scat-
tered over a wide expanse of dark territory—we are now entering a period
in which documentation is considerably more comprehensive and coherent.
Although the emerging picture is far from being as complete as we would
like, it nevertheless shows fairly well defined contours and some clearly
recognizable lines of development. It seems advisable to divide the whole
field of investigation into three areas: the first, concerning the cycle of
feasts throughout the year; the second, dealing with the texts of the chants
for the Masses and Offices of these feasts; and the third, with the melodies
for these chants. The failure to distinguish clearly between these three
aspects of the development has caused numerous erroneous conclusions
on the part of the scholars or, at least, erroneous impressions among their
readers. We may be able to show that a certain feast existed in the fifth
century, but this fact in no way implies that the Mass for this feast consisted of the same Introit, Gradual, etc., as in the eighth century. Nor can
we take it for granted that, assuming it did have these items, they were
sung to the same melodies that we find, for the first time, in manuscripts
of the tenth or eleventh centuries. To assume that the Introit *Ad te levavi*

dates from the same time as the institution of the First Sunday of Advent would be gratuitous; to assume that its melody is of the same or of similar antiquity would be foolish.

The cycle of feasts as it existed at the time of Gregory is well known to us from liturgical books of the seventh and eighth centuries such as the *Sacramentaries, Lectionaries,* and *Evangeliaries.* Through careful examination and comparison of these sources liturgical scholars have been able to establish which feasts were celebrated at the time of Pope Gregory. The annual cycle consisted of a *Temporale* of *circa* ninety-five feasts and a *Sanctorale* of about sixty.

The *Temporale* covered the year so completely that only a few additions were made in subsequent centuries. It is generally assumed that before Gregory it was considerably less complete and that the form in which we find it about 600 is the result of Gregory's work. Thus he would fully deserve his legendary fame in the field of liturgical organization. This "Gregorian Temporale" is represented in our table of the liturgical year [pp. 9ff] by all feasts not marked by a letter. No losses ever occurred in it, but a number of additions were made, and these concerned, for the most part, a number of Sundays and Thursdays. The Sundays are those following the four Ember Weeks; in other words, the Fourth Sunday of Advent, the Second Sunday of Lent, the First Sunday after Pentecost, and the Sunday after the Ember Week of September. According to an old tradition, the Saturdays of Ember Weeks were the proper time for the ordinations of priests, a ceremonial which greatly lengthened the liturgy so that it lasted until early Sunday morning. The Mass was celebrated at the end of the ordinations, so that no Mass formulary for the Sunday was needed. It was not until after Gregory that this custom changed and that special Masses for the Sundays were introduced; first for the two Sundays after Pentecost, then for that in Advent, and finally, in the tenth century, for that of Lent. It is perhaps not without significance that the process of filling in these gaps (in the old books they are frequently marked: *Dominica vacat)* started with the period after Pentecost, which liturgically was of least significance.

As for the Thursdays, it should be noted that the *Temporale,* although it consists essentially of Sundays, also includes a number of more or less complete weeks with special Masses and Offices for all or some of their days. These are the four Ember Weeks, the half Week before *Quadragesima,* the five weeks after *Quadragesima* (to Palm Sunday), Holy Week (before Easter), Easter Week (after Easter), and Whitsun Week (after Whit Sunday). Originally, Thursday *(Feria V.)* was excluded from all these weeks. By the time of Gregory, only two of them included Thursday as a liturgical day, that is Holy Week (Maundy Thursday) and Easter Week. The five weeks of Lent were complete except for the Thursdays, and the four Ember

Weeks included only three liturgical days, Wednesday, Friday, and Saturday. The process of adding the Thursdays to the liturgical calendar started
with the six Thursdays of Lent, introduced by Pope Gregory II (715-31),
and came to its conclusion with the introduction, about 900, of the Thursday after Pentecost. It never affected the Ember Weeks. Two of the above-
mentioned weeks, that before *Quadragesima* and the fifth week of Lent,
also lacked the Saturdays, which were not added until the eleventh century.

A final group of accessions is formed by a number of special feasts;
namely, the Vigil (Eve, day before) of Ascension, Trinity Sunday, the Feast
of the Circumcision, the Rogation Days, Corpus Christi, and the Feasts
of the Holy Name, the Holy Family, and the Sacred Heart, the last three
being late accretions from the seventeenth or eighteenth century.

There remains the question as to when these various accessions to the
Temporale were introduced. In some cases, for instance, for the Thursdays
of Lent and for Corpus Christi, the dates are known. In other cases they
can be determined approximately by comparing the calendars of *Graduals*
from different centuries, which represent the liturgical year in successive
degrees of completeness. The following chronological list is based on the
Graduals of Monza, Compiègne, and St. Gall *339*,[1] which indicate the
state of affairs at about 750, 850, and 950 respectively. The feasts of each
group are marked in the table of the liturgical year (pp. 9ff) by the corresponding letters, a, b, c, d, and e.

ADDITIONS TO THE GREGORIAN TEMPORALE

A. 600-750 (additions found in the *Gradual of Monza*):
   Six Thursdays of Lent (*Sextuplex* nos. 38, 44, 50, 57, 64, 71). Introduced
      by Gregory II (715-31)

B. 750-850 (additions found in the *Gradual of Compiègne*):
   Fourth Sunday of Advent (*Sext.* no. 7 *bis*)
   Vigil of Ascension (*Sext.* no. 101 *bis*)[2]
   Rogation Days (*In Letania; Sext.* no. 94). Adopted in Rome *c.* 800[3]

C. 850-950 (additions found in St. Gall *339*):
   Trinity Sunday. The Mass formulary *De Sancta Trinitate* occurs for

---

1 For Monza and Compiègne, see the tables in Hesbert's *Sextuplex*; for St. Gall *339*, in
Wagner I, 280ff.

2 Still absent in the *Gradual* of Corbie (*Sextuplex*) as well as in the *Cantatorium* St.
Gall *359* (*Pal. mus.*, Second Series, I), both from the end of the ninth century.

3 The Litanies of the Rogation Days were introduced in Vienne as early as 470, under
the bishop Mamertus, and were widely celebrated in Gaul long before they were officially
adopted in the Roman rite. See *Sextuplex*, p. lxv, fn. 2.

the first time in the *Gradual of Senlis* which dates from the second half of the ninth century (*Sext.* no. 172 *bis*)[4]

Thursday in Whitsun Week

D. After 950 (feasts not included in St. Gall *339*):

Second Sunday of Lent

Saturday after Ash Wednesday

Saturday before Palm Sunday

The Circumcision of Our Lord

Corpus Christi. The liturgy was written by St. Thomas Aquinas (d. 1274), and the feast was universally introduced in 1264, under Pope Urban IV

E. After 1600:

The Holy Name of Jesus. Universally adopted in 1721 by Pope Innocent XIII

The Holy Family. Universally adopted by Pope Benedict XV (1914-22)

The Sacred Heart of Jesus. Approved by Pope Clement XIII in 1765, and universally adopted by Pius IX in 1859. In 1929 Pius XI introduced a new Office and Mass (Introit *Cogitationes*)

It remains for us to add a few remarks about the *Sanctorale*. This presents an infinitely more complex situation than the *Temporale* because of the numerous additions, deletions, and replacements that took place in the calendar of the Saints. It is impossible (and, in fact, unnecessary from our point of view) to indicate even the main outlines of this involved process. Suffice it to say that the original nucleus, at the time of Gregory, consisted of about sixty feasts for the Saints, that at the end of the ninth century it had increased to about one hundred, and that it continued to increase until it reached the present-day number of close to four hundred.[5] It may also be noticed that the entire Common of Saints, which contains services for groups (e.g., Martyrs, Virgins, Abbots) rather than for individuals, is a later arrangement, which begins to appear in the twelfth century.

As for details, we shall confine ourselves to a consideration of the feasts that were added during the seventh century, namely, the Dedication of a Church, the Feasts of the Virgin, and the Feasts of the Cross.

The Dedication of a Church [L 1241ff; G [71]] originated with the consecration, on May 13, A.D. 609, of the ancient Roman *Pantheon* as a

[4] See p. 8, fn. 6.

[5] For the Gregorian *Sanctorale* see Gastoué, *Origines*, pp. 257-270 (*c.* 50 feasts), and W. H. Frere, *The Sarum Gradual* (1895), pp. xxiiff (*c.* 60 feasts); for the period about 900, see *Sextuplex*, p. 254, and *Wagner I*, 280ff. The latter list gives a good survey of the increase in the number of feasts, since the post-Gregorian accretions are marked by parentheses.

Christian church, renamed *Basilica S. Mariae ad Martyres*. It is the earliest feast definitely known to be post-Gregorian.

As far as can be ascertained, no feast of the Virgin Mary existed at the time of Gregory, a fact all the more noteworthy since several female Saints, for example, S. Prisca, S. Agnes, S. Agatha, had special feasts as early as the third or fourth century. The first feast of the Virgin that was introduced, probably shortly after Gregory's death, was a *Natale S. Mariae*[6] celebrated on January 1, one week after Christmas [*Sext.* 16 *bis*], at the stational Church of St. Mary, and therefore called *Statio ad Sanctam Mariam*.[7] This disappeared in the tenth century, when it was replaced by the Feast of the Circumcision. The four feasts of the Virgin which attained permanent importance are: the Purification, on February 2; the Annunciation, on March 25; the Assumption, on August 15; and the Nativity, on Sept. 8. All of these were imported from the Greek Church, and already existed in the time of Pope Sergius I (687-701), who ordered that solemn processions should be held on each of these days.[8] Very likely, the Purification is the earliest of these feasts. Originally it was the feast of S. Simeon, commemorating the day when the aging Simeon, shortly before his death, went to the temple to embrace the child Jesus (Luke 2:26-29). The Communion, *Responsum accepit Simeon,* and the Tract *Nunc dimittis* (from the Canticle of Simeon; Luke 2:32) still remind us of the original meaning of the Feast of the Purification. The Feast of the Nativity of the B. V. M., although it existed in the seventh century, was not generally accepted until the eleventh century. It does not occur in the *Sextuplex* nor in St. Gall *359* or *339*.

Also of Greek origin are the two Feasts of the Cross, the Exaltation *(Exaltatio Crucis)* on September 14, and the Finding *(Inventio Crucis)* on May 3. The former existed already under Pope Sergius, while the latter seems to be of a somewhat more recent date. Both of them, however, were celebrated centuries earlier in Jerusalem and Constantinople.[9]

6 *Natale* (old term for *Nativitas*) does not necessarily mean "birth" but possibly also "death" (heavenly birth) or, as a rule, any feast in honor of the Saint. The old manuscripts indicate several *Natale S. Mariae* on different days.

7 Stational Church is the name for the old churches in Rome in which the pope used to celebrate Mass on a given day. In commemoration of this usage many Masses still carry designations such as Station at St. Mary Major (First Sunday of Advent and others), Station at St. John of the Lateran (Holy Saturday), Station at the Holy Cross in Jerusalem (Good Friday), etc. See G. Lefebvre, *Saint Andrew Daily Missal* (1945), pp. 69ff, with city plan of Rome. As mentioned before [p. 44], the Stational Churches of Rome were built in imitation of those at Jerusalem.

8 The statement, occasionally found, that the feasts themselves were introduced by Pope Sergius is not correct. Of the processions only that for Purification survived.

9 See *Sextuplex*, p. lxxxii. The Feast of the Finding of the Cross is mentioned by Etheria [see p. 40, no. 27].

THE MASS FORMULARIES

We shall now begin the discussion of the second aspect, that is, the texts of the musical items for the various feasts. At the outset it may be remarked that we have to limit ourselves to the Mass, because of the almost complete lack of information concerning the development of the items of the Office. First of all, sources are considerably more scarce in this field than in that of the Mass repertory. The earliest collection of Office chants (texts only) is found in the Manuscript of Compiègne (ninth century) which actually consists of a *Gradual* and an *Antiphonal*. Although the *Gradual* is included and examined in Hesbert's *Sextuplex*, the *Antiphonal*, available only in Migne's *Patrologia latina*,[1] has received practically no attention on the part of musico-liturgical scholars. Much better known is the tenth-century *Antiphonal* commonly referred to as the Codex Hartker, or the eleventh-century Codex Lucca and the *Antiphonals* of Worcester and Salisbury, both from the thirteenth century.[2] However, no attempt has been made in the direction of a detailed comparative study of these sources. Such a study would be immensely more laborious than that of the Mass chants, not only because of the much greater number of Office chants (in the Codex of Compiègne the *Gradual* comprises thirty folios, the *Antiphonal* seventy), but also because of the much greater variability that existed in this field.

Turning to the Mass, we find ourselves in a rather fortunate situation since manuscripts containing the Mass formularies—that is, the texts of the Proper chants of the Mass—occur as early as the eighth century. The most ancient of these, the *Codex Monza*, is a *Cantatorium*, containing only solo chants, Graduals, Alleluias, and Tracts. For the Introits, Offertories, and Communions we have to turn to the slightly later *Graduals* of Mont-Blandin, Compiègne, and the others now conveniently available in Hesbert's publication, which forms the basis of the subsequent study.

There is good reason to assume that the Mass formularies given in these sources are, on the whole, those of the Gregorian era. We have no positive proof of this, to be sure, and therefore the statement remains to a certain extent hypothetical. However, considering the highly authoritative character of the Gregorian reform, it is very unlikely that changes were made in the matters he had fixed. Although his role in the purely musical field has often been regarded as uncertain, few scholars have seriously questioned that he codified not only the liturgical year but also the Mass formularies for it. An internal argument, often adduced to "prove" Greg-

---

1 *Patr. lat.* 78, pp. 725-850.
2 See List of Sources [p. 56], nos. 37, 38, 39, 40.

ory's role as "father of the chant," carries much more weight in connection with the textual aspect of the Mass. It proceeds from the fact that almost all the texts of the Mass chants are taken from the earliest translation of the Bible, the *Itala* of the second and third centuries [see List of Data, p. 39, no. 8], not from the Vulgate of *c.* 400 [see *ibid.,* no. 31]. The latter, made by St. Jerome and supported by Pope Damasus, enjoyed uncontested authority in Rome and was universally used in all the churches about 600, as we know from the testimony of Isidore of Seville [see *ibid.,* no. 54]. It is therefore practically out of the question that Mass items with an *Itala* text could have been introduced after 600.[3]

A basic trait of the Gregorian Mass repertory is its stability, at least in the *Temporale.* It is a most interesting and rewarding experience to examine sources dating from widely different periods, a purely textual *Gradual* of the eighth or ninth century, a musical source of the twelfth, or the present-day books, and to find them in full agreement as to the Mass formularies of the various feasts. W. H. Frere has succinctly summed up the matter by saying that "fixity means antiquity,"[4] and this statement is fully borne out by a comparative study of the oldest extant Mass formularies, contained and conveniently arranged in the *Sextuplex* publication.[5] Actually, these Mass formularies show a few cases of variability; but these confirm rather than contradict Frere's statement, since nearly all of them occur in feasts which, although forming a part of the Gregorian *Temporale,* are nevertheless of "lesser antiquity." In fact, these cases are of particular interest since they permit us to set apart certain feasts that represent additions to a still older nucleus, additions that must have been made shortly before Gregory or, more likely, by him.

Particularly revealing in this respect are the Graduals of the four Ember Saturdays. Each of these days had four Graduals [see p. 29], but the Saturday in Ember Week of Advent is the only one for which they are given

---

3 An example is the Gradual from the First Sunday of Advent, which has the text: *Universi qui te expectant, non confundentur.* ℣. *Vias tuas, Domine, notas fac mihi: et semitas tuas edoce me* [320]. The Vulgate text is found in Ps. 24, ℣. 2 and 4 [1788]: *Etenim universi qui sustinent te non confundentur. Vias tuas, Domine, demonstra mihi: et semitas tuas edoce me.* Some of the texts of the Mass chants, particularly those borrowed from the Psalms, are taken, not from the *Itala,* but from Jerome's first translation (made in 338) which is very similar to the *Itala* and which is known as *Psalterium romanum,* because it was immediately introduced into the Roman liturgy by Pope Damasus. The Vulgate is Jerome's second translation, also known as *Psalterium gallicanum,* because it was first adopted in Gaul. Jerome's third translation, made directly from the Hebrew, was not adopted for liturgical use. Cf. C. Marbach, *Carmina Scripturarum* (1907), p. 33*. In this most valuable book the sources for all the scriptural chants of the liturgy are indicated.

4 *Graduale Sarisburiense,* p. x.

5 See the *Table par Genres,* pp. 231ff.

identically in all the manuscripts.[6] The other three Saturdays often carry only general indications such as "Resp. Grad. quatuor quale volueris dic ad hunc diem pertinentes" (say [i.e., sing] whichever four Graduals you wish that pertain to this day); it is therefore not to be wondered at that this early *ad libitum* practice led to a certain amount of disagreement when, at a later time, specific Graduals were selected. Also of interest is the fact that these selections were limited to a nucleus of five or six graduals and that, in the eleventh or twelfth century, those for the Ember Saturday of Pentecost were replaced by Alleluias. The following table shows the Graduals given in the Mss Rheinau, Senlis [see *Sextuplex* nos. 46, 111, 192; the other sources either omit the feast or have no specific indication of Graduals], St. Gall *359*, and St. Gall *339*.[7]

GRADUALS FOR EMBER SATURDAYS

	Rheinau	Senlis	St. Gall 359	St. Gall 339	Liber usualis
Lent	*Miserere mihi*	*Propitius*	*Protector*	*Dirigatur*	*Propitius*
	Esto mihi	*Protector*	*Dirigatur*	*Convertere*	*Protector*
	Oculi omnium	*Dirigatur*	*Propitius*	*Propitius*	*Convertere*
		Salvum fac	*Salvum fac*	*Salvum fac*	*Dirigatur*
		Convertere			
Pent.	no Mass given	no Graduals	Resp. iiii	*Propitius*	All. *Spiritus est*
		indicated	Gradualia[(a)]	*Protector*	All. *Spiritus ejus*
				Jacta cogitatum	All. *Dum complerentur*
				Ad Dominum	All. *Benedictus es*
Sept.	no Mass given	Resp. iiii	Resp. iiii	*Propitius*	*Propitius*
		Propitius	Gradualia[(b)]	*Protector*	*Protector*
		(others not		*Dirigatur*	*Convertere*
		indicated)		*Salvum fac*	*Dirigatur*

(a) later entry: All. *Emitte spiritum;* All. *Spiritus domini;* All. *Paraclitus;* All. *Veni sancte;* All. *Benedictus;* All. *Sancti spiritus.*
(b) later entry: Gr. *Propitius;* Gr. *Protector;* Gr. *Dirigatur;* Gr. *Salvum fac.*

Almost complete fixity exists in the Introits, Offertories, and Communions. A special case of great interest is that of the Communions for the weekdays of Lent, from Ash Wednesday to Palm Sunday. We have seen that the series of feasts during this period of five and a half weeks originally did not include any Thursday nor the Saturdays after Ash Wednesday and before Palm Sunday. If we disregard these later additions (as well as the Sundays which stand outside the series), and consider the Communions

[6] The *Graduals* of Monza and Rheinau have only three, the former omitting *Excita Domine,* the latter, *Domine Deus virtutum.* See *Sextuplex,* no. 7; also the explanatory remarks, p. xl.
[7] The contents of St. Gall *339* are given at the end of *Wagner I.*

of the remaining twenty-six Masses, a most interesting fact appears: their texts are taken in numerical order from the first twenty-six Psalms. These Communions offer the most striking example of unified organization in the entire Mass repertory. It is perfectly obvious that they were introduced simultaneously, perhaps under Gregory, and that they represent an intermediate layer between that of the Sundays (except for the Sunday after the Ember Days) and that of the Thursdays and the two Saturdays.

Actually, the original series of twenty-six Communions taken from Ps. 1 to 26 did not remain entirely unchanged. Even in the earliest *Graduals,* such as Mont-Blandin or Compiègne, as well as in all the later sources, five of these psalmodic texts are replaced by texts taken from the Gospel read on that day. These changes must have taken place some time between *c.* 600 and *c.* 800. At a still later time, a similar substitution was introduced for Monday in the First Week of Lent. This, being the third day in the series, still has its original Communion, *Voce mea,* from Ps. 3, in all the *Graduals* of the *Sextuplex* as well as in St. Gall *359* and *339.* In the later sources, however, it is universally replaced by the Communion *Amen dico vobis,* taken once more from the Gospel (Matthew 25:31-46) read on that day. The following table, although not complete,[8] will suffice to illustrate the principle of organization as well as the later deviations from it.

COMMUNIONS OF THE WEEKDAYS OF LENT

1. Feria IV. Cinerum	Qui meditabitur	Ps. 1	
2. Feria VI. p. Cin.	Servite Domino	Ps. 2	
3. Feria II. p. Dom. I.	Voce mea	Ps. 3	
later:	*Amen dico vobis*		Matt. 25
....	......	....	
8. Feria II. p. Dom. II.	Domine Dominus	Ps. 8	
....	......	....	
12. Sabbato p. Dom. II.	*Oportet te*		Luke 15
13. Feria II. p. Dom. III.	Quis dabit	Ps. 13	
....	......	....	
16. Feria VI. p. Dom. III.	*Qui biberit*		John 4
17. Sabbato p. Dom. III.	*Nemo te condemnavit*		John 8
18. Feria II. p. Dom. IV.	Ab occultis meis	Ps. 18	
....	......	....	
20. Feria IV. p. Dom. IV.	*Lutum fecit*		John 9
21. Feria VI. p. Dom. IV.	*Videns Dominus*		John 11
22. Sabbato p. Dom. IV.	Dominus regit me	Ps. 22	
23. Feria II. p. Dom. Pass.	Dominus virtutum	Ps. 23	
....	......	....	
26. Feria VI. p. Dom. Pass.	Ne tradideris	Ps. 26	

8 For the complete list see, e.g., *Wagner I,* 283ff; *Sextuplex,* p. xlvii. The weekdays of Lent are not included in the *Liber,* but are found in the *Graduale romanum.*

If considered within the ample framework of the Gregorian Mass items, the few changes described only serve to give additional support to the previous statement regarding the fixity of the old repertory. The only chants that do not at all conform with this principle are the Alleluias, as distinguished from each other by their different verses. In this category variability prevails to such an extent, not only in the oldest sources but also down to the thirteenth and fourteenth century, that there are probably no more than a dozen feasts in the *Temporale* which have the same Alleluia in all the manuscripts. One has to turn to such truly old feasts as the first three Sundays of Advent, Nativity, Easter Sunday, Ascension, and Whit Sunday in order to find fixed Alleluias. Great variation exists in Easter Week, as well as in the Sundays after Easter to the end of the year.[9] Several of the older sources simply prescribe for a number of feasts *Alleluia quale volueris* (whichever you wish), to be selected from a list of Alleluias added in an appendix.[10] All this clearly indicates that the Alleluias, at least in their final form with verses, represent a relatively late accretion to the Mass repertory. We know that in the fifth and sixth centuries the Alleluia was used very sparingly, at one time only once a year [see List of Data, no. 37], and that it was Gregory who made it a standard item of the Mass. While it is usually stated that he extended its use over the entire year [see List of Data, no. 47], there is reason to assume that he introduced it only for the period from Advent to Lent, and that its general adoption is of a still later date [see pp. 380f].

In addition to their fixity, the Gregorian Mass formularies are characterized by what may be called "properness," this term being understood to mean that there exist individual ("proper") items for each liturgical day; in other words, that items are not borrowed from one feast to serve for another. Actually, there are not a few cases of borrowing in the Gregorian *Temporale,* and at least some of these provide additional evidence for the distinction between an old nucleus and more recent (though still Gregorian) accretions. Thus the assumption of a relatively recent date for the Ember Saturdays of Lent [541], Pentecost [900], and September [1052] is confirmed by the fact that they all have the same Offertory, *Domine Deus salutis,* and the same Tract, *Laudate Dominum,* the latter originally from Holy Saturday [760] and also transferred to Whitsun Eve [860].

Even more remarkable in this respect are the Sundays after Pentecost, nearly all of which borrowed their Graduals and Offertories from the weekdays of Lent.[11] Following are some examples:

9 See the tables in *Wagner I,* 300 and *Sextuplex,* pp. lxiv, lxvii, lxxiii.

10 See *Sextuplex,* pp. cxix, 198.

11 G has the reverse indication of borrowing, giving the chants in full for the Sundays [e.g., G 321] and referring to them on the weekdays [e.g., G 121], because the former are liturgically more important than the latter.

Dom. II	Grad.	*Ad Dominum dum*	from Fer. VI. p. Dom. II Quad.
	Off.	*Domine convertere*	Fer. II. p. Dom. Pass.
Dom. III	Grad.	*Jacta cogitatum*	Fer. III. p. Dom. II. Quad.
	Off.	*Sperant in te*	Fer. III. p. Dom. V. Quad.
Dom. IV	Grad.	*Propitius esto*	Fer. IV. p. Dom. II. Quad.
	Off.	*Illumina oculos*	Sab. p. Dom. II. Quad.
Dom. V	Grad.	*Protector noster*	Fer. II. p. Dom. I. Quad.
	Off.	*Benedicam Dominum*	Fer. II. p. Dom. II. Quad.

Needless to say, transfers are quite frequent in the Alleluias. On the other hand, they are practically non-existent among the Introits and Communions, which, as we have seen, are remarkable for their fixity. All the above-mentioned feasts have new Introits and Communions, introduced at a time (probably very close to or under Gregory) when the Graduals and Offertories had already become a closed repertory which could be expanded only by transfers.

The principle of borrowing, which makes its appearance toward the end of the Gregorian period, assumed much greater importance in the post-Gregorian development. Indeed, in turning to the Mass formularies for the feasts that were introduced after Gregory [see pp. 58f], the most significant fact is that nearly every one of them borrowed its items from the Masses of older feasts. This fact clearly shows that after 600 the entire repertory was considered a fixed formulary which was expanded mainly by borrowing. The following list is designed to provide a detailed insight into this process (for the meaning of * see p. 69, under c).

BORROWING OF MASS ITEMS IN THE POST-GREGORIAN TEMPORALE

A. 600-750

1. *Feria V. post Cineres* [*Sext.* no. 38; G 91].

    | Intr. | *Dum clamarem* | Dom. X. post Pent. |
    | Grad. | *Jacta cogitatum* | Fer. III. p. Dom. II. Quad. |
    | Off. | *Ad te Domine levavi* | Dom. I. Adv. |
    | Comm. | *Acceptabis* | Dom. X. p. Pent. |

2. *Feria V. post Dominicam I. in Quadragesima* [*Sext.* no. 44; G 104].

    | Intr. | *Confessio* | S. Laurentii Martyris |
    | Grad. | *Custodi me* | Dom. X. p. Pent. |
    | Off. | *Immittet* | Dom. XIV. p. Pent. |
    | Comm. | *Panis quem* | Dom. XV. (orig. XIV.) p. Pent. |

3. *Feria V. post Dominicam II. in Quadragesima* [*Sext.* no. 50; G 120].

    | Intr. | *Deus in adjutorium* | Dom. XII. p. Pent. |
    | Grad. | *Propitius esto* | Sabb. Q. T. Quad. |
    | Off. | *Precatus est Moyses* | Dom. XII. p. Pent. |
    | Comm. | *Qui manducat* | Dom. IX. (orig. XV.) p. Pent. |

4. *Feria V. post Dominicam III. in Quadragesima* [*Sext.* no. 57; G 134].

Intr.	*Salus populi*	Dom. XIX. p. Pent.[12]
Grad.	*Oculi omnium*	Dom. XX. p. Pent. (and others; today for Corpus Christi)
Off.	*Si ambulavero*	Dom. XIX. p. Pent.
Comm.	*Tu mandasti*	Dom. XIX. p. Pent.

5. *Feria V. post Dominicam IV. in Quadragesima* [*Sext.* no. 64; G 146].

Intr.	*Laetetur cor*	Feria VI. Q. T. Sept.
Grad.	*Respice Domine*	Dom. XIII. p. Pent.
Off.	*Domine in auxilium*	Fer. VI. p. Dom. II. Quad.
Off.	**Domine ad adjuvandum*	new (in Mont-Blandin and Senlis)
Comm.	*Domine memorabor*	Dom. XVI. p. Pent.

6. *Feria V. post Dominicam Passionis* [*Sext.* no. 71; G 162].

Intr.	*Omnia quae*	Dom. XX. p. Pent.
Grad.	*Tollite hostias*	new (early 8th cent.; cf. *Sext.* p. lvi)
Off.	*Super flumina*	Dom. XX. p. Pent.
Comm.	*Memento verbi*	Dom. XX. p. Pent.

B. 750-850

7. *Dominica IV. Adventus* [*Sext.* no. 7 *bis;* G 21].[13]

Intr.	*Veni et ostende* (R)	Sabb. Q. T. Adv.
Intr.	*Memento nostri* (C, G₁)	new
Intr.	**Rorate caeli* (S)	Fer. IV. Q. T. Adv.
Grad.	*A summo celo* (R, G₁)	Sabb. Q. T. Adv.
Grad.	**Prope est* (C, S, G₂)	Fer. IV. Q. T. Adv.
Off.	*Exulta* (R)	Sabb. Q. T. Adv.
Off.	**Ave Maria* (C, S, G₁, G₂)	Fer. IV. Q. T. Adv.[14]
Comm.	*Exultavit* (R)	Sabb. Q. T. Adv.
Comm.	**Ecce virgo* (C, S, G₁, G₂)	Fer. IV. Q. T. Adv.

8. *In Vigilia Ascensionis* [*Sext.* no. 101 *bis;* G 284].

Intr.	*Omnes gentes* (C, S)	new[15]
Intr.	*Narrabo* (R)	new
Intr.	**Vocem jucunditatis*	Dom. V. p. Pascha

[12] Since the Mass formularies for the 19th and 20th Sundays after Pentecost may also be post-Gregorian [see p. 71], there could be some doubt as to the direction of borrowing, also for *Feria V. post Dominicam Passionis* (above table, no. 6). In view of the general situation, as shown in the table, the borrowing indicated is much more likely than the reverse. Probably the complete series of Mass formularies for the Sundays of Pentecost was completed (with one exception, the Mass *Omnes gentes*) about 700, shortly before the Thursdays of Lent were introduced, under Pope Gregory II (715-31).

[13] See the explanations below, under (c).

[14] Originally (seventh century) for the Feast of Assumption; cf. *Sextuplex,* pp. xxxviiif.

[15] The Introit *Omnes gentes* is also used for the Mass of the Seventh Sunday after Pentecost which, according to recent research, is the latest of all the Mass formularies of the post-Pentecost series [see p. 70]. The question whether the Introit was originally destined for this Sunday or for the Vigil of Ascension is discussed in an article by Hesbert, "La Messe *Omnes gentes*" (*RG,* XVII, XVIII), and resolved in favor of the latter.

Off.	*Viri Galilei* (*C, S*)	Ascensio Domini
Off.	*Deus deus meus* (*R*)	Dom. II. p. Pascha
Off.	**Benedicite gentes*	Dom. V. p. Pascha
Comm.	*Pater cum essem* (*R, S*)	Dom. infra Oct. Asc.
Comm.	*Non vos relinquam* (*C*)	Sabb. Q. T. Pent. (today Feria **VI. Q.** T. Pent.)
Comm.	**Cantate Domino*	Dom. V. p. Pascha

9. *In Litaniis* (Rogation Days) [*Sext.* no. 94; G 282].

Intr.	*Exaudivit de templo*	new
Off.	*Confitebor*	new
Comm.	*Petite et accipite*	new

C. 850-950

10. *In Festo Ss. Trinitatis* [*Sext.* no. 172 *bis;* G 308].

Intr.	*Benedicta sit*	new; after *Invocabit me* from Dom. I. in Quad. [G 93]
Grad.	*Benedictus es*	new; after *Constitues* from S. Andreae Apostoli [G 392]
Off.	*Benedictus sit*	new; after *Constitues* from SS. Apost. Petri et Pauli [G 532]
Comm.	*Benedicimus Deum*	new; after *Feci judicium,* originally from S. Prisca, now Commune Virginis [G 59]

11. *Feria V. post Pentecosten* [G 302].   all items borrowed from *Dominica Pentecostes*

D. After 950

12. *Dominica II. in Quadragesima* [G 111].
All items borrowed from *Fer. IV. Q. T. Quad.* [G 102][16]

13. *Sabbato post Cineres* [G 93].
All items borrowed from *Fer. VI. post Cineres* [G 91]

14. *Sabbato post Dominicam Passionis* [G 165].
All items borrowed from *Fer. VI. p. Dom. Pass.* [G 163]

15. *In Circumcisione Domini* [G 49].
All items borrowed from *In Die Nat. Dom.* [G 33]

16. *Corpus Christi* [G 313].

Intr.	*Cibavit eos*	Fer. II. p. Pent.
Grad.	*Oculi omnium*	Dom. XX. p. Pent. [see under no. 4]
Off.	*Sacerdotes*	new; after *Confirma hoc* from Dom. Pent. [G 295]
Comm.	*Quotienscumque*	new; after *Factus est* from Dom. Pent. [G 296]

16 Once more, the reverse borrowing is indicated in G. Beneventan manuscripts have a new, proper Mass formulary for this Sunday as well as for the two Saturdays, nos. 13, 14, of our list. See *Pal. mus.,* XIV, 234.

Since this table involves a fairly large number of items, it may be advisable to sum up some of its contents.

a. The main sources for borrowing are the Sundays after Pentecost. This is interesting because the individual Mass formularies for these Sundays represent a relatively late accretion which, in its final form of twenty-three Masses, was not completed until perhaps *c.* 800.[17] It would then appear that items of a fairly recent date were considered more readily transferable than those which for a long time had been associated with an old feast.

b. Next in importance as a source for borrowing are the weekdays of Lent.

c. A case of special interest is that of the Fourth Sunday of Advent, for which the Mass formularies from the immediately preceding Ember Days of Advent were drawn upon. The borrowing, however, was far from uniform, and we have thought it worthwhile to present a complete picture of the state of affairs as it existed in the ninth and tenth centuries. The letters *R, C, S, G*$_1$ and *G*$_2$, indicate respectively the *Graduals* of Rheinau, Compiègne, Senlis, St. Gall *359* and St. Gall *339*,[18] while items marked * are those of the later manuscripts and of the present-day books, which simply transfer the entire Mass of the Wednesday to the Sunday. It appears that here (as well as in many other cases) the Codex Rheinau represents an exceptional usage.

d. A similar situation exists for the Vigil of Ascension. Here also the borrowing is far from uniform. The two St. Gall Mss do not give a Mass for this feast. The late-medieval and present-day books simply prescribe the Mass of the Fifth Sunday after Easter.

e. The Mass for Rogation Days, a feast that was probably introduced in the eighth century, is remarkable because its Mass formulary is entirely new, a fact for which the very special character of the occasion provides a plausible explanation.

f. The Mass for Trinity Sunday, which probably dates from the second half of the ninth century, is interesting because it is the first indication of another procedure to provide Masses for new feasts, that is, to use new texts suitable for the occasion and combine these with pre-existing melodies. This method, known as adaptation, was also used for the Offertory and the Communion of the twelfth-century feast of Corpus Christi, and was extensively employed in the nineteenth century (Dom Pothier and others) in connection with feasts of a recent date such as the Feast of the Holy Name of Jesus:

[17] See p. 71.
[18] The other *Graduals* of the *Sextuplex* do not include this feast.

In Festo Ss. Nominis Jesu [G 50]

Intr.	*In nomine Jesu*	new; after *In nomine Domine* from Fer. IV. Majoris Hebd. [G 190]
Grad.	*Salvos fac*	new; after *Benedicite Dominum* from In Dedicatione S. Michaelis [G 608]
Off.	*Confitebor tibi*	new; after *Jubilate Deo universa* from Dom. II. p. Epiph. [G 69]
Comm.	*Omnes gentes*	new; after *Domine memorabor* from Dom. XVI. p. Pent. [G 365]

g. A special explanation is needed for the Sundays after Pentecost, a series of feasts that underwent many changes and which has been the subject of numerous studies on the part of liturgists as well as musicologists. How involved the problem is appears from the fact that only a few years ago, in 1952, it was re-examined by A. Chavasse on the basis of all the available sources, such as *Sacramentaries, Lectionaries,* and *Graduals.*[19] In its final form, the series consisted of twenty-three formularies, a different one for each of the minimum number of Sundays after Pentecost. This stage was reached shortly before 800, as appears from the fact that the full series is found in the *Graduals* of Corbie and Senlis. In earlier centuries, however, it was less complete. The Gelasian *Sacramentary,* which goes back to a period a hundred years before Gregory [see List of Sources, p. 53, no. 2], contains prayers for sixteen Masses only. Very likely the corresponding musical items were those of Masses nos. 1 to 6 and 8 to 17 of the final series, Mass no. 7, with the Introit *Omnes gentes,* being a considerably later addition. An important characteristic of this original nucleus is that all of its Introits and Graduals have psalmodic texts, and that those of the Introits strictly preserve the order of the Psalter, beginning with Ps. 12, 17, 24, etc. The same principle of ascending numerical order prevails in the Offertories and Communions which, however, include a few non-psalmodic texts.[20]

To these sixteen Mass formularies, which can be considered as pre-Gregorian, Gregory added two; four more were added during the seventh century, so that about 700 the series numbered twenty-two. The last addition, made in the eighth century, was the Mass *Omnes gentes* which, according to recent research, is of Frankish origin and was not used in Rome until the thirteenth century.[21] In fact, this is the only Mass in the entire series concerning which the old *Graduals* show variation: some lack it completely (e.g., the Codex Monza and the Old-Roman *Graduals*); others

---

19 A. Chavasse, "Les plus anciens types du lectionnaire et de l'antiphonaire romains de la messe" (*Revue Bénédictine,* LXII [1952], 3-94).

20 For more details, see pp. 91 ff.

21 See Hesbert, "La Messe *Omnes gentes*" (*RG,* XVII and XVIII).

list it as no. 22; still others have it in two positions, as no. 7 and 22, while the majority have it only as no. 7.

As for the remaining Masses of the Pentecost series, that is, nos. 18 to 23, there is a certain probability that the two Masses added by Gregory were nos. 18 and 19, but no definite information about this seems to exist. Whichever they were, they do not seem to present special features distinguishing them from the other four.

Finally it should be noticed that the rather blurred picture of the post-Pentecost Masses is further complicated by a purely liturgical factor, that is, the presence within this period of two Ember Weeks. As was previously explained [p. 57], the Sundays after these Ember Weeks, that is, the first and (normally) the eighteenth in the series, were originally without a Mass formulary of their own, so that the series started on the second Sunday after Pentecost. At a later time, when the old tradition was changed, no new Mass formularies were introduced; the series was simply shifted back, so that the Mass for the Second Sunday became that of the First,[22] and those for the end of the series (if they already existed at that time) were employed two weeks earlier than originally. Unfortunately, we have no information as to the approximate time when this took place, except that it was completed before *c.* 750, as appears from the fact that in the Codex Monza the series starts with the First Sunday. Assuming, for the purpose of illustration, that the filling-in took place early in the seventh century and that the Ember Week of September falls between the Sundays XVII and XVIII, the various shifts can be illustrated as follows (the Masses are identified by their present-day numbers):

Sundays	A	B	C	D	E
I	*vacat*	*vacat*	1	1	1
II to VII	1 to 6	1 to 6	2 to 6; 8	2 to 6; 8	2 to 7
VIII to XVII	8 to 17	8 to 17	9 to 18	9 to 18	8 to 17
XVIII	....	*vacat*	19	19	18
XIX, XX	....	18, 19	....	20, 21	19, 20
XXI, XXII	....	....	....	22, 23	21, 22
XXIII	....	....	....	....	23

A. Before Gregory: 16 Mass formularies; 2 Sundays *vacat*
B. Under Gregory: 18 Mass formularies; 2 Sundays *vacat*
C. After Gregory: 18 Mass formularies; no Sundays *vacat*
D. *C.* 700: 22 Mass formularies; no Sundays *vacat*
E. *C.* 800: 23 Mass formularies; no Sundays *vacat*

We turn finally to a brief consideration of the Mass formularies for the feasts of the Saints. In its general aspect, the *Sanctorale* differs from the

[22] Eventually replaced by Trinity Sunday. The original Mass formulary for *Dom. I. p. Pent.*, now used on the next free weekday, is suppressed in *L,* but given in *G* 310.

Temporale by its considerably lesser degree of fixity and properness, even in its early portion as it existed before and under Gregory. Not infrequently the same formulary or, at least, the same item is prescribed in different manuscripts for different Saints, or in one and the same manuscript for a number of Saints. Nearly always, however, such variability is confined to Saints of the same rank or category. It will suffice to mention two examples, the Gradual *Dilexisti* and the Gradual *Gloriosus.* The former occurs in the Masses for three female Saints, S. Lucia, S. Pudentiana, and S. Praxedis, while the latter is prescribed for several feasts of two Saints—SS. Fabian and Sebastian, SS. Gervasius and Protasius, SS. Abdon and Sennen, SS. Felix and Adauctus, and SS. Dionysius and Rusticus. This practice is of interest because it foreshadows and represents the root of the formation of the Common of Saints, which began in the twelfth century. In fact, both the above mentioned Graduals now belong to the Common of Saints, *Dilexisti* being the Gradual of the Mass for a Virgin Martyr [1216], *Gloriosus* that of the Mass for Two Martyrs [1163].[23]

As for the post-Gregorian *Sanctorale,* we shall consider only those feasts which were introduced shortly after Gregory, that is, the Dedication of a Church, the Feasts of the Cross, and the Feasts of the Virgin. The Mass for the Dedication [1250], the earliest feast definitely known to be post-Gregorian (A.D. 608), is entirely new, and is often cited in modern writings as evidence that the "creative period," usually supposed to have come to its conclusion under Gregory, extended three or four years after his death (A. D. 604). As a matter of fact, creation continued sporadically through out the seventh and eighth century, as will be seen from our table of the post-Gregorian Temporale [pp. 66ff]. This contains a complete Mass, that for Rogation Days, and a number of single Mass items which, at least to the best of our knowledge, are "new."

The Masses for the two Feasts of the Cross are to a certain extent identical, and are largely borrowed from Maundy Thursday:

Exaltation and Finding of the Cross [1629, 1454]

Intr.	*Nos autem* (Exalt. and Find.)	Maundy Thursday
Grad.	*Christus factus* (Exalt.)	Maundy Thursday
All.	*Dulce lignum* (Exalt. and Find.)	new
All.	*Dicite in gentibus* (Find.)	Friday in Easter Week
Off.	*Dextera Domini* (Find.)	Maundy Thursday
Off.	*Protege Domine* (Exalt.)	new
Comm.	*Per signum* (Exalt. and Find.)	new

23 It may be noticed that most of the Mass items of the old *Sanctorale* have been transferred to the Common of Saints which, therefore, represents an ancient layer of the chant, while the Proper of Saints includes numerous chants of a late medieval date and even modern compositions (Pothier).

The original Communion for both feasts was *Nos autem gloriari opor-tet*. This was borrowed from the Mass for Tuesday in Holy Week, in which, however, it was at an early date replaced by the present-day Communion, *Adversum me*.[24]

The Masses for the four (originally five) Feasts of the Virgin present an interesting process of borrowing and exchange. The original material came from the Feast of S. Agnes on January 21 [*Sextuplex* no. 25; *G* 416; *L* 1339] and its Octave on January 28 [*Sextuplex* no. 28; *G* 421]. Their items provided the material for the old *Statio ad S. Mariam*, for the new feasts of the Virgin, as well as, at a later time, for the Commons of a Virgin [1215, 1220, 1225]. The details are shown in the following table.

MASSES FOR THE FEASTS OF THE B.V.M.

1. Statio ad S. Mariam [*Sext.* no. 16 *bis* and 23 *bis*]

Intr.	*Vultum tuum*	S. Agnes, Octave
Grad.	*Diffusa est*	S. Agnes
Off.	*Offerentur* (now *Afferentur*)	S. Agnes
Comm.	*Simile est*	S. Agnes, Octave

2. Purification [*Sext.* no. 29; *G* 428; *L* 1361]

Intr.	*Suscepimus*	Eighth Sunday after Pentecost
Grad.	*Suscepimus*	new
Off.	*Diffusa est*	S. Agnes, Octave
Comm.	*Responsum accepit*	new

3. Annunciation [*Sext.* no. 33; *G* 461; *L* 1415]

Intr.	*Vultum tuum*	S. Agnes, Octave
Grad.	*Diffusa est*	S. Agnes
Off.	*Ave Maria*	new
Comm.	*Ecce virgo*	Fer. IV. Q. T. Adv. [*G* 11], transferred to Fourth Sunday of Advent [356]

4. Assumption [*Sext.* no. 140; *G* 582; *L* 1601][25]

Intr.	(originally) *Vultum tuum*	S. Agnes, Octave
	(later) *Gaudeamus*	S. Agatha
Grad.	*Propter veritatem*	from a *Natale S. Mariae* represented only in Cod. Monza [*Sext.* no. 144 *bis*]
Off.	*Assumpta est*	new; after *Angelus Domini* from Easter Monday
Comm.	*Optimam partem*	new

5. Nativity [not in *Sext.*; *G* 593; *L* 1624]

Intr.	*Salve sancta*	new; after *Ecce advenit* from Epiphany
Grad.	*Benedicta et venerabilis*	new; after *Domine praevenisti*, originally Eve of St. John, now for the Common of Feasts of the B.V.M.

24 See *Sextuplex* nos. 97 *bis* and 150.

25 An entirely new Mass for Assumption was adopted in 1952, in connection with the definition of the dogma of the Assumption of the Virgin.

Off.   *Beata es Virgo*   new; freely after *Angelus Domini*
Comm.   *Beata viscera*   new[26]

Further details regarding the formation of the post-Gregorian Sancto-rale are beyond the scope of this book. In order to illustrate some of the processes involved, it may be mentioned that the Mass for St. George the Martyr became the Mass for the Common of One Martyr in Paschal Time [1146], while that of SS. Abdon and Sennen, two third-century martyrs of Persian origin, was transferred to the Common of Two Martyrs [1162], ex-cept for the Communion, *Posuerunt,* now used for the Mass of the Vigil of the Apostles Simon and Jude [G 644]. This Mass originally had a dif-ferent Communion, *Justorum animae,* which is now used for the Octave of SS. Peter and Paul [1547].[27]

THE MUSIC

From its inception the development that has just been traced in its liturgical and textual aspects was accompanied by music. Every writer who mentions the Psalms, whether Pope Clement in the first century, St. Athanasius in the third, or the abbess Etheria in the fourth, states that they were sung; and probably as early as the fifth century there existed an *annalis cantus,* a cycle of chants for the entire year which may have in-cluded Antiphons, Responsories, and other items of a musical nature. What do we know about the melodies that were used for the delivery of these texts? From our point of view this is the most interesting, the most burning of all the questions pertaining to the development of the Roman liturgy. Unfortunately, it is also the most difficult to answer.

We may begin with an attempt at a critical evaluation of the evidence mentioned at a previous occasion (p. 48), according to which the ec-clesiastical chant of the Roman Church goes back to Pope Gregory. The most obvious objection that can be—and has been—raised against this evidence is that it is not contemporary and therefore lacks documentary value: the earliest witness, Bishop Egbert, lived 150 years after Gregory. However, the admission of nothing but contemporary documentation would invalidate practically all our source material concerning the early history of the liturgy and the chant. In fact, one may wonder what would become of medieval research in general—and not only medieval—if such a rigid and somewhat pedantic yardstick were used. We may well admit

26 According to Gastoué, *Origines,* p. 269, fn. 6, all the chants of this Mass are "adapta-tions postérieurs," but I have been unable to find a model for the Communion *Beata viscera* [1268], except for an identical beginning in the Communion *Quicumque fecerit* [G 456] from the feast of SS. *Quadraginta Martyrum,* originally of SS. *Septem Fratrum* [*Sextuplex* no. 126].

27 For more details, see *Wagner I,* 178, fn. 1.

that there is sufficient documentation to warrant the assumption that a *liber antiphonarius* of Gregory did exist. The main difficulty, it seems to me, is one, not of documentation but of interpretation. What was this book like, and in which relationship does it stand to the earliest *Antiphonals* that are preserved? Can we assume that it had music in some primitive sort of notation? This is very doubtful indeed, since as late as the eighth and ninth centuries *Antiphonaries* included only the texts. Moreover, Isidore of Seville, who lived about 30 years after Gregory (*c.* 570-636) says that "unless the musical sounds are retained by the human memory, they perish, because they cannot be written down" (*Nisi enim ab homine memoria teneantur soni, pereunt, quia scribi non possunt; Patr. lat.* LXXXII, 163). Obviously, no notation existed at that time. But even regardless of whether "Gregory's" melodies were notated or orally transmitted, what reason do we have to assume that they were the same as those known to us from the extant musical sources?

The earliest manuscripts showing the melodies in a clearly readable notation (diastematic neumes) date from the mid-eleventh century. However, there exist manuscripts of the tenth century [see List of Sources, nos. 26-30] which enable us to trace the melodies back to a considerably earlier time. Extended comparative studies have shown that the staffless neumes of these sources fully agree with the diastematic neumes of the later sources as to type (e.g., ascending or descending), number of notes, grouping in extended melismas, etc. Clearly, the melodies are the same, although the possibility of minor changes, concerning ornamentations or the pitch of this or that note, will have to be admitted.[1] On the whole we are justified in assuming that the majority of the melodies existed about 900 or 850 in nearly the same form as they appear in the later medieval sources and in the present-day publications. We might well be satisfied with this state of affairs, were it not for the fact that we have considerably earlier documentation for the existence of the texts, and even earlier evidence for the feasts. We have seen that the former can be traced back to the middle of the eighth century, the latter at least to the time of Gregory. It has always been the aim of musical scholars to match this record, and to show or, more properly speaking, to maintain that the melodies are equally old, except for those that are connected with post-Gregorian feasts.

Obviously, this argument proceeds from the premise that the development of the liturgical calendar, of the liturgical texts, and of the liturgical music are strictly synchronous phenomena, in other words, that the permanent institution of a certain feast entails and insures equal permanence of the texts and the melodies that were originally used. Actually this is a highly uncertain and, in fact, entirely unwarranted premise. In spite of

[1] Such changes are demonstrable particularly in the Communions, which are often classified differently in the various tonaries. See pp. 167ff.

the close relationship that, no doubt, existed between the various layers of the liturgy, it would be nothing more than wishful thinking to assume that a liturgical melody is necessarily as old as the text to which, or the feast at which, it is sung. By its very nature a liturgical calendar has a much higher degree of fixity than a collection of prayers or other texts for the Masses and Offices, and this, in turn, has an incomparably higher degree of fixity than a collection of melodies, at least in a period in which, to the best of our knowledge, the preservation of music was exclusively a matter of oral tradition. It is entirely unthinkable that a collection of melodies even approximating the size and elaborateness of the "Gregorian" repertory could have been transmitted—to say nothing of "preserved"—orally over two or three centuries. The truly Gregorian and, even more, any pre-Gregorian repertory must have been of a much more elementary character. Possibly the melodies even for a Gradual were of a very simple type; possibly only one or a few melodies served for all Graduals; possibly the melodies were not fixed at all or only in their main outlines, much being left to improvisation; possibly only the Psalms and other basic scriptural texts had a musical delivery regulated to some extent by tradition: it is idle to speculate about these matters. If we rely on evidence rather than on wishful thinking or fantasy we cannot but admit that we know nothing about the liturgical melodies until we approach the period from which we have the earliest musical manuscripts, that is, the end of the ninth century.

Naturally, we cannot assume that the earliest musical manuscript that has come down to us from these remote times was actually the earliest ever written. The highly complex and intricate notation of a manuscript such as St. Gall *359* [see pp. 120f] marks it beyond doubt as one that was preceded by others, now lost. On the other hand, it is very unlikely that a fully developed system of neumatic notation existed long before the year 850. Otherwise it would be difficult to explain why all the eighth- and ninth-century *Graduals* (those of the *Sextuplex* publication) are written without music, or why such a thorough treatise as Aurelian's *Musica disciplina* (*c.* 850) lacks a chapter on notation. Only in his chapter XIX, dealing with the problem of distinguishing between high and low tones in the verses, does Aurelian mention the terms *acutus accentus* and *circumflexio,* thus indicating that he is still concerned with a primitive system of ekphonetic notation which may have served fairly well for simple recitation formulae, but was totally inadequate for the written fixation of such elaborate melodies as are recorded in St. Gall *359.* Thus it would appear that the evolution of neumatic notation can hardly have begun much earlier than 800. All in all, it is safe to say that paleographic evidence permits us to trace the Gregorian melodies back to the period around 800, and to think of them as having received their final form during the century from *c.* 750 to 850.

To sum up: it is a matter of scientific caution and prudence to assign
to the liturgical melodies, as we have them, a considerably later date than
has generally been done before. True enough, caution and prudence are
negative rather than positive virtues, preventing us from committing mis-
takes rather than helping us to establish the truth. In the present case,
however, they seem to have the latter property as well. Within the past few
years the Gregorian question has once more been scrutinized by various
scholars with entirely novel and most interesting results. Although the
results vary, they all agree in one aspect, that is, to assign to the "Gregorian" melodies a post-Gregorian date of origin.

About five years ago, B. Stäblein presented a theory proceeding from two
facts, both known for about fifty years but now for the first time brought
into close relationship.[2] The first of these is that the famous list of men who
"edited an *annalis cantus*" [see p. 47; Stäblein considers it as the work of
John the Archicantor] does not close with Gregory. There follows not only
Pope Martinus (649-53), but also, after him, three abbots of St. Peter's in
Rome—Catolenus, Maurianus, and Virbonus—whose activity in the field
of the cantus annalis is mentioned with especially distinctive words of
praise, "diligentissime," "nobile," and "magnifice."[3] The second fact is
that there exist, in addition to the numerous manuscripts of "Gregorian
chant," four (or possibly more) manuscripts of the eleventh to thirteenth
centuries which contain essentially the same liturgical repertory but with
noticeably different melodies. These form a striking contrast to all the
other sources in which the melodies, except for occasional minor variants,
are absolutely identical. Dom Mocquereau, who was the first to call attention to this special group of manuscripts,[4] considered and dismissed them
as variants from a decadent epoch. This assumption, however, is contradicted by the fact that their liturgical repertory is that of the oldest sources,
excluding, as it does, the feasts that were added in the ninth, tenth, and
later centuries. Dom Andoyer was the first to maintain that these special
manuscripts contain a musical repertory which, far from being "decadent,"
is actually older than the standard repertory commonly referred to as
Gregorian. He therefore designated it as "pre-Gregorian."[5] For the purpose of non-committal reference we shall distinguish the two repertories
as the "standard" and the "special."

[2] See "Zur Entstehung der gregorianischen Melodien" (*KJ*, XXXV, 5); "Zur Frühgeschichte des römischen Chorals" (*ACI*, p. 271); article "Choral" (*MGG*, II, 1272ff).

[3] *Catolenus abba, ibi deserviens ad sepulchrum sancti Petri, et ipse quidem annum
circuli cantum diligentissime edidit; post hunc quoque Maurianus abba, ipsius sancti
Petri apostoli serviens, annalem suum cantum et ipse nobile ordinavit; post hunc vero
domnus Virbonus abba et omnem cantum anni circuli magnifice ordinavit* (*Patr. lat.*
138, p. 1346; reprinted in Gastoué, *Origines*, p. 110, fn.3). Cf. Data, nos. 55, 56.

[4] *Pal. mus.*, II, 4, fn. 1. See the musical example on pp. 6ff.

[5] "Le Chant romain antégrégorien" (*RCG*, XX, 69, 107).

Stäblein (in common with all modern scholars) agrees with Andoyer's conclusion that the special repertory is older than the standard repertory, but changes their relative historical positions from "pre-Gregorian" and "Gregorian" to "Gregorian" and "post-Gregorian." According to him, the standard repertory is the work of the above-named abbots Catolenus, Maurianus and Virbonus, whom he believes to have been active between 653 and 680. This period coincides with the rule of Pope Vitalian (657-72), and Stäblein adduces some additional evidence for musical activity under this pope.[6] He concludes that the special repertory represents the chant that was used in Rome shortly before and at the time of Gregory, and that half a century later, under Pope Vitalian, the melodies received the form in which we find them in the standard repertory. He distinguishes the two versions as Old-Roman and New-Roman, associating the former with the service in the Basilica of the Lateran, the latter with that in the Papal palace.[7]

Stäblein's provocative theory is a most important contribution, because it once more brings the Gregorian problem into the open. I do not, however, believe that it represents the final answer. A weak spot is the *terminus ad quem* for the activity of the three Roman abbots, the year 680. This date is based on Silva-Tarouca's theory that the list of musical popes and abbots was written by John the Archicantor, a theory which is no longer considered tenable [see p. 46, fn. 1]. However, even if we admit Stäblein's dates as approximately correct, the main difficulty is not removed: we are still faced with a gap of 200 years between origin and written fixation—in other words, we still have no way of knowing what relationship the "Vitalian" melodies had to those that have been transmitted. Even greater difficulties exist with the Old-Roman repertory, if this is supposed to represent the true "Gregorian" chant. Here the gap amounts to almost 500 years, since the earliest manuscript containing the Old-Roman melodies is dated 1071.

A more promising avenue of investigation is suggested by a recent article, "Le chant 'vieux-romain'," by M. Huglo [*Sacris erudiri* VI (1954), 96], at the end of which he suggests the possibility that the two repertories might be representatives, not primarily of different periods, but of different locales. This remark may well turn out to be of crucial importance. It is highly significant that the manuscripts containing the special repertory are all of Roman origin, having been written for local churches such as St. Cecilia and the Lateran. Thus there can be no doubt that we are in the

---

6 Ekkehard V of St. Gall (fl. *c.* 1200) speaks of *cantores Vitaliani*. Radulph de Rivo (fl. *c.* 1400; dean of Tongern, near Liége), the last liturgist of the Middle Ages, says that both Gregory and Vitalian "received the Roman chant" (*cantum romanum receperunt;* see *MGG*, II, 1272).

7 See *ACI*, p. 275.

presence of a chant that originated and was mainly employed in Rome and therefore is properly called Roman Chant.

As for the early sources of the standard repertory (that is, of "Gregorian" chant), it has often been noticed, though only grudgingly admitted, that none of them was written in Rome or, for that matter, in Italy. They all come from such places in Western Europe as St. Gall, Metz, Einsiedeln, Chartres, Laon, and Montpellier, in other words, from the Franco-German empire. Surely this fact is also of the highest significance, particularly in connection with—or in contrast to—the exclusively Roman origin of the special sources. It leads to the conclusion that the standard repertory is of Frankish origin or, at least, that it received its final form—the only one known to us—in places of the West.

There is, indeed, a great deal of historical evidence in support of the view that what we call "Gregorian chant" represents an eighth-to-ninth-century fusion of Roman and Frankish elements. This fusion is of particular interest because of its political implication and motivation: it was one of the chief means by which the Frankish rulers tried to strengthen their relationship with the Church of Rome. The main events were:[8]

1. In 752-3 Pope Stephen II visited Gaul, accompanied by Roman clergy who celebrated Mass according to the Roman usage. Pepin (752-68), father of Charlemagne, determined to gain the support of the pope by introducing the Roman usage in his kingdom, in place of the old Gallican rites.

2. In 753, bishop Chrodegang of Metz was sent by Pepin to Rome and, upon his return, established the Roman use in the cathedral of Metz.

3. About 760, Pope Paul I sent to Pepin, upon the latter's request, an *Antiphonale (Gradual)* and a *Responsale (Antiphonal)*.

4. Charlemagne (768-814) issued numerous decrees designed to promote the introduction of the *cantus Romanus* and to protect it against becoming "corrupt."

5. *C.* 825 the abbot Wala from the monastery of Corbie went to Rome and received a copy of a Roman *Antiphonal* revised by Pope Hadrian (772-95).

6. In 831 or 832 Amalarius of Metz went to Rome in order to obtain an authentic Antiphonary. The pope (Gregory IV) informed him that he had none to spare, but referred him to the one at Corbie. Upon his return to France, Amalarius went to Corbie and found, to his great surprise, that it differed from the usage of Metz: "I compared the above-mentioned volumes [of Corbie] with our antiphonaries and I found them different not only in their [liturgical] order but also in their words and

[8] See, e.g., R. van Doren, *Étude sur l'influence musicale de l'abbaye de Saint-Gall* (1925), pp. 34ff.

in the great number of responsories and antiphons which we do not sing."[9]

One thing is certain: the efforts to introduce the Roman usage into the Frankish empire met with the strong resistance of the Gallican clergy and brought about a great confusion. The reports about Charlemagne's attempts to protect the *cantus Romanus* against becoming corrupt speak eloquently enough. Equally illuminating—if we may use such a word in this connection—are the reports about the various liturgical books (probably without musical notation) that were brought from Rome to France, one in 760 to Metz, the other in 825 to Corbie, obviously in order to bring about greater conformity with the Roman use. Yet, when Amalarius studied the book of Corbie, he found that it differed in many respects from the liturgy of Metz. How can we explain this? One explanation would be that the change took place in Rome, in other words, that the book sent to Metz was an Old-Roman, the one sent to Corbie a New-Roman (standard repertory, "Gregorian"). However, Huglo has shown conclusively that the Corbie book was of the Old-Roman type.[10] Perhaps a more plausible explanation is that Amalarius based his comparison, not on the book sent to Metz in 760, but on more recent Messine *Antiphonals* that already incorporated numerous changes. How confused the situation became appears from an interesting passage in Amalarius' *Liber de ordine antiphonarii* concerning the difference between the Roman and the Frankish use of Gospel Antiphons after the Feast of Dedication [ed. Hanssens, III, 99]:

> Deus scit si isti [Romani] fallant, aut si ipsi [nostri magistri] fefellissent qui gloriati sunt se eas [antiphonas de evangelio] percepisse a magistris Romanae ecclesia, aut si Romani propter incuriam et neglegentiam eas amisissent aut si nunquam cantassent eas.
>
> (God knows whether the Romans are in error; or whether our masters have erred, who boast of having learned the Gospel Antiphons from the masters of the Roman Church; or whether the Romans have omitted them because of carelessness and negligence; or whether they have never sung them.)

If even a contemporary observer like Amalarius despaired over the confused situation, how can we ever hope to untangle it?

One other thing is certain: although the Roman rite emerged from this struggle victorious, it certainly did not emerge unscathed or intact. Liturgical scholars have long been fully aware of this fact. Thus, J. A. Jungmann, in his standard work, *The Mass of the Roman Rite* (*Missarum Solemnia*), discussing the Roman Mass in France, says (p. 76): "Unconsciously of course, but nonetheless surely, profound alterations were made from the

---

[9] See Huglo, in *Sacris erudiri*, VI, 120.
[10] See *Sacris erudiri*, VI, 120ff.

very outset in the Roman liturgy, especially in the Roman Mass—in fact, fundamental transformations. The exotic seedling, when planted in a new soil and in a new climate, was still pliant enough to be reshaped and modified by these influences." And later (p. 95): "Thus we come to that episode which proved to be of such incalculable importance for the entire subsequent history of the Roman liturgy. About the middle of the tenth century the Roman liturgy began to return in force from Franco-Germanic lands to Italy and to Rome, but it was a liturgy which meanwhile had undergone radical changes and a great development. This importation entailed supplanting the local form of the Roman liturgy by its Gallicized version, even at the very center of Christendom."

It would be more than wishful thinking to assume that during this process of profound alterations in the liturgy the melodies remained unchanged.[11] Yet it is to the West that we owe the written fixation and preservation of what is now called "Gregorian chant." The conclusion is almost inescapable that this chant, as found in the manuscripts of St. Gall, Einsiedeln, Metz, Chartres, etc., received its final form in France, in the period about 800, a form that differed considerably from its Roman model. A very interesting confirmation of this state of affairs exists in the report of an anonymous monk of St. Gall who, about 885, speaks of the "exceedingly large difference between our chant and that of Rome" and tells us that, through the endeavours of a singer whom Charlemagne had sent to Rome for instruction and later assigned to the cathedral of Metz, the chant spread over all France, "so that it is even now called *ecclesiastica cantilena Metensis*.[12] Moreover, the non-Roman character of the Mss of St. Gall,

[11] There exist a number of reports which, taken together, give an interesting picture of the altercations and frictions between Roman and Frankish singers, particularly in the time of Charlemagne. See, e.g., H. Hucke, "Die Einführung des Gregorianischen Gesangs im Frankenreich" (*Römische Quartalschrift für Christliche Altertumskunde und Kirchengeschichte,* Band 49 [1954], pp. 172ff).

[12] Monachus Sangalliensis (Notker Balbulus?), *De vita Caroli magni;* see Ph. Jaffé, *Bibliotheca rerum germanicarum,* IV (1867), 639, 641. Monachus' book is to a large extent a collection of legends about Charlemagne and therefore of little historical value (e.g., he says that Charlemagne—who died in 814—assigned the singer to the cathedral of Metz at the request of his son Truogo, bishop of Metz; actually, Truogo did not become bishop of Metz until 823). However, this is no reason to doubt the accuracy of information that refers to his own time. Equally relevant is the following statement of Johannes Diaconus: "As much as, until now, the chant of Metz is inferior to that of Rome, so much are the chants of [the other] German and French churches inferior to that of Metz, as is conceded by all those who esteem the plain truth" (*Patr. lat.* 75, col. 91f). Of particular interest is the somewhat reluctant recognition ("until now"!) of the superiority of the chant of Rome, and also the remark about differences among the various churches in Germany (St. Gall?) and France. It is very unfortunate that no document of the *cantus Metensis* has been preserved. Long before the recent re-examination of the Gregorian problem the importance of Metz (rather than St. Gall) had been emphasized by R. van Doren (see fn. 8).

Einsiedeln, etc., is clearly demonstrated by the fact that they all include chants for the Feast of the Holy Trinity, a feast of unquestionably Western origin which was not officially adopted in Rome until the twelfth century [see p. 8, fn. 6]. None of the Old-Roman manuscripts include this feast.

Different though the theory of Stäblein and the one just outlined are, they agree in one point: the standard repertory of chant is not "Gregorian" in the historical sense of the word. This does not necessarily mean to dismiss the evidence proffered by Morin, Cagin, Wagner, and others [see p. 49], to show that a repertory of chant was formed at the time of Gregory. This may well have been the case, but we have no information as to what it was like; for instance, whether it was essentially identical with the Old-Roman chant. Nor can we say anything definite about the chant that was formed, fifty years later, under the Roman abbots Catolenus, Maurianus, and Virbonus. The chief difficulty in both cases is the absence of contemporary or approximately contemporary documentation by musical sources. Any attempt to relate repertories of such early periods to manuscripts at least two hundred years later in date is fraught with uncertainty and danger. This element of risk is almost completely eliminated if we regard the standard repertory as one that was formed in France between 750 and 850. A manuscript such as the Codex St. Gall *359* is close enough both to the time and to the place of origin to be considered as an authentic and reliable testimonial.

We may then assume that what we call Gregorian chant is the result of a development that took place in the Franco-German empire under Pepin, Charlemagne, and his successors. This does not mean to say that all the many thousands of melodies of the present-day repertory were composed during this time, in the same way as the symphonies of Mozart and Beethoven were composed during the fifty years from 1770 to 1820. It means that they represent the final stage, and the only one known to us, of an evolution, the beginnings of which may go back to the earliest Christian period and even to the chant of the Synagogue. What changes took place during the numerous pre-formative stages we cannot say. Some chants may have changed relatively little, others so much that their original form was obscured or completely lost. On grounds of probability and plausability we may assume that the simpler chants were much less affected by the vicissitudes of a purely oral tradition than those of a highly ornate character. We shall come back to this question in the final chapter of this book. For the present time it will suffice to say that it is probably safe to think of certain very rudimentary types, such as the psalm tones or the archaic *Gloria XV* [56] as being a heritage from early Christian, and ultimately pre-Christian days; of simple Antiphons as dating possibly from the time of Gregory; and of an Introit, a Gradual, a Tract as being, in its present-day form, a product of the eighth or ninth century. With such general ideas in his mind the reader may now turn to a study of "Gregorian chant."[13]

13 The reader's attention is called to Handschin's interesting discussion of "La Question du chant 'vieux-romain' " in *Annales musicologiques,* II (1954; published after the completion of our manuscript), 49ff.

2

General Aspects
of the Chant

CHAPTER ONE

The Texts

THE PSALMS

NOT WITHOUT justification has the Book of Psalms been called the most influential single source of texts in all music history. Indeed it is by far the most important textual source in Gregorian chant. Our previous explanations have made it clear to what an extent the Psalms prevail in the Office Hours; they are no less important in the Mass, although here their presence is less obvious. In the course of the centuries various methods of psalm-singing developed, leading to modifications which, in their final stages, bear scant resemblance to a Psalm. An historical analysis, however, clearly shows that nearly all the chants of the Gregorian repertory have a psalmodic background, the main exceptions being the Antiphons, the Responsories, and the Hymns.

The early custom of singing complete Psalms is fully preserved in the Office Hours, to every one of which is assigned a definite number of Psalms, as shown in the table, p. 23. The distribution of the Psalms among the various Hours is a matter of no small interest. The basic principle was that the entire Book of Psalms should be sung once every week. When the details of the distribution were worked out, the Hours of Matins and Vespers received primary consideration. The 150 Psalms were divided into two groups roughly corresponding in size to the number of Psalms, nine (originally, twelve) and five, prescribed for these two Offices. Thus, the group for Matins comprises approximately the first hundred Psalms, that for Vespers, the remaining fifty. To put it more precisely, the Psalms for Matins comprise Ps. 1 to 108, those for Vespers, Ps. 109 to 147. In both groups, a number of Psalms are omitted, and these occur in the other Office Hours, e.g., the long Ps. 118 which, divided into eleven parts, provides nearly all the material for the Little Hours, from Prime to None, of Sunday [226ff].

The distribution of the Vesper Psalms, as sung during the week from Sunday to Saturday, is as follows:

Sunday	[250]:	Ps. 109,	110,	111,	112,	113
Monday	[280]:	114,	115,	119,	120,	121
Tuesday	[285]:	122,	123,	124,	125,	126
Wednesday	[290]:	127,	128,	129,	130,	131
Thursday	[295]:	132,	135.I,	135.II,	136,	137
Friday	[301]:	138.I,	138.II,	139,	140,	141
Saturday	[307]:	143.I,	143.II,	144.I,	144.II,	144.III

It should be noticed that the numbering of the Psalms in the Latin version of the Bible (the so-called *Vulgata,* Vulgate) differs from that of the English King James version, since in a few cases two successive Psalms of one version appear as one Psalm in the other. The concordances are as follows: Lat. 1 to 8 = Engl. 1 to 8; Lat. 9 = Engl. 9, 10; Lat. 10 to 112 = Engl. 11 to 113; Lat. 113 = Engl. 114, 115; Lat. 114, 115 = Engl. 116; Lat. 116 to 145 = Engl. 117 to 146; Lat. 146, 147 = Engl. 147; Lat. 148 to 150 = Engl. 148 to 150.

On certain high feasts the above plan is slightly varied through the partial substitution of other Psalms, a fact already mentioned in our discussion of the Ordinary and Proper (p. 18). Invariably, however, the substitutions are made in such a manner that the ascending order of numbers is preserved.

At Matins, Ps. 1 to 108 were originally distributed over the week according to a plan similar to that for Vespers. On high feasts, however, the scheme underwent rather considerable variations, as appears from the following table based on the Psalms of Matins given in *L:*

		NOCTURN I	NOCTURN II	NOCTURN III
Nativity	[371]:	2, 18, 44	47, 71, 84	88, 95, 97
Maundy Thursday	[622]:	68, 69, 70	71, 72, 73	74, 75, 76
Good Friday	[666]:	2, 21, 26	37, 39, 53	58, 87, 93
Holy Saturday	[713]:	4, 14, 15	23, 26, 29	53, 75, 87
Easter Sunday	[771]:	1, 2, 3		
Whit Sunday	[868]:	47, 67, 103		
Corpus Christi	[923]:	1, 4, 15	19, 22, 41	42, 80, 83
Office for the Dead	[1782]:	5, 6, 7	22, 24, 26	39, 40, 41

The original plan of successive numerical order is most fully preserved on Maundy Thursday. The principle of ascending numbers is never violated.

A special place is reserved in the service of Matins for Ps. 94, *Venite, exsultemus Domino,* which is sung, as an Ordinary chant, at the very beginning of every Matins. Inviting to worship with the words, "O come, let us sing unto the Lord," it deserves this place as well as the name Invitatory Psalm.

In the foregoing explanations we have considered the singing of complete Psalms in the Office Hours. In the Mass, this ancient method survives only in the Tracts, all the other psalmodic chants having undergone drastic reductions, which will be considered subsequently (p. 180). As a matter of fact, this tendency toward reduction has also affected the Tracts, though not to such an extent as to obliterate their original character. Each Tract consists of a number of verses, all taken from a single Psalm. Among the most complete Tracts are *Qui habitat,* which omits only ℣. 8-10 of Ps. 90; *Eripe me,* which omits ℣. 11-13 of Ps. 139; and *Deus Deus meus,* which has twelve out of the thirty-four verses of Ps. 21.* Many Tracts, however, have retained only three or four verses, some only two. A few Tracts are derived from Canticles, namely, *Cantemus Domino* (Canticle of Moses), *Domine audivi* (Canticle of Habacuc), and *Nunc dimittis* (Canticle of Simeon), the first two much shortened and with altered versions, the last one complete and with the original text. In addition to the *Nunc dimittis,* several other Tracts, all of a later date (twelfth, thirteenth centuries, modern), use texts from the New Testament (*Ave Maria,* Luke 1; *Tu es Petrus,* Matthew 16), while non-scriptural texts also occur, as in *Gaude Maria* and *Tu es vas.*

PSALM VERSES

The use of a single psalm verse as text for a chant is of very frequent occurrence, particularly in the oldest layer of the Mass chants, that is, in the Introits, Graduals, Alleluias, Offertories, and Communions of the *de tempore.* Especially informative in this respect are the Graduals. Each of these consists of two sections, the respond and the verse. The very name for the latter suggests that it is a psalm verse, which indeed it is. However, the text for the respond also is nearly always a psalm verse, and if so, both respond and verse are taken from the same Psalm.[1] Only a few Graduals of the old, Gregorian repertory are non-psalmodic, the reason being that for certain feasts of a very distinct nature a particularly suitable text was found in other parts of Scripture. Thus, in the Mass of Christmas Eve the respond of the Gradual has a text, *Hodie scietis* [360], modelled after Exodus 16:6-7, which provides a most appropriate commentary for the day preceding the anniversary of Christ's birth: "This day you shall know that the Lord will come and save us: and in the morning you shall see his glory." Similarly, for the Mass of Epiphany, commemorating the arrival of

---

* It should be noticed that the indication of "Verses" in the Tracts, as given in the liturgical books, is somewhat misleading. Properly, the ℣. should appear also at the very beginning of the text, since this is a verse of the Psalm (often the first) like all the others. Briefly, each Tract has one more verse than the number suggested by the signs ℣.

[1] A rare exception is the Gradual *Tollite hostias* [G 162], with the respond taken from Ps. 95, the verse, *Revelavit Dominus,* from Ps. 28. For all the questions concerning the texts of the chants, whether from the Psalms or other parts of Scripture, C. Marbach's *Carmina Scripturarum* is an indispensable tool. Also useful is the table of contents, given in *Wagner I,* 280, of the Codex St. Gall *339,* where the textual source is indicated for each chant.

the gift-bearing kings, no more suitable text could be imagined than the one from Isaiah 60:6: "All they from Saba shall come, bringing gold and frankincense, and showing forth praise to the Lord."

In the Introits the selection of texts is guided by the same principles. These chants also consist of two sections (disregarding the addition of the *Gloria Patri;* see p. 228), the antiphon and the verse. In the old Introits, the latter invariably is a psalm verse, and a great majority of the antiphons are also psalmodic. If so, they are, without exception, taken from the same Psalm as the verse. Non-psalmodic texts for the antiphons occur in about one-third of the Masses (thirty out of eighty-six found in the Proper of the Time as given in *L*). The percentage of non-psalmodic texts is somewhat less in the Alleluias and Offertories (about one to five), and only in the Communions is the majority of the texts non-psalmodic. This reversal of preponderance is mainly due to the tendency to take the text for the Communion from one of the Lessons prescribed for the Mass, particularly from that of the Gospels. Thus, the text for the Communion of Holy Innocents, *Vox in Rama* [430], forms part of the reading from Matthew on the same day [429], and that for Whit Sunday, *Factus est repente* [882], occurs near the beginning of the reading from the Acts of the Apostles in the same Mass [879].

In the manuscripts of the tenth and eleventh centuries the Offertories— which today consist of only one section, the antiphon (or respond; see p. 363)—have a number of verses, two or sometimes three, added to the antiphon. Without exception, these verses are taken from the same source (mostly a Psalm) as the antiphon. Therefore, these Offertories represent the Psalms in about the same stage of reduction as do the Tracts with three or four verses.

For more complete illustration, the table at the top of p. 91 gives the textual sources for the chants of a number of Masses from the Proper of the Time. Plain figures signify Psalms, while other books of Scripture are expressly indicated.

A perusal of this table shows that on not a few occasions two or more chants of a Mass draw upon the same Psalm (sometimes even the same verse) for their text, examples in point being found in Advent I, Ember Saturday of Advent, the three Masses of Nativity, etc. The most striking example of a textually unified Mass is that of the First Sunday of Lent, based entirely on Ps. 90. This, however, is a unique case. Usually no more than two or three chants are based on the same Psalm, and even these cases occur in a minority of perhaps no more than ten per cent, if the entire cycle of Masses is considered.

Even more interesting than the examples of "horizontal" unification are some instances of seriation which appear if the Masses are considered "vertically," from one to the next. The most striking of these concerns the Communions of the weekdays of Lent. As has been explained previously

	INTROIT		GRADUAL		ALLEL.	OFF.	COMM.
	ANT.	V.	RESP.	V.			
Advent I	24	24	24	24	84	24	84
Advent II	Isa. 30	79	49	49	121	84	Bar. 5
Advent III	Phil. 4	95	79	79	79	84	Isa. 35
Ember Sat. of Advent	79	79	18	18	(Tr.*) 79	Zach. 9	18
			18	18			
			79	79			
			79	79			
Advent IV	Isa. 45	18	144	144	105	Luke 1	Isa. 7
Vigil of Nativity	Exod. 16	23	Exod. 16	79	Esdras IV	23	Isa. 40
Nativity, Mass 1	2	2	109	109	2	95	109
Nativity, Mass 2	Isa. 9	92	117	117	92	92	Zach. 9
Nativity, Mass 3	Isa. 9	97	97	97	?	88	97
St. Stephen	118	118	118	118	Acts 7	Acts 6	Acts 7
St. John	Eccles. 15	91	John 21	21	John 21	91	John 21
Sunday after Epiph.	Apoc. 4	99	71	71	99	99	Luke 2
First Sun. of Lent	90	90	90	90	(Tr.) 90	90	90
Ember Wed. of Lent	24	24	24	24	(Tr.) 24	118	5
Wednesday Holy Week	Phil. 2	101	68	68	(Tr.) 101	101	101
Easter Sunday	138	138	117	117	I Cor. 5	75	I Cor. 5
Ascension	Acts 1	46			46; 67	Acts 1	67
Whit Sunday	Wisd. 1	67			103; 67	67	Acts 2

* Tr. indicates Tract instead of Alleluia.

(pp. 63f), the original series of twenty-six days had the texts of its Communions taken in numerical order from Psalms 1 to 26. In order to illustrate this once more, the first seven Communions, with translations, are here reproduced. The verse indications are those of the King James version of the Bible.

	COMMUNION	PSALM
1. Ash Wednesday [529; G 90]	*Qui meditabitur in lege*	Ps. 1:2. He that shall meditate in the law
2. Feria VI. [G 93]	*Servite Domino in timore*	Ps. 2:11. Serve the Lord with fear
3. Feria II. p. Quad.	*Voce mea ad Dominum clamavi*	Ps. 3:4. I cried unto the Lord with my voice
4. Feria III. [G 102]	*Cum invocarem te, exaudisti me*	Ps. 4:1. When I called upon Thee Thou didst hear me
5. Feria IV. [G 104]	*Intellige clamorem meum*	Ps. 5:2. Hearken to my cry
6. Feria VI. [G 106]	*Erubescant et conturbentur omnes inimici mei*	Ps. 6:10. Let all mine enemies be ashamed and troubled
7. Sabbato [G 111]	*Domine Deus meus, in te speravi*	Ps. 7:10. Lord my God, in Thee have I put my trust

Another case of "vertical organization" is presented by the Masses for the Sundays after Pentecost, particularly the group of the first seventeen

Sundays up to the Ember Days of September. The basic principle exhibited here is not the strictly numerical succession which we found in the Communions of Lent, but an ascending numerical order, similar to what has been observed in the organization of the Psalms for Matins of the high feasts (see p. 88). This principle is most clearly evident in the Introits, the first ten of which have texts taken from Ps. 12, 17, 24, 26, 26, 27, 46, 47, 53, and 54. It also prevails in the Offertories and Communions in which, however, a few substitutions occur, from Daniel, Matthew, etc. As for the Alleluias, the great fluctuation that existed in this field must constantly be borne in mind, as well as the fact that in some of the earliest sources they occur as a separate group, without assignment to individual feasts. However, the tenth-century Codex St. Gall *339* contains at the end a group of *Alleluiae in Dominicis diebus per circulum anni* consisting of twenty-six Alleluias whose verses are once more taken from the Psalms in ascending numerical order: Ps. 5, 7, 7, 17, 30, 46, 58, 64, 77, etc.[2] Essentially the same arrangement occurs in most of the later sources and in the present-day books, although with some modifications resulting from various shifts and insertions that took place in the series of Sundays after Pentecost, so that what formerly had been the Mass formulary of the Second Sunday became that of the First, etc.[3] The only chants which stand completely outside this plan are the Graduals, as appears from the fact that the series of Psalms from which their texts are taken begins as follows: Ps. 40, 119, 54, 78, 83, 89, 33, 70, 8, etc. This series occurs as early as the eighth century, in the Codex Monza, as well as in all the later sources. There is, however, one exception, the Codex Rheinau (only slightly later than Monza), which has an entirely different group of Graduals for the Sundays after Pentecost, and this series shows the same organization according to ascending Psalm numbers as do the other chants for these Sundays. There can be hardly any doubt that this series is of a more recent date, resulting from an intention to make the Graduals conform to the other chants.[4] Although the Rheinau series did not attain permanent significance, it is interesting enough to justify inclusion in the subsequent table showing the first ten Masses after Pentecost.[5]

[2] Reprinted in *Wagner I,* 298. *Per circulum anni* (for the cycle of the year) means here, as elsewhere, the final part of the year, after Pentecost.

[3] See the explanations, pp. 70f.

[4] Cf. *Sextuplex,* p. lxxviii, where Hesbert points out that there is no reason why an original series showing psalmodic order should have been "volontièrement brouillé," nor, if this was done, why the Graduals only had been thus treated. However, Chavasse seems to consider the Rheinau series of Graduals as the old one (*Revue Bénédictine,* LXII, 62). The Rheinau series appears also in the Code Mont-Blandin, together with the normal series of Graduals; see *Sextuplex,* nos. 173-198.

[5] Items no longer in use for that day are in italics. For the complete series of post-Pentecost Masses, see *Wagner I,* 296; *Sextuplex* pp. lxxv, lxxviii; *RG,* XVII, 172 (Hesbert, "La Messe *Omnes gentes*").

SUNDAY	INTROITS	Ps.	GRADUALS	Ps.	GRADUALS (RHEINAU)	Ps.	ALLELUIAS	Ps.	OFFERTORIES	Ps.	COMMUNIONS	Ps.
1.	Domine in tua	12	Ego dixi	40	*Miserere mihi*	6	Verba mea	5	Intende voci	5	Narrabo omnia	9
2.	Factus est Dominus	17	Ad Dominum cum	119	*Domine Dominus noster*	8	Domine Deus	7	Domine convertere	6	Cantabo Domine	12
3.	Respice in me	24	Jacta cogitatum	54	*Adjutor in opportunitatibus*	9	Deus judex	7	Sperent in te	9	*Ego clamavi*	16
4.	Dominus illuminatio	26	Propitius est	78	*Exsurge Domine*	9	Deus qui sedes	9	Illumina oculos	12	Dominus firmamentum	17
5.	Exaudi Domine	26	Protector noster	83	*Ab occultis*	18	Domine in virtute	20	Benedicam Dominum	15	Unam petii	26
6.	Dominus fortitudo	27	Convertere Domine	89	*Unam petii*	26	In te Domine	30	Perfice gressus	16	Circuibo	26
7.	Omnes gentes	46	Venite filii	33	*Venite filii*	33	Omnes gentes	46	Sicut in holocausto	Dan. 3	Inclina aurem	30
8.	Suscepimus Deus	47	Esto mihi	30	*Liberasti nos*	43	Magnus Dominus	47	Populum humilem	17	Gustate et videte	33
9.	Ecce Deus	53	Domine Dominus noster	8	*Speciosus forma*	44	Eripe me	58	Justitiae Domini	18	*Primum quaerite*	Matt. 6
10.	Cum clamarem	54	Custodi me	16	*Benedictus Dominus*	71	Te decet hymnus	64	Ad te Domine levavi	24	Acceptabis sacrificium	50

The various instances of, shall we say, "psalm arithmetic," whether within one Mass (use of the same Psalm) or within a group of Masses (successive or ascending order of Psalms), are not only interesting in themselves but also of importance for the study of the historical development of the Mass repertory. They show beyond any doubt that the formation of this repertory was the result, not of a single act, but of multiple processes of one kind or another. Some of these processes had taken place before the time of Gregory, whose book, as Peter Wagner has pointed out, fully deserves its early title, *Antiphonarius cento*.[6] Others occurred later, between the seventh and tenth centuries. It is not impossible to separate these layers and thus gain a certain insight into the historical development of the Mass.

As has been previously pointed out, the earliest components of the Mass are the Lesson-chants, that is, the Graduals and the Tracts. We have just seen that, in the group of Sundays after Pentecost, the Graduals are the only chants that do not participate in the scheme of ascending psalm numbers. This statement is also true of the whole series of Graduals, which follow each other in an irregular manner from the beginning to the end of the liturgical year. As for the Tracts, the few that have survived in the Proper of the Time are not sufficient to justify definite statements. Those that remain show no evidence of numerical order, except perhaps the five Tracts for the Sundays of Lent and Passion Sunday, which are taken from Psalms 90, 116, 122, 124, and 128. As for "horizontal" agreement between Gradual and Tract, our table on p. 91 shows three instances: Ember Saturday of Advent (Ps. 79), the First Sunday of Lent (Ps. 90), and Ember Wednesday of Lent (Ps. 24).

When the other Mass chants, Introits, Alleluias, Offertories, and Communions, were introduced, their Psalms or psalm verses were selected to a certain extent in accordance with that of the Gradual of the same day. The result of this procedure is evident in a few Masses: e.g., that for the First Sunday of Advent (Introit, Offertory); for Ember Saturday of Advent (Introit, Communion; also Tract); for Nativity, Mass 1 (Communion) and Mass 3 (Introit verse, Communion); for the Feast of St. Stephen (Introit), and for that of St. John (Alleluia, Communion); for the First Sunday of Lent (all items); and for Ember Wednesday of Lent (Introit; also Tract). In Wednesday of Holy Week it seems to have been the Tract, from Ps. 101, which influenced the selection of the Introit verse as well as of the Offertory and the Communion. Possibly the same situation existed in other Masses in which it is no longer evident because of the replacement of the Tract by an Alleluia. In some cases the Tract may have been replaced by an Alleluia taken from the same Psalm; this surmise would explain the agreement that exists between the Alleluia and some other chants in Mass 2 of the Nativity and that for the First Sunday after Epiphany.

Yet another step in the formation of the Mass formularies was the assimi-

6 See List of Data, p. 42, no. 51.

lation of some of the Communions to the texts of one of the Lessons, particularly those from the Gospels (p. 90).

Finally, there are the two vertical series which obviously represent separate layers in the formation of the Mass formularies; that of the weekdays of Lent and that of the Sundays after Pentecost. The weekdays of Lent are a very old component of the liturgical year, and there is no doubt that the series of the Communions for these days was introduced before Gregory. As for the Sundays after Pentecost, a plausible assumption would be that the original Graduals are Gregorian and that the other chants were introduced after Gregory.

NON-PSALMODIC TEXTS

The foregoing considerations have shown that, aside from a negligible number of exceptions, the texts of the Mass chants are psalmodic. In a striking contrast to this are the Office chants, the great majority of which are non-psalmodic and even non-scriptural. One can hardly go wrong in interpreting this as a deliberate effort to provide a certain balance against the Psalms, which comprise the major part of the Offices.

The chants to be considered in this context are the Antiphons of the Psalms, the Responsories of Matins, and the Hymns. The Hymns are, of course, strictly poetic texts of a character entirely different from that of all other chants. A brief description will be given later (see pp. 423ff). As for the Responsories, they constitute a literature "the critical study of which has yet to be undertaken."[1] It is unfortunate that this statement, made in 1898, is still valid today, so that we have to confine ourselves to a few random remarks which do not give a complete and probably not an entirely correct picture. Very few Responsories are psalmodic. Many take their texts from the historical books of the Old Testament, such as Genesis, Kings, Esther, etc. Thus, a Responsory for Septuagesima Sunday [*LR* 398] begins with the first sentence of Scripture: *In principio creavit Deus caelum et terram* (Gen. 1:1) and continues with a later verse describing the creation of man: *et fecit in ea hominem ad imaginem et similitudinem suam* (Gen. 1:26); while the verse, *Formavit igitur Deus hominem de limo terrae, et inspiravit in faciem eius spiraculum vitae,* is taken from Gen. 2:7.[2] Other Responsories of the same type are *Locutus est Dominus ad Abram* (Gen. 12:1) for Friday and Saturday after Ash Wednesday [*LR* 402]; *Dixit Dominus ad Noe* (Gen. 6:13, 14) for Sexagesima Sunday [*LR* 399]; and the first three Responsories from the Feast of St. Joseph (Spouse of the Virgin) [*LR* 305ff] which are taken from the story of Joseph:

[1] P. Batiffol, *History of the Roman Breviary* (1898), p. 106. See, however, the remarks in Marbach's *Carmina Scripturarum*, pp. 75*ff.

[2] In the *Antiphonal* of Compiègne this is the first Responsory of Sexagesima Sunday, and is followed by eleven others based on the story of the Creation of Man, Adam, Eve, Abel, and Cain. See *Patr. lat.* 78, pp. 748f.

Fuit Dominus cum Joseph (Gen. 39:21), *Esuriente terra Aegypti* (Gen. 42:56), and *Fecit me Dominus quasi patrem regis* (Gen. 45:6, 7). Such "historical" Responsories were used particularly for the Sundays after Pentecost and were actually called *Historiae*. The *Antiphonal* of Compiègne includes, at the end, a number of Responsories for post-Pentecost Sundays, grouped together under such titles as *Responsoria de libro regum* (from the Book of Kings), *Responsoria de beato Job, de Tobia, de Judith,* etc.[3]

A number of Responsories belong to ecclesiastical literature of the fourth and fifth centuries and are of great interest as such. Written in an ecstatic language of great beauty, they often provide vividly impressive commentaries on a liturgical event, for instance, the Nativity:

Hodie nobis caelorum [375]: Today the King of Heaven has deigned to be born unto us, so that He may redeem the lost man into the heavenly kingdom. The host of angels rejoices, for the eternal salvation has appeared to mankind. ℣. Glory to God in the highest, and on earth peace to men of good will.

Hodie nobis de caelo [376]: Today the true peace has descended from the heavens, today the heavens have been made flowing with honey throughout the world. ℣. Today there shines for us the day of new redemption, of old reparation, of eternal felicity.

Quem vidistis [377]: Whom have you seen, oh shepherds? Tell us, announce unto us, who has appeared on earth? We have seen the Lord who has been born, and the choirs of angels praising Him. ℣. Tell us what you have seen, and announce unto us the birth of Christ.

As for the Antiphons, the general aspects of their textual sources are well known, owing mainly to the investigations of Gevaert who has used the textual categories as a basis for a chronological classification of the melodies.[4] A small number of Antiphons borrow their text from the Psalm with which they are, or originally were, connected. Following are some examples (full verses are indicated by numbers, 1, 2, etc.; 1a indicates the first, 1b the second half of the verse):

Tamquam sponsus [372]	Ps. 18, ℣. 5b [372]
Veritas de terra [380]	84, ℣. 12 [381]
Laetentur caeli [387]	95, from ℣. 11, 12 [388]
Notum fecit Dominus [388]	97, ℣. 3a [388]
Tecum principium [412]	109, ℣. 4 [128]
Redemptionem misit [412]	110, ℣. 8 [134]
Exortum est [412]	111, ℣. 4 [141]
Apud Dominum [412]	129, ℣. 7 [179]
De fructu ventris [412]	131, ℣. 11b [179]

3 *Patr. lat.* 78, pp. 832ff.
4 *La Mélopée antique dans le chant de l'église latine* (1895), pp. 160ff.

These examples illustrate a practice which, no doubt, is very ancient and which, at an early time, may have been almost universal. However, it survived in only a few instances, such as the Nativity, from which all the above examples are taken.[5] The great majority of Antiphons, according to Gevaert more than three-fourths of the total, borrow their texts from other parts of the Scriptures, mainly the Prophecies, the Histories, and the Gospels. In the Prophetic Antiphons the scriptural text is often condensed, modified, or amplified; as, for instance, in *Urbs fortitudinis* [332], which combines portions of Isaiah 26:1, 2 (Sion is the city of our strength, the Savior will be appointed in it as a wall and bulwark: open ye the gates) with a free "refrain," *quia nobiscum Deus* (for the Lord is with us). For the purpose of additional illustration it may suffice to mention the five Antiphons for Vespers of the First Sunday of Advent [323f], the first four of which are taken respectively from Joel 3:18, Zechariah 9:9, Zechariah 14:5, 7 (condensed), and Isaiah 55:1, while the last, *Ecce veniet*, seems to be a new text. As for the Gospels, they are drawn upon particularly for the Antiphons of the Magnificat. Thus, the first three Sundays of Advent have the following Magnificat Antiphons:

Ne timeas Maria [326]:	Luke 1:30b, 31a
Tu es qui venturus [333]:	Matthew 11:3-5 (condensed)
Beata es Maria [339]:	Luke 1:45

Finally a word about strictly poetic texts. These are, of course, omnipresent in the hymns, but otherwise so rare that they are noteworthy only as curiosities. Among these is the verse of the Gradual *Benedicta et venerabilis* [1264], a distich:

Vīrgŏ Dĕī Gĕnĭtrīx, quĕm tōtŭs nōn căpĭt ōrbŭs
īn tŭă sē clăusīt   vīscĕră făctŭs hŏmō.

The same Mass, for the Feasts of the Virgin Mary, has an Introit with a hexametric text, from the *Carmen paschale* of Sedulius:

Sālvĕ sānctă Părēns, ĕnīxă pŭĕrpĕră Rēgĕm
quī căelūm tĕrrāmquĕ tĕnēt pĕr sāecŭlă cūiŭs.[6]

While these are probably the only poetic texts of the Mass, a few more occur in the Office, among the Antiphons and Responsories. It will suffice to mention two Magnificat Antiphons, *Hic vir despiciens* [1199], a distich, and *Cum pervenisset* [1308], which contains the rhymed stanza:

[5] The same practice exists in the Vesper Psalms of Sunday, where the Psalms 109 to 113 are sung with the Antiphons *Dixit Dominus* (Ps. 109, ℣. 1), *Magna opera* (Ps. 110, ℣. 2), *Qui timet* (Ps. 111, ℣. 1), *Sit nomen* (Ps. 112, ℣. 2), and *Deus autem* (Ps. 113, ℣. 11).
[6] The conclusion of the second line is modified to: *regit in saecula saeculorum.*

O bona crux, diu desiderata
et jam concupiscenti animo praeparata:
securus et gaudens venio ad te:
ita et tu exsultans suscipias me,
discipulum ejus qui pependit in te.[7]

7 For a Responsory with a poetic text, see p. 240.

CHAPTER TWO

The Notation

Τ HE traditional notation of Gregorian chant employs a number of symbols called neumes. This name is derived from the Greek word *neuma* which means something like "a nod" or "a sign," a term that probably refers to the fact that originally these symbols were written representations of manual signs by which the up-and-down motion of the melody was indicated. In fact, the main difference between the neumatic notation and that of the present day is the employment, in the former, not so much of signs for single pitches as for groups of two, three, or more pitches in various combinations of upward and downward motion.

Another difference is that the neumes have a primarily melodic significance and lack the indication of rhythmic values which, in the modern system, is as basic as that of pitch. This does not necessarily mean that different note-values were non-existent in Gregorian chant; rather that they are not clearly and explicitly indicated in the notation, as is amply demonstrated by the fact that to the present day the problem of "Gregorian rhythm" remains disputed [see pp. 126ff]. In the following discussion the neumes will be considered exclusively as symbols of melodic motion.

All the hundreds of manuscripts of Gregorian chant, dating from the ninth to the thirteenth century or later, and written in France, Italy, Germany or other countries, are notated in neumes. This wide dissemination in time and space naturally entailed numerous modifications of the basic system. In the various localities where chant was cultivated we encounter notations showing strongly individual traits, and each of these was also subject to temporal changes. Some of the differences are differences of penmanship only, but there are also others of an essential nature. This opens up a wide and highly interesting field of investigation, a field that has been explored in great detail by a number of scholars.[1] Naturally, no attempt at a study even approximating completeness can be undertaken here. We shall begin with an explanation of what may be called the

[1] The basic books are P. Wagner's *Neumenkunde* (*Wagner II;* 2nd ed., 1912) and G. Suñol, *Introduction à la paléographie musicale grégorienne* (1935).

standard system of neumatic notation, that is, the system which is employed in the present-day books and which is essentially identical with one that evolved in France during the twelfth century. To this we shall add a survey of the earliest development as it manifests itself in the manuscripts from the ninth through the twelfth centuries, and shall close with a brief discussion of the problem of rhythm in Gregorian chant.

THE STANDARD NOTATION

The neumatic signs can be divided into three groups: the basic neumes, the liquescent neumes, and the repercussive neumes.

THE BASIC NEUMES

The following table shows the symbols of this group, arranged according to the number of notes they contain.[2]

FIGURE 5

One note:	*punctum*	
	virga	
Two notes:	*podatus (pes)*	
	clivis (flexa)	
Three notes:	*scandicus*	
	climacus	
	torculus (pes flexus)	
	porrectus (flexa resupina)	
Four notes:	*scandicus flexus*	
	porrectus flexus	
	climacus resupinus	
	torculus resupinus	
	pes subbipunctis	
	virga subtripunctis	
	virga praetripunctis	

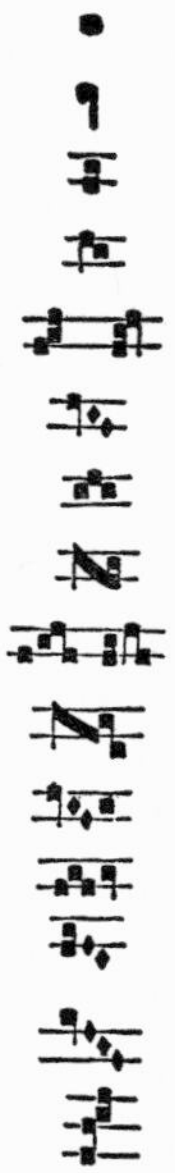

REMARKS:

a. Strictly speaking (that is, from the arithmetical point of view) there should be only one sign in the one-note category, as against two in the two-note, four in the three-note, eight in the four-note, sixteen in the five-note group, etc. However, even the earliest manuscripts employ two signs for single notes, one in the form of a slanting or vertical stroke (*virga,* i.e.,

2 The rudiments of the neumatic notation, staff, clefs, etc., are explained in *L* xviiff.

30541

rod, line), the other in the shape of a short horizontal dash or of a point (*punctum*), and it is from these that the two signs of our table developed. Originally the *virga* served to indicate a tone of high pitch or one reached in ascending motion; the *punctum,* a tone of low pitch or one reached in descending motion. Such a distinction was useful and necessary at a time when the neumes were not yet clearly notated on a staff. When this was introduced, the distinction lost its significance and, as a result, the *virga* tended to disappear. The process of its gradual elimination may be illustrated by an example, the Antiphon *Assumpta est Maria* [1606]. In a Ms of the early eleventh century (Paris, Bibl. Nat. *Cod. lat. 12601;* see *Wagner II,* 187) this Antiphon has *virga* signs on all the single notes of higher pitch:

> .   .   . /   / // . / .   / / .   . . / .
> Assumpta est Maria in caelum . . . . angeli . . . . benedicunt.

In a codex from the early twelfth century (Paris, B. N. *lat. 12044*) only two of these *virgae* are left, the one on "cae(lum)" and that on "(bene)di-(cunt)," while in the *Liber usualis* they are all replaced by the *punctum.* In the modern books the *virga* is found very rarely, and without a distinctive significance. It never occurs singly, but only within a melisma, as in the *Kyrie XI* [46; last "Kyrie"] or, more often, at its beginning: e.g., in the Tract *Ecce sic* [1290; on "(Ec)ce"], the Gradual *Laudate* [1275; on "(cae)-lis," "(excel)sis"], or the Alleluia *Dulce lignum* [1456; initial melisma]. Only in two of these instances does it represent a higher note.

b. The *podatus* (*pes*) has two squares written vertically one above the other. These are invariably to be read in an ascending direction, beginning with the lower note.

c. In the *porrectus* the first two tones are indicated, not by separate squares, but by a slanting stroke starting and ending at the pitches to be represented. This form is a mere convenience of writing, and should not be interpreted as involving any sort of *glissando.*

d. The designation of the *torculus* as *pes flexus* shows that this three-note neume was considered as a sort of combination of the *pes* and the *flexa* or, more proper, as a *pes* followed by a (downward) inflection. Similarly, the *porrectus* is a *flexa resupina,* that is, a *flexa* followed by an upward motion. The same terminology is used for the building-up of neumes with four notes, such as the *scandicus flexus* and the *torculus resupinus.* It can also be used for the formation of neumes with five notes. Thus, in the Gradual *Benedictus es Domine* [910] the first neume on "(Cheru)bim" is a *torculus resupinus flexus.*

e. Another method of building up complex neumes is indicated by the affixes *subbipunctis* and *subtripunctis,* terms which signify the addition, to a simple neume, of two or three notes in descending motion. These

Lincoln Christian College

invariably appear in the form of lozenges, as in the *climacus*. Such descending formations, usually in scalar succession, are extremely frequent in the Gregorian melodies, as a glance at almost any page of the *Liber usualis* shows. In fact, the addition of *sub-puncti* is the most common way of building up many-note neumes. Neumes with four *sub-puncti* are by no means rare (e.g., the *porrectus subquadripunctis* in the Alleluia *Loquebar* [1369], or the *podatus subquadripunctis* in the Alleluia *Non vos relinquam* [856]), and occasionally one finds examples of five *sub-puncta,* e.g., in the Alleluia *Levita* [1595] and in the Alleluia *Stabat sancta Maria* [1633ᵛ]. As will be seen later (p. 389), it is no mere chance that all these examples were quoted from Alleluias.

f. In striking contrast to the frequency of fairly extended groups of descending notes, ascending motion within a neume is usually limited to three degrees, as in the *scandicus* and the *scandicus flexus.* The *virga praetripunctis,* which consists of four ascending notes, is rather rare and, in fact, is not included among the neumes explained in *L,* although it occurs, without a special name, in the table of neumes found on p. x of *G.* Examples occur in the Antiphon *O sacrum convivium* [959, "me(moria)"] and in the Alleluia *Manum suam* [1695, "pal(ma)" and "su(as)"]; these are always written in the form of two closely joined *podatus* rather than of a *virga* preceded by three *puncta.* More frequent is a modification of this neume in which one of the two inner notes is replaced by a *quilisma,* an ornamenting sign to be explained later (pp. 113ff). See, e.g., the Introit *In nomine Domini* [612] on "id(eo)"; the Responsory *Angelus Domini* [774] on "(No)li(te)"; the Offertory *Holocaustum* [974] on "ca-(pite)" etc. The Alleluia *Tota pulchra* [1318] has, in the opening section, several examples of what would have to be termed a *virga praetripunctis subbipunctis,* as well as a *virga praequadripunctis.*

g. Among the eight possible combinations in the four-note group there is one, high-low-high-high, which never seems to have received a status of recognition and a name. It could be called *porrectus resupinus.* It is, in fact, extremely rare, and the few examples to be found in the *Liber usualis* (Tract *Qui confidunt* [561], on "(Jeru)sa(lem)" and "hoc"; Alleluia *Exsultate Deo* [1026], middle of the first line) all involve the *quilisma* modification. It will be noticed that this form closes with three ascending notes, and its scarcity (which is particularly striking if compared with the frequent occurrence of its inverted counterpart, the *pes subbipunctis*) is, no doubt, caused by the same disinclination for ascending motion which results in the *virga praetripunctis* being so much less frequent than the *virga subtripunctis.*

A special case of some importance is the succession of two neumes joined by a common pitch, e.g., of two *clivis* such as a-g g-e, or a *podatus* and *clivis* f-a a-g, or a *punctum* and *podatus* f f-a, etc. Such neumes (more correctly, combinations of two neumes) are known as *pressus* neumes. They are interesting mainly because they have been the subject of rather heated controversies among modern Gregorianists. The question involved may be illustrated by Fig. 6, showing three possible methods of performance:

The first of these possibilities (a) would seem to represent the "natural" method of performance, but this rarely enters into the discussion, it usually being assumed that the common pitch is held over from the first to the second neume.[3] The real issue is one of accentuation, that is, whether the accent should fall on the first note of the group (b) or on the joining note (c). The former interpretation was advanced by Pothier, whose general view was that in every neume a slight emphasis should be placed on the first note. Consequently, he explained the *pressus* neumes as an exceptional suppression of the normal accent, in other words, as a syncopation.[4] This view was strongly opposed by Mocquereau who, as we shall see later [p. 127], introduced a new theory of rhythm and accent in Gregorian chant, and stated that "the effect of syncopation is foreign to the Gregorian art."[5] Consequently, the *Liber usualis* (p. xxv) says that the accent (*ictus*) should fall on the doubled note. Gastoué and Wagner more or less adopt Mocquereau's view which, however, was vehemently attacked in a more recent publication by Juget.[6] We cannot help feeling that the whole controversy is, historically speaking, without point, since the two opposing camps take it for granted that the common pitch is to be performed as a sustained note, an assumption which can hardly be proved. At any rate, controversies about such fine details are somewhat in the nature of "much ado about nothing," particularly if we realize that we are ignorant about so many problems of infinitely greater importance concerning the performance of Gregorian chant.

[3] Cf. Mocquereau, "Étude et exécution de l'Apostrophe pressus . . ." (*Rass. Greg.*, VI, 199), an attempt to prove the correctness of this assumption, by citing examples where a *pressus* of one manuscript is represented in another manuscript as a single pitch or marked by the sign *cō*, i.e., *conjunctim*. See, however, the exceptions mentioned on pp. 219ff.

[4] Pothier, *Les Mélodies grégoriennes* (1881), p. 46: "un effet analogue à celui de la syncope en musique."

[5] *Le Nombre musical grégorien* (2 vols., 1908, 1927), I, 128.

[6] Gastoué, *Cours théorique et pratique de chant grégorien* (1917), p. 18 (exceptions, p. 19); Wagner, *Elemente des gregorianischen Gesanges* (2nd edition, 1916), p. 49; Juget, *Des Signes rythmiques de Dom Mocquereau et de leur malfaisance* (1931), pp. 6ff.

THE LIQUESCENT NEUMES

This is a group consisting not so much of new symbols as of variants of the basic neumes, characterized by the use of a smaller head for the last note. Some of these modified symbols received individual names, as follows:

FIGURE 7

epiphonus	(liquescent *podatus*)	
cephalicus	(liquescent *flexa*)	
ancus	(liquescent *climacus*)[7]	
pinnosa	(liquescent *torculus*)	
porrectus liquescens		
scandicus liquescens		

The liquescent neumes are also called *semivocales,* and both terms suggest that a special kind of voice production is involved, with the last note sung in a "fluid" or "half-voiced" manner, somewhat like a grace note that is only lightly touched upon. Their nature appears clearly from the fact that they are used almost exclusively when the text presents certain special phonetic conditions: either two successive consonants as in *angelus, inferni, ubertas, mundi, hosanna, tollis,* or two vowels forming a diphthong, as in *autem, euge,* also *alleluia.* Obviously the liquescent neumes were designed to facilitate the correct pronunciation of such words. In the case of two successive consonants this may have been done by the insertion of a mute *e* (half-vowel, *semivocalis*), e.g., *an(e)gelus, in(e)fer(e)ni,* which received the liquescent note. In the case of a diphthong the phonetic process obviously involves a separation of the diphthong into its component vowels, the second of which was pronounced weak: *a-u* instead of *au,* or *e-u* instead of *eu.* This, of course, is the correct Latin pronunciation [see *L* xxxvii]. It is interesting to notice that the liquescent neumes in a way form an exception to (or, at least, a borderline case of) the basic principle that a neume can never fall on more than one syllable. Actually, what appears in writing as a single syllable with a neume, is separated into two syllables, the second of which receives the last, liquescent note of the neume.[8]

7 In the table of the *Liber usualis* (p. xxii) the *ancus* as well as the liquescent *porrectus* are represented by the normal, non-liquescent forms. The correct form of the liquescent *porrectus* occurs on the first line of p. 961, while that of the *ancus* seems not to have been used.

8 Guido of Arezzo gives the following description: *Liquescunt vero in multis voces more litterarum, ita ut inceptus modus unius ad alteram limpide transiens, nec finiri videatur* (Often [the neumes] are made liquescent according to the letters [of the text], so that there seems to be a limpid transition from one pitch to another, without a finish); see Pothier, "La note liquescente d'après Guy d'Arezzo" (*RCG,* IX, 3).

Examples of liquescent neumes occur on almost any page of the *Liber,* e.g., in *Benedictus es Domine* [348ff] many times on "la-udabilis" as well as on "patrum(e) nostrorum," "tem(e)plo," "sanctum(e) reg(e)ni," "in-tuen(e)s," "om(e)nes," etc. It is not always used if one or both of the two consonants is a sharp labial (especially *t*), as in *benedictus, patrum, sanctum, nostrorum,* because these combinations present no difficulty of pronunciation.[9] Finally it may be noticed that, while a liquescent neume nearly always occurs in connection with the above-described phonetic peculiarity, the reverse statement is not universally correct. First of all, there are numerous cases in which a syllable of the type under consideration has a single note (not a two- or three-note neume) which, of course is not capable of liquescence. Thus, liquescence hardly exists in chants which are strictly or prevailingly syllabic, such as simple Antiphons, Hymns, the melodies for the *Credo,* etc. In the hymns the very fact that they are strophic chants militates against the consistent use of liquescence even when a syllable is sung to a *podatus* or *clivis.* However, the more elaborate chants also show not a few instances of inattention to liquescence. It will suffice to mention the Antiphon and the Introit *Dum medium silentium,* both for the Sunday after Christmas [433]; the Antiphon opens with a liquescent neume ("Dum(e) medium"), the Introit, with a normal *podatus.*

Particularly instructive for a study of the liquescent neumes are the cases in which one and the same melody is used for several chants with different texts. Such a situation exists in the verses of the Introits of a given mode which, as will be seen later (p. 228), are all sung to the same melody. The following table shows the beginning of the second half of the melody for the third mode, with different texts. Those in the left column employ the normal neumes, *clivis* and *podatus,* while in the others the *clivis* is replaced by its liquescent variant, the *cephalicus,* in accordance with the phonetic peculiarity offered by the words.

FIGURE 8

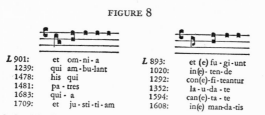

L 901:	et om-ni-a	*L* 893:	et (e) fu-gi-unt
1239:	qui am-bu-lant	1020:	in(e)-ten-de
1478:	his qui	1292:	con(e)-fi-teantur
1481:	pa-tres	1352:	la-u-da-te
1683:	qui-a	1594:	can(e)-ta-te
1709:	et ju-sti-ti-am	1608:	in(e) man-da-tis

A more extended table, from the Introits of Mode IV, is given in *Wagner II,* 28.

Attention may be called to an interesting study by H. Freistedt, *Die liqueszierenden Noten des Gregorianischen Chorals* (1929), in which the customary explanation of the liquescent neumes, as outlined above, is rejected. Freistedt points out that the term *semivocalis* as employed by the

[9] See the detailed study in *Pal. mus.,* II, 37ff.

Latin grammarians denotes, not a "half-vowel," but a certain group of consonants, namely, those that can be sustained in pronunciation, as *f, l, m, n, r,* and *s* (voiced consonants). Accordingly, he maintains that in a word like *angelus* the liquescent note falls, not on an inserted (*e*), but on the consonant *n* which is slightly sustained. This theory provides an explanation for the fact that in not a few cases a liquescent neume occurs in the early manuscripts in connection with a single consonant, e.g. in *dom-inus* or *tim-ore.* It also provides a more sensible explanation for the numerous cases involving a doubled consonant, e.g., *summo,* which according to the customary explanation would require the rather awkward rendition *sum(e)mo.* However, Freistedt fails to give a satisfactory explanation for the frequent occurrence of liquescence in connection with explosive (voiceless) consonants like *t* and *d,* which, of course, cannot be sustained.

THE REPERCUSSIVE NEUMES

Normally, a neume is a symbol for melodic motion, that is, progression from one pitch to another. There are, however, a few neumes involving the immediate repeat of a pitch, an effect known as repercussion. The most important of these are the *bistropha (distropha)* and *tristropha,* represented in the modern books by two or three *puncta* written close together and placed on one syllable. In the early St. Gall manuscripts, however, they appear not as two or three *puncta* but as two or three little hooks somewhat in the shape of an apostrophe: " or '". In a few recent publications, particularly the *Ambrosian Gradual (Antiphonale Missarum juxta ritum Sanctae Ecclesiae Mediolanensis,* 1935) and the *Antiphonale monasticum* (1934), the early form has been restored by the introduction of a special form for these neumes, a method that is, no doubt, preferable to that of the standard publications. Fig. 9 shows the various forms of the *bistropha* and *tristropha,* together with a few other neumes of the *strophicus*-family.

FIGURE 9

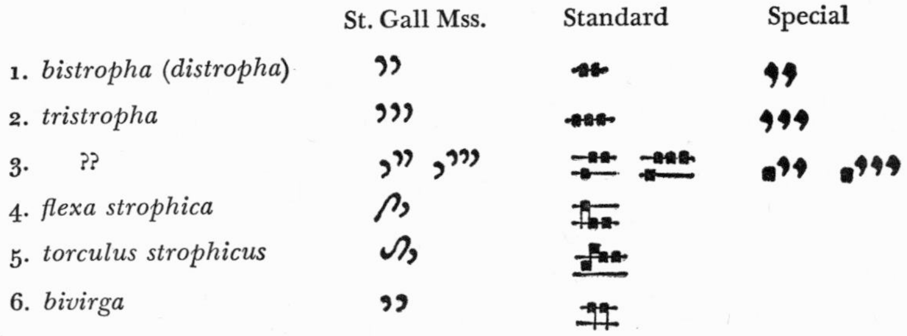

	St. Gall Mss.	Standard	Special
1. *bistropha (distropha)*			
2. *tristropha*			
3. ??			
4. *flexa strophica*			
5. *torculus strophicus*			
6. *bivirga*			

REMARKS:

a. Examples of the *bistropha* and *tristropha* can be found in practically every Gradual. Occasionally several of these neumes occur in immediate succession, resulting in a six- or seven-fold repercussion on the same pitch, as in the phrase E_1 of Fig. 106 (p. 354). This is a standard formula employed for the close of many Graduals of the third mode, e.g., *Exsurge autem* [604], *Salvos fac* [447; also end of the respond], *Eripe me* [570; end of the respond], *Benedicite* [1654], etc. Another repercussion of seven notes occurs at the beginning of the Offertory *Reges Tharsis* [461], and one of nine notes in the Gradual *Quemadmodum* [1478] on "(siti)vit."

b. The neumes given under no. 3, although not infrequent in certain chants (see, e.g., the Offertory *Exaltabo* [528] and the Tract *Qui habitat* [533, lines 2 and 4]) do not seem to have received an individual name. The editors of the *Liber usualis* consider the form as a variant of the *tristropha* (p. xxiii), while P. Wagner designates them respectively as *apostropha* with *bistropha* and *apostropha* with *tristropha*.[10] *Apostropha* is the name for the single hook of the St. Gall notation, exactly like our apostrophe. All the various *strophici* are derived from this sign which, however, hardly ever occurs singly.

c. The neumes nos. 4 and 5 show the addition of the *apostropha* at the end of some of the basic neumes, apparently only those that close in descending motion. Such formations are also referred to as *oriscus* neumes. Originally the sign of the *oriscus* was different from the *apostropha* and probably had a somewhat different meaning (see p. 111). At an early time, however, it disappeared and became identified with the *apostropha*.

d. The *bivirga* represents the high-pitch counterpart of the *bistropha*, to which it stands in the same relation as the *virga* to the *punctum*. It occurs very rarely in the old manuscripts as well as in the modern books. Examples are found in the Responsories *Jerusalem surge* [718], *Tenebrae* [680, "(excla)ma(vit)"], and *Animam meam* [681, "(adver)sa(rii)"], as well as in the Alleluia *Beatus vir Sanctus Martinus* [1747, in the melisma].

There can be no question that in medieval practice these neumes were performed as a real repercussion, that is, a fairly rapid reiteration of the same pitch. On this point we have the express testimony of a ninth-century writer, Aurelianus of Réomé, who tells us that the *tristropha* was sung as a rapid pulsation like a vibration of the hand.[11] Thus, the *bistropha* and *tristropha*, particularly if they occur in lengthy combinations as in the example given in Fig. 10, represent a true vocal *tremolo*, comparable to

[10] *Wagner II*, 123. In Suñol's *Paléographie*, p. 5, the name *distropha (tristropha) praepunctis* is used, which describes the neume very well.

[11] Referring to the *tristropha* in the third introit tone, on "Sancto" and "semper" [14] Aurelianus says: *Sagax cantor, sagaciter intende ut . . . trinum, ad instar manus reverberantis, facias celerem ictum* (Wise singer, understand wisely that you should make a quick pulsation, similar to the reverberation of the hand: *GS*, I, 57a). See C. Vivell, "Les sons répercutés dans le chant grégorien" (*TG*, XVIII, 43, 107); A. Mocquereau, "Étude des strophicus" (*Rass. Greg.*, VII, 96).

the violin *tremolo*. In modern singing this effect is never used, being contemptuously referred to as "goat's trill" (in German, *Bockstriller;* in French, *chevrotement*). It is not without interest, however, to notice that it was generally employed, under the name of *trillo,* as one of the most important ornamentations of the monodic style in the early part of the seventeenth century.[12] In the Solesmes books with modern notation the *strophici* are reproduced as shown in Fig. 10 under (a), and a note in the preface of the *Liber usualis* (p. xxiii) says that the most perfect manner of rendition would be a soft and delicate repercussion on each single note (*apostropha*). In actual practice, as taught by the Solesmes school, the reiterated pitches are combined into a single sound of double, triple, quintuple, etc., duration, with a slight emphasis (*ictus*) on the first note of each group, as shown under (b). Aside from the more or less complete suppression of the repercussive effect, this manner of rendition results in an undue prolongation of the sound. Aurelianus' reference to a "rapid vibration of the hand" clearly shows that the historically correct performance would be approximately as shown under (c).

FIGURE 10

There is reason to assume that at a certain period the *tristropha* involved a lowering of pitch on the middle note (e.g., f-e-f), since in not a few cases later manuscripts with diastematic notation reproduce it as a *porrectus.* Similarly, the *distropha* is sometimes reproduced as a *podatus* (e.g., e-f). Probably the interval involved was not exactly a full semitone, but smaller, close to a quarter-tone, so that in diastematic notation the group could with equal justification be represented as f-f-f (f-f) or f-e-f (e-f).[13]

THE EARLY NEUMES

Various theories have been offered in explanation of the origin of the neumes. The one generally accepted today interprets them as being derived from the grammatical accents of Greek and Latin literature, the same accents that survive to the present day in the French language as *accent aigu, accent grave,* and *accent circonflexe.* Originally these signs seem to have indicated not so much accentuation (dynamic stress) as slight inflections of the speaking voice. In fact, the very term *accentus* suggests such a semi-

[12] Caccini, in the preface to his *Nuove musiche* of 1602. See *HDM,* under "Tremolo."
[13] See P. Wagner, "Die Diatonisierung des gregorianischen Gesanges durch das Liniensystem" (*Rass. Greg.,* III [1903], 245; also in *Greg. Rundschau,* III [1904], 140, and, in French, in *TG,* X [1904], 144).

musical connotation, being derived from *ad cantum* (perhaps *signum ad cantum,* sign for the song). Thus, the *accentus acutus* (high accent) indicated a raising of the pitch, the *accentus gravis* a lowering, and the *accentus circumflexus* a combination of both, perhaps with the voice going first above, then below the normal pitch level. Some of the Latin grammarians of the fifth and sixth centuries also mention the *accentus anticircumflexus,* which would be the inversion of the *circumflexus.* Although the *anticircumflexus* played only a minor role in declamation, it survived in the neumes of Gregorian chant. The resemblance between the accents and the

FIGURE 11

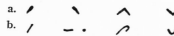

a. Accents   1. *acutus*   2. *gravis*   3. *circumflexus*   4. *anticircumflexus*
b. Neumes   1. *virga*   2. *punctum*   3. *clivis*   4. *podatus*

early forms of the neumes is so striking as to constitute convincing evidence of the evolutionary connection between the former and the latter. In fact, an anonymous writer of the ninth century tells us that "the notational sign called neuma originated from the accents."[1] The only sign that underwent a noticeable modification is the *accentus gravis,* obviously because it entailed a left-to-right motion of the pen which proved inconvenient in fluent writing. In the earliest neumatic manuscripts from St. Gall it appears as a little horizontal dash,[2] while later it was written as a dot or little square, hence the name *punctum* (point). It is easy to see how combinations of the four elementary signs led to the symbols for the various three-note and four-note neumes. All the "basic" neumes are nothing but combinations of the accent signs, and are therefore usually referred to as accent neumes.

In addition to these, the early manuscripts, particularly those from St. Gall, employ a number of symbols of a somewhat different graph, characterized by the use of rounded lines in the form of a hook or of a half-circle. These have been called hook neumes (G. *Hakenneumen;* Wagner), but actually only some of them show a graph reminiscent of a hook. Perhaps the term round neumes (G. *Rundneumen*) may be somewhat more appropriate, at least for those that do not clearly belong to the hook family.

---

[1] Vatican Library, *cod. lat. palat. 235,* f. 38′: *De accentibus toni oritur nota quae dicitur neuma* (cf. *Wagner II,* 355). Handschin, in an article entitled "Eine alte Neumenschrift" (*Acta musicologica,* XXII, 69) has called attention to a ninth-century fragment in which the *accentus acutus* indicates, not a high tone, but a *podatus.*

[2] This sign has played an important role in the controversies about Gregorian rhythm. Wagner considered it as a variety of the *virga,* called it *virga jacens* (horizontal *virga*), and interpreted it as a sign for length (quarter-note; see *Wagner II,* 381). Mocquereau regarded it as an early form of the *punctum,* called it *punctum planum* (level *punctum*), and opposed Wagner's rhythmic interpretation (*Nombre,* I, 159).

In this group we find the various *strophici* already mentioned as well as the early forms of the liquescent neumes shown in Fig. 12.

FIGURE 12

1. *epiphonus*   2. *cephalicus*   3. *pinnosa*   4. *scandicus liquescens*

Finally, there are a few signs calling for special consideration, mainly the *salicus, oriscus, pressus, quilisma,* and *trigon* [see Fig. 13].

FIGURE 13

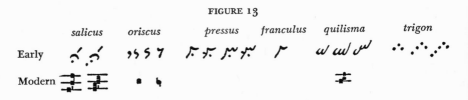

	salicus	oriscus	pressus	franculus	quilisma	trigon
Early						
Modern						

At the outset it may be remarked that all these neumes are of a more or less uncertain nature, as appears clearly from the conflicting interpretations they have received at the hand of modern scholars. We shall endeavor to present the different views as objectively as possible.

a. The *salicus* indicates three pitches (sometimes four, very rarely five) in ascending motion, as does the *scandicus*. It occurs almost exclusively in the St. Gall manuscripts. Its graph differs from that of the *scandicus* in that the middle pitch (in the four- or five-note forms, the penultimate pitch) is represented, not by a dot, but by a hook opening toward the bottom. Very likely this middle pitch was a "forbidden" chromatic tone, for instance, in d-f♯-g, or even a quarter-tone, as in e-e+-f. This assumption would explain the fact that the diastematic manuscripts represent the *salicus* either as a normal *scandicus* (changing d-f♯-g into d-f-g) or as a group with a unison at the beginning (changing e-e+-f into e e-f). Both these forms appear in the *Liber usualis* under the name of *salicus* [p. xxi], but a remark on p. xxiv warns the reader not to confuse the (ascending) *salicus* with the *scandicus,* the difference being that the former has the vertical *episema* placed under the middle note and that the note thus marked should be emphasized and lengthened. This interpretation goes back to Mocquereau, who explained and defended it in his *Le Nombre musical* (vol. I, 385ff). It is, however, open to doubt, and has indeed been rejected by such scholars as Wagner and Gastoué. It certainly cannot be reconciled with their supposition that this middle pitch was an unstable tone, chromatic or enharmonic. Such a tone would suggest a rather quick passing over, a manner of performance which is perhaps also implied in the term *salicus,* derived from Lat. *salire,* to jump. Gastoué, seconding Wagner, calls the Solesmes view a "fausse interprétation."[3]

b. The *oriscus* is a strange sign, in name as well as in meaning. The name has been explained as being derived from Greek *horos,* limit, end (cf. horizon). It is indeed usually a sign for a note added at the end of a neume, either in unison with the final note or a step above it. The standard Solesmes books represent the *oriscus* by the normal *punctum,* while a special sign, reminiscent of the early *oriscus,* is used in the *Antiphonale monasticum* [see p. xiii] and other publications. It is shown in Fig. 13. According to Mocquereau,[4] the St. Gall manuscripts employ most frequently the upper-degree *oriscus,* that is, at a pitch a semitone or a tone above that of the preceding note. However, the unison *oriscus* is also very common and occurs frequently between two *torculus* neumes, particularly on the sub-semitonal degrees, c' and f, e.g., c'-d'-c' *c'* a-b-a or f-g-f *f* d-e-d (*oriscus* in italics). Fig. 14 shows some examples from St. Gall *359,* together with the modern equivalents.[5]

FIGURE 14

Grad. *Gloriosus,* "sanctis"

Tract *Commovisti,* "mota"

Grad. *Tribulationes,* "-nes"

Grad. *Tribulationes,* "(me)-i"

Exactly what the *oriscus* means is very uncertain. Several scholars have come to the conclusion that, once more, an unstable pitch is involved, not in the *oriscus* itself but in the note that precedes it, because in a number of cases a *torculus*-plus-*oriscus* appears in the diastematic sources either as a *torculus*-plus-*punctum* (e.g., f-g-f f) or as a *torculus resupinus* (f-g-e-f). It is therefore generally assumed that the note preceding the *oriscus* was midway between the e and the f, so that it could be reproduced either way in diastematic notation.[6]

It is obvious, however, that there is more involved in the *oriscus* than this. To ascribe to a neumatic sign a "retroactive" function is certainly not a very plausible explanation in itself. Moreover, it applies only to the

[3] See *Wagner II,* 144; *Origines,* p. 175, fn. 2.
[4] *Nombre,* I, 371.
[5] For others, see *Nombre,* I, 371f.
[6] *Wagner II,* 143; *Origines,* p. 174, fn. 5; *Nombre,* I, 375.

unison *oriscus,* but does not account for the numerous cases where the
oriscus is a degree higher than the preceding note, as in the first two
examples of Fig. 14. Finally, it should be noticed that the *oriscus,* though
normally attached to a neume, also occurs as an individual sign, placed
alone over a syllable. Several examples of this usage occur in the Antiphons
of the Codex Hartker, e.g.:

FIGURE 15

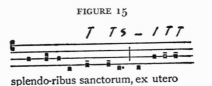

splendo-ribus sanctorum, ex utero

Ant. *Tecum principium* [412; *Pal. mus.,* II.i, 52]

Other examples are found in *Adhaesit,* on "(De)us" (*ibid.,* p. 59); in
Lapidabant judei, on "(Je)su" (p. 59); in the Responsory *Isti sunt sancti,*
on "su(a)" (p. 67), etc.

The striking and peculiar shape of this enigmatic symbol certainly suggests that it had a special meaning of its own, probably that of a short
ornament. The first scholar to propose such an explanation was Houdard,
who described the *oriscus* as a "broderie d'échappée," as an ornament involving the upper and the lower neighbor note, e.g., f-g-e for an *oriscus* on
f.[7] He based his explanation on the form of the *oriscus,* saying that the
symbol consists of an *epiphonus* and an inferior *apostropha:* ◡, = ꙮ.
Wagner tried to show that the *oriscus* consists of two notes, a main note of
normal duration and a short passing note at the lower second.[8] Fig. 16
shows an example of a unison -*oriscus* and its various interpretations.

FIGURE 16

Houdard   Wagner   Solesmes

c. The *pressus* was previously explained as a combination of two neumes
joined by the same pitch [p. 103]. Originally this effect was expressed by a
special sign, in the general form of an angular or wavy line with a dot
underneath. Mocquereau, who devotes an extended chapter to the study
of the "apostropha-pressus,"[9] always represents the *pressus* by the form

7 In *Le Rythme du chant dit grégorien* (1898), pp. 103ff. Concerning the main thesis of
this study, see p. 129.

8 See his article, "Quelques remarques sur la notation du Manuscrit *601* de la Bibliothèque Capitulaire de Lucques" (*TG,* XIV, 148).

9 *Nombre,* I, 300-332.

with the wavy line, while Wagner considers only the other form, which seems to be the one more widely used in the early manuscripts.[10] The *pressus* was known in two varieties, *major* and *minor,* the former distinguished by the addition of a little dash. In nearly all the tables of neumes these are listed at the very end, for instance, in a crude hexameter: *Ét pressús minór et máior, non plúribus útor* (and finally the minor and major *pressus,* other [neumes] I do not employ).[11]

According to Wagner, the *pressus* is derived from a more elementary symbol consisting of a *virga* with a hook attached to the upper end, and called *franculus* (from Lat. *frangere,* to break?). From concordances between chironomic and diastematic manuscripts it appears that the *franculus* is nearly always replaced by a *podatus,* occasionally by a single note. This would seem to indicate that the original *franculus* consisted of a main note and an ornamenting upper neighbor note, thus forming the counterpart of the *oriscus* which is characterized by an ornamenting lower neighbor note. The *pressus* results from the addition to the *franculus* of a dot, which always indicates a lower pitch. Accordingly, the *pressus* should have about the same significance as a *torculus,* e.g., a-b-g. Actually, its equivalent is always a *bistropha flexa,* e.g., a-a-g. Very likely, the seeming contradiction between the "a-b" of the *franculus* and the "a-a" of the *pressus* can be explained by assuming that the upper note of the *franculus* could vary from as much as a whole-tone to as little as a quarter-tone. Possibly it was such a microtonic interval that distinguished the *pressus* from seemingly identical forms.

Neither the *franculus* nor the microtonic intervals enter into the explanations given by Mocquereau. He adduces numerous examples showing that the special *pressus* symbol of the early sources is replaced, in other manuscripts, by an ordinary neume, e.g., a *clivis,* joined in unison to the preceding neume—in other words, that it is identical with the *pressus* forms of the modern publications. Fig. 17 shows an example from the Communion *Video* [418].[12]

FIGURE 17

fá-ci- unt

The neumes in the upper row are from Einsiedeln *121,* those below from St. Gall *339.* In the Solesmes editions the *pressus* formation is replaced by a simple *torculus,* g-a-g.

d. The *quilisma* is, no doubt, the most important among the special signs we are considering here. It is very frequent, particularly in the oldest

[10] *Wagner II,* 155ff.   [11] Cf., e.g., *Wagner II,* 106f.   [12] *Nombre,* I, 310.

manuscripts from the tenth and eleventh centuries. Accordingly, it was introduced into the modern editions, where it is represented by a special sign in the form of a jagged note occurring within a neume in ascending motion. Usually the neighboring notes are each at the distance of a second (e.g., f-*g*-a), but there are cases in which the lower neighbor is a third below the *quilisma* (e.g., e-*g*-a). Examples showing the upper note at a wider distance than a second apparently do not exist.

As for the performance of the *quilisma,* the *Liber usualis,* following Mocquereau,[13] makes the unqualified statement that "it must always be rendered lightly" and that "the note immediately before the *quilisma* should be notably lengthened and emphasized" [p. xxv]. This interpretation is, no doubt, entirely gratuitous, particularly in its first part. To consider the *quilisma* as a "lightly rendered" passing tone is a supposition that is refuted by the notational symbol itself. It is impossible to assume that a sign of such elaboration and striking appearance could have been used to indicate nothing but a single tone to be rendered lightly. There can be no question that it stands for a short ornamenting group involving several pitches, in other words, that it is a stenographic sign similar to those employed in modern notation to indicate a mordent, a turn, a trill, etc. Its exact meaning cannot be determined with certainty. The term is undoubtedly derived from the Greek word *kylisma* (rolling), and it is interesting to note that among the notational symbols of Byzantine chant there is a *kylisma* which shows a somewhat similar design (Fig. 18a) and indicates an ornament, perhaps a trill. Fig. 18b shows a number of interpretations given by Gastoué:[14]

FIGURE 18

A different explanation has been given by C. Vivell,[15] who observed that in early Italian manuscripts the *quilisma* is written in an ascending form [see Fig. 13], and that in later Italian manuscripts (eleventh-to-twelfth century; transition from chironomic to diastematic notation) the *quilisma* sign is replaced by two dots in ascending position. From this he concludes that the *quilisma* was an ascending *portamento* touching upon the chro-

13 *Nombre,* I, 404; see also his "La Tradition rythmique grégorienne à propos du *quilisma*" (*Rass. Greg.,* V, 225).
14 *Cours,* p. 19.
15 "Das Quilisma" (*Greg. Rundschau,* IV, V, several installments).

matic, or possibly even enharmonic, pitches between the fixed interval of the third:

FIGURE 19

As for the lengthening of the note(s) preceding the *quilisma* or, as Mocquereau puts it, the "effect rétroactif de retard ou même de prolonge-ment,"[16] this view is, on the whole, well supported by numerous examples from early manuscripts (St. Gall, Metz) in which the note before the *quilisma* carries a sign of prolongation, such as the Romanus letter *t* (*tenere*, to hold), the horizontal *episema,* or actual doubling of the pitch. Whether it is as universally valid as Mocquereau claims when he says "cette règle ne souffre aucune exception," is another question. Certainly there are cases where the "retroactive" prolongation is not indicated in the source, as in St. Gall *359,* where repeatedly the *quilisma* is preceded by a *clivis* (sometimes a *clivis* with *episema* which, however, affects only its first note, not the one before the *quilisma*):

FIGURE 20

a. *Pal. mus.*, II.ii, 25-45, line 11 (*bonum*); line 12 (*regi*)
b. *ibid.*, 11-31, line 2 (*egressio*); 12-32, line 1 (first neume)

At any rate, the question concerning the note before the *quilisma* is, it seems to me, of minor importance compared to that concerning the *quilisma* itself.

e. The *trigon* (L. *trigonum,* triangle) is a neumatic sign consisting, in its simplest form, of three dots outlining a triangle. Composite forms are the *trigonum* preceded and/or followed by one or two dots (*praepunctis, subpunctis*), in which one or both of the two sides of the "triangle" consist of four or even five dots. The *trigonum,* with its unusually "graphic" de-sign, clearly suggests a melodic motion identical with that represented by the *torculus*, e.g., b-c'-a. The difference between the two signs may have been one of performance, that is, *legato* for the *torculus* and *staccato* for the *trigonum,* or one of note-values, shorter in the latter than in the former. Of greater importance and of more lasting significance, however, was a difference of melodic description. While a *torculus* may indicate any pitches outlining a low-high-low motion, the *trigonum* is much more lim-

16 *Nombre,* I, 399.

ited in this respect. A comparison with its diastematic equivalents shows, first of all, that in the great majority of cases its highest tone is one of the subsemitonal degrees, f, c′, or b-flat. This suggests that its initial interval was always a semitone, e-f-(d), b-c′-(a), or a-b♭-(g). Actually, there is good reason to assume that it was a microtonic interval, approximately a quarter-tone. This is proved, almost beyond doubt, by the fact that the diastematic manuscripts nearly always represent the *trigonum* as a *bistropha flexa,* that is, as f-f-(d), c′-c′-(a), etc. Fig. 21 shows two examples of the *trigonum* (from St. Gall *359*), together with their later equivalents.

FIGURE 21

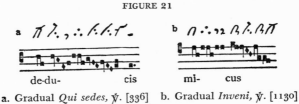

a. Gradual *Qui sedes,* ℣. [336]   b. Gradual *Inveni,* ℣. [1130]

The first example is interesting because it shows one of the very rare examples of a single *apostropha.*

The early neumes that have just been discussed represent the Franco-German notation of the ninth to eleventh centuries, best known through the Mss St. Gall *359,* St. Gall *339,* Einsiedeln *121,* and St. Gall *390-391* (Codex Hartker), all published in the volumes of the *Paléographie musicale.* It is mainly in these sources that we find the "special neumes," *salicus, oriscus, pressus, franculus, quilisma,* and *trigonum,* each of which involves a peculiar effect such as microtonic intervals, *staccato, portamento,* or ornamentations in the character of a trill or a turn. Such effects are also indicated in the case of neumes that are only recorded in medieval treatises under strange names such as *tremula, vinnula* (charming; pleasant; from *vinnus,* lock of hair?), *concinna* (well put together, elegant), *cincinnum* (from *cincinnus,* lock of hair?), *sirenimpha* (like the song of the sirens?), etc.[17] Naturally it is impossible to determine the meaning of these terms, if they ever had a definite one. There can be no doubt, however, that at a certain time and in certain localities the chant was performed in a manner which the later manuscripts and present-day books reflect only faintly.

17 In *c.* 1028, Adhémar de Chavannes (also known as the Monk of Angoulème) wrote: "All the French singers have learned the Roman notes *(notam romanam)* which they now call French *(franciscam),* except for the *voces tremulas* or *vinnolas* or *collisibiles* (from *collidere,* cf. collision) or *secabiles* (from *secare,* to cut apart?). These the French have not been able to express perfectly in their song, since, with their natural and barbaric voice, they break the sounds in their throat *(frangentes in gutture)* rather than bring it forward *(exprimentes)."* See, e.g., J. Handschin in *Acta musicologica,* XXII, 72.

Finally, we must mention certain subsidiary signs that are frequently added to the neumes in the above-mentioned sources in order to clarify the melodic motion or details of rhythm. These are the so-called Romanus letters and the *episema*. The former are named after a somewhat legendary Romanus who, according to the St. Gall chronicler Ekkehard IV (d. 1030), came from Rome to St. Gall at the time of Charlemagne and transplanted the Roman chant to the German monastery. A letter written by Notker Balbulus (d. 912) contains a table in which practically every letter of the alphabet is explained as the abbreviation of some significant word,[18] but only a few of these letters are actually encountered in the musical sources.

MELODIC LETTERS

a   ut *altius* elevetur admonet (warns to raise the voice)
l   *levare* neumam (lift the neume)
s   *sursum* scandere (step upward)
d   ut *deprimatur* (should be depressed)
i   *iusum* vel *inferius* insinuat (insinuates "below")
e   ut *equalitur* sonetur (should be sung in unison)

RHYTHMIC LETTERS

t   *trahere* vel *tenere* (to drag or to hold)
x   *expectare* (to await, to retard)
m   *mediocriter* moderari melodiam (moderation, retard?)
c   ut *cito* vel *celeriter* dicatur (should be sung quickly)

These letters occur in St. Gall *359* and, with particular frequency, in Codex Einsiedeln *121* (*Pal. mus.,* IV). The melodic signs are, on the whole, of little interest since they clarify only the direction of the motion without giving the exact intervals, for which we have to depend upon the later manuscripts in diastematic notation. The only exception is the sign *e* (*equaliter*) for a unison, and this has indeed proved valuable for the investigation of certain questions.[19] The rhythmic letters, on the other hand, have played a prominent role in the attempts to solve the problem of Gregorian rhythm, which will be discussed later.

Of as great significance as the rhythmic letters is the *episema*, a horizontal dash on top of a neume, especially a *virga* or a *clivis*. Several examples occur in the illustrations previously given, e.g., the *virgae* with *episema* in Figs. 14 and 15, or the *clivis* with *episema* in Figs. 17, 20, and 21. Scholars are generally agreed that this indicates a prolongation. A prolongation may also be indicated by the use of a horizontal stroke in the

[18] *GS,* I, 95. Also *Pal. mus.,* IV, 10; *Nombre,* I, 164.

[19] See R. J. Hesbert, "L'interprétation de l'*equaliter* dans les manuscrits sangalliens" (*RG,* XVIII, 161).

place of a dot, the *punctum planum* or *virga jacens,* as it has been called (see p. 109, fn. 2). This occurs not only as an individual sign (e.g., in Fig. 15 on "ex" or in Fig. 21 on "(dedu)cis"), but also in *scandicus* and *climacus* neumes, where frequently one or several of the dots are replaced by a stroke (cf. Fig. 22, p. 120, first column).

The extended use of such peculiarities as highly specialized neumes, significative letters, and episematic modifications occurs particularly in the St. Gall manuscripts, and sets them apart from other sources, written in Italy, France, and England, which employ a much simpler notation, often nothing but the basic neumes and their liquescent varieties. The historical evaluation of this contrast is one of the points of contention among scholars. In an interesting reversal of national interests, which certainly is to their credit, most French scholars—Houdard, Dechevrens, Mocquereau—have placed the greatest confidence in the St. Gall tradition, while some Germans, such as O. Fleischer (in his *Neumenstudien*) and Wagner, have considered them as hardly more than curiosities of local interest. Whatever their value is, they do, of course, represent a tradition, if only a special one, that cannot be disregarded.

THE DEVELOPMENT OF NEUMATIC NOTATION

Aside from a few eighth-century fragments, the earliest musical manuscripts date from the ninth century. In these, as well as in those of the next century, the neumes are written in such a manner as to represent only the general contour of the melodic motion, such as high-to-low (*clivis*), low-to high (*podatus*), etc., without in any way indicating the pitches or intervals involved. Thus, in the case of a *podatus* we can be sure that an ascending motion is involved, but we cannot tell whether this motion comprises the interval of a second, a third, or a fifth, nor whether it starts on c, on f, or on some other pitch. Evidently these signs served only as a guide for singers who knew the melodies more or less by heart, or for the choir leader who may have interpreted them to the singers by appropriate movements of the hand. Such neumes are called staffless, oratorical, cheironomic (Greek for hand sign), or *in campo aperto* ("in the open field," i.e., without clear orientation).

Shortly before the year 1000 we find the earliest traces of a more careful manner of writing, designed to give a clearer visual indication of pitches and intervals. Without actually writing a staff, the scribes imagined horizontal lines representing lower or higher pitches, and wrote the neumes not only in lower or higher positions, but also to a certain extent in various degrees of elongation, so that a *podatus* standing for an ascending fourth would reach up higher than one indicating an ascending second. Such neumes are called diastematic, heightened, or intervallic. Notation of a tentatively diastematic character appears for the first time in Italian and Aquitanian (southern-French) manuscripts of the late tenth century.[1] Later sources of this type often have one or two lines scratched into the parchment, lines which, however, have no fixed meaning, representing the pitches d, f, g, etc., depending upon the range of the melody. According to a sixteenth-century chronicler this innovation was made at the monastery of Corbie under its abbot Ratold (972-986): "In this time there started in our monastery a new method of singing, from signs arranged by means of lines and spaces. . . . Until then the Graduals and Antiphonals of our church had no lines."[2] This primitive method of diastematic notation persisted in some countries long after Guido of Arezzo (died c. 1050) had brought previous experiments to their final solution by introducing a system of four lines representing intervals of a third, and by indicating the pitch through colored lines (usually red for f, yellow or green for c′) or clef letters, mostly f and c′. To the present day, Gregorian chant is notated on a four-line staff, with the clef-letters f and c′.

As was pointed out at the beginning of this chapter, the numerous manuscripts of chant fall into national groups with strong characteristics of penmanship and notational details. And even within the same country there were individual schools centered around monasteries where the chant was especially cultivated. Thus in France we have to distinguish between neumatic manuscripts from Metz (in the East), Chartres (in the West), and St. Martial at Limoges (in the South, Aquitania); in Italy, between those from Novara (North-West), Nonantola and Bologna (North-East), and Benevento (South). Fig. 22 serves to illustrate the characteristic traits of five important schools: St. Gall (German neumes); Metz (Messine neumes); St. Martial (Aquitanian neumes); northern France (square neumes); and Benevento (Beneventan, Italian neumes).

The early neumes, particularly those from St. Gall and Metz, occur in varied forms which have rhythmic significance, indicating that one or another of the pitches involved is of longer duration. Especially conspicuous in this respect are the various forms of the *climacus* in the St. Gall manuscripts. The Messine notation indicates the tendency to dissolve the neumatic signs into signs for individual pitches, a tendency which was fully realized in the Aquitanian notation. Whenever single signs (dots, etc.) are

---

[1] Wagner believes that the diastematic notation is the original system, developed in Italy, and that the St. Gall Mss represent a deterioration of it. See Adler's *Handbuch der Musikgeschichte,* I (2nd ed., 1929), 96.

[2] Gerbert, *De Cantu,* II, 61. In an article, "The Musical Notation of Guido of Arezzo" (*MD*, V, 15), J. Smits van Waesberghe declares this text to be "not of the slightest historical value" (p. 49). It certainly lacks the authority of a contemporary document, and is included above only with the necessary reservation. On the other hand, it should be noticed that the report makes no claim for the fully developed Guidonian system with four lines, but only for a tentatively diastematic notation, such as probably existed before Guido.

written in a strictly vertical arrangement, they are to read from top to bottom [see the *climacus* under II and III]. For further details the reader is referred to the Plates, which show the Mass chants for Easter Sunday as they appear in manuscripts from the ninth to the twelfth century. The following remarks are designed to facilitate their study.

FIGURE 22

	I	II	III	IV	V	VI
punctum, virga						
podatus						
clivis						
scandicus						
climacus						
torculus						
porrectus						
scandicus flexus						
pes subbipunctus						

I. St. Gall   II. Messine   III. Aquitanian   IV. Northern French
V. Beneventan   VI. Modern

PLATE I. St. Gall *359* (c. 900). The earliest complete manuscript preserved. A *Cantatorium,* which gives the full text and music only for the solo chants, Graduals, Alleluias, and Tracts, the Introits, etc., being indicated by their incipits.

> *Incensum tantum* (only incense to be used)
> *Statio ad Sanctam Mariam* (Stational Church)
> *A*(ntiphon) *Resurrexi et adhuc* (Introit)
>   *Psalmus. Domine probasti me* (verse of the Introit)
> *R*(esponsorium) *G*(raduale) *Haec dies . . .*
>   *V*(ersus) *Confitemini Domino . . .*
>   *Alleluia Pascha nostrum . . .*

The neumes of the first row are: *clivis* with letter *t* (tenere); *climacus* (with *episema?*); *clivis*; a special form of the *podatus*, sometimes called *pes quassus* (*Nombre,* I, 159); *bistropha; climacus; porrectus; virga* with *episema; podatus; bivirga; bistropha; torculus; climacus; virga* with *episema; porrectus* with *episema;*

tristropha. Middle of line 2, on "(exul)te(mus)": *clivis; climacus praebipunctis; trigon* (in later sources modified into a *pressus,* c′-c′-b). Line 3, several instances of *c* *(celeriter).* Beginning of line 4: two *virga jacens (punctum planum)* with *e* *(equaliter),* probably meaning an a (today a c′); *epiphonus;* two *virgae; clivis* with *c* *(celeriter); climacus praebipunctis.* Line 5, on "bonus": *virga* (with *episema?*); *trivirga;* two *climacus* in which the *puncta* are replaced by *virga-jacens* forms; *clivis* with *episema.* Line 7, last neume, *quilisma* with *episema.*

Alleluia, line 1: three *puncta; pes quassus* with *episema, t,* and *f* *(cum fragore,* with a loud noise); *torculus resupinus* (probably b-d′-c′-d′; today b-d′ d′ d′); *pressus* with *t* (today omitted). Line 3: several *climacus* with one *punctum* and one *virga jacens.* Line 4: *punctum; salicus* "cum fragore."

PLATE II. St. Gall *339* (tenth century).

> *In die ad missam* (on the day for the Mass)
> A. *Resurrexi et adhuc* . . . *a*(ll)*e*(l)*uia a*(ll)*e*(l)*uia.*
> *Ps*(almus) *D*(omi)*ne p*(ro)*ba*(sti)
> RG. *Haec dies* . . . *V. Confitemini* . . .
> *Alleluia Pascha nostrum* . . .
> *V. Epulemur in azimis sinceritatis et veritatis.*[3]
> *Of*(fertorium). *Terra tremuit* . . .
> *V. Notus in Judea* . . . *V. Et factus est* . . .
> *V. Ibi confregit* . . .[4]
> *Co*(mmunio). *Pascha nostrum* . . .

The significant letters have completely disappeared, and only the *episema* is retained. The notational symbols are practically the same as in St. Gall *359*. Note that the second *clivis* on "(exul)te(mus)" (after the *trigon*) has an *episema,* which is missing in St. Gall *359*.

PLATE III. Codex Chartres *47* (*c.* 1000). Contents are the same as in St. Gall *339*. The captions *R., V., Of., Co.,* are written in color, which hardly shows in the photographic reproduction. Note that the *Alleluia Pascha nostrum,* ℣. *Epulemur* is only indicated, without music (line 7). The marginal signs indicate the mode and probably the initial tone, for example, for the Communion *Pascha nostrum: ut in vi,* that is: start with the first tone (*ut* of the hexachord) of the sixth mode.[5]

The notation shows the characteristic traits of the French system, particularly in the tendency to dissolve the neumes into single signs. Thus, the initial *clivis* of *Hec dies* is written as two dots placed in a vertical line; the first neume on "(exulte)mus" (beginning of line 5), a *podatus subbipunctis,* appears as a single dot followed by three dots written vertically from top to bottom; and the *scandicus* on "et" (same line) is given as two *puncta* and a *virga.* Of special interest is the transformation of the *trigon* into a rectangular form. Note that dots written in a vertical position are always to be read downwards, in contrast to those appearing

---

3 For Alleluias with two verses, see p. 185.

4 For Offertories with verses, see pp. 192ff.

5 The abbreviation *em* in the marginal note for the verse *Ibi confregit* stands perhaps for *emmeles,* an early term for the subfinal.

in a slanting position. In order to save space, longer melismas frequently extend beyond the syllable to which they belong, as for instance that for "(fe)cit" (line 4), which continues above the neumes for "dominus." Obviously, the notation is completely non-diastematic.

PLATE IV. British Museum, *Egerton 857* (late eleventh century). Contents are the same as in St. Gall *339,* but without the Offertory verses.

The neumes show a noticeable tendency toward diastematic writing. The notation is French (probably northern French), but does not show the characteristic traits noticed in the Chartres manuscript. The *climacus,* in particular, is always written in the earlier manner. This specimen is also interesting because it illustrates the beginning of the square neumes, particularly in the *podatus,* which always has a little square for each of the two pitches, the lower one to the left, the upper to the right of the connecting stroke (see, e.g., "quam" of *Hec dies*). In the twelfth century it became customary to place both squares to the left of the stroke, and this became the final form of the *podatus.* The *clivis,* on the other hand, appears in a strange form (somewhat like the figure 7) which completely fails to indicate or suggest the pitches involved. This appears from a consideration of the beginning of *Hec dies,* where the first clivis stands for a-g, the second for a-f.[6]

PLATE V. Paris, Bibl. nat. *lat. 776* (from Albi, 11th century). The beginning of the Introit, *Resurrexi et adhuc,* is written in a highly decorative manner, with the letters interspersed, for instance, *u* and *r* within the *S.* The Alleluia includes two tropes, which are designated as *P*(ro)*sa*.[7]

This is a pure example of the Aquitanian notation. Neumes of the earlier type, written in a continuous graph, have almost completely disappeared. The dots, into which they are segregated, are carefully arranged on lines scratched into the parchment.

PLATE VI. Montpellier *H. 159* (11th century). This is a famous manuscript, unique in its tonal arrangement of the Mass chants *(tonale missarum),* its "bilingual" notation, in neumes as well as in letters, and its signs for quarter-tones. Our page contains chants of the fourth mode, as indicated by the inscription *deuterus* and the marginal indication *pl*(agius). The first complete chant is the Introit *Resurrexi,* with the remaining portions of the Easter Mass, *Ps. Domine probasti,* ℞. *Hec dies, All. Pascha nostrum, Of. Terra tremuit,* and *Co. Pascha nostrum,* indicated on the right margin.

The neumes are similar to those of Plate IV. Notice the incipient square form of the *podatus,* e.g., on "sum" (line 2 of the page) and on "(mi)ra(bilis)" at the beginning of line 4. The most important feature is the letter notation, which transcribes the non-diastematic neumes in a clearly readable form, making this one of the earliest manuscripts that can be accurately deciphered. The letters have their present-day meaning, but continue, above g, with the subsequent letters of

6 The *cephalicus* appears in the shape of the figure 9. Repeatedly there occurs a strange symbol in the form of a reclining 8, which is always followed by a *punctum* in lower position. Both signs together replace a *clivis* of other Mss.

7 See pp. 433ff for a discussion of Alleluias with tropes.

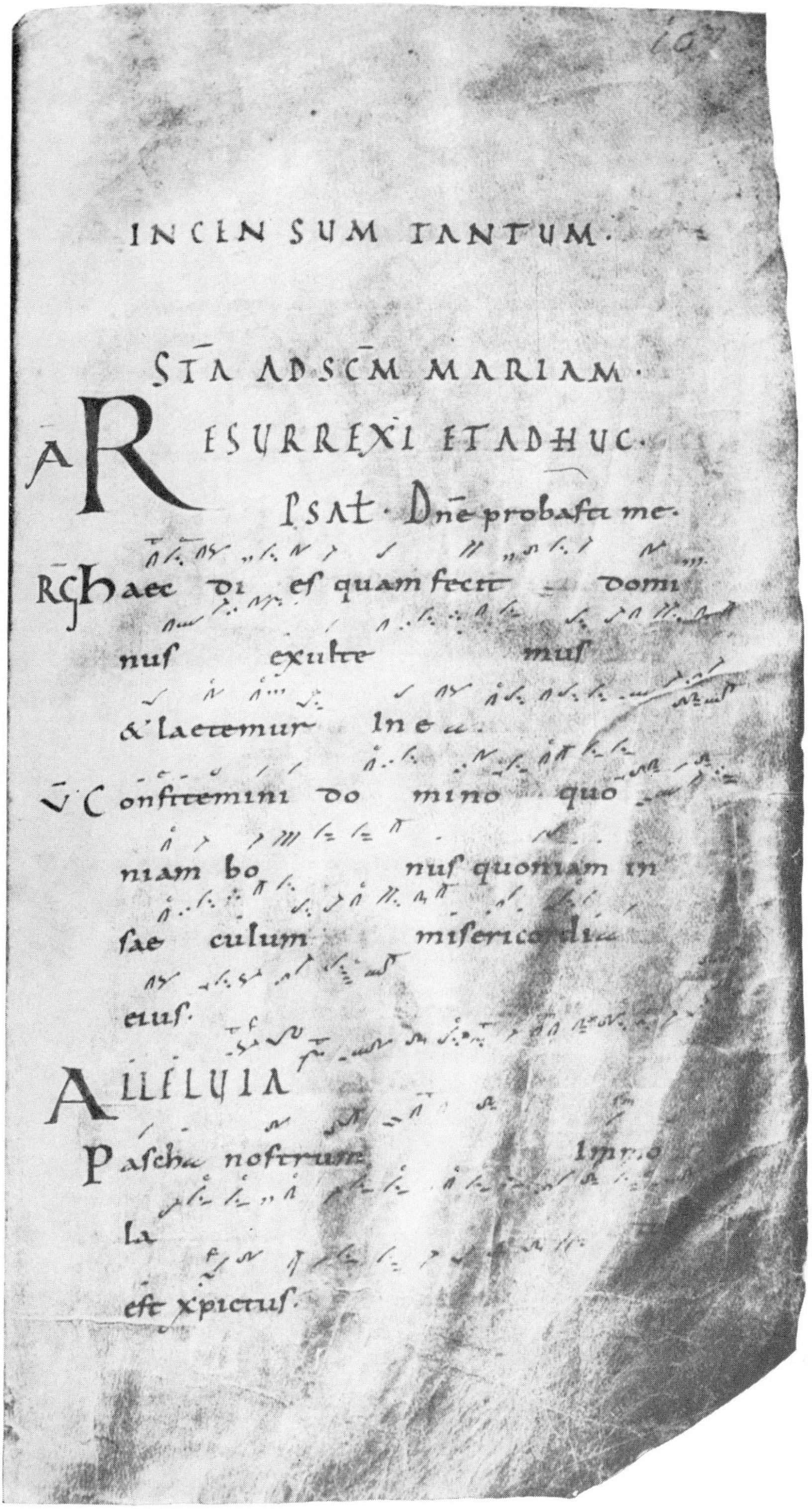

INCENSUM TANTUM.

STA ADSCM MARIAM.

AR ESURREXI ETADHUC.

PSAT. Dñe probasti me.

RC Haec di es quam fecit ~ Domi
nus exulte mus
& laetemur in e a.

V Confitemini do mino quo
niam bo nus quoniam in
sae culum misericordia
eius.

ALLELUIA

Pascha nostrum immo
la
est xpictus.

Plate I. St. Gall 359

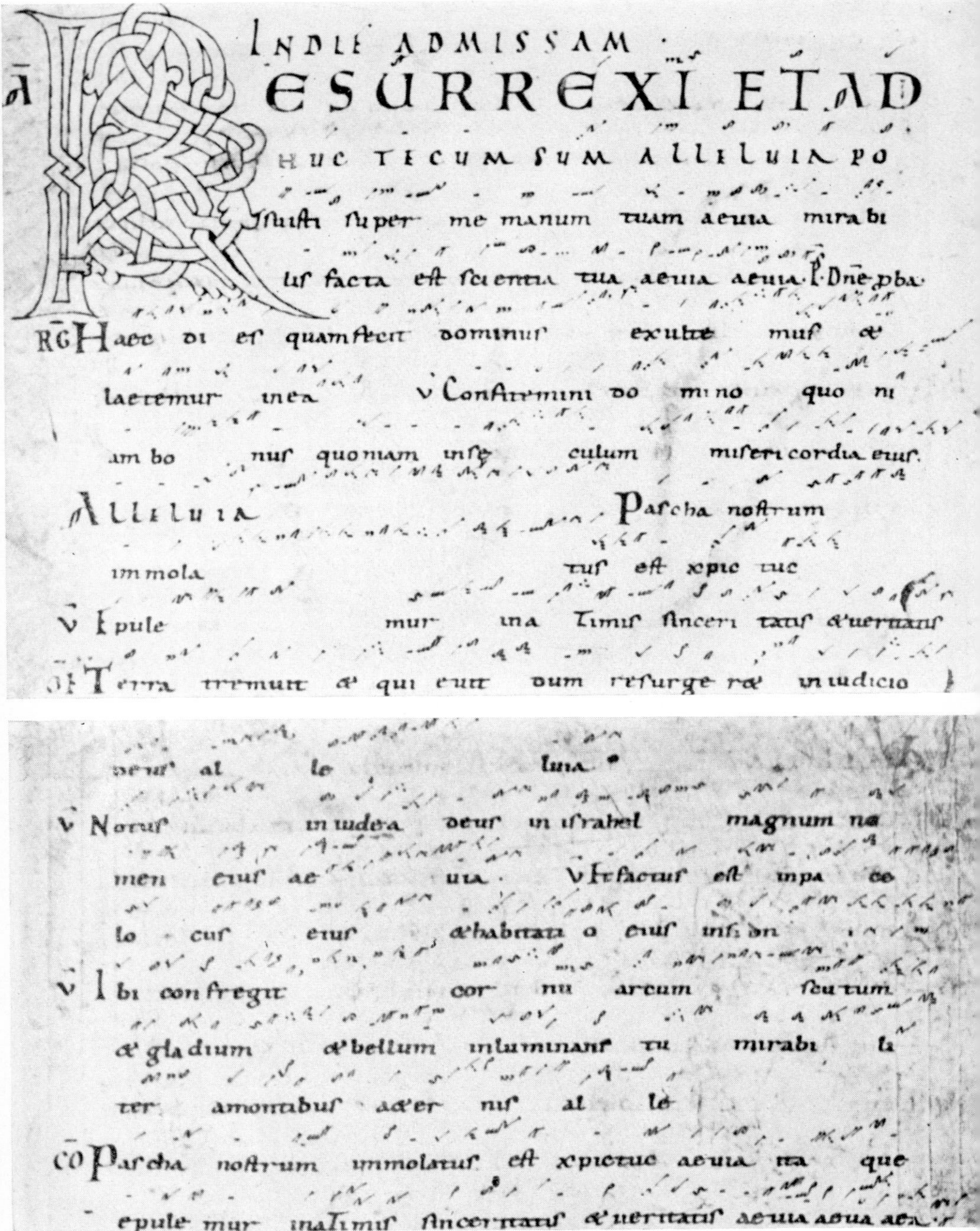

Plate II. St. Gall *339*

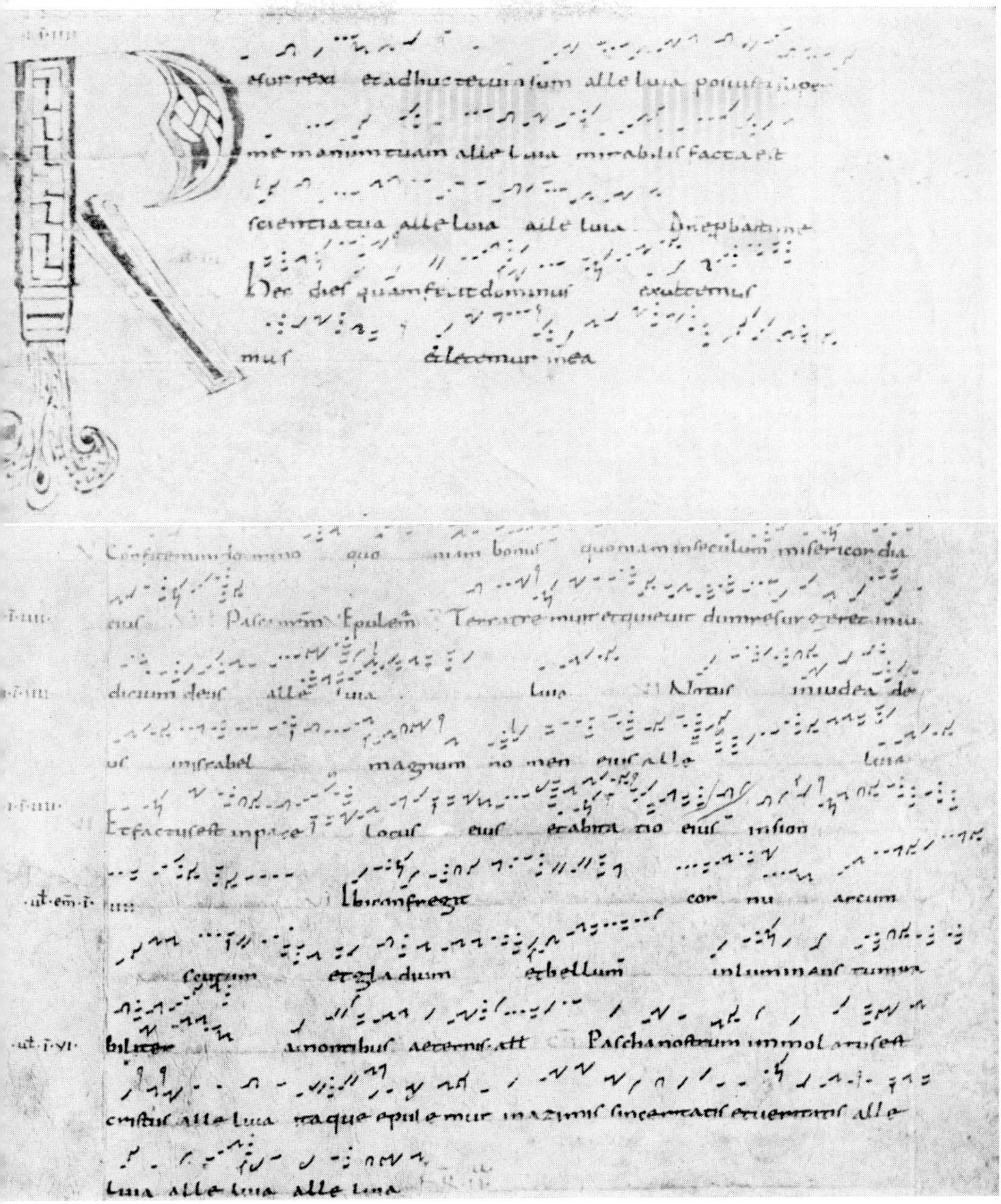

surrexa et adhuc tecum sum alleluia posuisti super
me manum tuam alleluia mirabilis facta est
scientia tua alleluia alleluia Dne probasti me
Hec dies quam fecit dominus exultemus
mur et letemur in ea

Confitemini domino quoniam bonus quoniam in seculum misericordia
eius Pascentium epulem Terrate mur et quieuit dum resurgeret inu
dicum deus alle luia luia Notus in iudea de
us in israhel magnum nomen eius allo luia luia
Et factus est in pace locus eius et habitatio eius in sion
ibi confregit cor nu arcum
scutum et gladium et bellum inluminans tu mira
biliter a montibus aeternis tatis Pascha nostrum immolatus est
cristus alleluia itaque epulemur in azimis sinceritatis et ueritatis euertimus alle
luia alleluia alle luia

Plate III. Chartres 47

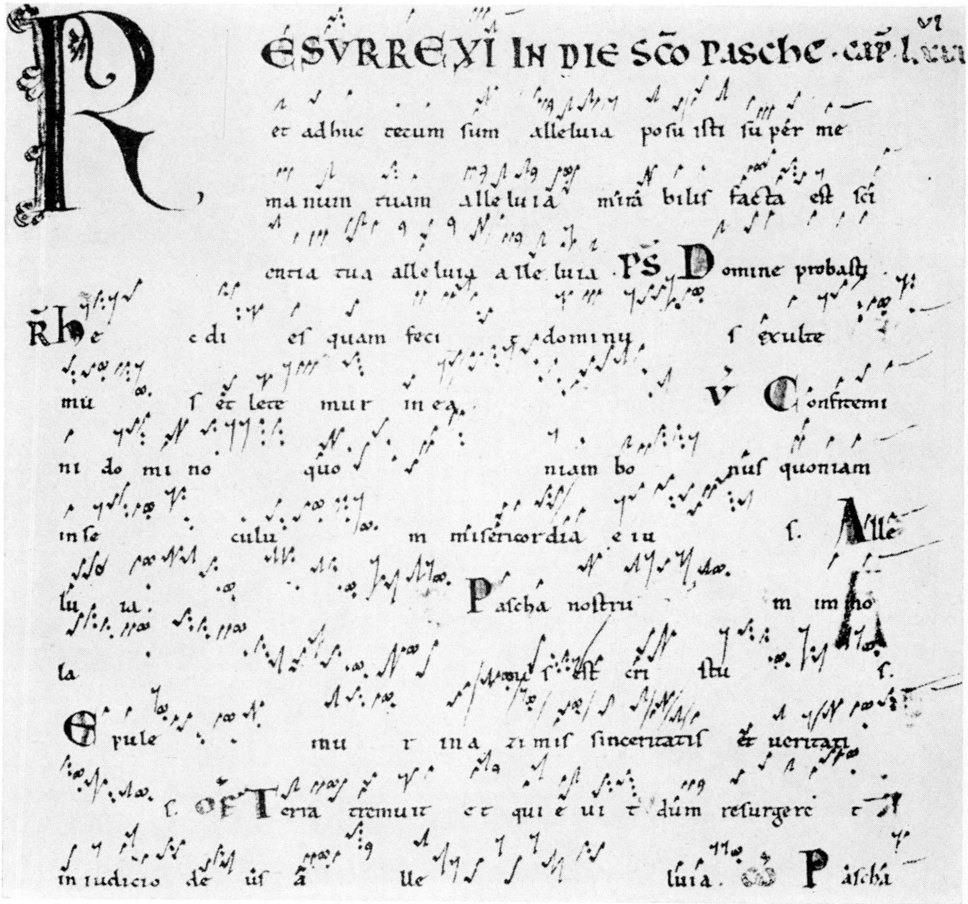

Plate IV. London, Brit. Mus. *Egerton 857*

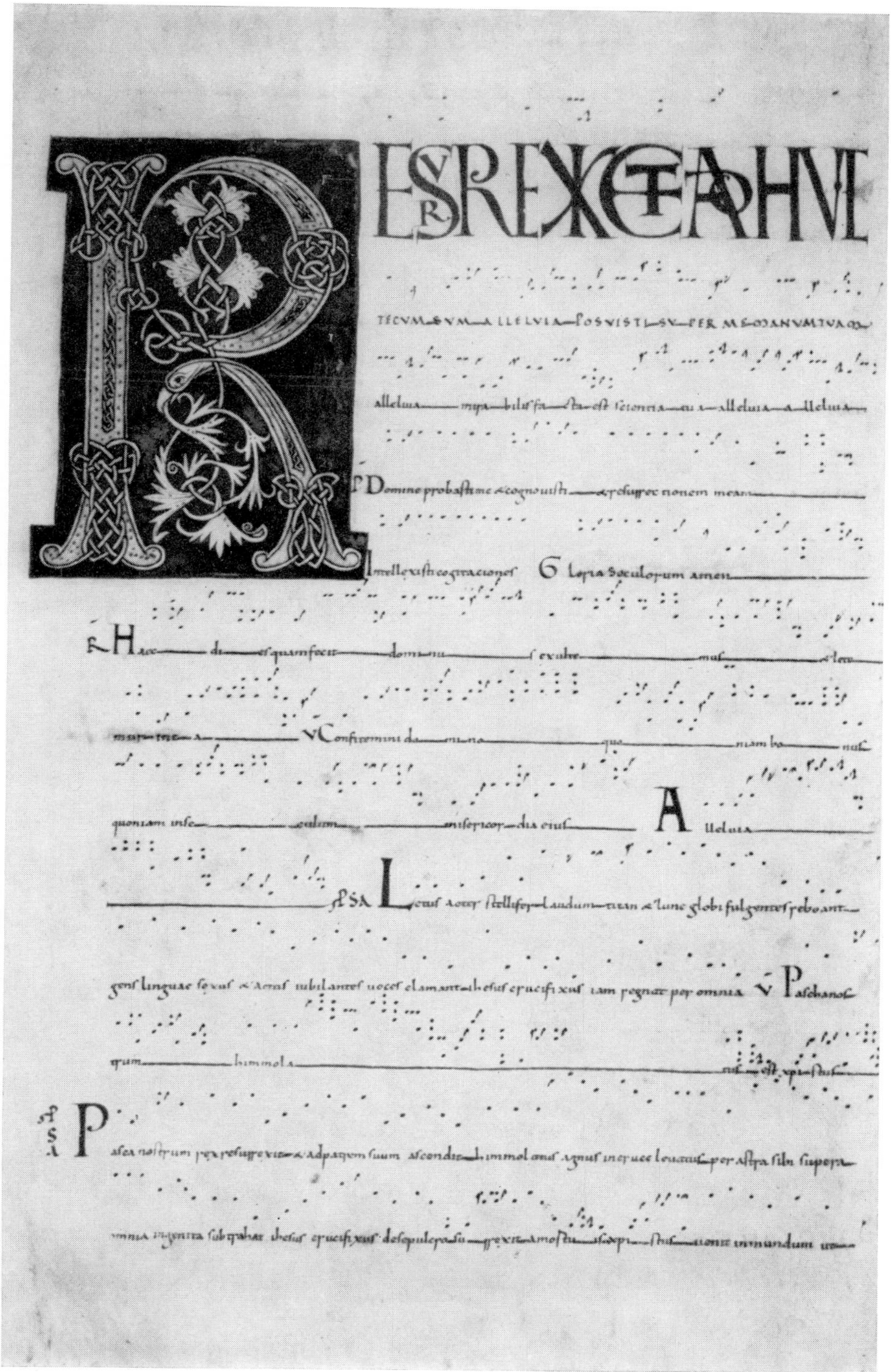

Plate V. Paris, Bibl. nat. *lat. 776*

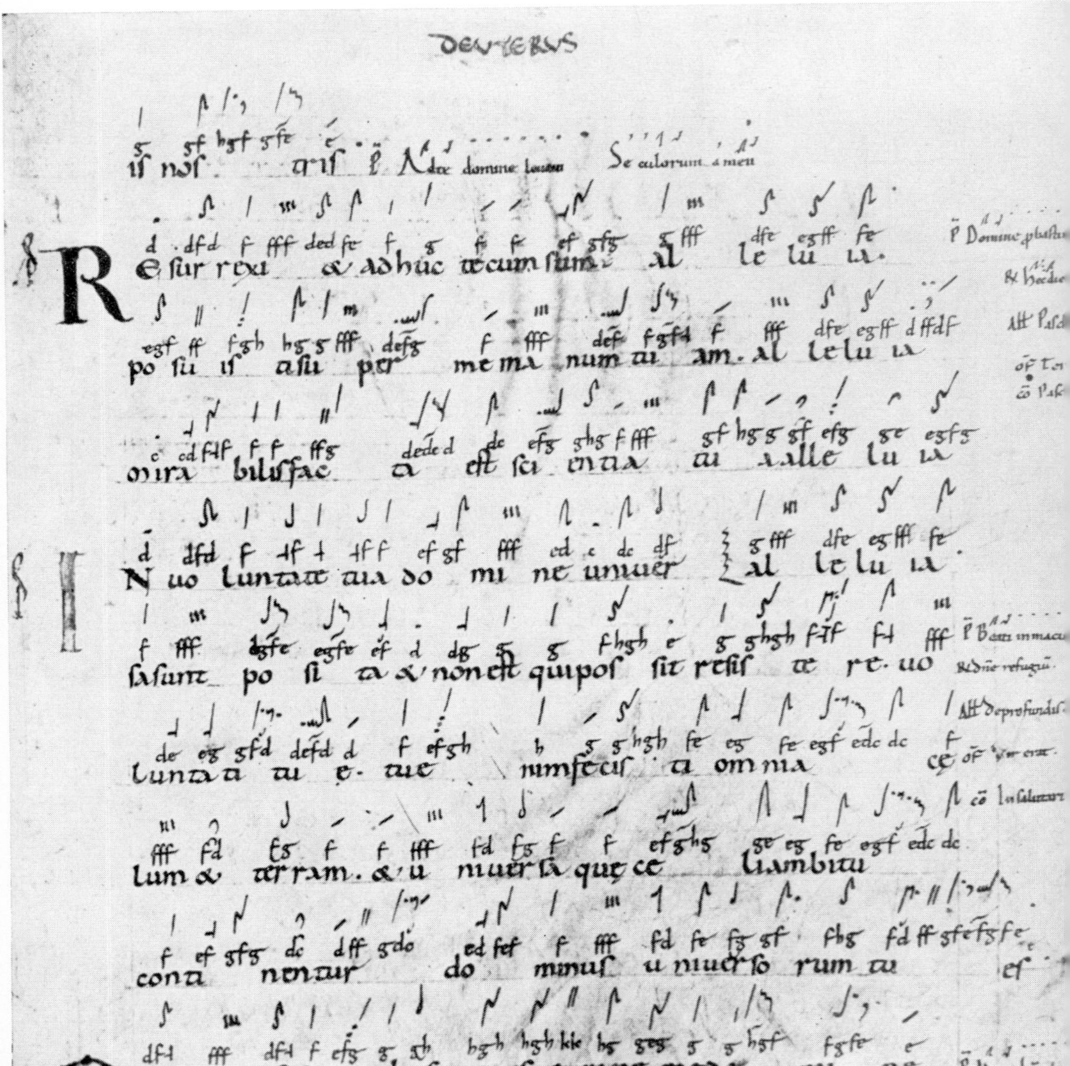

Plate VI. Montpellier, Bibl. de l'École de Méd. *H. 159*

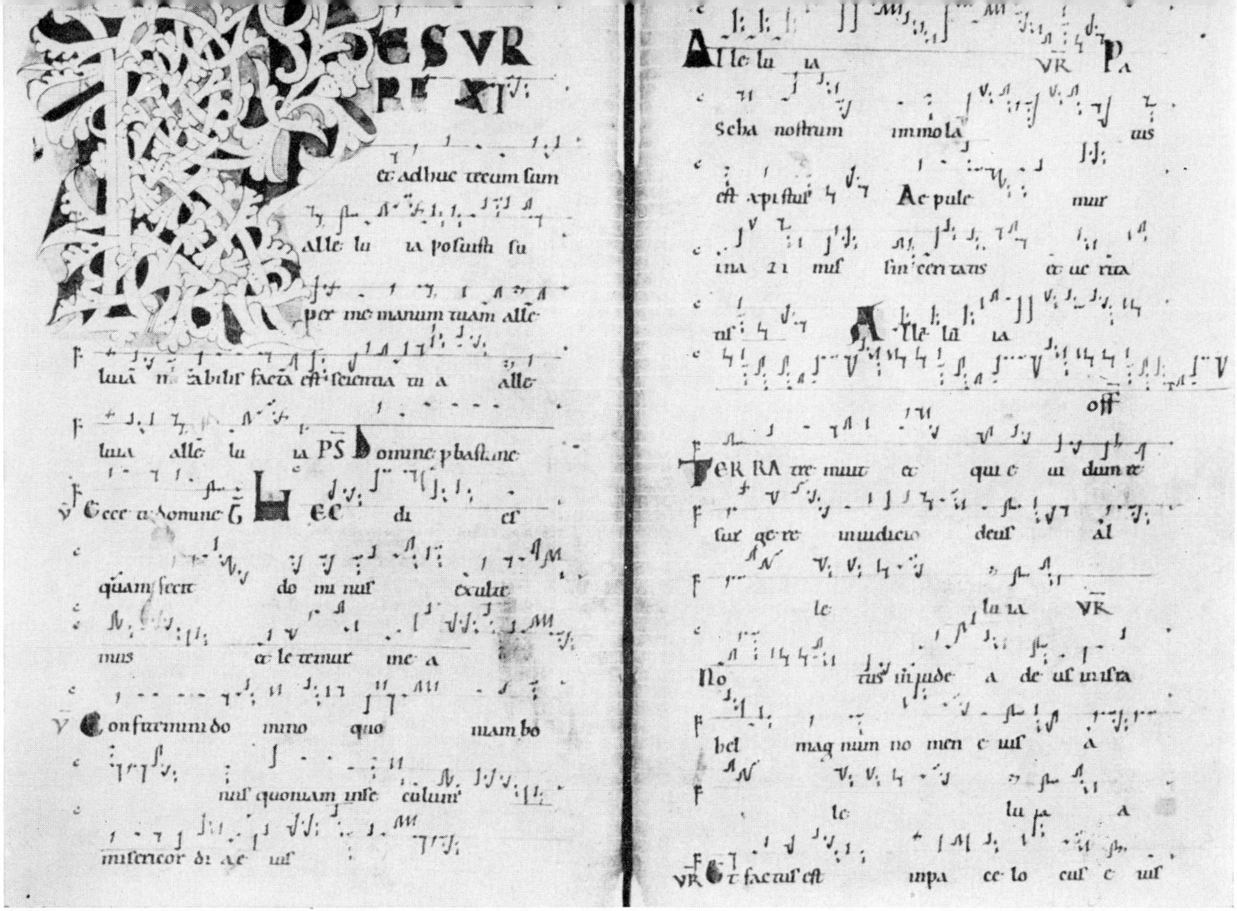

Plate VII. Rome, Vatican Libr. *lat. 5319*

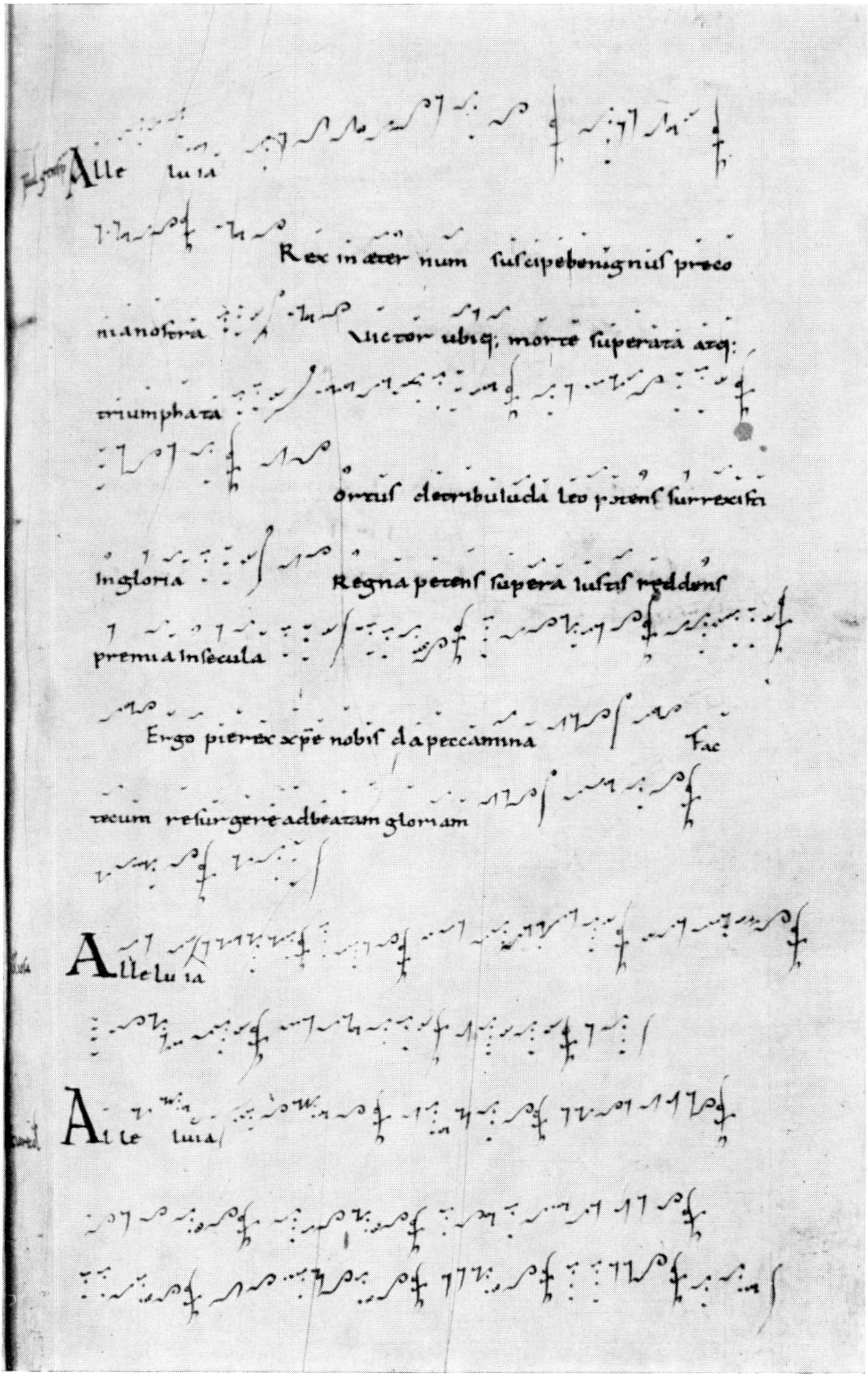

Alle lu ia

Rex in aeter num suscipe benignius preco
niano seria Victor ubiq; morte superata atq;
triumphata

ortus decoribuludia leo potens surrexisti
ingloria Regna petens supera lutas reddens
premia in secula

Ergo pie rex xpe nobis da peccamina fac
recum resurgere ad beatam gloriam

Alle lu ia

Alle lu ia

Plate VIII. Paris, Bibl. nat. *lat. 17436*

the alphabet, so that h, i, k, l, m, n, o, p stand for a, b, c′, d′, e′, f′, g′, and a′.[8] For instance, the letters fgh hg on "(posu)isti" (line 3) indicate f g a a g. The ornamental signs of the neumatic notation are reproduced in an interesting way, the *quilisma* by a short wavy stroke, [see "(su)per" on line 3], the *oriscus* by a small hook [see "(volunta)ti" at the beginning of line 7]. At the beginning of *In voluntate* (Introit for the Twenty-First Sunday after Pentecost [1066]) repeated use of the sign ┥ is made, which indicates, without doubt, the quarter-tone or some micro-interval below f.[9]

PLATE VII. Rome, Vatican Libr. *lat. 5319.* This is one of the four sources of the Old-Roman chant mentioned on p. 77. The Introit has two verses, *Domine probasti* and *Ecce a Domine,* the first, as usual, designated as *Ps*(almus). The *Alleluia Pascha nostrum* has the verse *Aepulemur,* as in St. Gall *339* (Plate II) and in most of the earlier sources.

The notation is an example of the Beneventan neumes, completely diastematic with lines and clef letters. In the original the F-line is red, the C-line yellow, the others are scratched in without color. The melodies, as will easily be seen, are completely different from those of the other manuscripts. (See the transcription of *Resurrexi,* Fig. 167, p. 488).

PLATE VIII. Paris, Bibl. nat. *lat. 17436* (*Antiphonal* of Compiègne, with musical entries of the eleventh century). This facsimile is given chiefly as an example of a *sequela* with *verba* [see p. 449]. It is written in an early, non-diastematic type of Aquitanian neumes, which may be compared with the later, diastematic type of Plate V. The elongated scrolls are signs of repeat, probably meaning *denuo* (again, twice). For further details the version of *Fulgens praeclara* in A. Hughes, *Anglo-French Sequelae* (1934), p. 41, may be consulted.

We need not carry this survey any farther, because with the beginning of the thirteenth century the square neumes were universally adopted. Only in Germany a special type of over-decorative script was cultivated, the Gothic neumes, also called *Hufnagelschrift* because of their resemblance to horse-shoe nails.[10]

THE NOTATION OF THE SOLESMES BOOKS

We owe the present-day books of Gregorian chant, such as the *Graduale Sacrosanctae Romanae Ecclesiae,* the *Antiphonale Sacrosanctae Romanae Ecclesiae,* and the *Liber usualis,* to the Benedictine monks of Solesmes who, under the leadership of Dom Guéranger (1805-75), Dom Pothier (1835-1923), and Dom Mocquereau (1849-1930), did the spadework which

8 See p. 152, system *Anonymus II.*

9 See J. Gmelch, *Die Vierteltonstufen im Messtonale von Montpellier* (1911). Also, e.g., G. Reese, *Music in the Middle Ages,* p. 136.

10 See the table of neumes in Grove's *Dictionary,* III, 648 (omitted in the new edition, 1954) or in *HDM,* s. v. "Neumes." They are obviously derived from the late (twelfth-century) Messine neumes.

led to the restoration of the medieval tradition. Without their efforts the study of Gregorian chant would be immensely more difficult, as would, for instance, the study of the works of Bach without the volumes of the *Bach Gesellschaft,* or that of Machaut, Josquin, and Palestrina without the modern editions of their complete works. Although none of these publications can wholly replace the original sources—least of all in the field of chant, the complete repertory of which far exceeds the contents of the modern books—they provide a reliable basis of ample proportions which the student may safely use for numerous investigations.

There is, however, a certain difference between the editorial principles and methods employed in the volumes of the *Bach Gesellschaft* (as well as in the other musicological publications just mentioned) and those adopted by the monks of Solesmes. Aware of their primary obligation which, of course, was to the Church rather than to musicology, they aimed at an edition that would not only restore the medieval tradition but also make it a part of the present-day liturgy, so that the old melodies would be sung again after more than a thousand years, as indeed they now are. Consequently it was felt necessary that some indications which would facilitate their performance by present-day singers and choirs should be added to the original melodies. Useful and perhaps indispensable though they may be, they tend to put the Solesmes books into the same category as, for example, a practical edition of Bach with its customary trappings of phrase marks, dynamic signs, etc. In either case it is important for the student to know what is authentic and what is an editorial addition.

The series of modern publications of Gregorian chant started with the *Liber gradualis* prepared by Dom Pothier and published, in two editions, in 1883 and 1895.[1] Here the only editorial signs are vertical strokes of two different lengths designed to indicate the end of phrases or of sections. They more or less agree with the full bar and the half bar of the later editions, prepared under the direction of Mocquereau, the author of a special theory and practice of Gregorian rhythm generally known as the Solesmes method. He obtained permission from the Sacred Congregation of Rites in Rome to incorporate his method into the new editions (Solesmes edition) which, consequently, contain considerably more material of an editorial nature. In addition to the above-mentioned phrase marks the Solesmes editions make consistent use of five other signs: the quarter bar, the comma, the dot, the horizontal *episema,* and the vertical *episema.* Following is a brief explanation of these signs.

a. The full bar, half bar, quarter bar, and comma are signs for phrasing or breathing [see, for example, the Gradual *In sole, L* 344]. Without questioning their practical usefulness, we may well (and often have to) disregard them in our analytical studies, except for the full bar, extending

[1] See p. 17.

through the entire staff like the modern bar line. This bar often serves to separate melodic units which are of basic importance particularly in the Tracts, Responsories, and Graduals, as will be seen later.[2] None of these signs occur in the medieval manuscripts.

b. The dot, called *punctum-mora* (L. *mora*, length, duration), is placed after a note or, occasionally in neumes, above it. It doubles the value of the affected note, making it a quarter-note rather than an eighth-note. Like the phrase signs, the dot does not occur in the early sources.

c. The horizontal *episema* (Gr. additional sign) is a horizontal stroke placed over a note or, occasionally, a group of two, three, or four notes [see the end of the Offertory *Posuisti, L* 438]. In the Solesmes system it indicates a slight lengthening of the notes above which it appears [see *L,* p. xx]. These horizontal *episemas* are not editorial marks, as are the other signs. They were adopted from the early St. Gall manuscripts which, as we have seen, frequently employ the *episema*—particularly in connection with the *virga* and the *clivis*—and also letters that pertain to details of rhythm. Mocquereau and his followers have given a prominent role to these manuscripts, which they have termed "rhythmic manuscripts."[3] The Solesmes *episema* is also used where the rhythmic manuscripts have the letter *t* or a specially formed neume believed to indicate lengthening of a note. For instance, in the Gradual *Haec dies* [778] the *episema* over the initial neume reproduces the *t* of the Codex St. Gall *359* [see Plate I]; that over the fourth neume stems from the special form of the *podatus;* those over the two *climacus* groups in the melisma "bo(nus)" stem from the *climacus* form with horizontal strokes (*punctum planum*) instead of dots. Now and then a rhythmic indication of the original is reproduced as *punctum-mora,* e.g., in the "special *podatus* with *episema*" near the beginning of the final melisma on "(e)jus."

d. Finally, extensive and consistent use is made of the vertical *episema,* a short vertical dash placed above or, occasionally, beneath a note. More than any other sign, this is bound up with Mocquereau's interpretation of Gregorian chant and the Solesmes method of singing derived from it. This method employs, in a very prominent position, the so-called *ictus,* i.e., a subtle emphasis or impulse which recurs on every second or third note, resulting in small rhythmic entities (feet) of two or three notes, often in irregular alternation. The rules for the placement of the *ictus* are fully explained on p. xxviii of the *Liber usualis.* The vertical *episema* serves to indicate the position of the *ictus* in all those cases in which it is not apparent from the general rules. Needless to say, there is no trace of the vertical *episema* in any of the medieval sources, and the historical validity of the *ictus* theory is, to put it mildly, highly questionable. We shall return

2 See, e.g., the tables on pp. 271, 273.

3 See, e.g., Suñol, *Paléographie,* pp. 131ff.

to this problem in the next section, dealing with the rhythm of Gregorian chant.

THE PROBLEM OF RHYTHM

Some time ago, when I told a friend of mine about my work on the present book he said: "How can you write a book on Gregorian chant; you don't know anything about its rhythm." It is true that I don't know anything about Gregorian rhythm, anything certain, that is—nor does anybody else. In contrast to my friend, however, I do not consider a knowledge of this matter a *sine qua non,* or ignorance of it a serious obstacle to fruitful and valid investigation in our field. On the contrary, I cannot help feeling that the importance of the rhythmic problem has been somewhat exaggerated. The numerous efforts made in this direction appear to me like so many answers to a question that was never raised. This does not mean to say that Gregorian chant had no rhythm. Music without rhythm is obviously a contradiction in itself. However, rhythm is not the same as a fixed rhythmic system, that is, a clearly formulated and consistently applied set of rules governing the duration of the notes and other matters pertaining to rhythm in the most general sense of the word. It is toward the discovery of some such system that the efforts of so many scholars have been directed—without any incontestable or generally accepted result. Could it be that they were chasing a phantom, that they were trying to find something that never existed? I believe so, for at least two reasons. One is that the melodies of the chant, in their specific melodic design, lend themselves to a rhythmic (or better, a-rhythmic?) rendition of the greatest flexibility and variability, similar to what we find in so many folkmelodies (e.g., American Indian) of a "rhapsodic" character. In such folkmelodies rhythm is present only as an accessory, not as a preconditioning element as it is in tunes pertaining to dancing. Their rhythmic structure, if that is what it should be called, is so evasive that it is bound to undergo variations from individual to individual, and even more so from generation to generation. It seems to me that Gregorian chant is equally susceptible to such vicissitudes.

The other reason is, that I am convinced there would be some tangible evidence of systematic rhythm either in the musical sources or in the medieval treatises if there ever had been a stable tradition in this field comparable to that which we find in the purely melodic aspect of the chant. True enough, there are the "rhythmic manuscripts" such as St. Gall *359,* which, no doubt, represent an effort in the direction of indication of some rhythmic details. However, they are extremely limited in number and locale, their importance as testimonials of the "true chant" has been contested, and their indications more than anything else have been the source of disagreement and controversy among scholars. The latter remark applies also to the few hints about rhythm that have been found in medieval treatises. Every one of them has been interpreted as evidence of opposite theories.

In view of this state of affairs—at least, the way I see them—I would like nothing better than to close this chapter right here. Since, however, the problem still looms large in the minds of scholars and students, it cannot very well be omitted in a book on Gregorian chant without inviting strong criticism. We shall therefore give a short resumé of the various theories that have been proposed.

It is customary to group these theories and their proponents into two categories—equalist and mensuralist. The chief difference is that the former admit only one basic time-value, while the latter insist that various time-values are involved. To the former group belong Pothier and Mocquereau; to the latter, Houdard, Riemann, Dechevrens, Fleury, Jeannin, Wagner, and, more recently, Lipphardt and Jammers.

I. *Pothier.* Pothier developed his ideas about Gregorian rhythm in his *Les Mélodies grégoriennes* (1881).[1] It is difficult to gain an entirely clear picture of his ideas from this book, and even more so from the writings of the few followers he had.[2] Although he is usually, and to a certain degree perhaps properly, considered an equalist, he repeatedly speaks about "des notes plus longues et d'autres plus brèves" (p. 184), and even says that there are "plusieurs sortes de longues, comme aussi plusieurs sortes de brèves" (p. 185). Obviously what he had in mind is a "free rhythm" admitting numerous subtle deviations from the basic time unit. Beyond this, he considered the Latin text with its accents a basic factor of the rhythmic life, particularly in the syllabic and neumatic chants or passages, in which the textual accent should make itself felt in the performance as a stress of the corresponding note of the melody. In melismatic passages the accent falls on the first note of each neume. His theory has been termed: "free oratoric rhythm."

II. *Mocquereau.* In opposition to Pothier, Mocquereau developed what has become known as the Solesmes system or, in distinction from Pothier's theory, as "free musical rhythm." He proposed this first in vol. VII of the *Paléographie musicale* and elaborated it in great detail in his *Le Nombre musical.* His system is incorporated in the modern publications of the Solesmes edition, which usually carry the remark: *rhythmicis signis a Soles-*

---

[1] Dom Gajard, in an article "Le Chant grégorien et la Méthode de Solesmes" (*RG*, XXIX, 22, etc.) mentions a book by Gontier, *Méthode raisonné de plainchant* (1859) as a first attempt in this direction (pp. 27f). This may have been in opposition to others who interpreted the neumes in terms of sixteenth-century mensural notation, e.g., the *climacus* as a *longa* followed by two *semibreves*.

[2] For instance, Dom Lucien David, *Le Rythme verbal et musical dans le chant romain* (1933). For a relatively clear summary see Gajard's article (fn. 1), p. 29.

mensibus monachis diligenter ornatum (carefully provided by the Monks of Solesmes with rhythmic signs). He is much more an "equalist" than Pothier, insisting, as he does, on a "rythme précis" as the foundation of the performance. All notes have equal value except for those marked by the horizontal *episema,* which are to be slightly lengthened, and those marked by the *punctum-mora,* which are to be approximately doubled. The latter occur only at the end of phrases or sections. However, doubled and even tripled values also result from unison groups, as in the *pressus* or in the *distropha* and *tristropha.* More fundamentally different and novel, however, are his views about accentuation. Completely discarding Pothier's idea of the text and of stress *(intensité)* as governing elements, he considers the rhythm as a purely musical phenomenon, as a motion consisting of *élan* and *repos* (arsis and thesis; approximately, up-beat and down-beat). These follow, not in regular patterns, but in irregular successions of groups of two or three notes. The constantly recurring "impulse" involved in this performance, the *ictus,* is indicated by the vertical *episema* whenever necessary. These elementary groups, always binary or ternary, are combined into rhythmic division of higher orders, incises, members, phrases, and periods. For the clarification of these ideas and for teaching purposes extensive use is made of cheironomic drawings *(chironomie),* wave-like lines drawn between and above the notes in order to give a visual impression of the *mouvement rythmique.*

Mocquereau's system has not only been universally adopted in the churches but has also found ardent admirers elsewhere. Perhaps its main merit lies in the field of musical education, where it has effectively counteracted the mechanizing influence of time-beating. In fact, Mocquereau himself seems to have considered it as such, rather than claiming historical correctness for it. Certainly, there is no historical foundation whatever for the central part of his theory, the binary and ternary groups with the *ictus.*[3] He devoted painstaking research to the "rhythmic manuscripts," from which he adopted the various signs for prolongation *(episema,* letters *t, x, m),* disregarding, however, the signs for acceleration *(c)* or those that indicate various degrees of intensity *(f, cum fragore; k, clange).* Thus, his work represents a mixture of historical exactitude and ingenious fancy. Considered aesthetically, its aim is to avoid manifest effects by introducing

3 Among his most outspoken critics were M. Emmanuel and Gastoué who, in a review of *Le Nombre musical (TG,* XIV, 258) said: "La tolérance que Dom M. a obtenue de Rome pour ses signes rythmiques lui permet—par un abus singulier—d'aller au bout de son dessin, qui est d'imposer 'au monde entier' son interprétation personelle des rythmes médiévaux. Il est temps de protester contre cette prétention, peu justifiée. Il ne faut pas que les practiciens du plain-chant se laissent régenter par un savant qui défend sa propre gloire, avec trop de partialité." An excellent presentation and well-balanced criticism of Mocquereau's method is found in G. Reese, *Music in the Middle Ages,* pp. 141ff.

various layers of emphasis that balance each other, such as the textual accent, the *ictus,* and the *episema.* In an ideal case (which is often realized) these three kinds of "stress" would appear each at a different place.

III. As for the mensuralists, we can only briefly indicate the appallingly different results they have arrived at, often upon the basis of the same sources (St. Gall *359;* Codex Hartker) and the same theorists (e.g., Guido).

a. *Houdard.* Each neumatic symbol has the same temporal value (quarter-note). Thus, the *punctum* and *virga* have the duration of a quarter-note; in the *podatus* and *clivis* each tone is an eighth-note; a *climacus,* etc., is reproduced as eighth-note triplets; a four-tone neume as sixteenth-notes, etc. See *Le rythme du chant grégorien* (1898).

b. *Riemann.* Transcription in strict 4/4-meter and phrases of four measures, on the basis of the text, which is arbitrarily forced into Ambrosian-hymn meter [see *Handbuch der Musikgeschichte* I.ii, (1905), p. 34]:

.   /   /   .   /   /   /   .   .   /   .   /   /
Da | *mi- hi in* | *dis- co* | *caput Jo- annis bap-/ ti- stae* |
/   /   .   /   .   .   /   /   .   /   .   /   /
/et contri-/ status est rex | *propter jusju- /ran- dum* |

c. *Dechevrens.* After an early attempt (*Études de science musicale,* 1898) he proposed in *Les vraies mélodies grégoriennes* (1902) a rendition of the Vesper Antiphons in regular meter (4/4, 2/4). The rendition is based on the neumes of the Codex Hartker, which are interpreted as variable depending upon the neighboring neumes. Thus, a *virga* with *episema* is a half-note if followed by a *virga* (quarter-note), but a dotted quarter-note if followed by a *punctum* (eighth-note). He makes extended use of grace notes, e.g., for the *quilisma* and for the liquescent *podatus.*[4]

d. *Fleury.* He emphasized the importance of the St. Gall *episema* and the Romanus letters for prolongation, interpreting them as indications for exactly doubled values (half-notes), the sign *c* (*celeriter*) as an indication for halved values (eighth-notes). The three note values are combined according to principles of the metrical feet. He gives no examples of transcription. [See *Ueber Choralrhythmus* (transl. by Bonvin, in *Publikationen der Internationalen Musikgesellschaft, Beihefte,* 1907).]

e. *Wagner.* Originally a champion of the Pothier-type of free rhythm (*Neumenkunde,* 1st edition, 1905), he later proposed an interpretation in measured values (eighth-note, quarter-note, dotted quarter-note), but without meter. His main tenet was that the *virga* as well as the *punctum planum* (which he called *virga jacens*) indicate doubled values, which are

---

[4] In the appendix to *Les vraies mélodies,* Dechevrens gives two transcriptions of the *Vespéral,* in *Notation rythmique ancienne* (I) and in *Notation rythmique moderne* (II). Both are practically identical, save for the addition of bar-lines and meter in the latter. He revised his theory once more in *Composition littéraire et composition musicale* (1910). For an example see Gajard's article (fn. 1), p. 23.

increased to triple values (dotted quarter-note) by the *episema*. He also assigned a fixed metrical scheme to each neume. [See *Wagner II*, 353ff; also Adler's *Handbuch der Musikwissenschaft* I, (1924), 93 and 102ff.]

f. *Jeannin*. He admits only two time values, quarter- and eighth-note, which are arranged in irregular measures, 3/8, 4/8, 5/8, etc., at least for simple chants such as Antiphons. [See *Études sur le rythme grégorien* (1926).]

g. *Lipphardt* studied the Antiphons on the basis of the Codex Hartker, and, in contrast to Dechevrens [see under c.], arrived at a rendition in triple meter, essentially an alternation of longs and short in the manner of the first rhythmic mode. [See "Studien zur Rhythmik der Antiphonen" (*Die Musikforschung* III, (1950), 47, 224).] Similar results had been formulated by Sowa, in *Quellen zur Transformation der Antiphonen* (1935).

h. *Jammers* also studied the Antiphons as found in the Codex Hartker, with more careful attention to the neumatic symbols. Like Dechevrens, he concludes that all the Antiphons are essentially in 4/4-meter. [See *Der Gregorianische Rhythmus* (1937).]

For the purpose of further illustration, examples from the various mensuralists are given in Fig. 23. In one case and another it has been possible to show the same melody in different rhythmic interpretations. These are grouped together.

If, in conclusion, I am permitted to express my own views, I would say that for the over-all tradition of the chant the method of Pothier comes as close to being a plausible and practicable solution as may be expected. It recommends itself by the fact that it involves no "difficult problem" and, for that reason, no "ingenious solution." Its main premises, the importance of the textual accent and of the first note of each neume, are clearly implied in, and easily intelligible from, the notation as we find it in the great majority of the manuscripts. I would not, however, advocate a strictly equalistic performance of the melodies. In the neumatic and melismatic chants particularly I would admit subtle nuances of rhythm on the basis of Houdard's theory, the merits of which, it seems to me, have been slighted or altogether overlooked. I would not go as far as to maintain that a five-note neume should be sung in exactly the same time as one of two or three notes, but the idea of subtly varying the speed according to the number of notes found in a neume appeals to me, because it is as simple and natural as the principles advocated by Pothier.

In offering these suggestions I do not mean to exclude the possibility of seeking, and perhaps finding, special solutions for individual rhythmic manuscripts, such as St. Gall *359* and *339*, Einsiedeln *121*, or the Codex Hartker. Here the main question is whether the rhythmic signs or letters indicate only nuances (Mocquereau) or really different note values (mensuralists). I agree with the position taken by practically every musicologist

FIGURE 23

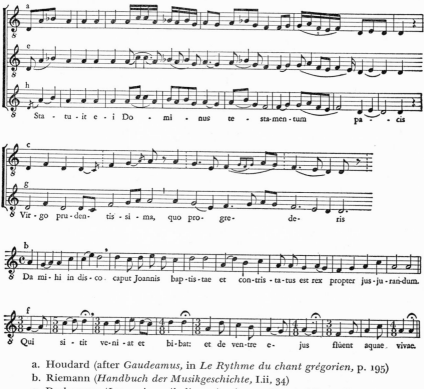

Sta - tu - te - i Do - mi - nus te - sta-men - tum pa - - cis

Vir - go pru - den - tis' - si - ma, quo pro - gre - de- ris

Da mi - hi in dis - co - caput Joannis bap - tis-tae et con-tris - ta-tus est rex propter jus-ju-ran-dum.

Qui si - tit ve - ni - at et bi-bat: et de ven-tre e- jus flùent aquae - vivae.

a. Houdard (after *Gaudeamus*, in *Le Rythme du chant grégorien*, p. 195)
b. Riemann (*Handbuch der Musikgeschichte*, I.ii, 34)
c. Dechevrens (*Les vraies mélodies grégoriennes,* Vespéral I, p. 78)
e. Wagner (Adler, *Handbuch*, I, 112)
f. Jeannin (*Études sur le rythme grégorien*, p. 26)
g. Lipphardt (*Die Musikforschung*, III, 235)
h. Jammers (*Der gregorianische Rhythmus*, Examples, p. 46)

that the latter interpretation is correct.[5] Of all the various renditions listed above it seems to me that those given by Wagner are by far the best, because they are free from preconceived notions such as regular meter, notions which belong to a considerably later period of music and which, if applied to the Gregorian melodies, always involve some deviation from, or forced interpretation of, the original. Wagner, on the contrary, has given rhythmic interpretations which reflect every detail and nuance of such highly com-

[5] To quote only one of the most recent statements: "The outstanding trait of Gregorian cantillation, mentioned through all the Middle Ages, though neglected today, is the mingling of short and long notes; the contemporary writers insist again and again on a careful distinction between the two values." (C. Sachs, *Rhythm and Tempo*, 1953, p. 152). See also the remarks in Stäblein's article "Choral" (*MGG*, especially pp. 1288ff).

plex notations as that of St. Gall *359* and of similar manuscripts of the ninth and tenth centuries. By the consistent application of the principle that the stroke (*virga* or *virga jacens*) represents a long value, the dot (*punctum*) a short one, he has succeeded in giving plausible explanations for the various modifications of the neumes, for instance, the different forms of the *podatus* or the *climacus* to which we have called attention in our description of Plate I [see p. 120]. His table showing the rhythmic equivalents of all the neumes[6] provides a solid basis for the interpretation of the early manuscripts, and his transcriptions of the Graduals *Sciant gentes* and *Specie tua,* as well as of other melodies, demonstrate the practical applicability of his method.[7]

I am less confident about Wagner's attempts to apply the same rhythmic interpretation to such a late source as a German manuscript of the fifteenth century.[8] All evidence points to the fact that the rhythmic performance of chant was an early practice which was lost after *c.* 1000. One of the most eloquent testimonies comes from Aribo, who, in his *De Musica* of *c.* 1070, says: "In earlier times not only the inventors of melodies but also the singers themselves used great circumspection that everything should be invented and sung in proportion (*proportionaliter et invenirent et canerent*). This consideration perished some time ago and is now entirely buried."[9]

6 *Wagner II,* 395ff; a short excerpt also in Adler's *Handbuch der Musikgeschichte,* I (2nd ed., 1929), 93.

7 See *Wagner II,* 405; Adler's *Handbuch,* pp. 105, 112f. Wagner points out that different early manuscripts, such as St. Gall *339* and Einsiedeln *121,* often show different rhythmic readings [*Handbuch,* p. 112]. This fact, however, does not invalidate the premise of Wagner's research. It only shows that rhythm (in the sense as we understand it here) was an accessory element which was greatly variable in time and locale. Each of the early manuscripts has its own rhythm.

8 See Adler's *Handbuch,* p. 107.

9 *GS,* II, 227a; also J. Smits van Waesberghe, *Aribonis De Musica* (1951), p. 49. Unless we admit the possibility that the melodies themselves underwent fundamental changes that caused them to lose their "proportion" (of phrases?)—a surmise never seriously considered by Gregorianists—Aribo's remark can only refer to proportional note-values.

CHAPTER THREE

The Tonality

THE CHURCH MODES

THE tonal basis of Gregorian chant is a system of eight tonalities, known as church modes. Each of these is an octave-segment of the diatonic (C-major) scale, with one of its tones playing the role of a central tone or tonic, comparable to the tone C in the C-major scale. The octave range is called *ambitus,* the central tone, *finalis.* There are four such *finales,* namely, d, e, f, and g. To each of these belong two modes which differ in their ambitus: one of them starts with the final and extends to its upper octave, while the other starts a fourth below the final and extends to the fifth above it. Those of the former type are called authentic, of the latter, plagal.[1] For the complete system, two sets of names were used. The older terminology employs the Greek terms *protus, deuterus, tritus,* and *tetrardus* (first, second, third, fourth) for the finals and uses the terms authentic or plagal for additional distinction. The other terminology, more commonly employed from the tenth century to the present day, simply numbers them from one to eight:

		MODE	FINALIS	AMBITUS
Protus authenticus	Primus tonus	1	d	d-d′
Protus plagius	Secundus t.	2	d	A-a
Deuterus auth.	Tertius t.	3	e	e-e′
Deuterus plag.	Quartus t.	4	e	B-b
Tritus auth.	Quintus t.	5	f	f-f′
Tritus plag.	Sextus t.	6	f	c-c′
Tetrardus auth.	Septimus t.	7	g	g-g′
Tetrardus plag.	Octavus t.	8	g	d-d′

Yet another terminology reverts to ancient Greek theory, in which the names *Dorian, Lydian, Phrygian, Mixolydian,* and others were employed to designate octave species or complete scales. Modern scholars have made

[1] Fom Gr. *plagios,* slanting, sideways, subsidiary. The *Commemoratio brevis* employs the terms *auctoralis* and *subjugalis.*

numerous attempts to solve the problem of the relationship between the two theoretical systems, the Greek and the medieval, without having been able to arrive at a universally accepted answer. For our purpose it suffices to say that the above names were applied in Greek theory to octave segments starting respectively on e, d, c, and B; while in the system of the church modes they denote octaves starting respectively on d, e, f, and g, so that they are synonymous with *protus, deuterus, tritus,* and *tetrardus.* The plagal varieties are indicated by the prefix *hypo-,* so that *hypodorian* is the second mode, *hypophrygian* the fourth, etc. Considering everything, it is probably best not to use the Greek names at all in connection with Gregorian chant.[2]

It is hardly necessary to point out that each of the eight modes represents a tonal realm of individual structure, the basic difference being the position of the half-tones with regard to the final. Thus, in mode 1 the half-tones (e-f and b-c′) begin at the second and sixth degrees; in mode 3 at the first and fifth; in mode 5 at the fourth and seventh; and in mode 7 at the third and sixth; while in the plagal modes one is above, the other below the final.

The four authentic modes are sometimes called Ambrosian, the others Gregorian, with the implication (or explicit statement) that the former were "invented" by St. Ambrose, the latter "added" by St. Gregory. There is not the least bit of evidence to support this story, nor even to make it appear probable or possible. First of all, there is no difference, as to tonal structure in general, between the Ambrosian and the Gregorian repertories, both of which employ the complete system of eight modes in generally the same way. Both repertories, moreover, give clear evidence of having been formed some time before the system of the eight modes was established. Otherwise there could not be so many melodies as there actually are that do not conform in one way or another with the theoretical system. The earliest allusion to this is found in a fragmentary treatise by Alcuin (735-804), friend and adviser of Charlemagne [see List of Sources, p. 54, no. 17]. Very likely it was in this period, sometimes called the "Carolingian Renaissance," that the tonal aspect of the Gregorian repertory became the subject of investigation and classification. The impulse for this may have come from Byzantium which exercised considerable influence on Western thought during the eighth century. Not only are the

2 Most of the important theorists employ the names *protus, deuterus,* etc., or *primus secundus,* etc. The earliest mention of the Greek scale designations is in the *Musica enchiriadis:* ". . . *protus autentus* or *plagis, deuterus autentus* or *plagis,* or *modus Dorius, Phyrgius, Lydius,* etc., names that have come from the vocabulary of the gentiles" (*GS,* I, 159b). Exceptional, because of its exclusive use of the Greek names, is a tenth-century treatise written in Old High German and ascribed to Notker, in which, however, the terms Dorian, Phrygian, Lydian, and Mixolydian denote the scales respectively on c, d, e and f, not on d, e, f, and g (*De octo modis; GS,* I, 98).

early designations, *protus, deuterus,* etc., *authenticus, plagius,* all derived
from Greek words, but the system of eight modes has an exact counterpart
in Byzantine theory, where it is known as *octoechos* (eight tones). In short,
the term "tonal basis" used in the first sentence of this chapter is correct
only in the technical, not in the historical sense of the word.

Occasionally we shall employ a term which occurs in some of the medieval treatises and which, although rarely used by modern musicologists
and Gregorianists, nevertheless is not devoid of usefulness. This is the term
maneria, which implies a classification, not of eight, but of four categories,
one for each of the finals. Thus, the four *maneriae* are the *protus, deuterus,
tritus,* and *tetrardus,* without the subdivision into authentic and plagal.[3]

The previous statement that the ambitus of each mode is an octave, is a
somewhat artificial simplification, for most of the Gregorian melodies require the addition of one degree below the bottom note of the octave segment, which thus becomes extended to a ninth. This additional tone is
required especially in the authentic modes, in which it represents the
degree below the final, a degree often touched upon in cadential or semi-
cadential formulae, but which may also occur elsewhere during the course
of the melody. It is called *subfinalis* or *subtonium modi,* the former name
being less commendable because it properly applies only to the authentic
modes.

While the earliest medieval theorists recognize only the octave ambitus—
dividing it into a fifth plus fourth (*diapente, diatessaron*) in the authentic
modes and into a fourth plus fifth in the plagal modes—a more realistic
point of view prevails in the tenth-century *Dialogus in musica* of Oddo of
Cluny (or one of his pupils; see List of Sources, no. 25). Here we find the
octave ambitus enlarged not only by the *subtonium modi,* in all the modes
except the sixth, but also often by one degree above the octave, so that
the total range becomes a tenth. The following table shows Oddo's explanations in a condensed form:[4]

AMBITUS ACCORDING TO ODDO

	AUTHENTIC			PLAGAL	
Mode:	1. c-d'	(ninth)		2. G-b	(tenth)
	3. d-e'	(ninth)		4. A-c'	(tenth)
	5. e-f'	(ninth)		6. c-d'	(ninth)
	7. f-a'	(tenth)		8. c-e'	(tenth)

In modern explanations the modes are usually described as having yet
another characteristic property, i.e., the so-called *dominant,* a secondary

[3] See G. Reese, *Music in the Middle Ages,* p. 153. Cf. *GS,* II, 266a (*Tonale S. Bernardi*)
and *CS,* II, 157a (Guido de Caroli-Loco, Guido of Cherlieu). Probably the *Tonale* is also
by Guido (d. 1158); see "Bernhard von Clairevaux" in *MGG.*
[4] *GS,* I, 259ff.

tonal center which, as a rule, is a fifth above the final in the authentic modes, and a third above it in the plagal modes. However, the dominant can hardly be said to be a characteristic of the mode, because the great majority of the melodies of a given mode fail to show any clear evidence of the dominant. Nor does the dominant occur in any of the medieval descriptions of the modes. Actually, the dominant is a characteristic property, not of a mode in general, but of a few special melodies associated with that mode, such as the psalm tones or other recitation tones. In these the dominant (more properly called *tenor*) does play a prominent role as the pitch for the recitation while, on the other hand, the basic characteristics of the mode, final and ambitus, are often absent. Naturally, among the many thousands of chants there are not a few in which the dominant is clearly recognizable. Particularly among the melodies of the second mode there are a number which emphasize the f as a reciting pitch, e.g., the Antiphon *Dominus Jesus* [661], the Introit *Dominus dixit* [392], the Communion *Dominus regit* [567], or the Offertory *Ad te Domine levavi* [321]. Many others, however, show no evidence of it. Moreover, in some chants with a recognizable recitation tone or pitch of emphasis this is not the pitch of the psalm-tone *tenor*. Thus, several Introits of the fourth mode, e.g., *Accipite* [890], *Involuntate* [1066], *Judica me* [603], or *Misericordia* [816], show recitation on f or g, rather than on the *tenor* of the psalm tone, which is a. On the whole, it cannot be said that the dominant is a characteristic of the mode; it is a characteristic of the recitation tones associated with the mode and of a number of melodies derived from or related to these recitation tones.

Finally, mention may be made of attempts to describe and define the church modes, not as abstract scale formations determined by final, ambitus, and possibly pitch of emphasis, but as categories characterized by a number of standard formulae or motives recurring in the melodies of that mode. This phenomenon, often referred to in modern musicological studies as "melody type,"[5] is fairly clearly evident in various musical cultures of the East; e.g., in the Byzantine and Armenian *echoi* (*octochos,* system of eight *echoi*), in the Syrian *risqolo,* the Javanese *patet,* the Hindu *raga,* and the Arabian *maqam.* Whether a similar state of affairs existed in Roman chant at an early time, as some scholars have maintained, is entirely conjectural. The repertory as we know it shows hardly any evidence for such a surmise. True enough, standard formulae play a prominent role in certain types of chant, particularly in the Tracts, Responsories, and Graduals; but the method employed in them seems to have little more in common with the "melody-type" phenomenon than the general principle of standard formulae which, of course, can be applied to widely different procedures. At any rate, the standard-formula method is a characteristic

5 See *HDM*, s.v. "Melody Type."

only of certain special categories, not of a mode. The Tracts of the eighth mode have different formulae from those of the Responsories of the eighth mode; and neither of these, nor any others, recur consistently in the over-all repertory of this mode.

MODAL CLASSIFICATION AND DISTRIBUTION

With the exception of some very simple chants such as the recitation tones for the prayers and readings [98ff], each Gregorian melody is assigned to one of the eight modes. The basis of this classification is the final note of the melody. According to whether this is d, e, f, or g, the chant is in the category of *protus* (modes 1 and 2), *deuterus* (3 and 4), *tritus* (5 and 6), or *tetrardus* (7 and 8). The range of the melody determines the choice between the authentic or plagal variety. In the modern books the mode is indicated by a figure placed underneath the title, e.g.: $\frac{\text{Offert.}}{5.}$ or $\frac{\text{Comm.}}{1.}$ [480, 481]. The modal classification is also indicated in the index (by the figure preceding the initial word of the chant), and this makes it easy to examine the frequency of each mode in the over-all repertory as well as in the various types of chant. The following table provides an insight into this question.

TABLE OF MODAL DISTRIBUTION[1]

	Maneria:	Pr.		Dt.		Tr.		Tet.	
	Mode:	1	2	3	4	5	6	7	8
1.	Introits (*L*)	29	18	34	18	12	12	16	18
2.	Introits (Cod. Einsiedeln)	29	18	26	20	10	12	19	13
3.	Graduals (*L*)	15	23	14	5	57	0	14	1
4.	Graduals (St. Gall Mss)	35		13		47		15	
5.	Alleluias (*L*)	48	25	14	23	6	2	28	24
6.	Alleluias (different melodies)	33	14	8	13	3	2	23	18
7.	Tracts (*L*)	0	18	0	0	0	0	0	29
8.	Offertories (*L*)	22	21	15	24	8	12	1	27
9.	Offertories (Codex Einsiedeln)	27		27		17		30	
10.	Communions (*L*)	39	17	10	17	14	18	16	29
11.	Communions (Cod. Einsiedeln)	25	18	9	18	14	21	15	25
12.	Antiphons (Cod. Lucca)	369	132	90	167	32	73	252	449
13.	Antiphons (Regino)	336	55	99	137	30	34	196	348
14.	Responsories (Codex Hartker)	91	79	62	78	38	22	125	139
15.	Hymns (*L*)	32	20	15	21	0	2	3	35

[1] The tabulations marked *L* are taken from the *Liber usualis*. Those referring to medieval manuscripts have been taken from the following books: nos. 2, 4, 9, 11, 12 from P. Ferretti, *Esthétique grégorienne* (1938), pp. 276, 161, 195, 276, 247; no. 12 from *Wagner III*, 303; no. 13 from *MGG*, s.v. "Antiphon" (B. Stäblein).

To start with the most numerous chants, the Antiphons, a glance at the table shows two facts: a decided preference for the modes 1 and 8, and a relatively weak representation of the modes 5 and 6, that is, of the f-tonality (*tritus*). Very close to the Antiphons in regard to modal distribution are the Alleluias, as appears from the following table showing the percentages for the four *maneriae*, i.e., authentic and modal combined in one group:

	D	E	F	G	
Antiphons	32	16	7	45	(%)
Alleluias	44	20	5	32	(%)

Most of the other chants show essentially the same picture, though with a tendency toward a more even participation of all the modes, a tendency which is particularly evident in the Introits and Communions. A striking contrast, however, is presented by the Graduals, Tracts, and Hymns. In the Graduals the *tritus* tonality, usually the weakest, becomes by far the strongest, represented by almost one-half of the total. No less striking is the complete absence within this *maneria* of the plagal variety, that is, of mode 6. Mode 8, which has a full share in all the other chants, is represented by only one example, *Dilexisti justitiam* [1216].[2] Yet another plagal mode, mode 4, is very rare in the Graduals. The five examples given in *L* are actually reduced to two melodies, that of *Domine praevenisti* [1207] which is also used for *Benedicta et venerabilis* [1264] and *Dolorosa et lacrimabilis* [1633ᵛ], and that of *Tenuisti manum* [591] which recurs, with some omissions, in *Memor fui* [1580].

A very peculiar situation exists in the Graduals of mode 2. This mode seems to be rather fully represented, its number being second only to that of mode 5. From the musical point of view, however, this number is highly deceptive, since all the Graduals of mode 2 employ one and the same melody or, to put it more correctly, a small number of fixed melodic phrases that recur in various combinations. They are all representatives of one and the same melodic type, usually referred to as the "Gradual-type *Justus ut palma*" [see p. 357]. An exception is the Gradual *Adjutor meus* [*G* 115], which, together with its modern adaptations, *Improperium* and *Repleta est*, is assigned to the second mode. Actually it is vaguely related to the Graduals of the first mode and could just as well be classified as such [see pp. 351f]. In any case, this does not affect the general picture of modal distribution in the Graduals, which can be briefly described as one in which the plagal modes are represented only by a very small number of melodies. It is tempting to speculate on the historical significance of this fact by interpreting it as evidence of an early stage of Gregorian tonality in which this was limited to the authentic modes, in other words, as evi-

---

2 In *G* also *Deus vitam* [*G* 128] and *Deus exaudi* [*G* 156], both having the same melody.

dence in favor of the "Ambrosian-versus-Gregorian-modes" theory previously alluded to. However, it should be noticed that the Gradual of Easter Sunday, *Haec dies*—unquestionably one of the oldest in the whole group —belongs to the second mode. Moreover, an entirely different picture of modal distribution is presented by another type of chant no less ancient than the Graduals, that is, the Tracts.

Turning to these, we are confronted with the most striking aspect of Gregorian tonality, there being Tracts in no modes other than the second and the eighth. As in the case of the Graduals of mode 2, the figures given in our table—eighteen for mode 2 and twenty-nine for mode 8—are deceptive, since in each of these two modes we find a situation quite similar to that presented by the Graduals of mode 2, characterized by the extensive use of standard phrases which recur in all the melodies [see pp. 315ff]. This method of "composition," often referred to as centonization, is the very opposite of "original creation" and unquestionably represents a very archaic technique. It bears a striking resemblance to the *ta' amim* technique which plays an important role in Jewish chant [see p. 363]. On the basis of these considerations P. Wagner has come to the conclusion that the plagal scales of the *deuterus* and *tetrardus* are the "urchristliche Tonarten" (arch-Christian tonalities).[3] In this connection it is interesting to notice that centonization plays an important role in yet another category of chants, the Responsories of Matins. Unlike the Tracts, Responsories exist in all the modes, but those of modes 2 and 8 stand apart from the others because of their much more extended and consistent use of standard phrases and centonization technique. Thus, the Responsories provide additional evidence for the theory that the plagal scales of the *deuterus* and *tetrardus* occupied a special place in the formative process leading to the fully developed system of the church modes.

The tendency, previously noticed in the Antiphons and Alleluias, to avoid the *tritus* is most fully realized in the hymns. Not a single hymn in the fifth mode is found in the *Liber,* and the more complete collections given in the *Antiphonals* include only one such melody, *Aeterne rector* [*AR* 867] = *Orbis patrator* [*AM* 1069], obviously of a late date, as appears from its cadential formula, e-c-d-e-f (e-c-d-f-f in *AM*). The two hymns in the sixth mode which are given in the *Liber* are *Stabat mater* [1424] and *Virgo virginum* [1424], both sung to the same melody, for the late Feast of the Seven Dolours. Originally, the *Stabat mater* (text by Jacopone da Todi, d. 1306?) was composed as a sequence [1634ᵛ]. The *Antiphonals* have three other hymns in the sixth mode.

The question is often raised as to whether there exists in Gregorian chant a tendency toward tonal unification between the chants sung during one and the same service, for instance, at Mass or at Matins of a given

3 *Wagner III,* 525.

feast. The answer is an unequivocal "no." As a rule, the chants show no attempt whatever at tonal organization. The only exceptions are certain Offices of late feasts, for which chants were occasionally written in a seriate arrangement of modes, starting with mode 1 and continuing with modes 2, 3, etc. Thus the five Antiphons for Vespers of Trinity Sunday [914] as well as those for Lauds and Vespers of Corpus Christi [939, 956] are successively in modes 1, 2, 3, 4, and 5. The same principle occurs in the nine Responsories of Matins which, for both feasts, employ the order of the eight modes in the first eight Responsories, the ninth being in mode 4 (for Trinity) or in mode 1 (for Corpus Christi).[4] In the present-day liturgy for Corpus Christi [926ff] the original order is somewhat modified, as shown here:

	4.	5.	6.
Original:	*Panis quem* (4)	*Coenantibus* (5)	*Accepit* (6)
Present:	*Coenantibus* (5)	*Accepit* (6)	*Ego sum* (7)

The last Responsory of the original series, *Unus panis* (1), is replaced by the *Te Deum*.

MODAL CHARACTERISTICS OF THE MELODIES

On the basis of the above-described system of the church modes and classification of the chants, we shall now turn to the important question concerning the "practical application of the system" or (to avoid any implication of precedence) the relationship between the modal theory and the melodies themselves. A comprehensive investigation of this problem would involve the individual consideration of nearly all the chants of the Gregorian repertory and, therefore, would require not only an excessive amount of labor and time but also a much greater portion of this book than can reasonably be allotted to it. On the other hand, to base the study on a limited number of examples picked at random here and there may mean to admit the dangerous element of chance or, even worse, of preconceived notions. Probably the best way out of this dilemma is to investigate the problem on the basis of a clearly circumscribed segment of the repertory, such as exists in the various types of chant. We shall select the Communions, which commend themselves for this purpose because of the relative shortness and simplicity of their melodies as well as by the fairly even distribution of the modes. Using these chants as a point of departure, we shall draw on other chants in order to make the picture more complete.

It may be stated at the outset that the answer to our initial question

4 See, e.g., *Wagner III*, 349, 351.

will be far less simple and unequivocal than may be expected; far less so, indeed, than would be the answer to an analogous question in a more recent period of music—for instance, the question as to the relationship between the system of major-minor tonalities and the compositions by Haydn or Mozart. While there are numerous chants that readily fall in line with the theory of the church modes, there are many others that do not. Examples of non-conformity are especially frequent in the Communions, and this fact is an additional reason for selecting them as the basis of our study. They represent, in a convenient frame, nearly all the aspects of Gregorian tonality, from the simplest to the most perplexing.

In the subsequent study we shall start with a consideration of the regular chants, those which fully conform with the theoretical system, proceeding thereafter to those that show some irregularity of tonal (or modal) behavior. Such irregularity may result from one or several of the following factors: limited ambitus, excessive ambitus, use of b-flat, transposition, each of which will be considered in a separate section. The material for the investigations are the chants as given in the modern publications, particularly the *Liber usualis*. This remark is not quite as superfluous as it may appear to be at first thought. It means that we shall rely on the Solesmes editions not only for the melodies as such, but also for their modal assignment. Can we assume that these data are entirely reliable? In general, the answer to this question is undoubtedly positive, since in the great majority of cases the mode is clearly apparent from the final and the ambitus. There are, however, not a few melodies, probably more than two hundred, whose modal assignment presents problems of one kind or another. The most problematic are those considered in our last section, entitled "Modal Ambiguity."[1]

THE REGULAR CHANTS

As a point of departure, there is indicated below for each mode one Communion which fully accords with the theoretical requirements of finalis and ambitus.

Mode 1: *Viderunt omnes* [410]	Mode 5: *Dico vobis* [984]
2: *Ego sum pastor* [439]	6: *Exsultavit* [352]
3: *Gustate* [1015]	7: *Dicite* [337]
4: *Quod dico* [1173]	8: *Modicum* [824]

[1] To my knowledge, this is the first attempt at a detailed description of Gregorian tonality, assuredly one of the most difficult problems of the chant. I am fully aware of its limitations, but I hope that it will provide a basis for further studies of a more ample scope and of a more definitive character. A very useful study of some of the aspects involved, especially of the theoretical foundation, is F. S. Andrews, *Mediaeval Modal Theory* (unpublished dissertation, Cornell University, 1935).

Although these eight melodies are certainly not sufficient in themselves to prove anything, they are nonetheless indicative of certain traits which we will find confirmed by the investigation of additional material. One of these is a contrast between the authentic and the plagal modes in the extent to which they utilize the degrees of their respective ranges. The melodies of the authentic modes move freely within their full ambitus, with perhaps the exception of the subfinal and the octave above the final, which are only occasionally touched upon. In the plagal melodies, on the other hand, the upper fifth is the only part of the ambitus fully exploited, while the notes below the final are rarely used, in some cases only once. The difference can be conveniently indicated by the modern term *tessitura* which "differs from range in that it does not take into account a few isolated notes of extraordinarily high or low pitch."[2] The difference, then, is that in the authentic modes the *tessitura* comprises most of the ambitus, while in the plagal modes it takes up only its upper fifth.

Another important trait, noticeable at least in some of the examples, is the tendency toward what may be called tonal (or modal) instability. The meaning of this term will become clear if we draw upon a modern (though not too modern) example for comparison. In a melody by Bach, Mozart, Beethoven we can take it for granted that its tonality is established not only by the final cadence but from the very outset, being achieved by the constant emphasis on the characteristic degrees of the scale, tonic, fifth, third, etc. Nowhere in the wide boundaries of major-minor tonality is there place for a melody such as shown here:

FIGURE 24

It is precisely this tonal behavior to which the term "tonal instability" refers, and which, though impossible in music of a more recent period, not only occurs frequently in Gregorian chant but actually forms a characteristic trait of some of its modes. As the reader may perceive from a perusal of the above eight Communions, and as can easily be confirmed by many other examples, the melodies of the *deuterus,* with the final on e (modes 3 and 4) are the ones most liable to tonal instability. There are numerous chants in this group whose opening phrases, through their outline and cadential points, suggest any other tonality than E; among the shorter chants there are not a few in which this tonality is never established until the very last note appears, the Introit *Intret oratio* [541] being an example in point. In fact, it is quite difficult to find a chant such as the Responsory *Omnes amici* [671] in which the E-tonality is indicated by the first cadence at least, though hardly by the opening notes.

2 *HDM,* s.v. "Tessitura."

In contrast to the peculiar evasiveness of the *deuterus*, tonal stability prevails in the *tetrardus*, particularly in the melodies of the seventh mode which, it will be noticed, comes closest of all the modes to the modern major. Of this, the Communion *Dicite* indicated above is a characteristic example, with its cadences on g, d', b, and g. In the two other groups, *protus* and *tritus*, the situation is more ambivalent although tonal stability seems to prevail. Possibly a detailed study of the complete repertory, divided according to types and modes, would lead to more definite statements than we are able to make. As a modest contribution to such a study, the Alleluias of mode 1 may be considered briefly. Each of these begins with a well-defined opening phrase accompanying the word "Alleluia." Among the thirty-three different melodies found in this group there are eighteen in which this opening phrase ends on d, seven on a, three on f, and five on g. The general impression is that of tonal stability established at the very beginning of the melody by a cadence either on the "tonic" or on the "dominant."

We must leave it to the reader to examine other chants of the "regular" type which will serve to put the previous explanations on a fuller and more secure basis. In order to facilitate this important task, there follows a list of additional examples for each mode.

Mode 1: Antiphon *Apertis thesauris* [463]; Alleluia *Laudem Domini* [448]; Introit *Exsurge* [504]; Hymn *Deus tuorum militum* [419].

Mode 2: Antiphon *Ante luciferum* [463]; Introit *Veni et ostende* [343]; Alleluia *Dies sanctificatus* [409]; Offertory *Ad te Domine* [321]; Responsory *Comedetis* [927].

Mode 3: Antiphon *Adhaereat* [297]; Gradual *Adjutor* [498]; Alleluia *Cognoverunt* [817]; Offertory *Domine exaudi* [620]; Responsory *O magnum mysterium* [382].

Mode 4: Antiphon *Candor est* [1380]; Hymn *Ad regias* [814]; Introit *Reminiscere* [545]; Responsory *Quem vidistis* [377].

Mode 5: Antiphon *Domine tu mihi* [661]; Introit *Loquebar* [1215]; Offertory *Expectans* [1043]; Responsory *Plange* [722].

Mode 6: Introit *Esto mihi* [511]; Offertory *Domine in auxilium* [1046].

Mode 7: Introit *Puer natus* [408]; Gradual *Benedictus Dominus* [478]; Alleluia *Exivi* [831]; Responsory *Beata* [383].

Mode 8: Introit *Ad te levavi* [318]; Alleluia *Angelus Domini* [786]; Offertory *Beata es* [1272]; Responsory *Astiterunt* [732].

The reader wishing to enlarge this list will soon discover that, except for a few groups such as mode 2 and mode 7, it is not too easy to find perfectly regular examples, that is, melodies fully conforming with the theoretical system. In the field of the Communions, which we selected as the basis of our study, an examination of the complete repertory shows that in two modes, mode 4 and mode 5, the examples previously given are the only ones that could be called regular; and that in all the other modes, with the sole exception of mode 7, the number of regular examples is less than that of melodies showing some irregularity of their tonal (or modal) behavior. We shall now turn to a consideration of the various aspects of this phenomenon.

LIMITED RANGE

The distinction between the authentic and the plagal mode of the same final (*maneria*) is based on the ambitus. Common to both is a range extended from the sub-final to the fifth above the final. Therefore the distinction depends upon the degrees above the fifth or those below the sub-final. If none of these degrees occur in a given melody, the situation is, *a priori,* ambivalent, as, for instance, in a melody closing on d and confined to the range from c to a (schematically represented by the symbol d:c-a), which theoretically could be assigned to mode 1 as well as to mode 2. One may be inclined to dismiss the whole question as rather moot, preferring in such cases simply to indicate the *maneria,* about which there is no doubt. Actually, the question has practical significance for chants such as Antiphons, Introits, and Responsories (formerly also Communions), since these are connected with a Psalm or a psalm verse sung to a standard "tone" (psalm tone, etc.), which is selected according to the mode of the chant.

As early as the beginning of the eleventh century, theorists discuss the problem presented by the small-range melodies, and inform us that they should be considered as plagal. Thus, Berno of Reichenau says: "If a chant does not reach up to the fifth nor include the lower fourth, it is customary to consider it as plagal because of its shortness and imperfection."[3] This means that chants of the type d:c-g and d:B-g should be regarded as plagal, as indeed they always are.[4] A little treatise, *Quomodo de arithmetica procedit musica,* states that a chant is authentic if it descends one or two degrees below the final and ascends one or more degrees above the fifth (e.g., d:c-b); plagal if it extends more than two degrees below the final, even though going up one or two degrees above the fifth (e.g., d:A-c′); and also plagal if it has a small range, not exceeding a fifth (e.g., d:c-g or d:d-a).[5]

An examination of the chants shows that these rules are by no means regularly observed. To start with the last statement, it suffices to point out that among the chants of the type g:g-d′ there are two, the Alleluia *Crastina die* [361] and the Antiphon *Terra tremuit* [641], which are assigned to

---

3 GS, II, 72b.

4 With the possible exception of some Antiphons, since in this category modal assignment depends primarily on melodic types. See pp. 223, 394ff.

5 GS, II, 60a.

mode 8, while the Antiphons *Magnificatus est* [364] and *Responsum accepit* [1366] are assigned to mode 7. The second statement of the *Quomodo* treatise concerns melodies with an excessive range (more than an octave), which will be considered in the next chapter. As for the first statement, we should like to postpone its consideration until after the study of a type which, although the most interesting of the various small-range configurations, is not mentioned by Berno nor in the *Quomodo* treatise: these are melodies which extend from the sub-final to the upper fifth (d:c-a), thus employing exactly that range common to both authentic and plagal ambitus. Turning to a study of these chants, we may begin once more with a list of the Communions that fall under this category:

Mode 1: *Petite* [843]; *Amen dico* [1206]; *Visionem* [1587].
    2: *Dominus Jesus* [657]; *Vos qui secuti* [1614].
    4: *Memento verbi* [1065].
    8: *Introibo* [508]; *Pater si non* [601]; *Spiritus ubi vult* [906];
        Panem caeli [1495].

It appears that most of the subfinal-to-fifth Communions occur in the *protus* and *tetrardus,* while, on the other hand, there are no examples of the *tritus.* This means that all the *Communions* with the final on f have an ambitus clearly indicative of either mode 5 or mode 6. As for the modal assignment, this is exclusively plagal in the *deuterus* (mode 4) and *tetrardus* (mode 8), but predominantly authentic in the *protus* (modes 1, 2).

Naturally, the number of chants included in this list is too small to serve as a basis for general conclusions. Interestingly enough, however, a fuller investigation confirms each of these findings. Following is a tabulation based on all the chants of the *Liber usualis:*[6]

CHANTS WITH SUBFINAL-TO-FIFTH RANGE

	MODE	TOTAL	ADVENT TO EASTER
Protus	1	*c.* 35	10 [331; 338; 365; 373; 443; 463; 466; 468; 550; 771]
	2	*c.* 22	7 [427; 590; 651; 657; 663; 736; 770]
Deuterus	3	0	0
	4	*c.* 10	2 [336; 443]
Tritus	5	0	0
	6	0	0
Tetrardus	7	0	0
	8	*c.* 50	17 [333; 376; 406; 474; 508; 513; 580; 622; 624; 630; 640; 666; etc.]

6 Hymns and Short Responsories have been disregarded. The preparatory work for this tabulation was done during a Seminar on Gregorian Chant (UCLA, Summer 1954) by Miss Diane Kestin and Messrs. Sidney H. Appleman, William P. Malm, and Clyde E. Sorensen. The figures of the "Total" column are approximate, while those from Advent to Easter have been checked and can be assumed to be correct.

REMARKS:

a. Chants of this type are completely absent in the *tritus,* relatively rare in the *deuterus,* and particularly frequent in the *protus* and *tetrardus.* Their absence in the *tritus* results largely from the fact that the *subtonium* below f is practically never used, so that chants in the *tritus* either stay above the final, in which case they are authentic, or go two or more degrees below it, thus becoming plagal. Naturally, for a proper evaluation of the figures given in the tabulation, the fact should be borne in mind that in the total repertory of chants the *protus* and *tetrardus* occupy a considerably more prominent place than the other two, there being approximately 750 chants in the *protus,* 450 in the *deuterus,* 250 in the *tritus,* and 900 in the *tetrardus.* This, however, changes the result only by degrees, without affecting its general validity. Percentage-wise, chants of the type under consideration are most frequent in the *protus* (*c.* 12%), about half as frequent in the *tetrardus,* and half again as frequent in the *deuterus.*

b. Another question of interest concerns the distribution of the small-range melodies among the various types of chant. As may be expected, the largest share, approximately one-half of the total, is held by the Antiphons which, because of their shortness and simplicity of style, are bound to include many melodies of a limited range. Contrary to expectation, however, the chants next in frequency are the Alleluias, with close to one-fifth of the total. The Alleluias are commonly thought of as highly ornate, melismatic chants. This they are indeed; nevertheless a surprisingly large number of them are confined to a rather small range.

c. As for the modal assignment within each *maneria,* our figures confirm what was suggested by the Communions, that is, a near-exclusive preference for the plagal assignment, except in the *protus* where assignment to the authentic mode clearly prevails. It is not easy to find a convincing reason for the strikingly different procedure encountered in the *protus.* Nearly all the "authentic" melodies are short Antiphons which move to a large extent within the third or fourth above the final, touching the fifth only a few times, as *Ecce in nubibus* [331], *Levate capita* [365; same melody], or *Erat Pater* [468]. In some cases the authentic assignment could perhaps be defended because of certain details of the melodic design, such as the ascending motion, from d to a, at the beginning of *Germinavit radix* [443] and of *Postulavi* [771]; the high beginning, with f-a, in *Diffusa est* [373]; or the jump d-a that occurs twice in *Tribus miraculis* [466].

We can now return to the statement of the treatise *Quomodo,* according to which chants ascending one or two degrees above the fifth are to be considered as authentic, even though they descend one or two degrees below the final. Without examining all the various configurations referred to in this statement, we shall confine ourselves to the simplest of them, that is, the one with an ambitus from the subfinal up to the sixth above the final (type d:c-b). Considering the fact that the sixth lies outside the plagal ambitus, one would expect to find the judgment of the treatise fully borne out by the facts. Actually this is far from being the case. The over-all picture presented by the subfinal-to-sixth chants is not much different from that of subfinal-to-fifth chants, only slightly more balanced in favor of the authentic assignment:

CHANTS WITH SUBFINAL-TO-SIXTH RANGE

	MODE	ADVENT TO EASTER
Protus	1	13 [356; 357; 357; 412; 420; 426; 483; 491; 494; 515; 652; 692; 694]
	2	2 [405; 474]
Deuterus	3	1 [333]
	4	6 [428; 462; 484; 654; 708; 781]
Tritus	5	0
	6	0
Tetrardus	7	6 [398; 491; 578; 588; 726; 782]
	8	6 [320; 371; 482; 557; 761; 783]

The strikingly large number of examples in mode 1 is explained by the fact that nearly all of them are Antiphons modelled after exactly the same standard theme which is characterized by a rising fifth (usually: c-d-a-b-a) at or near the beginning, and often by a recitation on the fifth degree.[7] By contrast, the two examples of the second mode, the Antiphon *Et Jesus* and particularly the Alleluia *Dominus regnavit,* show an emphasis on f, which is the reciting note (tenor) of the second mode (more correctly, of the second psalm tone). Thus the distinction between authentic and plagal chants is justified by inner criteria, that is, certain characteristics of the melodic line which often assume decisive importance in cases where the external criterion of the ambitus fails.

As for the assignments in the *deuterus* and *tetrardus,* most of them can be explained in a similar way. In the *deuterus* group, the Antiphon *Ecce Dominus* [333] is the only melody which shows an emphasis on the fifth degree (b), while all the others move mainly around the lower pitches, a, g, and even f [see the Introit *Omnis terra,* 484], touching only occasionally upon the c′ and upon the b which, moreover, is usually lowered to b-flat. Similar distinctions prevail in the *tetrardus* group. Several melodies of mode 7 begin with a rising fifth (Antiphon *Facta est* [398]; Responsory *Recessit* [726]), while others begin directly with the fifth degree and emphasize it during the further course of the melody (Antiphons *Cum angelis* [588] and *Et ecce* [782]). The melodies of mode 8, on the other hand, move mainly around the fourth degree, c′, which is the tenor of the eighth psalm tone.

[7] Gevaert, *Mélopée, thème 4* (p. 236) and *thème 5* (p. 238). The opening motive frequently appears with b-flat, see p. 153.

The foregoing explanations will suffice to illustrate the importance of the internal criteria in the question of modal assignment for melodies of an ambivalent ambitus. We may only add that occasionally they assume the decisive role even against the clear evidence of an unequivocal ambitus. An example in point is the Offertory *Benedixisti* [337] which, in view of its ambitus (e:d-d'), is clearly authentic; nevertheless it is assigned to mode 4 because of its internal characteristics, which are the same as the ones shown by the fourth-mode melodies of the above table.

Although in the great majority of cases the modal assignment of the small-range melodies is corroborated by internal evidence, this is not always so. There are a number of chants in which the inner criteria themselves are uncertain or ambivalent, so that they fail to provide a basis for a clear-cut decision. Moreover, in some cases the assignment is rather clearly contradicted by the melodic design, a striking example being the Communion *Mirabantur* [491], for which mode 8 would seem to be much more proper than mode 7. Following are a few other chants whose modal assignment could be challenged:

Mode 1 or 2: Antiphons *Venit lumen* [463]; *Postulavi* [771]; *Erat Pater* [468].
Alleluias *Repleti fructu* [1545]; *Ego sum pastor* [818]; *O quam bonus* [898]; *Dominus regnavit* [405].
Communion *Vos qui secuti* [1392].
Mode 7 or 8: Alleluias *Vos estis* [1548]; *Videbitis* [1483].

Most of these chants contain some phrases suggestive of the authentic, others of the plagal, mode. Usually the decision is made in favor of the mode indicated by the opening phrase. We shall see later [p. 173] that in the ninth and tenth centuries the mode of a chant, particularly of the Antiphons, was determined by its beginning, even if this was in contradiction to the mode (or rather, *maneria*) indicated by the final.

EXCESSIVE RANGE

This category includes chants whose range exceeds the authentic as well as the plagal ambitus. The minimal range for such melodies is that of an octave starting two degrees below the final and going up to the sixth above it—for instance, from c to c' in the *deuterus,* where the low c is outside the authentic ambitus, the high c' outside the plagal. By going one or two steps below or above the octave the range may increase to that of a ninth, tenth, or occasionally even an eleventh, as in the Gradual *Qui sedes* [335].[8] As may be expected, the modal assignment, whether authentic or plagal, of these chants is as variable as in the field of chants with a limited range.

---

[8] We are not considering here the case of an extended ambitus resulting from the combination of a lower-range respond and a higher-range verse, frequently encountered in the Graduals and Offertories. See pp. 150f.

No end would be served by entering into a detailed consideration of this question. We shall limit ourself to a list of examples which will enable the reader to form an idea as to whether, or to what an extent, the assignments find their justification in specific traits such as have been indicated for the small-range melodies.

CHANTS WITH EXCESSIVE RANGE

A. Extending Two Degrees below the Final

Protus: none

Deuterus:

e:c-c′	All.	*Beatus quem* [1479]	Mode 3
	Com.	*Exsulta* [406]	4
	Off.	*Doctrinam* [1513]	4
e:c-d′	Ant.	*Dixit autem* [1409]	3
	Com.	*Jerusalem* [563]	4
	Ant.	*Postquam surrexit* [660]	4

Tritus:

f:d-d′	Com.	*Intellige clamorem* [549]	5
f:d-e′	Com.	*Dicit Dominus* [487]	6
f:d-f′	Com.	*Quinque prudentes* [1228]	5
	Grad.	*Exaltent eum* [1331]	5

Tetrardus:

g:e-e′	Ant.	*Dixi iniquis* [640]	7
	Com.	*Hoc Corpus* [573]	8
	All.	*Haec est vera* [1508]	8

B. Extending Three Degrees below the Final

Protus:

d:A-b(♭)	All.	*Qui docti* [1466]	1
	Intr.	*De ventre* [1499]	1
	Com.	*Contra spem* [1353ᵛ]	2
	Com.	*Tu puer* [1502]	2
d:A-c′	Grad.	*Timete Dominum* [1726]	1
	Off.	*Stetit Angelus* [1656]	1

Deuterus: none

Tritus:

f:c-d′	Grad.	*Quemadmodum desiderat* [1478]	5
	Com.	*Ecce sic* [1292]	6
f:c-e′	Intr.	*Respice in me* [981]	6
f:c-f′	Com.	*Qui mihi* [1141]	5
	Com.	*Laetabitur* [1149]	5

Tetrardus:

g:d-e′	Ant.	*Ecce apparebit* [332]	7
	Com.	*Video caelos* [418]	8
	Ant.	*Fili quid* [477]	8
g:d-f′	Off.	*Precatus est* [1030]	8
	Ant.	*Beata Agnes* [1338]	8

A separate and particularly interesting category of melodies with an excessive range is formed by chants consisting of two or more distinct sections, each of which employs a different ambitus. Quite a number of examples of this type are found among the responsorial chants, consisting of a respond sung by the choir and one or more verses sung by a soloist. The types we have to consider in this connection are the Graduals and the Offertories.[9] The normal phenomenon in these chants is that the range of the verse is one or two tones higher than that of the respond. A typical example is the Gradual *Beatus vir* [1136], mode 5, which has the range d-e′ in the respond, f-f′ in the verse. Here, as in most of the Graduals of this mode, the difference in range is apparent to the eye by the use of two different positions for the c-clef. In a few cases the difference of range is more considerable:

	MODE	RESPOND	VERSE	TOTAL RANGE
Gr. *Jacta cogitatum* [982]	7	g:f-f′	d-g′	eleventh
Sciant gentes [506]	1	d:c-c′	d-f′	eleventh
Suscepimus [1362]	5	f:c-c′	f-f′	eleventh
Universi [320]	1	d:A-b	c-e′	twelfth
Domine praevenisti [1207]	4	e:c-c′	A-c′	tenth

In two of these Graduals, *Suscepimus* and *Universi,* the respond moves as clearly in the plagal ambitus as does the verse in the authentic. Naturally this precludes a "correct" assignment to either variety. The most sensible thing to do is to renounce this distinction altogether and indicate only the *maneria—protus, deuterus,* etc.—following the precedent of the Codex Montpellier [see p. 167]. More than any other Gradual, *Universi,* which stands at the very beginning of the liturgical year, has presented a thorny problem. Pothier, in his *Liber gradualis* of 1895, marked it *2.et 1.;* Wagner strongly insisted that it is in mode 2;[10] and in the *Graduale Romanum* it is given as mode 1. Perhaps it is not merely a printer's error that on p. 320 of the *Liber usualis* it is marked 1, while in the Index (p. 1895) it appears with the symbol 2. We shall briefly return to this question in the chapter on the Graduals [p. 352].

In the Offertories a difference of range between the respond and the verse or the verses (not a few Offertories have more than one verse) is even more frequent and more pronounced than in the Graduals. It will be sufficient to indicate a few particularly striking examples:[11]

9 From the stylistic point of view, the Offertories have to be considered as responsorial chants, although originally they belonged to the antiphonal type.

10 *Wagner III,* 375.

11 Page references are to C. Ott, *Offertoriale sive Versus Offertoriorum* (1935).

OFFERTORY	MODE	℞.	℣. 1	℣. 2	℣. 3	TOTAL RANGE
Super flumina (p. 119)	1	d:c-c′	c-e′	g-g′	a-g′	twelfth
Ad te Domine (5)	2	d:G-g	d-e′	d-e′		thirteenth
Laudate Dominum (40)	2	d:G-g	e-d′	f-d′	e-e′	thirteenth
Deus Deus meus (66)	2	d-c-a	A-a	c-c′		twelfth
Anima nostra (145)	2	d:A-b♭	d-e′	e-g′		fourteenth
Tollite portas (14)	2	a:e-f′	f-e′	F-g		two octaves
Dextera Domini (25)	2	a:d-d′	G-a	c-d′		twelfth
Sicut in holocausto (92)	5	f:f-c′	c-d′			ninth
Desiderium (90)	6	f:d-c′	c-b♭	c-a	f-f′	twelfth
Gloriabuntur (135)	6	f:d-c′	f-e′	f-f′		tenth
Immittit angelus (102)	8	g:f-d′	f-d′	f-d′	g-g′	ninth

Nowhere in the entire repertory of Gregorian chant (except in the late sequences) do we find melodies of such a wide range as among the Offertories of the second mode. Some of these, e.g., *Ad te Domine, Laudate Dominum,* and *Anima nostra,* exploit the lower part of their gamut in the respond, the higher part in the verses. Even more exceptional and remarkable are *Tollite portas* and *Dextera Domini* which start with a respond transposed to the upper fifth, and therefore moving in a high range, but descend to the lowest pitches in one of the verses. *Tollite portas* is unique in the entire repertory of Gregorian chant because of its two-octave range and of its use of the low F, a pitch not admitted by any of the theorists of the tenth or eleventh centuries:

d-B♭ c-B♭-A-G A-B♭-G G   G-F B♭ c-d-c
℣. 2. e-   um et   su-per

In some Offertories the contrast between the various sections becomes even more striking if we consider the *tessitura* rather than the range. For instance, in *Deus Deus meus* the last verse touches upon the lower notes of the range (c, d, e) only at the beginning and at the end, moving mainly within the fifth from f to c′, while the second verse rarely goes beyond the f or g. In chants like this one is almost led to assume that the verses were sung by different soloists.

Naturally, no "correct" modal assignment can be expected in chants of such an excessive range. Confronted with the problem of accounting for melodies moving in the authentic as well as in the plagal ambitus, later theorists coined the terms *tonus plusquamperfectus, mixtus,* and *commixtus,* thus merely conceding that the system of the eight modes is not applicable.[12] For melodies with an excessive range the simpler system of the four *maneriae: protus, deuterus, tritus,* and *tetrardus* provides a much

[12] See, e.g., Marchettus de Padua's *Lucidarium* of c. 1309 (*GS,* III, 101).

more suitable basis of tonal classification. True enough, the modal system does not work too well either for melodies with a limited range, but here it is indispensable because this group includes a considerable number of Antiphons, Introits, Communions, and Responsories—chants which have to be classified according to modes because of their connection with a psalm tone, introit tone, etc. Finally, the fact should not be overlooked that the chants with a limited or excessive range, numerous though they are, constitute only a fraction of the total repertory. In the great majority of chants the eight-mode system does provide a workable and valuable basis for tonal classification and investigation.

THE B-FLAT

Considering the admirable variety of tonal realms afforded by the eight-mode system on a strictly diatonic basis (a variety much greater than the major-minor system was able to elicit from the much fuller material afforded by the chromatic scale), one cannot help pondering about the reasons that led to the addition of the b-flat, the single "black sheep," as it were, among the "pure-white" flock of the Gregorian pitches. Whatever answer may be given to this question—the most obvious one being that it was added in order to avoid the tritone above f—it is interesting to notice that the b-flat is not officially recognized in the earliest treatises containing information about the tonal material of the chant. This appears most clearly from a consideration of the various systems of letter designation advocated by the theorists of the ninth century:[13]

Modern:	A	B	c	d	e	f	g	a	b	c′	d′	e′	f′	g′	a′	b′	c″
Scholia enchiriadis:			A	B	C	D	E	F	G	H	I	K	L	M	N	O	P
Anonymus II:	A	B	C	D	E	F	G	H	I	K	L	M	N	O	P		
Hucbaldi Musica:	F	G	A	B	C	D	E	F	G	A	B	C	D	E	F	G	

The first indication of the recognition of the b-flat occurs in the *Divisio monochordi* of the so-called *Anonymus de la Fage,* which employs the system of *Anonymus II,* adding the letter R for the b-flat.[14] The tenth-century *Dialogus de musica* generally ascribed to Oddo of Cluny [see List of Sources, p. 55, no. 25] is the earliest treatise to distinguish the b-flat from the b-natural by the use of two shapes of the letter b, the *b rotundum* (round b) for the former, and the *b quadratum* (angular b) for the latter, forms which persist in our present-day signs ♭ and ♮. Does this mean that the b-flat represents an innovation of the ninth century? We can only raise this question without trying to give an answer. At any rate, it should be realized that absence of official recognition does not necessarily mean absence *de facto.* As we shall see [pp. 162f], there is good reason to assume

13 *GS,* I, 209, 342, and 118.
14 J. A. de la Fage, *Essais de diphtérographie musicale* (1864), p. 73.

that originally the tonal material of the chant included also other chromatic notes, mainly the e-flat and the f-sharp, which, however, were never adopted into the theoretical system.

Turning from the theoretical to the practical sources, it is hardly necessary to state that the earliest musical manuscripts, that is those written in neumes without indication of pitch or intervals, never prescribe a b-flat. Perhaps the first manuscript to do so is the Codex Montpellier of the eleventh century which, in addition to staffless neumes, notates the chants by means of the letter system of *Anonymus II,* in which the degree of b is represented by the letter i. Similar to Oddo's two shapes of the b, the Codex Montpellier employs two shapes of the i, an upright (i) for the b-natural and a slanting (*i*) for the b-flat.[15] Diastematic manuscripts dating from about the same time, such as the Beneventan Gradual and the Codex Lucca of the eleventh century, indicate the b-flat in the usual manner, as do all the later sources.

A comparative study of these sources reveals a situation disconcertingly similar to the one that exists in polyphonic music of the thirteenth through the sixteenth centuries, where to the present day scholars argue about *musica ficta* and editorial accidentals. A detailed investigation of the b-flat in the medieval manuscripts of Gregorian chant still remains to be undertaken, but there can be little doubt that it would reveal hundreds of cases in which one manuscript shows a b-flat at a certain place where it is absent in another source of equal authority. An important preparatory study is J. Jeannin's "Du si bémol grégorien" [*TG* xxv, 1928, pp. 143, 175], in which he points to the numerous "contradictions . . . entre excellents témoins de la tradition," the contradictions between equally excellent sources.

The similarity between the Gregorian b-flat and that of early polyphonic music also extends to the modern publications which, in either case, show a tendency to conform with nineteenth-century principles of tonality by introducing numerous chromatic alterations that are, to say the least, of doubtful authenticity. Certainly, the basic Solesmes editions, *Liber usualis, Graduale,* and *Antiphonale,* contain numerous b-flats which cannot be justified. In a recent article, "Du rôle des principales familles de manuscripts" [*RG* xxx, 1951, p. 6], J. Gajard reproached the editors for their "déférence pour les habitudes de l'oreille moderne," the deference to the habits of the modern ear. The case most frequently noted is the formula c-d-a-b♭-a found at the beginning of many Introits and Antiphons of the first mode. According to the best manuscripts this should read: c-d-a-b-a. The faulty version of the standard Solesmes books has indeed been corrected in more recent publications based on more exacting principles of

---

[15] See, e.g., the facsimile in Suñol's *Paléographie,* p. 395: g h *i* h (line 1, "populi"); h i k i h (line 3, "e-os").

research and scholarship: e.g., in the *Antiphonale monasticum* (1934), which contains the Office Hours according to the Benedictine (not the official Roman) rites; the *Officium et Missa ultimi Tridui Majoris Hebdomadae* (1947), containing the Office and Mass for the last three days of Holy Week (also Easter Sunday) according to the monastic rites; and the *In Nocte Nativitatis Domini, juxta ritum monasticum* (1936), a similar edition of the liturgy of the Nativity. In these books the Antiphons *Traditor autem* [652], *Posuerunt* [694], *Tecum principium* [412], and others appear without a flat. Similar corrections should be made for many Introits, e.g., *Rorate* [353] and *Gaudeamus* [437], not only at the beginning but also at other places where the *Liber usualis* has a b-flat.[16]

Nor are the Solesmes editions always consistent in the application of the b-flat. This appears particularly from the study of chants employing standard phrases, that is, complete melodic units that are transferred from one chant to another, a procedure which is of basic importance in the Tracts, Responsories, and Graduals.[17] Occasionally such a phrase appears with a b-flat in one chant, without it in another. An example in point is a phrase employed for the close of several Responsories of the fourth mode (end of the respond), e.g., in *Aestimatus sum* [732], *Quem vidistis* [377], *Qui Lazarum* [1786], and *Subvenite* [1765]. In the first two chants this phrase appears with a b-natural, resulting in a tritone formation, f-g-a-b, which is changed into f-g-a-b♭ in the last two.

Earlier editions of the chant are even more inaccurate in this respect. Thus, the *Liber responsorialis,* published in 1895, shows the Responsory *Sicut ovis* (p. 339) with a flat for every note b, while the *Liber usualis* [716] and the *Officium . . . Tridui* (p. 196) have it entirely without b-flat, a version born out by the medieval manuscripts such as the Codex Worcester [*Pal. mus.,* XII, Plates, p. 126]. There are many similar cases in which future research will lead to a correct version. Many others, however, will probably always remain doubtful because of the lack of agreement between the sources.

In spite of the great uncertainty in details, some general principles concerning the b-flat can be unequivocally stated. First of all, the use of the altered pitch does not affect the classification according to *maneriae* and modes, which rests on the final. Thus, a melody on d was considered a *protus,* regardless of whether it employed the b-natural, the b-flat, or both. Theoretically speaking, each of the four standard scales is available in two varieties; one with the semitone b-c', the other with the semitone a-b♭,

---

16 In the Codex Lucca the Antiphon *Hodie Christus natus* [413] does not have a single flat (see *Pal. mus.,* IX, facsimiles, p. 39). The flat is extremely rare in this manuscript, but not entirely absent. Thus, it does occur in the Responsory *Oremus omnes* (*ibid.,* p. 494) in connection with a direct tritone, on "Dominum:"f-b♭ b♭-a-g . . .

17 See pp. 315f, 331ff, 345ff.

the former a fifth, the latter a fourth above the fixed semitone e-f (or, if this occurs in the higher octave, e′-f′, the former a fourth, the latter a fifth below it):

FIGURE 25

It will be noticed that each of these eight scales represents a different tonality, if this term is understood to indicate the position of the two semitonal intervals with respect to the final. The only exception is the b-flat *tetrardus* which, aside from a transposition at the distance of a fourth, is identical with the b-natural *protus*. However, this does not mean that, owing to the addition of the b-flat, the number of *maneriae* is raised from four to seven or that of the modes from eight to fourteen. Such an increase of tonalities would presuppose the existence of a number of chants making consistent use of the b-flat, side by side with others which employ the b-natural exclusively. Actually there is no such dichotomy. Practically all the chants are either strictly diatonic or show a fluctuation between the b-natural and the b-flat. There are a few chants in the *tritus* (particularly in the sixth mode; see p. 156) there are "completely flattened," but probably all of them are either of a late date or owe their "F-major" tonality to the conforming tendencies of modern editors. At any rate, their number is so small as to be negligible.

In order to provide a basis for the study of the b-flat, as it occurs in the various modes, a list of Communions follows:

Mode 1: *Data est* [803]; *Amen dico* [1077]; *Ecce virgo* [356].
    2: *Multitudo* [1337]; *Potum meum* [620]; *Tu puer* [1502].
    3: *Qui meditabitur* [529]; *Scapulis suis* [537].
    4: *Semel juravi* [1132]; *Tanto tempore* [1450].
    5: *Adversum me* [611]; *Non vos relinquam* [899]; *Intellige* [549].
    6: *De fructu* [1031]; *Diffusa est* [1572].
    7: none
    8: *Domine memorabor* [1046]; *Omnes gentes* [449]; *Dum venerit* [828].

From these examples, together with others found in various categories of chant (Graduals, Antiphons, etc.), the following general conclusions can be drawn:

Mode 1 shows fluctuation between b-natural and b-flat, the latter being often introduced when the b occurs as a peak tone (a-b-a) or in a tritone position (f-b or b-f). As was indicated previously (p. 153), the beginning of *Amen dico,* where the b occurs above the ascending fifth (c-d-a-b-a) should probably have a b-natural.

In mode 2 the b lies outside the proper ambitus. Whenever it occurs, as a peak tone, it is invariably b-flat.

The occurrence, not at all infrequent and documented by the best sources, of the b-flat in modes 3 and 4 is the strangest phenomenon in the field under consideration. In both these modes the b (natural), situated a fifth above the final, holds such an important position in the scale that it cannot be altered without impairing the very nature of the mode. However, we have already pointed out (p. 142) that the two modes of the *deuterus* are greatly given to instability and variability of tonal structure. Internal cadences on f are found in practically every melody of some extension, and these account for many of the b-flats, e.g., that on "ve-(ritas)" in *Scapulis suis.* However, even cadences on e quite frequently have a b-flat because of a preceding f, as on "ac nocte" in *Qui meditabitur* [529], or on "alleluia" in *Tanto tempore* [1450]. In fact, cadential formulae with the general outline of f-b♭-e are among the most characteristic traits of nearly all melodies in the modes 3 and 4. One of the most striking instances of the use of the b-flat occurs at the end of the initial phrase of *Tanto tempore,* which closes on the low b-flat (B-flat), thus employing for its cadential point a note foreign not only to the mode but also to the medieval gamut. Parenthetically, it may be remarked that the B-flat occurs in a standard formulae of the Responsories of mode 2 (see Fig. 94, p. 333: G1).

Mode 5 presents a situation similar to mode 1, that is, fluctuation between the b-natural and the b-flat. Not a few melodies employ the flat throughout, in which case the resulting tonality is the modern major. A nearly perfect example is *Adversum me* [611], the only b-natural occurring in the liquescent *clivis (cephalicus)* on "mul(titudine)."[18] *Intellige* [549], on the other hand, has b-natural throughout, except for the final cadence. The Responsory *Plange quasi virgo* [722] may be cited as one of the relatively few examples of an extended chant of mode 5 without a b-flat.

Mode 6 seems to be very similar to mode 5 in its use of the b-flat. Two extreme examples are the Responsories *Tradiderunt* [686] and *Accepit Jesus* [932], both of which are completely "flattened," the former by transposition on c′, the latter by its having (at least in *L*) a b-flat signature.

[18] For the rules governing the validity of the flat in the Solesmes editions, see *L,* p. xviii.

Mode 7 is the only one that remains virtually untouched by the b-flat, thus retaining its characteristic interval, the major third. The special problem presented by the Antiphon *Urbs fortitudinis* [332] will be considered later (p. 177f).

Mode 8, for which the major third would seem to be equally typical, does not show the same resistance. The difference is caused by the fact that, in the plagal mode, the subfinal frequently serves as an inner cadential point. These cadences on f entail the b-flat, as is shown by the Communions mentioned in our table as well as by numerous other chants, e.g., the Tracts of the eighth mode. One of the standard formulae of these Tracts (g3 of Fig. 89 on p. 320; see *Nunc dimittis* [1363], on "(popu)lo(rum)") shows the b-flat and the b-natural in such close succession as almost to convey the impression of true chromaticism.

TRANSPOSITION

The system of the church modes is built upon the foundation of four final notes, that is, d, e, f, and g. Properly, every chant should close on one of these pitches. There are, however, not a few melodies which employ higher notes for their finals, namely the so-called *affinales* (co-finals) a, b, and c'.[19] This phenomenon is generally referred to as transposition, the surmise being that originally such chants did close on one of the four basic finals and that, for some reason or other, they were later sung and notated at a pitch different from the original one. The evidence for this surmise and the reasons why some chants were transposed are questions to be considered later. Our first task is to acquaint ourselves with the facts, thus providing a basis for the discussion of the various problems involved in this matter.

The only transpositions that can cause a chant to close on a, b, or c' are those to the upper fifth or upper fourth, for instance, from d to a or from e to a. Theoretically, the co-finals could also be reached by transpositions up a second (from g to a) or up a major third (from f to a, or from g to b). However, these are impossible because of the chromatic tones that would result. For instance, transposition up a second would entail an f-sharp (for e) and a c-sharp (for b), or would presuppose an e-flat and b-flat in the original position. We shall see later that such transpositions probably did occur. However, they always involved a modification of some intervals and therefore are not transpositions in the strict sense of the word. Moreover, they seem to have taken place only within the four basic finals (e.g., from f to g), and therefore need not be considered here where we are concerned with transpositions leading from a *finalis* to an *affinalis*.

[19] A few chants, probably all of a late date, close on the low c, e.g., the Alleluia *Beatus vir Sanctus Martinus* [1747] and the processional Antiphon *Cum audisset populus* [586] for Palm Sunday.

Naturally, transpositions to the upper fourth and fifth also produce in-admissible chromatics, namely e-flat (upper fourth of b-flat) and f-sharp (upper fifth of b-natural). The difference is that here the chromatic tones have their origin in the degree of b, and therefore disappear if this is chromatically altered. Thus, transposition to the upper fourth is possible if (and only if) the basic scale has a b-natural, while transposition to the upper fifth is possible if (and only if) the basic scale employs the b-flat. In addition, certain transpositions are ruled out for other reasons, for instance inadmissible finals (b-flat, d′) or a range exceeding the Gregorian gamut. The diagram, Fig. 26, serves to illustrate the possibilities of transposing the modes (the symbols 1:♮, etc., stand for mode 1 with b-natural, etc.).

FIGURE 26

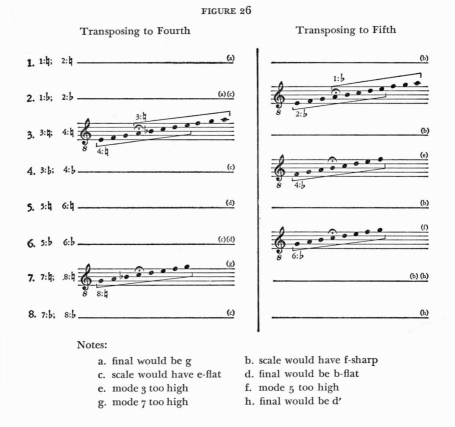

Transposing to Fourth   Transposing to Fifth

Notes:

a. final would be g
c. scale would have e-flat
e. mode 3 too high
g. mode 7 too high
b. scale would have f-sharp
d. final would be b-flat
f. mode 5 too high
h. final would be d′

To sum up: modes 1 and 2, with b-flat, can be transposed to the upper fifth; modes 3 and 4, with b-natural, to the upper fourth; mode 4, with b-flat, to the upper fifth; mode 6, with b-flat, to the upper fifth; and mode 8, with b-natural, to the upper fourth. Modes 5 and 7 cannot properly be transposed because the resulting range exceeds the Gregorian gamut. Transposition would be possible only for specific melodies with a limited ambitus. We have seen, however, that such chants are likely to be classified as plagal rather than as authentic. By grouping the transposed modes according to *affinales,* we arrive at the following picture:

Co-final a: Modes 1:♭; 2:♭; 3:♮; 4:♮
b: Mode 4:♭
c′: Modes 6:♭; 8:♮.

Turning now to the melodies themselves, we find the preceding theoretical demonstration fully borne out. There exist examples for each of the transpositions represented in the diagram, while, as far as I can see, there are none for those that have been ruled out.[20] A seeming exception is the Offertory *Eripe me . . . Domine* [605] which is in the third mode and closes on b. Actually, this is not a transposed chant at all, as appears from its range which extends from d to e′. The final b results from the incomplete reproduction in modern editions, which omit the verses of the Offertories. The complete version, given in Ott, p. 30, shows, after the second verse, a restatement of the respond with a different ending which correctly closes on e. As for the truly transposed chants, the following list of examples will suffice to give a general view of the situation.

TRANSPOSED CHANTS[21]

FINAL a

Mode 1:
    Com.   *Passer invenit* [556]
    Intr.   *Exaudi Domine* [854]

Mode 2:
    Com.   *Cantabo* [963]; *Cantate Domino* [833]
    Intr.   *Venite adoremus* [G 371]
    All Graduals, e.g., *Haec dies* [778], *Justus ut palma* [1201], etc.
    All.   *Confitemini . . et invocate* [1060]
    Off.   *Tollite* [362]; *Exaltabo* [528]; *Dextera* [656]; *Vir erat* [1069]
    Resp.   *Sancta et immaculata* [384]; *Locutus est* [LR 402]
    Ant.   *Magnum haereditatis* [444]

Mode 3:
    Com.   *Beatus servus* [1203]

[20] D. Johner, in his *A New School of Gregorian Chant* (1914), p. 57, includes mode 5 among those that can be transposed to the fifth. Perhaps there are some examples with a limited range, from b or c′ to g′. On the other hand, he omits mode 8, for which there is at least one example, indicated in our list of Transposed Chants.

[21] The asterisk indicates chants having a b-natural as well as a b-flat; see p. 163.

Mode 4:
   Ant.   *Factus sum* [730]; *Apud Dominum* [412]; *Ecce veniet* [324]; *Ex Aegypto* [1081]; and many others of the same type.[22]

FINAL b

Mode 4:
   Com.   *Tollite hostias* [1058]; *Dilexisti* [1241]; *Per signum* [1457]
   Off.   *Domine fac mecum* [G 133]
            Gloria I [16]

FINAL c'

Mode 6:
   Com.   *Circuibo* [1009]
   Off.   *In virtute* [1205]
   Resp.   *Tradiderunt* [686]; *Gaude Maria* [PM 146]
Mode 8:
   Resp.   *Jesum tradidit* [687]

It may be noticed that nearly all the transposed chants are plagal, and that transpositions to the final a are by far the most frequent.

We can now turn to the various questions and problems arising in connection with the transposed chants. The most urgent, of course, is: are we justified in considering the chants closing on a, b, and c' as "transposed?" If so, why were they transposed? The obvious answer to the second question would be that this was done in order to bring them into a more convenient range; but this answer is hardly satisfactory since hundreds of other chants continued to be sung at the lowest part of the medieval gamut. As for the first question, one might be inclined to answer it in the positive because the co-finals lie outside the system of the church modes. Once more, this argument carries little weight since it is universally recognized that this system is not the historical basis for the Gregorian melodies, but represents a relatively late attempt at tonal classification.

Fortunately, we can give a very definite answer to each of these questions. The question as to whether the chants are transposed is to be answered in the positive, provided this term is properly understood. It does not necessarily imply that they were originally sung at a lower pitch and later brought up to a higher one. In order to understand the issue involved we have to bear in mind that originally the chants were not notated at all, or if they were, that this was done in a staffless notation which, aside from

22 This group of Antiphons (*thème 29* of Gevaert's *Mélopée,* pp. 322-30) will receive our attention on several other occasions; see pp. 162, 399. They require for the Psalm the fourth tone in "another position of the same tone" [L 115], specified by the terminations c, A or A* (the normal terminations of the fourth tone are g and E). In the index of *AM* these Antiphons are distinguished by the use of the italic figure *4.* The corresponding psalm tone is called *Quartus modus "alteratus" seu cum alteratione chromatica* [*AM* 1215]. Actually, the "chromatic alteration" is present, not in the psalm tone, but in the Antiphons.

many other uncertainties, contains no indication of pitch whatsoever. This means that they could be sung at any pitch that was convenient or customary. The only things that mattered were the intervallic relationships—in other words, the position of the semitones with regard to the final—but these are, of course, entirely independent of the pitch, whether (to use modern equivalents) d, e, or f-sharp. This state of affairs underwent a radical change with the introduction of the staff and of diastematic notation. This made it necessary to allocate each chant in such a way that its semitones were properly represented on the staff. The majority of the chants apparently offered no great problems in this respect, or if there were problems (e.g., quarter-tones) they were solved by some compromise. In a number of cases, however, a satisfactory solution could be found only if the chants were notated at a higher pitch, so that they closed on one of the co-finals, and these are the chants that we usually call "transposed." Somewhat more properly we might say that they were notated so as to appear in transposition.

As for the reason for the "transposition," this was done, not in order to bring them into a more convenient range, but because of the intervallic structure of the melody, which could be represented in staff notation (or letter notation) only if the melody was interpreted as closing on one of the co-finals. The most convincing proof of this exists in a passage found in the *Prologus ad tonarium* by Berno [see List of Sources, p. 54, no. 16]. Because of their unusually informative character, we quote the major part of Berno's explanations:[23]

It should be noticed that there exists such a concordance between the lower finals and those a fifth above them that certain melodies are found to close on the latter as if they were regular finals. . . . In a miraculous way it happens that the [basic] finals have associates not only at the upper fifth, as we have said, but also comparable ones at the upper fourth.[24] . . . Indeed, each mode, whether authentic or plagal, is found to recur in a miraculous and divine concordance if considered at a fourth from its location, . . . in such a manner that a good number of melodies, if begun on their [proper] final—or, as the case may be, at some other tone above or below it—do not come out well because of the lack of semi-

[23] *GS*, II, 74b: "Notandum vero est . . ." We offer a somewhat simplified translation, in which, e.g., the Greek terms *mese*, etc., are replaced by their modern equivalents. The basic work on chromaticism in Gregorian chant is G. Jacobsthal, *Die chromatische Alteration im liturgischen Gesang der abendländischen Kirche* (1897). More than twenty years earlier, R. Schlecht had called attention to chromaticism in the chant, in *Caecilia* (ed. Hermesdorff, Trier), 1874. Chromaticism also plays a role in several articles by J. Borremans (*TG*, XIX, XX [1913/14]), in which he discusses Alleluias in versions of Cistercian and Premonstratensian manuscripts. Apparently he had no knowledge of the studies by Schlecht and Jacobsthal, since he says in conclusion: "Il y a dans la théorie actuelle du chant grégorien une lacune grave qu'il importe de combler à tout prix."

[24] The "concordance" at the upper fourth presupposes, of course, the use of the b-flat, e.g., d-e-f-g = g-a-b♭-c′ (or, of the f-sharp, e.g., d-e-f♯-g = g-a-b-c′?).

tones; if, however, they are begun at the higher level, then they continue smoothly without detriment to any pitch and close quite properly on the associated final.

In order to illustrate this more clearly, let us take as an example the following antiphons of the fourth mode: *Factus sum, O mors ero, Sion renovaberis, Sion noli timere,* and *Vade iam.* If you try to begin these antiphons on g, a third above their [proper] final [that is, e], your melody will be defective because you will not find a semitone at the place where it should be. If, however, you consider the tone a [as a final] and if, through the interposition of the b-flat and b-natural, you begin these antiphons on c′, you will notice that the entire melody can be sung without any damage, until it closes on the associate final a. Similarly, if you insist on beginning the antiphons of the same mode, *Ad te Dominum levavi* and *Ex Aegypto vocavi* on their (proper) final, you will see that in the middle part they won't come out right. If, however, you begin them on a, they can be sung without distortion (*dispendium,* loss) of the neumes, until they close on the same note [on which they began]. People who don't see this maintain that these antiphons and similar ones belong to the seventh rather than to the fourth mode, although they don't deny that they close in the fourth.

The same defect of notation (*defectus neumarum*) occurs in the communion *Beatus servus* of the third mode, unless it is transposed from e to a. . . . If you start to sing the communion of the eighth mode, *De fructu operum,* on its final [i.e., g], you will see that in the middle the melody does not come out properly, because of the semitones. If, however, it is started on c′, you will notice that the entire series [of tones] of this melody is related, in an orderly progression, to its associated final [i.e., c′].

The same thing may happen at the distance of a fifth. Unless the antiphons of the sixth mode, *Alias oves habeo* and *Domine qui operati sunt,* are transposed to the upper fifth (*in quintum transponantur locum*), that is, from f to c′, they in no way retain their order in the regular monochord.

The meaning of these explanations becomes immediately clear if we consider one of the transposed modes of our table, for instance, the *deuterus* raised to the fourth, and replace in this the b-flat by a b-natural. This means, in the original position, to replace the f by an f-sharp, and it is this f-sharp to which Berno alludes when he says, in connection with the Antiphons *Factus sum* and others, that "you will not find a semitone at the place where it should be." Obviously, there existed melodies which involved, at different places, progressions such as e-f-g and e-f♯-g, thus presupposing the availability of a semitonal cluster (e, f, f♯, g) which occurs in the medieval gamut only at a place a fourth above (a, b♭, b♮, c′). Thus it is only by transposing the entire melody to the upper fourth that the pitches involved can be expressed in the "regular monochord" and in writing. Conversely, it appears that originally these chants were sung a fourth below their notated pitch, e.g., *Factus sum:*[25]

[25] *Factus sum* as well as the other Antiphons mentioned by Berno together with it belong to the previously mentioned *thème 29* of Gevaert's *Mélopée.* Gevaert changes them into what he believes to be their original form, with a close on b instead of on a.

FIGURE 27

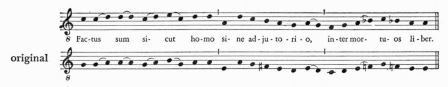

original

Perhaps it is not superfluous to remark that expressions such as "sung a fourth below" do not have quite the same meaning here as they have in present-day practice. The difference is in the frame of reference, which consists not so much of actual pitches but of the theoretical degrees of the diatonic scale as represented by the tone-letters.

If we apply the same line of reasoning to a transposition of a fifth, our table shows that normally all the modes involved include only the b-natural, the fifth above e. It is possible, however, to introduce into such a transposed mode a b-flat which, in the original position, would correspond to an e-flat. Assuming that there were melodies including d-e-f as well as f-eb-d, it appears that the degrees involved (d, eb, e, f) are available only in the semitonal group a, bb, bԁ, c′, in other words, only by transposition to the upper fifth. Since the examples, *Alias oves* and *Domine qui,* cited by Berno are not found in the modern books,[26] we reproduce here two relevant passages from the Communion *Circuibo* [1009]:

FIGURE 28

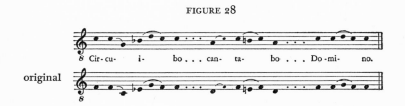

original

We can now make the following general statement: If a chant transposed to the upper fourth (modes 3 and 4 on a, mode 8 on c′) contains a b-natural, this indicates an f-sharp in the original melody. If a chant transposed to the upper fifth (modes 1 and 2 on a, mode 4 on b, mode 6 on c′) contains a b-flat, this indicates an e-flat in the original melody. Our table of Transposed Chants [p. 159] includes a number of additional examples, marked by an asterisk.

The earliest clear evidence of chromatically altered tones is found in the *Scholia enchiriadis* of c. 900, in which a considerable number of penta-chords (scale segments comprising a fifth) are accurately indicated by means

26 *Alias oves* is given in *A* and *AM,* but as an untransposed melody of the eighth mode. See, however, Gevaert, p. 199. *Domine qui operati sunt* occurs in the Codex Lucca (*Pal. mus.,* IX, Plates, p. 475), transposed on c′ but without b-flat.

of daseian signs.[27] In addition to diatonic pentachords such as c-d-e-f-g and d-e-f-g-a (both upward and downward) the author describes formations such as c-d-e♭-f-g (up and down), c-d-e-f♯-g (up and down), as well as others of a mixed type, e.g., ascending with e-flat and descending with e-natural. He calls these chromatic variants *absonia*. We may therefore assume that in the ninth century and possibly even earlier singers made use of the e-flat and f-sharp, probably without fully realizing that, in doing so, they were transgressing the boundaries of the tonal system which, for that matter, may not as yet have existed or have been universally recognized. Gradually, musicians must have become aware that such usage was not quite proper. The very name *absonia* (off-sound) which the author of the *Scholia enchiriadis* uses indicates a slight disapproval, and this attitude is even more evident when he calls them *vitium* (vice) and compares them to "barbarisms and solecisms" in poetry. Such designations are on a level with the terms *musica ficta* and *musica falsa* by which writers of the fourteenth century condoned the use of chromatic alterations in polyphonic music. After all, it was not until the twentieth century that the chromatic tones received a status fully equal to that of the diatonic tones.

Whatever the attitude toward the e-flat and f-sharp may have been in those early days, the development of musical theory was not favorable to them. The first obstacle must have occurred when the tone-letters were introduced. We have seen (p. 152) that the earliest systems of letter designation were purely diatonic. The first indication of recognized chromaticism exists in the addition, to the diatonic series A to P, of the letter R for b-flat. It would have been easy to add the letter S for e-flat and T for f-sharp, but apparently these tones were so rare in comparison with the b-flat (which, we must remember, is almost a diatonic degree in the *tritus*) that this was not done. When Oddo (who seems to have taken a hostile attitude toward the chromatic tones) introduced his new system of letters, from a to g, he provided for two b's, the *b rotundum* and the *b quadratum,* but neither for two e's nor for two f's.[28] The general acceptance of this system more or less implies the abolishment of the e-flat and the f-sharp. In many cases they were probably modified into some adjacent degree. Transposition into the recognized chromaticism of the b was their only means of survival, and it is in the few melodies of this type that we can trace them.

27 *GS,* I, 175ff. For an explanation of the daseian signs, see, e.g., W. Apel, *Notation of Polyphonic Music* (1942), p. 204.

28 In his tables showing the transpositions of the diatonic scale, G to a', Oddo consistently uses the letter *m* (*mysticum?*) whenever a chromatic tone occurs, e.g., A B m d for G A B c transposed a second upward [*GS,* I, 274]. Later he speaks about "quampluria mysteria" which he disregards "ne tenerum lectorem magis suffocare superfluis cibis, quam lacte nutrire videremur" (lest we should seem to suffocate the gentle reader with superfluous food, rather than nourish him with milk).

A second obstacle, even more definitive, was the staff notation which developed shortly after the letter notation. Essentially diatonic, like the oldest systems of letters, it borrowed from Oddo the two shapes of the letter b (♭ and ♮) which, whenever necessary, were placed in front of the note indicating the pitch b. Although the same signs could have been used equally well for the pitches e and f, this was never done in Gregorian chant.[29]

The theory that chants closing on an *affinalis* are transposed in order to accommodate (or disguise) chromatic pitches, does not necessarily apply to every chant closing on a, b, or c'. Our table of Transposed Chants contains a number of melodies (those lacking the asterisk) that do not include the crucial pitches—b-flat for transpositions of a fifth, b-natural for transpositions of a fourth—indicative of hidden chromaticism. It is perhaps no mere coincidence that most of these are Offertories, a type of chant characterized by numerous exceptional traits, among them a tendency to move in unusual ranges. It is entirely conceivable that some of the Offertories were originally and always sung at a high level of pitch and that, strictly speaking, they should not be listed with the chants which we have good reason to assume were transposed. The same line of reasoning applies even more cogently to certain chants of a late date, such as the *Kyrie IV* or the Antiphon *Ave regina* [274], the former closing on a, the latter on c'. With other melodies closing on one of the *affinales* the question of "transposed or not transposed" is difficult to decide. Examples in point are the numerous Graduals of the type *Justus ut palma,* all in the second mode and closing on a. In the Solesmes version each of these closely related melodies has one b-flat, e.g., *Justus ut palma* [1201] on "cedrus," *Haec dies* [778] on "Haec," and it is this b-flat that accounts for their being considered as transposed chants.[30] However, Ferretti states that the b-flat of *Haec dies* is not authentic, an assertion that would remove the only tangible evidence for transposition.[31] There is no point in quibbling over single examples. What matters is the general principle, and this is placed beyond doubt, mainly by Berno's testimony.[32]

[29] The only exception I have found is an e-flat in the final melisma of the second verse of the Offertory *In virtute*: c'-a-f f-g-e♭ f-d [Ott, p. 153].

[30] See *Wagner III,* 370. The b-flats occur in standard phrases, A_1 and A_4 of our table on p. 360.

[31] *Esthétique,* p. 163.

[32] In an article, "L'Insuffisance du système d'écriture guidonien" (*ACI,* p. 202), D. Delalande attempts to prove the existence of chromatic tones on the basis of evidence provided by certain variants found in German manuscripts, particularly the replacement of a second by a third (e.g., e'-f'-e' by e'-g'-e'), which have long been recognized as a peculiarity of the "German chorale dialect" (Wagner). According to Delalande, this phenomenon shows that originally there was a "note mobile" (f-sharp), which was lowered (to f) in the Latin, but raised (to g) in the German sources.

MODAL AMBIGUITY

In the preceding explanations we have considered what may be called "open transpositions," this term referring to the fact that the transposition is apparent from the use of the co-finals, a, b, and c'. There is reason to assume that transposition also occurred within the four basic finals, d, e, f, g, and these could be termed "hidden transpositions," because the melodies do not show any outward sign of being transposed. Obviously each such case involves a change of mode, a modal ambiguity. What we are concerned with, actually is not the problem of authentic-versus-plagal arising with melodies of a limited or excessive ambitus, but ambiguity of *maneria*. This is a most interesting, but also highly complex phenomenon. The whole problem arises from the fact that, in a considerable number of cases, the medieval sources show a striking disagreement of modal assignment, one and the same chant being classified as mode 1 in one source, 3 in another, 6 in a third, and 8 in a fourth (to quote an extreme example).

Before entering upon our explanations, it will be well to describe the source material pertinent to the question at hand. It falls into three categories: theoretical treatises, tonaries, and liturgical books (*Graduals, Antiphonals*). A typical example of a theorist providing information about modal assignment is Aurelianus, who in Chapters X to XVIII of his *Musica disciplina*[33] discusses the eight modes and indicates individual chants representative of each mode. Significantly, he limits himself to Antiphons, Introits, Offertories, Responsories, and Communions, that is, to those chants for which, because of their connection with a recitation tone (psalm tone, introit tone, etc.), the modal assignment is of practical significance, but excludes the Graduals and Alleluias for which it has only theoretical interest.[34] Considerably more extensive is the material provided by the tonaries, e.g., the *Tonarius* of Regino, from *c.* 900. They contain more or less complete lists of Antiphons, Introits, Communions, etc., grouped according to modes. Again, Graduals and Alleluias are disregarded, but also the Offertories. As for the liturgical books, the earliest source of information is the *Gradual* of Corbie of *c.* 900 which, although without musical notation, indicates the modes of the Introits and Communions by marginal signs, AP and PP for *authenticus protus* and *plagis proti* (first mode, second mode) and similar ones for the other six modes.[35] In the neumatic Codex Einsiedeln *121* (*Pal. mus.,* IV) the modes of the Introits and Communions are identifiable through their psalm verses, while the Codex Chartres *47* (*Pal. mus.,* XI) has marginal indications of the mode, as can be seen on Plate III [see the explanations, p. 121]. A central position in this question

---

[33] See the List of Sources, p. 54, also for the tonaries, etc., mentioned subsequently.

[34] The fact that Aurelianus includes the Offertories in his "catalogue of modes" is of great historical interest. See p. 512.

[35] See *Sextuplex*, p. cxxiii.

is held by the Codex Montpellier, in which the Mass chants are grouped according to their modes. Here we find modal indications for all the Mass chants, Introits and Communions as well as Graduals, Alleluias, and Offertories. The Graduals are grouped, not according to modes, but according to *maneriae,* and in many cases the respond and the verse carry individual modal designations, *Pl. (plagius)* and *At. (authenticus),* e.g.:

Pl. ℟. Adiutor meus. *At.* ℣. Confundantur.

The main source for the modal assignment of the Office chants is the Codex Hartker, in which the mode of each chant is indicated by Latin or Greek letters:

a = Mode 1	u = Mode 2
e = Mode 3	η = Mode 4
i = Mode 5	y = Mode 6
o = Mode 7	ω = Mode 8

The Codex Lucca adds to each Antiphon the *E u o u a e,* that is, the termination of the psalm tone,[36] thus giving an indirect indication of the mode of the Antiphon.

In the great majority of cases these sources agree in their modal designations, but the number of chants carrying different assignments is by no means inconsiderable. As for the Mass chants, a comprehensive study of modal ambiguity has been made by U. Bomm, in his important study, *Der Wechsel der Modalitätsbestimmung in der Tradition der Messgesänge im IX. bis XIII. Jahrhundert* (1929). This deals with close to one hundred Mass chants which occur with different designations of the mode, a number which represents a little less than one-tenth of the total Mass repertory (*c.* 1100 chants). No similarly complete study exists for the Office chants, but the number of cases is here probably even higher. Thus, there may be three hundred or more chants the modal assignment of which is problematic. It may be noticed that, at least in the Mass chants studied by Bomm, the ambiguity does not (or not primarily) involve that of authentic-versus-plagal, which we have considered in connection with the chants of limited or excessive ambitus, but rather a decision between different *maneriae.* The problems presented by these chants are not only of practical significance (in the Introits, Communions, etc.), but also important from the historical and analytical point of view. Their examination affords an interesting insight into the evolutionary processes of the chant and illuminates certain special traits of its tonal behavior.

For some unexplained reason, modal ambiguity prevails in the Com-

[36] See p. 220.

munions to a much larger extent (about one-fifth of the total) than in any
other type of Mass chant. It is least frequent in the Graduals. The list
of chants included in Bomm's study consists of fourteen Introits, four
Graduals (excluding duplications of a melody with different texts), seventeen Alleluias, nineteen Offertories, and thirty-eight Communions. From
this ample material we shall select a few examples which illustrate the
causes and reasons for the variation that exists in the field of modal assignment. In many cases these reasons are by no means clear, and we can
only speculate upon what this or that writer had in mind when he
ascribed a chant to this or that mode. One of the most striking examples
in point is the Communion *De fructu* [1031], which appears in the modern
books as an f:c-c′ melody properly assigned to mode 6. The medieval
sources, however, are by no means unanimous on this point. Both Aurelianus and Regino ascribe the melody to mode 3, as does also the *Gradual*
of Corbie. In Berno's *Tonarius* and in the *Graduale Sarisburiense* it appears as mode 8, and in Guido's *Tonarius* as mode 1, while the designation
as mode 6 occurs in the Codex Montpellier. It is very difficult, if not impossible, to say what caused such an appalling disagreement. The extended
commentaries which Jacobsthal and Bomm devote to this melody (the
former on pp. 52-58 and 136-178; the latter on pp. 60-61 and 97-103) are
sufficient evidence of the highly problematic character of this Communion
which, no doubt, underwent certain changes during the ninth, tenth, and
later centuries. Fortunately, there exist some examples of a less complex
nature, and it is on these that we shall draw for the subsequent explanations, which are designed to expose some of the reasons for differences in
modal assignment.

By far the simplest case is that of melodies with a small range. We have
already noticed that a small range is bound to lead to uncertainty in the
distinction between the authentic and the plagal mode of the same *maneria*
(p. 144). It may, however, cause more essential variations of modal assignment, involving a shift from one *maneria* to another. A case in point is that
of a melody using the scale segment known as the hexachord, that is, six
notes with a semitone between the third and the fourth degree. If this
hexachord occurs in the position g-a-b-c′-d′-e′ (*hexachordum durum*), the
melody would be a *tetrardus,* on g. However, the same hexachord occurs
on f: f-g-a-b♭-c′-d′, and in this position the melody would be a *tritus*. An
example in point is the Communion *Tu mandasti* [1062] which in *L* as
well as in most of the medieval sources (Corbie, Regino, Berno, Guido)
occurs as a *tritus* (mode 5), notated in f, g, a, b♭, c′, and d′. However, two
sources (Montpellier, Salisbury) have it notated on g, so that it becomes
a *tetrardus* (mode 7). The latter notation and assignment would seem to
be preferable because it does away with the continuous b-flat of the *tritus-*
version. Since, however, the *tritus*-designation is by far the older of the

two, we have to accept it as the original and proper one. Possibly, the Communion was not always sung with a "b-flat signature," but with vacillation between b-flat and b-natural, in which case it would have to be a *tritus.* A similar example is the Alleluia *Benedictus es* [904, 911), a purely pentachordal melody which occurs in *L* as mode 8 (*g*-a-b-c'-d'), in Montpellier as mode 6 (*f*-g-a-b♭-c'). The same ambiguity exists in its musical model, the Alleluia *Crastina die* [361], which, however, seems to have been universally assigned to mode 8.

The same ambiguity may occur in melodies of a more extended range, if the tonal material within this range shows a gap. Thus, c-d-*f*-g-a-b♭ (*f* is the final) is equivalent to d-e-g-a-b-c'. An example in point is the Communion *Venite post me* [1306], which *L* as well as most of the medieval sources notate as a *tetrardus* on g (mode 8). Corbie, however, designates it as *authenticus tritus,* and Berno lists it under the Communions of the *plagis triti,* which means that the melody is interpreted as being on f. Probably a number of similar examples occur among the Antiphons, many of which have a limited or defective range.

If a melody exploits the full range of a mode, ambiguity of assignment often involves some melodic variant or hidden chromaticism. The Antiphons *Postquam surrexit* and *Si ego Dominus* from Maundy Thursday [660, 662] are given in the standard Solesmes books as melodies with a range from c to d' and closing on e, and assigned to mode 4. In an appendix to the more recent *Officium . . . Tridui,* containing the chants of Maundy Thursday "ad fidem codicum restitutae," they appear transposed to the upper fourth and are labelled: 1 transp. The transposition alone would not, of course, account for the change of mode, from 4 to 1. This results from the fact that in the new version (which appears to be the original reading) the final is lowered from a to g or, if we disregard the transposition, from e to d, as shown in Fig. 29 (Antiphon *Postquam*):

FIGURE 29

Liber usualis   Officium tridui   untransposed

The difference of assignment not only extends to the *maneria,* which changes from the *deuterus* to the *protus,* but also involves a change from the plagal to the authentic variety. The plagal designation of *L* is obviously based on the fact that the melody, although extending as high as d', touches (only once, in the closing cadence) upon the c, which is a third below the final. With the final lowered from e to d, this c becomes the subfinal, with the result that the authentic designation becomes imperative.

As has been mentioned before, in many cases of multiple assignment its *raison d'être* cannot be definitely ascertained, particularly if the differing designation occurs in sources that fail to give the melody (as, e.g., the *Gradual* of Corbie or the tonaries) or which have it notated in nondiastematic neumes (e.g., the Codex Einsiedeln). To this group belong many of the examples discussed by Jacobsthal and Bomm, whose explanations are often necessarily tentative and inconclusive. There are, however, some chants in which the situation appears to be reasonably clear and unequivocal, among them the following:

1. Communion *Principes*. *L* [1238]: mode 1; Regino, Corbie, Einsiedeln: mode 3.

The melody, as it is given in *L*, extends from d to d', with b-flat and b-natural. The assignment to the third mode probably means that it was considered as extending from e to e', a position which requires the f-sharp for the second degree. Strictly speaking, a c-sharp would be necessary in place of the b-natural, but probably the c-natural was used throughout:

FIGURE 30

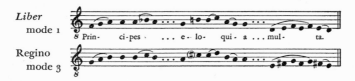

2. Communion *Ego clamavi*. *L* [1073], mode 8; Montpellier: mode 6.

In Montpellier the melody is a fifth higher, but with a different ending which closes, not on d', but on c'. Since the melody is assigned to mode 6, it will have to be transposed to close on f, that is, a fifth below the notated pitch. This leads to the same version as in *L*, except for the cadence. Moreover, this cadence includes a b-flat, which becomes an e-flat in the transposition:

FIGURE 31

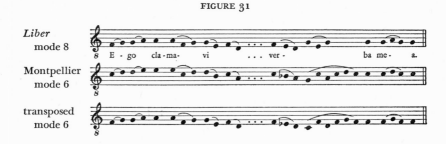

Thus, the transposition involves here a melodic variant as well as a chromatic degree.

3. Alleluia *Laetatus sum.* *L* [329]: mode 1; Montpellier: mode 3.

As in the previous case, Montpellier shows the melody notated a fifth higher, but otherwise identical (aside from minor variants), thus closing on a. Because of the designation as a *deuterus,* with a final on e, transposition to the lower fourth is required. In addition, the Montpellier melody fluctuates between b-flat and b-natural, the latter being used for the initial section of the verse, from "Laetatus" to "domum," the former, for the opening "Alleluia" as well as for the close of the verse, from "Domini" to "ibimus" (as in most of the Alleluias, the close of the verse restates the melody for the Alleluia). This "modulation," from b-flat to b-natural to b-flat, appears in the transposed version as one from f-natural to f-sharp to f-natural:

FIGURE 32

| *Liber* mode 1 |
| Montpellier mode 3 |
| transposed mode 3 |

A comparison of the first and the third version shows that the middle section (B) is transposed from d to e, while the first and last sections (A and C) change from the d-mode (*protus*) to the e-mode (*deuterus*). Exactly the same situation occurs in the Alleluia *Timebunt gentes* [1056], which Montpellier notates on a, with b-flat from the beginning to "reges," b-natural for "terrae gloriam tuam," and return to b-flat for the final melisma.

4. Communion *Circuibo.* *L* [1009], Guido, St. Gall *381:* mode 6; Corbie, Berno, Einsiedeln, Montpellier: mode 8; Regino: mode 2.

Although this example is somewhat more problematic than the others, it is worth considering because of the multiplicity of assignments and transpositions involved. Both *L* and Montpellier have it in transposed notation, on c′, with alternation of b-flat and b-natural, and with the same melody, except for an extra note on b-flat near the end, on "(di)cam," which does not occur in *L* (nor in Einsiedeln). However, while *L* and some of the medieval sources assign the melody to mode 6, Montpellier and others characterize it as mode 8. The former designation implies transposition to the lower fifth, on f, with alternation of e-flat and e-natural; the latter, to the lower fourth, on g, with f-natural and f-sharp. Finally, Regino assigns the melody to mode 2, which may mean that he heard it on d, a fourth below the g-position which perhaps could be considered as the original one. Thus, the melody may have occurred in four different positions:

FIGURE 33

Liber, Montpellier
notated

Cir-cu-   i-   bo ... can- ta-   bo-   ...-cam Do-mi-   no.

transposed to f
mode 6

transposed to g
mode 8

transposed to d
mode 2

The presence, in Montpellier, of the b-flat (transposed: f), i.e., of the *subtonium* (whole-tone below the tonic) shortly before the close justifies and, in fact, demands the assignment to the g-mode. Whether Regino's indication, mode 2, actually means that he heard the melody transposed down to d, is not certain.[37] If so, there is little doubt that the passage on "cantabo," which in strict transposition would show a c-sharp, was modified, perhaps as is indicated by the "editorial" accidentals.

It will be noticed that all our examples of ambiguous modal classification, whether resulting from incomplete range or from chromatic alterations, involve transpositions between neighboring *maneriae,* more specifically, between *protus* and *deuterus,* or between *tritus* and *tetrardus,* and this statement can be extended to all the melodies falling under this classification. The reason is, of course, that the two former *maneriae* are related to each other by having a minor third, while the other two have a major third. The essential character of these degrees practically precludes exchange from one pair to the other. The only exchange possible would be between the *protus* and the *tetrardus* with b-flat, but these scales are actually identical, so that, at least theoretically, any melody of the *protus* (particularly mode 2) could also be assigned to the *tetrardus* with b-flat (particularly mode 8 in which, as we have seen, the b-flat is quite common).

This does not mean that modal ambiguity between *protus* and *tritus* or between *deuterus* and *tetrardus* never occurs. Actually a number of such cases exist, but probably all of these belong to a different category, to which we shall now turn.

As has been pointed out previously (p. 142), a considerable number of chants show a vacillation between two or more tonal realms, a tonal instability which expresses itself most clearly in the use of intermediate cadences that are totally unrelated to the final cadence. This phenomenon is particularly frequent in, in fact characteristic of, the *deuterus* modes, but not at all confined to these.

[37] Cf. Jacobsthal, pp. 50ff; Bomm, pp. 58ff.

Less obvious than the phenomenon itself is its connection with the problem under consideration here, that is, ambiguity of modal assignment. No transposition is involved in the melodies of this group, nor variants of transmission resulting in a different final. What is the reason for assigning different modes (properly speaking, different *maneriae*) to a chant with an unvariable final? The answer is that in the earliest period of modal theory it was the beginning rather than the end of a melody which determined the modal assignment, at least in the Antiphons, Introits, and Communions. Strange though this may at first seem to be, there are good reasons for it. After all, the beginning of a melody is at least as important from the point of view of "tonal impression" as its conclusion, and if we consider an example such as the Offertory *Laetentur caeli* [394], which from the beginning almost to the end is a clear example of a second mode, it is rather incongruous to label it: mode 3, only because the final note is e.

There was, however, a more cogent reason for considering the beginning of a melody as the mode-determining factor, a reason most clearly apparent in the Antiphons of the Office Hours (Vespers, etc.), which today are sung before and after a Psalm, but originally were repeated after each of its verses (see p. 187):

$$A\ V_1\ A\ V_2\ A\ V_3 \ldots A\ V_n\ A$$

In this rondo-like concatenation foremost attention was given to tonal unity of the whole. This was achieved by providing, for the verses, eight recitation melodies (psalm tones), one for each mode, and by selecting the psalm tone according to the mode of the Antiphon; for example, the first psalm tone for an Antiphon in the first mode, the second tone for an Antiphon in the second mode, etc. Moreover, most of the psalm tones were provided with a number of different closing formulae (terminations) designed to make a smooth transition to the initial note of the subsequent Antiphon.[38] From this it appears that an important part of the scheme, namely, the selection of the psalm tone, depends upon the mode of the Antiphon. In the majority of the cases this poses no problem. If, however, the Antiphon is of instable tonality, starting in one mode and closing in another, a decision has to be made. The present-day practice, which developed in the mid-tenth century, is to consider the end of the Antiphon, in particular the final note, as the decisive criterion, a procedure which connects the Antiphon with the subsequent verse and gives the Antiphon somewhat the character of an introduction. Originally, however, it was the beginning of the Antiphon which determined the psalm tone, so that the Antiphon appears as a postlude to the verse, which, no doubt, is its proper function. Indeed, one might perhaps conclude that originally the

[38] For more details, see pp. 218ff.

Antiphon was not sung at all before the Psalm, and that the performance consisted purely of verse plus Antiphon:

$$V_1 + A, \quad V_2 + A, \ldots V_n + A.$$

This arrangement clearly reveals the importance of the beginning of the Antiphon, since it is this section that forms the point of connection with the preceding verse. Essentially the same situation existed in the Introits and Communions which, probably as late as the ninth century, were sung with a more or less complete Psalm exactly like the Office Psalms.[39]

The theorists of the ninth century speak very clearly about this point. Both Aurelianus and Regino insist that in the antiphonal chants it is the beginning that determines the mode, and that only in the elaborate chants of the responsorial type is the mode determined by the final.

AURELIANUS:

It should well be noticed that in the Offertories, Responsories [i.e., Responsories of Matins as well as Graduals] and Invitatories the mode (tonus) should be sought only at the point where the verses are inserted [i.e., at the end of the Offertory, Gradual, etc.]. . . . In the Introits, however, as well as in the Antiphons and Communions the mode should always be looked for at the beginning.[40]

REGINO:

The wise singer should observe most diligently to pay attention to the beginning of Antiphons, Introits, and Communions rather than to their end, in respect to their mode. In the Responsories, on the contrary, he should consider the end and close rather than the beginning.[41]

It is perhaps significant that Aurelianus, who wrote about 850, speaks only about the beginning of the Antiphons, etc., while Regino, some forty years later, mentions both the beginning and the close, although insisting that the former should be regarded as decisive. Yet another thirty or forty years later, Oddo clearly pronounces the modern point of view in the following words, placed right at the beginning of the *Prooemium* (Introduction) to his tonary, in which he obviously addresses himself to the monks of his abbey:

The formulae for the chant, which I have procured for you in writing, designed to show how every singer of the church should execute the tones for the Antiphons, Introits, or Communions, should be most diligently studied by whoever wants to attain the peak of mastery in the ecclesiastical chant. . . . Whoever

[39] See pp. 190ff.

[40] GS, I, 44b: *Notandum sane* . . . The somewhat puzzling *ubi fines versuum intromittuntur* has been translated as "where the verses are inserted." Cf. Bomm, p. 176.

[41] GS, I, 231b.

wishes to gain full knowledge of the chant, should read these formulae [i.e., the psalm tones and their terminations *(differentias)*] every day, and when he is about to begin the Antiphon, he should not look at its opening, but quickly run to its end, and whichever tone he finds there, in that he should begin the psalm. . . .[42]

Later writers are unanimous in adopting this view:

GUIDO:

If you begin a chant, you don't know what will follow; if, however, you have finished it, you know what has preceded. Therefore, it is the final tone which should rather be considered.[43]

COTTO:

One should not make hasty judgment about the modes, but rather should he cautiously wait until the end upon which all judgment about the mode depends. Otherwise, if he has judged the mode prematurely, he may repent not to have remained silent when the end refutes his pronouncement.[44]

From Cotto's statement it would appear that still in his day *(c.* 1080) there were musicians who considered the beginning of an Antiphon as the decisive mark of modality.

Regino's *De Harmonica Institutione* is particularly revealing for the question of tonal instability and the modal ambiguity that results from it. The above-quoted remark is only the concluding sentence of a whole paragraph in which he discusses Antiphons called *nothae* (bastards), that is, "degenerate and non-legitimate Antiphons which begin in one mode, belong to another in the middle, and finish in a third." For the purpose of illustration he enumerates fourteen Antiphons and twelve Introits, adding with each a remark such as: "a tertio tono incipiunt, sed octavo finiuntur." Among the Antiphons we find *Ex Aegypto, Ad te Domine, Sion renovaberis, O mors,* and *Vade iam,* that is, the same group of Antiphons which Berno uses in order to illustrate the presence of a chromatic f-sharp, saying that "some people maintain that they belong to the

---

42 *GS,* I, 248a.

43 *Micrologus,* cap. xi: *Incepto enim . . . (GS,* II, 12a; ed. by Hermesdorff, p. 68; ed. by Smits van Waesberghe, p. 144).

44 *De Musica,* cap. xvi: *Cantus toni . . . (GS,* II, 251b). See also J. Smits van Waesberghe, *Johannes Affligemensis, De Musica cum Tonario* (1950), p. 111. Waesberghe maintains that Johannes, usually called Cotto and regarded as an Englishman (Cotton), actually was a Belgian connected with the abbey of Afflighem. This theory has been disputed by Ellinwood [*Notes,* VIII (1950), 650] but once more defended by Waesberghe [*MD,* VI (1952), 139]. Although Waesberghe's arguments have considerable weight, we see no reason to drop the name Cotto by which the author of the treatise has been known for a long time.

seventh rather than to the fourth mode, although they don't deny that they close in the fourth" [see p. 162]. This remark is clearly addressed to Regino (or his disciples) who, about a hundred years before Berno, says indeed: "a septimo tono incipiunt, et in quarto finiuntur tono." The ambiguity of his modal assignment finds its justification in the fact that in all these Antiphons the first and second phrases of the melody definitely suggest the seventh mode, the cadences being respectively on d' and g, while it is only in the short concluding phrase that the fourth mode makes its appearance:[45]

Cadence on: d'	g	b♮-a
Factus sum sicut homo	*since adjutorio*	*inter mortuos liber*
Ex Aegypto . . . meum	*veniet ut salvet*	*populum meum*
Sion renovaberis	*et videbitis . . . tuum*	*qui venturus est in te*
O mors, ero mors tua	*morsus tuus*	*ero inferne*
Sion noli timere	*ecce Deus tuus*	*veniet, alleluia.*

Regino's interpretation is entirely convincing if we read these Antiphons in their present-day notation. It is rather less so if, following Berno, we consider this as a transposition from an original notation a fourth below, as we did in the section on Transposition [p. 162]. Here the cadential points of the beginning change to a and d, tones both of which are foreign to the seventh mode. However, the melodic line, with its characteristic f-sharp, remains, of course, the same, regardless of the pitch. In this connection it is interesting to notice that in the *Commemoratio brevis* [see List of Sources, no. 23] the Antiphon *Ex Aegypto* is assigned to the second mode.[46] The simplest explanation for such an assignment is to consider the melody transposed to the lower fourth [as in our illustration for *Factus sum*, p. 163], but with an f-natural instead of the f-sharp and, of course, with the beginning as the mode-determining element.

In addition to the group of Antiphons we have just considered, Regino mentions several others as "imbued with ambiguity and doubt" (*ambiguitatibus et dubietatibus permixtae*), but judging from his description all of these must have existed in his day with melodies different or varying from those that have reached us. Relatively clear cases are the Antiphons *Qui odit* [262] and *Et respicientes* [783], both of which he describes as beginning in mode 3 and closing in mode 8 (final g), while the preserved melodies close on e. We must assume that there existed an earlier version in which they had g as a final. Similar examples are mentioned by Aurelianus who says that the Antiphons *Puer Jesus* [437] and *Vobis datum est* [510] begin in

[45] See the reproduction of *Factus sum*, Fig. 27, p. 163; also p. 160, fn. 22.

[46] *GS*, I, 217. Later manuscripts, such as the Tonary of Oddo, the Codex Hartker, and the Codex Montpellier assign the Antiphons of this type to mode 4. See *Mélopée*, pp. 205-12.

mode 6 but close in mode 1 (final d), in contrast to the present versions which have them in mode 6 throughout, with f as a final.[47] Actually, these versions are suspicious because they involve a cadential motion from the lower fourth, c-f (c-d-f for *Vobis datum est*), which is extremely rare in Gregorian chant[48] and which strikes one as being out of place, especially in such simple chants as these Antiphons. Fortunately, Aurelianus' explanations permit us to state with a high degree of probability how these changes came about. He says that, as long as the Psalm is sung, the Antiphons should be sung with their proper ending which, in his day, was in the first mode, hence on d. For the last repeat, however, i.e., after the last verse of the Psalm, they should close in the same mode in which they begin, that is, on f. The reason for this modification is obvious. Since for him (as well as Regino) it is the beginning of the Antiphon which is the decisive tonal criterion, the Antiphons *Puer Jesus* and *Vobis datum est* both require the sixth psalm tone (actually that of the *Magnificat*) for each verse. Thus, the entire chant, with its alternation of verses and Antiphons, proceeds in the sixth mode, except for the d-cadences of the Antiphons. These matter little as long as they occur in the middle, where they have the function of an inner cadence, resulting in a momentary modulation which actually introduces a rather desirable element of tonal variation. In the last statement, however, the inner cadence becomes the final cadence and, as such, constitutes a violation of the basic principle of tonal unity. It is therefore necessary to change the final note in the last statement of the Antiphon:

FIGURE 34

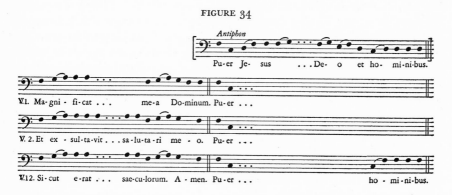

It is only natural that, with the omission of all the inner repeats of the Antiphon, its melody survived in the varied form of the final statement.

One of the thorniest problems (discussed at length by Jacobsthal) is presented by the Antiphon *Urbs fortitudinis* [332], a chant of mode 7 with b-flat in the first half, b-natural in the second. Oddo lists it under the

[47] *GS*, I, 50a, b.
[48] See p. 266.

"Quinta differentia septimi toni," but Regino assigns it to mode 1 (there-fore with f and f-sharp), and in the *Alia musica* it is said to begin in the first and to end in the eighth mode (*GS*, I, 140a). Perhaps we have here a similar case to that of *Puer Jesus*: Originally *Urbs fortitudinis* started on d and closed on g, but a modified ending was employed for its final state-ment, after the Psalm (sung to the first psalm tone). It survived with this modified ending as an Antiphon of mode 1 (Regino), but since it also had an f and f-sharp, it was finally transposed to mode 7 (Oddo).

It remains to consider briefly some of the other *cantus nothi* mentioned by Regino, namely, the Introits. As with the Antiphons, several of his examples are no longer clear to us, no doubt because of changes that oc-curred after him. Four or five of them, however, are quite clear, and these are listed below, together with two Communions that belong to the same class of *cantus nothi,* although they are not mentioned by Regino:[49]

Intr.	*Deus dum egrederis* [892]:	Modes 8 and 4 (or 3)
	Victricem manum [796]:	Modes 3 and 8
	Accipite jocunditatem [890]:	Modes 8 and 4
	Eduxit Dominus [804]:	Modes 4 and 8 (as to mode 4, transpose the beginning to the lower fifth).
Com.	*Domus mea* [1253]:	Modes 7 and 5
	Unam petii [1005]:	Modes 5 and 7

To conclude these lengthy and often involved explanations we should like to call attention to a relatively little-known treatise of the late eleventh century, preserved in the Codex *lat. 1492* of the University Library of Leipzig, and published in H. Sowa, *Quellen zur Transformation der Anti-phonen* (1935). Its first part is a tonary of Antiphons, a number of which receive commentaries indicative of modal changes.[50] The tonary is fol-lowed by a short treatise, in which the author distinguishes between *trans-formatio* and *transpositio,* saying that there is between these "a great but rather useful difference." *Transpositio* is caused by the "lack of a semi-tone" and involves change into a co-final (*affinis*), while *transformatio* means a change "into the final of another mode" (*vox alterius modi*). It appears that what we have called "modal ambiguity" could well be sub-sumed under the term "transformation."

49 Additional examples are given by Berno [see *GS,* II, 73b]. See also *Pal. mus.,* XIV, 208, 211, for Introits and Communions which occur in Beneventan *Graduals* with end-ings and, therefore, modal indications different from those of the Roman books.

50 Some of these "ambiguous" Antiphons are discussed in Sowa's publications, which thus forms a counterpart to Bomm's study of the Mass chants.

CHAPTER FOUR

Methods and Forms of Psalmody

IN A PREVIOUS chapter we have discussed the importance of the Psalms as a source of texts for the Gregorian repertory, Office as well as Mass. We shall now examine the musical aspect of this phenomenon, as reflected in the various methods of psalm singing and in the resulting forms.

DIRECT PSALMODY

The simplest method of psalm singing is the so-called direct psalmody, which means that the Psalm is sung straight, without any additional text such as occurs in the other types of psalmody. Natural though it is, this method is rarely employed in Gregorian chant. It is most clearly represented by the *psalmus directaneus* (*psalmus in directum*, sometimes misspelled *indirectum*) which is used for some Psalms sung during the Little Hours of certain days of a somber character, for which an especially simple manner of singing was deemed proper:

Ps. 145, *Lauda anima mea:* Vespers of the Office of the Dead [1776]
Ps. 129, *De profundis:* Lauds of the Office of the Dead [1805]
Ps. 69, *Deus in adjutorium:* Procession of Rogation Days [839]
Ps. 4, 90, and 133 at Compline of Holy Saturday [762][1]

In all of these cases the music consists of a very elementary recitation formula which is repeated for every verse, somewhat similar to a strophic song. The resulting form can be indicated by the scheme:

A A A . . . A.

In addition to this type of direct psalmody, which belongs to the Office, there is another which occurs in the Mass, namely, the Tracts. Originally,

---

[1] According to Ferretti, *Esthétique,* p. 155, direct psalmody was also prescribed for the Psalms of the Lesser Hours of Maundy Thursday, Good Friday, and Holy Saturday, which in present-day usage are merely said [*L* 654, etc.].

each Tract also was a complete Psalm sung in essentially the same manner as the Psalms *in directum* of the Office. However, in keeping with the much greater liturgical importance of the Mass, the melodies were, or became considerably more elaborate and extended, including numerous melismas and showing only scant traces of the recitation style characteristic of the Office Psalms. With melodies of such richness—which, for a single verse, easily take ten times as long to perform—it became impossible to sing complete Psalms, not a few of which have twenty or more verses. The resulting conflict between music and text was solved in favor of the former, as it was also in all the other departments of psalmody where a similar situation arose. As the melodies grew more and more elaborate, the Psalms were reduced by omitting more and more verses, so that none of the extant Tracts, except the very short *Laudate Dominum* (Ps. 116), represents a complete Psalm; most of them consist of four or five verses. As for the music, the simple repeat scheme of the *psalmus in directum* was replaced or, at least greatly modified by a complex process based on the interchange of standard phrases, which will be studied in detail later [see pp. 315ff].

RESPONSORIAL PSALMODY

This is a type of psalmody characterized by the alternation of a soloist and a group of singers, originally the congregation, later the church choir (*schola cantorum*). The ancient Jewish roots of this method are clearly recognizable in Ps. 136, whose every verse closes with the words: "for his mercy endureth for ever"; in Ps. 118, which has the same refrain at the end of ℣. 1 to 4 and 29; or in Ps. 32 and 87, several verses of which close with the word "Selah." That responsorial singing was not limited to the choral-refrain practice nor to the few Psalms for which this is expressly indicated, appears from a number of passages found in the Talmudic writings in which various methods of singing a Psalm with congregational participation are described.[1] One method is for the leader to sing the first half of each verse, while the group answers with the second. Another is to have each half-verse immediately repeated by the group. Yet another is the use of a choral refrain consisting of a short exclamation such as "Alleluia" or "Selah." Finally there is the possibility of having the first half-verse restated by the group after each of the subsequent half-verses. Here the congregation participates by singing a refrain which is taken from the Psalm itself. This method is of particular interest because it is the one that was adopted in Christian practice. In the earliest examples

[1] See A. Z. Idelsohn, *Jewish Music in its Development*, pp. 20f and, particularly, H. Avenary, "Formal Structure of Psalms and Canticles in Early Christian and Jewish Chant" (*MD*, VII, 1).

of Christian responsorial psalmody, especially in the Graduals, the choral refrain (respond) is indeed taken from the Psalm itself.[2] Later, however, sentences from other parts of Scripture were used for the responds.

Turning from Jewish to early Christian sources, the Church Father Tertullian (*c*. 155-*c*. 222), St. Athanasius (d. 373), the Spanish pilgrim Etheria (fl. *c*. 380) and St. Basil (*c*. 330-79) are among those who tell us about responsorial psalm singing in Carthage, Alexandria, Jerusalem, and other places of the Orient.[3] Particularly illuminating are the words of Isidore of Seville (*c*. 570-636): "Responsorial songs were adopted by the Italians a long time ago, and are thus called because the chorus in consonance gives answer (*respondeat*) to the solo singer (*uno canente*)."[4] Such psalms must have been performed according to a rondo-like scheme such as:

$$R \; V_1 \; R \; V_2 \; R \; V_3 \ldots R \; V_n \; R,$$

where V_1, V_2, etc. are the verses of a psalm, sung by a soloist, and R a refrain sung by the chorus.

At some time, possibly as early as the fourth century, when the Church, having been officially recognized by Constantine the Great (ruled 306-337), entered into its first period of flowering, elaborate methods of singing developed, resulting in more extended melodies not only for the psalm verses but also for the respond which, originally sung by the congregation, was now entrusted to the trained church choir. Also from the textual point of view there was a tendency toward extension, since responds in the character of short exclamations such as "For his mercy endureth forever," or "Selah" disappeared, being universally replaced by complete sentences adopted from, or similar to, a psalm verse. Obviously it was impossible to sing entire Psalms, with ten or more verses, in this manner. The remedy taken was the same we observed in the Tracts, that is, a reduction of the number of psalm verses. Probably because of the presence of the respond, the reduction here went much further, so that in most cases only one psalm verse remained. It is in this stage that responsorial psalmody survives in the Office, where it is represented by the Responsories of Matins, and in the Mass where it is represented by the *responsorium graduale,* that is, the Gradual. The latter consists now of a respond followed by a single verse, R V, but the fuller form R V R, which represents the medieval practice, is also permitted [see *L* 320]. The Responsories of Matins have forms such as R V R' (*Immolabit,* 926), R V R' R (*Plange,* 722), R V_1

---

[2] See the table on p. 91.

[3] See List of Data, pp. 39f, nos. 10, 15, 24, 27.

[4] Ibid., no. 53.

R′ V₂ R″ (*Subvenite,* 1765), R V R′ D R (*Hodie,* 375), or R V R′ D R′
(*Quem vidistis,* 377).[5]

R′, R″, etc., indicate successively shortened versions of the respond, resulting
from the omission of its first half, two-thirds, etc., so that only the concluding
section is retained. The corresponding places are indicated in the text of the respond by the signs *, †, ‡. Rather confusingly, the asterisk is also, and more
generally, used in the modern books for an entirely different purpose, that is, to
indicate where in performance a solo incipit comes to an end and the chorus
picks up. This is the meaning of the first asterisk in *Subvenite,* while the second
(at "Suscipientes") indicates the beginning of R′. The letter D in the above and
in several subsequent schemes stands for the so-called Doxology (word of praise):
*Gloria Patri et Filio et Spiritui Sancto: Sicut erat in principio, et nunc, et semper,
et in secula seculorum. Amen* (literally: Glory be to the Father, the Son, and the
Holy Ghost: as was in the beginning, and [is] now, and always, and in the ages of
ages. Amen). At an early time this was added to Psalms as a final verse, and it
survives in this position in various types of psalmody. In the Responsories it occurs in its older form, comprising only the first sentence, *Gloria . . . Sancto.*[6]

Among the various forms given above for the Responsories, the shortest,
R V R′, is the normal one. The more extended forms are usually reserved
for the last Responsory of each Nocturn, as appears from the following
table:

R V R′ R: Nos. 3, 6, 9 of Maundy Thursday [628ff], Good Friday
    [671ff], Holy Saturday [716ff]
R V R′ D R′: Nos. 3, 6, 8 of Nativity [375ff] and Corpus Christi [926ff];
    Nos. 2 of Easter Sunday [775] and Whit Sunday [875][7]
R V₁ R′ V₂ R′: Nos. 3, 6, 9 of the Office of the Dead [1785ff]
R V R′ D R: No. 1 of Nativity [375] and Easter Sunday [774]

The *Liber responsorialis,* which contains the service of Matins for
numerous feasts, usually in the fuller, monastic structure with four Responsories for each Nocturn, has the form R V R′ for the first three, and
R V R′ D R′ for the fourth Responsory of each Nocturn.

There survive a few chants showing the rondo structure of responsorial
psalmody in a more complete form. One of the most interesting examples
occurs in Easter Week. There are six Graduals in this week, from Easter
Sunday [778] to Friday [801], each showing the simple form R V (R). The

---

5 Properly speaking, the Responsories do not fall under the category of responsorial
psalmody, since their texts, responds as well as verses, are rarely taken from the Psalms.
See pp. 95f.

6 This text is known as the Lesser Doxology, in distinction from the Greater Doxology,
the *Gloria in excelsis* from the Mass Ordinary.

7 On these feasts the last Responsory is replaced by the *Te Deum.* See p. 22, fn. 5.

remarkable fact, however, is that they all use the same respond: *Haec dies, quam fecit Dominus: exsultemus and laetemur in ea,* and that this, as well as all the verses (except for one), is taken from the same Psalm, Ps. 117:

Respond:	*Haec dies*	Ps. 117:23
Verse, Sunday:	*Confitemini Domino*	117:1
Monday:	*Dicat nunc Israel*	117:2
Tuesday:	*Dicant nunc qui redempti sunt*	106:2
Wednesday:	*Dextera Domini*	117:16
Thursday:	*Lapidem quem reprobaverunt*	117:21
Friday:	*Benedictus qui venit*	117:25

Moreover, the melodies used for the different verses are nearly identical. The conclusion is almost inescapable that originally these six Graduals formed one extended *responsorium graduale* with six verses that was sung on Easter Sunday, but later distributed over the whole Easter Week. Unequivocal confirmation of this theory is found in the *Gradual* of Mont-Blandin, which indicates for Easter Sunday the *Haec dies* with six verses as above, the only difference being that the third verse is *Dicat nunc domus Aaron,* that is, ℣. 3 of Ps. 117, so that we have here the original form in which all the verses are taken from the same psalm in ascending order.[8]

Another interesting case is the Gradual *Tenuisti* [591] from Palm Sunday, which is striking for its unusually long verse, *Quam bonus.* Actually this verse comprises ℣. 1 (*Quam bonus Israel Deus rectis corde*), ℣. 2 (*Mei autem pene moti sunt pedes, pene effusi sunt gressus mei*), and ℣. 3 (*Quia zelavi in peccatoribus, pacem peccatorum videns*) of Ps. 72, while the respond is ℣. 23 of the same Psalm [see *L* 635f]. Probably these were originally treated as separate verses, with repeat of the respond, either full or in part, after each verse.[9]

Nor are these the only indications of an early Gradual with several verses. The Gradual *Ecce quam bonum* [1071] from the Twenty-Second

[8] See *Sextuplex,* p. 100, no. 80. The theory regarding the Easter Gradual was advanced by Wagner (I, 79). However, his statement (*ibid.,* fn. 1) that the complete *Haec dies* with all its original verses occurs in the *Graduale Compendiense* of Migne's *Patrologia latina* vol. 78, p. 678, is erroneous. The text given in Migne under the title *Liber antiphonarius* is actually taken from the Codex of Mont-Blandin, not from the Codex of Compiègne, in spite of Migne's repeated references to *Compendiensis.* The mistake goes back to earlier editions which Migne used as his source. See the explanations in *Sextuplex,* p. xvi, fn. 1.

[9] Gastoué, who proposed this reconstruction (*Cours,* pp. 141f), states that the Gradual *Tenuisti* "fut, au moyen âge, exécuté conformément à la coupe du texte original, et avec autant de reprises." I am not aware of any documentary evidence that would justify the unequivocal statement "it *was* executed," since all the early manuscripts give it with only one long verse. However, Gastoué's interpretation is certainly a plausible and even probable conjecture.

Sunday after Pentecost was sung with two verses, *Sicut unguentum* and *Mandavit Dominus,* as late as the eleventh century.[10] Only the first of these survived. Furthermore, there is good reason to believe that originally a number of Tracts of the second mode, perhaps all of them, were Graduals; in other words, that they were sung, not *in directum* as they were later, but with the first verse repeated, like a refrain, after each of the subsequent verses. The clearest example occurs in the Mass of Wednesday in Holy Week, which today has the Gradual *Ne avertas* and the Tract *Domine exaudi* [614]. However, the *Ordo Officii in Domo S. Benedicti* says that at this Mass there were "read two lessons, and sung two graduals, each one with five verses." No traces of a five-verse Gradual *Ne avertas* survive, but the Tract *Domine exaudi* has indeed five verses and is actually called *graduale* in the *Graduals* of Monza and Compiegne. Moreover, one of the most important early liturgists, Amalarius, in describing the ceremony of Wednesday in Holy Week, calls the *Domine exaudi* a *responsorium* and states that it has five verses. In the *Consuetudines* of the monastery of Corbie this chant appears already under the name of *tractus,* but is described as having the form of a Gradual, with repeats of the initial verse sung by the entire "conventus monachorum." Similar evidence exists in the case of other chants, now classified as Tracts of mode 2, which originally were Graduals with several verses, as appears from the designations *responsorium* or *responsorium graduale* with which they occur in the earliest manuscripts. From this it has been concluded that the whole group of Tracts of the second mode originally were Graduals, with several verses and choral refrains, and that at some time before the tenth century the repeats of the first verse were omitted, a process by which the chant adopted a form similar to that of the real and original Tracts, that is, those of the eighth mode.[11]

Among the Responsories there are several with more than one verse (not counting the Doxology verse). Three examples with two verses, all from the Office of the Dead, have been mentioned previously in our table showing various forms of the Responsories [p. 182]. The most complete Responsory on record is the *Libera me . . . de morte* from the Burial Service which has five verses in the Codex Hartker, six in the Codex Worcester, and seven in the Codex Lucca.[12] In its late-medieval and present-day form it has three verses. Next in completeness is the *Aspiciens a longe* from Matins of the First Sunday of Advent, with three verses and the Doxology. Following is a list of Responsories with two or more verses:

[10] Thus in the *Graduals* of Compiègne, Senlis (*Sextuplex,* p. 136, no. 120b), St. Gall *339 (Wagner I,* 296), Lucca *(Pal. mus,* IX), etc.

[11] For fuller discussions of this question see *Wagner I,* 78; Ferretti, *Esthétique,* pp. 148ff; *Sextuplex,* p.li.

[12] Cf. *Pal. mus.,* Ser. 2, I (Hartker), 392; XII (Worcester), 438; IX (Lucca), 557.

Domine quando veneris [1787]:	R V_1 R′ V_2 R′
Ne recorderis [1792]:	R V_1 R′ V_2 R′
Libera me . . . de viis [1798]:	R V_1 R′ V_2 R′
Aspiciens a longe [PM 18]:	R V_1 R′ V_2 R″ V_3 R‴ D R
Libera me . . . de morte [1767]:	R V_1 R′ V_2 R″ V_3 R
Iste Johannes [PM 33]:	R V_1 R′ V_2 R′ V_3 R′
Media vita [PM 45]:	R V_1 R′ V_2 R′ D R′

Brief mention only need be made here of the short Responsories (*responsoria brevia* or *responsoriola*), which are sung after the Chapter of the Lesser Hours and of Compline. These are short chants in a simple style, with repeat forms such as R R V R′ D R or simply R V D. The complete form is used for Prime [229], Compline [269], and normally for Terce [237], the short one for Sext [243], None [247] and Terce during Advent, Lent, and Paschal Time [238f]. The short Responsories of the Proper of the Time generally follow the same scheme, e.g., on Christmas Eve [359, 363, 364] and Nativity [407, 411, 411]. Each Responsory is followed by a so-called versicle, consisting of two short sentences sung to the same melody, a very simple recitation formula. These versicles, however, are not really a part of the Responsory, since they are also sung after hymns [see, e.g., *L* 118].

In addition to the Graduals and Responsories, the Alleluias are usually placed in the category of responsorial psalmody. They have the form A′ A V A, where A′ stands for the word "Alleluia," and A for the same word (and melody) followed by a melisma, the so-called *jubilus*. It should be noted, however, that in the Alleluias the verse is probably not a remnant of an earlier, more complete form (as is the case in the Graduals and Responsories), but results from a later addition. Originally, the Alleluia was not a psalmodic chant. As late as the sixth century it was nothing but the word Alleluia itself followed by an extended *jubilus,* as we know from Cassiodorus (*c.* 485-*c.* 580).[13] Perhaps it was not until the time of St. Gregory that a full text, usually taken from the Psalms and therefore called verse, was added to the Alleluia. In the earliest Mss we find a few Alleluias with two verses, as, e.g., in the Codex St. Gall *359* which contains twelve such Alleluias, mostly for high feasts. Thus the Easter Alleluia has the verses *Pascha nostrum* and *Epulemur* [see Plate I], that for Easter Monday the verses *Angelus Domini* and *Benedictus es,* and that for Holy Innocents the verses *Laudate pueri* and *Sit nomen Domini*. None of these Alleluias with two verses survived in later practice.

ANTIPHONAL PSALMODY

While direct psalmody is entirely soloistic and responsorial psalmody calls for alternation of a soloist and the choir, antiphonal psalmody is

[13] See List of Data, p. 41, no. 45.

characterized by the use of alternating half-choruses. Such singing is occasionally mentioned in the Bible: for instance, after David's return from the victory over the Philistines, "And the women answered one another as they played" (Sam. 18:7); or at the celebration after the wall of Jerusalem had been built, "Then I . . . appointed two great companies of them that gave thanks, whereof one went on the right hand upon the wall . . . and the other . . . went over against them . . ." (Neh. 12:31-38).[1] Philo of Alexandria (born *c.* 20 A.D.) gives an interesting description of antiphonal singing among the *Therapeuts,* a Jewish sect near Alexandria: "After the meal . . . they form two choruses, one of men, the other of women. . . . Then they sing hymns to God in many meters and melodies, partly together and partly alternating (*antiphonois*)." About A.D. 300 Eusebius, bishop of Caesarea in Palestine, mentions Philo's report and says that the same practice exists among the Christians of his time. In the early fourth century, antiphonal singing flourished in eastern Syria in the secluded Christian communities that form the root of monastic life. Two monks transplanted it to the orthodox Church of Antioch in order to combat the Arians who had found in the hymns of Bardesanes (d. 223) a very popular form of worship. Apparently antiphonal singing, with its characteristic element of liveliness and active participation, proved effective. Near the end of the fourth century St. Basil introduced it in Nicea, St. Chrysostom in Constantinople, and Ambrose in Milan, whence it spread to all the other centers of the Latin church.[2]

The traditional term for this method of singing, antiphony, is derived from the Greek word *antiphonos* (literally, counter-sound), which in Greek theory denoted the octave in contradistinction to *symphonos,* the unison, and *paraphonos,* the fifth. The original meaning of the term suggests that, in the earliest days of antiphonal singing, the second of the two alternating groups consisted of women or children singing an octave higher than the men. In fact, Philo expressly says that one chorus was formed by men, the other by women.

Aside from this, nothing specific is known about the early manner of antiphonal singing. St. Basil is the first to mention it as a method of singing the Psalms. It is plausible to assume that all the verses of the Psalm were sung to the same melody, probably nothing more than a simple recitation formula, and that the two choruses, under the guidance of their leaders, alternated either from verse to verse or in half-verses. It is this method that survived in the *psalmus in directum,* which at an early time may well have been performed by two groups.

At some time, possibly as early as the fourth century, the *cantus anti-*

[1] There is, however, no evidence for the antiphonal singing of Psalms. See the article by Avenary mentioned on p. 180, fn. 1.

[2] See List of Data, pp. 38ff, nos. 1, 17, 21, 30.

phonarius was enriched by the addition of a short text sung before and after each verse, and called *antiphona*. There resulted a refrain-like structure similar to, and perhaps suggested by the *cantus responsorius:*

$$A \ V_1 \ A \ V_2 \ A \ V_3 \ldots A \ V_n \ A.$$

Usually, the report of Etheria (*c.* 380) is regarded as the first evidence for this stage of antiphonal singing. Previously [see pp. 45f] we pointed out that the evidence is not entirely convincing, but there can be hardly any doubt that the method of singing Psalms with an interspersed Antiphon originated at about this time. In fact, the church historian Sozomenos informs us that *c.* 362, because of the anti-Christian edicts of Julian the Apostate (361-363), the relics of the Martyr St. Babylas were brought to a safe place in Antiochia, and that during the accompanying procession the "experts" sang a Psalm (Ps. 96?), while the people repeated after each verse: *Confusi sunt omnes* (Ps. 96, ℣. 7).[3] This report is also interesting because it shows the popular, one might almost say, "activistic" nature of early antiphonal psalmody.

The introduction of the additional text (and melody) brought about a noteworthy change in the meaning of the term antiphonal psalmody, that is, the change from a term descriptive of performance (alternating choirs) to one indicative of structure (refrain form). How completely the original meaning of the term was lost appears from the fact the *psalmus in directum* is generally considered as a type in opposition to antiphonal (as well as responsorial) psalmody, although actually it is the purest representative of antiphonal psalmody in the proper meaning of the term.

While in responsorial psalmody the refrain is a natural part of the structure, it forms a rather extraneous and arbitrary element in antiphonal psalmody, a willful addition which may well be regarded as the earliest instance of troping. Responsorial psalmody is impossible without a refrain, the respond, which provides that contrast between solo and choral performance that is essential in responsorial singing. Antiphonal singing, on the other hand, is in no way predicated upon the use of a refrain. In fact, it is not at all clear how this refrain, the Antiphon, was fitted into the antiphonal (that is, double-chorus) method of performance. We can only speculate whether it was sung by both choirs combined, or whether it was also sung antiphonally by being divided into two phrases, a method which seems to have been practiced in the ninth or tenth century under the name of *ad antiphonam respondere*.

---

[3] Migne, *Patr. graeca* 67, p. 1275. Sozomenos also reports that under Theodosius (379-95) the Arians, divided into groups, sang Psalms antiphonally, with the addition of "closing sentences" (*akroteleutia*) written according to their dogma, and that St. John Chrysostom (d. 407) "urged the people of his flock to sing Psalms in a similar way" (*Patr. graeca* 67, p. 1535). Perhaps *akroteleutia* is the Doxology.

The extraneous character of the Antiphons is also clearly noticeable in their musical style. In the responsorial chants both the responds and verses are rather similar to each other and, in fact, are often closely related through the use of identical or similar musical material. No greater contrast, on the other hand, can be imagined than that between the monotone recitation of a psalm verse and the free melodic flow of an Antiphon. It is this very contrast which provides both an historical explanation and an aesthetic justification for the introduction of the Antiphons.

As in the case of responsorial psalmody, the full form of antiphonal psalmody, with its refrain-like repeat of the Antiphon, proved too long; therefore it was reduced by omitting either verses of the Psalm or repeats of the Antiphon. The full form, however, may still be seen in a few special chants, such as the Invitatory Psalm, *Venite exsultemus,* of Matins [368, etc., with varying Antiphons]; the Canticle *Nunc dimittis* as sung during the distribution of the candles at Purification [1357; with the Antiphon *Lumen ad revelationem*]; or the *Versus Psalmi 44. cum Antiphona, in tono olim usitato* (in the tone formerly used) as given in *Variae Preces* for the Feast of Assumption [*VP* 201]:[4]

Venite exsultemus:	A A V_1 A V_2 A′ V_3 A V_4 A′ V_5 A D A′ A
Nunc dimittis:[5]	A V_1 A V_2 A V_3 A D_1 A D_2 A
Eructavit cor meum:	A V_1 V_2 A V_3 V_4 A V_5 V_6 A V_7 V_8 A D_1 D_2 A

By far the most frequent type of antiphonal psalmody is that represented by the Office Psalms sung during the Office Hours, from Matins to Compline. Here the Psalms are sung complete, with the Doxology added at the end to form two additional verses; but the Antiphon is sung only before the first and after the final verse:

$$A \; V_1 \; V_2 \; V_3 \ldots V_n \; D_1 \; D_2 \; A,$$

and its initial statement is often reduced to an *incipit* [see p. 217]. However, even in this greatly curtailed form the Office Psalms betray their original refrain structure by an interesting detail, that is, the *differentiae,* a number of different formulae provided for the conclusion of the psalm tone (i.e., the recitation melody employed for all the verses) for the purpose of making a smooth connection between the end of the Psalm (D_2) and

---

4 Ferretti (*Esthétique,* p. 215) and others (e.g., Batiffol, *History of the Roman Breviary,* p. 100) consider the Invitatory as a responsorial, not an antiphonal Psalm. True enough, it is sung today (and probably was in medieval practice) in a responsorial manner, but so are all the antiphonal Psalms. Certainly, from the point of view of musical style the Invitatory is as close to antiphonal psalmody as it is different from the responsorial types. Moreover, all the responsorial types are post-lesson chants, while the Invitatory has the function of an "introit" for Matins.

5 D_1 and D_2 stand for the first and the second half of the Doxology, each of which is treated as a single verse.

the beginning of the Antiphon sung thereafter [see p. 218]. According to this function, the specific *differentia* would be required only for the last verse of the Doxology. Actually it is used at the end of every verse, thus showing that originally the Antiphon was indeed repeated after each verse.

The antiphonal chants of the Mass are the Introit, the Offertory, and the Communion, or, as they are occasionally called in the early books, *Antiphona ad Introitum, Antiphona ad Offertorium,* and *Antiphona ad Communionem.* Each of these items is a chant accompanying a liturgical action: entrance of the priest, offering of the gifts, and distribution of the Holy Wafers. This puts them into a marked contrast to the responsorial chants, the Graduals, Alleluias, and Responsories (as well as to the purely solo Tracts), which are contemplative postludes to the reading from Scripture. There can be no doubt that this distinction is the result, not of coincidence, but of careful planning guided by a fine feeling for the liturgical property and propriety of each type, a feeling which also manifests itself in a basic difference of the musical styles: the responsorial "lesson-chants" are highly melismatic, while the antiphonal "action-chants" employ a relatively simpler style. An exception are the Offertories which, in the course of time, acquired richly ornate melodies so that from the stylistic point of view they belong to the responsorial category.

Considering the fact that the melodies of the antiphonal Mass chants are simpler (and, consequently, shorter) than those of the responsorial group, one might expect to find here fuller forms, with several verses and refrain-like repeats of the Antiphon. Such forms did indeed exist at a relatively late date, between the eighth and twelfth centuries, when the responsorial chants had long since been reduced to their simple form. Eventually, however, the tendency toward reduction caught up with the antiphonal chants as well, leading to even more severely curtailed forms. The Introit was reduced to one verse and the Doxology, preceded and followed by the Antiphon: A V D A. In the Communion the Psalm was completely eliminated, so that only the Antiphon remained—a complete reversal of its original function. The Offertories retained their verses, from one to four, throughout the Middle Ages, and did not lose them until the twelfth century. Today the Offertories are similar to the Communions in that they consist only of the Antiphon. Only in the Mass of the Dead do we find a Communion, *Lux aeterna,* and an Offertory, *Domine Jesu Christe,* with a verse.

Evidence of the early, more complete forms just alluded to is found, first of all, in certain literary documents called *Ordo Romanus,* which contain rather detailed descriptions of the Mass as celebrated by the pope. The earliest of these, usually referred to as *Ordo Romanus Gerbert,* dates from the early eighth century (c. 700-730); the next, universally called *Ordo*

Romanus primus, was written in the second half of the eighth century; and the third, known as the *Ordo of St.-Amand,* dates from the ninth century.[6] The first of these sources describes the Introit as consisting of the first verse of a Psalm, the first and second half of the Doxology, and another psalm verse, each of these in alternation with the Antiphon which is also taken from the same Psalm:

$$A \ V_1 \ A \ D_1 \ A \ D_2 \ A \ V_2 \ A$$

The *Ordo Romanus primus* contains a minute description of the ceremonial that opened the pontifical Mass: the pope arriving at the sacristy and being clothed with the sacred vestments; the dignitaries gathering there and entering the nave of the church; the solemn procession to the altar; the pope inspecting the "Sancta" (consecrated bread), prostrating himself in prayer and giving the kiss of peace to the priests, after which he gives the sign for the *Gloria,* that is, the beginning of the Doxology; another prayer by the pope who kneels before the altar together with the priests; the priests rising and saluting the altar, during which ceremony the *Sicut erat,* that is, the second part of the Doxology, is sung by the choir; finally the pope also rising, kissing the Gospel and the altar, and returning to his throne. No doubt the major part of this long ceremonial was accompanied by the singing of the Introit, and it is obvious that even the fuller form indicated above would not nearly have sufficed to fill the time. Probably the Introit started with an indefinite number of verses of the Psalm, sung in alternation with the Antiphon until the pope gave the signal to sing the *Gloria* and, somewhat later, the *Sicut erat.* The final part of the ceremony was once more accompanied by psalm verses, the so-called *versus ad repetendum* (or, simply, *repetenda*), that is, one or two additional verses added *ad libitum* depending upon the time required to finish the action. An Introit sung according to this scheme must have had a form somewhat like the following:

$$A \ V_1 \ A \ V_2 \ A \ V_3 \ A \ D_1 \ A \ D_2 \ A \ V_4 \ A \ V_5 \ A \ (V_4, V_5 = \textit{repetenda})$$

It is interesting to notice that this form shows the same structure as the one actually described in the earlier *Ordo Romanus* (the *Anonymus Gerbert*), but in greater fullness. In each case the Doxology appears in the middle, preceded and followed by one or several verses of the Psalm.

Naturally, the elaborate ceremony of the pontifical Mass in Rome was a unique phenomenon. In other churches the introductory celebrations were much simpler and less time-consuming, so that considerably shortened Introits were sufficient. The early form is still partly preserved in the

---

[6] See List of Sources, p. 53, nos. 4 to 6. The following explanations are taken from J. Froger, *Les Chants de la messe aux VIIIe et IXe siècles* (1950).

eleventh-century Ms St. Gall *381*, in which the initial Psalm is already reduced to a single verse, but one or two verses *ad repetendum* after the Doxology are fully indicated.[7] In the later codices these disappear, but occasionally we find evidence that the Antiphon was repeated, not only at the end, but also between the verse and the Doxology: A V A D A.[8] Finally it may be observed that to the present day the verse of the Introit is marked, not ℣. (Verse), as in the Graduals, Responsories, Tracts, etc., but Ps. (Psalm), a last reminder of the fact that originally it was a complete Psalm.

The magnificent prelude of the pontifical Mass, as described in the sources of the eighth and ninth centuries, is matched by a scarcely less impressive postlude, the Communion, during which everyone present received a piece of the consecrated bread and a sip of the consecrated wine, in representation of the flesh and blood of Christ. First the pope, seated on his throne, received the communion from the archdeacon (*archidiaconus*); then the bishops received theirs from the pope; the first bishop attended to the other members of the clergy; and finally the bread and wine was given to the people. Except for the communion of the pope, which took place in silence, the whole ceremony was accompanied by the choir singing the chant called Communion. Like the Introit, this consisted of a whole Psalm or as much of it as was needed, followed by the *Gloria Patri* and a final verse *ad repetendum,* the whole enframed by the Antiphon: "If there are many clerks participating in the communion, the entire Psalm is sung with the Antiphon, until the priest makes the sign of the cross on his forehead to sing the *Gloria Patri*. And after the *Gloria* a verse of the Psalm is repeated and finally the Antiphon is sung."[9] Although this description does not specify the repeat of the Antiphon after each verse, there is little doubt that this was actually done. The early form of the Communion, therefore, corresponded in every detail to that of the Introit. Like this, it was greatly curtailed in the ensuing centuries, because the practice of giving Communion individually to every member of the clergy and to the people was abandoned. For a while the Communion underwent the same process of reduction as the Introit, as appears particularly from the previously mentioned Codex St. Gall *381*, in which the Communions have exactly the same form as the Introits—one verse, the Doxology, and one or two verses *ad repetendum*. For instance,

---

[7] The *Gradual* of Laon (*Pal. mus.*, X) had a *versus ad repetendum* for every Introit, but these were carefully erased at a later time. Some of them are still visible, e.g., Intr. *Esto mihi;* Ps. *In te Domine;* Ad R. *Inclina* (p. 34).

[8] The *Consuetudines antiquae Cluniacensium* prescribed for the Mass of Sunday that the Antiphon should be sung half after the verse, and full after the Doxology.

[9] Froger [fn. 6], pp. 37f.

the Communion *Circuibo* from the Sixth Sunday after Pentecost [1009] appears there in the following form:[10]

C(ommunio): *Circuibo et immolabo . . .*
(Ps.): *Dominus illuminatio mea et salus mea quem timebo.*
ad R(epetendum): *Dominus protector vitae meae a quo trepidabo.*
ad R.: *Exaudi domine vocem meam qua clamavi: miserere mei et exaudi me.*

The Doxology is not indicated, but its insertion after the Psalm was taken for granted, as well as the repeats of the Antiphon. For the Communion of Easter Sunday, *Pascha nostrum* [781], the same codex prescribes as many as six *versus ad repentendum,* after the initial verse (Ps.) and the Doxology:

$$\text{A Ps A D A V}_1 \text{ A V}_2 \text{ A V}_3 \text{ A V}_4 \text{ A V}_5 \text{ A V}_6 \text{ A}$$

In the twelfth century only the initial verse (Ps.) and the Doxology remained, at least in some sources, leading to a form exactly like that of the present Introit. Moreover, the parallelism between the Introit and the Communion is enhanced by the fact that the verses of the latter were always sung to the same eight recitation melodies (one for each mode) that were, and still are, used for the verses of the former [see p. 228]. Eventually, however, the Communions lost the last vestiges of psalm verses, the only exception being that of the Mass for the Dead, *Lux aeterna,* which to the present day has retained a verse, *Requiem aeternam,* as well as the repeat of the second half of the Antiphon, *Cum sanctis* [1815].[11]

Finally we have to consider the Offertory, that is, the chant which accompanies the offering of bread and wine at the altar. Originally every member of the clergy and of the congregation participated in this pious act by bringing gifts which were consecrated and of which they received a part during the Communion. The usage of singing a Psalm during this action existed in Carthage as early as the fourth century, as we know from St. Augustine who speaks about "the custom, just started at Carthage, of singing hymns from the Book of Psalms, either before the offering or during the distribution of what has been offered."[12] The *Ordines romani*

10 See the facsimile reproduction in *Wagner II,* 264. In the *Gradual* of St. Yrieix (eleventh century) the Communion *Viderunt omnes* [410] appears in the following form: *Viderunt omnes fines terrae salutare Dei nostri. Ps. Jubilate Domino omnis terra, cantate et exultate et psallite. Viderunt (. . . nostri). (Gloria Patri . . .) seculorum amen. Salutare (. . . nostri):* A V A D A' (*Pal. mus., XIII,* Plates, p. 21).

11 The Sacred Congregation of Rites has recently approved the reintroduction of the full Introit, with several verses (see *RG,* XXVI [1947], 146). Attempts in the same direction are made for the Communion.

12 See List of Data, p. 41, no. 33.

give little specific indication about the chant of the Offertory. All we hear is that "the pope descends to receive the offerings of the people, and gives a sign to the archdeacon of the *schola* (choir) to say the offertory" [*Ordo of St. -Amand*], and that for the conclusion, "the pope inclines a little to the altar, looks at the *schola,* and gives them the sign for silence" [*Ordo Romanus primus*]. The express reference to the *schola* suggests that at this time the Offertory was still an antiphonal chant, probably an entire Psalm or the major part of it sung antiphonally, similar to the Introit and the Communion. In the earliest musical manuscripts, however, it appears already as a responsorial chant, with highly florid melodies, and with from one to three verses. It was not until the twelfth century that the Offertories lost their verses, the only exception being that of the Mass for the Dead, *Domine Jesu Christe,* which to the present day has retained one verse, *Hostias et preces* [1813].

The Offertories with their medieval verses have been published by C. Ott under the title of *Offertoriale sive versus Offertoriorum* (1935). Among the 110 Offertories of this collection, we find about a dozen with one verse, *c.* seventy with two, twenty-five with three, and one, *Vir erat* from the Twenty-first Sunday after Pentecost, with four. In most of them repeat of the Antiphon or, usually, of its second half is indicated, so that the following form emerges as the normal one:

$$A \ V_1 \ A' \ V_2 \ A'$$

Those for the highest feasts usually have three verses, e.g.:

NATIVITY: *Tui sunt caeli,* ℣. 1. *Magnus et metuendus,* ℣. 2. *Misericordia,* ℣. 3. *Tu humiliasti*

EPIPHANY: *Reges Tharsis,* ℣. 1. *Deus judicium,* ℣. 2. *Suscipiant montes,* ℣. 3. *Orietur in diebus*

SEPTUAGESIMA SUNDAY: *Bonum est confiteri,* ℣. 1. *Quam magnificata,* ℣. 2. *Ecce inimici;* ℣. 3. *Exaltabitur*

ASH WEDNESDAY: *Domine exaudi,* ℣. 1. *Ne avertas,* ℣. 2. *Quia oblitus sum,* ℣. 3. *Tu exsurgens*

EASTER SUNDAY: *Terra tremuit,* ℣. 1. *Notus in Judaea,* ℣. 2. *Et factus est,* ℣. 3. *Ibi confregit* [cf. Plates II, III, IV, etc.]

PENTECOST: *Confirma hoc,* ℣. 1. *Cantate Domino,* ℣. 2. *In ecclesiis,* ℣. 3. *Regna terrae*

Also those for the oldest of Saints, e.g., St. John the Baptist.

In a number of Offertories with several verses the repeat of the Antiphon is not indicated, or not indicated after each verse. In the great majority of the cases, this is probably due to scribal negligence. For instance, it can safely be assumed that in *Scapulis suis* [Ott, p. 32] the second part of the

Antiphon, from *Scuto,* is repeated, not only after ℣. 1 and ℣. 3, where it is prescribed, but also after ℣. 2, where it is not. In other cases the repeat is necessary in order to bring the piece to its proper close, on the final of its mode. An example in point is *Bonum est confiteri* [Ott, p. 26] which, being in mode 8, requires g as the final, which indeed appears as the last note of the Antiphon. The last verse, however, closes on e, an obvious impossibility for a composition in the eighth mode. It appears that the Antiphon has to be repeated after the last verse, as well as after the two others which employ the same cadential formula as the final verse. Still other Offertories reveal their repeat structure through the presence of a peculiarity that could be called musical rhyme. This consists in the use, at the end of each verse, of the same cadential formula which, in the Antiphon, immediately precedes its second part (that is, the part which is repeated after each verse), as follows (A′, A″ are the first and second part of the Antiphon):

$$A' + e \rightarrow A''; \quad V_1 + e \rightarrow A''; \quad V_2 + e \rightarrow A''$$

Thus the repeated refrain (A″) each time is introduced and announced by the same connecting formula. An example is the Offertory *Confortamini* [Ott, p. 9], from which the three passages pertaining to the present question are reproduced in Fig. 35. Others are *Deus tu convertens, Laeten-*

FIGURE 35

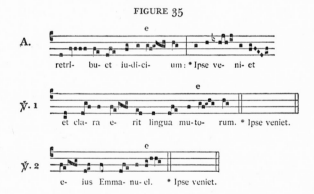

tur caeli (in which each verse terminates with the complete A′), *Tui sunt caeli, Domine vivifica* (℣. 1 only), *Domine fac mecum* (℣. 2), *Eripe me . . . Domine,* etc. While in these Offertories the repeat of the Antiphon (or, rather, its second half) is properly indicated, there are others lacking this indication but showing exactly the same peculiarity of identical cadential formulae in the middle of the Antiphon and at the end of the verses; e.g., *De profundis* [Ott, p. 126], from which three passages are reproduced in Fig. 36, the first from the inner melisma, "meam," of the Antiphon, the others from the close of the two verses. It is obvious that the respond

FIGURE 36

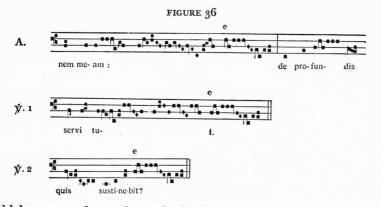

should be repeated, not from the beginning but after the melisma [for more details regarding this Offertory see p. 371]. A similar example is *Super flumina* [Ott, p. 119], the first verse of which borrows its ending from the melisma "flevimus" of the Antiphon, thus suggesting repeat of its closing section, "dum recordaremur tui, Sion."

Finally it should be noticed that in a few Offertories the refrain is taken, not from the Antiphon, but from the closing section of the first verse. Thus, after the third verse of *Benedictus es . . . in labiis* [Ott, p. 28] the indication for repeat reads: "*In labiis *vel* *Aufer a plebe," giving an option between the repeat of the closing section of the Antiphon or that of the first verse.[13] Similar cases are *Super flumina* [Ott, p. 119], where the repeat "*Qui dixerunt" after ℣. 3 refers to the closing section of ℣. 2; *Mihi autem* [Ott, p. 128; repeat "*Nimis" from ℣. 1], and *Anima nostra* [Ott, p. 145], where the melody indicated for the repeat "*Laqueus" shows that this is the "Laqueus contritus est nos, liberati sumus" from the end of ℣. 1, not from the end of the Antiphon which closes with the same words, but set to a different melody.

These and other structural peculiarities[14] place the Offertories in a category all their own. No other type of chant shows so many variants of its basic structure. In reality these variants are even more numerous than appears from a study of Ott's publication, since not a few Offertories occur in different manuscripts with different numbers of verses or with divergent indications for the repeat of the Antiphon. It is not easy to give a satisfactory explanation for the great amount of structural variability found in these chants. Froger tries to account for their "physionomie si originale" by considering them as representatives of "poésie lyrique,"[15]

[13] Musically, the refrain "In labiis" is preferable, since it starts with e, thus making for a smooth connection with the verses, all of which close on e. The refrain "Aufer a plebe" starts with c' and therefore would produce an upward leap of a sixth.

[14] For more details, see pp. 370ff.

[15] Froger [fn. 6], p. 29.

but it is difficult to see how this designation, if at all applicable to Gregorian chant, could serve to distinguish the Offertories from the Introits or
Graduals, in which we find texts no less "poetic" and "lyrical" than those
of the Offertories. A more prosaic, but probably more reasonable, explanation is that the Offertories have survived only in a relatively late form,
dating from the second half of the ninth century [see pp. 375, 513].

QUESTIONS OF PERFORMANCE

Originally and properly, the terms responsorial and antiphonal pertain
to matters of performance, the former indicating the alternation between
a soloist and a choir, the latter, between two choirs. In later usage they
acquired somewhat different meanings, becoming primarily associated
with differentiations in the field of musical style (responsorial = elaborate;
antiphonal = simple) or of forms and types (responsorial = Graduals,
Alleluias, etc.; antiphonal = Introits, Communions, etc.). The question
arises whether and to what extent the original meaning survived in the
practice of the Middle Ages and of the present day; in other words, whether
all or some of the responsorial chants continued to be sung responsorially,
the antiphonal chants antiphonally.

As for the responsorial chants, the answer is clearly in the positive. As
far as can be ascertained, the Graduals, Alleluias, and Responsories of
Matins were always, and are at present, sung responsorially, the verse or
verses being entrusted to the soloist, the respond to the choir; e.g.,

$$\underline{R} \ \underline{V} \ \underline{R} \ \underline{D} \ \underline{R},$$

(straight lines indicate choral, dotted lines solo performance). In the twelfth
century, if not earlier, this method was modified in such a way that the
beginning of the respond was sung by the soloist, and the conclusion of the
verse by the choir. Each of these contrasting sections comprise from one
to three words, marked off from the rest by an asterisk, e.g. [409]:

R̲. *Viderunt omnes * fines terrae . . . omnis terra.* V̲. *Notum fecit
Dominus . . . ante conspectum gentium revelavit * justitiam suam.*[1]

The use of a solo opening means that the chant is intoned by the solo
singer, a practice which is justifiable not only aesthetically but also from
a practical point of view, the soloist assuming the role of one who gives
the pitch to the choir. It is equally imperative, on aesthetic grounds, that
each chant should be closed by the choir, and this principle is also universally observed. It operates automatically if the Gradual is sung in its

[1] This manner of performance is of basic importance in the organa of the School of
Notre-Dame (Leoninus, Perotinus; *c.* 1200), in which the solo sections only have polyphonic music, the choral sections being sung in plainsong.

early, fuller form, with the respond repeated after the verse. In this case the verse is sung entirely by the soloist. The later custom of omitting the repeat of the respond necessitated the introduction of a choral close for the verse. The present-day Roman rite permits both the full and the shorter form of the Gradual. Following is a schematic representation showing the alternation of soloist and choir in the responsorial chants (the sign .___ indicates a choral section with solo opening, the sign ....___ a solo section with choral close):[2]

Gradual: R V_   or R V. R

Responsory: R V. R′ or R V. R′ .R

Alleluia: A A + j V   A + j (A = Alleluia; j = jubilus)

Turning now to the question of antiphonal singing, we face a more difficult problem. As far as the authorized present-day practice is concerned, antiphony has completely disappeared in what is called "antiphonal" chants. The Psalms are sung in alternation between the cantor (soloist) and the choir, the former singing the first, the latter the second half of each verse.[3] Some monasteries, particularly in Germany, employ an antiphonal performance—two half-choirs alternate with full verses, while the Antiphon is sung by both groups together, except for a solo incipit. As for the medieval practice, this seems to have varied. As has been previously pointed out, antiphonal singing was introduced as a decidedly "popular" (perhaps, more precisely, popularizing) method of worship. It found its way into the Church because of its activistic, even propagandistic qualities, not dissimilar to those found today in the Salvation Army. It is easy to understand that these qualities were of the highest value for the Church when she was fighting for survival, but it is also understandable that they lost their importance when the victory was won, and when the general character of the worship changed from exuberant jubilation to pious devotion. According to recent investigations, the Psalms were sung, in the sixth century and later, in a responsorial manner, the verses by a soloist and the Antiphon after each verse by the entire group of monks.[4] In the ninth century, however, Amalarius says that "the antiphon is begun by one singer of one choir, and in accordance with its mode the psalm is sung by the two choirs (in alternation); but in the antiphon itself both choirs join."[5] Thus, both the "responsorialists" and the "antiphonalists" of the

2 See the indications *L*, p. xv, also pp. 320ff.

3 See *L* 251.

4 Cf. C. Gindele, "Doppelchor und Psalmvortrag im Frühmittelalter" (*Die Musikforschung*, VI [1953], 296).

5 *De Ecclesiastico Officio*, IV, 7: *Antiphona inchoatur ab uno unius chori; et ad eius symphoniam psalmus cantatur per duos choros; ipsa enim, id est antiphona, coniunguntur simul duo chori* (ed. Hanssens, II, 433).

present day can cite historical authority for their views, the former from the sixth to the eighth, the latter from the ninth and possibly the fourth century.

Turning to the antiphonal chants of the Mass, the Introit is the only one of sufficient extension to permit alternation of performing bodies. Nothing definite seems to be known about the medieval practice. At present, it is performed responsorially; e.g.:

	Cantor	Choir
Ant.	*Ad te levavi *animam meam . . . non confundantur.*	

	Cantor	Choir
Ps.	*Vias tuas, Domine demonstra mihi: *et semitas tuas edoce me.*	

	Cantor	Choir
Dox.	*Gloria Patri . . . Sancto. *Sicut . . . saecula saeculorum. Amen.*	

	Choir
Ant.	*Ad te levavi . . . non confundantur.*

The Roman usage prescribes one cantor on weekdays and Simple Feasts, two on other Feasts and Sundays, and four on Solemn Feasts.[6] Thus, on the last-mentioned occasions, the effect approaches antiphony.

Antiphonal singing is employed today mainly for chants that have no connection with antiphonal psalmody; e.g., the *Kyrie,* the *Gloria,* the Hymns, the Sequences, or the bilingual *Sanctus* of Good Friday [705]. It is also used for the Tracts which have completely lost their solo character. The verses of the Tract are sung alternately by two choirs (or by the cantors and the full choir), except for the opening and the closing passage (marked off by an asterisk), the former of which is given to a soloist, the latter to both choirs combined.

6 *L,* p. xv.

3

Stylistic Analysis

CHAPTER ONE

The Liturgical Recitative

GENERAL OBSERVATIONS

WITH this chapter we turn from a consideration of the more basic and general aspects of Gregorian chant—liturgical structure, notation, tonality, types, and forms—to the study of its inner organism, in other words, of its style.

The basis of stylistic analysis of Gregorian chant is the customary distinction of three styles, syllabic, neumatic (group), and melismatic. The syllabic chants are those in which each syllable of the text receives one, occasionally two or three notes. In a neumatic chant the majority of the syllables are sung to a group of two, three, four, or more notes, each group being represented by a single neume (hence the name neumatic style for this class). In a melismatic chant there are a number of syllables carrying a true melisma, consisting of ten, twenty, thirty, or more notes. As is implied in these definitions, the neumatic chants also include syllables having only one note, and the melismatic chants consist of a mixture of single notes, short groups, and extended melismas. If we select an example of each class and count the number of notes appearing with, e.g., fifteen syllables, this number may be about twenty in a syllabic, thirty to forty in a neumatic, and close to one hundred in a melismatic chant.

The style of a given chant is determined by the liturgical category to which it belongs. Each category, whether part of the Office or of the Mass, has its distinct style from which there is a hardly ever a deviation, and which conforms with its liturgical importance and solemnity. Thus, starting with the Offices of weekdays and going on to the Day Hours of Sundays and feast days, to Lauds and Vespers, to the night service (Matins), and finally to the Proper of the Mass, we proceed from the simplest to the most elaborately adorned melodies.

Following is a table which illustrates this point in greater detail, the various types of chant being listed approximately according to the position they hold in the stylistic order of rank:

Syllabic: Lesson and Prayer Tones
                Psalm Tones; Tones for the Introit Verses
                Psalm Antiphons; Short Responsories; Hymns; Sequences;
                    Glorias; Credos
Neumatic: Sanctus; Agnus Dei
                Introits; Communions
                Processional and Marian Antiphons
Melismatic: Kyries
                Great Responsories; Offertories; Tracts
                Graduals; Alleluias.[1]

The statement that the individual chants closely adhere to the general style of their class is particularly evident in the psalm Antiphons, Short Responsories, Hymns, and in the Proper of the Mass. Some of the Great Responsories show neumatic rather than melismatic style; e.g., *Qui Lazarum* [1786]. Particularly striking is the considerable variation found in the *Kyries*, as, for instance, between the highly melismatic *Kyrie I* and the very modest *Kyrie XVIII*. With good reason the former is used today (and probably was in medieval practice) for Solemn Feasts, the latter for the weekdays of Advent and Lent.

Although the classification according to syllabic, neumatic, and melismatic style is basic, it is, needless to say, by no means sufficient to account for the whole range of stylistic variety found in Gregorian chant. We have only to consider the fact that the syllabic group includes such widely heterogenous chants as the lesson tones, the psalm Antiphons, and the Hymns in order to realize that many other points of view enter into the picture. The most important of these aspects are those resulting from the innumerable manifestations of melodic motion: which may be stationary, oscillating, or scalar; narrow or wide in range; conjunct or disjunct, the latter with intervals ranging from a third to a sixth or more, with or without leaps in the same or in a changed direction; involving variation of a basic design, recurrence of standard formulae, etc. On another level we have to consider structural elements such as over-all length, division into phrases, repeat of phrases and sections, symmetry of phraseology, etc. Finally, as to the relationship between the music and the text, the consideration of the number of notes assigned to a syllable is only the beginning of investigations of a more subtle nature, such as accentuation, emphasis placed on important words, word painting, and others.

[1] A famous example illustrating the close relationship between musical style and liturgical category is provided by the psalm verse *Justus ut palma* which, at different occasions, is sung to melodies ranging from a monotone recitation to the most profusely ornamented type of chant; L 1125: Versicle (tones on p. 118); 735: psalm tone (℣. 12); 1204: Introit; 1193: Offertory; 1201: Gradual; 1207: Alleluia. See *Wagner III*, 7ff.

Turning now to a study of all these aspects, we shall largely follow the outline of Wagner's *Gregorianische Formenlehre,* in which the repertory is divided into two categories, the "Gebundene Formen" and the "Freie Formen." The former category includes the chants having the character of a recitative; the latter those having (or, at least, including) freely invented melodies. In each group we shall proceed from the simplest to the more complex types, in somewhat the order given in the table shown on the preceding page.

THE TONES FOR THE READINGS AND PRAYERS

The most elementary stage of the liturgical recitative is represented by the melodic formulae used for the musical delivery of the readings and prayers that form a part of the Office and of the Mass. In view of the close relationship which generally exists between degrees of musical elaboration and degrees of liturgical significance, it is perhaps surprising to encounter such rudimentary types of chant not only in the Office Hours, but also (in fact, much more prominently) in the solemn liturgy of the Mass. The explanation is that these are not musical items in the proper sense. They are essentially spoken texts, the meaning of which would be destroyed by any but the simplest manner of musical delivery. Here, as well as in the slightly more developed formulae used for the Psalms, the music has no independent significance and value, but only serves as a means of obtaining a distinct and clearly audible pronunciation of the words, so that they will resound into the farthest corners of the church. Today, these texts are often recited *recto tono,* that is, on one unchanged pitch, and with a slight pause to mark the end of phrases or sentences.[1] This, however, is not a medieval practice. It was introduced, together with many other modifications, through the reforming work of Giov. Guidetti (1530-92), whose *Directorium chori* of 1582 is perhaps the most important of the various reform editions of that period, much more so than the notorious *Editio Medicea* of 1614.

The formulae used for the musical delivery of such texts as readings and prayers (also the Psalms; see p. 208) are called tones, in translation of the Latin term *tonus* commonly used for them in the Middle Ages. As may be expected in the case of such semi-musical chants, the medieval books show considerable variation in the details of the various *toni.* These variants have been fully studied by Wagner,[2] but they are hardly important enough to be included in the present book. The basic principles are always the

[1] See *L,* p. 99.
[2] See *Wagner III,* 37-82.

same, and become sufficiently evident from a consideration of the tones given in the modern books of chant.

The *Liber usualis* prescribes tones for the prayers (collects) and the readings from Prophecy, Epistles, or Gospels that form a part of the Mass, as well as for the short Chapters of the Day Hours and the more extended Lessons of Matins.[3] All these tones are essentially monotone recitations sung at a certain pitch called *tenor* (in medieval books also *tuba*, in characterizing reference to its loudness, like that of a trumpet), and with downward inflections at the various points of punctuation, as indicated in the text by a comma, colon, semicolon, interrogation mark, or period. In the earliest manuscripts the recitation is made preferably on a, with inflections down to g and f. In twelfth-century sources we find the first examples of a tenor on c′, with inflections down to b and a, or on f with inflections down to e or d. This change is an indication of a tendency, often noticeable in Gregorian chant, to replace a subtonal tenor by a subsemitonal tenor; that is, a tenor having a whole-tone below it (g, a, b) by one forming a semitone with its lower neighbor (f, c′). We shall see later that the tendency toward subsemitonal tenors also plays an important role in the formation of the psalm tones. As for the tones of the prayers, etc., the liturgical books of the present day prefer the subsemitonal tenors, listing the others as "Ancient Tones." Nearly all the tones given in *L* have a tenor on c′, the only exceptions being the ancient tones for the Prayer given on pp. 100f, for the Gospel on p. 108, and for the Lessons of Matins on p. 121.

The melodic punctuations where the singer deviates from the monotone recitation are called *positurae* or *pausationes*. They are chiefly four, namely, flex (*flexa*, originally *punctus circumflexus*), metrum (usually called *punctus elevatus* in medieval sources), the interrogation (*punctus interrogationis*), and the full stop (*punctus versus*, i.e., final stop of the verse). The flex usually involves a simple downward motion to the lower note, such as a-g, and roughly corresponds to a comma of the text. The metrum involves a down-and-up motion, as a-g-g-a or a-g-f-a, and generally occurs at the place of a colon. Interrogative sentences usually call for a recitation at the pitch below the tenor, but with a final rise up to the tenor, for example, g . . . g-a, or g . . . g-f-g-a. The full stop normally involves a final motion down to a lower pitch, e.g., from a tenor on a to g: a-g-f-g, or down to d: a-f-g-d. Most of the tones also provide a somewhat more extended formula for the Conclusion, that is, the very last words of the text.

For further illustration a table follows which shows the punctuation formulae for some of the ancient tones given in *L*.[4]

---

[3] See *L*, pp. 98ff, 120ff, etc.

[4] The dashes serve to indicate the position of the accented syllable. Cf. *Wagner III*, 46, for a number of instructive examples.

FIGURE 37

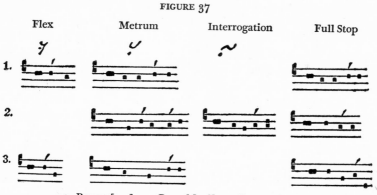

1. Prayer [100]   2. Gospel [108]   3. Lessons [122]

The signs given at the top of the figure are the ones used in the medieval books to indicate the various punctuations—*punctus flexus, elevatus, interrogativus*—and the corresponding inflections of the melody. The reader will easily recognize that the sign for the *punctus interrogativus* is an early form of our question mark, which thus reveals an interesting musical ancestry. While this sign only underwent a modification of its form, the medieval signs for the flex and the metrum were abandoned about 1500, and were replaced by the signs + and * which are still in use today.[5]

Finally, we reproduce in Fig. 38 [from *L* 108] an excerpt showing how the punctuation formulae were applied to a text, in this case from the Gospels:

FIGURE 38

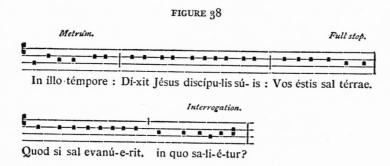

In illo témpore : Díxit Jésus discípu-lis sú- is : Vos éstis sal térrae.

Quod si sal evanú-e-rit. in quo sa-li-é-tur?

On the three days preceding Easter, that is, on Maundy Thursday, Good Friday, and Holy Saturday, the lessons of Matins take on a more solemn form than usual. On each of these days the three lessons of the first Nocturn are taken from the Lamentations of Jeremiah, and are sung to a tone of a

[5] See *L*, p. 124.

slightly more elaborate character than the one normally employed for the lessons of Matins.[6] The recitation is made throughout on the subtonal tenor a, with three inflections which can be said to represent the flex (F), the metrum (M), and the full stop (S). The normal succession of these inflections within a verse is F M : F S, the verse being divided, in the manner of the psalm verses, in halves, the first of which closes with the metrum, the second with the full stop, both of them being subdivided by the flex. In verses whose text is not long enough to accommodate the full scheme, either the first or the second half is sung without the flex, so that the inflections occur in the succession M : F S or F M : S. A special feature, adopted from the original text, is the enumeration of the verses by the letters of the Hebrew alphabet: *ALEPH: Quomodo sedet sola . . . BETH: Plorans ploravit in nocte . . .* , etc. Each of these letter names is sung to a special formula.

FIGURE 39

F: Flex	M: Metrum	S: Full Stop	Letters

ALEPH.

Brief mention only need be made of the tones for the Absolutions and Blessings [119], which are sung at Matins [e.g., 375], and which are very similar to the tones just described. They are preceded by a versicle, i.e., a short text consisting of two lines of similar length designated ℣ (verse) and ℟ (respond), which are sung to the same melodic formula consisting of a straight recitation with a closing melisma of eight to ten notes [374]:

FIGURE 40

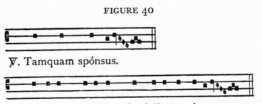

℣. Tamquam spónsus.

℟. Dóminus procédens de thálamo sú-o.

Similar versicles, usually sung to the same tone, occur after each Vesper hymn [e.g., 259], and after each Short Responsory [e.g., 229]. A more extended versicle, concluded by the *Gloria Patri,* is the *Deus in adjutorium,* which is an invariable opening chant of every Office Hour. Three melodies

---

[6] See *L,* pp. 626, 669, 715. A detailed study of the Lamentations is found in *Wagner III,* 235ff.

are provided for it, a Simple Tone for the Little Hours and Compline [263], a Festal Tone for Matins, Lauds, and Vespers [250], and a Solemn Tone for Vespers of very solemn feasts [112]. The last differs from the others (in fact, from all the tones we have so far considered) by its having an intonation, that is, an initial motion, f-g-a, leading up to the tenor on a. In this respect it resembles the psalm tones and other tones of a more elaborate character which will be studied later. Another tone opening with an intonation is that of the Prefaces [109], which serve as introductions to the reading of the Canon of the Mass [5]. An extended study of the various melodies with which the Prefaces occur in the medieval books is given in *Wagner III,* 69-80.

Among the various other recitatives used for special occasions—the *Te Deum* [1832], the *Exsultet* [739],[7] etc.—we shall consider only one which is interesting, and unique in Gregorian chant, because of its dramatic character; that is, the tone (or tones) for the Passions. The four versions of the Passion story are recited during Mass on four days shortly before Easter: that from Matthew on Palm Sunday [596], from Mark on Tuesday in Holy Week [607], from Luke on Wednesday [616], and from John on Good Friday [700]. Today these are generally read, but the medieval practice was to sing them in a manner designed to bring out the contrast between the participants of the story: Christ, the Jews, and the Evangelist who narrates the events. This was done by providing for a recitation at three different pitch levels and speeds, low and slow for the words of Christ, high and fast for those of the Jews, and medium for those of the Evangelist. The earliest manuscripts (ninth and tenth century) distinguish only between the words of Christ and the rest of the text by marking the former *t* (*tarde,* slowly), the latter *c* (*celeriter,* quick). Later the letter *s* (*sursum,* high) was added to characterize the *turba Judaeorum,* the crowd of the Jews. Finally, the letter *t* was interpreted as the sign of the Cross, **†**, and the two others adopted a different meaning, that is, *C* for *Chronista* and *S* for *Synagoga.*

The complete chant for the Passion according to St. John, on Good Friday, is included in the *Officium et Missa ultimi tridui Majoris Hebdomadae* (1947), pp. 149-169. The *Chronista* has a recitation on c′, with a mediant down to a (c′ b a c′) and a termination down to f (c′ g a f or, before the words of Christ, c′-b♭-a g f). The words of Christ are recited on f, with inflections down to c, while those of the *Synagoga* are sung an octave higher. Fig. 41 shows a section of this dialogue chant, which contains the roots of the liturgical drama.

---

[7] The *Praeconium Paschale* (Paschal laudation), a *psalmus idioticus* similar to the *Te Deum,* sung on Holy Saturday during the Blessings of the Paschal Candle [L 739]. For the music see *Officium . . . Tridui,* p. 227.

FIGURE 41

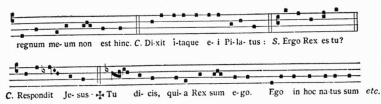

regnum me-um non est hinc. C. Di-xit i-taque e- i Pi-la- tus : S. Ergo Rex es tu?

C. Respondit Je- sus · ✠ Tu   di- cis, qui- a Rex sum e- go.   Ego in hoc na-tus sum etc.

As early as c. 1300 Johannes de Grocheo remarked that *lectio, epistola, evangelium,* and *oratio* "ad musicum non pertinet" (does not concern the musician), because they are governed only by the rules of accent and grammar.[8] In particular, they are practically the only chants that stand outside the system of the church modes. The very narrowness of their range, often including only three pitches, prevents their being assigned to a definite mode. In spite of their primitive style and limited tonality, however, they are not without artistic interest and significance. They certainly represent an admirable solution of the difficulties involved in the loud and clear delivery of a prose text, achieving, as they do, with a minimum of means a remarkably high degree of liturgical propriety, artistic order, and aesthetic satisfaction. Needless to say, they are extremely interesting from the historical point of view. They represent a stage in which music is shaped exclusively and in every detail by the requirements of textual pronunciation. Forgoing any attempt at musical elaboration for its own sake, they are the purest embodiment of that principle which, more than a thousand years later, when the recitative was reborn, Monteverdi expressed in the famous words: *L'orazione sia padrona dell'armonia e non serva* (The word should be the mistress of the music, not the servant).

THE PSALM TONES

The psalm tones are the melodic formulae used for the singing of the complete Psalms which form the nucleus of the service in all the Office Hours. In their essential traits they are very similar to the tones discussed in the previous chapter, consisting of a tenor recitation with inflections at the places of punctuation. The similarity is particularly striking in the case of one special psalm tone, the so-called *tonus in directum* (*tonus directaneus*), employed on a few occasions for a Psalm sung without antiphon [see p. 179]. It consists of a recitation on c' or on f (in medieval sources also on a) with two inflections identical with the flex and the metrum of the lesson tone shown in Fig. 37 [p. 205]. It is even simpler than this tone, because it lacks the interrogation (hardly ever required in a Psalm) and employs the formula of the flex also for the full stop. Fig. 42

8 E. Rohloff, *Der Musiktraktat des Johannes de Grocheo* (1943), p. 59.

shows the elements of the *tonus in directum* [see *L* 1776; the white notes are designed to take care of extra syllables in dactylic words]. As in all

FIGURE 42

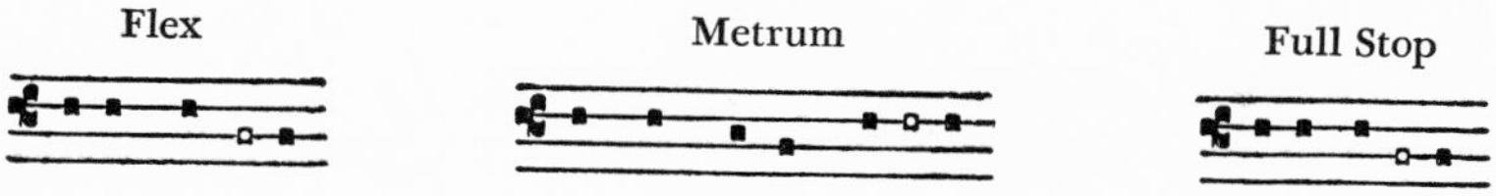

Flex	Metrum	Full Stop

Psalms, this formula is repeated for each verse, the flex being used only for the relatively few verses in which the length of the text requires a division into three phrases.

Psalms without an Antiphon also occur around Easter, namely, at Compline of Holy Saturday [762] and at the Little Hours of Easter Sunday and Easter Week [777, 784]. Also included in this group are the Psalms of the Little Hours (Prime to None) of Maundy Thursday and Good Friday, which, however, today are merely said [654]. All these Psalms are sung to one and the same tone, also called *tonus in directum* [see *L*, p. 118], which differs from the one previously mentioned mainly because it has an intonation:

FIGURE 43

The same melody is also employed for the Canticle *Nunc dimittis* at Compline of Easter Sunday [784].

We now turn to the regular psalm tones, that is, those employed for the Psalms sung with an Antiphon. Considered individually, these tones closely resemble those for the lessons, etc. True enough, they all begin with an intonation, but this is used for the first verse only, so that all the subsequent verses start directly with the tenor and thus employ formulae very similar to those considered above. As a group, however, the psalm tones present a new aspect because they became an integral part of the system of the church modes. Even the earliest sources containing detailed information about the singing of Psalms, e.g., the *Commemoratio brevis de tonis et psalmis modulandis* of the ninth century,[1] present the psalm tones as a fully developed system of eight *toni*, one for each mode. The reason for this organization is the ancient usage of connecting the Psalm with an Antiphon sung at the beginning and end of the Psalm, originally also between the verses [see p. 187]. These Antiphons are freely composed chants which vary from feast to feast and which show definite modal characteristics, some being in the first mode, others in the second, etc. It was con-

[1] See List of Sources, p. 55, no. 23. The musical examples for the psalmody are transcribed in Ferretti, *Esthétique*, pp. 303ff.

sidered necessary to sing the Psalm in such a way as to produce a tonal unity of the two constituent parts. By devising a different psalm tone for each mode a very ingenious solution was found for the problem presented by the combination of a fixed element, the psalmodic recitative, and a variable one, the Antiphon. Eight psalm tones were sufficient to accommodate the several thousands of Antiphons.

Each psalm tone consists of a tenor with three main inflections, the intonation (*intonatio, initium*) at the beginning, the mediant (*mediatio*) in the middle, and the termination (*terminatio*) at the end. The mediant corresponds to the metrum, the termination to the full stop of the prayer and lesson tones, while the consistent use of the intonation introduces a new element into the liturgical recitative. As is well known, nearly every psalm verse falls into halves, which often express the same thought in two different ways (*parallelismus membrorum*), as in Ps. 83:17: "Let them be confounded and troubled for ever; yea, let them be put to shame, and perish." The tenor recitation with three inflections fully corresponds to this binary structure of the text. The intonation falls on the initial syllables (usually the first two) of the verse, the mediant on the closing syllables of its first half, the termination on those of its second half, while all the other syllables are recited on the tenor note. Occasionally there are psalm verses of such length that a strict application of the general method would lead to an overly protracted recitation. For these the first half of the verse is subdivided by a small inflection, the flex. The general scheme of a psalm tone therefore is as follows:

Intonation—Tenor—(Flex—Tenor)—Mediant—Tenor—Termination

e.g., in the eighth tone:

FIGURE 44

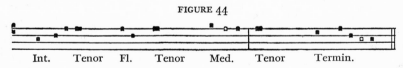

Int.   Tenor   Fl.   Tenor   Med.   Tenor   Termin.

The previous statement, that the psalm tones are integrated into the system of the eight church modes, should not be interpreted to mean that a given psalm tone is a melody of the corresponding mode. That this is not the case appears from the fact that often a psalm tone does not conform with the most basic requirement for a melody of a given mode, that is, that it close on its final. As we shall see later (p. 219), the terminations of the psalm tones are variable, and if one or the other closes on the tonic of the mode, this results from entirely different considerations than adherence to modal characteristics. The decisive element of the psalm tones is not the final, but the tenor, which is determined by the rule that it falls on the fifth above the final in the authentic modes, and on the third above the final in the plagal modes:

		final	tenor
Mode 1	protus auth.	d	a
2	plag.	d	f
3	deuterus auth.	e	b*
4	plag.	e	g*
5	tritus auth.	f	c′
6	plag.	f	a
7	tetrardus auth.	g	d′
8	plag.	g	b*

This, however, is not entirely the actual state of affairs. In present-day practice as well as in the common usage of the Middle Ages the three tenors marked by an asterisk are each a tone higher; for the third psalm tone the tenor is on c′, for the fourth on a, and for the eighth on c′. The reason for this deviation from the regular scheme is perhaps to be found in the aversion to making prominent use of the tone b, a scale degree suspect to the medieval mind because of its association with the tritone (f-b) and because of its chromatic variability (b-natural or b-flat). This line of reasoning would explain at least the change of the two tenors on b into tenors on c′, in the third and eighth psalm tone. As to the fourth tone, it has been suggested that its tenor was raised in consequence of the raise made in the third tone, in order to preserve in the *deuterus* group the normal relationship between the plagal and the authentic tenors, at the distance of a third. We shall, however, see soon that this explanation is not tenable.

The present-day system of the psalm-tone tenors, as just described, appears as early as the eleventh century, in the *De Musica* of Johannes Cotto,[2] and remained unchanged thereafter. It is only when we turn to the earliest source, the *Commemoratio brevis* of c. 900, that we get an insight into the original state of affairs. The *Commemoratio* describes two series of psalm tones, one requiring a "slower tempo, as in the canticles of the New Testament" (*ubi moriosori cantu opus est, utpote ad cantica Evangeliorum*), and another, somewhat simpler in style, for the Day Offices (*ad cursum canendum*). In both of these the third psalm tone has a recitation on b, not on c′.[3] The fourth psalm tone of the first series has a tenor on a; but for that of the second series a recitation on g is clearly indicated, at least for the first half of the verse, while a similar indication for the second half is unfortunately missing because of the shortness of the text, so that it is difficult to decide whether, for a more protracted text, the recitation would have been made on g or on a. We reproduce here the

---

[2] *GS*, II, 243. Also Waesberghe, *Johannes Affligemensis, De Musica cum Tonario* (1950), pp. 82ff.

[3] See the tables in *Wagner III*, 89, 90, and in Ferretti, *Esthétique*, pp. 303 and 307. The recitation on b for the third psalm tone has been restored in *AM*, p. 1212: "Tonus in tenore antiquo."

original notation (replacing the *daseia* signs by their equivalents in staff notation) together with two interpretations for the second half.[4] Both

FIGURE 45

Tu mandasti   manda - ta tu - a: cu -sto - di - ri   ni - mis.

Wagner and Ferretti [p. 308] interpret the second half as under (b), so that the psalm tone has two different tenors, as in the *tonus peregrinus.* The fact that in the original notation the tone a appears twice in succession (in Wagner's transcription three times), while the pitch g is reached only once, would seem to favor this interpretation. It should be noticed, however, that this interpretation leaves only two syllables, *nimis,* for the termination, while the terminations of all the other psalm tones in the *Commemoratio* have four or five syllables, either the standard *(secu)lorum amen,* or *lege Domini, (man)data tua,* etc. This certainly is a fairly convincing argument in favor of the interpretation (a), with the termination *-diri nimis* and, consequently, with the recitation on g in the second as well as in the first half of the psalm tone. At any rate, it appears that at the time of the *Commemoratio* the tenor of the fourth psalm tone was either g or g-a. It also appears that the change to a, adumbrated here and established not long thereafter, could not possibly have been made in consequence of the raise of the tenor in the third psalm tone, since this tenor had not yet changed. Finally, as to the eighth psalm tone, all the examples of the *Commemoratio* have the tenor on c'. However, traces of a recitation on b occur in certain chants of psalmodic derivation, e.g., in the verses of the Responsories.[5]

In addition to the eight regular psalm tones there is the *tonus peregrinus* (foreign, strange tone), characterized by the use of two different tenors, on a for the first half of the verse, and on g for the second [117]:

4 The transcription in *Wagner III,* 90, with a recitation on a in the first half and with the mediant closing on a, is wrong.

5 See p. 236. There can be no doubt that in the Tracts of the eighth mode the recitation was originally on b, not on c' [see, e.g., the Tract *Cantemus, L* 745, on "Dominus conterens"]. The clearest evidence for the recitation on b is found in the Beneventan Mss published in *Pal. mus.,* XIV, in which the above passage reads: *Do-*   g-a-b-c' b b   b b c' *mi-nus con-te-rens* [*Pal. mus.,* XIV, Plates, p. 67; Pl. xix, xxiv; also XV, Plates, p. 119ᵛ].

FIGURE 46

This tone is used today for Ps. 112, *Laudate pueri* [152] and Ps. 113, *In exitu Israel* [160], on certain occasions, e.g., Vespers of Sunday [254], Vespers of the Common of Two or More Martyrs [1154], and Second Vespers of the Dedication of the Church of St. Michael [1660]. Actually, its use is predicated not so much on liturgical occasions or specific Psalms as on the Antiphons with which these Psalms are sung in the cases just mentioned. All these Antiphons, *Deus autem, Martyres Domini, Angeli Domini,* as well as others no longer in general use, belong to the same melody type which escapes modal classification and which was considered problematic as early as the ninth century.[6] Aurelianus [*GS,* I, 51b] lists this group of Antiphons under the eighth mode as an "eleventh division which in all respects stands apart from the normal track (*orbita,* wheel-rut) of the eighth mode." Indeed, it is easy to see that the eighth psalm tone, with its g-a-c'-b-c'-a-g outline, does not harmonize at all with a melody such as that of *Deus autem* [256], which starts on the low c and includes a characteristic a-bb-a near the end. Obviously the *tonus peregrinus,* with its a-bb-a beginning and its close on d, was "made to order" for these Antiphons. In fact, Aurelianus [*GS,* I, 52a] refers to it, with obvious disapproval, as a *neophytus tonus* (a new-fangled tone), thus indicating that this tone, generally considered by modern scholars as an archaic formula,[7] was a late addition to the system of psalm tones. The author of the *Commemoratio* reproduces it [*GS,* I, 218] under the name of *tonus novissimus.* This tone, shown in Fig. 47, differs from the later version not only in the mediant but also in the tenor of the second half, which is predominantly on a. Thus it appears that the distinctive trait of the *tonus peregrinus* is (or was) not the two different tenors, but the special intonation and termination formulae made to harmonize with the melodic outline of the Antiphons.

FIGURE 47

Afférte Dómino, fí-li- i De- i : * afférte Dómino fí-li- os a-rí- etum.

The medieval books contain several other "irregular" psalm tones, which apparently were used only for certain occasions and in certain localities. The *Antiphonale monasticum* indicates a *tonus irregularis* [*AM*

6 Gevaert's *thème 28;* see p. 400.

7 H. Gaisser, in "L'Origine du *tonus peregrinus*" (*Congrès d'histoire de la musique, 1900,* ed. by Combarieu [1901], p. 127), derives it from Byzantine models, while C. Vivell, in "Le tonus peregrinus" (*RCG,* XVIII, XIX), declares it to be of Hebrew origin. See also the study of the *tonus peregrinus* in Ferretti's *Esthétique,* pp. 324ff.

1219] which, like the *tonus peregrinus,* is used in connection with a few Antiphons of a certain type, e.g., the Antiphon *In matutinis* [*AM* 372]. Particularly interesting are two psalm tones reproduced in the *Variae preces* collection. One of them—used for Ps. 50, *Miserere mei Deus,* during Lent—is a *tonus in directum* (without Antiphon) with two different tenors (like the *tonus peregrinus*), on f and on e [*VP* 108]. The other is a *tonus solemnis* for Ps. 46, *Omnes gentes,* on the Feast of the Ascension, which actually employs two different psalm tones, both of the double-tenor type: one, with recitation on e and f, for the odd-numbered verses; the other, with recitation on a and g, for the even-numbered ones [*VP* 153]. Fig. 48 shows the beginning of this Psalm, in which the Antiphon, *Alleluia,* is repeated after each verse.

FIGURE 48

Alle- lu- ia.   Alle-lú- ia, al-le- lú- ia.   Omnes gentes plaudi-te ma-nibus : ju-bi-la-te De- o

in vo-ce exsulta-ti- o-nis.   Alle-lu-ia, alle- lu-ia.   Quo-ni- am Domi-nus excelsus, terri-bi- lis:

rex magnus su- per omnem terram.   Alle-lu- ia : alle-lu-ia, alle- lu- ia.   Subje-cit popu-los *etc.*

PSALM TONES AND PSALM TEXTS

As was stated at the beginning of the preceding section, the psalm tones are the melodic formulae used for the singing of the complete Psalms. This is done by repeating the formula for every verse of the Psalm, as well as for the two verses of the *Gloria Patri* added to it as a conclusion.[1] Thus the over-all form of a Psalm is not unlike that of a strophic song, a hymn, for example, every stanza of which is sung to the same melody. In the hymns the repeat of the melody presents no problem, since they have poetic texts with identical versification in every stanza. The Psalms, however, are prose texts, and each verse differs greatly from the other as to number of syllables and distribution of accents. In order to sing all these verses to the same melodic formula (we purposely avoid using the term "melody" in this context), special methods of adaptation have to be devised. It is not within the scope of this book to enter into a detailed explanation of all the rules pertaining to this matter, since they are important chiefly from the practical point of view.[2] The general principles will appear from the consideration of a typical example, that is, the first psalm tone applied to Ps. 111, *Beatus vir* [140f; see Figure 49].

---

[1] The Doxology is omitted from Passion Sunday to Easter [see *L* 568].

[2] See, e.g., *L* 113ff and D. Johner, *A New School of Gregorian Chant* (1914), pp. 69ff.

FIGURE 49

FIRST PSALM TONE: PS. 111

Int.	Tenor	Flex	Mediant	Tenor	Termination
1. Be-a-	tus vir qui		ti- met Dó-mi-num	*in mandatis ejus	vo-let ní- mis.
2.	Potens in terra erit		sé- men é- jus:	*generatio rectorum be-	ne-di-cé- tur.
3.	Gloriae et divitiae in		dó- mo é- jus:	*et justitia ejus manet in saé-	cu-lum saé - cu - li.
4.	Exortum est in tenebris		lú- men ré- ctis:	*misericors et miserá-	tor, et jú- stus.
5.	Jucundus homo qui †disponet ser- miseretur et cóm-mo-dat, mones suos		in ju-di-ci- o:	*quia in aeternum non	commo-vé- bi- tur
6.	In memoria aeterna		é- rit jú- stus:	*ab auditione mala	non ti-mé- bit.
7.	Paratum cor ejus †confirmatum sperare in Dó-mi- no,		cor é -	*non commovebitur donec dispiciat ini-	mí-cos sú- os.
8.	Dispersit, dedit pau- †justitia ejus pé-ri- bus manet in		est sáe-cu-lum saé-cu- li ·	*cornu ejus exaltábi-	tur in gló- ri - a.
9.	Peccator videbit et ira- †dentibus suis scé- fremet		et ta-bé- · scet:	*desiderium peccató-	rum per-í- bit.
10.	Gloria		Pá- tri et Fí- li - o,	*et Spirí-	tu - i Sán- cto.
11.	Sicut erat in principio,et		nunc et sém- per,	*et in saecula saecu-	lórum. A- mén.

REMARKS:

(a) The intonation of this psalm tone takes care of the first two syllables of the first verse, the first syllable being sung to the initial pitch, f, the second to the *podatus* g-a. With the third syllable the recitation on the tenor begins, and this continues until we come to the flex or, if there is no flex, to the mediant. The intonation is employed only for the first verse. All the subsequent verses start directly with the tenor recitation.[3]

(b) The flex is used only for unusually long verses, such as ℣. 5 of the Psalm under consideration. It may be noticed that in Ps. 115, *Credidi propter quod* [161f], ℣. 7 has a flex while ℣. 8 has none, although this actually has a considerably longer text. The reason is that this verse cannot be readily divided into three distinct phrases. The flex calls for a lowering of the pitch on the last two syllables of the phrase if the third syllable from the end has an accent, so that the phrase closes with a dactylic group of syllables, /.., such as *Dómino* or *(pau)péribus* (℣. 7, 8). Here the flex takes on the form of a-g-g. In all other cases the pitch is lowered for the last syllable only, so that the flex appears as a-g. Usually this means that the phrase closes with a trochaic group of syllables, /., such as *(iras)cétur* (℣. 9). However, the two-note flex is to be used also for a phrase ending with a group, such as *vivífica me* or *éripe me,* in which the last accent is further away from the end than the third syllable. In other words, the flex can have no other form than a-g or a-g-g, the latter exclusively for dactylic groups of syllables. The extra tone required in the latter case is indicated by a white note.

(c) The rules governing the mediant are essentially the same as those given for the flex. The tones 2, 5, and 8 have a "mediant of one accent," and this is treated exactly like the flex. Tone 4 has a "mediant of one accent with two preparatory syllables," which means that the two syllables preceding the accent are sung to the pitches g-a. Tone 1 (as well as 3, 6, and 7) has a "mediant of two accents," and the rules to be followed here can be most easily understood if such a mediant is considered as consisting of two successive flexes, first from b♭ down to a, then from g up to a. The second "flex" takes on the form g-a-a or simply g-a depending upon whether the last three syllables form a dactyl or not, and the same criterion is applied to the preceding syllables in connection with the first "flex." Usually the textual accentuation clearly indicates the form of the mediant, e.g.: b♭-a-a g-a-a for *Dómine Dóminus* or *saéculum saeculi* (℣. 8); b♭-a-a g-a-a for *tímet Dóminum* (℣. 1) or *(mise)rátor Dóminus;* b♭-a-a g-a for *Dómino*

---

[3] Originally, particularly at the time when the Antiphon was repeated after each verse, all the verses started with the intonation. This practice is still preserved in the *Commemoratio,* where the three first verses of Ps. 97, *Cantate Domino,* are given each with the intonation; see *GS,* I, 217, and Ferretti, p. 309. The custom disappeared later (eleventh century?), but survived in the Canticles [see p. 226].

méo or *scíto cor méum;* b♭-a g-a for *dómo éjus* (℣. 3) or *núnc, et sémper* (℣. 11). Occasionally, however, the textual accents cannot be used as a guide, because they are more than two syllables apart from each other, e.g., in *exaltábitur in glória.* Here the last three syllables are dactylic, while the three preceding syllables are nondactylic. The mediant therefore is b♭-a g-a-a, for *-tur in glória.* In *diligéntibus te* or in *singuláriter in spe* there is no dactyl at the end. Therefore the mediant closes with g-a, preceded by b♭-a in the former case, by b♭-a-a in the latter.[4]

(d) The termination of our example is "of 1 accent with 2 preparatory syllables." It consists of four units, the single note g, the single note f, the *podatus* g-a and the *virga subtripunctis* g-f-e-d, with an optional g placed between them. These two neumes are treated like the flex. They are sung to the last two syllables except in the case of a dactylic group at the end, which calls for the interpolated tone, so that the *clivis* falls on the third syllable from the end. The two preparatory notes are sung to the two syllables preceding the one that falls on the *clivis,* regardless of their accents. From this it appears that the termination covers the last five syllables if there is a dactylic group at the end, as in *(sáe)culum saéculi* (℣. 3) or in *commovébitur* (℣. 5); otherwise the last four, as in *volet nímis* (℣. 1) or in *(be)nedicétur* (℣. 2) or in *(saecu)lórum. Amen* (℣. 11). In the *Liber usualis* all syllables falling on what is called an "accent of the mediant or the termination" (not identical with an accent of the text) are printed in boldface, and the preparatory syllables of the termination in italics. It may be noticed that the fourth psalm tone has a mediant with two preparatory syllables, which is treated exactly like the termination just described.

PSALM TONES AND ANTIPHONS

Aside from a few cases mentioned on pp. 208f, each Psalm is sung in connection with an Antiphon. The standard medieval practice was to sing the Antiphon before and after the Psalm, omitting all the internal restatements inherent in the original form of antiphonal psalmody. In the late Middle Ages it became customary to reduce the initial Antiphon to its *incipit,* consisting often of no more than one or two words. This method has been adopted in present-day practice [see, e.g., *L* 224-228], al-

---

[4] According to *Wagner III,* 124, the strict application of these rules is an innovation of the Solesmes School, derived from their principle of the *ictus* which permits only groups of two or three notes in the melody, as well as from their propensity for a conflict between the textual and the musical accent. In medieval practice the two accents of a two-accent mediant simply fell on the two last accents of the text:

b♭ a a   a g a   a a b♭   a g a
Medieval: Dóminum de cóelis   Solesmes: Dóminum de cóelis

though it amounts to a mutilation generally deplored by liturgists. Only on feasts of the double class (marked d. or D. in the Roman Calendar [pp. xliiff]) is the full Antiphon sung at the beginning.

From the earliest time about which we have documentation, the connection between the Antiphon and the Psalm was made with a distinct view toward tonal unity. Each Antiphon was assigned to one of the eight modes, and the Psalm was sung to the corresponding psalm tone. Thus, if the Antiphon is in the first mode, the Psalm (or Psalms, if several of them are grouped together under one Antiphon, as is the case in the Little Hours) is invariably sung in the first tone. It was this close connection between Antiphon and Psalm that led to the establishment of the two parallel systems, that of the eight modes and that of the eight tones.

It appears that in the case of the Antiphons the modal classification is not only of theoretical interest (as it is, for example, in the Graduals or hymns), but also, and primarily, of practical importance, serving to indicate the correct psalm tone. An interesting illustration of this aspect is provided by the tonaries of the ninth, tenth, and later centuries, such as the *Tonarius* of Regino, the *Intonarium* of Oddo, and the *De modorum formulis* ascribed to Guido.[1] These are catalogues in which the Antiphons are grouped according to their mode, in order to enable the singer to select the proper psalm tone. Such assistance was, of course, particularly important at a time when the chants were still written in staffless neumes, so that the singers were largely dependent upon their memory. Usually the tonaries group the Antiphons not only according to their modes but also in subdivisions—three, four, or more for each mode—which, as we shall see, served a no less important practical purpose: that is, to bring about a smooth transition at the points where the Antiphon and the Psalm are joined.

As appears from the general scheme Antiphon—Psalm plus Doxology—Antiphon, there are two places of joining: one at the beginning, between the end of the Antiphon and the intonation of the psalm tone, the other at the end, between the termination of the psalm tone (sung to the last words of the Doxology, *seculorum. Amen*) and the beginning of the Antiphon melody. The first of these presents no problem, since all the Antiphons of a given mode close at the same pitch, the final of the mode. It can easily be seen that in every mode the intonation does indeed make a smooth connection between this final tone and the recitation pitch of the psalm tone:[2]

---

[1] See List of Sources, nos. 13 to 16.

[2] This simple and natural state of affairs is, of course, completely destroyed if the Antiphon is reduced to its beginning, so that it may well close on a different pitch, a third, a fourth, or even a fifth higher than the final.

FIGURE 50

The other connection, however, at the end of the Psalm, does present a difficulty since it involves the beginning of the Antiphon, which is not at all an unalterable pitch. An Antiphon of the first mode, for instance, may start on such different notes as c, d, f, g, or a, and similar divergences occur in most of the other modes. Obviously, no one termination can serve satisfactorily in all these cases. The problem was ingeniously solved by providing, under the name of *differentiae,* a number of terminations closing on different pitches, and by selecting for a given Antiphon that termination the closing notes of which harmonized with the initial notes of the Antiphon. The number of terminations varies greatly from mode to mode, there being as many as ten in the first mode, three or five in others, while a few have only one ending. All the terminations are fully listed in the *Liber usualis* on pp. 113ff, and are identified by a letter indicating the final note, this letter being written as a capital if the final note is the final of the mode. Thus, for the first psalm tone there exist terminations labelled D, f, g, etc., while the third tone has terminations E and g. Some tones have several terminations ending on the same pitch, and these are distinguished from the main termination by superior figures, e.g., a, a^2, a^3, etc.

Accordingly, each Antiphon carries an indication not only for the psalm tone but also for the termination. For instance, the five Vesper Psalms of Sunday [251ff] are sung with five Antiphons (1. Ant., 2. Ant., 3. Ant., etc.) each of which is accompanied by a symbol such as $7.c^2$, 3.b, 4.g, etc. This means that the first Psalm is to be sung in the seventh tone with the second termination on c; the second Psalm, in the third tone with the termination on b; the third, in the fourth tone with the termination on g, etc. After each Antiphon the Psalm follows, with the psalm tone and its proper termination given in full, and with the formula for the flex added at the end for those Psalms in which the flex is needed for one or more verses, as, for example, in Ps. 110 [252]. Properly speaking, only one of the two ways in which the psalm tone and its termination are indicated would be required. In fact, this double method is used in the *Liber usualis* only for Vespers and Compline of Sunday and Saturday, in order to facilitate the psalmody at these Offices which are of greater importance and more

regularly observed, even in small churches, than the others. Another con-
cession to "popular demand" is the exact indication as to how and when
the Antiphon should be sung; i.e., partly before the Psalm and in full after
the Psalm, e.g. [252]:

    2. Ant.   *Magna opera Domini.*
    3.b
          Psalm 110

    Ant.   *Magna opera Domini, exquisita in omnes voluntates ejus.*

A more common way of writing Antiphon and Psalm is that used, for
instance, for the Vesper Psalms of Monday [28off]. Here the Antiphon is
given only once, before the Psalm, with an asterisk marking off that short
initial portion that is to be sung before the Psalm. Following an old medieval tradition, the termination to be used for the psalm tone is indicated,
aside from the figure-and-letter symbol, at the end of the Antiphon, notated above the letters *E u o u a e.* These are the traditional abbreviation
of *seculorum. Amen* (represented by the vowels), the last words of the
minor Doxology, *Gloria Patri,* which is nearly always added to each Psalm
and forms its last two verses. Thus, the words *seculorum. Amen* are invariably sung to the termination formula and have therefore become asso-

FIGURE 51

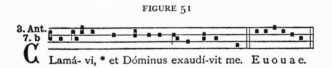

    Lamá- vi, * et Dóminus exaudí-vit me. E u o u a e.

ciated with it. The above example illustrates this manner of writing which,
it is perhaps not superfluous to state once more, does not mean that the
entire melody is sung as it stands. The performance starts with the passage
Clamavi, then follows the Psalm with every verse employing the termination indicated above *E u o u a e,* and after this the entire Antiphon is sung
(of course, without the *E u o u a e*).

    In the Proper of the Time, the Common of Saints, and the Proper of
Saints, i.e., for individual feasts, the Psalms are sung with proper Antiphons. Here the Psalms are not printed, but are only indicated by their
number, with the termination to be used and with reference to the page
where the complete text can be found; e.g., for Second Vespers of the
Nativity [411]:

    Psalms. 1. Dixit Dominus. 1.g. *p.* 128.—2. *Confitebor tibi.* 7.a.
    p. 139.—3. *Beatus vir.* 7.b. *p.* 146—(etc.).

Then the five Antiphons follow in the same style as in the above example.

The usage of prescribing for a given Antiphon not only the psalm tone but also its termination is as old as the earliest documents about psalm singing, such as the *Musica disciplina,* the *Alia musica,* or the *Commemoratio brevis.* Although the details underwent some changes and fluctuations, there has never been a deviation from the principle that special terminations should be used in order to provide for a smooth transition from the end of the Psalm to the beginning of the subsequent Antiphon. This raises the question as to what methods were employed in order to effectuate this smooth transition, in other words, which rules govern the relationship between the end of the psalm tone and the beginning of the Antiphon. A possible solution would have been to make consistent use of one interval, such as the unison or the upper second, and to provide a different termination for each initial note that may occur in the Antiphons of a given mode. For instance, in the first mode we find Antiphons starting on c, d, f, g, and on a. Consequently, a "smooth transition" could be effected by providing five terminations closing on the same tones or, perhaps, on their upper seconds. It is easy to see that no such methodical procedure was followed. The mere fact that in some psalm tones the number of terminations is considerably greater than that of initial notes in the Antiphons (e.g., in Tone 1), in others smaller (e.g., Tone 5), shows that the situation is more complex than outlined above. Moreover, an inspection of a handful of Antiphons shows that the intervallic relationship between the two crucial notes is far from being uniform. The juncture can be made by any interval from the unison to the fifth, most of them either ascending or descending. A tabulation of about one half of all the Antiphons in the *Liber usualis* shows that the connection is made most frequently by the unison or by the descending second, the former accounting for about one half, the other for an additional one third of the total. The remaining part, about one fifth of the total, includes junctures at the ascending second, descending and ascending third, descending fourth, and descending fifth. The ascending fourth and fifth do not occur:

INTERVALS FROM TERMINATION TO ANTIPHON

Unison	287	Fourth down	27
Second down	180	Fourth up	o
Second up	64	Fifth down	26
Third down	77	Fifth up	o
Third up	23	Total	684

The general conclusions to be drawn from this tabulation are: first, that the wider an interval is, the more rarely is it used, except for the fourth and fifth which are about equally frequent; second, that every interval is used much more often to make a downward connection than one leading upward, the fourth and fifth occurring exclusively in downward motion.

As to further details, an examination of the medieval treatises is very informative and interesting. An early description of the *differentiae* is found in the *Alia musica* of *c.* 900, particularly in its commentary entitled *Nova expositio* [see List of Sources, p. 55, no. 22]. Here each *tonus* is described as having a number of *differentiae* as well as *loca*.[3] The *loca* (places) turn out to be the initial notes of the Antiphons, as appears from the examples given. For the purpose of illustration we reproduce here the detailed indications for the first mode:

Diff. I.	closes on a	*locum* 1 on a:	*Veniet Dominus* [338]
		locum 2 on f:	*Apertis thesauris* [463]
Diff. II.	closes on g	*locum* 1 on g:	*Canite tuba* [356]
		locum 2 on d:	*Ecce nomen* [317]
		locum 3 on c:	*Intempesta nocte*
Diff. III.	closes on f	*locum* 1 on c:	*O beatum pontificem* [1750]
Diff. IV.	closes on e	*locum* 1 on e:	*Inclinans se Jesus* [1092]
Diff. V.	closes on c	*locum* 1 on c:	*Euge serve* [1181 or 1195]
		locum 2 on d:	*Sint lumbi*

The archaic character of this system appears clearly from the fact that it includes only five terminations for the first tone, while the later sources indicate ten or even more. Moreover, it does not give the impression of being a workable solution, because it does not provide an unequivocal correlation between the *loca* and the *differentiae*. Our table shows that for an Antiphon beginning with c there was a choice of three different terminations, II, III, and V; and for an Antiphon beginning with d, a choice of two, II, and V. Unless there were additional rules or practices not mentioned by the author of the *Nova expositio,* his system was bound to be ambiguous and confusing.

The later treatises reveal quite a different and more realistic approach to the problem. The underlying principle of the system as it appears in the tenth century and later was to make a connection, not so much between two notes (which seems to have been the governing principle of the *Alia musica*), as between two groups of notes, that is, the termination formula of the psalm tone and the initial passage of the Antiphon. Evidently such a method would be impossible or, at least, highly impracticable

---

3 For instance, the first tone "habet 5 differentias et 9 loca in nocturnis" (*GS,* I, 130a). "In nocturnis" seems to refer to Lauds, Vespers, Compline, and Matins; "in diurnis" to the Day Hours. In this treatise the pitches are indicated by the so-called Boethian letters, A B C E H I M O, etc., an early designation for A B c d e f g a, etc. *Canite tuba* begins in *L* on f, in *AM* 226 on e, in Codex Lucca *(Pal. mus.,* IX, 21) on g. *Euge serve* begins (in all these sources) on c, *Inclinans se Jesus* (later *Inclinavit se Jesus*) on d. *Sint lumbi vestri* begins in Cod. Lucca (p. 534) on g. The indication "sesquioctavum remissum" for *Sint lumbi* should probably read: "sesquioctavum elevatum" (a whole-tone up).

if the Antiphons were entirely free melodies, each beginning (and continuing) in its own way. Actually, this is not the case. As has been shown
in a famous study by Gevaert,[4] the many thousands of Antiphons can be
grouped into a relatively small number of types (called *thèmes* by Gevaert),
perhaps thirty or forty, each of which includes many Antiphons of somewhat similar design and, in particular, with an identical or nearly identical
beginning. It is therefore possible to classify the Antiphons not only as to
modes but also, within each mode, in subdivisions characterized by a common initial motive, which we shall call *incipit*. The basic principle of the
standard system of terminations is to assign to each *incipit* a suitable
termination.

The clearest evidence of this principle is found in the medieval tonaries.
In these the Antiphons (occasionally also Introits and Communions) are
arranged, within each mode, according to subdivisions, one for each *differentia*. These tonaries, therefore, are a very convenient and indispensable
tool for the study of the Antiphons and of their connection with the psalm
tones. Particularly useful is the aforementioned *Intonarium* of Oddo which
seems to have had considerable authority in the tenth and eleventh centuries. The copy (probably dating from the twelfth century) which Cousse-
maker used for his edition bears the inscription: *Incipit intonarium a
Domno Octone (Oddone) abbate diligenter examinatum et ordinatum, a
Guidone sanctissimo monaco, optimo musico, examinatum, probatum
legitime, approbatum et autenticatum . . .* (Here begins the tonary diligently examined and put together by the abbot Oddo, and examined,
legitimately approved and authenticated by Guido, most holy monk and
excellent musician.)[5] We have used it as a basis for the subsequent study
of the termination-*incipit* question.

Significantly, Oddo prefaces his catalogue with the motto: *Omnes antiphone habentes tale principium debent habere tale seculorum* (All the
antiphons having such an *incipit* must have such a termination), thus
clearly indicating its aim and purpose.[6] Minor variations notwithstanding,
his system of terminations is much the same as that of present-day use. For
the first mode he lists nine *differentiae,* saying, however, that often ten or
eleven are prescribed. In accordance with the late medieval practice, the
Liber usualis has ten terminations for this mode. For the modes 3 and 4
Oddo indicates four terminations, while the *Liber usualis* has five; for
mode 7 he has six, two of them nearly identical and treated later as one;

[4] *La Mélopée antique,* pp. 225ff: "Catalogue thématique des antiennes." Gevaert
distinguishes 47 *thèmes.* See p. 394.

[5] *CS,* II, 117.

[6] In Guido's *Tonarius* (*CS,* II, 80b) the same principle is stated as follows: "The
differentiae of these modes are disposed according to the beginning of the antiphons
(*cantuum*) . . . so that there may be a good connection (*pulchra connexio*) between the
two parts through an appropriate intervallic motion (*motus*)" [free translation].

and for mode 5 he indicates two, only one of which has survived. The other three modes have the same number of terminations as today, one for modes 2 and 6, and three for mode 8. As to the formulae themselves, most of them are identical with those of present-day use, the greatest variation being found in mode 4, which in every respect is the most irregular of all the modes. Nearly complete agreement as to number and design of *differentiae* exists in mode 7, and it is for this reason that we have selected the seventh mode for a detailed presentation of its psalm-tone terminations and the Antiphon *incipits* connected with them. Fig. 52 shows Oddo's six terminations (with their present-day designations) as well as the *incipits* associated with them.[7]

FIGURE 52

Terminations and *Incipits*, mode 7

REMARKS:

a. Following Gevaert, we have indicated subdivisions for the two terminations most frequently employed, II and IV, in order to illustrate the modifications that occur within the basic design of the *incipit*. Although, from his point of view, Gevaert was justified in distinguishing between groups such as his *thèmes* 22, 23, and 24, the close relationship of their *incipits* is apparent, as is also the case with the groups under IV.

b. Some of the Antiphons in group IIa start out with the note d' twice, three times, four times, and even six times in succession, e.g., *Ecce sacerdos* [1176] with d'-d'-b, *Annulo suo* [1340] with d'-d'-d'-b, and *Gratias tibi*

[7] *CS*, II, 131a. For a list of Antiphons for the various groups, see pp. 396f.

[1371] with d'-d'-d'-d'-b. For such cases Oddo allows special divisions entitled *ad duo, ad tres, ad quatuor, ad sex.* They also occur in other groups.

c. Oddo's *sexta differencia* (VI) was later identified with his *tertia differencia* (III), from which it differs only in the grouping of the last three notes. Today all the Antiphons of group VI and group III have the same termination, 7.c², although the former begin with b, the latter, with c'. Gevaert considers them, not without reason, as two different groups (*thèmes* 20, 21), as does Oddo.

d. Oddo's *quinta differencia* (V) is slightly different from the present-day 7.d, which closes with b-d' instead of c'-d'—hardly an improvement, whether considered in itself or in relationship to the subsequent *incipit*.

e. Naturally, the *incipits* also underwent modifications in the course of time. For instance, the Antiphon *Magnificatus est* appears in *L* [364] with the beginning g-b-c'-d'-c'-a, while in Oddo's *Tonarium* this is given as g-a-c'-d'-c'-a. For the same *incipit* Oddo gives three more examples, *De celo veniet, Cantate Domino,* and *Afferte Domino.*[8] None of these are in general use today. The first two are included in the Benedictine Antiphonary (*Antiphonale Monasticum,* pp. 199 and 202) but with the *incipit* g-b-c'-d'-e'-d' (group IVa of our tabulation). It seems that Oddo's formula, so interesting for its archaic flavor, has completely gone out of use. It is perhaps also worth noticing that, on the other hand, the most "modern" of all the *incipits,* that of our group IVc, does not occur among the examples given in the *Tonarius.*

By way of a summary it can be said that in the seventh mode the *incipits* of the Antiphons and the terminations of the psalm tone form two very closely corresponding systems. One cannot help feeling that in every instance the termination is well adapted to the ensuing *incipit,* somehow anticipating its outline and indeed providing a "smooth transition" between the Psalm and the subsequent Antiphon.

It is not necessary to consider the corresponding formulae of the other modes, since they generally follow the same principles. We cannot, however, pass over the question as to why there exists such a striking variation in the number of terminations, ranging from a single one in modes 2, 5, and 6 to as many as ten in mode 1. Although there is no entirely satisfactory answer to this question, it is not difficult to see that, in general, the number of terminations provided for a given psalm tone agrees with the number of different *incipits* found among the Antiphons of the corresponding mode. This appears from the subsequent table showing the number of terminations in various sources as well as the number of *thèmes* according to Gevaert.[9]

[8] *CS,* II, 133.

[9] For possibilities of revising Gevaert's catalogue, see p. 395, fn. 8.

MODE	NUMBER OF TERMINATIONS				THÈMES (Gevaert)	
	L	Od	Re	Lu[10]		
1	10	9	5	10	12	(Th. 1-11, 31)
2	1	1	1	1	3	(Th. 45-47)
3	5	4	6	5	5	(Th. 34-38)
4	4	4	5	8	4	(Th. 29, 30, 32, 33)
5	1	2	3	3	3	(Th. 42-44)
6	1	1	1	1	3	(Th. 39-41)
7	5	6	6	7	9	(Th. 19-27)
8	3	3	3	3	7	(Th. 12-18)

THE TONES OF THE CANTICLES

The method used for the chanting of the Canticles is very similar to that employed for the Psalms. The main difference is that the intonation is used not only for the beginning of the first verse but for that of all the other verses as well. Obviously the Canticles were considered as a some-what more solemn type of chant than the Psalms.

This special character is also apparent in the medieval tones for the Canticles, eight recitation formulae similar to but slightly more elaborate than the psalm tones, as are also the Antiphons for the Canticles. Today these medieval canticle tones are used for the highest feasts only. In the *Liber* they are given under the title of Solemn Tones for the *Magnificat* [213-218], but are also used for the other major Canticles on high feasts, e.g., for the *Benedictus* at Lauds of Nativity [402] and of Maundy Thurs-day [652]. Actually therefore these are the solemn tones for all the Can-ticles, of which the *Magnificat* is the most important and the only one fully represented in the *Liber*.[1] A similar remark applies to the simple tones for the *Magnificat* [207-212], which are used for the *Magnificat* throughout the year, but also for the other Canticles except at the highest feasts. They are identical with the psalm tones, except for a somewhat more elaborate intonation (borrowed from the solemn tones) of the second and the eighth tone.

The solemn (or medieval) tones employ the same tenors as the psalm tones and also the same terminations, but have more ornate formulae for the intonations and particularly for the mediants, with *podatus* and *clivis* groups instead of single notes. Fig. 53 shows the various formulae of both systems, together with those of the Introit tones, which will be studied later (p. 228). It will be seen that the essential outlines are the same. The

---

[10] L = *Liber usualis;* Od = *Tonarius of Oddo;* Re = *Tonary of Regino;* Lu = *Codex Lucca.*

[1] In the Roman and Benedictine *Antiphonale* the *Benedictus* of Lauds is as fully repre-sented as is the *Magnificat* of Vespers.

substitution of two-note neumes for single notes is especially evident in the intonations of modes 2 and 8, and in the mediants of modes 3 and 7. In modes 1, 4, 5, and 6 the mediant is expanded by the addition of one unit, while in modes 2 and 8 the number of units is increased by three. A striking exception occurs in mode 5, whose formulae were taken over, virtually without change, for the Canticles as well as for the Introits. The accentual structure of the mediants is the same in the psalm tones and canticle tones, except for modes 1 and 6 (which employ identical formulae). Here the two-accent mediant of the psalms is changed into a one-accent mediant with three preparatory syllables. The rules for the adaptation to dactylic and non-dactylic groups of syllables are the same as in the psalm tones.

FIGURE 53

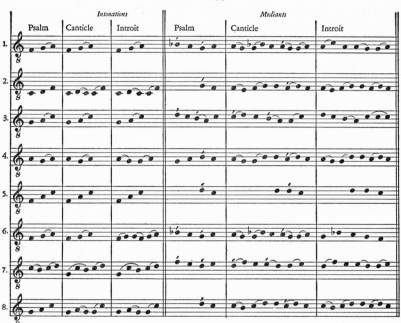

It may be noticed that on three occasions the *Nunc dimittis* appears with melodies different from those just described. At Compline of Holy Saturday [764] it is sung to the psalm tone 8.G., that is, without the more elaborate intonation prescribed for the canticle tones (both normal and solemn) of this mode. On Easter Sunday [784] it occurs with that special *tonus in directum* which is employed for the Psalms (sung without Antiphons) at Compline of Holy Saturday and at the Day Hours of Easter Sunday and Easter Week [see p. 209]. At Compline of the Commemoration of All the Faithful Departed (All-Souls' Day, November 2) the *Nunc dimit-*

tis is sung to a special tone [1735] which is also indicated (*ad libitum*) for the Psalms sung at that service [1733]. There is some logic in the last case, and it is interesting to notice that the same logic would also prevail in the two other cases if the two tones for the *Nunc dimittis* were exchanged, that of Holy Saturday being employed for Easter Sunday, and *vice versa*. As it is, the Compline Psalms of Holy Saturday are sung in the *tonus in directum* and the Canticle *Nunc dimittis* in the psalm tone 8.G., while on Easter Sunday the Compline Psalms are sung in the psalm tone 8.G. and the Canticle in the *tonus in directum*.

THE TONES FOR THE INTROITS

As was pointed out in our study of the psalmodic forms [p. 190], the Introits originally were full Psalms combined with an Antiphon which was repeated after each verse. Later the Psalm was reduced to one verse and the Doxology, the Antiphon being sung only at the beginning and at the end: A V D A. The reduction, however, did not affect the musical style of the Introit. It always was, and still is, sung essentially like an Office Psalm, that is, with a free melody for the Antiphon and with a recitative formula for the verse and the Doxology. The analogy goes even further. Similar to the psalm tones and canticle tones, the melodies for the verses of the Introits form a system of eight tones, organized along the same lines as the other systems. Until the twelfth century the Communions had the same form as the Introits, with a verse and the Doxology. However, no new system of "Communion tones" was ever used (as far as we can ascertain), since the Communion verses were always sung to the tones of the Introits. Thus, the author of the *Commemoratio brevis,* after having briefly enumerated the eight *toni* (meaning here modes), says: "According to the properties of these eight modes (*tonorum*) we employ individual tones (*modulationes*) for the responsories, and others for the major antiphons, that is, those sung in the introit of the Mass or at the end of the celebration in the communion."[1] Only one of the Communions, *Lux aeterna* of the Mass for the Dead [1815] retained a verse, *Requiem aeternam dona eis Domine, et lux perpetua luceat eis* (not a psalm verse), but this is sung to the eighth psalm tone, not to the eighth tone for the Communions (or Introits).

The structure of the Introit tones (more correctly, of the tones for the verses of the Introits) is essentially the same as that of the psalm tones. The main difference is that an opening formula is provided not only for the beginning of the verse but also for its second half. These formulae are usually distinguished as intonation and second intonation. The general scheme therefore is:

[1] *GS,* I, 213.

Intonation—Tenor—Mediant; Second Intonation—Tenor—Termination.

As for the Doxology, this is treated as a single verse (not as two verses, as in the psalm tones and canticle tones) divided into three phrases:

> *Gloria Patri, et Filio, et Spiritui Sancto.*
> *Sicut erat in principio, et nunc, et semper,*
> *et in saecula saeculorum. Amen.*

Consequently the melody falls into three distinct sections, each consisting of an opening and a closing formula with a tenor recitation in between. Properly such a scheme would require six different formulae, but actually the four mentioned above are made to serve for all the sections, the second intonation being used for sections 2 and 3, the mediant, for 1 and 2. This tripartite scheme is employed only for the *Gloria,* never for the verses, although some of these are at least as long as the Doxology, for example, *Dominus regnavit* from the Introit *Dum medium* [433]. Following is an example illustrating the method of singing the verse and the Doxology (I_1 = intonation; I_2 = second intonation; M = mediant; Tr = termination; T = tenor):

		I_1	T	M
{	℣:	Dominus	regnavit, de-	corem indutus est:
	D:	Gloria	Patri et Filio et Spi-	ritui Sancto:
		I_2	T	M
	D:	Sicut	erat in principio	et nunc et semper
		I_2	T	Tr
{	℣:	indu-	tus est Dominus fortitudi-	nem, et praecinxit se.
	D:	et in	saecula sae-	culorum. Amen.

A minor deviation from this method is encountered in the sixth mode, since here the intonation for the middle phrase of the Doxology (*Sicut*) is not identical with the second intonation, only similar to it. As we shall see later, the sixth introit tone differs in various respects from the normal scheme.

Since the introit tones are conveniently arranged on p. 14 of the *Liber usualis,* it is unnecessary to reproduce them here in full. The pitches for the tenor recitation are the same as in the psalm tones, except for the sixth tone, which we shall consider separately.[2] The formulae for intonation and mediant show a degree of elaborateness very similar to that of the canticle tones, with *clivis* and *podatus* groups. In fact, most of them are nearly identical, as appears from the table, Fig. 53, on p. 227. The only essential difference occurs in mode 6, where the mediant for the Psalms and Canticles closes on a, that for the Introits on f. As in the psalm tones

[2] See pp. 233f.

and canticle tones, the intonations of the introit tones are invariable, that is, they are sung to the first two or three syllables regardless of the textual accents. The mediants are variable, depending upon the textual accents, as are those of the psalm tones and of the canticle tones. In Fig. 53 the mediants are given in their simplest form, as used in connection with two trochees, e.g., *et núnc et sémper*. If the passage in question (that is, the end of the first half of the verse) includes one or two dactyls, one or two notes are added, but the rules concerning these additions are not as simple and uniform as they are in the psalm tones [see p. 216]. This will appear from Fig. 54, showing the mediant of the first and of the eighth tone, each with a number of different texts:

FIGURE 54

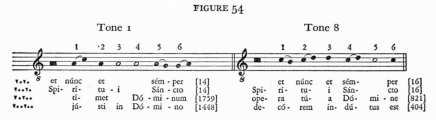

It appears that in both cases additional notes are provided to account for a maximum of six syllables, as required by two dactyls. Aside from this, the two methods of adaptation are strikingly different. The mediant of the eighth tone clearly represents a formula of "one accent with three preparatory syllables," like the mediants of the canticle tones 1, 2, 4, 6, and 8 [see p. 227]. Unit 4 invariably receives the last accent, while the preceding syllables are underlaid without regard to accent. The mediant of the first tone, however, is treated in a very special manner, not encountered elsewhere in the Gregorian recitative. The only regularly accented unit is the first (1), bearing the penultimate accent, while the position of the last accent varies. If the final group of syllables is trochaic, it falls on the *clivis* 5, if dactylic, on the additional note preceding it. For texts ending with two dactyls the formula provides for the use of two additional notes in succession, in contrast to the psalm and canticle formulae which never have more than one additional note at a time. Perhaps the mediant under consideration could be described as having "one accent with three, four, or five subsequent syllables."[3]

To the type of mediant 1 belong also mediants 3 and 7; to the other, mediants 2 and 4. All the mediants of the first group (authentic modes) close with two neumes, while those of the second group (plagal modes) close with one neume and a single note. Very likely, this is the inner reason

---

[3] Ferretti (p. 284) describes the mediant of tone 1 (as well as 3 and 7) as "à deux accents, sans préparation."

for the different treatment. The mediants of the *tritus,* 5 and 6, present special cases.[4]

We turn finally to the terminations of the introit tones. Here we find a situation considerably simpler than in the psalm tones. *Differentiae,* that is, different terminations for one tone, do exist, but to a much lesser degree: three for the first tone, two for the tones 4, 5, 6, and 8, while the remaining three tones have only one termination. The medieval sources show some fluctuation in the number of *differentiae* of the introit tones, but always within the same limits—never more than three.[5] The formulae are more elaborate than those previously encountered, some of them including neumes of three, four, and occasionally even six notes. Their main interest, however, lies in the field of relationship between text and music, where they represent a new principle, that of non-adaptation. This places them in a different category from the terminations of the Psalms or Canticles (as well as from the mediants), which admit modifications according to the prosodic structure of the text. Such formulae are called tonic. The terminations of the Introit, on the other hand, are invariable formulae of five units which always accommodate the last five syllables of the text, regardless of its prosodic structure. Formulae of this type are called cursive. Fig. 55 illustrates the principle of cursive formulae, showing the termination of the third tone with a number of texts.

FIGURE 55

	1	2	3	4	5	
▾•▾•	Domi -	no	óm-	nis	tér - ra	[1594]
▾••▾•	a	fá-	ci-	e	é- jus	[893]
▾•▾••	in	lé-	ge	Dó-	mi- ni	[1239]
▾••▾••	saé-	cu-	lum	saé-	cu- li	[1150]
		et	e-	rí-	pe me	[897]
	con-	gre •	ga-	ti-	ó- ne	[1544]

In such cursive formulae the consideration of the textual accent, which is an essential trait of the tonic formulae, is not present. The music becomes autonomous and follows its own course, forcing the text into submission. In order to justify such a role of leadership, the music must offer

---

[4] Mediant 5, the simplest of all, consists of three elements, d′ d′ c′, and is treated like a flex, with the accented syllable on the second d′ and with an inserted c′ for dactyls, e.g., *in Dómino:* d′ d′ c′ c′ [970]. Mediant 6, on the other hand, is the most complex as well as the most variable in treatment. According to Ferretti (p. 284), it is not always correctly treated in the Vatican edition.

[5] See the table in *Wagner III,* 167, compiled from nine sources ranging from the ninth-century Aurelianus to the seventeenth-century *Graduale Medicaeum* (1614-15) and the Vatican edition of 1908. The late medieval and present-day practice is to employ the secondary endings, if at all, only for the Doxology, not for the psalm verse which always closes with the main termination. See, e.g., the Introit *Exclamaverunt* [1448], at "collaudationes" and at "E u o u a e."

sufficient interest of its own, and it is hardly necessary to say that this aesthetic law is carefully observed in Gregorian chant. Without exception, the cursive formulae show an elaborate musical design (particularly in the tones of the Responsories; see pp. 235f), while the elementary formulae, of little interest in themselves, derive their validity largely from the careful attention to prosodic declamation. In fact, it is this principle which accounts for an exceptional case among the Introit terminations, that of the fifth tone. This is purely syllabic, c'-d'-b-c'-a, consequently it is treated as a tonic formula, as may be seen from the following examples:

c' c' d' b c' a	d' b c' a a
libe- rá- tor mé- us [497]	*col- lau- dá- ti- o* [970]

d' b b c' a	d' b b c' a a
fá- ci- e é- jus [1024]	*Dó- mi- ni i- bi- mus* [560]

A formula like this is "tonic" in the proper sense of the word because, as they frequently do in Gregorian chant, the accented syllables fall on higher pitches, a phenomenon known as tonic accent.[6] If the termination of the fifth tone were treated cursively, like the others, the tonic accent would disappear in the case of dactylic groups:

c' d' b c' a	c' d' b c' a	c' c' d' b c' a
col- lau- dá- ti- o	*fá- ci- e é- jus*	*Dó- mi- ni i- bi- mus*

It is more difficult to account for the fact that tonic treatment is also used, at least partly, for the termination of the eighth introit tone, as the following table shows:

	1	2	3	4	5	
	c'	c'c'b	ga	c'b	a	(a)	g
u-	*ni-*	*vér-*	*sa*	*tér-*		*ra*	[910]
fortitudi-	*nem*	*et*	*prae-*	*cin-*	*xit*	*se*	[404]
Domi-	*no*	*in*	*lae-*	*ti-*	*ti-*	*a*	[478]
cae-	*li*	*com-*	*mo-*	*rá-*	*bi-*	*tur*	[532]
in	*á-*	*tri-*	*a*	*Dó-*	*mi-*	*ni*	[1645]

Here the five-syllable termination is extended into one of six units for texts closing with a dactylic group, so that the last accent always falls on unit 4. Judging from the few available examples, the termination of the sixth mode is treated in the same manner [see *L* 1133, 1190]. One is tempted to explain this peculiar method by the fact that the two final units of this

---

6 See p. 277. It may be noticed that most of the psalm-tone formulae are tonic in this specific sense of the word, though not all of them; e.g., the terminations 1.a and 2, or the mediants 6 and 7.

termination are single notes, not neumes. However, the termination of the fourth tone, which also closes with two single notes, is always treated as a cursive formula [see, e.g., *L* 1067, 1162, 1433]. The only noticeable difference is that in terminations 6 and 8 these two notes form a descending second, while in termination 4 they are a third apart.[7]

We close our study of the introit tones with an examination of the sixth tone which holds a special position within the system, mainly because it employs two different tenors, a in the first half, and f in the second half of the verse. In this respect it is similar to the *tonus peregrinus* and other early psalm tones with two recitation pitches, and even more so to the plagal tones of the Responsories [see p. 235], because the second recitation takes place on the tonic of the mode. Also exceptional is the second intonation, which consists of four units, f-ga-ac'-g, while all the other tones have only two units for this formula, e.g., gf-ga in the first tone, fd-df in the second.[8] Since the termination has five units, the three components of the second half of the verse, i.e., second intonation, tenor, and termination, require at least ten syllables. In not a few cases the second half of the verse simply is not long enough for this scheme. Here the second intonation is reduced to a-ac'-g, occasionally even to a two-unit formula, ac'-g, or completely omitted. For unusually long verses, on the other hand, it is expanded by the insertion of a tenor recitation on a between the second and the third unit, f-ga-a . . . -ac'-g, with the result that the second half of the verse has two tenors, first a, then f. It will be noticed that all these irregularities occur in the second half of the verse. Fig. 56 shows a number of typical examples.

FIGURE 56

Additional examples (from the 13th-century *Gradual* of St. Thomas, Leipzig) showing the initial recitation on a are given in Wagner's vol. III, p. 161. Unfortunately these are incomplete, and do not show to what an extent the second recitation, on f, is employed. Finally it may be noticed that the Introit of the Mass for the Dead, *Requiem aeternam* [1807], employs a "sixth tone" all its own, with recitation on a throughout, and with

[7] I am not in a position to say whether this is the explanation, nor whether the exceptional treatment of terminations 6 and 8, as evidenced in the Solesmes editions, has medieval authority.

[8] The fifth tone has only one, g.

special formulae for the mediant, the second intonation, and the termination.

A study of the medieval sources shows that the tones of the Introits are nearly identical in all the manuscripts.[9] They were much less subject to fluctuations than were those of the Psalms. It was not until the sixteenth century that the old tradition deteriorated and that many variants were introduced which, fortunately, were eliminated in the Solesmes editions.[10]

THE TONES FOR THE GREAT RESPONSORIES

The Great Responsories (*responsoria prolixa*) of Matins consist of an opening chant, the respond, and one or several verses alternating with the repeated response in schemes such as R V R', R V R' V R', R V R' D R', etc. [pp. 181f]. While the responds (like the antiphons of the Introits) belong to the category of free melodies, the verses are sung to fixed recitatives similar to those for the verses of the Psalms or Introits (though considerably more elaborate), and form a complete system of eight tones, one for each mode. Full tables of these tones are available in Grove's *Dictionary*, under "Psalmody" (vol. IV, 266); in W. Frere's *Antiphonale Sarisburiense* (I, 4); in the Solesmes books, *Liber responsorialis* (*LR*, p. 50) and *Processionale monasticum* (*PM*, p. 14) with the text *Gloria Patri;* in Wagner's *Gregorianische Formenlehre* (pp. 190ff); and in Ferretti's *Esthétique grégorienne* (pp. 248ff). The first two tables, both prepared by Frere, are essentially identical, as are also those given in the Solesmes publications. Aside from these duplications, all the tables differ slightly in some particular or other because they are based on different sources.[1] Thus they illustrate the fact that the medieval tradition of the responsorial tones is not entirely uniform. It is less stable than that of the introit tones, though not as variable as that of the psalm tones. The subsequent explanations are based on the versions given in the Solesmes publications.

Structurally, the responsorial tones are similar to those of the Introits. They consist of two phrases: intonation, tenor, and mediation for the first, and second intonation, tenor, and termination for the second. An im-

[9] That is, approximately from the eleventh century on. However, Aurelianus (*GS*, I, 55b) gives a description of the *Gloria* for the Introits of the first mode which, although rather vague, clearly results in a strikingly different melody, tentatively as follows:

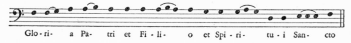

Glo - ri-   a Pa-   tri et Fi - li-   o et Spi - ri-   tu - i San-   cto

[10] A detailed study of the vicissitudes of the Introit psalmody is found in *Wagner III*, 139-175.

[1] Frere: *Antiphonale Sarisburiense;* Wagner: Antiphonary of St. Maur-des-Fossés (Bibl. Nat. *12044);* Ferretti: not indicated.

portant difference, however, is that there are two recitation pitches, one for the first half and another for the second half, similar to the *tonus peregrinus* and to the exceptional introit tone of the sixth mode. The basic principle is, that in the authentic modes the first tenor is at the fourth above the tonic, the second at the fifth, while in the plagal modes the first tenor is at the third, and the second at the tonic. It will be seen that the sixth introit tone, with its tenors on a and f, conforms to the rule for the plagal tones of the Responsories. The principle just indicated is not strictly observed in the fifth mode, for good reason—the fourth degree forms a tritone with the tonic. Here the b is invariably replaced by the c′, so that this tone has the same recitation pitch in both parts. Recitation on b is also required in the second half of tone 3 (fifth above e) and in the first half of tone 8 (third above g). In both of these cases it forms a normal and permissible interval with the tonic, and is therefore often employed. However, the tendency toward elimination of b as a tenor, which played a decisive role in the final formation of the psalm tones [pp. 211f], made itself felt in the responsorial tones also, with the result that in most Responsories the recitation takes place on c′ rather than on b. Probably as a concomitant of this change, the second tenor of the fourth tone was usually raised by a semitone, from e to f. No plausible explanation, however, can be given for the fact that the first tenor of the sixth tone is a third higher than it should be, c′ rather than a. In the following table the original tenors are given in parentheses.

TENORS OF THE RESPONSORIAL TONES

	AUTHENTIC			PLAGAL	
1.	g	a	2.	f	d
3.	a	(b) c′	4.	g	(e) f
5.	c′	c′	6.	(a) c′	f
7.	c′	d′	8.	(b) c′	g

Since the responsorial tones have extended formulae for their intonations, mediant, and termination, often only one or two syllables, sometimes none, remain for the recitation. An example in point is the *Gloria Patri* text which is used in the tables of the responsorial tones in *LR* and *PM*, but which is too short to show all the details of these tones. It is only in connection with extended texts that their structure appears clearly. An additional difficulty encountered in the study of the responsorial tones is the fact that only a small fraction of the Responsories (c. 70 out of more than eight hundred found in the medieval manuscripts) are reproduced in the *Liber usualis* and that not a few of these have their verses set to different melodies of later origin [pp. 239f]. For instance, the *Liber usualis* contains not a single good example of the first tone. For this reason we reproduce in Fig. 57 the verses of three Responsories of mode 1:

FIGURE 57

1. *Dum iret Jacob* [LR 406]   2. *Ego ex ore* [LR 266]   3. *Confirmatum est* [PM 166]

This figure illustrates a typical trait of the responsorial tones, that is, the animation of the recitative by means of inflections which invariably fall on accented syllables. The first tenor may have one, two, or even three such inflections, depending upon the length of the text, while the second tenor rarely has more than one.

The "original" tenors mentioned previously are of considerable importance because they are among the few remnants of that early psalmody in which the tenors were consistently a fifth or a third above the final of the mode. Responsories showing the original tenors are very rare, but the few which are preserved are for that reason of great interest. Following are all the examples I have found:[2]

Tone 3, tenors a and b:
  ℟. *Omnes amici,* ℣. *Inter iniquos* [671]
Tone 4, tenors g and e:
  ℟. *Ecce quomodo,* ℣. *Tamquam agnus* [728]
  ℟. *Sicut ovis,* ℣. *Tradidit in mortem* [716f]
Tone 8, tenors b and g:
  ℟. *Unus ex discipulis,* ℣. *Qui intingit* [640]
  ℟. *Vinea mea,* ℣. *Sepivi te* [675]

[2] The study is based on the Responsories found in L, LR, and PM, with occasional consultation of the *Antiphonals* of Lucca and Worcester. Here, as in all studies concerned with the Responsories, the absence of a complete and reliable modern edition is a great handicap. Both LR and PM are early Solesmes publications which probably do not always represent the best tradition. I have been unable to find an example of the "original" tenors, a and f (rather than c′ and f), in the sixth tone. Ferretti (p. 250) gives a formula for the sixth responsorial tone which, in the first half, includes a recitation on c′ followed by one on a, and gives three examples, ℣. *Ecce in pulvere (from* ℟. *Paucitas dierum),* ℣. *Supra montem (from* ℟. *Clama in fortitudine),* and ℣. *Si ascendero (from ?;* the responds are not indicated). My attempts to verify Ferretti's versions have been unsuccessful.

It is interesting to notice that all these Responsories belong to the *triduum* before Easter, Maundy Thursday, Good Friday, and Holy Saturday. Even such an old feast as the Nativity did not remain immune to the change, as appears from the Responsory of mode 4, *Quem vidistis* [377], whose verse, *Dicite quidnam,* has the recitation on f (rather than on e) in the second half. In *Hodie nobis* [376] of mode 8, however, a trace of the original tenor seems to have survived on the word "illuxit" (ab-b-ba), while the continuation, "nobis dies" shows the raised tenor (c'd'-c'-c'd'-c'-c'). This intermediate stage, with a recitation starting on b and continuing on c', is more clearly indicated in the version of *Hodie nobis* as given in *LR*, as well as in a few other Responsories of the eighth mode shown in Fig. 58:

FIGURE 58

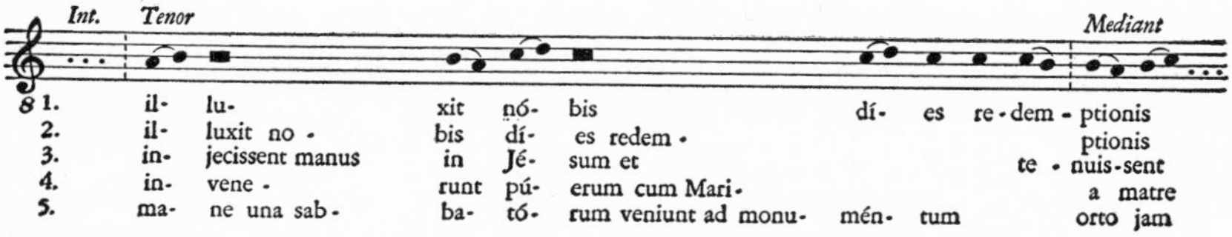

1. *Hodie nobis* [376]   2. *Hodie nobis* [LR 57]
3. *Tamquam latronem* [679]   4. *Stella quam* [LR 78]
5. *Maria Magdalena* [LR 85]

The foregoing study of the tenors of the responsorial tones may be supplemented by a brief consideration of their opening and closing formulae. Because the *Liber usualis* includes a relatively high number of Responsories of the eighth mode, we shall use the eighth tone as the basis of our discussion. Fig. 59 shows its four formulae in connection with the verse *Insurrexerunt* of the Responsory *Animam meam* [681], with fragments of other texts added underneath. A is the intonation, B the mediant, C the second intonation, and D the termination. Each of these four formulae consists of several units which are here numbered successively for convenient reference.

FIGURE 59

A. Intonation. In its shortest form this consists of the two units 2 and 3, as used for the word *Quá-re.* If the text starts with a dactylic word, the formula is amplified by a prefixed c' (unit 1), as in *Hó-di-e.* For one or more syllables preceding the first accent this initial c′ is repeated, so that the intonation starts with a short recitation, as in *Insurre-xé-runt*. Not a few Responsories reveal a tendency to postpone the main units, 2 and 3, so that they appear on the second rather than on the first accented syllable, a practice which leads to a fairly extended initial recitation. Thus, in the verse *Et intrántes dómum* [*LR* 79] the unit 2 falls on *dó-*, preceded by a four-note recitation on c′.[3] An extreme example occurs in the Responsory *Constantes estote*,[4] where the verse, *Vos qui in púlvere éstis*, has initial recitation for six syllables, with unit 2 falling on *és-*.

B. Mediant. The mediant belongs to the type of formulae with "one accent and three preparatory units" which we have repeatedly encountered in the tones for the Canticles and the introit verses [see p. 227]. The three syllables preceding the last accent fall on units 4, 5, and 6. If the accent is followed by two syllables (dactylic), units 7, 8, 9 are employed, otherwise only 8 and 9. All the mediants of the responsorial tones show this structure. Actually the mediant of Tone 8 forms to a certain extent an exception, since it often occurs with four preparatory syllables, i.e., with a *clivis* c′-b (rather than the simple reciting note c′) on the fourth syllable before the accent. Once more, the medieval sources are not consistent in this detail.

C. Second Intonation. This is a very simple formula, always consisting of two units (10, 11) for the first two syllables of the second half of the verse.

D. Termination. The terminations of the responsorial tones are five-unit formulae of an elaborate design, often with seven or eight notes to one unit, and with as many as twenty-five notes for the whole group. Their structure is invariable and strictly cursive, without regard for the prosodic accents of the text. Within the Gregorian recitative they represent the clearest manifestation of the principle of musical autonomy. It is very interesting to observe that this principle was fully recognized in the ninth and tenth centuries, and perhaps more generally practiced in this period than later. Thus, the anonymous author of the *Instituta patrum de modo psallendi vel cantandi* says:[5]

[3] In *LR* the intonation starts, not with c′, but with a *podatus* g-c′ (in the *Gloria Patri* verse on p. 51 as well as in the individual psalm verses). This variant, obviously intended to make a connection from the end of the respond, is, on the whole, not borne out by the medieval sources. The *Liber usualis* has the g-c′ beginning only for the Responsories from the Office of the Dead, *Credo quod* [1785], *Domine quando* [1787], and *Domine secundum* [1798]. Only the first and second of these have this beginning in the Codex Lucca, while in the Codex Worcester all three start without the *podatus*. In *Wagner III*, 197, the eighth tone starts with a *podatus* a-c′, following Cod. *12044* of the Bibl. nat.

[4] From the Vigil of the Nativity; Lucca, p. 29 (with initial *podatus* g-c′), Worcester, p. 25 (starting directly with c′).

[5] *GS*, I, 6b/7a. Smits van Waesberghe (*Muziekgeschiedenis der Middeleeuwen*, II, 197ff) considers the *Instituta* as a work of Ekkehard V, while S. A. van Dijk ascribes it to St. Bernard (1091-1153) [see *MD*, IV, 99]. Judging from its contents, I have no doubt that it actually describes a considerably earlier practice.

We shall now say how the tones should be treated in their cadences (*in finalibus*) with regard to varying accents (*diversos accentus*). All the adaptations of the tones in the mediants as well as terminations (*in finalibus mediis vel ultimis*) are to be made, not according to the word accent, but according to the musical melody of the tone (*musicalem melodiam toni*), as Priscius says: "Music is not subject to the rules of Donatus, as little as are Holy Scriptures."[6] If accent and melody agree, they should be treated accordingly; if not, the tone of the chant or psalm should be concluded according to the melody. Nearly all the tones are treated in such a manner that the music, through its melody, disregards (*supprimit*, suppresses) the syllables and obscures (*sophisticat*) the accent in the cadences of the verses, and this particularly in the psalmody. If therefore the close of a verse is made according to a tone (*deponitur tonaliter*), it is often necessary to infringe (*infringatur*) upon the accent. For instance, if we have the six syllables *saeculorum amen,* they have to be adapted in the treatment (*depositione*) of words and syllables to six notes of the tone.

It is very unusual, as well as highly interesting, to find in so early a document such a clear statement about a specific detail. From the author's insistent reiteration of the same point one has the impression that he worked in a place (St. Gall?) where a different practice prevailed. Of particular interest is the fact that he speaks about *toni* in general and that he expressly mentions the mediant together with the termination as formulae not subject to the rules of the word accent. Very likely in his time the use of cursive terminations was much more common than is indicated in the musical manuscripts of the twelfth century. Another interesting detail is the fact that he describes the *saeculorum. Amen* as a six-syllable formula, in contrast to the later (and present) practice of treating it as one of five syllables (*u o u a e*), the first syllable of *saeculorum* being included in the tenor recitation.[7]

The classical system of the responsorial tones does not include any *differentiae*. There is only one termination for each tone. Attempts in the direction toward different endings can be traced in some of the earliest *Antiphonaries*, e.g., in the twelfth-century *Antiphonal of St. Maur-des-Fossés* (Paris, B. N. *12044*), in which the termination of the fourth tone occurs not only with the normal close on *d,* but also in variants closing on *e* or *f*.[8] That this was not a general practice appears from other Mss of the same period (e.g., the *Codex Lucca*) in which these differences are absent.

Of greater importance and of lasting significance was the tendency to employ for the verses of the Responsories free variants of the responsorial

[6] Donatus, a Roman grammarian of the late fourth century, teacher of St. Jerome. Priscius lived *c.* 500.

[7] Thus Aurelianus: "We beseech the singer that in the nocturnal responds he start the close of all the verses at the fifth syllable before the last" (*GS*, I, 58a: *Id autem oramus . . .*).

[8] *Wagner III,* 210.

tones or new melodies of a completely different design. A decisive impulse
for this practice came from the introduction, in the ninth century and
later, of new feasts such as the Annunciation of the Virgin Mary or Corpus
Christi, and of special rites such as the Burial Service and the Office and
Mass for the Dead. The most striking examples are the Responsories of
Corpus Christi. Not a single one of their verses is sung to the standard
tones. Two of them, *Comedetis* [927] and *Coenantibus* [931], employ the
first half of their responsorial tones, but continue with considerable modification in the second half. In *Accepit* [932] the entire melody of the verse
is a free variant of the responsorial tone (the sixth) or, at least, could be
interpreted as such. In all the others the verses are sung to entirely free
melodies, conspicuously different from the responsorial tones in their wide
range and fluctuating design which shows no trace of recitation. An example is the verse of the Responsory *Misit me* [938]—adapted from *Verbum caro* [*LR* 67] for Nativity—which may be compared with the eighth
responsorial tone that would normally be used in connection with it.
Even more radically free is the melody used for the verse of *Immolabit*
[926]. Its unmistakable emphasis on the degrees of tonic and dominant
(d, a, d′) clearly marks it as a late product. The Office for the Dead has a
Responsory, *Peccantem* [1797], whose verse employs the second half of the
first responsorial tone but has a different recitation in its first half, in
opposition to the just-mentioned Responsories of Corpus Christi in which
the second half of the tone is modified. The last Responsory of the same
Office, *Libera me . . . de viis* [1798], has a free melody, used for both of its
verses, *Clamantes* and *Requiem,* while the celebrated *Libera me . . . de
morte* [1767] has a different melody for each verse, *Tremens, Dies illa,* and
Requiem. Another famous example is the Responsory *Gaude Maria Virgo*
for the Annunciation of the Virgin [*PM* 146f]. Its verse, *Gabrielem Archangelum,* is remarkable not only for its free melody but also for its rhymed
text, consisting of three extended lines:

Gabrielem Archangelum scimus divinitus esse affatum:
uterum tuum de Spiritu Sancto credimus impregnatum:
erubescat Judaeus infelix, qui dicit Christum ex Joseph semine esse natum.

Yet another example of a free verse occurs in *Descendit de caelis* from
the Nativity. Famous for the *neuma triplex* in the repeats of the respond
[see p. 343], this Responsory is also unique in having a long melisma at the
beginning of the verse, *Tamquam sponsus,* and the *Gloria:*[9]

FIGURE 60

Glo-   ri- a Patri

[9] See *PM* 27. In *LR* 59 all the melismas are omitted.

Less exceptional but also interesting is the verse of *Ecce jam* for the Feast of St. Stephan [*PM* 31]. It is sung to a recitative showing the general characteristics of the first responsorial tone, but with a tripartite structure (similar to the Doxology of the Introits) and with individual formulae for intonation, mediant, and termination. Other examples of a "free" recitative occur in the *Responsoria de Tempore* (Responsories for Sundays); e.g., in *Jerusalem cito veniet* for the Second Sunday of Advent [*LR* 392], *Domine ne in ira* for the Sundays after Epiphany [*LR* 398], *Cum turba plurima* for Sexagesima Sunday [*LR* 400], and *Videntes Joseph* for the Third Sunday in *Quadragesima* [*LR* 408]. There is no reason to assume that these are melodies of "decadent days."[10] Their liturgical connection as well as their style suggest that they come from a preparatory period in which the system of responsorial tones was not yet fully established and standardized.

Finally, mention may be made of a number of Responsories which appear in early manuscripts with two verses, the first of which is set to a standard tone, while the second is free. An example in point is the ℟. *Iste est Joannes* from the Feast of John the Apostle and Evangelist [*PM* 33], for which there exist three verses, *Fluenta Evangelii, Joannes hic Theologus,* and *Gloria sit Altissimo*. The first verse is in prose and is sung to the first responsorial tone. The two others, however, are hymn stanzas, textually as well as musically, e.g.:

> *Gloria sit Altissimo*
> *genitori ingenito*
> *ingenitique Genito*
> *et flamini Paraclito.*

These, of course, are additions from decadent days, probably not earlier than the twelfth century.[11]

THE TONES OF THE INVITATORY PSALM

The Night Office, during which the Great Responsories are sung, includes another chant representing the Gregorian recitative in its most elaborate form, that is, the Invitatory Psalm, *Venite exsultemus Domino* [see pp. 20, 88]. The special esteem accorded this psalm is evident in its unique liturgical position, at the very beginning of what was formerly the most important Office Hour, as well as in the fact that to the present day it has retained its full rondo form, with repeat of the Antiphon after

[10] As Frere implies (Grove's *Dictionary*, IV, 369b): "In decadent days even the responsories of the Office have their verses set to a special melody and not to the common tone."

[11] The *Antiphonals* of Hartker, Lucca, and Worcester have only one verse, *Valde honorandus,* sung to the standard tone.

each verse [see p. 188]. It also stands apart from the other Office Psalms, e.g., those of Vespers, in having a set of special tones for the verses, different from, and much more elaborate than the ordinary psalm tones.

In the medieval sources the Invitatory is represented by numerous Antiphons, one for each feast, and a number of tones for the Psalm. For instance, the eleventh-century Codex Hartker contains over sixty, the Codex Worcester of the thirteenth century close to one hundred Invitatory Antiphons. The latter also has thirteen Invitatory tones. In other manuscripts the number of tones is sometimes smaller, sometimes greater. In fact, the Invitatory tones never became organized into a standard system of eight tones, one for each mode, as we find it in the tones of the ordinary Psalms, Canticles, Introits, and Responsories. Several modes are represented by a number of tones while, on the other hand, there are no tones for two modes, the first and the eighth. Their absence conforms with the fact that there exist no Invitatory Antiphons in these two modes. Most sources have one tone for modes 2, 3, 5, and 7, but several for modes 4 and 6. The *Liber responsorialis* [pp. 6ff] restricts itself to eight tones, three for mode 4 (distinguished as 4.g, 4.E, and 4.d), and one for each of the other modes (except, of course, 1 and 8), as does also the Codex Lucca of the twelfth century. Since this set is fully sufficient for a study of the methods employed in the Invitatory tones, we have selected it as the basis of the subsequent presentation.[1] The *Liber usualis* includes only four Invitatory tones: 4.g. for Nativity [368; Antiphon *Christus natus*], 4.E. for Corpus Christi [918; Antiphon *Christum regem*], 5. for Whit Sunday [863; Antiphon *Alleluia Spiritus Domini*], and 6. for Easter Sunday [765; Antiphon *Surrexit Dominus*], and the Office of the Dead [1779; Antiphon *Regem cui*].[2]

The archaic character of the Invitatory appears also from the fact that its text is taken, not from the standard Latin translation of St. Jerome known as the Vulgate, but from an earlier translation referred to as the *Itala*. Aside from several variants, this includes the words "*Quoniam non repellet Dominus plebem,*" which are missing in the Vulgate (as well as in the English translation, O come, let us sing, Ps. 95). Also different is the division of the text into verses, the *Itala* text having only five verses, each of which corresponds to two or three of the eleven verses of the Vulgate. As a result, the verses of the Invitatory psalm are considerably more extended than the ordinary psalm verses, and are therefore treated as a tripartite recitative, similar to the Doxology of Introits, with an initial

---

[1] Ferretti, *Esthétique*, pp. 227ff, offers a list of fifteen tones; *Wagner III*, 177) gives one of ten. A Solesmes publication, *Psalmus Venite exsultemus per varios tonos cum invitatoriis* (1895), has not been available for the present study. See also *Pal. mus.*, IV, 165ff.

[2] Because of its joyful character, the Invitatory is omitted during Holy Week, e.g., on Maundy Thursday.

and a closing formula for each of the three sections. We have seen [p. 229] that in the introit Doxology only four different formulae are employed, the first intonation (I_1) being used for the opening of the first section, the second intonation (I_2) for the openings of the second and third section, the mediant (M) for the close of the first two sections, and the termination (T) for the close of the third section. Several of the Invitatory tones follow a similar procedure, but with the first intonation used twice. Others, however, have three intonations, a different one for each section (I_1, I_2, I_3). There is always only one mediant, but in some tones this occurs in two modifications (M, M′) differing in their final notes, not dissimilar to the *ouvert* and *clos* endings of the fourteenth-century ballades and virelais (Machaut) or to the modern *prima* and *seconda volta*. The two final notes are always at the intervallic distance of a second, as is also normally the case in the *ouvert* and *clos* of the fourteenth century.

Between each opening and closing formula the tone continues with recitation. This shows not only occasional inflections such as occur in the responsorial tones, but also major deviations suggestive of half-cadences in the middle of a section, or fluctuations from one tenor pitch to another. No other type of Gregorian recitative shows such varied modulation, such flexible treatment of the reciting voice as is found in the Invitatories.[3] The following table shows the outlines of the eight Invitatory tones given in the *Liber responsorialis*. The closing notes of the mediants are added in parentheses.

		TENOR				TENOR				TENOR	
Tone 2	I_1	f	M (d)	I_1	f	M (d)	I_2	d	T
3	I_1	a	M (c′)	I_2	d′-a	M′ (b)	I_3	c′	T
4.g	I_1	a-g	M (g)	I_2	a-g	M (g)	I_3	g	T
4.E	I_1	a	M (e)	I_1	a	M′ (d)	I_2	f	T
4.d	I_1	g	M (d)	I_2	g	M′ (e)	I_3	f	T
5	I_1	c′	M (d′)	I_2	c′	M′ (c′)	I_3	c′	T
6	I_1	c′-a	M (f)	I_1	c′-a	M (f)	I_2	f	T
7	I_1	d′	M (c′)	I_2	d′	M (d′)	I_3	d′	T

For the purpose of more detailed illustration it will suffice to consider two examples, tones 4.E and 5. The former is used in the Night Office of Corpus Christi [918], the latter in that of Whit Sunday [863]. In order to show all the details, it is best not to use the first verse, *Venite*, because it is relatively short and therefore lacks the recitation in the third section. In Fig. 61 both tones are given with the fourth verse, *Hodie*, divided into its three sections.

[3] The versions of Ferretti (given without sources) have even more inflections than those of *LR* and the *Liber usualis*, particularly the version of the third tone.

FIGURE 61

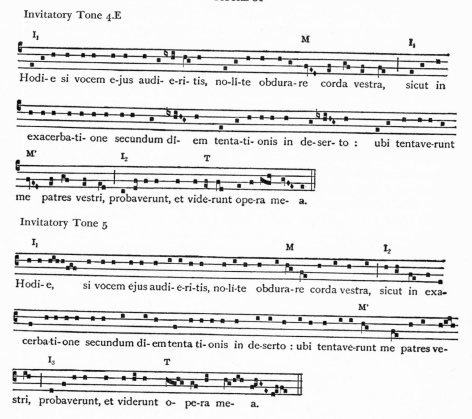

It is not necessary to enter into a detailed analysis of the intonations, mediants, and terminations of the invitatory tones, as this would add nothing new to our previous explanations. Suffice it to say that the terminations are all cursive, applied to the last five syllables of the text (*opera mea* in the verse of our illustration). For some reason, tone 2 has two different terminations, one for the odd-numbered verses, the other for the even-numbered verses. This probably has to do with the fact that the Antiphon is repeated in full after ℣℣. 1, 3, 5, while after the others its second half only recurs. However, there is no obvious reason why this principle, universally observed in all the Invitatories, should have affected only one of its tones.

THE SHORT RESPONSORIES

The difference, in liturgical importance, between Matins and the other Office Hours is clearly reflected in the Responsories assigned to them.

Those of Matins, the *responsoria prolixa* or Great Responsories, are extended and elaborate chants which, at least in their responds, often approach the highly melismatic character of the Graduals. Quite different from these are the *responsoria brevia* or Short Responsories, which are sung after the Chapter of the Lesser Hours, from Prime to None, and of Compline.[1] These are extremely short and almost completely syllabic, in their responds as well as in their verses. Their normal structure is R R V R' D R or simply R V D [see p. 185]. As in the Great Responsories, the Doxology is reduced to its first half, *Gloria Patri et Filio et Spiritui Sancto.*

The music of this rubric follows principles quite different from those encountered in the previous categories. In the Office Psalms, Canticles, Introits, and Great Responsories the music for the verse is prescribed by a standard formula, while that of the antiphon or respond is essentially free. The Short Responsories, however, have fixed melodies for the respond as well as the verse, the text being the main element of variety. Three main melodies are provided and assigned to different seasons, one being used "during the year," the other during Advent, and the third during Paschal Time [229f]. The Paschal melody is also used for high feasts, for instance, Nativity [407, 411], Holy Name [446, 450, 451] Epiphany [458, 462, 463], and Corpus Christi [942, 955].

In addition to the three standard melodies, each of which is used for a considerable number of texts, there are a few special ones which seem to be limited to a single text. Two examples of this kind are prescribed for Sunday at Terce; namely, *Inclina cor meum* for "During the Year" [237] and *Erue a framea* for Passion Sunday and Palm Sunday [239]. The medieval books of chant contain numerous other melodies for the Short Responsories, often more elaborate than those in present-day use, and occasionally approaching the ornate design and extension of the Great Responsories. Little is known about the medieval repertory of the Short Responsories, except for a brief, but very informative study contained in Wagner's *Formenlehre* [pp. 217ff].

[1] At the other Hours the Responsory is replaced by a hymn. See the table on p. 23.

CHAPTER TWO

The Free Compositions: General Aspects

IN THE foregoing chapter we have studied the liturgical recitative, that is, fixed melodies consisting essentially of a monotone recitation with opening and closing formulae, each designed to serve for a great number of texts. Turning now to the free compositions, we shall deal with chants having a distinctive and individual melodic line, and each composed for one special text. The latter statement could be challenged by pointing to the fact that some of these chants, particularly among the Alleluias and Hymns (later also the Sequences), occur with different texts, sometimes as many as ten or more. This, however, is not part of the original intention but rather the result of a subsequent emergency, arising from the introduction of new feasts for Saints in the eleventh century and later. For these the older melodies were used, and provided with a new text suitable to the occasion. As was observed in a previous chapter, the earliest indications of this method, known as adaptation, occur in the Mass for the Feast of the Holy Trinity [see p. 69].

At the outset it should be noted that the designation "free" applied to the chants of the Gregorian repertory should not be taken at its face value, that is, in the sense it would have in the case of a composition by Bach or Beethoven. Some of the chants have melodies which, in spite of their seemingly free design, may be elaborate versions of a recitative. Such melodies, then, would be "free" only at the level of variation or decoration technique, not of their thematic substance. Another restriction of free invention exists in the use of standard phrases (migrating melismas), i.e., phrases recurring in numerous chants of a certain group (as in the Tracts or Graduals of a given mode), sometimes to such an extent that the entire chant consists of a succession of such formulae.[1] Finally, it should be borne

---

[1] This technique is commonly called centonization, from L. *cento*, patchwork. *Antiphonarius cento* is the term used by Johannes Diaconus (John the Deacon) in his *Vita S. Gregorii Magni* of *c.* 870 to describe Gregory's activity in the field of music: "Then, in the house of the Lord, like another wise Solomon, because of the compunction (*compunctio*) inspired by the sweetness of music, he compiled, in the interest of the singers, the *antiphonarius cento* [i.e., collection called *Antiphonal*], which is of the greatest usefulness" (*Patr. lat.* 75, p. 90: *Deinde in domo Domini*).

in mind that in several liturgical categories each chant is a combination of a free melody and a recitative, the former being the respond or the antiphon, the latter, the verse. In the Introits and Great Responsories the verses are recitatives and, therefore, have been studied in the previous section of this book. Their antiphons or responds, on the other hand, are essentially free compositions and thus find their place in the present chapter. There is, of course, a certain awkwardness in this method of dividing a chant into its two constituent parts and treating each separately. However, the advantages of this procedure outweigh its drawbacks, in spite of the fact that in not a few instances the free and the recitative sections of a chant are musically related to each other. Moreover, the opposite procedure also leads to some awkward consequences, for instance, in the case of the Office Psalms where it would mean that the Antiphons should be studied simultaneously with the psalm tones, obviously a highly impracticable proposition.

A different situation exists with the Graduals, Offertories, and Alleluias, since here both the respond and the verse are freely composed melodies (within the limitations outlined above). Musical correlations between the two sections are quite frequently encountered in these chants, and actually are a normal feature in the Alleluias. It is therefore necessary to study these chants as a unified whole. The same remark applies to the Tracts which are psalms *in directum,* without antiphon or respond, and, of course, to the various types of non-psalmodic chant, such as the Hymns, the Ordinaries of the Mass, the Sequences, etc.

CHARACTERISTICS OF MELODIC DESIGN

The free chants of the Gregorian repertory cover a wide range of formations. At one end of the gamut we find Antiphons consisting of no more than a dozen notes, one for each syllable of the text; while at the other there are Tracts occupying more than two pages and including many melismas, each of which has more notes than are found in one of the shortest chants. Whether short or long, simple or elaborate, they all exhibit a keen feeling for melody as a living organism or, to use another metaphor, for the kinetic and dynamic qualities of the musical line. These qualities are, of course, present in all great melodies, whether by the unknown masters of the Roman chant or by outstanding composers of later centuries, from Leoninus to the present day. The uniqueness of the Gregorian work consists in the fact that here dynamic melody is created out of a purely melodic substance, unassisted (or, should we say, unencumbered) by two other factors essential in the shaping of later melodies, that is, regular meter and harmonic implications.

TOTAL RANGE

The over-all range in which the Gregorian melodies move is essentially that of the combined eight modes, that is, from the low A of the second mode to the high g' of the seventh. Examples of the low A occur particularly in the Tracts of the second mode, most of which start with the formula d-c-d-c-A . . . , and occasionally also touch upon the low pitch in the further course of the melody as, for instance, in *Qui habitat* [533]. There are a few chants, naturally all in the second mode, in which the melody descends to the low G, a pitch first recognized in the *Dialogus de musica* by Oddo of Cluny (d. 942), who designated it by the Greek letter Γ (*gamma; gamma-ut* in the terminology of Guido of Arezzo). Following is a list which, although not necessarily complete, probably includes most of the chants in which the G occurs:

TRACTS:
   Emitte Spiritum [1279]   Votive Mass of the Holy Ghost
   Gaude Maria [1266]   Feasts of the Virgin Mary
   Tu es vas [1346]   Conversion of St. Paul
RESPONSORIES:
   Collegerunt [579]   Palm Sunday (Procession)
   Repleti sunt [875]   Whit Sunday
   Emendemus [524]   Ash Wednesday (Procession)
   Obtulerunt [1360]   Purification (Procession)
OFFERTORIES:
   De profundis [℣. 2; Ott, 127]   23rd Sunday after Pentecost
   Protege [℣. 1; Ott, 169]   Exaltation of the Holy Cross
ALLELUIAS:
   Stabat Mater [1633ᵛ]   Feast of the Seven Dolours

All these chants belong to later feasts or to ceremonies of a later date, such as the Processions on Palm Sunday and Ash Wednesday. The only exception is the Responsory *Repleti sunt* of Whit Sunday, but in view of all the other evidence it is probably admissible to interpret the single G of this chant (on "dicentium") as a later variant, all the more since it occurs in a formula which appears in other Responsories of the second mode without this low tone.[1] It seems reasonable to conclude that the G was added to the Gregorian gamut at a relatively late date, perhaps some time during the ninth century, not too long before it was officially recognized by Oddo.

There is one single chant (at least, no other is known to me) in which the melody descends to the low F. This occurs in the second verse of the Offertory *Tollite portas,* where the word "et" is sung to the *clivis* G-F [Ott,

---

[1] Cf. the standard phrase F₁ in Fig. 94, p. 333.

p. 15]. This is one of the many traits indicative of the exceptional tonal behavior of the Offertory verses, for which we shall encounter numerous examples in our further studies.

Turning now to the upper limit of the gamut, there is no need to give special attention to the high g′, because this occurs very frequently in melodies of the seventh mode. Of greater interest is the fact that not a few chants go up to the a′:

GRADUALS:

Laetatus sum [560]	Fourth Sunday of Lent
Dirigatur [1060]	19th Sunday after Pentecost
Liberasti [1075]	23rd Sunday after Pentecost

ALLELUIAS:

Pascha nostrum [779]	Easter Sunday
Domine exaudi [1049]	17th Sunday after Pentecost
De profundis [1076]	23rd Sunday after Pentecost

INTROITS:

Aqua sapientiae [789]	Easter Tuesday
Exsultet [470]	Holy Family

There is at least one chant whose ambitus extends one or even two degrees higher, namely, the Responsory *Gaude Maria* from the Feast of the Annunciation [*PM* 146], the verse of which includes the following passage:

FIGURE 62

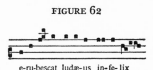

e-ru-bescat Judæ-us in-fe-lix

In the thirteenth-century Codex Worcester this passage reads: e′ e′ g′-a′-b′ a′ a′ a′-g′ g′,[2] but probably there are some manuscripts showing the version which is reproduced in the Solesmes publication. It may be noticed that this chant is not in the seventh mode but in the sixth, transposed a fifth up, from f to c′.

PHRASE STRUCTURE

The basic design of a Gregorian melody is that of an arch whose apex is reached and left in wavy lines formed mostly by ascending and descending seconds, but often also including larger intervals, particularly thirds. The most elementary embodiment of this design exists in the psalmodic recitative with its upward-leading intonation, its tenor recitation, and its downward-leading termination. It represents the prototype of the Grego-

2 *Pal. mus.*, XII, Plates, p. 271. Similarly in the Codex Lucca, *Pal. mus.*, IX, Plates, p. 354: c′ e′ f′-g′-a′-b′ a′ a′ a′ g′.

rian phrase, from the analytical and probably also from the historical point of view.

Some of the shortest chants consist of only one arch, e.g., the *Alleluia* Antiphon [304] shown in Fig. 63, while the Antiphon *Angeli eorum* [431] may be cited as an example of a double arch. Among the more extended

FIGURE 63

Alle-lu-ia,   alle-lu-ia, alle-lu- ia.

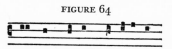

Ange-li e-orum   semper vident faci-em Patris.

chants there are many which consist of a succession of such arches, for instance the Responsory *Emendemus* [524], the Introit *Misereris omnium* [525], the *Alleluia Dominus regnavit* [405], or the Offertory *Domine Deus* [544].[3]

Side by side with such curves, however, there are others of a different design, suggesting an inverted arch or a more or less straight line with wave-like inflections. The prototype for the latter design could be found in recitatives such as the first phrase of the Invitatory Tone 5 [see p. 244]. It occurs occasionally in free compositions, e.g., at the beginning of the Communion *Vox in Rama* [430] from the feast of the Holy Innocents

FIGURE 64

Vox in Rama   audi-ta est

(see Fig. 64). Other examples are the phrase "posuisti super manum tuam" from the Introit *Resurrexi* [778], the beginning of the Offertory *Oravi* [1050], or that of the Gradual *Domine refugium* [1067].[4]

The inverted arch is found at the beginning of several chants, e.g., the Responsory *O vos omnes* [727]; the Antiphons *Ecce Dominus veniet* [324],

FIGURE 65

Ecce Dominus veni- et,   et omnes sancti ejus cum e-o :

[3] Other examples, quoted from *Wagner III*, 286f are: Intr. *Ecce advenit, Cibavit eos, Repleatur os meum;* Grad. *Ecce sacerdos;* All. *Benedictus es;* Off. *Meditabor;* Com. *Beatus servus, Confundantur superbi.* See also Ferretti, pp. 43ff.

[4] Ferretti (*Esthétique,* p. 46), following Gevaert (*Mélopée,* p. 126), calls this form "circulaire," i.e., circling around a center tone.

Stephanus autem [413], and *Hoc est praeceptum* [1111]; the Communion *Domine Deus* [544]; the Introit *Exaudi* [1002]; the Alleluia *Loquebar* [1369]; or the Communion *Cor meum* [1474]. Other chants start with a downward motion without continuing into a reversed arch; e.g., the Antiphons *Ecce quam bonum* [295] and *O magnum pietatis bonum* [1459], or the Introit *Deus in loco* [1024]. Such downward motions occurring at the beginning of chants have been explained by Wagner and Ferretti as a deliberate means to emphasize an initial word of particular importance, a "bedeutsames Anfangswort" or an "affirmation ou une pensée solennelle, énergique."[5] We find it difficult to accept this explanation, because of its vagueness (what is an "important" word?) and because there are, of course, hundreds of chants starting with an equally "important" word set to a melodic line of an ascending motion.

We also would prefer to avoid the term "law" in connection with this phenomenon of the Gregorian arch, as well as with others to be discussed subsequently.[6] There is no question that we are concerned with a very important principle of Roman chant, but to call it a law would mean to confer upon it the appearance of a universal validity which it actually does not have. If we interpret this law to indicate that all Gregorian phrases show the design of an arch, it is simply not correct. If we admit variations such as the reversed arch, descending motion at the beginning of a phrase, or wavy motion, then the law becomes commonplace because such designs are common characteristics of practically all musical phrases. Finally it should be borne in mind that definite statements regarding the design of phrases in a chant are often difficult to make because it is not always easy to say what constitutes a phrase in a given chant. It is obvious that by combining and dividing melodic units in different ways various kinds of basic design can be construed. As we shall see later, the indications of phrases or periods given in the Solesmes books are based on the divisions of the text [see pp. 267f]. However, there are cases in which the "law of the arch" would suggest a different division. An example in point is the section "et judica causam tuam" from the verse of the Gradual *Respice me Domine* [1033f], reproduced in Fig. 66. Here we find a sweeping ascending

FIGURE 66

et ju-   di-ca   cau-   sam tu-   am

[5] *Wagner III*, 287; Ferretti, p. 45. Even more untenable is Wagner's statement (*Elemente des gregorianischen Gesanges*, p. 159) that "the end of the period moves upward only when the text closes with a question." Of the four examples he adduces (Com. *Dominus Jesus* [657], at "Magister?"; Com. *Quis dabit* [G 129] at "Israel?"; Ant. *Fili quid fecisti* [477] at "quaerebatis?"; Ant. *Dixit paterfamilias* [503] at "otiosi?") only one or possibly two are convincing. Moreover, there are the numerous examples of the inverted arch, all closing with an upward motion without involving a question in the text.

[6] *Wagner III*, 286, fn.: "Konstruktionsgesetz aller choralischen Melodik."

motion to the words "et judica," an inverted arch for "causam," and a descending motion for "tuam." However, two perfect arches would result if we were to divide the melody in the middle of the melisma for "causam." Whether such a purely musical interpretation of the melody is admissible, it is difficult to say.

In the syllabic and neumatic chants the principle of the arch is generally valid at least to the extent that the musical line approaches a major division of the text in descending motion and continues in ascending motion, forming the beginning of a new curve. Occasionally one encounters an exception to this rule, for instance, in the Introit *Intret oratio* [541], in which a melodic arch encompasses both the end of one textual division and the beginning of the next, so that the apex of the bow coincides with the dividing point:

FIGURE 67

in conspe-   ctu tu- o :   incli- na   aurem tu-   am

Considering the entreating character of the text, one cannot help feeling that this departure from common practice is deliberate. It certainly causes the melody to stand in an almost gestic relationship to the words. Somewhat similar, although less impressive, are the following examples:

> Introit *In nomine* [612]
> . . . *et infernorum: quia Dominus factus obediens* . . .
> Introit *In virtute* [1135]
> . . . *exsultabit vehementer: desiderium animae ejus* . . .
> Antiphon *Dicebat Jesus* [1097]
> *Qui ex Deo est, verba Dei audit: propterea vos non auditis* . . .

MELODIC PROGRESSIONS[7]

If we consider the Roman repertory from the point of view of progressions from one note to the next, the basic role of stepwise motion is self-evident. There is no chant in which the number of steps would not be, by far, greater than that of all other progressions combined. The only exception, if it can be so considered, is the simple recitative with prevailing unison repeat. Unison repeats of a special character occur in some of the elaborate chants, where we find the same pitch repeated, up to eight times, on one syllable; e.g., three unisons in the gradual *Haec dies* [778] on "(Do)mi(nus)," five in the Offertory *Perfice gressus* [508] on "gres(sus),"

[7] A short study of this important aspect (the only one known to me) is found in Wagner's *Elemente*, pp. 129f.

eight in the Offertory *Anima nostra* [430] on "(libera)ti." Actually, it would be misleading to consider these formations under the aspect of melodic progression. As explained previously [p. 107], they represent an ornament, the vocal counterpart of the violin tremolo.

Among the disjunct progressions ascending and descending, major or minor thirds occur very frequently. Numerous chants consist of nothing but unisons, seconds, and thirds, for instance the just-mentioned Offertory *Anima nostra*. Next in frequency is the ascending or descending fourth, examples of which are found, for instance, in the Offertory *Perfice gressus* and in the Communion *Introibo ad altare* from the same feast. The fifth is decidedly more rare, particularly descending. Its ascending form, however, occurs with surprising frequency as an opening interval, imparting an impressive sweep to the beginning of a chant or one of its phrases. Examples are the Introit *Rorate caeli* from the Fourth Sunday of Advent [353], the intonation of the Invitatory Psalm of Nativity [368], an entire group of Antiphons of the first mode (e.g., *Fontes* [884], *Vado* [825]), the Communion *Factus est* [882] which also shows a descending fifth, the Alleluia *Te decet* [1022], the Offertory *Ascendit* [849], the *Kyrie IV* [25], etc. It is interesting to notice that in all these examples the fifth is either d-a or g-d', and that fifths on other degrees are much more difficult to find. For instance, one would expect to find examples of the fifth f-c' in the numerous Graduals of the fifth mode. This motion is indeed found in many of them, particularly at the beginning of the verse, but invariably in the form of the triad, f-a-c', as in *Anima nostra* [1167] or in *Beatus vir* [1136]. The fifth c-g occurs in the Gradual *Dilexisti* [1216], the only Gradual in the eighth mode; the fifth a-e' in the *Gloria* and *Sanctus* of Mass I [16ff].

Intervals larger than the fifth are exceedingly rare, and probably limited to chants of a late date.[8] A descending sixth, e'-g, occurs in the *jubilus* of the Alleluia *Multifarie* [441], and an ascending seventh in the final melisma of ℣. 2 of the Offertory *Domine Deus meus* [Ott, 175]:

FIGURE 68

The octave occurs only as a dead interval in some very late chants which have no connection with the Gregorian repertory, e.g., the fifteenth-cen-

---

8 Guido, in his *Micrologus*, cap. iv, recognizes six intervals (*sex vocum consonantias*): *tonum, semitonium, ditonum, semiditonum, diatessaron,* and *diapente,* saying that "in no chant is there any other way of connecting one tone with the next, whether ascending or descending" (*GS*, II, 6a; ed. Smits van Waesberghe, p. 105). In several copies of the *Micrologus* there are later insertions stating that the *diapente cum semitonio* and the *diapente cum tono* (minor, major sixth) are also used, as well as the *diapason* (octave), though rarely.

tury *Credo IV* [71, after "caelis"] or the seventeenth-century *Credo III* [70, after "finis"], probably also in some late sequences. The complete absence of real octave leaps is one of the numerous details setting the chant apart from Palestrinian melody which has often been described as being based upon the principles of Gregorian melody.[9]

The difference between these two idioms becomes even more apparent from a study of successive progressions, to which we now turn. Two successive thirds in the same direction (3 + 3) are, needless to say, quite common, upward as well as downward, and probably equally frequent in the major- and minor-triad form. Occasionally they outline a diminished fifth as, for instance, the e-g-bb in the Alleluia *Surrexit Dominus* [790], in the melisma on "Surrexit"; the bb-g-e in ℣. 3 of the Offertory *Domine exaudi,* on "misereberis" [Ott 54]; and the f'-d'-b which is found in every Gradual of mode 2—for instance, *Haec dies* [778] on "ea"—since it occurs in two standard phrases of the Gradual-type *Justus ut palma,* to which all the Graduals of mode 2 belong [see the phrases A3 and D10 of Fig. 108, p. 360].

As to the various combinations of a third and a fourth, only one of them can be said to belong to the language of Roman chant, that is the one outlining a descending sixth-chord, 4 + 3 downward. Even this is far from being frequent, being practically limited to a small number of Graduals and Offertories. The most striking example is a standard phrase used for the beginning of the verses of about eight Graduals in the fifth mode, a phrase in which the formation d'-a-f occurs three times in rather close succession.[10] A somewhat similar phrase including two statements of d'-a-f opens the verse of five other Graduals of the same mode.[11] In addition, the Gradual *Sacerdotes* [1187] (now used for the Common of a Confessor Bishop, but originally for the old feasts of St. Simplicius and St. Xystus) shows the progressions c'-g-e and bb-f-d. The presence, among the Graduals just alluded to, of *Viderunt omnes* from the Nativity clearly shows that the "descending sixth-chord,"[12] rare though it is, belongs to the old layer of the chant. As for the Offertories, the only example from the *Liber usualis* which I can indicate is the bb-f-d at the end of *Erit vobis* [803] from Friday of Easter Week. Not a few examples, however, are found in the verses of the Offertories; e.g., f'-c'-a in *Scapulis suis* ℣. 3 [Ott 33]; d'-a'-f in *Domine in auxilium* ℣. 2 [Ott 107]; c'-g-e in *Lauda anima* ℣. 2 [Ott 68],

[9] Many formations that "will be sought in vain in Palestrina music" (K. Jeppesen, *The Style of Palestrina and the Dissonance,* 1946, p. 74), e.g., e'-c'-b-a or a-b-d'-c', are, needless to say, ubiquitous in the chant.

[10] E.g., *Anima nostra* [1167], on "Laqueus." Cf. the standard phrase A10 in Fig. 104, p. 348.

[11] E.g., *Omnes de Saba* [459], on "Surge." Cf. the standard phrase M.

[12] This term and similar ones are used here only for the sake of convenience, without implying any "harmonic" connotation. To interpret Gregorian chant in terms of harmonic analysis is, to put it mildly, an inexcusable anachronism.

Oravi Deum ℣. 2 [Ott 109], *Afferentur* ℣. 2 [Ott 156]; and several others. They nearly always occur within an extended melisma, as in the above-mentioned standard phrases of the Graduals. The relative frequency with which the "descending sixth-chord" occurs in the Offertory verses is one of the various traits which give them a character all their own.[13]

As for the other combinations of a third and a fourth, they are so rare that they are scarcely more than curiosities. For the descending 3 + 4 ("six-four-chord") I can offer only three examples, none of them "pure," that is, the e′-c′-c′-c′-g which occurs twice in the Tract *Commovisti* [507],[14] the e′c′-c′-g in the final "alleluia"-melisma of the last verse of the Offertory *Confitebuntur caeli* [Ott 140], and the e′-d-c′-g in the melisma on "gloria" in the last verse of the Offertory *Perfice gressus* [Ott 91]. As for the two ascending combinations, 3 + 4 upward does not seem to exist; for 4 + 3 the following examples are all I have found: c-f-a in the melisma "Adducentur" in ℣. 2 of the Offertory *Afferentur* [Ott 164; originally *Offerentur*]; c-f-f-a in the melisma "meo" in ℣. 2 of the Offertory *Veritas mea* [Ott 149]; and G-c-d-e at the beginning of ℣. 1 of the Offertory *Protege Domine* [Ott 169] (this last example is added here only because "none better could be had"—as was said of Bach when he was appointed cantor of St. Thomas).

The almost complete absence of such a relatively familiar progression as the upward fourth-plus-third (or third-plus-fourth) is all the more note-worthy because the combination 5 + 3 upward, outlining a seventh, is not at all uncommon in Roman chant. It forms part of the beginning of a fairly numerous group of Antiphons including, among others, *Vos amici* [1111], *Fontes* [884], and *Vado* [825].[15] Other examples occur in the Alleluias *Surrexit* [790: d-a-a-a-c′], *Justus germinabit* [1192: d-a-c′], and *Virgo Dei* [1684: d-a-c′]; in the Offertory *Justorum animae* [1172: d-a-c′]; and in the Graduals *Liberasti* [1075] and *Benedictus Dominus* [478], both of which employ the same closing formula starting with g-d′-f′. The descending 3 + 5 I have found only in the "jucunda"-melisma of ℣. 2 of the Offertory *Confitebor* [Ott 46], and in the Gradual *Qui sedes* [335], where a seventh, g′-e′-e′-a, is sung to the word "super."

No less interesting is another combination outlining an ascending seventh, that is, 4 + 4. It occurs in a standard formula, opening with d-g-c′, which is used in a number of Tracts of the eighth mode; e.g., *Commovisti* [507], *Qui confidunt* [561], and *Ego autem* [G 566; see beginning of p. 568]. Other examples occur in the Introit *Ego clamavi* [GR 130: d-g-g-c′] and in the Offertory *Benedictus es Dominus* [514: d-g-g-c′ on "omnia"]. Once more, the final verses of the Offertories provide by far the best hunting ground for these formations, as in *Deus enim,* ℣. 2 [Ott

---

13 See p. 375.
14 See Fig. 90, p. 323. Also in others, e.g., *Tu gloria* [1378], on "Tota."
15 Gevaert's *thème* 3, 4, 5.

18, "Domine"]; *Tui sunt,* ℣. 3 [Ott 20, "dextera"]; *Portas caeli,* ℣. 2 [Ott 61, "loquar"]; *Benedictus sit,* ℣. 2 [Ott 82, "Cherubim"]; and *Posuisti,* ℣. 2 [Ott 137, "gloria"]. It will be noticed that all the examples of two ascending fourths involve the same pitches, d-g-c′. Again, the descending variety of this formation is much rarer, only two examples having been found, one in the Alleluia *Scitote* [1296], the other in the Offertory *Posuisti,* ℣. 2 [Ott 138, "eius"], both on c′-g-d.

The important role which the interval of a seventh plays in the melodic formations of the chant becomes even more apparent from a study of the rather frequent cases in which it is outlined through several intermediate pitches, as, for instance, d-f-a-c′ or d-g-a-c′. Fig. 69 shows a number of examples.

FIGURE 69

1. Offertory *Jubilate Deo omnis* [480, "terra"]; Offertory *Justorum animae* [1172, "et"]; Alleluia *In conspectu* [1276, "Angelorum"][16]
2. Alleluia *Cognoverunt* [817, "Cognoverunt"]; Offertory *Deus enim* ℣. 2 [Ott 18, final melisma]
3. Alleluia *Christus resurgens* [827, "mors"]
4. Graduals *Viderunt omnes* [409, "omnis"]; *Tribulationes* [547, "Domine"]; *Anima nostra* [1167, "Laqueus"]
5. Gradual *Laetatus sum* [561, "abundantia"]
6. Alleluia *Post dies octo* [810, "alleluia" and *jubilus*]
7. Graduals *Exsurge Domine non* [553, "homo"]; *Spera in Domino* [1352ᵛ, "ipse"]
8. Alleluia *Angelus Domini* [786, *jubilus*]; Tract *Gaude Maria* [1266, "Gaude" (G-f)]
9. Introit *Protector* [1036, "millia"]; Offertory *Jubilate* [487, "animae"]; Graduals *Exsurge Domine non* [553, "homo"; likewise at the end of the melisma "facie"] and *Tenuisti* [592, "corde"]
10. Gradual *Deus vitam* [G 128, "tuo" and final melisma]

There is little doubt that by means of a thorough search the number of such examples could at least be doubled. If, however, this seems like a rather insignificant yield, we have only to turn to the Offertory verses which have already proved to be a store of interesting formations. Here seventh-formations occur so frequently that they become a characteristic trait of the musical style. We can indicate here only a small number of examples (reference to Ott by page and system):

A-c-d-d-g [10, 9]; f-g-b-c′-d′-e′ [13, 8]; f′-d′-c′-c′-a-g [33, 8]; (d)-c-d-f-e-f-g-b♭ [40, 2]; f′-d′-e′-c′-c′-b-g [47, 2]; d-g-a-c′ [80, 8]; f-g-a-c′-d′-e′ [96, 2]; c′-b-a-g-f-e-d [116, 2]; e-g-a-c′-c′-d′ [133, 3].

Melodic formations encompassing an octave are noticeably less frequent than those moving within the distance of a seventh. An example (unique,

[16] The Alleluia *Venite* [1726, "omnes"] has the formation f-a-c′-e′, comprising a major seventh.

as far as I can see) of the succession of a fifth and a fourth occurs in the second verse of the Offertory *Constitues,* where we find c-g-g-c′ to the word "Speciosus" [Ott 132]. Equally rare are examples of the octave with two intermediate pitches, the d-a-c′-d′ from the verse of the Offertory *Viri Galilei* [Ott 173, "euntem"] being the only one that has been found. Octave formations with three or more intervening notes occur in greater number and variety, as Fig. 70 shows:

FIGURE 70

1. Gradual *Christus factus est* [655, "illum"]
2. Communion *Unam petii* [1005, "hanc"]
3. Communion *Ecce virgo* [356, "pariet"]
4. Offertory *Angelus Domini* [787, "descendit"]; also Graduals *Si ambulem* [G 137, "tua"] and *Sapientia* [G 398, "ejus"]
5. Offertory *Afferentur* ℣. 1 [Ott 164, "meum"]
6. Offertory *Precatus est Moyses* ℣. 2 [Ott 100, "Accedite"]
7. Alleluia *Multifarie* [441, *jubilus*]
8. Alleluia *Domine in virtute* [1004, "vehementer"]
9. Alleluia *Qui docti* [1466, "quasi"]
10. Alleluia *Beatus vir* [1747, "Beatus"]
11. Alleluia *Veni Domine* [355, final melisma]
12. Kyrie XIII [51]
13. Kyrie II [19]

Although this random selection is insufficient to provide a basis for definite conclusions, one can hardly go wrong in saying that octave formations are not only considerably less frequent than those encompassing a seventh, but also that they belong to a later stage in the development of the chant. Aside from the Offertory verses, which abound in unusual formations of any kind, the most prolific source for octave formations are the Alleluias which, on the whole, constitute one of the latest accretions to the repertory of Roman chant. Of a yet later date are the majority of the *Kyrie* melodies, and it is probably no mere coincidence that the two examples cited from this category are the only ones emphasizing the fifth as the most important intermediate pitch within the octave, so that the ear receives the familiar impression of a 1-5-8 outline. Usually the octave formations emphasize the fourth, the sixth, or some other degree between the lowest and the highest note.

In order to round off our discussion of the melodic motion in Gregorian chant, a few examples representing the utmost degree of boldness encountered in its tonal language are given in Fig. 71. These show arduous rises and precipitate falls, utterly unlike the smoothed-out contours of a Palestrinian melody, and, as may be expected by now, they are found particularly in the Offertories (many more examples occur in their verses). That from *Jubilate* is one of the most celebrated passages in the entire repertory.

FIGURE 71

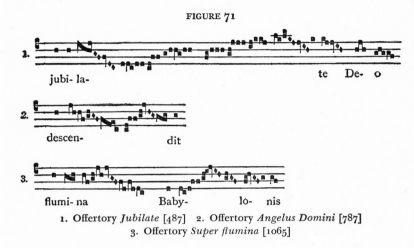

1. Offertory *Jubilate* [487]   2. Offertory *Angelus Domini* [787]
3. Offertory *Super flumina* [1065]

REPETITION OF MELODIC UNITS

While, on the whole, Gregorian melody is highly variable and unpredictable, exhibiting a tendency toward constant change of design, it is not entirely devoid of the opposite principle of melodic construction, that is, repetition in one form or another. We are not dealing with repetition as applied to entire melodies or sections, a procedure which, as has been shown earlier [pp. 181ff], is a basic element of formal structure in Gregorian chant. Rather are we concerned with small units occurring within a melody which are repeated and thus made to stand out within the general series of different units. Such repeats may occur in immediate succession (a a), after a contrasting unit (a b a), or at separate places of a chant, either at the same or at a different pitch. Immediate repetition takes on the character of imitation (as we may call it without danger of confusion with polyphonic imitation) if the pitch remains the same, of sequential progression if the pitch goes up or down by degrees. Repetition at separate places often takes on the character of a musical rhyme, occasionally one involving transposition, for instance, at the upper fifth. As for the extension of the repeated unit, this may vary from a short motive of three or four notes to longer groups and occasionally even to complete phrases.

We do not intend to enter into a detailed study of this aspect, but will confine ourselves to a brief presentation of the most typical cases, illustrating each of these by a few examples, the number of which could easily be augmented.[17] We do not include here the melismas of the Alleluias and Offertory verses purposely, because in these melodic repetition is so frequently encountered that it becomes a characteristic trait calling for separate study [see pp. 368ff, 386ff].

FIGURE 72

Repetition of Melodic Units

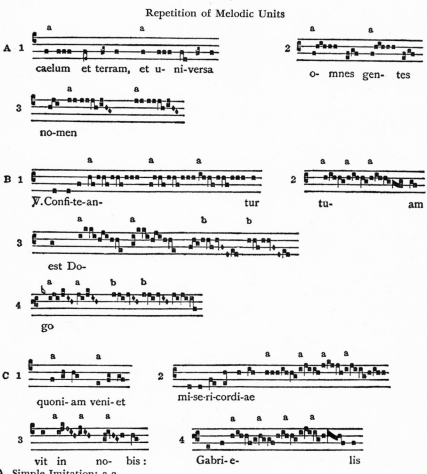

A. Simple Imitation: a a
    1. Introit *In voluntate* [1066]; 2. Offertory *Reges Tharsis* [461]; 3. Gradual *Benedicite* [1654].
B. Multiple Imitation: a a a, a a b b, etc.
    1. Gradual *Misit Dominus* [485]; 2. Gradual *Respice Domine* [1033]; 3. Gradual *Clamaverunt* [1170]; 4. Tract *Gaude Maria* [1266; see formula D7 of Fig. 93].
C. Sequence
    1. Antiphon *Montes et colles* [332]; 2. Gradual *Misit Dominus* [485]; 3. Responsory *Verbum caro* [390]; 4. Tract *Gaude Maria* [1266].

17 See Ferretti, *Esthétique,* pp. 49ff; Johner, *New School,* pp. 252ff; Wagner, *Elemente,* pp. 148ff.

It will be noticed that nearly all these examples come from chants of a highly ornate character, such as Graduals, Tracts, Responsories, and Offertories. While a repeat involving no more than two statements is usually exact, the repeated motive is subtly modified if occurring for a third or fourth time, as in the examples given under B and C. In example no. 3 of group C the three sequential statements, although exact as to pitches, undergo a most gratifying modification because of the shift of accent resulting from the irregular neumatic groups.

A number of chants employ the same motive at separate places for the close of different periods or sections, a phenomenon known as musical rhyme. Following are some examples:

1. Com. *Memento verbi* [1065]: "dedisti" = "mea"
2. Off. *Scapulis suis* [537]: "tibi Dominus" = "(ve)ritas ejus"
3. Intr. *Ego autem cum justitia* [G 121]: "tuo" = "tua"
4. Off. *Domine fac mecum* [G 133]: "(miseri)cordiam tuam" = "(miseri)cordia tua"
5. Intr. *Requiem aeternam* [1807]: "(do)na eis Domine" = "luceat eis"
6. Ant. *Nativitas tua* [1627]: "(annunti)avit universo mundo" = "(justi)tiae, Christus Deus noster" = "nobis vitam sempiternam"

Occasionally the musical rhyme corresponds to, and is obviously prompted by, a "textual rhyme," as in examples 3 and 4. Usually, however, it is a purely musical device of structural organization and unification. Particularly interesting from this point of view are chants showing a musical rhyme in transposition, e.g. (the transposition is indicated by the pitch of the final note):

7. Intr. *Populus Sion* [327]: "gentes" (g) = "suae" (d′) = "vestri" (g)
8. Intr. *Laudate pueri* [G 550]: "Dominum" (d) = "Domini" (f) = "(lae)tantem" (d)
9. Com. *Beati mundo corde* [1727]: "videbunt" (d) = "vocabuntur" (f) = "justitiam" (f) = "caelorum" (d).

It is probably no mere coincidence that examples of musical rhyme occur almost exclusively in the less ornate and shorter types of chant, such as Introits, Antiphons, and Communions, in which this device is obviously much more noticeable and effective than it would be, for instance, in a Gradual.

In addition to the repeat, either immediately or at separate places, of short motives, there are instances showing the repeat of fairly extended phrases or segments. The best-known examples occur in a number of Offertories, where they are predicated upon a peculiarity to be considered later, i.e., the repetition of words or sections of the text [see p. 364]. A somewhat similar situation exists in the Gradual *Hic est qui venit* [1533] from the Feast of the Most Precious Blood of Christ, in which the sections "Tres sunt, qui testimonium dant in caelo" and "Tres sunt, qui testimonium dant in terra" are sung to the same melody. That this Gradual does not belong to the medieval repertory appears from its non-psalmodic text as well as from its affiliation with a rather recent feast. In the Introit *Resurrexi* [778] from the Mass of Easter Sunday the repeat of an entire musical phrase could be explained by the textual rhyme of "et adhuc tecum sum, alleluia" and "alleluia, alleluia," but this explanation loses some of its weight because of the fact that a different melody is used for "manum tuam, alleluia," which occurs between the two other exclamations. In order to illustrate these and a few other cases of repetition of entire phrases, the texts (as complete as necessary) with indication (a_____) of those sections which are sung to the same melody are reproduced below.

1. Gradual *Hic est qui venit,* ℣ [1533]:
   a_____
   Tres sunt, qui testimonium dant in caelo: Pater, Verbum, et Spiritus Sanctus:
                   a_____
   et hi tres unum sunt. Et tres sunt, qui testimonium dant in terra: Spiritus,
   Aqua, et Sanguis: et hi tres unum sunt.

2. Introit *Resurrexi* [778]:
                   a_____
   Resurrexi, et adhuc tecum sum, alleluia: posuisti super me manum tuam,
                               a_____
   alleluia: mirabilis facta est scientia tua, alleluia, alleluia.

3. Antiphon *Innocentes* [432]:
                   a_____
   Innocentes pro Christo infantes occisi sunt, ab iniquo rege lactentes interfecti
   _____   a_____
   sunt: ipsum sequuntur Agnum sine macula, et dicunt semper: Gloria tibi
   _____
   Domine.

4. Antiphon *Virgo gloriosa* [1757]:
            a_____   a_____
   Virgo gloriosa semper Evangelium Christi gerebat in pectore suo, et non diebus
   _____
   neque noctibus, a colloquiis divinis et oratione cessebat.

5. Antiphon *Cum pervenisset* [1308]:
                                       a_____
   Cum pervenisset beatus Andreas ad locum ubi crux parata erat, exclamavit et
   _____ b_____
   dixit: O bona crux, diu desiderata, et jam concupiscenti animo praeparata:
   a_____a_____ b_____
   securus et gaudens venio ad te: ita et tu exsultans suscipias me, discipulum ejus
   qui pependit in te.

In the preceding explanations we have dealt with what may be called the "obvious" manifestations of the principle of repetition. Although assuredly not without importance and interest, these are, on the whole, exceptional. Only in certain special categories, such as the melismas of the Alleluias and Offertories, or in the hymns and sequences, do they attain the status of a characteristic trait. Much more significant and, in fact, decidedly typical of numerous chants is a repetition technique of a more subtle and evasive nature, a certain type of melodic design which may be described by the term "reiterative style." It is this style which bestows upon a large segment of Gregorian chant that special character which, rightly or wrongly, has often been called "oriental." Whether oriental or not, it is indeed far removed from the basic concepts of the Western mind, as appears from the fact that our vocabulary has only more or less derogatory terms to indicate it: pleonasm, prolixity, diffuseness, etc., all indicative or suggestive of a lack of conciseness. It is not easy to describe this style in definite terms or to illustrate it by specific examples, because it involves subtle allusions rather than demonstrable data. No one, however, can help noticing it in many chants of the responsorial type particularly, with their numerous instances of redundancy, of insistence on minute melodic turns or even single notes. Perhaps the most obvious examples are the cadential formulae which occur in nearly all the chants except those employing a simple syllabic style (Antiphons, hymns). To give one example out of hundreds, a cadential motion descending from a to e may appear in the following forms:

FIGURE 73

a. Introit *Cognovi* [1239]   b. Alleluia *Emitte Spiritum* [879]
c. Gradual *Speciosus forma* [434]

Obviously, such formulae cannot be adequately described by any term suggesting a "lack," the absence of a principle. They possess a decidedly positive quality, a richness and fullness which makes the elementary form appear meager and empty by comparison. At any rate, they are as inseparable from Gregorian chant as are tautologies and circumlocutions from ancient Greek, Jewish, or Hindu literature.

While traces of the reiterative style can be found on practically every page of Gregorian chant, it is particularly characteristic of, and all-pervasive in, the Graduals. We shall have more to say about this in the special section devoted to the study of these chants.

CADENCES

If one were to describe the evolution of musical style in terms of one single element, it is difficult to think of one more suitable for such a task than the cadence. Not only is it present in all periods of Western music history, but it fully participated in the major changes of style, adopting a great variety of forms which may well serve as earmarks of the main periods of musical development.

In Gregorian chant the cadences are purely melodic formations, lacking the harmonic element that was to play a decisive role in their later development. In spite of this restriction, the Gregorian cadences are far from being uniform or of limited variability, as is usually the case in later strata of monophonic music, for instance, in the sequences or in the songs of the trouvères. On the contrary, they are so diversified that a complete study of their forms, considered *per se* as well as in relationship to such categories as modes or types of chant, would easily require a fairly large book.

In a previous chapter [p. 142] we have considered the Gregorian cadences briefly from the point of view of tonality, examining the closing degrees of the inner cadences in relationship to that of the final cadence. This aspect, which provides an insight into the tonal instability of numerous Gregorian melodies, will again receive our attention in the study of the Tracts, Graduals, and Responsories [pp. 324, 336]. The object of the present study is the cadential formulae as such, that is, the different ways in which the final note is approached and prepared. The first question arising in this connection is that of the motion leading from the penultimate to the final pitch, and it is this question which we propose to investigate, being well aware of the fact that the result will be no more than an initial step.

It can easily be seen that, in the great majority of cases, the final pitch is reached in a descending motion. Most often this is stepwise, the penultimate note being one degree above the final, but examples in which these two notes are at the distance of a third are not at all infrequent. Ascending motion is much rarer and practically limited to the ascending second. A general impression as to the relative frequency of these three types may be gained from the fact that among the 131 chants occurring in the Temporale between Advent and the end of Nativity [317 to 414] there are ninety closing with a descending second, twenty-six with a descending third, and fifteen with an ascending second.[18] The picture changes, however, to a

[18] Throughout the subsequent study of cadential motion we have disregarded what could be called a unison cadence, that is, the preparatory anticipation of the final pitch. Thus cases like a-g-g or b-g-g are considered as mere variants of a-g or b-g. Only the final cadences are considered.

Wagner, in his *Elemente*, p. 142, says that the main cadences of the chant are those involving stepwise motion, descending or ascending. I cannot understand what caused Wagner to make this statement. The main cadences are, beyond doubt, the descending second and the descending third.

certain extent and receives more significant traits if the various types of chant are considered separately. This appears from the following table in which the same chants are listed as to types:

	INTR.	GRAD.	ALL.	OFF.	COMM.	RESP.	ANT.	HYMN
Desc. Second	7	3	5	9	9	8	45	4
Desc. Third	2	11	3	0	0	0	10	0
Asc. Second	0	0	0	1	1	0	9	4

Naturally, this tabulation is not sufficiently comprehensive to give an adequate picture of the over-all situation in the various categories of chant. However, it accurately reflects exceptional tendencies in at least two of them, i.e., in the Graduals and in the hymns. In the former it indicates a strong emphasis on the descending third for the cadential motion, and this indication is fully confirmed by a study of the entire repertory of Graduals, although not to the same degree as in the above table. Following is a tabulation of the cadences in all the Graduals found in the *Liber usualis*. Since, depending upon the manner of performance (R V or R V R), either the verse or the respond form the closing section of the Gradual, both of them have been included:

	RESPOND	VERSE
Desc. Second	75	63
Desc. Third	55	67

It appears that in the responds of the Graduals the descending third is almost as frequent in the cadences as is the descending second, and that both intervals are equally frequent in the verses. Ascending motion is completely absent in the cadences of the Graduals.

In the hymns, on the other hand, our table indicates a remarkably different situation, the descending third being not represented at all, and the ascending second being as frequent as the descending. A survey made on a larger scale[19] gives reason to assume that in the total repertory of the hymns the former cadence is actually about twice as frequent as the latter, and that the descending third is highly exceptional. An even more decided preference for the ascending second exists in the field of the sequences, where this cadential motion is so common as to assume the character of a standard trait.

In connection with the cadence formed by an ascending second the question arises as to how frequently it takes on the modern form of the leading tone cadence, characterized by a semitonal progression. The answer is, as may almost be expected, that this hardly exists in Gregorian

[19] Based on the hymns of the Ordinary and Proper of the Time up to Palm Sunday, as given in the *Antiphonale monasticum*, which has better versions for the hymns than the other editions. The final *Amen*, which invariably closes with an ascending second, has been disregarded.

chant. Obviously, within the system of the church modes, a leading-tone cadence is possible only on f, that is, in modes 5 and 6. Since, on the other hand, the hymns constitute the most fertile field for cadences with an ascending second, we are naturally led to the hymns of the fifth or sixth mode for an answer to our question. Actually, hymns on f are so rare that there is only one melody in the *Liber usualis*[20] and only six in the more comprehensive collections, the *Antiphonale Romanum* and the *Antiphonale Monasticum*. Only one of these has a leading-tone cadence, namely, *Aeterne Rector* [A 867], sung at the Feast of the Holy Guardian Angels, which was introduced by Pope Paul V in 1608. It evidently belongs to what have been called Baroque or Rococo hymns. Outside the hymns, I can indicate only three examples of the leading-tone cadence, the Communion *De fructu* [1031], the Antiphon *Virgo potens* [1679], and the Antiphon *O quam gloriosum* [A 903]. The only old chant in this group is *De fructu*, but its present cadence is, without doubt, the result of the manifold changes it underwent [see p. 168].

Since the Graduals belong to the old layer of chants, one is led to the conclusion that the descending third is an archaic cadence, no less so than the descending second which, from an over-all point of view, appears to be *the* cadence of the Gregorian chant. The ascending second, on the other hand, is definitely a late cadential formation, probably not in general use earlier than the tenth or eleventh centuries. This statement could be challenged by pointing to our table on p. 264 which shows a relatively high number of ascending seconds in the Antiphons, chants which, on the whole, belong to the older repertory of Gregorian chant. Actually, the nine examples given there represent only one single case, since they all close with the same melodic formula, e.g.:

a	g	fg	gfd	f	fg	g	g	
lac	*et*		*mel,*	*al-*	*le-*	*lu-*	*ia*	[323]
Je-	*ru-*	*sa-*	*lem,*	*al-*	*le-*	*lu-*	*ia*	[324]
a	*Do-*	*mi-*	*no,*	*al-*	*le-*	*lu-*	*ia*	[339]

In this connection it is interesting to notice that in the Alleluias, many of which are fairly recent chants, the ascending second is completely absent, while the descending third is about half as frequent as the descending second. Obviously they were composed at a time when the descending third had not yet been generally replaced by the ascending second.

In the Responsories the descending second is practically the only cadential motion ever used, a statement which applies even more unequivocally to the Tracts. Since these two types of chant, as well as the Graduals, make extensive use of standard phrases, they provide a safe basis for the investigation not only of their final cadences but also of numerous inner cadences.

[20] The twelfth-century *Stabat mater* [1424]. The same melody in *Virgo virginum* [1424].

A glance at the various tables of standard phrases that are given in the later course of this book [see pp. 319, 326f] fully bears out the statements just made.

It remains for us to comment briefly upon some cadential motions of very rare occurrence, that is, the descending fourth, the ascending fourth, and the ascending third. The first of these occurs in a few chants which belong to the old, though perhaps not the oldest, layer of the repertory: the Responsory *Angelus Domini* [774] from Easter Sunday; the Communion *Erubescant* [605] from Monday in Holy Week; the Invitatory Antiphon *Christus natus* [368] from the Nativity; the Offertory *Gloria et honore* [1137] from the Common of a Martyr not a Bishop (originally from the Feast of St. John and others); and the Alleluia *Dicite in gentibus* [801] from Friday in Easter Week. For the ascending fourth I can indicate only three examples; the last verse of the Offertory *Gloria et honore* [Ott 135], the Alleluia *In multitudine* [1513] from the Feast of St. Irenaeus, and the Antiphon *Puer Jesus* [437] from the Sunday after Christmas. The last of these is unquestionably old, but we have seen upon a former occasion that its cadence is probably the result of a later modification [see p. 177]. The same remark applies to the Antiphon *Vobis datum est* [510] from Sexagesima Sunday, which closes with the same phrase as *Puer Jesus,* but with the cadential motion c-f modified into c-d-f. This then could be considered as an ascending-third cadence, for which only one other example can be indicated, the Communion *Jacob autem*.[21] As for a more extended use of this cadence, one will probably have to turn to sequences, e.g., the *Ave Maria* [VP 46], in which a number of sections close with the formula d-f-f. No examples of the fifth, whether descending or ascending, have been found.

In conclusion it must be said once more that the preceding study, in which we have limited ourselves, somewhat artificially, to the consideration of the penultimate pitches, is no more than a beginning or an outline of a complete investigation, which would have to include the examination of the antepenultimate pitches and of full cadential formulae. Such a study cannot be attempted here. It may be pointed out, however, that fixed cadential formulae of considerable extension play a basic role in the formation of various chants, particularly the Graduals, Responsories, and Tracts. We shall have occasion to examine these formulae in the special chapters devoted to these chants.

MELODY AND TEXT

Intimate relationship between melody and text is a trait so fundamental in Gregorian chant that it needs no substantiation. Relationship, how-

---

[21] L 1442. This is a late adaptation from the Communion *Dicit Andreas* [G 392], originally for the Feast of St. Andrew, now for its Vigil.

ever, is not the same as dependency or subjection. While it is true that in certain types of chant, such as the recitation tones or the psalm tones, the melody is nothing more than a means to achieve a clear and impressive delivery of the text, it is equally undeniable that in many other cases the music assumes a degree of autonomy not dissimilar to that which exists in an aria by Bach or in a song by Schubert. In a Gradual, Alleluia, or Offertory word and song join hands in the rendition of the liturgical prayer, one contributing the thought, the other what Thomas Aquinas called the "exsultatio mentis, de aeternis habita, prorumpens in vocem"—the exultation of the mind, derived from things eternal, bursting forth in sound. It is not without interest to notice that in the early centuries of Christian worship music occasionally exercised this function completely independent of a text. St. Augustine (as well as other church fathers) repeatedly expressed the idea that the highest rejoicing of the soul calls for music without words: "If somebody is full of joyful exultation, . . . he bursts out in an exulting song without words;" or: "For whom is this jubilation more proper than for the nameless God? . . . And since you cannot name him and yet may not remain silent, what else can you do but break out in jubilation so that your heart may rejoice without words, and that the immensity of your joy may not know the bounds of syllables."[1] Such wordless jubilations of great extension, including up to three hundred notes, occur in Ambrosian chant. Although nominally attached to the syllable of a word, they actually attain independent status as purely musical formations. No vocalizations of comparable length exist in the Gregorian repertory, but there is only a difference of degree, not of essence, between the endless Ambrosian *melodiae* and the fairly extended melismas so frequently found in Gregorian chant, particularly in the Graduals and in the verses of the Offertories. They are the most obvious indication of the fact that the music of the chant stands in the relationship of a peer, not of a servant, to the text. In our subsequent studies we shall find this statement corroborated in many ways.

TEXTUAL AND MELODIC PHRASES

In a previous section [p. 249] the phrase structure of Gregorian chant has been studied from the purely musical point of view. Here we are concerned with the relationship between the structure of the music and that of the text; that is, with the question whether the melodic phrases agree with the syntactical divisions of the text, the latter as indicated by the various signs of punctuation, the former, by the vertical strokes indicating rests of shorter or longer duration. In order to approach this question properly, it must first be understood that both the grammatical and the musical signs of division are post-medieval additions. Even a source as

[1] Explanations of Ps. 99 and 32; *Patr. lat.* 37, p. 1272, and 36, p. 283.

relatively late as the Codex Worcester (13th century) contains no punctuation sign (except for the final dot), nor any of the division strokes found in the Solesmes editions.[2] No one will seriously question the propriety of the punctuation signs, since they are intrinsically present in the syntactic structure of the sentences. The musical phrase marks, however, present a more serious problem, not only because (like the bar lines in modern publications of medieval polyphony) they are editorial additions but because (unlike these) they are inserted on the basis of the textual divisions. Therefore, the complete agreement existing in the modern books between the divisions of the text and the divisions of the melody results from definition and thus has no evidential force.

This does not mean to question seriously the propriety of the division marks of the Solesmes editions. The longer strokes, particularly the "half bar" and the "full bar" [see *L*, p. xxv], are valid signs of musical syntax; only the "quarter bar," marking the end of "unimportant phrases," should be disregarded in connection with the present investigation. The melodic sections thus marked off usually turn out to be what may well be called "phrases," by virtue either of their design or of their cadential points, or both. In sum, there can be no doubt that agreement between the textual and the melodic divisions is a basic principle of Gregorian chant. Examples illustrating this fact are so frequent that specific references are not necessary.

It is, however, not unimportant to point out that there exist exceptions or deviations from this principle. In not a few cases one could argue about the validity of the phrasing marks of the Solesmes editions. In our previous study, in which we have considered the phrase structure from the purely musical point of view, we have indicated a few examples in which the musical principle of the "Gregorian arch" leads to a different division from that suggested by the text. Since, however, this principle in itself cannot be considered as infallible, it does not provide a solid basis for an objective investigation of the relationship between the musical and textual phrases. More reliable material for such a study is found in those fairly numerous chants which employ one and the same melody or melodic phrase with different texts.

Re-employment (or, as it is also called, adaptation) of complete melodies is particularly frequent in the Alleluias. For instance, the melody of the Alleluia *Dies sanctificatus* [409] from the Nativity recurs in each of the following Alleluias: *Video caelos* [416] from the Feast of St. Stephen, *Hic est discipulus* [422] from the Feast of St. John, *Vidimus stellam* [460] from the Epiphany, *Hic est sacerdos* [1184] from the Common of a Confessor Bishop, *Sancti tui* [1336] from the Feast of St. Fabian, *Magnus sanctus*

---

[2] Grammatical punctuations rarely occur in Latin manuscripts before the fifteenth century, even then with little consistency.

[1346] from the Conversion of St. Paul, *Inveni David* [1489] from the Feast of St. Basil (originally St. Silvester), *Tu puer* [1501] from the Nativity of St. John, and *Tu es Petrus* [1520] from the Feast of SS. Peter and Paul. The assumption, plausible on liturgical grounds, that the original text is that from the Nativity is strengthened by the fact that here melody and text are in perfect coordination, both of them being clearly tripartite. The following table shows how this as well as the other texts fit into the three major divisions of the melody:

I	II	III
Dies sanctificatus illuxit nobis:	*venite gentes, et adorate Dominum:*	*quia hodie descendit lux magna super terram.*
Video caelos apertos,	*et Jesum stantem*	*a dextris virtutis Dei.*
Hic est discipulus ille,	*qui testimonium perhibet de his:*	*et scimus quia verum est testimonium ejus.*
Vidimus stellam ejus	*in Oriente,*	*et venimus cum muneribus adorare Dominum.*
Hic est sacerdos,		*quem coronavit Dominus.*
Sancti tui, Domine,	*benedicent te:*	*gloriam regni tui dicent.*
Magnus sanctus Paulus, vas electionis,	*vere digne est glorificandus,*	*qui et meruit thronum duodecimum possidere.*
Inveni David	*servum meum:*	*oleo sancto meo unxi eum.*
Tu, puer, propheta	*Altissimi vocaberis:*	*praeibis ante Dominum parare vias ejus.*
Tu es Petrus, et super hanc petram	*aedificabo*	*Ecclesiam meam.*

It appears that only two of these texts, *Hic est discipulus* and *Magnus sanctus,* have the same syntactic structure as the original and, therefore, show the same complete agreement between textual and musical phrases. All the other texts are bipartite, and thus do not fall naturally into the tripartite scheme of the melody. While in *Video caelos* and *Sancti tui* a satisfactory adaptation has been achieved, this cannot be said of *Vidimus stellam* and even less of *Inveni David,* both of which are rather too short for a melody consisting of three extended phrases. Here the procedure adopted in *Hic est sacerdos,* that is, omission of the second phrase, would have resulted in a more "correct" agreement between text and music.

Finally, in *Tu puer* and *Tu es Petrus* the melodic divisions actually do violence to the textual structure, a fact all the more noteworthy since at least in the latter case a more suitable division is possible:

I	II	III
Tu es Petrus,	*et super hanc petram*	*aedificabo Ecclesiam meam.*

Naturally, in problems of this type the chronological facts have to be taken into consideration. If it can be shown that all the examples of poor adaptation occur in chants of a relatively later date, the situation appears in a different light from what it would be if they were found in old chants as well, or even exclusively in these. Unequivocal chronological evidence is provided by the earliest extant manuscripts, such as the eighth-century *Gradual* of Monza or the slightly later *Gradual* of Mont-Blandin.[3] Only three Alleluias from our group do not occur in the Codex Monza, namely, *Hic est sacerdos, Magnus sanctus,* and *Tu puer.* Our table shows that the adaptation is excellent in the first and second of these chants, and rather poor in the third. As for the remaining seven Alleluias, liturgical considerations make it likely that the four occurring between Nativity and Epiphany belong to the oldest layer. These are *Dies sanctificatus* (Nativity), *Video caelos* (St. Stephen), *Hic est discipulus* (St. John), and *Vidimus stellam* (Epiphany).[4] The adaptation is excellent in the first three of these, somewhat less good in the fourth, whose text has a bipartite rather than a tripartite structure. The other three, *Sancti tui, Inveni David,* and *Tu es Petrus,* are possibly of a slightly later date, but still belong to what is often called the "Golden Age" of Gregorian chant, since they are included in the Codex Monza of *c.* 800. In at least one of these, *Tu es Petrus,* the adaptation is extremely poor. In conclusion, it appears that the separation of this group of Alleluias along the lines of "good" and "poor" adaptation does not—or, at least, not entirely—conform with the division into "old" and "late."

Instead of studying other groups of Alleluias with identical melodies (for instance, the ten or more Alleluias of the type *Dominus dixit* [see p. 381]), it seems more profitable to turn to different types of chant. The most comprehensive material for adaptation exists in the twenty or more Graduals of the second mode collectively referred to as the "Gradual-type *Justus ut palma,*" all of which employ essentially the same melody. A musical analysis of this interesting group will be given later [see p. 357]. For the present purpose it will suffice to note that a tripartite division of the respond, musically as well as textually, is clearly indicated in most

3 See Hesbert's *Antiphonale missarum sextuplex.*

4 These are among the relatively few Alleluias that are both invariable (assigned to their feasts in all the sources) and proper (not assigned to any other feast). See pp. 378f.

of these Graduals; e.g., in *Haec dies* [778] from Easter Sunday and in the four Graduals from the Saturday in Ember Week of Advent, *A summo caelo* [343], *In sole posuit* [344], *Domine Deus* [345], and *Excita Domine* [347]. The majority of the other Graduals of this group have texts of a similar structure underlaid in conformity with the musical phrases. There are, however, at least four Graduals in which the principle of conformity is violated; namely, *Hodie scietis* [360] from the Eve of the Nativity, *Tecum principium* [393] from the Midnight Mass of the Nativity, *Justus ut palma* [1201] from the Mass of a Confessor (originally from the Feast of St. John the Evangelist), and *Dispersit dedit* [1608] from the Feast of St. Joachim (originally from that of St. Lawrence). The following table shows the texts of three of these Graduals (*Tecum principium* will be considered later), together with that of *In sole posuit* which may serve as a model of perfect adaptation:[5]

I (A₁)	II (A₂, or F₁)	III (A₃)
In sole posuit ǀ *taberna-culum suum:* ǀ	*et ipse tamquam sponsus* ǀ	*procedens de thalamo suo.*
Hodie scietis ǀ *quia veniet Dominus,* ǀ	*et salvabit nos:* ǀ *et mane* ǀ *videbitis* ǀ	*gloriam ejus.*
Justus ut palma florebit: ǀ *sicut cedrus Libani* ǀ	*multiplicabitur* ǀ	*in domo Domini.*
Dispersit, dedit pauperi-bus: ǀ *justitia ejus* ǀ	*manet in saeculum*	*saeculi.*

The following distribution would have led to a considerably better agreement between the musical and the textual units:

I	II	III
Hodie scietis quia veniet Dominus	*et salvabit nos:*	*et mane videbitis gloriam ejus.*
Justus ut palma florebit:	*sicut cedrus Libani*	*multiplicabitur in domo Domini.*
Dispersit, dedit pauperi-bus:	*justitia ejus*	*manet in saeculum saeculi.*

In *Tecum principium* the tripartite scheme is enlarged to one consisting of four phrases, as is also the case in *Tollite portas* [1269]. While in the latter the syntactic divisions agree with those of the music:

[5] In order to facilitate comparison with the musical analysis [p. 360] the symbols employed there for the various standard phrases (A₁, etc.) have been added. The shorter and longer strokes inserted in the texts represent the half bars and full bars of the Solesmes editions. It may be noticed that in *Dispersit* the full bar after "pauperibus" results in a musical phrase (ending on g) that does not exist in the Graduals of mode 1, which employ only d, a, f, and c as their cadential points.

I	II	III	IV
Tollite portas, principes vestras:	*et elevamini portas eternales,*	*et introibit*	*Rex gloriae,*

the text of the former is divided as follows:

Tecum principium in die virtutis tuae:	*in splendoribus sanctorum, ex utero*	*ante luciferum*	*genui te,*

although the following distribution would have been possible:

Tecum principium in die virtutis tuae:	*in splendoribus sanctorum,*	*ex utero*	*ante luciferum genui te.*

As for the verses of the Gradual-type *Justus ut palma,* they also consist of a small number of well-defined musical units. The textual divisions are nearly always in good agreement with these, except for one case of striking disregard, that is, in the verse of *Domine refugium* [1067] from the Twenty-first Sunday after Pentecost, which includes the following passage:

FIGURE 74

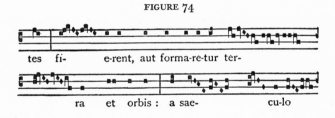

Musically, the correct division would be, not after "orbis:" but after "terra" (end of phrase A_{10}). The recitation on "et orbis:" forms the opening of the next phrase (F_{10}).

What do these analytical facts mean in terms of chronology? Nearly all the Graduals of our group, and all those considered above, appear in the Codex Monza and therefore existed about 750 at the latest. All attempts in the direction of finer chronological distinctions can be based only on circumstantial evidence derived from liturgical considerations, and such evidence is necessarily somewhat inconclusive. There can be no doubt, however, that the Graduals for Easter Sunday (*Haec dies*), for the Eve of the Nativity (*Hodie scietis*) and for the Midnight Mass of the Nativity (*Tecum principium*) belong to the oldest layer of the entire repertory of Graduals. It is therefore somewhat disconcerting to find both *Hodie scietis* and *Tecum principium* among those which leave something to be desired as to the coordination of textual and musical phrases. Naturally, this statement could be challenged by questioning the validity of the musical phrases as indicated above and in other modern studies. Although they are unmistakably indicated in all the Graduals of the group *Justus ut palma,* an attempt could be made to modify their beginnings and ends so that at least such truly venerable Graduals as those of the Nativity are no longer suspect of "poor adaptation of the text," an epithet that has often been conferred on chants of the "Silver Age" or of "decadent days." Unfortunately, no solution is possible that would lead to a satisfactory result in all three Graduals, as appears from the following table in which the disputable sections of their texts are shown as they occur in connection with small portions of the melody:[6]

	1	2	3	4	5
Tecum:	... *in splendoribus*	*sanctorum,*	*ex utero*	*ante luciferum*	*genui te.*
Hodie:	... *et salvabit nos:*	*et mane*	*videbitis*	....	*gloriam ejus.*
Haec dies:	*Haec dies*	*quam fecit*	*Dominus:*	*exsultemus*	*et laetemur in ea.*

As can easily be seen, *Tecum* would require a phrase closing after 2, *Hodie* a different one closing after 1, and *Haec dies* yet another closing after 3.

Ample material for the study of our problem exists in the Tracts, in which a limited number of standard phrases recur, not only in the various Tracts of one and the same mode, but also in the different verses of one and the same Tract [see p. 315]. As for the numerous texts connected with any of these standard formulae, a detailed investigation would, no doubt, confirm the general validity of the principle of conformity between the musical and the textual units. As an illustration we reproduce the text of the Tract *Confitemini* [547] divided according to the succession of the standard phrases of the Tracts in the second mode:[7]

Confitemini Domino | *quoniam bonus:* | *quoniam in saeculum* | *misericordia ejus.* ℣. *Quis loquetur* | *potentias Domini:* | *auditas faciet* | *omnes laudes ejus?* ℣. *Beati* | *qui custodiunt* | *judicium* | *et faciunt justitiam* | *in omni tempore.* ℣. *Memento* | *nostri, Domine,* | *in beneplacito populi tui:* | *visita nos* | *in salutari tuo.* |

It appears that there is nearly always a satisfactory conformity between the musical and the textual units or, at least, no contradiction between them. The only exception occurs at the beginning of the last verse, where

6 The melody for *Haec dies* has a different beginning, but the same cadences at 2. and 3.

7 The division marks given here do not necessarily agree with those of the Solesmes editions.

the text is divided *Memento | nostri, Domine,* rather than *Memento nostri, | Domine.*

A similar case occurs in the Tract *Deus Deus meus* [592] for Palm Sunday, at the beginning of the second (actually the third) verse. The *Liber usualis* divides the text as follows: *Deus meus | clamabo per diem, | nec exaudies: | in nocte, et non ad insipientiam mihi.* Sensible though this division is from the grammatical point of view, the musical units indicate a different one, as follows: *Deus meus clamabo | per diem, nec exaudies: | in nocte, et non | ad insipientiam mihi.*

All the examples considered so far belong to the old, if not to the oldest layer of the Gregorian repertory. Although it is possible and even probable that a thorough search would uncover additional cases of non-conformity between textual and musical phrases, there can be no doubt that they represent no more than rare exceptions to the general rule. The situation changes somewhat if we turn to chants of a later period, of "decadent days," as they have been called. A case in point is the Responsory *Ornatam monilibus* [*LR* 253] from the Night Office of Feasts for the Virgin Mary (originally for the Feast of the Assumption). This chant contains a passage which appears in the *Liber responsorialis* as follows:

FIGURE 75

The melody consists of two standard formulae of the Responsories of the eighth mode, the first closing on d (D₁), the second on f (F₁) [see p. 338], which are indicated in the figure. It appears that the musical units cut right across the textual divisions, and that the Solesmes edition, in observing the latter, shows musical phrases which do not exist among the standard formulae of the Responsories.

Particularly interesting in this respect is the Mass for Trinity Sunday, a feast locally introduced toward the end of the eighth century, and for which Alcuin (753-804) wrote the liturgy. His texts were adapted to pre-existent melodies [see p. 68] and it is interesting to note that, except for the Alleluia, every item of this Mass shows an instance of poor adaptation, that is, of disagreement between textual and musical phrases. This is shown in the subsequent table. The upper line of each item gives the original text and, by implication, the correct musical phrases (marked a. and b.), while the lower line shows the new text arranged as it appears with the same musical phrases:

1. Introit *Benedicta sit* [909]; from *Invocabit* [532]:
   a.   b.
   Invocabit me et ego exaudiam eum: eripiam . . .
   Benedicta sit sancta Trinitas atque in- divisa . . .

2. Gradual *Benedictus es* [910]; from *Constitues* [1519]:
   a.   b.
   . . . *super omnem terram: memores erunt* . . .
   . . . *qui intueris   abyssos, et sedes* . . .

3. Offertory *Benedicta sit* [911]; from *Constitues* [1520]:
   a.   b.
   . . . *memores erunt nominis tui, in omni progenie* . . .
   . . . *Dei Filius, Sanctus quoque Spiritus: quia* . . .

4. Communion *Benedicimus* [912]; from *Feci judicium* [1224]:
   a.   b.
   . . . *ad omnia mandata tua dirigebar, omnem viam* . . .
   . . . *confitebimur ei: quia fecit   nobiscum* . . .

Another late-medieval feast is that of Corpus Christi (twelfth century). Its Mass received two new texts, the Offertory *Sacerdotes* and the Communion *Quotienscumque*, both of which were set to earlier melodies, the former to *Confirma hoc*, the latter to *Factus est* [see p. 68]:

5. Offertory *Sacerdotes* [949]; from *Confirma hoc* [882]:
   a.   b.
   . . . *quod operatus es in nobis: a templo tuo* . . .
   incensum et panes offerunt Deo: et ideo . . .

6. Communion *Quotienscumque* [950]; from *Factus est* [882]:
   a.   b.
   . . . *ubi erant sedentes, alleluia: et repleti sunt omnes* . . .
   . . . *donec veniat: itaque quicumque manducaverit panem* . . .

The consistency with which the original phrases are disregarded in the new settings of Trinity and Corpus Christi is generally considered as an indication of approaching decadence, of the change from the "Golden" to the "Silver" age of the chant. We have seen, however, that such practice also occurs in undeniably old layers of the repertory, although only as an exception from the rule.

THE TEXTUAL ACCENT

Few aspects of Gregorian chant have been so often investigated and discussed as the problem of the accent, that is, the question as to how and to what extent the accent of the Latin text is reflected in the musical line. Several medieval writers speak about this question or allude to it in more or less clear terms. As early as the sixteenth century the Gregorian melodies were scrutinized from this point of view and found wanting—a discovery which more than any other consideration led to the abandoning of the traditional melodies and to the adoption of the "purified" versions of the *Editio Medicea*. After the restoration of the medieval tradition the question was taken up again, naturally from an entirely different point of view. Objective investigation took the place of high-handed criticism, and efforts were directed toward discovering the principles that govern the relationship between the textual accent and the music. Among the scholars working in this field were Dom Pothier in his *Les Mélodies grégoriennes d'après la tradition* (1881), Dom Mocquereau in several volumes of the *Paléographie musicale* (1893-1901) and in *Le Nombre musical grégorien* (1908), Gastoué in his *Cours théorique et pratique de plain-chant romain grégorien* (1904), Wagner in his *Gregorianische Formenlehre* (1921), and Ferretti in his *Esthétique grégorienne* (1938).

Several of these authors, particularly Mocquereau, preface and support their investigations by detailed explanations of the Latin accent as a purely philological phenomenon and problem. Although very little of this has a direct bearing on the question, a few remarks outlining the situation may be in place, particularly since the terms involved are frequently mentioned without always being correctly understood.

Each Latin word of more than one syllable has one, and only one accent, which falls either on the penultimate or on the antepenultimate syllable, that is, the first or the second before the last. This universal law distinguishes the Latin language from most of the others, in which the accent may also fall on the last syllable (e.g., Greek ἀνήρ [man], English *commánd*, French *choisi*, German *Gesétz*), or on a syllable farther removed from the last, as in *reáctionary*, or on two syllables, as in *répresentátion*.[8] Returning to Latin, the choice between the two possibilities of placing the accent depends upon the character of the penultimate syllable. If this is long, it carries the accent; if short, the accent falls on the antepenultimate. For instance, in *audite* the *i* is long, hence *audíte*; while in *Domino* the *i* is short, hence *Dómino*. There exist a number of rules which determine whether a syllable, especially the penultimate, is long or short, but this is not the place to explain them. Nor is it necessary to do this since in every case of doubt (i.e., for every word having more than two syllables) the accentuation is indicated in the modern books of chant. Suffice it to say that a syllable is always long if its vowel is followed by two consonants, e.g., *eréctus, secúndum, benedíctus*, etc.

The previous remarks pertain to the position of the Latin accent. Some-

---

8 The Solesmes scholars maintain that long Latin words have a secondary accent, e.g., *règpresentátio, còntinéntur*. This is an arbitrary interpretation resulting from the *ictus* principle (groups of no more than three notes).

what more involved and controversial are the questions concerning its character. Generally speaking, an accent, i.e., a stress, an emphasis, can be produced in three ways, which may conveniently be distinguished as dynamic, sustaining, and tonic accent. The first of these results from greater loudness, the second from longer duration, and the third from higher pitch:

FIGURE 76

| Dó-mi-nus | Dó-mi-nus | Dó-mi-nus |
| Accent: dynamic | sustaining | tonic |

All these accents are believed to have played a role in the Latin language, but in different degrees during the various periods of its development. Usually four such periods are distinguished: an archaic (prior to the second century B.C.), a classical (second century B.C. to the fourth century of the Christian era), a post-classical (fifth and sixth centuries), and a late period during which the Romance languages were formed (seventh and eighth centuries). French Latinists and, as a consequence, some Gregorian scholars,[9] say that in the classical period (nothing definite is known about the archaic period) the accent was essentially of the sustaining kind (usually called accent by quantity, or metric), but also tonic; that during the post-classical period (the period in which Gregorian chant was formed) a complete transformation took place with the result that the accent became predominantly tonic and dynamic, but lost the quantity so that now all syllables are short; and that in the late period the accent became pronouncedly dynamic but also, under certain circumstances, long, a character which was preserved in some of the Romance languages. The majority of Latin scholars (German, English, American) prefer to think that the accent of the classical period also had the quality of a stress (dynamic accent) and that the only change that took place was the loss of quantity.

Although we are mainly interested in post-classical Latinity, a few remarks about the classical accent as applied to poetry are in place, because a number of hymns of the Gregorian repertory are modelled after the principles of classical poetry. We have previously alluded to the distinction between long and short syllables that played an important role in this period, resulting in a manner of speech in which certain syllables were held almost twice as long as others. In the poetry of the classical era (Virgil, Ovid, Horace) this principle was so rigidly applied that it frequently led to a shift of the position of the accent. An instructive example is the following line from Horace, shown (a) with the normal accentuation (quality,

[9] Mocquereau, *Nombre*, II, 111ff; Ferretti, *Esthétique*, pp. 6ff.

indicated by ´), (b) with the poetic accentuation (quantity, scansion, indicated by –):

(a) *Partúriunt móntes et náscitur ridículus mús*[10]
(b) *Pārturiŭnt montēs ēt nāscitur rīdiculūs mus*

The striking difference results, among others, from the fact that the "rule of prolongation by two subsequent consonants" was also observed when these two consonants appeared in separate words, so that *et* becomes long (by position, as it is called) because there follows an *n,* and *-lus* of *ridiculus* becomes long because it is followed by an *m.*

The influence of this principle of versification is still evident in some of the Christian hymns, e.g., in:

Deús creátor ómniúm   (normally *Déus*)

or in:

*Glória laús et honór, tibi sit Rex Chríste Redémptor
Cui pueríle decús prómpsit hosánna píum*
(normally *hónor, décus, pium*).

Such examples of artificial accentuation are, however, exceptional in late Latinity and, as far as the Gregorian repertory is concerned, are practically confined to hymns.[11] In the prose texts the position of the accent is invariably governed by the previously explained rule of the three final syllables. It is probably correct to say that in this period the syllables were all pronounced equally long (or equally short) and that the accent was tonic and dynamic.

Transferred from their literary connotations to the field of music, tonic accent means that an accented syllable is distinguished by higher pitch; sustaining accent, that it has longer duration, which may result either from the prolongation of a single pitch (doubled or tripled values) or from the use of longer groups of notes (melisma).[12] Both these possibilities of "musical accentuation" have played a role in the study of Gregorian chant. In fact, they have been the issues of numerous controversies, conducted with arguments derived from Latin prosody, medieval treatises, or Oriental

10 The mountains labor, and bring forth a ridiculous mouse.

11 In the Solesmes editions the poetic accentuation (scansion) is disregarded. For poetic texts outside the hymns, see p. 97. For the versification of the hymns, see pp. 423ff.

12 Modern writers often employ a somewhat confusing terminology by speaking of the "quantity of the tonic accent" (Ferretti, p. 24: "quantité de l'accent tonique;" *Wagner II,* 497: "der tonische Akzent . . . nicht als eine Länge empfunden"). Here the term "tonic" refers only to the text, and could just as well be omitted or replaced by "textual."

church music, as well as from the musical sources themselves.[13] No end would be served by going into the details of all these disputes. Suffice it to say that, according to the basic tenet of the Solesmes school, the word accent of medieval Church Latin is high and short and that these qualities are reflected in the music. Therefore it is maintained that Gregorian chant, on the whole, displays a positive attitude toward the tonic accent, a negative attitude toward the sustaining accent. A somewhat different and less rigid view is evident in Ferretti's *Esthétique grégorienne*. Here the tonic accent receives the status of a fundamental law of Gregorian chant while, on the other hand, the melodies are said to be indifferent as to the sustaining accent.[14] It seems to us that even these statements, though more considerate than those found in earlier studies, fail to give a correct impression of the actual state of affairs. They tend to exaggerate the importance of one method at the expense of the other. We would prefer to say that both the tonic and the sustaining accent are formative principles of the chant, the former more fully than the latter, neither of them, however, attaining the status of a "law." The subsequent explanations are given in support of this view.

THE SUSTAINING (MELISMATIC) ACCENT

As was stated above, the sustaining accent may, *a priori*, take on two different forms, either that of a prolonged note or that of a group of notes. In Gregorian chant, the former interpretation is predicated upon the mensuralist theory of rhythm according to which the melodies include numerous notes of double or even triple the duration of the basic value (i.e., quarter- or dotted-quarter-notes, if the basic value is represented by an eighth-note), these notes being indicated either by the neumes themselves (Wagner's theory) or by special symbols such as the *episema* or the Romanus letters. Since, to the present day, this is the most controversial problem of Gregorian chant, it is plainly impossible to consider the sustaining accent from this point of view. Consequently, we are concerned only with its alternative manifestation, in which it presents itself under the form of a group of notes, that is, a shorter or longer melisma. In view of this limitation it seems advisable to use the term melismatic accent

---

13 A. Dechevrens, *Les vraies mélodies grégoriennes* (1902); A. Fleury, *Ueber Choralrhythmus* (1907); J. C. Jeannin, *Études sur le rythme grégorien* (1926); also the writings of Wagner, Gastoué, Mocquereau, Ferretti, Gajard, and others. The sustaining accent has been repeatedly considered in connection with the problem of Gregorian rhythm. Practically no attention has been paid to the possibility of a dynamic accent, except by P. Aubry who, in *Le Rythme tonique* (1903), p. 55, speaks of "l'accent d'intensité qui donne à la syllabe accentuée, ni plus d'acuité ni plus de durée, mais plus de force."

14 See *Esthétique*, pp. 14ff and 333ff.

rather than sustaining accent, because the latter suggests primarily that aspect with which we are not concerned.

The views held by scholars regarding the importance and proper role of the melismatic accent vary considerably, and a certain fluctuation is noticeable even within the work of one outstanding Gregorianist, Dom Mocquereau. In his first study of the problem of the accent, contained in vol. III of the *Paléographie musicale* and devoted primarily to the tonic accent, he touches briefly upon the melismatic accent by calling attention to an "erreur moderne," that is, of "décharger les syllabes non accentuées des notes, pour les amasser sur la syllabe marquée de l'accent tonique et très improprement dite syllabe longue" (the modern error of relieving the non-accented syllables of notes and piling them up on the accented syllable, which very improperly is called long; *Pal. mus.*, III, 29). The "modern error" refers to the Ratisbon (Latin-French for Regensburg) edition of F. X. Haberl (1871-81) which presented the chants in the utterly corrupt version of the *Editio Medicea* of 1614. As we shall see later [p. 288], one of the main principles of this edition was the strict observance of the melismatic accent, with the result that here indeed the notes were gathered on the accented syllables. Mocquereau justly takes a strong stand against this illicit procedure, pointing out that frequently the final syllable, which in Latin is invariably weak, is provided with long melismas. Nevertheless, on p. 30 of the same volume he says that "toutes les syllabes des mots latins sont susceptibles de dilatation musicale, mais la syllabe plus propre, *après la dernière*, à recevoir cette extension, est encore celle qui porte l'accent" (all the syllables of the Latin words are susceptible to musical expansion, but the one most proper to receive this extension is, aside from the final, the one that carries the accent). This statement (rather typical of Mocquereau in its fairly complete reversal of another made before) seems to indicate a positive attitude toward the melismatic accent, since melismas are said to fall most properly on the accented syllables. The same attitude is evinced in a chapter of vol. IV of the *Paléographie musicale*, entitled: *Les Pénultièmes bréves non accentuées chargées de notes* (pp. 69ff), in which he shows that in words with a weak penultimate syllable (*Dóminus, hódie, congregátio*) this syllable is nearly always treated as short, with only one or a few notes (see, e.g., the words "Dominus" and "justitiam" in the Gradual *Viderunt omnes*). We are not concerned here with the question whether this thesis is tenable (by dividing the whole field into three categories: *Prééminence du texte, Transaction entre le texte et la mélodie,* and *Prééminence de la musique,* Dom Mocquereau somehow succeeds in proving it, without proving anything). Suffice it to say that in his final statements he recognizes the validity of the melismatic accent by emphasizing its absence on certain weak syllables:

"Aussi les maîtres ne se permettaient-ils pas d'adapter, sauf des exceptions extrèmement rares, à un long melisma d'accent une pénultième brève non accentuée" (Thus the masters did not permit themselves, aside from very rare exceptions, to adapt a short, unaccented penultimate syllable to a long accent melisma; p. 103), and "Le répertoire grégorien contient quelques mélismes assez longs, une vingtaine peut-être, sur des pénultièmes non accentuées; mais ces faits rares n'infirment en rien les règles . . ." (The Gregorian repertory contains some rather long melismas, perhaps about twenty, on non-accented penultimates, but these rare occurrences in no way invalidate the rules . . . ; p. 108).

In contrast to these statements which, on the whole, are favorable to the principle of the melismatic accent, we find a completely reversed attitude in vol. VII of the *Paléographie*, in which Mocquereau proposes an entirely different thesis, that is, that Gregorian chant shows the tendency to treat the accented syllable as short, the non-accented final syllable as long. Thus, an example like the following:

$$\overset{1}{S}c\overset{3}{i}\text{-}\overset{1}{o}\ c\overset{5}{u}\text{-}i \quad \text{or} \quad \overset{1}{c}\overset{5}{o}n\text{-}\overset{1}{t}i\text{-}n\overset{7}{e}n\text{-}tur \quad [1344;\ 1066]$$

(the figures indicate the numbers of notes per syllable) would represent the normal or, at least, the ideal treatment in Gregorian chant, in opposition to the modern treatment in which the greater number of notes would be given to the accented syllable. Numerous examples are given in order to demonstrate "la brièveté de l'accent et aussi la durée de la dernière syllabe" (the shortness of the accent and also the length of the last syllable; *Pal. mus.*, VII, 225). Naturally, Mocquereau is not unaware of the fact that there exist many examples that do not conform with this principle, but these he considers as legitimate exceptions.

Considered aesthetically, Mocquereau's thesis is, no doubt, very attractive. The method of making the accented syllable short, the weak syllable long, results in a fine balance between the force of stress and the force of duration, a balance that is perhaps superior to the modern treatment in which one force adds its weight to the other. However, in spite of the numerous examples which Mocquereau adduces, his thesis cannot be maintained, because of the equally large, if not even larger number of examples showing the opposite treatment or indicating an attitude of indifference. Gastoué in his *Les Origines du chant Romain* (p. 177, fn.) pointed out that the axiom proposed by Mocquereau is just as wrong as the opposite axiom which had been suggested by others, and that actually the Gregorian musicians followed the procedure that seemed best to them, sometimes the one, sometimes the other. The same view is held by Ferretti who emphasizes the "indifférence à la quantité" of the Gregorian accent (*Esthé-*

tique, p. 24) and, at the end of the book, devotes an entire chapter to the refutation of differing views proffered by Dom Jeannin and others (pp. 333ff).

It appears that practically every possible theory regarding the melismatic accent has been championed by one scholar or another, some claiming it to be a positive force (melismas preferably on accented syllables), others emphasizing the negative or balancing role of the melismas (preferably on non-accented syllables), and yet others maintaining that there is complete indifference in this matter. Naturally, it is very easy to support each of these views by a great number of examples. Considering the fact that the texts of the Gregorian chants contain perhaps between 40,000 and 50,000 words with an accent, it is not surprising that a hundred or more examples can easily be adduced to support any one of these theories—a remark which also applies to other theories to be considered later. Such examples, impressive though they often look if gathered together on a couple of pages,[15] prove nothing, since it is just as easy to present an equally impressive list of examples supporting the opposite view. Much though we personally dislike statistical surveys, they are, in cases like these, the only method through which such questions can be decided and an objective picture can be obtained.

The natural basis for such a survey are the five standard chants of the Mass, the Antiphons being unsuitable because of their essentially syllabic character which practically excludes larger groups of notes, whether on accented or on unaccented syllables. In fact, even in the Mass chants it seems advisable to disregard the smallest groups—of two or three notes—because of their omnipresence and because of the almost negligible effect they produce. The difference between:

$$\overset{3}{D\acute{o}}\text{-}\overset{2}{mi}\text{-}\overset{1}{ne} \quad \text{and} \quad \overset{2}{D\acute{o}}\text{-}\overset{3}{mi}\text{-}\overset{1}{ne}$$

(the figures stand for number of notes per syllable) is so slight that to insist on it would be rather too pedantic.[16] The following study, therefore, is based on the examination of groups of four or more notes (per syllable), the question being what relationship there is between these groups and the textual accents in the chants of the above-named categories. As is customary and necessary in all studies dealing with the Latin accent, monosyllabic words such as *et, cum, te,* are excluded, because they have no accent in the proper sense of the term, and the presence of only one group (or one single note) precludes that comparison with neighboring groups

---

[15] See, e.g., *Nombre,* II, 215ff; *Esthétique,* p. 340ff.

[16] It can, however, be definitely stated that the inclusion of these groups would in no way change the final result.

which, of course, is basic in problems involving questions as to "larger or smaller" and "higher or lower." In any case, monosyllabic words are too rare in Latin to change the outcome one way or another. There remains the large number of words with two or more syllables, and these, considered from the present point of view, will fall into the following categories:

1. Positive: The accented syllable has four or more notes, and each unaccented syllable has fewer notes than the accented syllable. Examples:

4 1 2   4 6 3   5 3   5 3 9 4
Dó- mi- ne; ex- aú- di; súm- mo; e- ru- bés- cit.

2. Negative: An unaccented syllable has four or more notes, and the accented syllable has fewer notes than the unaccented syllable. Examples:

3 4 2   5 1 5   6 9   3 7 5 2
Dó- mi- ne; ex- aú- di; súm- mo; e- ru- bés- cit.

3. Indifferent: The accented syllable has four or more notes, but an unaccented syllable has the same number of notes. Examples:

6 2 6   3 4 4   6 6   5 1 5 3
Dó- mi- ne; ex- aú- di; súm- mo; e- ru- bés- cit.

In the practical application of this system we have considered only those words as positive or negative in which the numerical preponderance on the accented or unaccented syllable is sufficiently large to constitute an obvious and indisputable case. While a four-note group has more weight than one or two notes, it would be foolish to insist that a group of twelve notes has more weight than one of eleven or ten. Such cases (which are not frequent) have been considered as indifferent rather than positive or negative.

Another point that needs to be discussed here briefly concerns the final melismas which almost regularly occur over the last syllable of Graduals, Alleluias, and Tracts, occasionally also of Offertories. Since words with an accent on the last syllable do not exist in the Latin language, these final melismas invariably fall on a weak syllable. To include such cases among the "negative" count would obviously be unfair since we are here in the presence of a general principle deriving its authority from a different realm of thought. This statement applies to the final melismas not only of the complete chant but also of its basic sections, such as the responds of a Gradual (immediately before the verse) or the different verses of a Tract. In the latter chants the principle of the final melisma is even more fully present, since each verse falls into smaller units most of which close with a melisma (see pp. 315ff). Therefore, it seems best to exclude the Tracts from the study of the melismatic accent. It is also advisable to disregard Hebrew words such as *Joseph, Jacob, Cherubim, Jerusalem,* since their accentuation is ambiguous. This is particularly true of the word *alleluia,* whose accent may fall on its second or third syllable. Although the Solesmes books always give the word as *allelúia,* the melodies often suggest *alléluia* as the intended pronunciation, as, for example, in the Alleluias *Repleti* [1545], *Potestas* [1711], *Posuisti* [1148], *Veni Sancte Spiritus* [880], *Amavit* [1191], *Exivi* [831], etc.[17] At any rate, no end is served if this controversial point is permitted to enter into the discussion of the melismatic accent.

Turning to an examination of the Mass chants with these premises in mind, we should like to start with a concrete example in order to demonstrate the application of the principles outlined above. The first Mass chant of the liturgical year, the Introit *Ad te levavi* [318] gives the following result:

Positive:
$$\overset{4}{me}\text{-}\overset{2}{us;}\ \overset{1}{con}\text{-}\overset{4}{fi}\text{-}\overset{2}{do;}\ \overset{1}{in}\text{-}\overset{1}{i}\text{-}\overset{4}{mi}\text{-}\overset{2}{ci;}\ \overset{1}{u}\text{-}\overset{1}{ni}\text{-}\overset{4}{ver}\text{-}\overset{1}{si;}\ \overset{3}{ex}\text{-}\overset{4}{pec}\text{-}\overset{3}{tant}$$

Negative:
$$\overset{2}{e}\text{-}\overset{4}{ru}\text{-}\overset{3}{bes}\text{-}\overset{1}{cam;}\ \overset{1}{ne}\text{-}\overset{7}{que;}\ \overset{1}{con}\text{-}\overset{4}{fun}\text{-}\overset{3}{den}\text{-}\overset{1}{tur}$$

Indifferent:
$$\overset{1}{ir}\text{-}\overset{3}{ri}\text{-}\overset{2}{de}\text{-}\overset{3}{ant}$$

Final score: 5 positive; 3 negative; 1 indifferent.

Proceeding now to investigations on a larger scale, the following table shows the result of a count based on twelve successive Mass chants, beginning with those of Christmas Eve:

Introits	POS.	NEG.	IND.	Alleluias	POS.	NEG.	IND.
Hodie scietis	2	2	0	*Crastina die*	0	3	0
Dominus dixit	3	1	0	*Dominus dixit*	3	1	0
Lux fulgebit	7	2	0	*Dominus regnavit*	4	2	1
Puer natus	7	1	0	*Dies sanctificatus*	3	4	0
Etenim sederunt	6	1	0	*Video caelos*	4	1	1
Ex ore	2	1	1	*Hic est*	3	1	0
Dum medium	4	6	0	*Laudate pueri*	2	2	0
Gaudeamus	4	3	0	*Ego sum*	6	1	0
In nomine	5	0	1	*Multifarie*	6	2	0
Ecce advenit	4	2	0	*Laudem Domini*	6	2	0
Exsultet gaudio	4	0	2	*Exaltabo te*	3	3	1
In excelso	5	3	0	*Vidimus stellam*	3	2	1
	53	22	4		43	24	4

17 See the table in Ferretti, p. 344.

Graduals

Hodie scietis	3	4	2
Tecum principium	8	6	2
Benedictus	2	4	1
Viderunt	7	6	1
Sederunt	3	4	0
Exiit sermo	3	4	0
Anima nostra	3	4	1
Speciosus	8	6	4
Salvos fac	6	9	2
Omnes de Saba	7	2	0
Unam petii	5	3	1
Benedictus	3	5	3
	58	57	17

Offertories

Tollite portas	7	0	1
Laetentur	4	1	3
Deus enim	5	2	1
Tui sunt	8	1	2
Elegerunt	8	8	0
Anima nostra	3	4	1
Posuisti	7	0	1
Confitebor	11	0	1
Reges Tharsis	9	3	1
Tulerunt	3	0	3
Jubilate	12	6	0
Jubilate	13	3	0
	90	28	14

Communions

Revelabitur	3	1	2
In splendoribus	1	1	1
Exsulta filia	4	0	0
Viderunt omnes	2	1	0
Video caelos	3	1	0
Exiit sermo	1	3	0
Vox in Rama	2	1	0
Tolle puerum	2	2	1
Ego sum	3	1	0
Omnes gentes	7	2	1
Vidimus stellam	0	3	0
Descendit Jesus	2	0	1
	30	16	6

Although the basis of this tabulation is too small to give definite results, it nevertheless clearly reveals certain tendencies. It appears that in the Introits, Alleluias, Offertories, and Communions the number of melismatically accented words is far greater than that of the opposite category, and that it always exceeds even the number of the negative and indifferent cases combined. In the Graduals, however, we find an essentially different state of affairs, the positive and negative cases being equally numerous, and the indifferent cases taking a considerably larger share of the total than in the other chants. These tendencies are fully confirmed by investigations carried out on a larger scale, as appears from the following table, based on the Mass chants from Advent to the end of Paschal Time (Whit Sunday):[18]

[18] We claim no absolute correctness for these figures (or for those presented in similar tabulations). Slightly different figures will probably be obtained by whoever may wish to check them. These will not, however, affect the result and the correctness of our conclusions.

	POS.	NEG.	IND.
Introits	146	75	20
Graduals	158	165	53
Alleluias	110	59	8
Offertories	240	108	47
Communions	91	57	9

Is there a deeper reason for the strikingly similar behavior of the Introits, Alleluias, Offertories, and Communions, and, on the other hand, for the no less strikingly different situation encountered in the Graduals? Perhaps it is to be found in the fact that the Gradual is the only truly and originally responsorial type of chant in our group. The Alleluia verses are of a later date, and this may account for their greater attentiveness to melismatic accentuation. The Offertories were originally Antiphons, and although they acquired a style similar to that of the Responsories, it would appear that this change did not destroy the tendency toward melismatic accent which seems to have been a characteristic trait of the antiphonal chants; whereas in the responsorial types purely musical considerations, inevitably leading to a greater negligence of textual requirements, were permitted to prevail.

This view is fully confirmed by a study of the only other type of truly responsorial chants, the Responsories of Matins, as appears from the following tabulation of the eight Responsories of Nativity:[19]

	POS.	NEG.	IND.
Responsories			
Hodie . . . caelorum	8	6	1
Hodie . . . de caelo	4	1	2
Quem vidistis	4	5	1
O magnum	3	3	6
Beata Dei	4	3	2
Sancta et immaculata	1	3	3
Beata viscera	3	8	4
Verbum caro	5	3	1
	32	32	20

We may sum up the preceding investigations by saying that Mocquereau's thesis of the "brièveté de l'accent" as a governing principle of chant is entirely without foundation, and that the more recent theory of "indifference," proposed by Gastoué and Ferretti, is correct for the responsorial chants (probably also the Tracts), while the other chants, considered as a whole, show a decided preference for the melismatic accent.

[19] The figures refer to the responds, not to the verses, most of which are standard tones and, moreover, subject to the principle of cursive terminations in which the accent is disregarded.

We cannot leave this subject without emphasizing once more that the statistical method employed is not of our own choosing, but has been forced upon us as the only means of correcting misleading statements made by others. However, our tabulation of the Mass chants from Nativity to Epiphany [pp. 284f] will be useful for a more important purpose too, that is, to form an impression about individual chants or characteristic groups of chants. Most of these include melismatically accented words side by side with others in which the melisma falls on unaccented syllables, usually the former in a greater number than the latter, except in the Graduals and Responsories where they appear with equal frequency. Chants showing a near-perfect score of melismatic accents occur primarily (in fact, almost exclusively) among the Offertories and Alleluias. Our list contains three particularly impressive examples of the first group, that is, the Offertories *Tollite portas* [362], *Posuisti* [438], and *Confitebor tibi* [448; originally for Passion Sunday, 572], to which we may add *Domine exaudi* [620], *Angelus Domini* [787], *In die solemnitatis* [798], and others.[20] As for the Alleluias, those contained in our list do not give a correct impression of the general picture. Actually, there are a great number of Alleluias in which nearly every accent is adorned with a melisma, often of considerable extension; e.g., *Ostende nobis* [320], *Laetatus sum* [329], *Video caelos* [416], *Angelus Domini* [786], *Ego sum pastor* [818], *Exivi* [831], *Deus qui sedes* [1000], *Domine refugium* [1034], *Quoniam deus* [1042], *Cantate Domino* [1045], *Qui timent* [1072], *Justi epulentur* [1168], *Adorabo* [1251], *Benedicat vobis* [1290], *Diffusa est gratia* [1323], *Qui ad justitiam* [1467], *Candor est* [1586], and many others. It is a well-known fact that the Alleluias, even those of the *Temporale*, belong to a later stratum of Gregorian chant than the Graduals, Responsories, Introits, and Communions. All the evidence gathered in the preceding pages seems to combine into an evolutionary picture starting with a phase of complete indifference toward the melismatic accent (Graduals, Responsories, Tracts), proceeding to one of preference (Introits, Communions), and leading to one of unmistakable emphasis (Offertories, Alleluias).

The negative or indifferent attitude toward the melismatic accent apparent in many chants of the Gregorian repertory was critically noticed probably as early as *c.* 900. In Chapter 19 of his *Musica Disciplina* Aurelianus of Réomé repeatedly makes remarks which, although not too clear, seem to indicate that he was not satisfied with the manner in which the chants were sung by "ignari cantores" (unexperienced singers), who did not pay sufficient attention to the length or shortness of the syllables. Thus he says that in a dactylic word like *sanguine* the middle syllable should be "correpta" (short), which probably means that it should have only one

---

[20] Several of these Offertories close with the word "Alleluia," which in every case has a melisma on the second syllable, not the third.

note.[21] The details of his explanations are not always clear. However, a remark like the following can hardly be misunderstood: "It is particularly in this tone [Aurelianus speaks about the *authentus tetrardus,* i.e., the seventh mode], oh wise singer, that so many, not being careful and adopting improper usage, lengthen what is short, and shorten what is long."[22]

Indications of a critical attitude toward the treatment of long and short syllables have been found in a Franciscan *Gradual* of the late fourteenth century.[23] Certain it is that in the sixteenth century this aspect of the Gregorian tradition became the center of attention and the point of departure for far-reaching reforms. Blasius Rossetti, author of a *Libellus de rudimentibus musicae,* published in 1529,[24] deals at length with this problem, saying that very frequently a syllable that should be short is made long, which ill agrees with the rules of grammar, and that many abuses of this type could or should be eliminated. He adds, however, that this should not be done in the Responsories, Graduals, and Introits, because in these the grammar is the servant-maid of the music: *hic grammatica ancilla est musicae.* As an example he quotes the Introit *Gaudeamus omnes* [437], in which "the syllable *mi* on *Domino* is textually short, but seems to become long because of the ligature [neume, a-g-a-b♭-a-b♭] above it." Rossetti makes a distinction between the simple chants, such as Antiphons, Hymns, and Sequences (often referred to in the sixteenth century under the common designation of *accentus*) and the ornate chants, Introits, Graduals, etc. (*concentus*), insisting that in the former category the syllables should be correctly treated according to their length and shortness, but at the same time recognizing in the latter group the superiority of purely musical considerations.

This conservative and sensible attitude did not prevail. To the musicians of a later generation, imbued with the humanistic tradition of classical Latinity, the appalling disregard of quantity, of the length and brevity of syllables, appeared as plain "barbarism." They regarded the Gregorian treatment as a violation of "nature," a heritage of the dark middle ages which could not be tolerated in an enlightened era. The reform editions of Gregorian chant, starting with Guidetti's *Directorium chori* of 1582 and culminating with the *Editio Medicaea* of 1614, clearly show evidence of this line of thought. For curiosity's sake we show in Fig. 77 an excerpt (Gradual *Haec dies*) from the *Graduale . . . cum cantu Pauli V. Pont. Max. jussu reformato* of 1896, which is essentially a reprint of the *Editio Medicaea.*

21 Rather than two; cf. *Wagner III,* 268f.

22 *GS,* I, 58b/59a: *Est hoc in tono, o prudens cantor, quod plerique non devitantes* [*errorem?*] *usu improbo consectantes correptiones producunt, et corripiunt productiones.*

23 Cf. *Wagner II,* 482ff, especially 496.

24 Cf. R. P. Molitor, *Die nach-tridentinische Choralreform* (1901), I, 121ff.

FIGURE 77

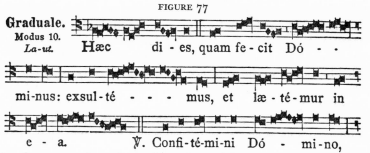

Graduale.
Modus 10.
La-ut. Hæc di - es, quam fe - cit Dó - -
mi-nus: exsul-té - - - mus, et læ - té-mur in
e - a. ℣. Confi-té-mi-ni Dó - mi-no,

In not a few cases the reformed version, although generally tending toward a drastic reduction of the Gregorian melismas, has an even longer group of notes on an accented syllable than the medieval sources, but always at the expense of the "unnatural" melismas on the weak syllables.

It is interesting to note that even such a profound Gregorianist as Wagner felt ill at ease in the presence of the "misplaced" melismas. He says that this procedure (of emphasizing a secondary, rather than the main syllable) "seems to be in contradiction to the congruence of word and tone, which constitutes the supreme law of all vocal music," and that "the modern musician cannot help criticizing the agglomerations of tones on a short syllable following an accented one" [*Formenlehre*, p. 291]. Later [p. 293] he expresses the view that this method is understandable in connection with the "early medieval rhythmic system with its various combinations of long and short values," but "lost all its justification when the groups of tones were performed in even values." It is difficult to see how this change of rhythm (assuming that it took place) could affect the picture. There is no other way of dealing with it than to admit frankly that the "supreme law of vocal music" had no validity, certainly no universal validity, in Gregorian chant; in other words, that here, as in so many cases, the medieval mind simply did not function as we would like. Examples of downright mis-accentuation are not rare even in fifteenth-century polyphonic music, a striking example being the passages "angé-lorúm" (correctly *angelórum*) and "salvé radíx sanctá" (instead of *sálve rádix sáncta*) in one of Dufay's settings of *Ave regina celorum*.[25] In cases like this one cannot help feeling that the seemingly "bad" accentuation is actually a "good" one, dictated by the intention to counteract rather than over-emphasize. Whether the "barbaric" melismas in Gregorian chant result from such an intention or from plain indifference, it is impossible to say.

THE TONIC ACCENT

We shall now turn to a consideration of the second method of musical accentuation, the so-called tonic accent, that is, emphasis by means of

25 See W. Apel, *The Notation of Polyphonic Music*, p. 118.

higher pitch.[26] This accent has received even greater attention on the part of Gregorianists than the melismatic accent—undoubtedly with justification because it is of considerably more fundamental importance. Nearly the entire third volume of the *Paléographie musicale* (published in 1892) is devoted to a study of the tonic accent, and practically every book dealing with Gregorian chant contains a shorter or longer exposition of its nature and function. Thus, Wagner formulates a "very important law of composition: in the syllabic and semi-syllabic chants the melodic line carefully follows the arses and theses (strong and weak syllables) of the text, and particularly the accented syllable of an important word is made to stand out by a higher tone, a melodic peak" [*Wagner III*, p. 289]. More recently, Ferretti devoted a large segment of his book to a study of this problem, giving it the form of a strict and universal law, applicable to ornate as well as simple chants, though subject to certain exceptions.[27]

In view of such definite and authoritative statements it is hardly necessary to say that we are indeed in the presence of a very basic principle, verifications of which can be found on any page of the *Liber usualis*. We could even let the matter rest here, were it not for the fact that both Wagner and, especially, Ferretti have formulated this principle in such a way as to create an impression which is not in agreement with the actual state of affairs. Particularly the use of the term "law" (Wagner: *Kompositionsgesetz;* Ferretti: *la loi de l'accent*) is misleading, because there are simply too many cases that do not agree with the "law," even if we admit exceptions resulting from the superior force of other laws, such as have been formulated by Ferretti.

First of all we will have to define the exact meaning of tonic accent. This is not as easy as it seems to be at first glance. No doubt it involves a higher pitch on the accented syllable, but higher than what? Higher than the pitch of the preceding syllable, of the subsequent syllable, or of both? What if the preceding or the subsequent syllable shows the same pitch as the accented syllable? And which criterion shall we use if some or all of the syllables to be considered carry a group of notes, so that the accented syllable is sung to different pitches, some lower and some higher than those in the neighboring groups? This last question is so involved that we had better exclude it from our investigations or, rather, postpone it for later consideration [see pp. 296f]. This means restricting the present investigation to syllabic chants, especially the Antiphons. Naturally there is no reason to exclude examples involving short groups of notes (neumatic

[26] The term "tonic accent" is employed exclusively with reference to the music, not as a term of prosody (e.g., "l'accent tonique latin").

[27] *Esthétique*, pp. 14-38. Partly translated in Reese, *Music in the Middle Ages*, pp. 166ff. Mocquereau deals with the tonic accent *(acuité de l'accent)* in *Nombre*, II, 161ff.

style), provided that they present a clear-cut situation. Thus, if we consider a-f as an example of tonic accent, examples such as ag-f, a-gf, or gag-fe
obviously fall under the same category.

Ferretti's explanations as to what constitutes a tonic accent are not entirely clear and unambiguous. His initial statement is that "the accented
syllable of each word is nearly always relatively higher than the weak syllable that follows, and often even higher than the preceding one,"[28] to
which he adds a footnote saying that "strictly speaking, it is not necessary
that the accented syllable should be higher than the *preceding* one." Later,
however, referring to a great number of examples given previously, he
remarks that in the great majority of the cases "the Latin accent is brought
out in an *absolute* manner, in the sense that the accented syllable is nearly
always higher than the syllable or syllables which precede or those which
follow" (p. 17.) Finally, he indicates three types of motion in which the
Latin accent has "only a relative, not an absolute value": (1) if the preceding note is in unison and the subsequent note lower; (2) if the preceding
note is lower and the subsequent in unison; (3) if the preceding note is
higher and the subsequent note lower (pp. 18f).

On the basis of these statements it is not easy to form a clear idea as
to what constitutes a tonic accent, and in which case this is "absolute" or
"relative." If the musical pitch of an accented syllable is considered in
relation to the pitches of both the preceding and the subsequent syllables,
it appears that nine types of motion are possible, which can be diagrammed
as follows:

FIGURE 78

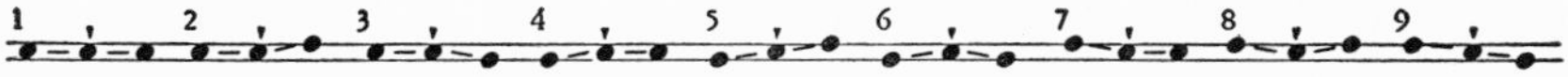

As far as I can make out, Ferretti's explanations would mean that a tonic
accent exists:

according to p. 15: in cases 3, 6, 9
according to p. 17: in cases 3, 4, 5, 6, 9 } absolute
according to p. 18: in cases 3, 4, 9   relative

Naturally no valid investigation or profitable discussion can proceed from
such uncertain premises.

Actually, the Latin word—which is the very basis of all these investigations—provides an entirely accurate and, at the same time, the only valid
definition of the tonic accent. Since, without exception, all Latin words

28 *Esthétique*, p. 15. Reese, in his translation (p. 166) says "higher than the one that
precedes it." Probably this is only due to an oversight, since otherwise he follows Ferretti
closely.

(of more than one syllable) have the accent on a syllable followed by one or two weak syllables, a tonic accent (in the musical sense of the word) exists only if the accented syllable is higher in pitch than the subsequent weak syllables or, at least, than the first of these. In other words, only cases 3, 6, and 9 of the above diagram constitute a tonic accent. Cases 4 and 5, in which the accented syllable is higher than the preceding one, in no way agree with, or reflect the Latin accent. To include them under the rubric of tonic accent is no more than wishful thinking. This would be different, for instance, in the English language, in which many words end on the accented syllable. For a word like "below" a melodic motion rising up to the accented syllable would constitute a tonic accent. In Latin, where this kind of accentuation does not exist, melodic motion descending from the pitch of the accented syllable is the only condition under which a tonic accent can be said to exist. Briefly, tonic accent is predicated upon what follows, not on what precedes.

Before we turn to an examination of the tonic accent as just defined, we must mention what Ferretti calls the "exceptions à la loi de l'accent" (p. 25), that is, formative principles of a higher order which prevent the tonic accent from functioning. Ferretti's explanations can be summed up as follows:[29]

1. Certain types of chant are to be disregarded, namely: (a) the psalm tones (also introit tones and, of course, the simple recitation tones) because they are based on the principle of monotone recitation; (b) chants of a later date, such as hymns, sequences, tropes, because they were written at a time when the rules of Latin prosody were carelessly treated; (c) late adaptations of new texts which were underlaid without regard to the original principles.

2. Cadences are subject to special laws which often overrule the application of the tonic accent. This is particularly the case in cadences closing with one or two notes of the same pitch, e.g., e-d-d or f-d-d-d (e.g., "cor mé-um" [690], or "dicit Dó-mi-nus" [494]).[30]

3. Another exception results from the "phrase accent" (accent phraséologique), that is, an accent formed by the melodic peak of a phrase and coinciding with an important word. If, as is often the case, this peak is

[29] See the summary in Reese, p. 167, where, however, cases nos. 2 and 4 of our summary are omitted.

[30] A much more important source of exceptions are the cursive terminations of the tones for the Introits and Responsories [see pp. 231, 238], in which the five last syllables are underlaid without regard to the position of the accent. It is one of the many indications of Mocquereau's unscholarly methods that he presents even these cursive terminations in such a manner as to make them appear (at least, for the credulous reader) as evidence in favor of his theories. See Nombre, II, 193, where the termination of the fourth responsorial tone is given with eight texts, all (except one) of the same textual structure, /../.

reached in a straight ascending motion, the tonic accent cannot be observed in the corresponding words. An example, cited by Ferretti, is the phrase "et cól-les flú-unt" from the Antiphon *In illa die* [323], sung to the melody f-g-a-c′-g, i.e., without tonic accent on "cól-." Another example is the phrase "et mág-no Ré-gi" from the Antiphon *Stella ista* [464].[31]

4. Another exceptional case is presented by the "dédoublement de podatus d'accent." This occurs in Antiphons of a given melodic type, a *podatus* placed on one syllable being split into two separate notes in order to accommodate two syllables in a different text. An example is found in the Antiphons *Videntes stellam Mági* [481] and *Dixit Dóminus* [252], in which $\overset{de\ \ d}{Má\text{-}gi}$ is transformed into $\overset{d\ \ e\ \ d}{Dó\text{-}mi\text{-}nus,}$ with the result that the tonic accent of the former disappears in the latter.

5. Defective accentuation may be caused by erroneous versions of a later date in which there is a tendency to replace certain pitches by higher ones, e.g., the e by f, and the b by c′. As an example Ferretti cites the Introit *Domine ne longe* [590], saying that the original version was not $\overset{bc′\ \ c′}{defensi\text{-}o\text{-}nem}$ but $\overset{bc′\ \ b}{defensi\text{-}o\text{-}nem,}$ in conformity with the principle of the tonic accent.

If we examine these exceptions objectively, those given under nos. 1 and 2 can readily be accepted as legitimate principles of a higher order. No. 5 is somewhat suspect, because it involves a surmise which cannot always be proved. However, examples of this type are relatively rare.

It is more difficult to accept the cases given under nos. 3 and 4 as legitimate exceptions. Ferretti's "phrase accent," being predicated upon two such rather uncertain factors as "phrase" and "important word," is one of those modern concepts that are very difficult to grasp with any degree of certitude. Nor is it easy to see why the cases falling under this category should be admitted as legitimate exceptions of the principle of the tonic accent. The "loi supérieure" involved here is entirely of Ferretti's making. In the same way, any case where the tonic accent is disregarded could be explained as the result of some superior law, if only the "superior law of the composer's freedom to choose what he considers best." The fact that accented syllables do occur in a straight ascending motion simply show that here, as in many other instances, the tonic accent is disregarded, not because of the presence of a higher law, but simply because it does not represent a law of such universal validity as some writers would have us believe.

The same remark applies to the exception no. 4. The very ease and fre-

---

31 It will be noticed that, from Ferretti's point of view, these cases actually need not be listed as exceptions, since they all represent the motion type no. 5 of our diagram on p. 291, which Ferretti regards as a tonic accent, even an "absolute" one. They do not, however, fall under our definition of the tonic accent.

quency with which a tonic-accent formula is transformed into one without tonic accent only shows one of two things: either that "poor adaptations of a new text" occur even in the old repertory of Gregorian chant, or that, once more, the principle of the tonic accent was not considered as vitally important. After all, the composer of *Dixit Dominus* was under no compulsion to "split the *podatus*." He could easily have inserted an extra note for the additional syllable, e.g., $\overset{\text{de}}{D}o\text{-}\overset{\text{d}}{mi}\text{-}\overset{\text{d}}{nus}$, as is done a thousand times in Gregorian chant. If he preferred to split the *podatus*, we can only conclude that the law of the tonic accent was to him of no supreme importance. Finally, Ferretti's argument is predicated on the assumption that *Videntes stellam* is the model, *Dixit Dominus* the adaptation, an assumption for which, of course, there is neither proof nor basis. If a decision of priority can be made at all, it would certainly be in favor of *Dixit Dominus*, because of its psalmodic text derived from the Psalm which it enframes.

On the basis of these explanations, we shall now turn to an examination of the Gregorian repertory in an attempt to determine the extent to which the tonic accent influences the formation of the melodic line.[32] Because of the difficulties of definition that arise in the case of melismatic chants [see p. 290], the Antiphons represent the natural basis for such an investigation. The following study is based on the Proper of the Time from Advent to the end of the Nativity [317-414], undoubtedly one of the earliest portions of the Gregorian repertory. This includes fifty-eight Antiphons (the Great Antiphons for the week before Christmas [340ff] have been omitted because they are all adapted to the same melody) with close to five hundred instances of accented words (i.e., words of more than one syllable), certainly a sufficiently comprehensive material for a valid investigation. Only two or three of these Antiphons can be said to be perfect examples for the use of the tonic accent, for instance the following:

FIGURE 79

Omnes si-ti-én-tes, vení-te ad áquas : quaéri-te Dómi-num,

dum v5 invení-ri pótest, alle-lú-ia.

or the Antiphon *Gloria in excelsis* [402], the latter with the exception of the "alleluia," one of the several Hebrew words whose accentuation (allelúia or alléluia?) is doubtful. The great majority contain one or two words for which the tonic accent is not present in the melody, and in some of them the negative cases actually outnumber the positive ones. Particularly striking in this respect are the Antiphons *Quem vidistis* [395] from Lauds of the Nativity, and *Crastina die* [363] from Sext of Christmas Eve, the second of which is shown in Fig. 80 (plus, minus, and zero signs indicate positive, negative, and indifferent cases):

FIGURE 80

In order to clarify the over-all picture, there follows a tabulation based on the entire group of Antiphons from Advent to the end of the Nativity. The legitimate exceptions mentioned previously have been disregarded, and the remaining cases are grouped under three rubrics: (a) positive, i.e., accented syllable higher than the following; (b) negative, i.e., accented syllable lower than the following; and (c) indifferent, i.e., accented syllable on the same pitch as the following:

	POSITIVE	NEGATIVE	INDIFFERENT
Number:	259	114	84
Percentage:	57	25	18

These figures throw a clear light upon the question of the importance of the tonic accent as a formative principle of Gregorian chant. The extent of its validity depends, in no small degree, upon the evaluation of the "indifferent" group. If, as Ferretti does in a tabulation of a similar kind,[33] these cases are reckoned on the side of the positive ones, the result is favorable to the extent of three-fourths of the total. If not, the balance is reduced to slightly over one half, and this seems to be the correct attitude in our question. After all, the point at issue is to demonstrate the importance of the tonic accent, not the unimportance of the "non-tonic accent" (*sit venia verbo*).[34] In a way, the indifferent cases indicate an "indiffer-

[33] *Esthétique*, p. 26. This tabulation is based on the same premises as ours (Antiphons from Advent to Christmas; tonic accent *a parte post*), but is limited to *proparoxytones* (words having the accent on the antepenult).

[34] To put it differently: it is correct to say (as Ferretti does) that only the negative cases constitute a real exception of the law; but it is incorrect to say (or imply, as Ferretti does also) that all the others represent a proof of it.

ence," a disregard of the tonic accent even more clearly than the negative cases, because in nearly all of them it would have been very easy to bring about a positive result by raising or lowering a single pitch by no more than one degree, e.g.:

$$
\begin{array}{lll}
& \text{g g g} & \text{g a g} \quad\quad \text{g g f} \\
\textit{In illa die} \ [323]: & \textit{stillábunt} \ \text{change to} \ \textit{stillábunt} \ \text{or} \ \textit{stillábunt}
\end{array}
$$

$$
\begin{array}{lll}
& \text{g g gfd} & \text{a g gfd} \quad \text{g f gfd} \\
\textit{Ne timeas} \ [326]: & \textit{fí- li- um} \ \text{change to} \ \textit{fí- li- um} \ \text{or} \ \textit{fí- li- um}
\end{array}
$$

The purpose of this study is not to assign to the tonic accent a statistical figure, but to present a picture of its role in Gregorian chant. That this role is important, nobody will deny; but it is equally undeniable that this role does not amount to a law, however hedged in by exceptions. True enough, we have not admitted all the exceptions which Ferretti considers legitimate and admissible. It may be noticed, however, that it is not difficult to find, even in our limited group of Antiphons, a considerable number of negative examples that are not covered by any of the exceptions admitted by Ferretti:

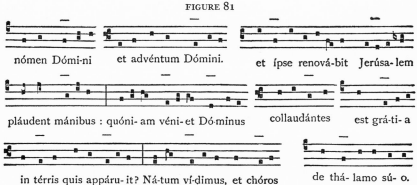

FIGURE 81

nómen Dómi-ni   et advéntum Dómini.   et ípse renová-bit Jerúsa-lem

pláudent mánibus : quóni- am véni-et Dó·minus   collaudántes   est grá-ti- a

in térris quis appáru- it? Ná-tum ví-dimus, et chóros   de thá- lamo sú- o.

See, in this order, *L* pp. 317, 339, 324, 332, 396, 373, 395, 372.

If, finally, we try to subject the more elaborate chants, such as Introits, Graduals, Alleluias, Offertories, Responsories, to a similar study, a serious obstacle arises because of the difficulty of obtaining a clear definition as to when a tonic accent is present in the case of groups of notes. If, for instance, in the following example (Fig. 82; from the Gradual *Clamaverunt*):

FIGURE 82

liberá- vit

the peak notes of the groups are considered, we have a negative case. If, on the other hand, the initial notes of the groups, or (to suggest another approach) the motion leading from one group to the next is taken into account, it is a positive example. Ferretti does not offer any explanations on this point, but merely reproduces the Offertory *Jubilate Deo* [486] as an impressive example of the tonic accent in the "style fleuri," which, in a way, it is.[35] In fact, the difficulty of finding a clear and unequivocal definition of the tonic accent in florid chants makes a systematic study comparable to the one we have given for the Antiphons all but impossible. Since unmistakable and often very impressive examples of tonic accent can be found on nearly every page, we shall limit ourselves to a selected list of negative cases, only in order to make clear that the "law" has its limitations in the neumatic and melismatic chants as well as in Antiphons (reference to *L* by pages and staves):

> 328,5: *decoris;* 330,4: *misericordiam;* 345,5: *occursus;* 351,2: *deducis;* 356,2: *vocabitur;* 375,1: *caelorum;* 375,2: *dignatus;* 375,5: *apparuit;* 377,4: *vidistis;* 377,5: *apparuit;* 384,1: *virginitas;* 384,2: *efferam;* 384,4: *mulieribus;* 384,5: *fructus;* 384,5: *ventris.*[36]

I may add, however, that from the study of numerous chants of the florid type I have gained the impression that clearly negative cases are, on the whole, less frequent here than in the Antiphons. This result (if confirmed by a detailed investigation) would contradict the opinion of Wagner who, it will be remembered, singled out the syllabic and semi-syllabic chants for their attention to the tonic accent.

THE CURSUS

The *cursus* is an oratorical principle of Latin antiquity designed to confer upon prose a certain feeling of the harmonious relationships that govern poetry. This was done by giving careful attention to the end of sentences, which had to comply with certain rules of rhythm, rules that are fully explained by Cicero (*De oratore,* 107 B.C.) and Quintilian (*Institutiones oratoricae,* A.D. 42). Since Latin poetry was based on the principle of quantity (or meter), that is, of long and short syllables [see p. 277], this also forms the basis of the *cursus* of Latin antiquity or, as it is called,

35 Reproduced (from Ferretti, pp. 16f.) in Reese, p. 166. I am not certain whether the asterisks that appear over each accented syllable are also meant to convey the impression that each of these syllables has a tonic accent. Even from a very liberal point of view it is difficult to find a tonic accent on "timétis" and on "Dóminus."

36 The reader's attention is called to the tables in Ferretti, pp. 340f, showing numerous settings of the words *Déus, Dóminus, Miserére,* and others, examples intended to prove the indifference of the chant in regard to the melismatic accent. Actually, they also demonstrate (against Ferretti's intention) the indifference in regard to the tonic accent. For instance, the group *Dóminus* includes 16 positive, 17 negative, and 19 indifferent examples of tonic accent. See also among the examples pp. 342ff: *oblivisci, continéntur, sitiéntes, sapiéntiae,* etc.

the metrical *cursus*. Various combinations of long and short syllables were considered as proper, the following in particular:

1. *cursus velox* (quick)   glōriăm congrĕgĕntŭr

2. *cursus planus* (even)   mēmbră firmăntŭr

3. *cursus tardus* (slow)   īră victōriae [37]

When, about A.D. 400, the classical principle of quantity was replaced by that of accentuation, a corresponding modification of the *cursus* took place, which changed from the metrical to the rhythmical *cursus*.[38] The corresponding forms are:

1. *cursus velox*   glóriam congrégéntur

2. *cursus planus*   mémbra firmántur

3. *cursus tardus*   ira victóriae

In an extended study, comprising the major part of vol. IV of the *Paléographie musicale*, Mocquereau has tried to show that the rhythmical *cursus*, particularly the form of the *cursus planus*, plays an important role in the formation of the cadential formulae of Gregorian chant in such a way that the accented members of the group are sung to a higher pitch, that is, receive a tonic accent. As he is wont to do, he adduces a wealth of material in support of this theory, material which, however, is often irrelevant and even, if properly evaluated, in contradiction with his theory. Actually, he proves nothing but the fact that, among the thousands of cases there are many hundreds that conform to the principle. As an illustration of his argumentation, we cite here three examples of what he calls *cadence plana*:[39]

FIGURE 83

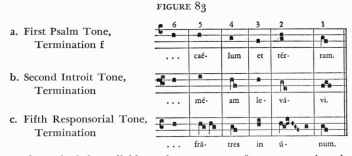

a. First Psalm Tone, Termination f

b. Second Introit Tone, Termination

c. Fifth Responsorial Tone, Termination

[37] It may be noticed that syllables such as *-am, con-, firm-*, etc., are long by position, the vowel being followed by two or more consonants.

[38] According to the investigations of the monks of Solesmes, evidence of the rhythmical *cursus* exists in the Papal Bulls from *c.* 450 to 600, while the Leonine and Gelasian Sacramentaries show the use of the metrical *cursus*.

[39] *Nombre*, II, 190, 191, 194.

To this we remark the following:

a. Considered from the purely musical point of view, this could be called a *cadence plana* because its peak tones fall on the fifth and on the second syllable from the end, in conformity with the position of the two accents in the *cursus planus*. It would provide a strong argument in favor of the *cursus* theory if it were used only, or mainly, in connection with texts closing with a *cursus planus*, e.g., *pédum tuórum, (inimi)córum tuórum, térra multórum, (Spi)rítui sáncto,* all of which occur in Ps. 109 [128].[40] However, the same termination formula is also used for the other verses of the same psalm (as well as many other psalms), all of which close with a different "cursus," e.g. *déxtris méis, génui te, súae réges, exaltábit cáput,* not to mention the ubiquitous *(saecu)lórum. Amen* which, because of the Hebrew word, presents an ambivalent case. In all these verses, the accentual structure of the text is in disagreement with the tonic-accent scheme of the musical formula, and agreement is reached only by modifying this scheme, placing the accent on the fourth rather than on the fifth note from the end, or inserting a note between the penultimate and the final member (for dactylic endings, as in *nómen Dómini*). In short, it seems to us that this cadential formula can only with reservation be considered as evidence for the *cursus* theory.

b. This formula shows a design similar to the previous one, that is, with higher pitches on the fifth and the second syllable from the end. However, it could also, and, in fact, more properly, be considered as one emphasizing the fifth and the third syllable, because it is the third rather than the second member that shows a melodic peak. Apparently, the formula can be interpreted in two ways, only one of which would make it a *cadence plana*. Do the texts, with which this formula appears, give a clue as to its meaning? Of course not, since, like all the introit terminations, this is a fixed formula which always receives the five last syllables of the text, regardless of their accentual structure. Thus, we have correct tonic accents with *méam levávi* as well as with *lége Dómini* [1220], but only the former is a *cursus planus*. Moreover, the first tonic accent completely disappears in connection with texts such as *univérsa térra* [428].

c. The remarks just made apply *a fortiori* to the last example, the termination of the fifth responsorial tone which, like the terminations of the introit tones, is a fixed formula in which the textual accents may fall on the members 5 and 2, 5 and 3, 4 and 2, or 6 and 3. Only in the first case do we have a *cursus planus*.

One of the main weaknesses of Mocquereau's demonstration is that he bases it primarily on formulae designed to be used with many texts (*automela,* to borrow a term from Byzantine nomenclature), formulae which,

---

[40] Strictly speaking, *(Spi)rítui sáncto* is not a correct example, since in the true *cursus planus* a new word should begin after the trochee, as in *pédum tuórum.*

whether of the tonic or of the cursive type, are subject to modifications of their accentual structure. A different approach to the *cursus* problem was made by H. Bewerunge and, on a much larger scale, by Ferretti.[41] Both of these studies proceed from the metrical *cursus* of Latin antiquity which is based upon the distinction between long and short syllables. Consequently, the Gregorian melodies are investigated from the point of view of the melismatic accent, as indicated by longer or shorter groups of notes. Bewerunge's material consists of the concluding formulae of Introits (not the introit tones), Communions, and Offertories from the First Sunday of Advent to the Saturday after Passion Sunday. These are all essentially different melodies, each with its own text (*idiomela*), and therefore provide a much more reliable basis of investigation than Mocquereau's tone terminations. However, instead of limiting himself to the few formulae given by Cicero and Quintilian, Bewerunge proceeds from the long list of metrical-*cursus* formations (twenty-four) which the Solesmes monks have found in the Leonine and Gelasian Sacramentaries. Such variety includes practically all the combinations that are arithmetically possible and is therefore confusing rather than clarifying. Nevertheless, the most frequent combination is the *cursus planus,* $- \smile \mid - - \smile$, and this also takes the first place among the "instances resembling forms of metrical cursus" which Bewerunge has found in the melodies. He gives only one example $\overset{2\ \ 1\ 8}{lu\text{-}ce\text{-}at}$ $\overset{6\ 2}{e\text{-}is}$ from the Introit of the Requiem Mass [1807], which, he admits, is not too satisfactory, because only the music suggests, by the number of notes in each of the five members, the scheme long-short long-long-short, while the text has the scheme long-short-short long-short. Moreover, the reservation implied in the word "resembling" makes for additional difficulty. A cursory check of the chants mentioned by Bewerunge brought to light only a few clear examples, nowhere close to the number of 112 which he indicates. A few meet the textual requirement, without, however, meeting the musical requirement, while others meet the latter but not the former.

As for Ferretti's extended study, it is very difficult (at least, for me) to grasp its implications and to summarize its conclusions. He formulates its basic thesis as follows: "The literary *cursus* that has influenced the formulae of the solemn psalmody and the recitatives as well as the cadences of the Antiphons and all the other Gregorian chants is the *metrical,* not the *tonic* [i.e., rhythmic]" [pp. 9f]. His aim seems to be not to demonstrate a relationship between the music and the text but to analyze the musical formulae themselves in terms of metrical feet in such a way that a single note stands for short, a *clivis* or *podatus* for long, a three-note neume

41 H. Bewerunge, "The Metrical Cursus in the Antiphon Melodies" (*Zeitschrift der Internationalen Musikgesellschaft,* XIII, [1910-11], 227); Ferretti, *Il cursu metrico e il ritmo delle melodie gregoriane* (1913).

(*scandicus*) for long-plus-short, a four-note neume for long-plus-long, etc. Thus, the Antiphon *Rex pacificus* [364] shows the following patterns:[42]

$$m\breve{a}gn\breve{i}f\breve{i}c\breve{a}t\breve{u}s\ \bar{e}st$$

$$(vul)t\bar{u}m\ d\breve{e}s\bar{i}d\breve{e}r\bar{a}t$$

$$\bar{u}n\breve{i}v\breve{e}rs\bar{a}\ t\bar{e}rr\bar{a}.$$

In the final chapter of his book [pp. 252ff] Ferretti transcribed some melodies in a manner similar to (though not based on the same premises as) that of some mensuralists (Jeannin), namely in metrical divisions, 2/4, 5/8, 3/8, etc. This, of course, brought him into conflict with the School of Solesmes. According to Gajard, he later renounced his theories: ". . . l'auteur, mieux avisé, reconnut son erreur et se rallia complètement à Solesmes."[43]

EXPRESSION, MOOD, WORD-PAINTING

Is Gregorian chant "expressive"? Yes and no. The answer depends on what is meant by "expressive." If this term is understood as the opposite of "dry," "pedantic," "intellectual," or what others words may be used to suggest "absence of artistic inspiration," the answer is, of course, in the positive. No one will deny that the chants are the product of artistic inspiration, although it is equally undeniable that whatever spiritual, emotional, or even intellectual forces involved in the process of musical creation in the eighth and ninth centuries were not the same as they were in the eighteenth and nineteenth. While Bach, and even more, Beethoven or Schumann bestow upon their compositions expressive values of a markedly personal and individual character, values that often have their origin in the composer's own experience and are as variable as these experiences, the unknown creators of the Gregorian melodies produced works carrying the stamp of supra-personal feelings, of spiritual values predicated upon a hieratic order which exists by its own—or, rather, divine—authority, and which neither needs nor admits justification in terms of personal experience.

Usually, however, the term "expressive" has a different meaning, particularly as applied to vocal music. It refers, not to an intrinsic quality of the music as such, but to its capacity of "expressing something," namely, the general mood of the text or the specific feelings associated with certain words of the text. The question is whether this capacity, so amply demonstrated in the songs of Schubert, Schumann, and Brahms, is also evident in Gregorian chant. My answer is an almost unqualified "no." Deliberate

---

[42] P. 202. The metrical signs refer to the music, not to the text. The dotted single notes (at the end) are considered as long.

[43] *RG,* XXIX, 26.

expression of the text, of its general mood or of single words, is, it seems to me, as contrary to the basic premises of the chant as is expression of personal feelings, if these two categories can be at all clearly separated. With this view, however, I find myself decidedly in the minority. Several of the outstanding Gregorianists as well as many of their "minor brethren" have attributed to certain chants specific expressive values derived from the text or related to the occasion. Thus, Gevaert finds that in the Antiphon *Ecce ancilla Domini: fiat mihi secundum verbum tuum* (Behold the handmaid of the Lord: be it unto me according to thy word; Luke 1:38) "the melodic line, sweetly bowing until the end of the chant, renders with a charming naïvety the profound reverence of the Virgin before the messenger of God."[44] To Frere, the Responsory *Angelus Domini apparuit Joseph* . . . (The angel of the Lord appeared unto Joseph . . . ; Matthew 1:20) "represents the quiet appearance of the angel to Abraham on Mt. Moriah."[45] Gérold sees in the first two melismas of the Tract *Commovisti, Domine, terram, et conturbasti eam* (Thou hast made the earth to tremble; thou hast broken it; Ps. 60:2) "the tendency to express in music the action of the Eternal shaking the earth."[46] Johner feels that in the Communion *Vox in Rama audita est, ploratus et ululatus: Rachel plorans filios suos noluit consolari, quia non sunt* (In Rama was there a voice heard, lamentation, and weeping, and great mourning, Rachel weeping for her children, and would not be comforted, because they are not; Matthew 2:18) "the inception on the fifth of the mode, the emphasis on the dominant and the *pressus* over *ploratus* are expressions of gripping sorrow; they almost sound like a shrill outcry," while at the end "through this harmony [close on d'-b-g] the grief is tempered."[47] Ferretti feels that in the Antiphon *Montes Gelboë* "the melodic line of *Quomodo,* with its descent from the dominant to the tonic, is an excellent rendition of David's stupor upon hearing the horrible news" [of Saul's and Jonathan's death; II Samuel 1:21-23], and that in the Communion *Video caelos* from the Feast of St. Stephen "la retombée mélodique sur *Dei* traduit, pour ainsi dire, la vision extatique du Premier Martyr chrétien, et son tranquille abandon à Dieu."[48]

Nobody will question the right, if not the duty, of Catholic writers to interpret the chants in such a way as to bring them close to the minds and hearts of the faithful. Descriptive explanations designed to achieve this goal have, no doubt, a legitimate place in books of a popularizing nature where, in fact, they are found in great number. If, however, they occur in

---

44 *Mélopée,* p. 153: "La ligne mélodique . . ."

45 *Antiphonale Sarisburiense,* Dissertation, p. 59.

46 *Histoire de la musique des origines à la fin du xive siècle* (1936), p. 213: "Ces deux passages . . ."

47 *The Chants of the Vatican Gradual* (1940), p. 69.

48 *Esthétique,* pp. 99, 97.

scholarly writings such as the above-quoted works (possibly with the exception of Johner's), they adopt the connotation, not of a modern exegesis, but of a historical statement, the implication being that they reflect the thinking of the men who wrote the melodies or, at least, the mentality of the period in which they were written. Assuming that this is what Gevaert, Gérold, Frere, and Ferretti wanted to say, I can only register my opposition against attempts to explain Gregorian chant as the result of mental processes so obviously indicative of nineteenth-century emotionalism, so obviously derived from an acquaintance with the art of Wagner and Brahms. Nor is it difficult to disprove the validity of such explanations by pointing to the basic role which the methods of adaptation and centonization play in so many categories of the chant, the Tracts, Antiphons, Graduals, Responsories, Alleluias, etc.—all of which show numerous examples of the same melody or the same melodic unit being used for a great number of texts of the most diverse contents. Moreover, the reader checking the above-mentioned examples will be probably very much disappointed in his expectations to find in them a suggestion, to say nothing of an unmistakable expression, of "reverence," "quiet appearance," "earth-shaking," "shrill outcry," "tempered grief," or "stupor."

Hardly more convincing are the examples of direct word painting that have been found in the chant. Perhaps the best-known of these occurs in the Communion *Passer invenit* [556] where, to the words *et turtur* (and the turtle-dove) "the cooing of the turtle-dove is imitated through the use of liquescent neumes."[49] Actually the liquescent neumes are the result, not primarily of the imagery of the words, but of their spelling, there being always two consonants after each vowel. Naturally, this purely external fact somewhat lessens the validity of this passage as an example of word painting. Another well-known example exists in the Alleluia *Angelus Domini* [786] from Easter Monday, where the "turning of the stone" (*revolvit lapidem*) is pictured by a revolving figure. The validity of this case is lessened by the fact that the revolving figure is not indicated in the neumatic notation of St. Gall *359* (pp. 141-*161*); obviously it is an innovation of the tenth or eleventh century.

The most likely candidates for word-painting are words suggesting "high" or "low," and it is not too difficult to find cases where the music shows a corresponding design. One of the most convincing examples exists in the Introit *Rorate caeli* [353], in which the melody reaches its highest position to the words *caeli desuper,* its lowest to the word *terra.* Another instance of correspondence occurs in the Alleluia *Angelus Domini* [786], which has a descending figure on *descendit.* Whether these conformities are intentional or the mere result of chance, it is difficult to say. Words suggesting "high" or "low" are so frequent in Gregorian chant that they

49 Reese, *Music in the Middle Ages,* p. 169.

are bound to appear occasionally with musical figures of a corresponding character. Certainly it is not difficult to find examples where they occur in connection with figures of the opposite character, for instance, the word *terrae* in the Communion *Viderunt omnes* [410] from the Nativity, or *terra* in the Offertory *Jubilate Deo* [480].

We should like to close this chapter with a particularly neat demonstration of the pitfalls besetting the realm of expression and word-painting in Gregorian chant. Among the Antiphons of the seventh mode there is a well-defined group characterized by an initial motive g-b-c'-d'-e'-d'. Among the *circa* 50 Antiphons of this group (Gevaert's *Thème* 19) there is one in which the standard motive is modified to extend up to the high g', g-b-c'-d'-e'-g'-d', and this is the Antiphon *Ascendo ad Patrem* [845] from Lauds of the Feast of the Ascension. Certainly this would seem to be as clear an example of deliberate word painting as one might hope to find. Unfortunately, exactly the same extended motive occurs in the Antiphon *Descendi in hortum* assigned in the medieval manuscripts (e.g., Codex Lucca, p. 458) to the Feast of the Assumption. We leave it for the reader to draw his own conclusions.

CHAPTER THREE

The Free Compositions According to Types

Ⅰ N THE present chapter we are concerned with a study somewhat
similar in design and purpose to that of the works of a composer
such as Palestrina, Bach, or Beethoven. Naturally, the very quantity of
material available in Gregorian chant excludes the possibility of considering each piece individually, as would be possible or even mandatory in
the case of the just-mentioned composers. Nor would such a consideration
be of any value, because it would proceed on a wrong premise, namely,
that each work of art has individual significance, a premise that did not
attain unquestioned validity until Beethoven. The sonatas of Mozart, and
even more so the cantatas of Bach, the motets of Palestrina, Josquin, or
Machaut, are primarily representatives of a type and reveal their significance only if considered as such. The further we retrogress in the history
of music, the more does artistic production take on the quasi-anonymous
character of group-creation, until finally the individuality both of the work
and of its creator becomes absorbed into the full anonymity of musical
types. Nowhere in music is this state of affairs so clearly indicated as in
Gregorian chant, where each single composition belongs to a liturgical
class from which it receives the general characteristics of musical form and
style that set it wholly apart from an item belonging to a different class.
In an earlier part of this book we have seen that even within the fairly
limited province of the Gregorian recitative there exist a number of different types—prayer tones, psalm tones, introit tones, etc.—that show
well-defined distinctive traits. Such traits, common to a group, but differing from one group to another, appear even more clearly in the field of
free compositions.

THE INTROITS

By way of general characterization, the Introits can be described as
chants of moderate length and of a moderately ornate style. In both these

respects they are remarkably uniform, considerably more so, for instance, than the Offertories or Communions. It will take some searching to find an Introit less than three lines long (such as *Justus es Domine* [1047] with only slightly over two lines), and practically none occupies more than four staves (we consider, of course, only the Introit proper, not the psalm verse). As for their style, which we have just described as moderately ornate, the Introits represent, no doubt, the most consistent use, in the entire repertory, of the neumatic or group style. In any given Introit, the great majority of syllables carry a group of notes numbering from two to five. Groups of more than five notes occur only exceptionally, mostly in the final cadence; and a group of eleven notes, such as occurs in the cadence of *Dum clamarem* [1020] probably represents the maximum of melismatic ornateness to be found in the Introits.[1]

Interspersed between these groups are single notes, perhaps in an average ratio of one to two (e.g., 21 single notes against 32 groups in *Ad te levavi* [318], and 15 single notes against 30 in *Populus Sion* [327]). Occasionally, such single notes occur in succession over three, four, or five syllables, but practically always on the same pitch, thus introducing a snatch of psalmodic recitative into the melodic motion of the neumes. Single notes forming a melodic line are so rare in the Introits (in contrast to the Antiphons, for example) that a reader familiar with their style definitely feels surprised when he happens upon passages like the following ones:

FIGURE 84

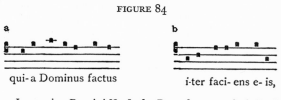

a.   b.

qui- a Dominus factus   i-ter faci- ens e- is,

a. *In nomine Domini* [612]   b. *Deus dum egrederis* [892]

The simplest neumes, that is, those with two or three notes, are of course by far the most frequent. Relatively rare is the *climacus* with its three notes in descending motion, and even more so *climacus* neumes with four notes. On the other hand, many Introits, probably the majority of them, contain a few examples of short *strophici*, usually in the form of the *tristropha* with its triple repercussion. Thus, *Ad te levavi* [318] has four *strophici*, one with four notes (on "neque"); *Veni et ostende* [343] has three *bistrophae*; *Dominus dixit* [392] has five, three of them of the variety

---

1 The entire cadence is borrowed from the Responsories; see p. 310.

involving an ascending third: d-f-f(-f); *Puer natus* [408] has four *tristro-phae,* and *Resurrexi* [778] as many as ten.

The combination of all these elements bestows upon the melodic design of the Introits a general character of gentle and moderate motion, undulating rather than striving, and often held stationary by recitative passages and repercussive groups. Boldly ascending or descending formations, such as are frequently encountered in the Graduals, Alleluias, or Offertories, are practically absent. Formations such as e'-f'-c'-a (*Audivit Dominus* [G 91], on the second "Dominus") and d-g g-c'-a-g (*Ego clamavi* [G 130], on "clamavi"), which in a Gradual or Offertory would hardly be worth noticing, impress one as almost a foreign element in the Introits.

Not a few Introits are striking for the stationary character of their entire melodic line, for their continuous insistence on a given pitch by means of single notes, *strophici,* and neumes emphasizing this pitch. Such Introits give the overall impression of a slightly ornamented recitative. Particularly interesting in this respect are a number of Introits of the second mode, namely, *Veni et ostende* [343], *Dominus dixit* [392], *Ecce advenit* [459], *Sitientes* [565], *Dominus illuminatio* [998], *Dominus fortitudo* [1006], and *Venite adoremus* [1052]. All these are essentially a recitation on f (*Venite* is transposed to the upper fifth), with d as a final, and occasionally touch upon c as a sub-final and g as a flex. Thus their melodic line, reduced to its essentials, is strikingly similar to that of the introit tone of the same mode, as used in the subsequent psalm verse and Doxology.

Additional examples of melodic similarity between Introits and introit tones occur also in other modes:

Mode 3, recitation on c': *Intret oratio* [541]; *Deus dum egrederis* [892]; *Tibi dixit* [G 117]; *In nomine Domini* [612] (= *In nomine Jesu* [446]); *Omnia quae fecisti* [1063]; the last three mainly in their first half.

Mode 5, recitation on c': *Circumdederunt* [497]; *Domine refugium* [G 101]; *Loquebar* [1215, originally for the Feast of St. Prisca; see also 1309, 1618].

Mode 8, recitation on c': *Miserere mihi* [1044]; *Laetabitur justus* [1138, originally from the Feasts of St. Vincent and St. Agapitus]; *Ad te levavi* [318]; *Lux fulgebit* [403]; etc.

Recitation-like Introits also occur in other modes, but with the recitation taking place on a pitch other than that of the tenor of the tone. For instance, there are several Introits of mode 4 which show an unmistakable emphasis, not on the tenor of the fourth tone (a), but on f or, less frequently, on g. One of the most striking examples is the Introit *Resurrexi* [778] from Easter Sunday:

FIGURE 85

Other examples are *Reminiscere* [545], *Judica Domine* [603], *Misericordia* [816], *In voluntate* [1066], and *Sicut oculi* [G 99], the last with a continuous emphasis on g, which very likely was the original tenor note of the fourth tone.

A very interesting state of affairs exists in mode 6. The normal tenor of the various tones (psalm, canticle, etc.) in this mode is a. None of the Introits of the sixth mode shows an unmistakable emphasis on this pitch. The sixth tone for the Introits, however, is exceptional in its having two tenors, a in the first half and f in the second (see p. 233), and there are, in fact, a considerable number of Introits that clearly suggest a recitation on f; for instance, *Quasimodo* [809], *Cantate Domino* [826], *Dicit Dominus: Ego* [1074], *In medio ecclesiae* [1190; originally for the Nativity of St. John], and *Exsultate* [G 368; this is transposed a fifth upward, so that c′ becomes the tonic]. Others, like *Hodie scietis* [359], *Omnes gentes* [1009], *Os justi* [1200; originally for the Feasts of St. Matthew, St. Felix, and others], and *Sacerdotes Dei* [1132; St. Xystus, St. Gregory, and others], show the emphasis on the tonic less consistently, but still with sufficient clarity.

As to the Introits of mode 7, there are several that are suggestive of recitation, but in a rather flexible and irregular manner. Two of them, *Puer natus* [408][2] and *In virtute* [1135], show a rather consistent emphasis on c′, that is, the tone below the normal tenor, d′. *Viri Galilei* [846], *Respice* [1032], and *Ne derelinquas* [G 118] would seem to indicate the presence of two tenors, d′ and c′, a phenomenon reminiscent of the *tonus peregrinus* and of the authentic responsorial tones (see p. 235), all of which employ the fifth as well as the fourth degree of the scale. Finally, there are some Introits in which the pitch f′ appears in a prominent position; for example, *Aqua sapientiae* [789; cf. the passage "potavit . . . flectetur, alleluia"], *Deus in adjutorium* [1027; f′ and c′], and *Ne timeas* [G 521; f′, d′, c′].

Turning finally to the Introits of mode 1, we find a strikingly different

2 Mentioned by Hucbald in his *De harmonica institutione* among the examples of *aequales voces* (i.e., unison); *GS,* I, 104b.

picture because of the almost complete absence of the "recitation type."
The only indisputable example is *Justus ut palma* [1204; originally for
St. Stephen and St. John the Baptist] with its continuous emphasis on f.
However, *Gaudete* [334] and *Exsurge* [504] could perhaps also be included
in this group. Both of them include passages suggesting a melodic stress
on f and on a.

The rather considerable number of Introits having a melody suggestive
of a recitative raises several interesting questions. Is it permissible to consider them as a well-defined and special group not only analytically, but
also historically? If so, can we assume that originally they actually were
simple recitatives, similar to that of the Introit verses, which in the course
of time became considerably more florid, without losing their pristine character? If so, can we derive any conclusions regarding the primitive stage
of psalmody from the fact that, in some modes, they seem to employ a tenor
different from that of the standard system? Finally, can we assume that
they represent an earlier type than the Introits having a freely moving
melody? It would be a rash undertaking indeed to answer these questions
one way or another. That there existed a close relationship between the
Introit and the psalm verse is sufficiently attested by the fact that, in the
great majority of cases, they draw upon the same Psalm for their texts.
Nearly all of the Introits listed above belong to this category, but not all
of them. The text of *Sitientes* is from Isaiah 55, of *Lux fulgebit* from Isaiah
9, of *Omnia quae* from Daniel 3, of *In voluntate* from Esther 13, and a few
even draw upon the New Testament, e.g., *In nomine* (Philippians 2),
Quasimodo (I Peter 2), and *Viri Galilei* (Acts 1:11).

Although, on the whole, the musical line of the Introits tends toward
moderation, some of them are famous for the impressive design of the
opening motion, suggestive of a bold gesture at the very beginning of the
Mass. Perhaps the most brilliant example is the Introit *Rorate caeli* [353]
from the Fourth Sunday of Advent (originally Wednesday in Ember Week
of Advent), with its characteristic upward sweep comprising the fifth, d-a,
as well as the two neighboring tones, c' and b-flat, a motion which impressively underlines the imperative "Rorate," although it is entirely out
of place from the point of view of word-painting.[3] Several other Introits
of the first mode, e.g., *Gaudeamus* [437, 1368, 1571), *Factus est Dominus*
[961], *Suscepimus* [1361], *Justus es Domine* [1047], *Da pacem* [1056], and
Inclina Domine [1040], employ the same initial formula, which is also
found in other chants of the first mode, for instance, in a well-characterized
group of Office Antiphons, in which the b-flat is often raised to b-natural
or to c'.[4] Other examples of an impressively designed initial motion occur

[3] *Rorare* means "to drop dew."
[4] Gevaert's *thèmes 3, 4, 5*. See p. 153. The motive d-a-b-a or d-a-c'-a has often been
considered as a typical motive of the first mode. It does, however, occur in the fourth
mode, as the intonation of the Invitatory tone 4.g [368].

in some Introits of mode 3, e.g., *Dispersit* [1607], *Cognovi Domine* [1239], and *Confessio* [1593].

While many of the Introits give the impression of having individual, freely composed melodies, musical relationships within the field as well as between this and other repertories are not entirely missing. An example in point is the just-mentioned opening formula of the first mode which, as we have seen, recurs in several Introits as well as in numerous Antiphons. Even more striking is the musical relationship between the Introits and a group of chants of an entirely different nature, that is, the Responsories of Matins. In not a few cases the cadential formulae of Introits are identical with those of Responsories of the same mode. There can be scarcely any doubt that this is a borrowing of the Introits from the Responsories, not *vice versa*. Not only are the Responsories probably an older type of chant but they also employ the cadential formulae under consideration in a much more prominent position, that is, as standard formulae that recur in a great number of Responsories, while in the Introits they appear only here and there. Finally, their melodic design, somewhat in the character of two or three turns on successively lower degrees, is as typical of the Responsories as it is out of line with the general style of the Introits. The following table, Fig. 86, gives a number of examples.

FIGURE 86

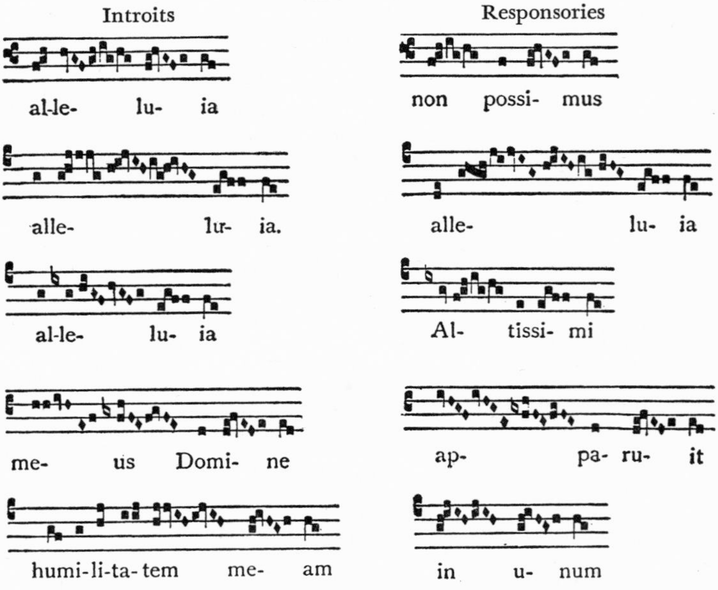

Introits   Responsories

al-le-   lu-   ia   non   possi-   mus

alle-   lu-   ia.   alle-   lu-   ia

al-le-   lu-   ia   Al-   tissi-   mi

me-   us   Domi-   ne   ap-   pa- ru-   it

humi-li-ta-tem   me-   am   in   u-   num

Introits   *Cibavit* [887]   *Repleatur* [897]   *Misericordia* [816]   *Ecce Deus* [1016]
            Domine [590]
Responsories   *Emendemus* [524]   *Cum complerentur* [873]   *Subvenite* [1765]
            Hodie [375]   *Astiterunt* [732]

The individual character of the introit melodies appears also from the fact that the technique of "migrating phrases" (i.e., of phrases transferred from one chant to another), which plays a basic role in the Graduals, Tracts, Responsories, and other chants, is practically absent in the Introits. The only example I can indicate is from the Introits *Quasimodo* [809] of Low Sunday and *Cantate Domino* [826] from the Fourth Sunday after Easter, which have the same melody for "alleluia: rationabilis, sine dolo" and "alleluia: quia mirabilia fecit Dominus."

THE COMMUNIONS

The chants sung during the closing ceremony of the Mass are essentially similar to those that accompany its beginning. There is, however, a marked difference of degree between the Introits and the Communions, the latter tending even more toward moderateness, not to say modesty, of design and style. Perhaps it is also permissible to say that the Communions, considered as a group, are somewhat less uniform, less conforming to a standard type, than is the case with the Introits. In this respect they are similar to the Offertories, which also show considerable variation of character.

In respect of length, the Communions vary not inconsiderably, certainly more than the Introits. Probably the shortest is *Inclina aurem* [1012] with just a little over one line, the longest, *Potum meum* [620] with over five lines. Also very short are *Tu es Petrus* [1122[6]] and *Lux aeterna* [1815],[1] in contrast to *Domine quinque* [1311] and *Adversum me* [611], both of them longer than any Introit.

Most of the Communions show a simple, neumatic style similar to that of the Introits, perhaps with an even greater preference for the shortest neumes with two or three notes. In several of them, however, syllabic style prevails to such an extent as to produce a marked similarity with the Office Antiphons. A Communion such as *Lux aeterna* [1815], *Vos estis* [1468], *Quod dico* [1173], *Oportet* [G 122], *Lutum fecit* [G 146], or *Videns Dominus* [G 148] is practically indistinguishable from an Antiphon for Vespers. On the other hand, fairly extended melismas are occasionally encountered, e.g., in *Communicantes* [1436], *Ab occultis* [G 142], *Dominus*

FIGURE 87

a.   et quod in aure   audi-tis, praedi-ca-te super te- cta.

b.   pro sae-   cu-   li   vi-   ta.

a. Communion *Quod dico*   b. Communion *Panis quem*

[1] Disregarding its verse. Originally, all the Communions had one or more verses.

virtutum [G 157], and particularly *Panis quem* [1043]. A comparison of *Quod dico* and *Panis quem* clearly indicates the variation of style encountered in the Communions, which ranges from that of the Office Antiphons to that of the Graduals (see Fig. 87).

The "responsorial" cadences which we observed in the Introits are also found, in slightly varied forms, in some of the Communions, e.g.:

Mode 3: *Cum esset* [G 624]
Mode 5: *Intellige* [549]; *Non vos relinquam* [899]; *Adversum me* [611]; *Tu mandasti* [1062]; *Justus Dominus* [G 120]
Mode 6: *Honora* [1026]; *Diffusa est* [1572]
Mode 7: *Unam petii* [1005]; *Domine quinque* [1311]
Mode 8: *Mense septimo* [1055].

The most remarkable aspect of the Communions is their tonal behavior. No other type of chant includes such a large percentage of melodies showing tonal instability and, as a result, ambiguity of modal assignment. The reader is referred to the chapter on the church modes, in which the various aspects of Gregorian tonality are explained with particular reference to the Communions.[2]

THE TRACTS

The Tracts belong mainly to the Masses of the pre-Easter period, from Septuagesima to Holy Saturday, and of the four Ember Saturdays [see the Table of Exceptional Masses, p. 30]. In the former they hold the position normally occupied by the Alleluia, i.e., a chant following the Gradual, between the Epistle and the Gospel:

Epistle—Gradual—Tract—Gospel

In the older type of Mass, which had three readings, the Tract was separated from the Gradual by the second reading. Thus, the Mass of Wednes-

---

[2] A very interesting but rather puzzling remark concerning the Communions is found in a treatise, *De musica*, by Oddo (or Berno?). After extolling Pope Gregory's achievements in various categories of chant—Responsories, Antiphons, Introits, Alleluias, Tracts, Graduals—the author continues: "In the Offertories and their verses, and especially *(maximeque)* in the Communions did he [Gregory] show what he could accomplish in this art. For in these there are the most varied kinds of ascent, descent, repeat *(duplicatio)*, delight for the *cognoscenti*, difficulty for the beginners, and an admirable organization [I read here *dispositio* for *depositio*] that differs widely from other chants; they are not so much made according to the rules of music *(secundum musicam)*, but rather evince the authority and validity *(auctoritatem et argumenta)* of music" (*CS*, I, 276a). While these remarks are very apt for the Offertories and their verses, they hardly make sense in connection with the Communions. Could we assume that there existed in the tenth century a repertory of highly elaborate Communions which has been completely lost except, perhaps, for traces surviving, e.g., in *Panis quem*?

day in Holy Week [613] probably is an example of the early state of affairs:

Lectio Isaiae—Gradual—*Lectio Isaiae*—Tract—*Passio Domini*

The group of medieval Tracts is relatively small. The oldest sources (*Sextuplex;* also St. Gall *359*) have Tracts for the following Masses:

1. The Sundays from Septuagesima to Palm Sunday, except for the Second Sunday of Quadragesima, which is of a later date:
   Septuagesima: *De profundis;* Sexagesima: *Commovisti;* Quinquagesima: *Jubilate;* Quadragesima I: *Qui habitat;* Quadragesima III: *Ad te levavi;* Quadragesima IV: *Qui confidunt;* Passion Sunday: *Saepe expugnaverunt;* Palm Sunday: *Deus Deus meus*
2. Wednesday in Ember Week of Lent: *De necessitatibus*
3. Saturday in Ember Week of Advent: *Qui regis*
4. Saturday in Ember Week of Lent and of September: *Laudate Dominum*
5. Wednesday in Holy Week: *Domine exaudi*
6. Good Friday: *Domine audivi; Eripe me*
7. Holy Saturday: *Cantemus; Vinea; Attende; Sicut cervus; Laudate Dominum* (see no. 4)
8. St. Gregory (today Common of a Martyr-Bishop, Mass II): *Beatus vir qui timet*
9. St. Valentine (today Common of a Martyr-Bishop, Mass I): *Desiderium*
10. St. Prisca (today Common of Two Martyrs): *Qui seminant*

This small group of tenth-century Tracts was enlarged in subsequent centuries by the following additions:[1]

Domine non secundum: for Ash Wednesday and all Mondays, Wednesdays, and Fridays thereafter until Monday in Holy Week
Effuderunt: Holy Innocents
Nunc dimittis: Purification
Absolve Domine: Mass for the Dead
Confitemini: Second Sunday of Lent (Quadr. II)
Audi filia: Common of a Virgin not a Martyr
Gaude Maria: Feasts of the B.V.M.
Ave Maria: St. Gabriel (originally for Annunciation?)
Tu es Petrus: St. Peter's Chair
Tu es vas: Conversion of St. Paul

1 See W. H. Frere, *The Sarum Gradual . . .* (1895), p. lxxxii. The eleventh-century *Gradual* of St. Yrieix (*Pal. mus.,* xiii) has all these additions except *Absolve, Audi filia,* and *Gaude Maria.* It also has eight Tracts not adopted in the modern books.

Thus we arrive at a group of thirty-one Tracts that can be considered as authentic. The number of Tracts found in the modern books is, however, considerably larger, there being forty-seven in the *Liber usualis* and eighty-seven in the *Graduale Romanum*. They are all for feasts of Saints which may fall in the period of Lent (e.g., *Spera in Domino* for St. John Bosco, on January 31) or for Votive Masses if celebrated during this period (e.g., *Benedicite Dominum* for the Votive Mass of the Holy Angels). In the absence of a critical and musicological edition of Gregorian chant it is impossible (at least, for this writer) to say which of these Tracts are taken from medieval sources and which are modern compositions that originated at Solesmes. At any rate, the medieval repertory is large enough to provide a solid basis for our investigations.

Aside from the rather unimportant case of the *tonus in directum* [see p. 179], the Tracts are the only surviving examples of direct psalmody, that is, of a Psalm sung without the addition of an Antiphon or Respond. Each Tract consists of a number of verses, from two to fourteen, taken from one and the same Psalm. Exceptions occur only in the group of later medieval additions, where we find non-psalmodic texts, e.g., *Ave Maria, Gaude Maria, Tu es Petrus,* as well as a textual compilation, *Domine, non secundum.*[2] It should be noticed that in the liturgical books the indication of the verses, by the sign ℣, is somewhat misleading, since this sign does not appear at the very beginning of the Tract, thus giving the impression that the opening portion might be something in the nature of a respond, followed by a number of verses. Actually, the initial section of the text is also a verse, often the first verse of the Psalm. The number of verses, therefore, is always one more than is suggested by the signs ℣. The longest Tract is *Deus Deus meus* with fourteen verses, the shortest, *Laudate Dominum* with only two, which, however, constitute the entire Psalm (Ps. 116).[3]

The musical style of the Tracts is considerably more ornate than that of the Introits. Every Tract includes a number of fairly extended melismas, and occasionally one comes upon melismas which are among the longest to be found in the entire repertory of chants, as, for instance, in *Commovisti* [507] at the close of the first and of the last verse. Fairly extended passages in monotone recitation occur in several Tracts, particularly in *Attende caelum* [751]. Between these extremes of syllabic recitation and long melismas the melodies move in a richly neumatic style, frequently employing groups of four, five, or six notes for one syllable.

One of the various unique aspects of the Tracts is that they are confined to two modes, the second and the eighth, a restriction for which there exists

---

2 ℣. 1 from Ps. 102:10; ℣. 2 from Ps. 78:8; ℣. 3 is non-scriptural.
3 The Tract *Nunc dimittis* has the entire text of the Canticle.

no parallel in the Gregorian repertory. In fact, there is some reason to assume that originally there existed only one mode for Tracts, the eighth.[4] Certain it is that the Tracts of the eighth mode prevail among the old group of twenty-one Tracts, fifteen of which are in the eighth mode. In the later additions, on the other hand, the second mode takes first place, with seven out of ten:

	OLD	ADDITIONS	TOTAL
Mode 8:	15	3	18
Mode 2:	6	7	13
	21	10	31

Considered from the point of view of tonal material, the Tracts are even much more restricted than is suggested by the limitation to two modes, because of the extensive use of standard phrases which not only recur within the various verses of one and the same Tract, but are also transferred from one Tract to others, so that, in each mode, the entire group is closely bound together by the use of identical thematic material. The Tracts are not the only type of chant in which standard phrases (or, as they are also called, migrating formulae) occur. Nowhere, however, is this technique carried out so systematically as in the Tracts, each of which consists almost completely of a succession of standard phrases.

THE TRACTS OF THE EIGHTH MODE

To this group belong most of the old Tracts and, in particular, all the five Tracts of Holy Saturday. These constitute a core of special interest and importance, which will serve as the basis of the analytical study of the melodies. Most of the Tracts of mode 8 have three verses, and several have four. *Laudate Dominum* is the shortest with only two verses, while *Attende* and *Ad te levavi* are the most extended, with five. Each verse falls into a small number of well-defined musical phrases, normally three, but occasionally two or four. Common to all these phrases is the cadential point, which is either the tonic, g, or the subtonic, f. The only exception is a phrase closing on c′ which occurs twice in *Commovisti*. The normal arrangement of cadential points, to be observed particularly in the central group of the Tracts from Holy Saturday, is g f g, that is, the verse begins with a phrase ending on g, continues with one ending on f, and closes with a third ending on g. Verses with four phrases usually close with two phrases on g, so that the arrangement of cadences becomes g f g g. Other schemes, such as f g g or g g g also occur.

These fairly fixed schemes of cadential notes represent the framework

4 See p. 184 for the theory that the Tracts of mode 2 originally were Graduals.

for a melodic structure which consists of a limited number of standard phrases. The principle involved is particularly apparent in the central group of Holy Saturday, a group which includes five Tracts with sixteen verses and fifty-one phrases. Actually, there are only eight different phrases which, recurring in various combinations, provide the material for the complete melodies. Six of these standard phrases close on g, and two on f. The g-group includes one phrase for the beginning of the first verse, one for the close of the last verse, one that is normally employed for the beginning of verses other than the first, and one that usually appears at the end of the verses, including the last in which it precedes the final phrase. The following scheme shows, by means of asterisks, how the sixteen verses are "composed" out of this basic material. The phrases are marked G or F (with inferior letters or numbers; a for the initial phrase, n for the final), depending upon whether they close on g or on f:

TRACTS OF HOLY SATURDAY

		G_a	G_1	F_1	F_2	G_2	G_3	G_4	G_n	
Cantemus [745]	℣. 1	*		*		*				(F_1, G_2 restated)
	2		*	*		*				
	3		*						*	
Vinea [748]	℣. 1	*			*	*				
	2		*	*		*				
	3			*		*			*	
Attende caelum [751]	℣. 1	*			*	*				
	2		*	*		*				
	3			*		*				
	4		*	*		*				
	5					*			*	
Sicut cervus [753]	℣. 1	*		*		*				
	2		*	*		*	*			
	3		*	*		*			*	
Laudate [760][5]	℣. 1	*			*	*	*			
	2		*	*				*	*	

It appears that this group of Tracts is a perfect example of centonization, a unified aggregate of eight elements variously selected and combined.

An analytical study similar to the one given above has been made by Ferretti, in his *Esthétique grégorienne* (pp. 135ff). Ferretti gives several examples showing how the standard phrases are modified according to the

[5] In *Laudate* some of the phrases are modified. See p. 322.

exigencies of the text, either by the interpolation of recitation passages or, occasionally, by splitting a neume into two shorter neumes:

FIGURE 88

a. Phrase G_2 in *Cantemus*, ℣. 2 and *Vinea*, ℣ 2.
b. Beginning of Phrase G_n in *Laudate*, ℣. 2 and *Cantemus*, ℣. 3.

Ferretti also states certain principles governing the succession and function of the standard phrases, but the reader must be warned that most of his statements are incorrect. Thus, on p. 136 he says (we translate and replace his symbols, A, B, C, by the corresponding symbols of our system, that is, F_1, G_1, G_2):

These two initial formulae of the verses [F_1 and G_1] serve also as mediants, but in such a way that the formula F_1 is never omitted. Thus, if a verse begins with the formula G_1, this must be immediately followed by F_1, except in the case of the final verse.

Actually there is no verse in any of the Tracts under consideration (nor in any of those to be studied later) in which G_1 serves as a mediant, that is, as an inner formula. More than any other formula (except for G_a and G_n) it has an invariable position, at the beginning of verses other than the first.

Later on (pp. 137ff) Ferretti says:

a) The mediant formula F_1 can never be missing, as we have said. . . .
b) The mediant formula G_1 is employed if the text is long. In this case the formulae follow in this order: F_1 G_1 G_2.
c) If the text has four divisions, the composers tend to let the formula F_1 alternate with the final formula [G_2], as follows: F_1 G_2 F_1 G_2.
d) The closing formula of the entire piece [G_n] . . . is usually preceded by the mediant formula G_1, if the text has only two divisions, or by the final formula G_2, if there are more than two divisions.

To these statements we offer the following remarks which should be regarded as constructive contributions given in order to obtain a correct picture:

a. The formula F_1 (or F_2) is missing in the final verses of *Cantemus* and *Attende;* also repeatedly in *Jubilate, Ad te levavi,* etc.; see the tabulation on p. 319.

b. The sequence F_1 G_1 G_2 never occurs. We have already remarked that G_1, far from being a "formule médiane," is always found at the beginning of a verse. There are, however, several instances of the sequence G_1 F_1 G_2 (*Cantemus*, ℣. 2; *Vinea*, ℣. 2; *Attende*, ℣. 2 and 4).

c. The alternating sequence, F_1 G_2 F_1 G_2, occurs only once in all the Tracts of the eighth mode, that is, in ℣. 1 of *Cantemus*, which actually has five divisions, G_a F_1 G_2 F_1 G_2. The verses with four divisions show the structure G F G G.

d. The sequence G_1 G_n occurs only once, in *Cantemus*, ℣. 3.

As in so many other cases, Ferretti has become a victim of his tendency to formulate exact rules and laws. Usually the picture is more complex than he presents it, and often too complex to be expressed at all in the form of concise statements. However, it is not too difficult to formulate a few general principles outlining the function and position of the standard phrases in the above group of Tracts, such as the following:

1. The basic structure of each verse is one consisting of three elements: an "intonation" formula closing on g, a "mediation" formula closing on f, and a "termination" formula closing on g. Normally, these formulae are G_1, F_1, and G_2.

2. Intonation: G_1 is invariably replaced by G_a in the first verse. Occasionally it is omitted.

3. Mediation: F_1 is occasionally replaced by F_2. In two verses it is omitted.

4. Termination: Some verses have a "doubled" termination consisting of two G-formulae, e.g., G_2 G_3. The last verse always closes with G_n.

We shall now proceed from the central group provided by the Tracts of Holy Saturday to the other Tracts of the eighth mode. The general picture presented by them is rather similar, though richer and more varied in detail. A few of the additional Tracts employ the same material that make up the central group, but in most of them the original phrases are varied or new elements are added to them. Following is a schematic representation of the eighteen medieval Tracts of the eighth mode:

TRACTS VIII: TABULATION

	℣. 1	℣. 2	℣. 3	℣. 4	℣. 5
Cantemus	$G_a F_1 G_2 \mid F_1 \mid G_2$	$G_1 \mid F_1 G_2$	$G_1 \mid G_n$		
Vinea	$G_a F_2 \mid G_2$	$G_1 \mid F_1 \mid G_2$	$F_1 \mid G_2 G_n$	$G_1 \mid F_1 \mid G_2$	$G_1 \mid G_n$
Attende	$G_a F_2 \mid G_2$	$G_1 \mid F_1 \mid G_2$	$F_1 \mid G_2$		
Sicut cervus	$G_a F_1 \mid G_2$	$G_1 F_1 \mid G_2 G_3$	$G_1 F_1 \mid G_2 G_n$		
Laudate	$G_a F_2 \mid G_2 G_3'$	$10+g_1 F_1 \mid G_4 G_n$			
Absolve	$G_a F_1 \mid G_2$	$F_1 \mid G_2$	$F_1 \mid G_n$		
Beatus vir qui	$G_a F_2 \mid G_2 G_3'$	$G_1 \mid G_2 G_3$	$G_1 \mid G_2 G_n$		
Qui regis	$G_a' F_3 \mid 10+F_2$	$G_1 G_3 \mid G_1 G_3$	$14+F_2 \mid G_n$		
De profundis	$G_a f_3 \mid g_2 G_3'$	$G_1 4+f_4 \mid G_2 G_3'$	$14+f_4 \mid 6+g_3$	$11+F_2 \mid G_2 G_n$	
Commovisti	$G_b G_5 \mid G_6 G_3'$	$C_1 5+F_2 \mid G_7$	$C_1 5+F_2 \mid G_2 G_n$	$10+f_2 \mid G_2 G_n$	
Jubilate	$G_a F_2 \mid G_6 G_3'$	$G_1 G_2$	$G_4 G_3'$	$C_9 G_5 7+f_2 \mid G_2$	
Ad te levavi	$G_c C_5 \mid G_6$	$G_8 G_3$	$G_8 G_3$		$9+f_4 \mid G_n$
Qui confidunt	$G_a 5+f_2 \mid 6+F_1 \mid G_2$	$g_7 F_1 \mid 13+f_3 \mid g_2 G_n$	$G_1 4+F_2 \mid 3+g_2 G_3$	$G_1 4+F_2 \mid G_2 G_n$	
Saepe expugnaverunt	$G_d G_3$	$G_9 F_2 \mid 4+g_2 G_3$	$8+f_4 \mid G_2 \mid G_n$		
Qui seminant	$G_c G_3$	$...g \mid G_3$	$10+f_4 \mid g_2 G_n$		
Desiderium	$G_e 3+F_2 \mid G_2 G_6$	$7+g_1 \mid ...g$	$12+f_4 g_2 \mid G_n$		
Effuderunt	$G_e G_6$	$5+g_6$			
Nunc dimittis	$G_d G_3$	$G_1 \mid F_2$	$G_1 \mid G_3$	$G_9 F_2 \mid g_2 G_n$	

1. A capital letter indicates a complete standard phrase terminating on the pitch suggested by the letter, g, f, or c'. 2. Opening phrases are indicated by inferior letters a, b, c; the closing phrase by n (G_a, G_b ... G_n). 3. All other phrases are designated by inferior numbers: G_1, G_2, F_1, F_2, etc. 4. Small letters are used to indicate the closing formula of the corresponding standard phrase, as marked off in Fig. 89. Thus f_1 indicates the closing part of F_1, etc. 5. A figure preceding one of the letter symbols stands for a free section comprising as many syllables as the figure indicates, and followed by a standard phrase. Thus, $10+F_1$ means that there is a free section of ten syllables closing with the standard phrase F_1. 6. The symbol ... is employed for complete phrases that do not recur in another Tract or verse. The cadential note of these phrases is added, e.g., ...g. 7. The separating strokes, |, represent the "full bars" of the *Liber usualis*. They are added mainly in order to facilitate the identification of the phrases. See, however, p. 320, fn. 6.

Fig. 89 shows the standard phrases used in the first seven Tracts of this tabulation. Underlining indicates portions that are variable.

FIGURE 89

Tracts VIII: Standard Phrases

In order to illustrate this method of representation, there is shown below the text of the Tract *Cantemus* [745] with the symbols for the various phrases.

G_a F_1 G_2
Cantemus Domino: gloriose enim honorificatus est: equum et ascensorem[6]
F_1 G_2
projecit in mare: adjutor et protector factus est mihi in salutem.
    G_1 F_1 G_2
℣. *Hic Deus meus, et honorabo eum: Deus patris mei, et exaltabo eum.*
    G_1 G_n
℣. *Dominus conterens bella: Dominus nomen est illi.*

Similarly for *Laudate* [760]:

[6] The passage *honorificatus . . . ascensorem* in ℣. 1 is another example of disagreement between the textual and the musical phrase (see pp. 273f), with the result that the Solesmes full bar (after *est*) appears right in the middle of the standard phrase G_2. Naturally, these bars are disregarded in our Tabulation on p. 319.

G_a $\qquad$ F_2 $\qquad$ G_2 $\qquad\qquad$ $G_3{}'$
Laudate Dominum omnes gentes et collaudate eum omnes populi.

$\quad$ 10 $\qquad\qquad\qquad\qquad$ $+g_1$ $\quad$ F_1 $\qquad\qquad$ G_4
℣. *Quoniam confirmata est super nos misericordia ejus: et veritas*

$\qquad$ G_n
Domini manet in aeternum.

Following are some observations about the "medieval" group of Tracts, with occasional remarks about the "late" Tracts included in the *Liber usualis* and *Graduale Romanum:*

1. In addition to the basic opening formula, G_a, there are four others employed for the beginning, G_b, G_c, G_d, G_e. The formula G_b of *Commovisti* does not recur in any other medieval Tract, but is used in some of the late (probably modern) Tracts, namely, in *Exsurge Domine* [G [101]] and *Magnificat anima mea* [G 50**]. There are only two Tracts, both late, that do not begin with one of the five formulae G_a to G_e. These are *Filii hominum* [L Supplement, Feast of the Eucharistic Heart of Jesus, p. 7] and *Ego diligentes* [G 61**], both of which start, highly irregularly, with an F-phrase.

2. Without exception, all Tracts close with one and the same formula, G_n which, moreover, occurs only in this position (in contrast to the Tracts of mode 2, in which the final phrase is occasionally used also for the close of inner verses). Sometimes the formula is slightly modified, e.g., in *Commovisti* (variant at the beginning) and in *Laudate* (shorter version near the end).

3. The group of medieval Tracts has nine recurring G-phrases (G_1 to G_9) other than those for the opening and the close. A few more could be added if the analysis is extended to include also the late Tracts. For ex-example, the "free" opening phrase, ...g, of ℣. 2 of *Qui seminant* recurs in ℣. 2 of *Notus in Judaea,* probably a Solesmes composition for the Mass to Beg for Peace [1286].

4. The four F-phrases are related to each other by having an identical conclusion. They are of special interest because they, or their concluding sections, frequently appear at the end of extended free passages, as indicated in our tabulation by symbols such as $14+F_2$, $14+f_4$, $10+f_4$, etc. Sometimes these passages are in the character of a monotone recitation, as in ℣. 3 of *Qui regis* where, however, an exuberant melisma somewhat incongruously interrupts the recitation on c'. More frequently, they move up and down freely in a moderately neumatic style, as in ℣. 1 of the same Tract. Most of these free passages occur at the beginning of a verse, where they take care of a considerable portion of the text.

5. The medieval Tracts include only one C-phrase, which occurs in *Commovisti* at the beginning of ℣. 2 and 3. It has, however, been incorporated in some of the modern Tracts, e.g., in *Notus in Judaea,* ℣. 3 [1286, on "potentias"; Mass to Beg for Peace], *Ecce sic,* ℣. 3 [1290, on "Et videas"; Nuptial Mass], and *Tu gloria,* ℣. 2 [1378, on "Tota"; Apparition of Our Blessed Lady at Lourdes].

6. Most of the "inner" G-phrases (G_1, etc.) have fairly well-defined functions. G_1 appears only at the beginning of verses, except for ℣. 2 of *Qui regis,* which is treated as if it consisted of two verses, "Qui sedes super Cherubim, appare coram Ephraim" and "Benjamin et Manasse," each set to $G_1 G_3$. G_2 is used mainly for the close of a verse, but is sometimes followed by G_3 (or by G_n in the last verse). G_3 is always a terminal formula. An F-phrase is included in most of the verses, but not in all of them (see *Beatus vir qui, Jubilate, Ad te levavi*). The other G-phrases occur only a few times, which makes it difficult to say whether they were considered as initial, mediant, or terminal formulae. It may be noticed that, e.g., G_4 appears in *Laudate,* ℣. 2, as a penultimate, and in *Jubilate,* ℣. 3, as an initial phrase.

7. Some formulae, notably G_1, G_2, and F_1, are often used to accommodate extra syllables in monotone recitation. The pitches are c' for G_1 and F_1, g for G_2. A good example is *Attende caelum,* which includes seven such passages.

8. Our schematic representation provides a good insight into the thematic relationship between the Tracts which, in fact, have been arranged according to this point of view. Naturally, the tabulation starts with the nucleus of the five tracts of Holy Saturday, which appear in their liturgical order. It is perhaps not merely incidental that the first three of these are the ones most clearly unified, since they employ only the formulae G_a, G_1, G_2, G_n, F_1, and F_2. The fourth Tract, *Sicut cervus,* introduces a new formula, G_3, and the fifth, *Laudate,* not only employs a variant of this formula, G_3' and a new phrase, G_4, but also starts out, in ℣. 2, with a free section, terminating in g_1. Closely related to this central group are the Tracts *Absolve* from the Mass for the Dead and *Beatus vir qui timet* from the feast of St. Gregory (now for the Common of a Martyr), both of which employ only the material of the Holy Saturday Tracts. A "modern" Tract belonging to the same class is *Laudate Dominum omnes angeli,* from the Feast of St. Raphael, Archangel [G 636]. The next two Tracts of our list, *Qui regis* and *De profundis,* include two new F-phrases, F_3 and f_4 as well as extended free passages. Decidedly new material appears in *Commovisti,* singular among the medieval Tracts in its use of G_b and C_1, and perhaps the progenitor of three new G-phrases, G_5, G_6, and G_7. The phrase C_1, shown in Fig. 90, includes a triadic progression, e'-c'-g, which, as has been previously noted [see p. 255], is extremely rare in Gregorian chant. Only

FIGURE 90

two additional formulae appear in the remaining Tracts, G₈ in *Ad te levavi* and G₉ in *Saepe expugnaverunt*.

THE TRACTS OF THE SECOND MODE

The old nucleus of Tracts of the second mode is very small. It consists of the following pieces:

Qui habitat [533] for First Sunday of Lent
Deus Deus meus [592] for Palm Sunday
Domine exaudi [614] for Wednesday in Holy Week
Domine audivi [695] for Good Friday
Eripe me [697] for Good Friday
De necessitatibus [G 102] for Wednesday of Ember Week in Lent

In a way, this small number is compensated for by the exceptional extension of three of these Tracts: *Deus Deus meus* with fourteen verses, *Qui habitat* with thirteen, and *Eripe me* with eleven. These are by far the longest chants in the Gregorian repertory, each covering three pages of the *Liber usualis*. *Deus Deus meus* alone includes almost as many verses as all the five eighth-mode Tracts of Holy Saturday together, so that this single Tract could well serve as a point of departure for an analytical study. Except for *De necessitatibus* which, with three verses, is the shortest, all the Tracts of the old repertory are closely related structurally as well as thematically and, with a total of sixty verses, provide a broad basis for investigation. In addition, we shall consider seven Tracts found in later medieval sources, namely, *Domine non secundum, Confitemini, Audi filia, Gaude Maria, Ave Maria, Tu es Petrus,* and *Tu es vas.*

The emerging picture is very similar to the one presented by the Tracts of mode 8. In a way it is even more impressive, because of the great number of elements involved, *c.* eighty verses with almost three hundred phrases, which can be reduced to only twenty different standard formulae. It is also structurally clearer, since the great majority of verses, *c.* sixty out of eighty, show an identical organization consisting of four phrases which terminate respectively on d, c, f, and d. In order to promote clarity and facilitate reference we shall designate these segments of a verse by terms borrowed from the psalm tones, namely, intonation (d), flex (c), mediation (f), and termination (d), reserving the term "opening" for the intonation of the first verse, and "closing" for the termination of the last. About a half dozen of the verses lack the mediation, and a similar number lack the flex, while a few show other deviations from the basic scheme.

In his *Gregorianische Formenlehre* (p. 353), P. Wagner characterized the Tracts as "psalmodie-ähnliche Variationen." Although to a certain extent this designation is applicable to all the Tracts, it is particularly suitable for those of the second mode, which indeed show an interesting relationship to psalmody as well as to variation technique. The consistency with which the cadential scheme, d-c-f-d, is employed is so obvious that one is tempted to reconstruct a psalmodic formula which could be considered as the skeleton melody for all the verses:

FIGURE 91

Int.   Flex   Med.   Term.

It is hardly necessary to say that this reconstruction is entirely hypothetical, and is given here only for the purpose of demonstration, without implying that it represents the "original form" of the tract melodies. Considered analytically, however, there can be no doubt that nearly all of the eighty verses found in the Tracts of the second mode are highly complex variations of a psalmodic theme such as the one just indicated. The method of variation would consist in replacing each of the "recitation pitches" of the theme by one or another of a group of standard phrases, all closing on the corresponding cadential note. It is not without interest to correlate this "Gregorian" variation technique to that employed, in the sixteenth and seventeenth centuries, in connection with certain themes of a somewhat similar character. We are referring to the descending tetrachord which occurs in the *Romanesca,* the *passamezzo antico,* the Spanish *Guardame las vacas,* and numerous passacaglias of the seventeenth century. Particularly suitable for the comparison are some of the sixteenth-century passamezzos, in which each tone of the tetrachord serves as the basis of four, six, or even eight measures, thus being extended into a passage comparable in length to those of the Tracts.[7] The difference in treatment is that in these variations the "thematic tone" appears at the beginning of the passages, while in the Tracts it appears at the end:

FIGURE 92

Passamezzo   Tract

[7] For instance, the Pass'e mezzo by Giovanni Picchi, reproduced in *HAM,* no. 154b.

Considering the fact that in the sixteenth-century variations as well as in the Tracts the theme is continuously repeated a number of times, one might push the analogy even one step further and designate a Tract, somewhat speciously, as a kind of ostinato. An especially good example would be *Eripe me,* in which the theme is restated eleven times without any change of its substance.[8]

The transition from the "theme" to the "variations" involves the introduction, at their proper places, of a limited number of standard formulae, most of which recur in different verses of the same or of some other Tracts. The repertory of recurring standard phrases consists of:

> two for the opening (D_a, D_b)
> ten for the intonation (D_1 to D_{10})
> three for the flex (C_1, C_2, occasionally C_3)
> one for the mediant (F_1, also in a variant F_1')
> five for the termination (D_{11} to D_{15})
> one for the close (D_n).

A tabulation of the Tracts of the second mode is shown on pp. 326f.

In order to facilitate the identification of the standard phrases, part of the text of *Deus Deus meus* follows, with the symbols added:

D_a 8 $+c_1$ 3 $+D_{11}$
℣. 1. *Deus, Deus meus, respice in me: quare me dereliquisti?*

D_1 C_1 f_1 D_{12}
℣. 2. *Longe a salute mea verba delictorum meorum.*

C_1 F_1 D_{13}
℣. 5. *In te speraverunt patres nostri: speraverunt, et liberasti eos.*

D_3 C_2 F_1
℣. 7. *Ego autem sum vermis, et non homo: opprobrium hominum*
D_{14}
et abjectio plebis.

D_7 3 $+C_2$ 3 $+d_2$ F_1 D_{13}
℣. 11. *Libera me de ore leonis: et a cor-nibus unicornuorum humilitatem*
meam.

... d ... f D_n'
℣. 14. *Populo qui nascetur, quem fecit Dominus.*

Fig. 93 shows some of the standard phrases, mainly those that have a variable beginning (indicated by underlining) or occur in a shortened form (indicated by small letters).

---

8 Concerning the date of this Tract, see p. 511.

(read horizontally to facing page)

TRACTS II: TABULATION

	℣. 1 (6, 11)				℣. 2 (7, 12)			
	Int.	Fl.	Med.	Term.	Int.	Fl.	Med.	Term.
Deus Deus meus	D_a	$8+c_1$		$3+D_{11}$	D_1	C_1	f_1	D_{12}
	D_4	$5+c_1$	F_1	D_{14}	D_3	C_2	F_1	D_{14}
	D_7	$3+C_2$	$3+d_2F_1$	D_{13}	D_8	C_1	F_1	D_{13}
Qui habitat	D_b	$9+c_1$		...d	D_8	C_1	$9+f_1$	D_{12}
	D_2	$c_1\ 13+c_1$		...d	$D_9\,d_2$	C_2	$3+d_3\ 4+c_1$	$3+D_{14}$
	D_3	C_1	F_1	$3+d_{13}$	$D_{10}\,d_2$	$5+c_1$	F_1	D_{13}
Eripe me	D_a	$4+c_1$	F_1	D_{11}	D_1	C_1	F_1	D_{12}
	$D_9\,d_2$	$8+c_1$	F_1	D_{14}	D_8	C_1	F_1	$4+d_{13}$
	D_8	C_1	$F_1{'}$	D_n				
Domine audivi	D_b	$C_1\ 3+c_1$	$F_1{'}$	D_{15}	$D_1D_5...$	$12+c_1$	$F_1{'}$	D_{15}
Domine exaudi	D_b	$3+C_1$	$F_1{'}$	D_{15}	D_1	$6+c_1$	$F_1\ 4+c_1$	d_{15}
	$D_{10}D_5$	C_3	$F_1{'}$	D_n				
Confitemini	D_a	$3+c_1$	F_1	d_{13}	D_1	C_1	F_1	D_{13}
Domine non	D_b	$6+c_1$	F_1F_1	$4+d_{14}$	$D_9\,d_2$	C_1	F_1	D_{13}
Audi filia	D_a	$7+c_1$	F_1	D_{11}		$C_1\ 4+c_1$	F_1	D_{11}
Gaude Maria	...d	$5+c_1$	F_1	D_{11}	D_1	...c		D_{11}
Tu es Petrus	D_a	$4+c_1$	F_1	D_{11}	D_1	C_1	F_1	D_{11}
Tu es vas	...d	$3+c_1$	F_1	$7+d_{12}$	$4+d_2$	C_3	$f_1...$	$3+d_{12}$
Ave Maria	D_a	$2+c_1$	F_1	D_{11}	D_8	$4+c_1$	F_1	$4+d_{14}$
	D_3D_5	C_3	$F_1{'}$	D_n				
De necessitatibus	...d $6+c_1$...d	$5+c_3\ 5+c_3\ D_{15}$			d_2 ...d $3+c_3$...C_3	$F_1{'}\ D_n$		

TRACTS II: TABULATION

℣. 3 (8, 13)

Int.	Fl.	Med.	Term.
D_2	$7+c_1$	F_1	$...d$
D_5	C_2	F_1	D_{14}
D_8	C_1	F_1'	D_{12}
D_3D_5	$7+c_1$		d_{13}
D_6	$4+c_1$	F_1	$2+d_{13}$
D_4	$C_1 3+C_1$	F_1'	D_n
D_2	$4+c_1$	F_1	D_{13}
D_8	C_1	F_1	D_{14}
$3+D_5$	$4+c_1$	F_1	D_n
		F_1	$...d$
$D_9 d_2$	C_2	F_1	d_{13}
$9+d_2$	C_1	F_1'	D_n
D_2	C_1	F_1	D_{11}
$D_7 d_2$	C_2	F_1'	$6+D_{11}$
D_3	C_1	F_1	D_{11}
$...c$		F_1	$3+d_3$
$D_9 d_2$	C_2	F_1	D_{11}
$...d$	C_3	F_1'	D_n

℣. 4 (9, 14)

Int.	Fl.	Med.	Term.
D_3	$5+c_1$		$...d$
D_6	$5+c_1$	F_1	D_{14}
$...d$		$...f$	D_n
D_6	$5+c_1$		$...d$
$D_{10}D_5$	$5+c_1$		$4+d_{13}$
$D_{10}D_5$	$6+c_1$	F_1	D_{11}
$D_7 4+d_2$	C_2	F_1	D_{14}
D_7	$6+c_1$	F_1'	D_n'
$4+d_3 D_5$	C_3	F_1	D_n'
$D_7 d_2$	C_1	F_1'	D_n
D_8	C_1	F_1'	D_n
		$...f$	D_n
D_7	C_2	F_1'	D_n
$D_7 d_2$		F_1'	D_n
D_2	$5+C_2$	F_1	D_{11}

℣. 5 (10, 15)

Int.	Fl.	Med.	Term.
	C_1	F_1	D_{13}
	C_1	F_1	$17+d_{14}$
D_5	$4+c_1$	F_1	D_{14}
$D_{10}D_5 C_3$		F_1	$4+D_9$
D_3D_5	C_2	F_1	D_{14}
D_9	C_1	F_1	D_{14}
D_{10}	$6+c_1$	F_1'	D_n
$D_{10}D_5$	$6+c_1$	F_1	D_n'
$D_7 d_2$	C_3	F_1	D_{14}

FIGURE 93

Tracts II: Standard Phrases

REMARKS:

1. The normal scheme for the verse, found in the great majority of cases, is a division into four phrases, with fixed formulae for the first and third, and fixed formulae or endings for the second and fourth. In a number of cases one of the four elements, particularly the intonation, includes two phrases in succession, e.g., $D_3 D_5$ in *Qui habitat*, ℣. 3; or a phrase followed by the conclusion of another, e.g., $D_9 d_2$ in ℣. 7 of the same tract. ℣. 11 of *Qui habitat* is one of several verses with a doubled flex $(2 + c_1$ $13 + c_1)$, while ℣. 1 of *Domine non* is a unique example of a doubled mediant, $F_1 F_1$.

2. In *Qui habitat*, ℣. 7, and in *Domine exaudi*, ℣. 2, the basic cadential scheme is amplified by the insertion, between mediant and termination, of a flex, $4 + c_1$. More frequent are reductions, such as omission of the mediant (*Deus Deus meus*, ℣. 4; *Qui habitat*, ℣. 1, 3, 4, 9; *Gaude Maria*,

$\mathbb{V}$. 2), of the intonation (*Audi filia,* $\mathbb{V}$. 2; *Tu es vas,* $\mathbb{V}$. 3; *Deus Deus meus,* $\mathbb{V}$. 5, 10), of the flex (*Deus Deus meus,* $\mathbb{V}$. 14), or even of intonation and flex (*Domine exaudi,* $\mathbb{V}$. 3; *Gaude Maria,* $\mathbb{V}$. 4).

3. In the field of the d-formulae there is a strict separation between those for the intonation (D_1 to D_{10}) and those for the termination (D_{11} to D_{15}). Notice, however, two cases in which an intonation formula is employed as a termination: *Qui habitat,* $\mathbb{V}$. 10, and *Tu es vas,* $\mathbb{V}$. 3.

5. The formula for the mediant, F_1, exists in a slightly more elaborate variant, $F_1{}'$ (characterized by a rise up to b-flat), which is often used in the last or in the penultimate verse. *Domine exaudi* also has it for $\mathbb{V}$. 1, *Domine audivi* for $\mathbb{V}$. 1 and 2.

6. As in the Tracts of mode 8, there is only one closing formula, D_n. The two Tracts just mentioned, *Domine exaudi* and *Domine audivi,* employ this formula also for the two verses preceding the last. This is the only instance in which the Tracts of mode 2 are less consistent than those of mode 8.

7. Three complete C-phrases can be distinguished, two of which, C_1 and C_2, have the same ending. This ending, designated as c_1, occurs frequently in connection with free passages ($8+c_1$, etc.). The standard phrase C_1 begins with an interesting passage, essentially a recitation on d with inflections up to f, which often occurs as a repetitive *distropha* or *tristropha*. A clear example is found in $\mathbb{V}$. 3 of *Domine non.*[9] Occasionally recitation passages on d occur within the F_1-formula, e.g., in *Confitemini* $\mathbb{V}$. 1 ("quoniam in") and $\mathbb{V}$. 3 ("faciunt"); in *Domine non* $\mathbb{V}$. 1 ("neque secundum iniquitates") and $\mathbb{V}$. 2 ("anticipent nos misericordia"); etc. A very unusual recitative occurs in *Qui habitat* $\mathbb{V}$. 2, where six consecutive syllables, "-gium meum, Deus," are each sung to a *podatus* d-e.[10]

8. Conspicuously different from the other Tracts is *De necessitatibus,* which, for this reason, we have placed at the end of our table, although it belongs to the old group. Its first and second verses consist of at least six phrases with a highly irregular sequence of cadential notes. Each of its verses includes at least one phrase that does not recur in any other Tract. Equally abnormal is the frequent use of the C_3-formula, which occurs five times in *De necessitatibus,* while it appears only seven times in all the other Tracts together.

After these detailed and lengthy explanations of the two groups of

[9] Ferretti, p. 141, interprets these *strophici* as indications of a "teneur cachée et sous-entendue" on f. While recitation on d is not infrequent in the Tracts of mode 2 (see *Confitemini,* $\mathbb{V}$. 1, 3, 4; *Qui habitat,* $\mathbb{V}$. 13; *Eripe,* $\mathbb{V}$. 9, 11), there is only one clear example of a recitation on f, that is, in *Domine non,* near the end of $\mathbb{V}$. 2, *quia pauperes facti sumus.*

[10] A recitative consisting of reiterated *torculi* is found quite frequently in the Old-Roman chant. Cf. p. 491, Fig. 170.

Tracts, one in the eighth, the other in the second mode, a few concluding remarks may be in place, mainly regarding the question of similarities and dissimilarities in their structural aspect and technique of composition. Essentially they employ the same method of "composing" all the verses from a limited repertory of standard formulae. The relative amount of standard material is about the same, as appears from our two tables of Standard Phrases, which show nineteen formulae for the sixty verses of Tracts VIII and twenty-two for the eighty verses of Tracts II.

As to differences of treatment, the most striking is the much greater regularity of structure displayed by Tracts in mode 2, in which quadripartite verses with cadences on d, c, f, and d occur so frequently as to constitute a norm. Nothing comparable exists in the Tracts in mode 8. Here the closest approximation to a "normal structure" would be a tripartite verse with cadences on g, f, and g, but a glance at our tabulation shows that this occurs only in a relatively small number of verses, even if we admit cases with a doubled cadence, such as g f g g.[11]

THE GREAT RESPONSORIES

The Great Responsories (responsoria prolixa) belong to Matins, where they have a function similar to that of the Gradual and Alleluia (or Tract) in the Mass, that is, as musical postludes to the lessons. In the Roman rite the liturgy of Matins requires nine Responsories, three for each Nocturn. While for the weekdays a common fund of ordinary chants is drawn upon, the Sundays and feasts have proper chants, varying from one occasion to another. As a result a large repertory of Responsories has accrued, which has been still further expanded by local usages. Even larger is the number of Responsories prescribed for the monastic rite of the Benedictines, because here each Nocturn has four Responsories. An idea of the total repertory can be formed on the basis of early Antiphonals. The eleventh-century Codex Hartker includes over 600 Responsories, the twelfth-century Codex Lucca over 700, and the thirteenth-century Codex Worcester—a monastic Antiphonal—close to one thousand. Thus, from the point of view of quantity, the Responsories are second only to the Antiphons.

A considerable portion of this repertory is available in modern publications. The Liber usualis includes eight services of Matins: Maundy Thurs-

---

11 Once more I find it impossible to agree with Ferretti, who says that the Tracts of mode 2 are "very rich in formulae, and do not have the simplicity" of the Tracts of mode 8 (p. 139). Ferretti considers only the central group of the latter type, the five Tracts from Holy Saturday, passing over the others with a brief remark about "formules de rechange" (exchange formulae; p. 138). Naturally, it is unfair to draw a comparison between a group of five Tracts with a total of sixteen verses, and a group of more than twenty tracts with a total of eighty verses.

day, Good Friday, Holy Saturday, and the Office of the Dead, each with nine Responsories; the Nativity and Corpus Christi, each with eight Responsories, the ninth being replaced by the *Te Deum;* [1] and Easter Sunday and Pentecost, both of which have only one Nocturn, with two Responsories and the *Te Deum.* The *Liber responsorialis (LR)* includes the service of Matins for the Nativity, Epiphany, Easter Sunday, Ascension, Pentecost, Corpus Christi; for seven Commons of Saints; and for eleven special Feasts of Saints. Each of these services has twelve Responsories, in addition to which there are given *c.* 40 Responsories for the Sundays of the year. Yet other Responsories are contained in the *Processionale monasticum (PM)*, published for use in French Benedictine monasteries, where it is customary to sing Responsories during the procession from the place of assembly to the church. Finally, the *Variae preces (VP)* contain *c.* 25 Responsories not found in the publications just mentioned. Altogether, these books contain close to 500 Responsories, certainly a sufficiently large number to serve as a basis for investigation and, in fact, one much larger than can be considered in our study. A very complete and detailed investigation of the Responsories found in the *Antiphonale Sarisburiense* and other early sources has been made by W. H. Frere.[2]

Each Responsory consists of two different sections, the respond and the verse, after which the respond is repeated either complete or, more frequently, from some point within its course. The verses are normally sung to one of eight standard tones, i.e., the responsorial tones which have been studied previously.[3] The following study deals only with the music for the responds and, to a certain extent, with that of verses having individual melodies.

There exist Responsories and, consequently, responds in each of the eight modes. Those of the *protus* and *tetrardus* modes are the most frequent, and those of the *tritus* are relatively few in number, as appears from the table on p. 137. Within each mode there exist standard phrases which recur in a number of different melodies, similar to what has been observed in the Tracts. However, the centonization method, which plays such a basic role in the Tracts, is considerably less prominent in the responds. Certainly, there is no parallel in the responds to the completely unified picture presented by nearly all the Tracts of the second mode. In the Responsories each modal group includes a number of melodies showing fairly close thematic relationship, but in addition to these there are many others that differ more or less radically from the main type. Even in those that can be grouped together on the basis of common material,

1 See p. 22, fn. 5.
2 *Antiphonale Sarisburiense,* Dissertation, pp. 5-61.
3 See pp. 234ff.

this is often considerably modified and intermingled with free elements. The two most fully unified groups of Responsories are those of the second and eighth modes, that is, the same modes to which all the Tracts belong. We can only speculate whether there is a historical relationship between these two phenomena.

THE RESPONSORIES OF MODE 2

This mode has an easily recognizable main melody. P. Wagner gives the Responsory *Dominator Domine* as its representative, saying that "more than two-thirds of the Responsories of mode 2 follow this type, whose variants are not numerous and are easily recognized as such."[4] W. H. Frere opens his detailed investigation with *Domine Deus* (which is musically identical with *Dominator Domine*) and indicates forty specific melodies in the Sarum Antiphonal, the Lucca Ms, and the Codex Hartker, which belong to this type.[5] For our purpose it will suffice to consider the examples that are easily accessible in the previously mentioned publications. Responsories associated with recent feasts, such as *S. Joseph, Sponsus B. Mariae V*. [*LR* 301], have been excluded.

RESPONSORIES II, MAIN TYPE: TABULATION[6]

PM 113	*Dominator Domine*	$C_1 D_1$	D_2 $C_2{}^*$	$10+d_1$
	Domine Deus[7]	$C_1 D_1$	D_2 $C_2{}^*$	$11+d_1$
PM 174	*Levita Laurentius*	$C_1 D_1$	D_2 $C_2{}^*$	G_1 d_1
L 1360	*Obtulerunt*	$C_1 d_1$	$3+d_2$ $C_2{}^*$	G_1 $2+d_1$
LR 143	*Constitues*	$C_1 D_1$	D_2 $C_2{}^*$	G_1 $4+d_1$
LR 201	*Amavit eum*	$C_1 D_1$	d_2 $C_2{}^*$	$11+d_3$
L 639	*Judas Mercator*	$C_1 D_1$	D_2 $C_2{}^*$	F_1 $3+d_4$
L 590	*Ingrediente*	$C_1 D_1$	D_2 $C_2{}^*$	f_1 $6+d_4$
LR 425	*Domine mi*	$C_1 D_1$	d_2 $C_2{}^*$	f_1 d_4
LR 322	*Domine non aspicias*	$C_1 d_1$	d_2 C_2	$...d \mid 9+d_2{}^* \mid 6+d_1$
LR 395	*Emitte agnum*	$C_1 D_1{}^*$	D_2	$4+d_4$
VP 262	*Tua est potentia*	$C_1 D_1$	$C_2{}^*$	$8+d_1$
LR 422	*Si bona*	$C_1 d_1$	$...d$ $C_2{}^*$	$...f \mid G_1 \mid 4+d_1$
LR 71	*In columbae specie*	$C_1 D_1$	$D_2{}^*$ $...d$	$6+d_3$
LR 321	*Inito consilio*	$C_1 D_1$	D_2 F_1	$G_1 \mid C_2...c^* \mid D_1$
L 524	*Emendemus*	$C_1 D_1$	$...a$ $5+d^{1*}$	G_1 $5+d_1$

4 *Wagner III*, 336.

5 *Ant. Sarisb.*, I, 6.

6 The symbols have the same meaning as in the tabulation of the Tracts. For the meaning of *, see below under (4).

7 *Ant. Sarisb.*, I, 6.

FIGURE 94

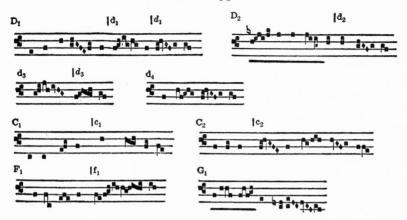

Responsories II: Standard Phrases

REMARKS:

1. The melodies show a tripartite structure, normally with two well-defined phrases in each of the three devisions. *Levita Laurentius, Obtulerunt,* and *Constitues* are the best representatives of this full form, which also prevails among the other Responsories, regardless of the mode.

2. Of the three divisions, the first is rigidly fixed. This is, of course, the result of our selection which includes only those Responsories that begin with $C_1 D_1$. Frere lists about twenty-five additional Responsories with the same beginning (O D^1 in his symbols). Ten of the Responsories of our tabulation also have an identical melody for the second division, and sixteen others of this type are indicated by Frere (O D^1 d^1 C). Variability in this division ranges from the omission of one of the two standard phrases (*Emitte agnum, Tua est potentia*) to a completely new melody, as in *Emendemus.* The third division shows the greatest amount of variability. The "normal" form, $G_1 d_1$, is found in only four Responsories of our tabulation. In others the first phrase is omitted or replaced by a standard F_1-phrase. Particularly irregular are the closing sections of *Domine non aspicias* and *Inito consilio,* as well as of many examples given by Frere.

3. In the material that has been available for this study, monotone recitation occurs only rarely. The main place for it is at the beginning of the formula F_1, which, in its complete form, includes a recitation on d—as in *Judas Mercator* and *Inito consilio* as well as in some Responsories of mode 2 that do not belong to the main type, e.g., *Repleti sunt* [875: "dabat eloqui"] or *Via recto* [LR 332: "cujus esset via quam cernerent, inqui-"]. The latter Responsory also shows a passage, "ab ejus cella in caelum usque," in which the recitation takes place on f, that is, on the

normal tenor of the second mode; but examples like this are rather exceptional. In this connection it should be noted that the responsorial tone used for the verses of the Responsories employs two tenors, f for the first half and d for the second half.[8] Although the melodies for the responds rarely show exact recitation on f, they frequently emphasize this pitch, thus making some of the melodies appear as free elaborations of a psalmodic formula with recitation alternating between f and d. A good example is *Ingrediente* [590].

4. An even clearer indication of a relationship between respond and verse exists in the fact that the formula C_2 of the former is identical with the termination of the latter.[9] This identity is of special interest because of its structural significance in the performance of the entire Responsory. This performance calls for the repeat, after the verse, of the concluding section of the respond, normally its third division, as is indicated in our schematic representation by the asterisk. It will be seen that in nearly all the Responsories, invariably in all those having the normal structure, this repeat starts after C_2. If we distinguish the two sections of the respond as R_1 and R_2 and designate the formula C_2 by the letter e (ending), the overall form becomes:

$$\overbrace{\substack{\text{R} \\ R_1 + e \to R_2}} \quad \overbrace{\substack{\text{V} \quad \text{R}' \\ V + e \to R_2}}.$$

Thus, the connection between R_1 and R_2 (indicated by the arrow) is made by the same cadential formula as that between V and R'. It appears that in all these cases the melody for the respond is written with a view to its being repeated, not in full, but only partly. This seemingly minor detail has considerable historical significance.[10]

If, on the basis of the schematic representations, the general structure of the Responsories is compared with that of the Tracts, e.g., those of mode 8, the extended use, in either category, of standard phrases seems to indicate a common principle of composition. Both can be, and usually are, regarded as examples of centonization. Actually, however, the two cases are quite different, as appears from the fact that in the Tracts the standard phrases occur in a great variety of combinations, while in the Responsories they occur mostly in an invariable sequence, $C_1 D_1 D_2 C_2 \ldots$ thus forming an extended melody which recurs at the beginning of each of the Responsories, each time with a different text. Only in the third division are standard phrases employed in various combinations. Therefore the entire group must be regarded as an example primarily of adapta-

8 See p. 235.
9 See any of the tables of the responsorial tones mentioned on p. 234.
10 See p. 513.

tion, with centonization being employed only for the closing section of the melodies.

In view of this state of affairs, the question may be raised whether there is any point in considering the four initial formulae of our tabulation as individual entities rather than as mere subdivisions of one and the same melody. In order to answer this question we must consider not only the special group which served as a point of departure but the entire repertory of Responsories of mode 2. This includes a number of examples in which one or another of the standard phrases occurs singly, in variable positions and in connection with other phrases. Some of the latter may also be termed "standard" because of their recurrence in different melodies. In fact, in his detailed analysis, Frere indicates, in addition to the main group (II^a), several other groups of Responsories having some material in common (II^b, II^c, II^d), but none of these are nearly as well defined as the main group. For our purposes it will suffice to indicate some Responsories in which one or another of the standard phrases recurs. Short and long strokes, representing the half-bar and the full bar, have been added in order to facilitate orientation.[11]

L	733	*Sepulto Domino*	C_1 ... ∣ ... ∣ ...
LR	138	*Fuerunt sine*	C_1 ∣ ... ∣ ... ∣ G_1 ∣ ... ∣ ...
L	673	*Velum templi*	... ∣ D_1 ∣ ... ∣ ... ∣ $6+d_3$
LR	72	*Reges Tharsis*	... ∣ $2+d_1$ ∣ ... ∣ D_1
L	384	*Sancta et immaculata*	$3+D_1$ ∣ $6+C_2$ ∣ G_1 ∣ ...
L	875	*Repleti sunt*	... d_1 ∣ ... ∣ F_1 ∣ $9+f_1$ ∣ $2+d_3$
LR	113	*Loquebantur*	... d_3 ∣ ... ∣ F_1 ∣ $2+d_3$
LR	354	*Innuebant*	... ∣ D_1 ∣ $6+d_2$ ∣ C_2 ∣ $5+d_1$
L	1791	*Hei mihi*	... ∣ ... ∣ F_1 ∣ $8+d_1$
L	1791	*Memento mihi*	... ∣ $5+d_4$ ∣ ... ∣ d_4
LR	105	*Ponis nubem*	$6+d_4$ ∣ ... ∣ C_2 ∣ ...
LR	195	*Ecce vere*	$6+d_3$ ∣ $2+d_3'$ ∣ ... ∣ C_2 ∣ ... ∣ ...
PM	249	*Benedicta*	... ∣ $6+d_2$ ∣ C_2 ∣ G_1 ∣ D_1
PM	117	*Homo Dei*	... ∣ $5+d_1$ ∣ ... ∣ ... (transposed to a).

This tabulation shows that standard phrases do occur in many Responsories of the second mode, but that their role is rather limited, most of the phrases being free. Actually, the number of free phrases is somewhat less than is suggested by the symbols of the table. For instance, *Velum templi* and *Reges Tharsis* employ the same c-formula for the beginning, and

11 Most of the D-phrases close with the same cadential formula, e-f-e-d-e e-d. This also occurs frequently at the end of sections which in this tabulation are represented by the symbol ..., that is, as free sections. Thus, all the free sections of *Sepulto Domino* close with this standard cadence. This and other details of a similar nature have not been included in the tabulations, in order to avoid their becoming even more complex as they already are.

another recurs at the beginning of *Repleti sunt, Loquebantur,* and *Innuebant.* Both could well be added to the store of standard phrases, and fuller investigations would yield several others, mainly d-formulae, that recur more or less frequently. We can dispense with the consideration of these details, not only because they are fully explored in Frere's study, but also because they do not add any new features to the picture.

It is, however, important to realize that all the afore-mentioned Responsories as well as many others, although frequently employing free material, nevertheless exhibit certain general traits that make them appear as members of one and the same family. What binds them together is, first of all, the cadential structure which, in spite of numerous variations and deviations, reveals a general principle; that is, emphasis on the tonic and subtonic, with occasional cadences on the third above, or on the fifth below the final, both of which occur, if at all, only toward the end of the melody. Hand in hand with this goes a certain "family resemblance" of nearly all the phrases, whether standard or free, that close on the same note. Common to them is a relatively narrow range, in which they move almost exclusively in the smallest intervals, seconds and thirds. It would be entirely possible to reduce all of them to two skeleton melodies, one closing on c, the other, on d:

FIGURE 95

C-phrase   D-phrase

W. H. Frere expresses this idea of family relationship by using the term "typical" for all the Responsories showing the same basic design. The validity of such a designation appears even more clearly if, in conclusion, we turn our attention to what he calls "original" Responsories, that is, a small group of melodies that show essentially different traits. The most striking example is *Collegerunt pontifices* [579], which is sung during the Blessing of the Palms on Palm Sunday. The ample melisma on "Collegerunt," with its repeated scale formation rising through a full octave, from G to g; the ascending and descending leaps of a fifth on "Quid facimus"; the descent from a to A on "veniant," with its quasi-sequential pattern: these are traits never encountered in any of the typical Responsories of the second mode. Equally exceptional is the verse, which is not sung to the responsorial tone but to a free melody that incorporates, on "Ab," the melisma on "veniant" from the respond.

Another "original" Responsory of mode 2 is *Stirps Jesse* [PM 186] from *Nativitas B.M.V.,* the melody of which recurs almost note for note in the late adaptation, *Comedetis* [927], for Corpus Christi. Its most striking feature is the long melisma on "almus" ("vescendum" in *Comedetis*), similar in its outline and sequential design to the "veniant" melisma of *Collegerunt*. The verse employs the responsorial tone only for the first half, closing with a free, melismatic termination.

It will suffice to indicate one more example, that is, *Circumdederunt* [*PM* 52] from Passion Sunday. Like *Collegerunt,* it has a free melody for both respond and verse, with some material common to both:

FIGURE 96

THE RESPONSORIES OF MODE 8

This mode includes more Responsories than any other, almost twice as many as mode 2. In spite of this, it does not have a central group of striking preponderance such as is found in the second mode. Instead, there are several "main melodies," each of which recurs, with modifications mainly in the final division, in a number of Responsories.

RESPONSORIES VIII: TABULATION

GROUP I

PM	153	*Hic est Michael*	F_1 G_1	G_2 F_2	$6+d_1$		g_1
PM	213	*Orante S. Clemente*	F_1 G_1	G_2 F_2	$8+f_1$		G_3
LR	114	*Disciplinam*	F_1 G_1 g_5	G_2 F_2	...		$6+g_5$
LR	76	*Magi veniunt*	F_1 G_1	G_4 F_2			$7+g_1$
PM	30	*Stephanus servus*	F_1 G_1	G_4' F_2	C_1		G_3
LR	90	*Tulerunt Dominum*	F_1 $9+g_1$	G_4 F_2	$5+d_1 \mid F_1 \mid ... \mid 6+g_5$		
L	732	*Astiterunt*	F_1 G_1	G_4	D_1		g_1
L	938	*Misit me*	F_1 G_1		$4+d_1$		g_1
L	1841	*Ecce sacerdos*	F_1 G_1	$6+g_5$	...		g_1

GROUP II

L	390	*Verbum caro*	F_1 G_3	...	$11+d_1$		$2+g_1$
LR	384	*In conspectu*	F_1 G_3	G_2 F_2	D_1	F_1	g_3
LR	272	*Ostendit mihi*	F_1 $7+g_3$	G_2	$14+d_1$		$3+g_5$
LR	253	*Ornatam monilibus*	F_1 $4+g_3$	G_4 ...	D_1	F_1 $4+g_1$	

GROUP III

LR 81	Hic est dies	F_1 A_1	G_2 F_2	D_1	F_1 G_1			
LR 159	Domine praevenisti	F_1 A_1	G_2 F_2		$2+g_5$			
LR 199	Iste est qui ante	F_1 A_1	G_2 F_2	D_1	$7+G_3$			
LR 331	Sexto die	F_1 A_1	G_2 F_2	D_1	g_1			
PM 183	Misit Herodes	F_1 A_1	G_2 F_2		$6+G_1$			
LR 390	Vidi angelum	F_1 A_1	G_2 F_2	$D_1 \mid F_1 \mid \ldots \mid 12+c_1 \mid 9+g_5$				
LR 80	Venit lumen	F_1 A_1	G_2 $3+f_2$	D_1	g_1			
LR 238	Orantibus in loco	F_1 A_1	G_2 $2+f_2$	D_1	g_1			
LR 235	Benedic Domine	F_1 A_1	G_2	D_1	$3+g_1$			
LR 257	Beatam me dicent	F_1 $3+a_1$	G_4 F_2		$4+g_1$			

GROUP IV

L 376	Hodie nobis	C_1	G_3	$\ldots \mid 6+g_3$	
L 580	In monte Oliveti	C_1	G_3	$6+g_5 \mid \ldots \mid G_4 \mid F_2 \mid G_2$	
L 630	Tristis est	C_1	G_3	$\ldots \mid \ldots \mid C_1 \mid 4+f_1 \; G_3$	
L 640	Unus ex discipulis	C_1	G_3	$3+f_2 \; f_2 \mid C_1 \mid 2+g_1$	
L 675	Vinea mea	C_1	G_3	$G_4 \; 3+f_2 \mid \ldots \mid 4+g_1$	
LR 145	Isti sunt qui	C_1		$6+f_1 \mid 2+g_3 \mid \ldots \mid 5+g_3$	
LR 401	Caecus sedebat	C_1 $3+g_1$	G_3	$G_4 \mid F_2 \mid 8+g_5$	

FIGURE 97

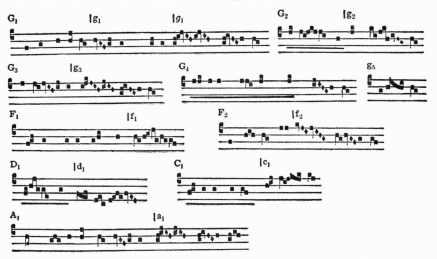

Responsories VIII: Standard Phrases

REMARKS:

1. Group I is remarkably similar in its cadential outline to the main type of the Responsories of mode 2, both employing subtonic and tonic

in the first division, tonic and subtonic in the second, and in the last a somewhat variable cadence point followed by the tonic.

FIGURE 98

Mode 2   Mode 8

2. Group II differs from group I in th̲   ̲t the end of the first division. Its cadential structure is essentially the same.

3. Group III, the largest and most stable of all, is characterized by the phrase A_1, which replaces the G_1 of group I. Actually, both these formulae are identical except for their final notes. If this difference is disregarded, as it may well be, the entire group III would combine with group I, resulting in a large central theme. In fact, Frere considers both groups as identical, employing the same symbols ($O^a + G_5$) for the beginning of *Magi veniunt* (p. 54) and of *Hic est Michael* (p. 52).[12] Wagner points out that the use of one variant or the other has a certain structural significance, being conditioned by the beginning of the subsequent phrase, G_2 or G_4. Both of these occur either with or without the "intonation" f-a. If this is present, the preceding phrase ends on a (A_1), if not, on g (G_1):

FIGURE 99

A_1 G_2 G_1 G_2

All our examples follow this rule, except for *Disciplinam* (group I), in which a short formula separates the two standard phrases in question.

4. Group IV is represented almost exclusively by Responsories from the highest feasts, the Nativity, Palm Sunday, Maundy Thursday, and Good Friday. It may well be of more ancient origin than the others. Only its first division is fixed, the continuation lacking a definite cadential pattern and frequently employing free material. Yet another detail that sets this group apart from the others is the complete absence of phrases closing on d.

5. The various g-phrases have well-defined functions in the over-all structure. G_1, G_3, and g_5 occur only at the end of a division, G_2 and G_4 only at the beginning. Similarly, F_1 is essentially an opening phrase, F_2 a closing phrase. In not a few cases, however, F_1 recurs as a mediant formula in the third division, e.g., in *Tulerunt, In conspectu,* and *Ornatam monilibus.*

[12] See also the musical illustration, *Ant. Sarisb.*, p. 53, where, in the second column, the formula G_5 appears twice closing on g, twice on a.

The general picture presented by these Responsories is very interesting and instructive, because it illustrates the interpenetration of two basic principles of Gregorian composition, adaptation and centonization. Within each group, the various Responsories are related to each other by adaptation, particularly in their first and second divisions. Centonization prevails in the concluding sections of the Responsories, and also relates the various groups to each other.

As in the Responsories of mode 2, many more examples of centonization occur in the large number of melodies that differ more or less radically from the types indicated above. Many of these melodies can also be combined in groups, on the basis of common opening phrases. It will suffice to indicate one such group characterized by a new opening phrase, G_6:[13]

FIGURE 100

LR 217	Specie tua	$G_6 \,	\ldots	\, 9+g_1$
LR 222	Fallax gratia	$G_6 \,	\, 4+g_5 \,	\ldots	\, g_1$
LR 295	Cumque perfusis	$G_6 \,	\, 13+f_2 \,	\, 7+g_2 \,	\ldots g_5$
LR 316	Descendit Jesus	$G_6 \, \ldots	\, 3+g_1$
LR 413	Quid me quaeritis	$G_6 \,|\, 6+g_1 \,|\ldots| \, 7+f_2 \,|\, 3+d_1 \,|\, g_1$
PM 20	Ecce dies	$G_6 \,|\ldots|\ldots|\ldots|\ldots| \, 9+g_5 \,|\, 5+g_5$
PM 269	Ecclesiae sponsum	$G_6 \,	\, 5+g_5 \,	\ldots	\, 7+g_5$
VP 259	Iste est de sublimibus	$G_6 \,|\ldots|\ldots|\ldots|\ldots$

The absence of a fixed cadential scheme, and the extended use of free material or of standard cadences rather than complete standard phrases, are quite typical for all the peripheral groups. Finally, it may be noticed that there are practically no Responsories in mode 8 that could be termed original. The closest approximation to such a melody is that of *Videntes Joseph a longe* [LR 408], with its exceptionally high-pitched melisma (c' to f') on "longe" and the ascending-seventh formation (d-e-f-g-a-c') on "somnia."

THE OTHER RESPONSORIES

As to the Responsories of the other modes, we shall limit ourselves to some general remarks. To treat them in the same detailed manner as those of modes 2 and 8 would demand a considerable amount of space without adding new traits to the general picture. In each mode there can be found a main melody which is used, with some modifications, for a number of

13 See *Wagner III*, 343, for additional Responsories of this group.

different texts. These form a central group governed chiefly by the method of adaptation. The basic melody consists of a number of phrases, and some of these recur in other Responsories where they are combined with other phrases, in a process of centonization. One or the other of these derivative melodies may again be used for different texts, or some of their constituent elements may recur in yet other Responsories. On the basis of identical material, mainly in the opening phrase, the repertory can be divided into a number of groups. Hardly any of these, however, is as well defined and as fully represented as are the groups of modes 2 and 8. Considered as a whole, all the Responsories that can be classified under one or another of these groups form a family of "typical" Responsories which are related to each other through some fixed method of composition, such as adaptation, centonization, or free modification of basic formulae.

Interesting though these processes of "musical synthesis" are, they should not be permitted to obscure the quantitative share, much less the artistic significance of original creation in the Responsories. It is perhaps no mere coincidence that this element is rather inadequately represented in the two modes that have been discussed. Both the second and the eighth mode seem to have been so strongly under the influence of formulism that free invention could hardly gain a foothold in them. It found an abode mainly in the authentic sister-modes, particularly in the first mode, which is by far the most prolific source for Responsories with individual melodies.

Among the free Responsories of the first mode is the *Libera me* from the Burial Service [1767], one of the most celebrated chants of the Gregorian repertory. It employs free melodies, impressive in their somber solemnity, for the respond as well as for each of its three verses, which are conspicuous for their syllabic style, similar to that normally found in the Antiphons. Of much the same character is the *Libera me . . . de viis* from Matins of the Office of the Dead [1798], which, however, employs for the verse the standard responsorial tone, though with a special termination. While both these Responsories move essentially within the limited range common to the authentic and plagal *protus,* much more strikingly free and uninhibited melodies are found in other Responsories of the first mode, for instance, *Filiae Jerusalem* [LR 169], *Ecce apparebit* [LR 393], *O beata Trinitas* [PM 91], and *Duo Seraphim* [PM 107]. The former two move above the authentic ambitus up to f', while the latter descend below it down to A, so that they could almost equally well be assigned to the plagal mode. Next to the first mode, the seventh is the main source for original melodies, such as *Aspiciens a longe* [PM 18], *Signum magnum* [PM 120],[14] or *Crux fidelis* [PM 152], or *O beate Johannes* [VP 210]. Among the Responsories included in the *Liber usualis* those of Corpus Christi are

14 For the late Feast of the Immaculate Conception, but in all probability with the new text adapted to a medieval melody.

noteworthy for their free melodies, particularly *Immolabit haedum* [926], *Coenantibus illis* [932], *Accepit Jesus* [932], and *Ego sum panis* [933].[15] We have previously pointed out that nearly all of these Responsories employ free melodies also for their verses [p. 240].

A particularly interesting trait of many Responsories is an extended melisma that occurs near the end of the respond, much longer and more exuberant than the "standard" or normal melismas, and therefore constituting a strikingly extraneous element within the over-all course of the melody. Two examples found in the *Liber usualis* occur among the Responsories from Corpus Christi, in *Comedetis* [927] on "vescendum" and in *Coenantibus* [931] on "corpus." Others are:

> Mode 1: *Unus panis* [LR 129]: "participamus"
>   *Terribilis est* [LR 235]: "Vere"
>   *Intempestae noctis* [LR 328]: "Omnem"
>   *Hodie Maria* [LR 379]: "regnat"
>   *Civitas Jerusalem* [PM 24]: "feret"
>   *Sint lumbi* [PM 228]: "a nuptiis"
> Mode 3: *Quis Deus* [LR 342]: "mirabilia"
> Mode 4: *Ego pro te* [LR 365]: "fratres"
>   *Judaea et Jerusalem* [PM 25]: "erit"
> Mode 6: *Homo quidam* [LR 419]: "omnia"
> Mode 7: *Moram faciente* [LR 297]: "volabo"[16]

Not a few of these melismas or, as they are called, responsorial *neumata,*

FIGURE 101

1. *Intempestate noctis* [LR 328]   2. *Moram faciente* [LR 297]

[15] The melodies for the Responsories of Corpus Christi were all borrowed, as were those for the chants of the Mass [see p. 68]. For example, *Immolabit* is from *Te sanctum* [PM 109; St. Michael], *Comedetis* from *Stirps Jesse* [PM 186; Annunciation], *Respexit Elias* from *Videte miraculum* [PM 251; Purification]. They were selected according to successive modes [see p. 140].

[16] According to *Wagner III*, 345, these melismas occur only sparingly in the tenth-century Codex Hartker, but much more frequently in the eleventh-century Codex Lucca where, however, they are restricted to the first and the eighth modes. They were used primarily for the last Responsory of the second and third Nocturn of feasts of Saints.

show a repeat structure, a a b, which we shall encounter again in numerous melismas of the Offertories and Alleluias.[17]

The most famous of the responsorial *neumata* is the *neuma triplex* which, so Amalarius tells us, was sung, "contrary to the custom of other Responsories," in the "novissimo responsorio" *In medio ecclesiae* for the Feast of St. John the Evangelist, and was introduced by the *moderni cantores* into the Responsory *Descendit de caelis* from the Nativity.[18] While it largely disappeared in the former, it was preserved in the latter, where it occurs on the penultimate word, "fabricae," in the form of three melismas, one for each of the three repeats of the respond (*Descendit de caelis* has the form R V R' D R' R; see *PM* 27). The first of these is comparable in extension and ornateness to the longest melismas found in the previously mentioned Responsories. The second is of about the same character, but the third is a vocalization of truly staggering dimensions, such as one expects to find in Ambrosian chant. Fig. 102 shows these three *neumata,* together with the corresponding passage in the initial respond.

FIGURE 102

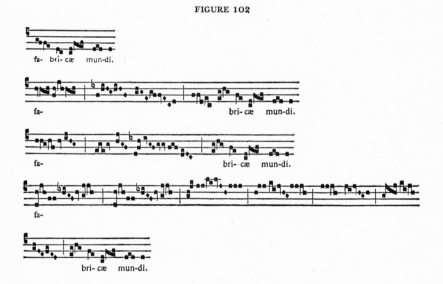

Only the first of these three *neumata* survived in the Responsory *In medio ecclesiae* (in Paschal Time; *PM* 227), where it appears at the end of the Respond, to the word "Alleluia."

17 See pp. 368f, 386ff.

18 *Liber de ordine antiphonarii,* cap. xviii (ed. Hanssens, III, 54-56; *Patr. lat.* 105, pp. 1273-5). F. Handschin points out that "the words 'in novissimo responsorio' . . . do not mean that it was a recent Responsory but that it was the last in the cycle of Responsories belonging to the Nocturns of St. John" (*New Oxf. Hist. of Mus.,* II, 142).

These responsorial *neumata* play an interesting role in the problem of the tropes. We shall return to them in the chapter dealing with this aspect of the chant [see p. 441].

THE GRADUALS

The Graduals are sung at Mass after the first lesson. Like the Responsories they consist of two sections, the choral respond and the solo verse, with the respond repeated, always in full, after the verse. Differing from the verses of the Responsories, those of the Graduals are sung, not to standard tones, but to individual melodies which, however, are closely interrelated by an extended use of standard phrases, as will be shown later.

Stylistically the Graduals are the most fully melismatic chants of the Gregorian repertory. Every Gradual contains a number of extended melismas, with from ten to thirty and more notes. These occur not only at the beginning or the end but often also in the middle of a phrase, sometimes emphasizing an important word, but mostly as a purely musical adornment, a sudden outburst of unrestrained vocality. Not infrequently the verses are even more melismatic than the responds, obviously because they were entrusted to the soloist. An extreme case is the Gradual *Clamaverunt* [1170] from the Common of Two Martyrs (originally for the Feast of SS. Cosma and Damian), the verse of which contains some of the longest melismas found in the Graduals and, for that matter, in the entire repertory of chants—one with fifty-six and one with sixty-six notes.

A tendency to set the verse off from the respond is noticeable in the difference of range or, at least, of tessitura that often exists between the two sections, the verse being slightly higher than the respond [see p. 150]. On the whole, however, the responds and the verses are rather similar in style, certainly much more so than in the Responsories in which there is a pronounced difference between the "free" melodies of the responds and the standard tones used for the verses. Moreover, there are not a few Graduals which employ the same material both in the respond and in the verse, particularly for their closing sections [see p. 355].

More than any other type of chant, the Graduals make use of the "re-iterative style," which has been described previously [see p. 262]. This manifests itself most clearly in the frequent use of repercussive neumes, such as the *bistropha* and *tristropha*, which are often combined into tremolos of five, six, or seven notes, or the *pressus*, mostly on c'-c'-c'-a, which may be immediately repeated three or four times.[1] The most striking example is the following passage from the Gradual *Misit Dominus* [485]:

[1] See the formula F_{11} of Fig. 104, p. 349.

FIGURE 103

℣.Confi-te-an-   tur

Nearly every Gradual includes melismas of this kind, or other formations indicative of the reiterative style. Thus, *Universi* [320] shows repercussive melismas on "expectant," "Domine," and "mihi"; *Ex Sion* [328] on "Congregate" (notice also the repeated use of motives such as e'-d'-c', d'-e'-d'-c' and b-c'-b-a, b-c'-a-g); *Qui sedes* [335] is remarkable for its several examples of freely sequential formations, e.g., on "regis" (essentially e'-c' d'-b c'-a b-g a-f g) and on "Joseph" (d'-b f'-d' f'-d' e'-c' d'-b d'-b c'-a a-f g); etc. Many of the standard phrases to be discussed later show a reiterative design, and since these phrases recur in numerous Graduals of the same mode, the entire repertory becomes permeated by such formations.

The most interesting aspect of the Graduals as a group is their use of standard phrases. These play an important role particularly in the verse sections, where centonization occasionally approximates the extent to which it occurs in the Tracts. However, this technique is also evident in the responds. The study of this aspect involves, of course, a separate investigation of the various modes. We have seen that the Graduals are almost entirely limited to the four authentic modes, with those of the fifth mode outnumbering all the others together.[2] If only because of their quantity, the Graduals of mode 5 afford by far the best insight into the various problems of structure and style that arise. They are therefore placed at the beginning of our study.

THE GRADUALS OF MODE 5

The *Liber usualis* contains about fifty Graduals of the fifth mode, the *Graduale romanum c.* sixty. Like the Tracts, a number of these are recent compositions or adaptations made at Solesmes; e.g., *Confiteor tibi* [1668] for the Feast of St. Teresa of the Child Jesus, *Flores apparuerunt* [1376] for the Feast of the Apparition of Our Blessed Lady at Lourdes, or *Nova bella* [Supplement] for the Feast of St. Joan of Arc. The medieval repertory, as represented by the manuscripts from the tenth to the twelfth centuries, includes about 45 Graduals in the fifth mode; these form the basis of the subsequent analysis.[3] Following is a schematic tabulation, arranged according to the initial formulae of the verses.

[2] See p. 137. As for the seemingly large number of Graduals in mode 2, see the remark on p. 138.

[3] See also the studies in *Wagner III*, 383ff, and in Ferretti, pp. 117ff, the latter limited to the verses.

		RESPOND	VERSE
GROUP I			
L 1037	*Bonum est confidere*	$F_a \mid \ldots \mid f_4$	$A_{10} \mid A_{15} \mid F_{10}$
L 1547	*Justorum animae*	$F_c \mid G_1 \mid \ldots$	$A_{10} \mid A_{15} \mid F_{10}$
G 92	*Unam petii, V̷. Ut videam*	$F_a \mid \ldots \mid \ldots \mid f_5$	$A_{10} \mid A_{15} \mid F_{10}$
L 471	*Unam petii, V̷. Beati*	same	$a_{10} \mid A_{15} \mid F_{10}$
L 1139	*Justus cum ceciderit*	$\ldots \mid F_1 \mid 3 + f_{10}$	$a_{10} \mid A_{15} \mid F_{10}$
G 311	*Ego dixi*	$\ldots c_1 \mid \ldots \mid c_1 \mid \ldots f_{11}$	$a_{10} \mid A_{15} \, c_{12} \mid F_{17} \mid \ldots (a)$
L 1167	*Anima nostra*	$C_1 \mid A_1 \mid \ldots a_2 + f_{11}$	$A_{10} \mid A_{15} \, c_{12} \mid 11 + c_{13} \mid 7 + f_{11}$
L 1602	*Propter veritatem*	$\ldots G_1 \mid \ldots$	$A_{10} \mid C_{12} \mid 6 + F_{12} \mid F_{13}$
GROUP II			
L 655	*Christus factus*	$F_b \mid F_1 \mid F_2$	$i_1 + A_{11} \mid C_{12} \mid F_{10}$
L 422	*Exiit sermo*	$F_b \mid F_1 \mid F_2$	$i_1 + A_{11} \mid F_{12} \mid F_{10}$
L 1183	*Ecce sacerdos*	$F_b \mid F_1 \mid F_2$	$i_1 + A_{11} \mid A_{15} \mid F_{10}$
L 999	*Propitius esto*	$F_a \mid \ldots \mid \ldots f_6$	$i_2 + A_{11} \mid A_{15} \mid F_{10}$
L 1251	*Locus iste*	$\ldots \mid \ldots f_4$	$i_3 + A_{11} \mid F_{14} \mid F_{10}$
L 1041	*Bonum est confiteri*	$C_1 \mid A_1 \mid \ldots \mid F_{11}$	$i_3 + A_{11} \mid A_{15} \, c_{12} \mid F_{17} \mid F_{10}$
G 643	*Vindica Domine*	$C_1 \mid \ldots f_3 \mid \ldots \cdot f_7$	$i_3 + A_{11} \mid A_{15} \, c_{12} \mid 6 + f_{18} \mid 5 + f_{11}$
L 1025	*In Deo speravit*	$\ldots \mid C_1 \mid \ldots$	$i_3 + A_{11} \mid C_{12} \mid \ldots \mid F_{10}$
GROUP III			
L 1007	*Convertere*	$F_a \mid \ldots \mid \ldots f_{10}$	$A_{12} \mid F_{14} \mid F_{10}$
L 1519	*Constitues*	$\ldots \mid \ldots f_4$	$A_{12} \mid F_{14} \mid 12 + f_{16}$
G 910	*Benedictus es*	$= Constitues$	$A_{12} \mid F_{14} \mid 6 + f_{16}$
L 1010	*Venite filii*	$\ldots \mid \ldots f_4$	$A_{12} \mid \ldots \mid 11 + f_4$
GROUP IV			
L 1362	*Suscepimus Deus*	$F_d \mid \ldots \mid \ldots \mid F_2$	$A_{13} \mid C_{12} \mid F_{10}$
G 158	*Discerne causam*	$F_b \mid \ldots f_5$	$A_{13} \mid C_{12} \mid \ldots \mid F_{10}$
L 1017	*Domine Dominus*	$F_d \mid \ldots f_6$	$A_{13} \mid \ldots \mid F_{10}$
G 164	*Pacifice loquebantur*	$F_b \mid \ldots a_1 \mid \ldots f_6$	$A_{13} \mid \ldots \mid F_{10}$
G 522	*Fuit homo*	$C_1 \mid \ldots \mid \ldots \mid \ldots f_{10}$	$A_{13} \mid F_{12} \mid a_{10} \mid F_{11}$

GROUP V			
L 354	*Prope est Dominus*	$C_1 \mid \ldots f_3 \mid \ldots \mid \ldots f_{11}$	$A_{14} \mid C_{12} \mid i_1 + a_{10} \mid 5 + f_{11}$
L 489	*Timebunt gentes*	$F_b \mid F_1' \mid \ldots f_3 \mid \ldots f_7$	$i_1 + A_{14} \mid a_{12} \mid F_{18} \mid F_{10}$
G 162	*Tollite hostias*	$\ldots \mid \ldots f_{10}$	$i_1 + C_{14} \mid \ldots \mid \ldots \mid F_{10}$
L 485	*Misit Dominus*	$F_b \mid F_1 \mid \ldots \mid \ldots$	$\ldots C_{14} \mid F_{15} \mid A_{16} \mid 6 + c_{13} \mid F_{11}$
GROUP VI			
L 416	*Sederunt principes*	$\ldots \mid \ldots \mid \ldots f_4$	$C_{10} \mid C_{12} \mid F_{10}$
L 1003	*Protector noster*	$C_1 \mid \ldots \mid \ldots$	$C_{10} \mid F_{14} \mid F_{10}$
L 404	*Benedictus qui venit*	$\ldots \mid \ldots$	$C_{10} \mid F_{12} \mid \ldots \mid F_{11}$
GROUP VII			
L 1226	*Specie tua*	$C_1 \mid \ldots \mid \ldots c_1 \ldots a_2 + f_{11}$	$C_{11} \mid F_{15} \mid C_{16} \mid C_{12}' \mid 3 + c_{13} \mid F_{11}$
L 546	*Tribulationes*	$\ldots \mid \ldots \mid \ldots$	$C_{11} \ldots \mid A_{10} \mid C_{12} \mid F_{11}$
GROUP VIII			
G 369	*Quis sicut*	$F_b \mid \ldots \mid \ldots f_{10}$	$M + c_{10} \mid \ldots \mid 4 + a_{10} \mid F_{10}$
L 1345	*Qui operatus est*	$\ldots \mid \ldots \mid \ldots f_5$	$M + c_{10} \mid \ldots \mid \ldots \mid F_{10}$
L 459	*Omnes de Saba*	$\ldots \mid \ldots \mid \ldots f_5$	$M + c_{10} \mid \ldots \mid a_{17} \mid 3 + F_{10}$
L 409	*Viderunt omnes*	$\ldots \mid \ldots \mid \ldots f_4$	$i_1 + M + a_{17} \mid \ldots \mid 5 + a_{17} \mid F_{12} F_{13}$
OTHERS			
L 1033	*Respice Domine*	$\ldots \mid A_1 \mid \ldots f_3 \mid \ldots$	$F_{15} \mid c_{10} \mid 1 + A_{16}' \mid 7 + f_{17} \mid F_{10}$
L 1136	*Beatus vir qui*	$\ldots \mid \ldots$	$\ldots \mid \ldots F_{10}$
L 961	*Ad Dominum*	$C_1 \mid \ldots \mid \ldots f_5$	$\ldots \mid A_{16} + c_{13} \mid \ldots \mid f_{11}$
L 1221	*Adjuvabit*	$\ldots \mid \ldots \mid \ldots f_5$	$\ldots \mid \ldots \mid 5 + f_{18} \mid F_{10}$
L 1013	*Esto mihi*	$\ldots c_1 \ldots a_2 + f_{11}$	$\ldots \mid A_{15} \mid F_{10}$
L 328	*Ex Sion*	$\ldots \mid \ldots$	$\ldots \mid \ldots \mid 4 + A_{16} \mid \ldots$
L 1500	*Priusquam*	$F_a \mid \ldots$	$8 + c_{12} \mid \ldots \mid F_{10}$
L 1594	*Probasti*	$F_c \mid G_1 \mid \ldots$	$\ldots \mid \ldots f_{11}$
L 1133	*Gloria et honore*	$= Probasti$	$= Probasti$

347

EXPLANATIONS:

1. Standard phrases of the responds are indicated by inferior letters (F_a, etc.) or by inferior figures 1 to 7, the former for initial phrases, the latter for the others. Standard phrases occurring mainly in the verses have inferior numbers beginning with 10 (A_{10}, etc.).
2. The standard phrase A_{11} of group II is preceded by different intonations, i_1, i_2, i_3.
3. The standard phrases A_{14} and A_{16} also occur in a slightly shortened form closing on $c\prime$ (C_{14}, C_{16}).
4. The opening phrase of group VIII is an extended melisma (M) which occurs with two different endings, c_{10} or a_{17}.

FIGURE 104

Graduals V: Standard Phrases

RESPONDS

VERSES

VERSES (*continued*)

REMARKS:

A. The Verses

1. The standard phrases are rather strictly divided into initial, final, and intermediate formulae. To the first category belong A_{10}, A_{11}, A_{12}, A_{13}, $A_{14}(C_{14})$, C_{10}, C_{11}, and M. Exceptionally, A_{10} appears as an intermediate phrase in *Tribulationes* (group VII). Nearly all the verses close with either F_{10} or F_{11}. Notable exceptions are *Viderunt* (VIII) and *Propter veritatem* (I), which close on F_{13}; *Ex Sion* (final group) with a singular ending; and *Ego dixi* (I), which closes on a.

2. The phrases of the verses employ only three cadential notes, that is, f, a, and c'.

3. The sections which, in our analysis, are marked as "free" (. . .) occasionally include short recurrent motives such as c'd'c' c' aba [*Venite filii* on "(illuminami)ni" and *Tollite hostias* on "(conden)sa"] or fgagf g gf [*Domine Dominus* on "tua" and *Discerne causam* on "(deduxe)runt"] that belong to the common language of our Graduals. These and several others of an even more "commonplace" nature are indicated in Ferretti's analysis (*Esthétique*, p. 117; formulae 34a, 34g, etc.) which, it seems to us, goes a bit too far in breaking down musical entities into small particles.

B. The Responds

4. The analysis shows that the responds, although much freer than the verses, nevertheless make considerable use of standard phrases or of their endings, particularly at the beginning and at the end. It should be noticed that most of the formulae of the responds are somewhat variable, as is indicated by underlining in the table of standard phrases. Among the very few responds that are entirely idiomelic is *Viderunt omnes* from Nativity, which, for liturgical reasons, one is inclined to regard as one of the earliest.

5. A number of Graduals employ the two main verse endings, F_{10} (f_{10}) and F_{11} (f_{11}) also for the close of the respond. In most, though not all, of these the formula of the respond is the same as that of the verse, resulting in a musical rhyme between the two sections, as in *Justus cum ceciderit* (f_{10}, F_{10}) or in *Prope est* (f_{11}, f_{11}). Actually, the number of Graduals with a short rhyme is even greater than appears from the tabulation, since the respond formula f_4 is very similar to the verse formula f_{10} and could well be considered as a variant thereof.

THE GRADUALS OF MODE 1

The medieval repertory of Graduals includes fifteen of the first mode. The modern books contain in addition about ten adaptations—e.g., *Omnes gentes* [G 78**] from *Sciant gentes* or *Dulcis et rectus* [971] from *Concupivit*, ℞ and *Ecce quam*, ℣—not considered in the following study.

GRADUALS I: TABULATION

		RESPOND	VERSE
30	*Inveni David*	$\ldots\mid 7+d_3\mid\ldots\mid\ldots$	$A_{10}\mid F_{10}\mid\ldots\mid 4+D_{13}\mid G_{10}\,D_{10}$
63	*Gloriosus Deus*	free	$A_{10}\mid 6+D_{13}\mid 3+D_{13}\mid G_{10}\,D_{10}$
87	*Sacerdotes*	$A_1\mid\ldots\mid\ldots$	$A_{10}\mid\ldots d_{13}\mid G_{10}\,D_{10}$
6	*Miserere mei*	$\ldots\mid\ldots\mid 7+c_1\mid D_1$	$A_{10}\mid\ldots\mid D_{13}\mid 2+g_{10}\,d_1$
▸5	*Salvum fac servum*	free	$A_{10}\mid g_{10}\mid D_{10}$
▸71	*Ecce quam*	$A_1{}'\ldots\mid A_2\mid D_2$	$A_{11}\mid F_{10}\mid\ldots\mid D_{12}$
30	*Concupivit*	$A_1\ldots\mid A_2\,D_2$	$A_{11}\mid F_{10}\mid g_{10}\,D_{10}$
26	*Timete*	$\ldots\mid\ldots\mid 5+d_{12}$	$A_{11}\mid\ldots\mid\ldots\mid D_{12}$
▸48	*Beata gens*	$\ldots\mid 9+c_1\mid 8+d_2$	$A_1\,F_{10}\mid\ldots\mid 7+c_1\mid 2+D_{10}$
▸21	*Custodi me*	$\ldots\mid 4+d_3\mid\ldots\mid D_1$	$A_1{}'\,F_{10}{}'\mid\ldots\mid D_{13}\mid G_{10}\mid D_{10}$
91	*Os justi*	$\ldots\mid 4+c_1\mid 6+d_4$	$F_{10}\mid 5+f_{10}\mid 6+c_1\mid D_{11}$
▸0	*Universi*	free	$\ldots\mid 4+f_{10}\mid 6+D_{11}$
▸6	*Sciant gentes*	$\ldots\mid 7+c_1\mid\ldots$	$\ldots\mid\ldots\mid 2+g_{10}\,D_{10}$
▸7	*Si ambulem*	$\ldots\mid 5+c_1\mid 9+d_4$	$\ldots A_1\mid\ldots\mid\ldots d_4$
5	*Adjutor meus*	$\ldots\mid\ldots\mid 5+d_4$	$\ldots d_4{}'\mid\ldots d_4{}'$

FIGURE 105

(*continued*)

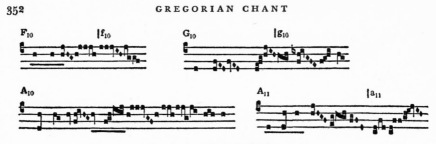

Graduals I: Standard Phrases

REMARKS:

1. The general picture is about the same as for the Graduals of mode 5: rather extended use of standard phrases in the verses, and in the responds occasional employment primarily of short standard terminations.

2. Several formulae are common to both respond and verse; namely, c_1 (*Miserere* ℟; *Beata gens* ℟, ℣; *Os justi* ℟, ℣; *Sciant gentes* ℟; *Si ambulem* ℟), A_1 (*Sacerdotes* ℟; *Ecce quam* ℟; *Concupivit* ℟; *Beata gens* ℣; *Si ambulem* ℣), d_4 (*Os justi* ℟; *Si ambulem* ℟, ℣; *Adjutor meus* ℟, ℣), and, on a smaller scale, D_1 (*Miserere* ℟, ℣; *Custodi* ℟) and D_{12} (*Timete* ℟, ℣). In the verse of *Beata gens* the formulae A_1 and F_{10} are combined into a single phrase (for "Verbo Domini") in such a way as to constitute another example of non-conformity between text and music: A_1 is sung to "Verbo Domi-," while F_{10} becomes the melisma over the syllable "-ni."

3. Some of the Graduals have responds that, more or less clearly, belong to the second mode. They are included here because their verses clearly belong to the first mode regarding their range as well as their standard phrases. Moreover, they differ essentially from the typical Graduals of the second mode which form a closely unified group. Thus the question as to the "correct" mode of *Universi* may be decided in favor of mode 1.[4]

THE GRADUALS OF MODES 3 AND 4

The Graduals of mode 3 belong mostly to the pre-Easter period, from Septuagesima Sunday (*Adjutor*) to Tuesday in Holy Week (*Ego autem*). Outside this period fall *Speciosus* for the First Sunday after Christmas, *Benedicite* for the Dedication of the Church, and *Juravit* for St. Clement, St. Felix, and St. Gregory. The last of these is found in all the early sources (e.g., in the *Sextuplex* Mss) and was given in the earlier Solesmes editions for the feast of St. Gregory (e.g., *Liber usualis,* edition of 1938, p. 1399), but has recently been replaced by the Gradual *Exaltent eum,* which is probably a modern composition.

---

[4] See p. 150. In the same category are *Gloriosus Deus* (assigned in *L* to mode 1, but considered in *Wagner III*, 379, under mode 2) and *Adjutor meus* (see pp. 138, 167).

		RESPOND	VERSE
L 570	*Eripe me*	$D_1\|G_1\|\ldots\|3+E_1$	$D_{10}'\|B_{10}\|7+e_{10}\|\ldots\|\ldots\|\ldots\|5+e_{10}$
L 1654	*Benedicite*	$D_1\|G_1\|5+d_1\|6+e_1$	$3+G_1\|4+G_{10}\|M+d\|2+e_1$
G 160	*Juravit*[5]	$D_1\|2+G_1\|\ldots\|3+d_1\|\ldots e_1$	$G_{11}\|E_{10}\|3+e_1$
L 553	*Exaltabo*	$D_1\|\ldots g_1\|\ldots\|3+B_1\|2+e_1$	$G_1\|5+G_{10}\|E_{10}\|\ldots e_{10}\|\ldots\|M+g\|B_1\,2+e_1$
L 566	*Exsurge . . . non*	$D_1\|5+D_2\|5+d_1\|3+E_1$	$G_{11}\|8+g_1\|M+d\|1+e_1$
L 498	*Tibi Domine*	$5+e_3\|\ldots\|D_2\|\ldots$	$D_{10}\|\ldots\|7+g_2\|\ldots\|\ldots$
L 512	*Adjutor*	$7+g_2\|\ldots\|\ldots e_2$	$D_{10}\ldots\|\ldots\|\ldots B_{10}'\|\ldots e_2$
L 604	*Tu es Deus*	$\ldots d_1\|\ldots d_1\|2+E_1$	$9+g_1\|\ldots e_3\|B_{10}\|D_{10}'\|\ldots e_{10}$
L 606	*Exsurge . . . et*	$6+e_3\|4+C_1\|4+C_1\|E_3$	$\ldots G_{10}\|M+g\|2+e_1$
L 591	*Ego autem*	$\ldots c_2\|\ldots\|3+e_3\|5+c_1\|E_3$	free
L 1207	*Tenuisti*	$\ldots c_2\|\ldots\|5+c_2\|\ldots e_1$	free
L 434	*Domine praevenisti*	free	$\ldots\ldots D_{12}$ (of mode 1)
G 143	*Speciosus*	free	free
	Exsurge . . . fer	= *Speciosus*	= *Speciosus*

[5] See last paragraph on p. 352.

353

FIGURE 106

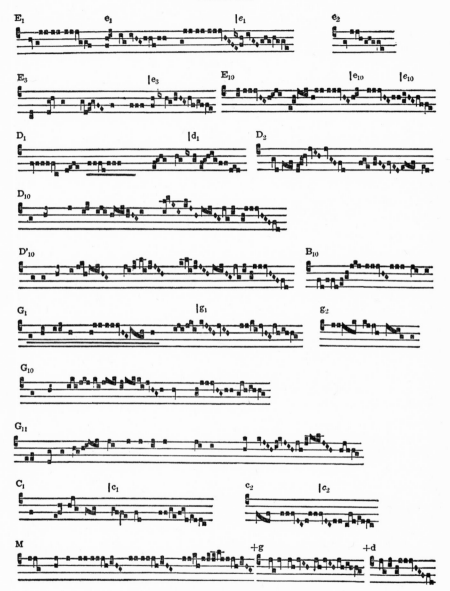

Graduals III, IV: Standard Phrases

1. The Graduals of mode 3 are, on the whole, considerably longer than is normally the case. Some of their standard phrases are among the most extended and most highly melismatic to be found in the entire repertory of centonized chants. They are also noteworthy for their almost excessively reiterative design, such as in E_1, E_{10}, D_1, D_{10}, and G_{10}.

2. In distinction from the other Graduals (excepting the special group *Justus ut palma*), their responds make as full use of standard phrases as do the verses.

3. Yet another unique trait is the high degree of unification between the responds and the verses. Not only is the main closing formula, E_1, common to both, but also other formulae occur in either section, e.g., G_1 (℞. *Eripe, Benedicite, Juravit;* ℣. *Benedicite, Exaltabo*), E_3 (℞. *Exsurge . . . et, Ego autem, Tibi Domine;* ℣. *Tu es Deus*), and g_2 (℞. *Adjutor;* ℣. *Tibi Domine*).

4. The first eight Graduals of our list form a main group of the third mode, unified by common material and with cadences on the tonic (e), subtonic (d), and mediant (g), occasionally also on the dominant (b).

5. A separate group is formed by the next three Graduals, *Exsurge . . . et* from Monday in Holy Week, *Ego autem* from the Tuesday, and *Tenuisti manum* from Palm Sunday. They are the only ones to employ cadences on c, two degrees below the final. Considering this as well as their ambitus, they could all be classified as mode 4—*Exsurge* for its respond, the two others for both respond and verse. Actually, *Tenuisti* is the only one assigned to mode 4, but Wagner considers *Ego autem* also as being in the fourth mode,[6] no doubt with justification. Aside from these, the fourth mode is represented among the medieval Graduals by only one other melody, *Domine praevenisti* from the Common of Abbots (originally from the Eve of St. John the Evangelist). This is a unique case of a Gradual employing a different tonality in the respond and in the verse. While the former is in mode 4, the latter shows all the characteristics of mode 1 and, in fact, closes with the standard phrase D_{12} of this group. The melody of *Tenuisti*, the longest of all the Graduals, reappears (with some omissions) in *Memor fui* [1580] and *Mihi autem* [G 481], both modern compositions; that of *Domine praevenisti* in *Benedicta et venerabilis* [1264] and *Dolorosa et lacrimosa* [1633ᵛ], the former (for Feasts of the Virgin Mary) possibly late-medieval, the latter (for the Feast of Seven Dolours) a modern composition.

6. The last two Graduals of our list employ one and the same melody, which has nothing in common with those of the other Graduals. The melody is remarkable for the amount of its material common to respond and verse, e.g., in *Speciosus:* ℞. "(homi)num: diffusa est gratia in labiis tuis" = ℣. "(Re)gi: lingua mea calamus scribae velociter scribentis." Notice also in the verse: "verbum bonum" = "mea Regi."

6 *Wagner III,* 382.

THE GRADUALS OF MODES 7 AND 8

GRADUALS VII: TABULATION

		RESPOND	VERSE
L 335	*Qui sedes*	...|...	$D_{10}+6$|...|G_{10}
L 478	*Benedictus Dominus*	...|$11+F_1$|...g_1	$5+B_{10}$|...|...|...g_{12}
L 560	*Laetatus sum*	...d_1|...	$2+d_1$|...|$5+d_1$|$6+g$
L 944	*Oculi omnium*	...d_1|...G_3	...|...G_3
L 982	*Jacta cogitatum*	...|$3+F_1$|...	$5+d_{11}$|...g_4|$4+G_{10}$
L 1028	*Benedicam*	$4+G_2$|...|...(a)	G_2|$8+f_1$|$6+F_1$|G_{11}
L 1060	*Dirigatur oratio*	...|...g_4|...	...|...g_{11}
L 1075	*Liberasti nos*	...g_4|...	D_{10}|$7+b_1$|$5+g_4$|$9+$
L 1170	*Clamaverunt*	...B_1|$14+F_1$|...	...|...|$6+B_{10}$|...
L 1755	*Audi filia*	$7+B_1$|$3+b_1$|$3+F_1$|...|$3+G_1$	...|$6+d_{11}$|$8+F_1$|G_{11}
G 119	*Salvum fac*	...B_1|$3+F_1$|$5+G_1$	...|...|$11+G_{11}$
G 133	*Miserere mihi*	free	D_{10}'|$6+b_1$|$4+g_4$|G_{10}

FIGURE 107

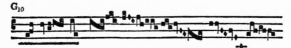

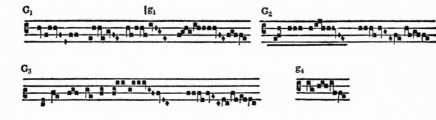

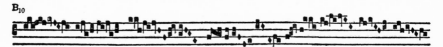

Graduals VII: Standard Phrases

This group of Graduals is similar to that of mode 3 in various respects: in their length, their highly florid style, the almost equal amount of centonization in respond as well as verse, and the unification of both sections by the use of common formulae (F_1, d_1, G_2, g_3, and b_1). The B_{10}-phrase, in *Benedictus Dominus* and *Clamaverunt,* includes what probably is the longest melisma in the present-day repertory of chant, equalled and surpassed only by some melismas in the verses of the Offertories or the *neuma triplex* of the Responsory *Descendit de caelis* [see p. 343]. The free sections of the Graduals also contain many extended melismas of individual design. A specially remarkable one is that at the beginning of the verse of *Clamaverunt* ("Dominus"), because it shows a repeat structure (a a b b) which, although frequent in the melismas of Offertories and Alleluias, is quite unusual in a Gradual. *Benedicam* is noteworthy because its respond does not close on the final of the mode. Thus it forms a counterpart to *Ego dixi* [p. 346] and *Domine praevenisti* [p. 355], in both of which the verse fails to close on the tonic. Repeat of the respond is as clearly required in these as it is out of place in *Benedicam.*

The eighth mode is represented by only two melodies, *Dilexisti justitiam* [1216; originally for St. Lucia], and *Deus vitam meam* [G 128] for Monday after Third Sunday of Quadragesima, which recurs, virtually unchanged, in *Deus exaudi orationem* [G 156] for Monday after Passion Sunday. The former melody is as remarkable for its initial phrase, which shows the outline c-g-c-e-g-c'-g. Very likely, such a triadic design is indicative of a relatively late date.

THE GRADUAL-TYPE *Justus ut palma*

It remains for us to consider a group of Graduals which, for various reasons, stand apart from all the others, representing an isolated class governed by its own rules. This group consists of nineteen medieval Graduals all of which belong, or originally belonged, to very ancient feasts, mostly from the Proper of the Time. Listed in the order of the liturgical year, these are:

PROPER OF THE TIME

1. *Tollite portas:* Wednesday in Ember Week of Advent [G 9]; now used for Masses of the B. V. M. on Saturdays [1269]
2. *Ostende nobis:* Friday in Ember Week of Advent [G 11]
3. *A summo caelo:* Saturday in Ember Week of Advent [343]
4. *In sole posuit:* Saturday in Ember Week of Advent [344]
5. *Domine Deus virtutum:* Saturday in Ember Week of Advent [345]
6. *Excita Domine:* Saturday in Ember Week of Advent [347]
7. *Hodie scietis:* Christmas Eve [360]
8. *Tecum principium:* The Nativity, Midnight Mass [393]
9. *Angelis suis:* First Sunday of Lent [533]

10. *Ab occultis:* Tuesday after the Third Sunday of Lent [G 130]

11. *Ne avertas:* Wednesday in Holy Week [613]

12. *Haec dies:* Easter Sunday [778] and, with different verses, during Easter Week [786, 790, 793, 797, 801][7]

13. *Domine refugium:* Twenty-first Sunday after Pentecost [1067]

PROPER OF SAINTS

14. *Justus ut palma:* St. John the Evangelist, now for Common of a Confessor not a Bishop [1201]

15. *In omnem terram:* Apostles Peter and Paul, now for St. Barnabas [1486]

16. *Exsultabunt:* St. Primus and Felicianus, now for the Vigils of All Saints [G 646]

17. *Dispersit:* Vigil of St. Lawrence, now for St. Joachim [1608]

18. *Nimis honorati:* Apostles Simon and Jude, now for St. Thomas [1326]

19. *Requiem aeternam:* Mass for the Dead [1808]

The melodies for these Graduals form the most closely unified group in the entire repertory of chant. They all appear in what is generally regarded as a transposition, with *a* as a final for both the respond and the verse. The transposition is usually considered as being at the interval of the fifth, the "original" final being *d*. Thus they are assigned to the second mode. However, some of the earliest writers, Aurelianus and the author of the *Alia musica,* assign them to the fourth mode, on *e,*[8] in which case the transposition would be at the interval of a fourth. The authenticity of the b-flat at the very beginning of *Haec dies* has been questioned and is indeed doubtful, this being the only b-flat in the entire Gradual. If it is disregarded, the version on *d* would appear with an e-natural, while that on *e* would call for an f-sharp. However, it is possible, perhaps even probable, that the melody was originally on *a,* and that no transposition is involved.

The group under consideration is usually called the Gradual-type *Justus ut palma,* with reference to one of its representatives. The designation "gradual-type" is very appropriate, because all the melodies employ centonization and adaptation to such an extent that they lose all individuality and become nothing but different manifestations of a basic type. There is, however, no compelling reason to name the group after the Gradual *Justus ut palma* which belongs to the Proper of Saints (St. John). Musically, nearly every one of its representatives has an equally good claim to be the model, and from the liturgical point of view a selection from the Proper of the Time would certainly be preferable. Actually, no single Gradual contains all the material that occurs in the group. A musically correct designation would be "gradual type *A summo caelo—Excita Domine—*

---

7 See the remarks on p. 183.

8 Aurelianus mentions *Exsultabunt sancti, A summo caelo, Tollite portas* and *Haec dies* in his chapter on the *Plagis Deuteri* (GS, I, 47f). The *gradale responsorium Haec dies* is mentioned in the chapter *De Quarto Tono* of the *Alia Musica* (GS, I, 135a).

Haec dies," because all the melodies of the entire group can be almost completely derived from the standard phrases provided by these three Graduals. Since, however, the name Gradual-type *Justus ut palma* has been universally accepted, we do not insist on replacing it by another name which, although more proper and correct, is, at the same time, a good deal more cumbersome.[9]

As for rigidity of centonization technique, there is only one parallel in the entire Gregorian repertory, that is, the Tracts of Holy Saturday. Like these, the Graduals of the type *Justus ut palma* consist exclusively of a number of standard phrases, so that their structure could be indicated by the same mechanical system of designation used for the Tracts:

	RESPOND					VERSE							
	A_1	A_2	$A+c_1$	F_1	A_3	D_{10}	D_{11}	A_{10}	A_{11}	C_{10}	F_{10}	F_1	A_{12}
A summo caelo	*	*			*	*		*			*		*
Tecum principium	*		*	*	*	*		*		*		*	*
Haec dies			*	*	*		*		*			*	*
Justus ut palma	*			*	*	*		*				*	*

A tabulation of the entire group in a more readable form follows on p. 360:[10]

REMARKS:

1. Each of the standard phrases recurs almost identically, aside from the adjustments required by the varying number of syllables and the varying positions of the accents. Variants of a more essential nature are indicated by the symbols A_1' (*In omnem terram, Ne avertas, Tecum principium*), A_1'' (*Exsultabunt sancti*), F_1' (*Ostende nobis*), and A_{10}' (*Ne avertas*). A_1' results from A_1 by an enlargement of the middle section, while A_1'' is a shortened version of A_1'.

2. In *Hodie scietis, Tollite portas,* and *Tecum principium* the a-phrase A_2 is changed into a c-phrase by the addition of closing formula, c_1, which, in *Haec dies,* serves as the termination for a unique a-phrase, A_4.

3. The Gradual *Haec dies* differs from the others not only in its individual opening phrase, but also in the phrase A_{11} employed for some of its verses, a phrase which, however, has the same ending as the normal phrase A_{10}. The verse intonation D_{11} is also employed in *Tollite portas.*

[9] Two entire volumes of the *Paléographie,* II and III, are devoted to a study of "Le répons-graduel *Justus ut palma.*" Ferretti, *Esthétique,* pp. 164ff, gives a number of illustrations showing the adaptation of different texts for the various standard phrases. A large table, "Analyse mélodique par Formules des Répons Graduels (1re part.) du IIe mode" is given in G. Suñol, *Introduction à la paléographie musicale grégorienne,* Planche F (appendix).

[10] Modern adaptations are, e.g., *Deriventur* [1562], *Uxor tua* [1289], *Nihil inquinatum* [G 48**], and *Qui ambulat* [G 30**].

GRADUAL-TYPE *Justus ut palma:* TABULATION

			RESPOND			VERSE			
1.	L 343	*A summo caelo*	A_1 A_2		A_3	D_{10}	A_{10}		F_{10}
2.	L 344	*In sole*	A_1 A_2		A_3	D_{10}	A_{10}		F_{10}
3.	L 345	*Domine Deus*	A_1 A_2		A_3	D_{10}	A_{10}		
4.	L 1608	*Dispersit*	A_1 A_2		A_3	D_{10}	A_{10}		F_{10}
5.	L 1486	*In omnem terram*	A_1' A_2		A_3	D_{10}	A_{10}		F_{10}
6.	L 347	*Excita Domine*	A_1	F_1	A_3	D_{10}	A_{10}	C_{10}	F_1
7.	L 533	*Angelis suis*	A_1	F_1	A_3	D_{10}	A_{10}		
8.	L 1201	*Justus ut palma*	A_1	F_1	A_3	D_{10}	A_{10}		F_{10}
9.	L 1067	*Domine refugium*	A_1	F_1	A_3	D_{10}	A_{10}		F_{10}
10.	L 1326	*Nimis honorati*	A_1	F_1	A_3	D_{10}	A_{10}		
11.	L 1808	*Requiem aeternam*	A_1	F_1	A_3	D_{10}	A_{10}		F_{10}
12.	G 130	*Ab occultis*	A_1	F_1	A_3	D_{10}	A_{10}		F_{10}
13.	L 613	*Ne avertas*	A_1'	F_1	A_3	D_{10}	A_{10}'	C_{10}	
14.	G 646	*Exsultabunt sancti*	A_1''	F_1	A_3	D_{10}	A_{10}		F_{10}
15.	G 11	*Ostende nobis*	...	F_1'	A_3	D_{10}	A_{10}		F_{10}
16.	L 360	*Hodie scietis*	A_1 A_2+c_1		A_3	D_{10}	A_{10}	C_{10}	F_1
17.	L 1269	*Tollite portas*	A_1 A_2+c_1	F_1	A_3	D_{11}	A_{10}		F_{10}
18.	L 393	*Tecum principium*	A_1' A_2+c_1	F_1	A_3	D_{10}	A_{10}	C_{10}	F_1
19.	L 778	*Haec dies, ℣. Confitemini*	A_4+c_1	F_1	A_3	D_{11}	A_{11}		F_1
20.	L 786	*Haec dies, ℣. Dicat nunc*	same			D_{11}	A_{11}		F_1
21.	L 790	*Haec dies, ℣. Dicant nunc*	same			D_{11}	A_{10}		F_{10}
22.	L 793	*Haec dies, ℣. Dextera*	same			D_{10}	A_{10}		F_{10}
23.	L 797	*Haec dies, ℣. Lapidem*	same			$D_{11} \mid$ ... $\mid 3+a_{10}$	c_{10}		
24.	L 801	*Haec dies, ℣. Benedictus*	same			D_{10}	A_{10}		F_{10}

FIGURE 108

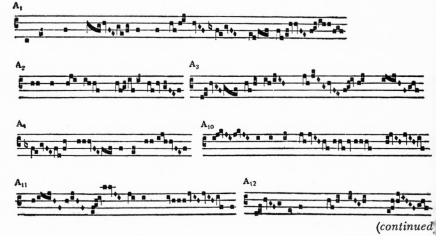

(continued)

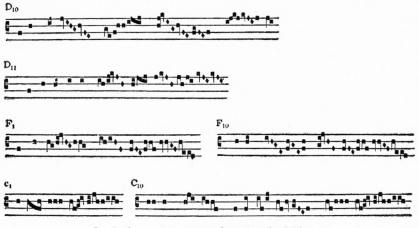

Gradual-type *Justus ut palma:* Standard Phrases

4. On the whole, the standard material for the responds is different from that of the verses. An exception is the mediant phrase F_1, which is used, in the same position, in the verses of *Excita, Hodie scietis, Tecum principium,* and in *Haec dies* ℣℣. *Confitemini* and *Dicat nunc.*

5. The Graduals of this group frequently employ a complete standard melody rather than standard phrases variously combined. Disregarding variants, the nineteen responds and twenty-four verses can be grouped as follows:

RESPOND:

					examples	
A_1	F_1	A_3			9 examples	(nos. 6 to 14)
A_1	A_2	A_3			6	(nos. 1 to 5, 16)
A_1	A_2	F_1	A_3		2	(nos. 17, 18)
$A_4 + c_1$	F_1	A_3			1	(no. 19)
$\ldots F_1$	A_3				1	(no. 15)

VERSE:

D_{10}	A_{10}	F_{10}	A_{12}		13 examples	(nos. 1, 2, 4, 5, 8, 9, 11, 12, 14, 15, 17, 22, 24)
D_{10}	A_{10}	C_{10}	F_1	A_{12}	3	(nos. 6, 16, 18)
D_{10}	A_{10}	A_{12}			3	(nos. 3, 7, 10)
D_{11}	A_{11}	F_1	A_{12}		2	(nos. 19, 20)
D_{10}	A_{10}	C_{10}	A_{12}		1	(no. 13)
D_{11}	A_{10}	F_{10}	A_{12}		1	(no. 21)
D_{11}	$\ldots$	a_{10}	c_{10}	A_{12}	1	(no. 23)

6. Attention may be called to our previous discussion of the relationship between musical and textual phrases in the Graduals of our group. It was shown that in four Graduals, *Hodie scietis, Tecum principium, Dispersit,*

and *Justus ut palma,* the textual phrases are underlaid with a certain disregard of the musical phrases.[11]

7. Considering liturgical, musical, and textual evidence, one may come to the conclusion that our gradual-type originated in the Mass of Saturday in Ember Week of Advent. All the four Graduals of this Mass belong to our group (nos. 1, 2, 3, and 6), and thus form a liturgico-musical nucleus comparable to that of the five Tracts of Holy Saturday. The first and fourth of these Graduals, *A summo caelo* and *Excita Domine,* contain nearly all the material of the entire group. Naturally, from the liturgical point of view the Easter Gradual *Haec dies* has an equally valid claim to be considered as the mother chant. However, its specific formulae (D_{11}, A_{11}, A_4) were not used elsewhere in the group.

At the end of his study devoted to the Graduals,[12] Peter Wagner makes some general observations which, like so many other of his ideas, deserve to be incorporated in this book. He first raises the question as to whether the mere conglomeration of melodic units, as revealed by his "anatomical" method, can possibly result in a satisfactory work of art: "It is possible to gather gems which, considered individually, delight us by their cut, brilliance, and rareness; if, however, they are to form a precious piece of jewelry, they must receive a splendid mounting, an ingenious connection, and a tasteful arrangement. Are the old melismas combined in this manner?" Wagner's answer is, of course, in the positive, and no one will hesitate to concur with him to the fullest extent. These melodies, fascinating in their analytical detail, are equally admirable for their synthetic quality, for their cohesion and union. In fact, the perception of their structural properties greatly enhances their significance as unified works of art, no less so than in the case of a sonata by Beethoven. True enough, there is the difference that in Beethoven the analytical details occur within one individual work, whereas in Gregorian chant they appear only upon comparison of a sufficient number of different pieces. To state this is only to emphasize once more, and demonstrate with special clarity, that a Gregorian melody is not an individual creation but a representative of a type.

Wagner then raises the question as to the origin of the centonization technique of the Graduals, a technique so diametrically opposed to the prevailing concept of musical composition. "Only one answer is possible: the technique of migrating melismas functioning as punctuations is a heritage from the psalmody of the Synagogue." Certainly there is a striking similarity between the Gregorian centonization technique and the Jewish method of singing a text to a number of short ornamenting figures indi-

---

11 See p. 271. The fact that *Justus ut palma* is in this group is another reason against considering it as the prototype.

12 *Wagner III,* 395.

cated stenographically by signs, the *ta'amim*.[13] Wagner observes that it would be entirely possible to sing a Gradual (or, for that matter, a Tract) with the mere help of figures or some other signs that would indicate to the singer which formulae to select from a memorized repertory. His contention that we are in the presence of a "heritage from the Synagogue" is perhaps a little too strongly worded to be accepted without reservation. After all, the earliest preserved manuscripts showing the Jewish *ta'amim* date from the ninth century.[14] On the other hand, there is scarcely any doubt that the practice as such is much older, possibly synagogal. Wherever encountered, it is obviously rooted in, or, at least, strongly influenced by a practical consideration, that is, to facilitate the task of the singer by reducing the melodies to a limited fund of formulae that can be memorized and applied according to the requirements of the texts.

THE OFFERTORIES

From the liturgical point of view, the Offertories belong in the same class as the Introits and Communions, i.e., chants accompanying an action, as opposed to the purely contemplative lesson chants, the Graduals, Alleluias, Tracts, and Responsories. The earliest mention of a chant accompanying the offering of gifts is found in St. Augustine who speaks about "the custom, just started at Carthage, of singing hymns from the Book of Psalms, either before the offering or during the distribution of what has been offered." This remark leaves hardly any doubt that at this early time the "Offertory" (if we may use this term in connection with such an ancient practice) was a complete Psalm, possibly with an Antiphon. It is certain that at some later time the Offertory adopted an entirely different character from that of the Introits and Communions. It acquired a rich melismatic style similar to that of the Graduals, Responsories, and Alleluias, and was entrusted to a soloist, thus becoming a responsorial chant. Until the twelfth century it retained a number of verses, usually two or three, with the antiphon (or respond) repeated after each verse.[1]

The change from an antiphonal to a responsorial type is not the only trait that gives the Offertories a unique position in the Gregorian repertory. In our previous discussions we have repeatedly pointed out other exceptional traits of the Offertories, especially of their verses. It may not be amiss to restate them here briefly, as a preliminary to a fuller study of their stylistic characteristics:

[13] See the example in *HAM*, I, 8.
[14] See A. Z. Idelsohn, *Jewish Music in its Historical Development*, p. 68.

[1] See the chapter on Methods and Forms of Psalmody, p. 179. In this discussion, dealing with problems of form, the Offertories were considered as antiphonal chants. In the present chapter, where the emphasis is on style, we prefer to designate the Offertory antiphon as a respond—not that this makes any difference. The verses are found in, and quoted after C. Ott's *Offertoriale*. Cf. L. David, "Les versets d'Offertoire" (*RCG*, XXXIX).

1. Extraordinarily large range of the combined respond and verse, in one case (*Tollite portas*) two octaves [p. 151].
2. The unique case of the low F in *Tollite portas*, ℣. 2, on "et" [p. 151].
3. The unique case of a leap of a seventh in *Domine Deus meus*, ℣. 2 [p. 253].[2]
4. The unique (?) example of a fifth-plus-fourth progression (cg gc') in *Constitues eos*, ℣. 2 [p. 257].
5. The only examples of an ascending fourth-plus-third progression [p. 255].
6. The unique case of an e-flat in *In virtute*, ℣. 2 [p. 165, fn. 29].
7. The relatively frequent occurrence, in the final verses, of fourth-plus-fourth progressions, which are very rare in other chants [pp. 255f].
8. The exceptionally great frequency of other progressions outlining a seventh [p. 256] and of unusually bold formations in general [p. 258].

Perhaps the most striking peculiarity of the Offertories is the fact that in not a few of them single words, groups of words, or entire phrases of the text are repeated, once or several times. Outside the Offertories there exists only one example of this procedure, that is, in the Gradual *Ecce quam bonum* [1071], the verse of which reads: *Sicut unguentum in capite, quod descendit in barbam, barbam Aaron* (like the ointment on the head, that ran down upon the beard, the beard of Aaron). Since, however, this is the original text of Scripture (Ps. 132), it cannot be considered on the same level with the repeats in the Offertories (italics indicate that the melody also is repeated):

A.

1. *Benedictus es ... in labiis* [514; Ott 28]
   ℞. *Benedictus es Domine, doce me justificationes tuas: benedictus es Domine, doce me justificationes tuas:* in labiis meis pronuntiavi omnia judicia oris tui.
2. *Jubilate Deo omnis* [480; Ott 23]
   ℞. *Jubilate Deo omnis terra: jubilate Deo omnis terra,* servite Domino ... quia Dominus ipse est Deus.
3. *Jubilate Deo universa* [486; Ott 69]
   ℞. *Jubilate Deo universa terra: jubilate Deo universa terra:* psalmum dicite nomini ejus: ... quanta fecit Dominus animae meae, alleluia.
   ℣. 1 Reddam tibi vota mea, reddam tibi vota mea, quae distinxerunt labia mea.
   ℣. 2 *Locutum est os meum in tribulatione mea: locutum est os meum in tribulatione mea:* holocausta medullata offeram tibi.

---

[2] This Offertory does not occur in the oldest Mss (e.g., in the *Sextuplex*) nor in the modern editions. Ott reproduces it from an unspecified source with the remark: "Olim paenultima et ultima Dominica post Pentecosten."

4. *Precatus est* [1030; Ott 97]

℞. *Precatus est Moyses in conspectu Domini Dei sui, et dixit. Precatus est Moyses in conspectu Domini Dei sui, et dixit:* Quare, Domine, irasceris in populo tuo? . . . quam dixit facere populo suo.

℣. 2 Dixit Moyses et Aaron, dixit Moyses et Aaron ad omnem synagogam . . . et exaudivit murmurationem vestram in tempore.

5. *Domine exaudi* [620; Ott 53]

℣. 1 *Ne avertas faciem tuam, ne avertas faciem tuam* a me.

6. *Exsultabunt sancti* [1169; Ott 143]

℣. 1 Cantate Domino canticum novum, cantate Domino canticum novum: laus eius in ecclesia . . . exsultent in Rege suo.

7. *Afferentur* (originally: *Offerentur*) *regi* [1219; Ott 155].

℣. 1 Eructavit cor meum *verbum bonum*, eructavit cor meum *verbum bonum:* dico ego . . . velociter scribentis.

℣. 2 Diffusa est gratia in labiis tuis, diffusa est gratia in labiis tuis: propterea benedixit te Deus in aeternum.

B.

8. *De profundis* [1076; Ott 126]

℞. *De profundis clamavi ad te, Domine:* Domine exaudi orationem meam: *de profundis clamavi ad te, Domine.*

9. *Domine in auxilium* [1046; Ott 106]

℞. *Domine, in auxilium meum respice:* confundantur et revereantur qui quaerunt animam meam, ut auferant eam: *Domine, in auxilium meum respice.*

C.

10. *Vir erat* [1069; Ott 122]

℣. 1 *Utinam appenderentur peccata mea: utinam appenderentur peccata mea, quibus iram merui, quibus iram merui, et calamitas* et calamitas *et calamitas,* quam patior, et gravior appareret.

℣. 2 Quae est enim, quae est enim, quae est enim fortitudo mea, ut sustineam? *Aut quis finis meus, ut patienter agam? Aut finis meus, ut patienter agam?*

℣. 3 Numquid fortitudo lapidum est fortitudo mea? *Aut caro mea aenea est? Aut caro mea aenea est.*

℣. 4 Quoniam, quoniam, quoniam non revertetur oculus meus, ut videat bona, *ut videat bona, ut videat bona,* ut videat bona, *ut videat bona, ut videat bona,* ut videat bona.

REMARKS:

1. Group A comprises the cases representing what may be considered the normal procedure, that is, the immediate repeat of the initial portion of the text. Counting responds and verses separately, our list includes eleven examples of this method. In six of these the repeated portion of the text is sung to the same melody, resulting in the musical form a a b which

was destined to play such a prominent role in the later development of music: in the hymns [see p. 426], in the music of the troubadours and trouvères,[3] in the polyphonic music of the fourteenth century (ballades of Machaut), in the music of the minnesingers and mastersingers (barform), in the Lutheran chorales, and in the sonata-form of the Viennese classics. In most cases the second statement is considerably expanded by the insertion of long melismas, either at the end (e.g., *Benedictus, Jubilate Deo universa,* ℣. 2) or at the beginning (both *Jubilate* on "Jubilate").

2. In group B the initial portion of the text is repeated at the end, in both cases with the same melody, thus resulting in the form a b a.

3. Entirely unique are the repeats in *Vir erat*. Whatever the ultimate cause of the textual repeats in the Offertories and their verses may have been—possibly nothing more than the necessity of prolonging the chant in conformity with the duration of the service—it is apparent that the aim was usually pursued in a well-ordered and aesthetically comprehensible manner, by repeating the initial portion of the text (and often also its music) either immediately or at the end. No such organizing principle is at work in *Vir erat,* except for its third verse which, textually as well as musically, has the form a b b, a form no less admissible and comprehensible than a a b or a b a. The same form occurs in ℣. 2, but this also shows, at its beginning, a triple statement of the exclamation *Quae est enim.* Even more numerous are the repeats in ℣. 1, in which three successive fragments of the text, *Utinam appenderentur peccata mea, quibus iram merui,* and *et calamitas,* appear in double or triple statements. The ultimate of this method—if it can thus be called—is reached in ℣. 4 [Fig. 109], which starts

FIGURE 109

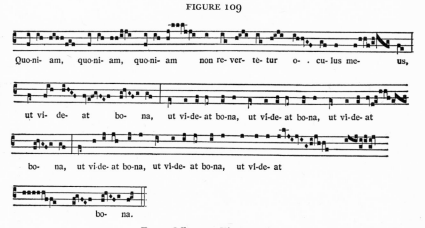

From Offertory *Vir erat,* ℣. 4

3 See W. Apel, "Rondeaux, Virelais, and Ballades in French 13th-Century Song" (*Journal of the American Musicological Association,* VII [1954], 121).

with a threefold *Quoniam,* and closes with seven statements of *ut videat bona.*[4] No doubt the reason for this highly reiterative treatment is found in the text, which deals with the illness and grief of Job. The numerous repeats are a graphic description of a man tormented by pain and anguish, and crying out again and again to "see the good things" of his earlier days.[5] The dramatic character of the text is paralleled and even surpassed by the music which transforms these outcries into a most stirring crescendo of expressiveness. Certainly, we are here in the presence of a composition which, for its subjective and dramatic character, is without parallel in the Gregorian repertory.

The Offertory responds vary considerably in length, being similar in this respect to the Communions. One of the shortest and simplest is *Laetentur caeli* [394] from the Midnight Mass of the Nativity, with hardly more than two lines. The other extreme is represented by *Precatus est Moyses* [1030] from the Twelfth Sunday after Pentecost, which occupies over ten lines of music. In medieval practice, when the respond was followed by two or more verses and repeated after each of them, chants of exorbitant dimensions, hardly second to the longest Tracts, resulted. Not a few of the full Offertories, as reproduced in Ott's publication, occupy close to three pages, and would cover four pages if the repeats were written out in full.

The style of the Offertories is neumatic-melismatic; in fact, more consistently so than that of the Graduals or Alleluias, because of the almost complete absence of short syllabic passages such as are usually found in these. According to Wagner, no Offertory contains a syllabic passage of more than five syllables, and the entire repertory includes only eight cases of syllabic passages of four or five syllables.[6] In most of the Offertories moderate groups of from two to ten notes are spread rather evenly over the entire text. Many of them, however, include a few extended melismas, occasionally in the respond, but more frequently in the verses. One of the most celebrated Offertory melismas is found in *Jubilate Deo universa* [487], upon the repeat of the initial word [see Fig. 71, p. 258]. Quickly

---

[4] Certain Mss have ℣. 4 in an even longer form, with nine statements of *ut videat bonum;* cf. the version, from a twelfth-century *Gradual* of Reims, in Gevaert's *Mélopeé,* p. 429 and in Ott, p. 195. Yet other versions are given in *Wagner III,* 431; Ferretti's *Esthétique,* p. 202; and Gastoué's *Origines,* p. 155 (final melisma, with f'-sharp). The above figure is from Ott, pp. 124f.

[5] Amalarius, commenting upon the fact that the repeats occur only in the verses, aptly remarks that the Offertory itself contains the words of the historian, while the verses contain those of the sick and complaining Job, adding that a sick man, whose breath is weak, is wont to repeat "verba imperfecta" (*Liber officialis* [*De officio*], iii, 39; ed. Hanssens, II, 373; *Patr. lat.* 105, p. 1157).

[6] *Wagner III,* 418, fn. 2. Monotone recitations of some extension occur only in later adaptations, e.g., *Exsultabunt sancti,* ℣., on "Laetetur Israel in eo, qui fecit . . ." [Ott 144; from *Afferentur,* ℣. 1, "lingua mea," Ott 155].

descending through an octave, and slowly rising from the low c to the high f', it is universally admired as one of the most impressive embodiments of what has been called the classical-Roman style in Gregorian chant. It is interesting to notice, however, that the verses of *Jubilate* include two melismas which are not only much longer than that of the respond, but also of an entirely different character, static-reiterative rather than kinetic, and strikingly similar to the melismas of the Graduals [see pp. 344f]. One of them, a profuse elaboration of the triad f-a-c', is shown in Fig. 110.

FIGURE 110

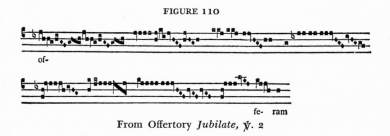

From Offertory *Jubilate*, ℣. 2

Extended melismas, say of thirty or more notes, are not too frequent in the Offertory responds. In addition to that of *Jubilate* there are perhaps ten others, for instance in *Jubilate Deo omnis* [480], *Super flumina* [1065], *Justorum animae* [1172], *De profundis* [1076], and *Erit vobis* [802]. In the verses, on the other hand, they occur almost regularly, particularly near the end of the last verse, and often they are of much the same length as that from the last verse of *Jubilate*, on "offeram." Some show a similar, vaguely reiterative design, for instance the final melisma of *Deus enim* [Ott 18], which could be described as a profuse elaboration of the fourth-chord, d-g-c':

FIGURE 111

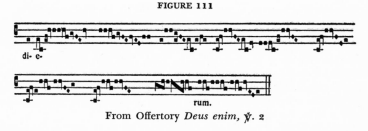

From Offertory *Deus enim*, ℣. 2

Many of them, however, have a different physiognomy, that is, of a clearly defined repeat structure. Particularly frequent is the form a a b, which may be illustrated by two examples:[7]

---

[7] See also: *Super flumina*, ℟. on "Sion" [1065; Ott 120]; *Tollite portas*, ℣. 2. "eum" [Ott 15]; *Benedictus es*, ℣. 3. on "cor meum" [Ott 30]; *Domine exaudi*, ℣. 1 on "me" [Ott 54]; *Angelus Domini*, ℣. 2 on "stetit" [Ott 58]; *Precatus est*, ℣. 2 on "tempore" [Ott

FIGURE 112

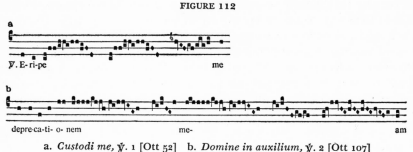

a. *Custodi me, ℣. 1* [Ott 52] b. *Domine in auxilium, ℣. 2* [Ott 107]

Other melismas show multiple repeats of one type or another, e.g.:[8]

FIGURE 113

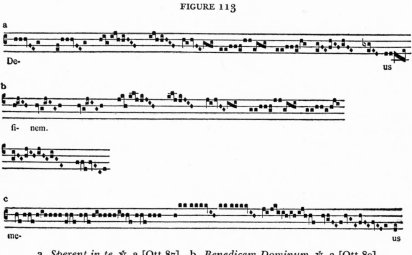

a. *Sperent in te, ℣. 2* [Ott 87] b. *Benedicam Dominum, ℣. 2* [Ott 89]
c. *Expectans expectavi, ℣. 2* [Ott 106]

Melismas with such clear-cut repeat structures are totally absent in the Responsories, Tracts, or Graduals. They occur, however, with even greater frequency and clearer formal definition in the Alleluias. There can be hardly any doubt that such formations are the product of a relatively late

100]; *Sanctificavit, ℣. 2* on "terra" [Ott 117]; *Posuisti, ℣. 2* on "gloria" [Ott 137]; *Laetamini, ℣. 1* on "Beati" [Ott 140]; *Justorum animae, ℣. 1* on "coram" [Ott 145]; *Justus ut palma, ℣. 3* on "florebit" [Ott 151]; *Domine Deus, ℣. 1* on "Dominus" [Ott 160]; *Stetit angelus, ℣. 1* on "conspectu" [Ott 171]; *Erue Domine, ℣. 1* on "Deus" [Ott 178]; *Tu es Petrus, ℣. 1* on "Beatus es," "tibi," and "qui est" [Ott 187f]; *Felix namque, ℣. 1* on "venerabilis" [Ott 189].

[8] See also Ott: p. 46, line 4/5: a b a c a'; p. 88, 3/4: a a a b b; p. 94, 5/6: a a b c c d; p. 121, 8/9: a b a; p. 136, 6/7: a a b b c; p. 148, 5/6: a b b; p. 169f: a a.

period, and that they appeared first and tentatively in the Offertory verses, whence they were adopted for the Alleluias.

We finally turn to a consideration of the Offertories and their verses as musical entities. Essentially, each of the constituent parts of a complete Offertory is a free melody. The technique of transferable standard phrases, which plays such a conspicuous role in the Tracts, Responsories, and Graduals, is practically non-existent in the Offertories. Whatever relationship there exists between one Offertory and another (excepting, of course, the cases of complete adaptation; see p. 69) is limited to the occasional recurrence of some shorter or longer melisma, for example:

FIGURE 114

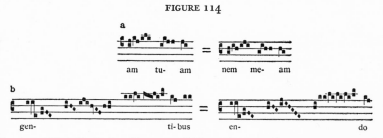

a. *Miserere mihi* ℟. "(misericordi)am tuam" [Ott 35] = *Exaudi Deus* ℟. "(deprecatio)nem meam [Ott 36]
b. *Eripe me* ℟. "(insur)gentibus" [Ott 46] = *Exaudi Deus* ℣. 2 "(retribu)endo" [Ott 37]

There exist, on the other hand, not a few cases of musical relationship and references within a given Offertory, particularly between its respond and its verses, in fact, a sufficient number to make this a rather typical trait of these chants. They serve to a certain extent to integrate the different portions of an Offertory into a unified whole. Thus, in turning from the Tracts or the Graduals to the Offertories, we seem to witness a shift of allegiance, the emphasis on group characteristics giving way to concern with individual organisms.

The most interesting of these unifying devices is the employment of the same cadence for the verses and for the first half of the respond (R′). This is a principle of structural organization, by means of which the second half of the respond (R″), which is repeated after each verse, is introduced and announced by the same formula each time it is sung:

$$R' + e \rightarrow R''; \quad V_1 + e \rightarrow R''; \quad V_2 + e \rightarrow R''$$

This method has been mentioned earlier in our discussion of the forms of responsorial and antiphonal psalmody [see p. 194]. It occurs in the following Offertories [indication by numbers refers to Ott's publication; the length of the identical ending is indicated either by number of notes or, if they are of considerable extension, by quotation of the portions of the text with which they appear]:[9]

Deus tu convertens (no. 2): six notes

Confortamini (no. 4): "-et judicium" = "lingua mutorum" = "Emmanuel" [see Fig. 35, p. 194]

Laetentur (no. 8): here the common ending consists of the entire R':
"Laetentur . . . terra" = "cantate . . . terra" = "de die . . . eius"

Tui sunt caeli (no. 10, three verses): six notes

Eripe me Domine (no. 30): the common ending of R', $\mathcal{V}_1$, and $\mathcal{V}_2$ comprises five or six notes; however, $\mathcal{V}_1$ and $\mathcal{V}_2$ have a longer ending in common: " (ser)vo tuo Domine" = "spiritus meus"[10]

Jubilate Deo universa (no. 42): nine notes

Viri Galilei (no. 102): "in caelum" = "dixerunt"

Ascendit Deus (no. 45): nine notes (modified)

De profundis (no. 73): the common ending, comprising eleven notes, occurs in the respond at the end of the melisma on "meam," but there is no asterisk after "meam," nor is there an indication for the repeat of the respond (or its second half) after either of the two verses. Nevertheless, the occurrence of the verse ending in the middle of the respond leaves no doubt that the second part of the respond, "de profundis . . . Domine," is to be used as a refrain [see Fig. 36]. Since this portion of the text (and melody) occurs also at the beginning of the respond [see p. 365], the entire Offertory shows strict rondo form:

```
        r              a                r                    b
R': De . . . Domine: Domine . . . meam: de . . . Domine. V. 1: Fiant . . .
      r                      c                  r
 tui. R': de . . . Domine. V. 2: Si . . . sustinebit? R': de . . . Domine.
```

In a number of Offertories only some of the verses employ the internal ending of the respond (before the asterisk):

Domine vivifica (no. 16), V. 1: eight or nine notes

Domine fac mecum (no. 21), V. 2: "propter . . ." = "ego . . ."

Eripe me . . . Deus (no. 27), V. 1: the common ending begins ten notes before " (insurgen)tibus in me" and " (for)tes in me"

Benedictus es . . . non tradas (no. 28), V. 2: six notes

Intonuit (no. 35), V. 1: "vocem suam" = "meus"

Si ambulavero (no. 69), V. 2: eleven notes

Super flumina (no. 70), V. 1: the ten-note ending occurs in the middle of the respond, at "flevimus" (no asterisk). See p. 195.

[9] In the respond the common ending appears, of course, immediately before the asterisk. It will be recalled that a similar practice occurs in the Responsories [see p. 334].

[10] This Offertory, as shown in *L* 605, has the unusual feature in that its respond closes on b, a fifth above the final. In its full form, with two verses, this ending is employed before ỹ. 1 and before ỹ. 2, while for the concluding repeat, after ỹ. 2, a *seconda volta* ending is indicated which correctly closes on the final, e.

Desiderium (no. 90), ℣. 1: "ei, Domine" = "ei, Domine" (notice the identity of both text and music)
Domine Deus meus (no. 103), ℣. 2: seven notes
Repleti sumus (no. 104), ℣. 1: eight notes

In all these Offertories the verses borrow their endings from the internal cadence of the respond, a phenomenon resulting from (or indicative of) the refrain structure. In a number of Offertories it is the final cadence of the respond that recurs in some or all of the verses, resulting in a "musical rhyme" similar to that found in some of the Graduals, e.g., those of the fifth mode [see p. 350]. Thus, in *Protege Domine* (no. 100) the cadence of the respond recurs in ℣. 1 and 2:

		d-c-d-e-f e-d
℟.:	*Protege . . .*	*alle- luia*
℣. 1:	*Te sancta . . .*	*in te*
℣. 2:	*Qui pro mundi . . .*	*se- curus,*

while ℣. 3 has a different ending. Other examples are:

Terra tremuit (no. 33): the respond and the three verses each close with an "alleluia" sung to the same melody in ℟. and ℣. 3, to a modified melody in ℣. 1 and ℣. 2.

Immittet angelus (no. 61): same ending for ℟. and ℣. 1, 2, 3.

Mihi autem (no. 74): both ℟. and ℣. 1 close with the words "principatus eorum" sung to the same melody.

Confitebuntur caeli (no. 80), ℣. 1, 2: the respond closes with "alleluia, alleluia." The second "alleluia" recurs at the close of ℣. 1, and both "alleluia, alleluia" at the close of ℣. 2. For another melodic repeat, between respond and ℣. 1, see p. 374.

Anima nostra (no. 85): the respond and ℣. 1 both close with the words "et nos liberati sumus" sung to the same melody, but transposed to the upper fifth in the verse.

Justus ut palma (no. 88): the entire second half of the respond, "Sicut cedrus, quae in Libano est, multiplicabitur," recurs with the same text and with the same melody (aside from an enlarged melisma) at the end of ℣. 3. ℣. 1 and 2 have a common ending of eleven notes.

O pie Deus (no. 107): Both respond and verse have the same ending of seven notes.

Finally, there are a considerable number of Offertories in which two or more of the verses have a common ending which, however, does not occur in the respond. Considered *per se,* this phenomenon is not unusual; in fact, it occurs in nearly all the chants employing several verses—in the ordinary Psalms, in the Introits (verse and Doxology), and in the Tracts. The difference is that in all these chants the various verses are sung to the same melody (psalm tone, introit tone, etc.), a method which necessarily and automatically implies the use of the same closing formula (termination, etc.). In the Offertories, however, each verse is sung to a free and individual melody. The cases in which these different melodies have a common ending are therefore noteworthy as additional evidence of the use of unifying devices in the Offertories. Since the common ending does not occur in the respond, it cannot be explained as resulting from the refrain structure. It is a purely musical phenomenon, a "musical rhyme," such as also occurs in many later strata, e.g., in the sequences, the estampie, etc. A good example is the Offertory *Perfice gressus* (no. 54):

$$g \quad g\text{-}b\text{-}a\text{-}b\text{-}a\text{-}a\text{-}a$$

℣. 1: *Exaudi*, . . .   *orationem me- am*
2: *Custodi* . . .   *ab im- pi- o*
3: *Ego autem* . . .   *gloria tu- a*

Following is a list of the Offertories showing musical rhyme:

(a) of all the verses:

Exsulta (no. 5); *Jubilate . . . omnis* (no. 12); *Portas caeli* (no. 36); *Benedicite gentes* (no. 43); *Confitebor* (no. 44); *Emitte spiritum* (no. 46); *Confirma hoc* (no. 47); *Benedictus sit* (no. 48); *Sperent* (no. 51); *Illumina* (no. 52); *Benedicam Dominum* (no. 53); *Perfice gressus* (no. 54); *Sanctificavit Moyses* (no. 68); *Mirabilis Deus* (no. 82); *Afferentur* (no. 96); *Confessio et pulchritudo* (no. 98);

(b) of some of the verses:

Reges Tharsis (no. 11; ℣. 2 and 3); *Bonum est confiteri* (no. 14; ℣. 2 and 3); *Improperium* (no. 29; ℣. 1 and 2); *Custodi me* (no. 31; ℣. 2 and 3); *Constitues eos* (no. 76; ℣. 2 and 3).

The length of the common ending varies from as few as five notes, as in *Sperent,* to the extreme case presented by *Emitte Spiritum* in which the common ending extends, with some variants, over the entire second half of each of the three verses.

While the tendency toward motival unification expresses itself most clearly in the closing formulae of the responds, the verses, or both, it also manifests itself in other details:

Confitebor tibi, Domine (no. 26): three short passages, "corde meo," " (ver)bum tuum, Domine," and "in lege Domini," the first two in the respond, the third in ℣. 1, employ the same melodic formula.

Eripe me . . . Domine (no. 30) has the same short melisma on "tuam" and "es tu," both in the respond [see *L* 605].

Custodi me (no. 31): the respond employs the same melody for the penultimate and the final phrase, "Et ab hominibus iniquis" and "eripe me, Domine," resulting in the form a b b. Moreover, ℣. 2 and 3 have not only a common ending [see above], but also the same melody for their initial phrases, "Qui cogitaverunt" and "Dixi Domino."

Domine exaudi (no. 32): two subsequent phrases in the middle of the respond, "orationem mean" and "et clamor meus," employ the same melody, so that the form becomes a b b c [620].

Benedictus qui venit (no. 39) has the same musical phrase for the two subsequent words "Domini" and "Deus" [806]. ℣. 1 shows the form a b b c, the extended melisma of "exsultemus" being immediately restated on "et laetemur."

Lauda anima (no. 41): The same melodic formula occurs at two separate places of ℣. 2, " (extermi)nabit" and " (Si)on."

Jubilate Deo universa (no. 42): the melody of the beginning of the respond, "Jubilate Deo universa terra," recurs, with minor variants, at the beginning of ℣. 2, "Locutum est os meum in tribulatione mea." In addition, both the respond and the second verse repeat the initial phrase of their texts, with nearly the same melody [see above, p. 364].

Ascendit Deus (no. 45): a short motif, d-a-b-a, occurs seven times: ℟. "in," "Do (minus"; ℣. 1. "Om (nes)," "in"; ℣. 2, "Rex," "su (per)"; ℣. 3, "sub."

Confirma hoc (no. 47): a short motif, d-g-a-c′-a-g-f, occurs repeatedly (with variants) in ℣. 2, "Domi (no)," and in ℣. 3, "cantate," "psal (lite)," and "ascendit."

Domine in auxilium (no. 63): ℣. 1 employs the same melisma on " (re)trorsum" and " (eru)bescant."

Si ambulavero (no. 69): a short motif, g-a-b-c′-d′-c′-b-a, recurs five times in ℣. 2, as a part of the melismas on "tuum," " (confi)te (bor)," "Do (mine)," "tu (a)," and " (veri)ta (te)."

Confitebuntur caeli (no. 80): the melody for "in ecclesia sanctorum" in the respond recurs in ℣. 1 with a similar text, "in consilio sanctorum." In addition, this Offertory has common endings for the closing "alleluia" of the respond and both verses [see above, p. 372].

In virtute tua (no. 89): the second half of the melisma on "ei" (close of the respond) recurs in four melismas of ℣. 1, on "pe (tiit)," "ei," " (di)e (rum)," and "sae (culi)."

Domine Deus meus (no. 103): The respond and ℣. 1 begin with the same text, "Domine, Deus meus," and the two melodies accompanying this text have the same beginning as well as the same closing formula. A short motif, g-a-c′-c′-a-g-g-f, forms not only the common ending of ℟′ and ℣. 2 [see above, p. 372], but recurs, altogether, nine times in the course of the entire chant. Notice also the identity (or near identity) of the three melismas on "meus," "me fac," and " (persequentibus) me" in the respond. Here, as in numerous other cases, it is obviously the recurrence of the same word which suggested the employment of the same melodic phrase.

Repleti sumus (no. 104): Most of the melodic material of ℣. 2 is derived from that of ℣. 1. Aside from the four opening notes, which reiterate the opening of ℣. 1, the entire beginning of ℣. 2, "Priusquam fierent montes," is sung to the melody of the section "refugium factus est nobis" of ℣. 1, and " (sae)culo et in saeculum" of ℣. 2 has the same melody as " (generati)one et progeni (e)" of ℣. 1.

Misit rex (no. 105): This Offertory, which is probably of a more recent date (it is not contained in the *Sextuplex* Mss.), is remarkable for its repeated use of a "dominant-seventh" motif, g-d'-f'-d' (twice in the respond) or g-b-d'-f'-d' (twice in the verse). Notice also the four recurrences of the motif d'-f'-e'-f'-g'-f'-e'-d' in the two verse melismas on "aliud" and "caput."

These lengthy explanations, although perhaps tiring in all their details, were necessary in order to establish clearly the peculiar character of the Offertories and their verses. Unique and exceptionally bold melodic progressions, repetition of entire portions of the text, profuse melismas of the reiterative type as well as melismas showing a clear-cut repeat structure, unifying devices such as common endings or recurrent phrases and motifs: all these traits combine to put these chants in a class entirely their own. Nor is the interest of the Offertories limited to the field of analytical investigation. They are equally remarkable and extraordinary if regarded from the aesthetic point of view, from which they appear indeed as outstanding embodiments of medieval art. We are, of course, speaking of the Offertories in their complete form, with their verses which, in fact, reveal the specific character of these chants much more clearly than the responds. It is a great pity that these verses are so little known. In the preface of his publication, Ott aptly extols them for their magnificent flow, the harmony of their parts, the elegance of their lines, the originality of their formulae, the ever-varying forms of their melismas, adding that "nobody will deny their being superior to the verses of the Graduals." Certainly they represent a dramatic climax in the development of the chant which stands in marked contrast to the quiet greatness of the earlier melodies, a contrast not dissimilar to that between Beethoven and Bach.

THE ALLELUIAS

The Alleluia is the third chant of the Proper of the Mass, and is sung immediately after the Gradual. It is omitted during the pre-Easter period beginning with Septuagesima Sunday but, as if in recompense for the omission, doubled during Paschal Time—more correctly, from Saturday in Easter Week to Friday after Pentecost (Ember Friday), when two Alleluias are sung instead of the normal Gradual-plus-Alleluia. The Saturday after Pentecost (Ember Saturday) has five Alleluias, instead of the normal

sequence of four Graduals and Hymn *(Benedictus es Domine)* for the
Saturdays of Ember Weeks [see p. 29].

Taken over directly from the Jewish rites (alleluia = *hallelu Jah,* praise
ye Jehova), the Alleluia was widely used as an expression of joyful praise of
the Lord, not only in the liturgy but also at many occasions of daily life.
St. Jerome gives a vivid description of this practice, saying that "wherever
you turn, the ploughman with the plough-handle in his hand sings the
Alleluia, the perspiring reaper relieves himself with a Psalm, and the vine-
yardist, cutting the vine with a curved knife, sings something from David."[1]
He also tells us that the Alleluia was sung at festive meals, and that a
young girl, barely able to speak, sang it to the joy of her grandfather.
Sidonius Apollinaris (born *c.* 430) speaks in a poem of the Alleluia being
sung by the boatmen and resounding from the banks of the river (Loire);
while Bede tells us that in a battle of 448 the priests of the Britons intoned
three times the Alleluia, to which the soldiers responded as with a single
voice, thus discomfiting the army of the Saxons and Picts.

As for the liturgical Alleluia, this occurs not only in its specific connotation as a Mass chant but also, and possibly much earlier, as an addition
to other chants. St. Jerome strongly recommended to Pope Damasus that
he add the Alleluia to all the Psalms of Matins, and St. Benedict prescribed
it for all the Psalms and Responsories during Paschal Time, as well as for
the last six Psalms of Matins and the Canticles of Sundays outside of Lent.[2]
The later and present-day practice is to add it at the end of every chant
sung during Paschal Time.

At present, we are concerned only with the Alleluia of the Mass. It is
usually stated that this was introduced in Rome by Pope Damasus, on the
advice of St. Jerome and for Easter Sunday only. Recent investigations,
however, have revealed an entirely different picture.[3] It seems that before

1 See for this and subsequent quotations: I. Glibotić, "De cantu 'Alleluia' in patribus
saeculo VII anterioribus" *(Ephemerides liturgicae,* L [1936], 99); J. Froger, "L'Alleluia
dans l'usage romain" *(ibid.,* LXII [1948], 6); and the article "Alleluja" (Stäblein) in *MGG.*

2 See, for St. Jerome, *Patr. lat.* 130, p. 659: *Alleluia semper cum omnibus psalmis affi-
gatur . . .;* for St. Benedict, *Patr. lat.* 66, pp. 451ff, or *The Holy Rule of . . . Saint Benedict* (St. Meinrad's Abbey, 1937), p. 32.

3 See the articles by Glibotić and Froger (fn. 1). The change results from a correction
in a famous letter by Gregory including the words *Nam ut alleluia hic diceretur* (The
custom to sing the Alleluia here, i.e., in Rome), which actually should read *Nam ut alleluia hic* non *diceretur* (The custom *not* to sing the Alleluia here). The whole passage is
as follows: "Somebody came to me from Sicily and told me that some of his friends . . .
grumbled about my dispositions, saying: although he wants to suppress the Church of
Constantinople, he nevertheless follows all its customs. When I asked him: which
customs do we follow? he said: that the Alleluia should be sung at Masses outside of
Paschal Time. . . . I answered him: In none of these matters have we followed another
Church. Tradition has it that our custom not to sing the Alleluia was adopted, through

Damasus the Alleluia was used in Rome as widely as in the Churches of the Orient, although we cannot be certain whether or to what extent it was used as a chant of the Mass. Exactly what happened under Damasus is not entirely clear. If we are to believe the famous passage in one of Gregory's letters (in its correct form; see fn. 3), we must conclude that Damasus actually abolished it. Strange though this conclusion may be, it is confirmed in a way by the statement of the Greek church historian Sozomenos, according to which the Alleluia was sung in Rome, about 450, only once during the year, on the first day of Easter [see List of Data, no. 37]. There can hardly be any doubt that this single Alleluia was the Alleluia of the Easter Mass. In the ensuing 150 years the use of the Alleluia was extended over the entire Easter period, a process that was completed by the time of Gregory, as appears from his above-mentioned letter written in 598 to the Bishop Johannes of Syracuse in answer to a complaint about several innovations he had introduced, among them the "singing of the Alleluia at Masses outside of Paschal Time." From this letter we learn two facts: first, that before Gregory the Mass Alleluia was sung only during the period from Easter to Pentecost; second, that he extended its use beyond this period. The latter is usually interpreted to mean that he ordered the use of the Alleluia for the entire year, excepting, of course, the pre-Easter period [see List of Data, no. 47]. Actually, there is reason to assume that he introduced it only for the first season of the year, from the first Sunday of Advent to the last Sunday after Epiphany [see pp. 380f].

It is usually said that during the pre-Easter period and on other occasions of penitence or mourning, "the Alleluia is replaced by the Tract."[4] Although this is a convenient way of describing the present-day state of affairs, it is not correct in the historical sense for the simple reason that an Alleluia never existed on those days. Perhaps a case could be made for the reverse statement, namely, that the Tracts were replaced by the Alleluia on all days except those of a penitential character. If we recall the early form of the Mass with three readings and two Psalms between them [see pp. 24f], it is certainly a plausible assumption that the first Psalm was

---

St. Jerome, from the Church of Jerusalem at the time of Pope Damasus of blessed memory . . ." (*Patr. lat.* 77, p. 956; the complete letter is reproduced in Gastoué, *Origines*, p. 283).

After the completion of my manuscript an article appeared, by E. Wellesz, "Gregory the Great's Letter on the Alleluia" (*Annales musicologiques*, II [1954], 7), in which the older reading without the word *non* is defended with an array of evidence no less impressive than that brough forward by Glibotić and Froger in support of the version with the word *non*. I am not in a position to take sides on this issue.

4 *Wagner I*, 86: "On days of mourning . . . the Alleluia is replaced by the Tract." Ferretti, *Esthétique*, pp. 133f: ". . . le *Trait* . . . remplace le chant de l'*Alleluia.* . . ."

a *psalmus responsorius,* that is, a Gradual, the second a *psalmus direc-taneus,* that is, a Tract. Indeed, more than any other Mass chant the Tract has a valid claim to be considered as a Psalm.[5]

The Alleluia, on the other hand, is not a psalmodic chant in the proper sense of the word, in spite of the fact that in its final form it consists of the word *Alleluia* followed by a verse usually taken from a Psalm. Although this structure is similar to that of the Gradual, Responsory, Introit, etc., in which the respond (or antiphon) is followed by a verse, it probably resulted from a process of addition, rather than reduction from a complete Psalm as was the case in the truly psalmodic chants. None of the early writers make any allusion to a Psalm in connection with the Alleluia, but describe it as being nothing but the word *Alleluia* itself, sung in a more or less melismatic manner. St. Augustine (*c.* 400) compares it to the *celeusma,* the far-sounding cry of the Roman sailors, and Cassiodorus (*c.* 550) describes it in some detail but without any reference to a full text, saying only that it is "an ornament for the tongue of the singers" and that, "like an inexhaustible treasure, it is renewed in ever-varying melodies.[6]

It is not known at what time the verses were added to the Alleluia. Since the earliest sources for the Mass formularies show the Alleluia invariably connected with a verse (e.g., the Codex Monza of the eighth century), it appears that this step must have been taken some time between *c.* 550 and *c.* 750. Wagner surmises that this was done by Gregory, but there is no proof for this assumption. In fact it seems rather unlikely, because of the considerable variability that exists in the assignment of the verses to the various feasts of the liturgical year. If, in addition to extending the use of the Alleluia over the entire year, Gregory had also provided individual verses, the combined result of the two steps would have been similar to that in the other Mass chants, that is, a definite and invariable assignment of a given verse to a given feast would exist. Actually, this is far from being the case. In no other class of chant is there so much variability and lack of conformity as in the Alleluias. We cannot possibly enter into a detailed description of this extremely complex picture, nor would this serve any useful purpose from our point of view.[7] It will suffice to describe briefly the state of affairs as it exists in the earliest sources, the six manuscripts of Hesbert's *Sextuplex* publication. In the *Temporale,* the following feasts are the only ones having an invariable Alleluia verse:

5 As has been mentioned previously [p. 184], there is good reason to assume that at least some of the Tracts originally were Graduals.

6 St. Augustine: "Our *celeusma,* that we sing, is the miraculous Alleluia" (*Patr. lat.* 40, p. 680). Cassiodorus, see *Patr. lat.* 70, p. 742.

7 The Alleluia is the only chant of the Mass Proper for which new texts and melodies were written as late as the fifteenth century. See the article "Alleluja" in *MGG.*

SEXT.	FEAST	VERSE	L
1	Dom. I. Adv.	*Ostende nobis*	320
2	Dom. II. Adv.	*Laetatus sum*	329
4	Dom. III. Adv.	*Excita Domine*	336
7bis	Dom. IV. Adv.	*Veni Domine*[8]	354
9	Nat., Nocte	*Dominus dixit*	394
10	Nat., Mane	*Dominus regnavit decore(m)*	405
11	Nat., Die	*Dies sanctificatus*	409
17	Dom. I. p. Nat.	*Dominus regnavit decore(m)*	435
18	Epiphania	*Vidimus stellam*	460
19	Dom. I. p. Ep.	*Jubilate Deo*	479
21	Dom. II. p. Ep.	*Laudate Deum*	486
26	Dom. III. p. Ep.	*Dominus regnavit exultet*[9]	490
79	Sabb. Sancto	*Confitemini Domino*	759
80	Dom. Paschae	*Pascha nostrum*	779
81	Fer. II. p. P.	*Dominus regnavit decore(m)*	...
86	Sabb. p. P.	*Laudate pueri*[10]	805
94	Letaniae	*Confitemini Domino*	841
102	Ascensa	*Ascendit Deus; Dominus in Sina*	848
105	Vig. Pent.	*Confitemini Domino*	860
106	Pentecosten	*Emitte Spiritum; Veni Sancte Spiritus*	879f

This list covers the complete *Temporale* from Advent up to Easter (nos. 1 to 80), disregarding, of course, the pre-Easter period in which there is no Alleluia. After Easter, however, the picture changes, only five Masses existing with an invariable Alleluia; i.e., for Saturday in Easter Week, Litany Days, Ascension, Vigil of Pentecost, and Pentecost. For Monday in Easter Week the *Sextuplex* Mss are still in agreement among themselves (no. 81), but in the earliest musical sources, such as St. Gall *359* and *339,* the original *Dominus regnavit decorem,* adopted from the Nativity, is replaced by *Surrexit Dominus vere,* which eventually gave way to *Angelus Domini descendit.* For the subsequent days of Easter Week even the *Graduals* of the *Sextuplex* are in disagreement. A typical example is the Wednesday in Easter Week (*Sextuplex* no. 83):

[8] Only in Compiègne and Senlis. In Monza, Mont-Blandin, and Corbie this Sunday, which is a later addition, is not represented. Codex Rheinau has a Mass for it, but omits the Alleluia, as it does in a number of other Masses.

[9] Mont-Blandin has *Alleluia: Beatus vir.*

[10] The other Alleluia of this day, ℣. *Haec dies,* is clearly indicated only in Corbie. The other Mss prescribe the Gradual *Haec dies.* Monza has the rather puzzling indication: *Resp. Grad. All. Hec dies.*

Codex Monza:	All. *Quoniam Deus magnus*
Codex Rheinau:	All. *Redemptionem misit*
Codex Mont-Blandin:	All. quale volueris (whichever you wish)
Codex Compiègne:	All. *Dominus regnavit*
Codex Corbie:	All. *Jubilate Deo*
Codex Senlis:	All. *Jubilate Deo*
Liber usualis:	All. *Surrexit Dominus.*

Similarly for the Second Sunday after Easter (*Sextuplex* no. 88):

Codex Monza:	Alleluias II
Codex Rheinau:	All. *Confitemini Domino et invocate;* All. *Confitemini Domino quoniam*
Codex Mont-Blandin:	All. II quale volueris
Codex Compiègne:	All. *Surrexit Altissimus;* All. *Dominus regnavit decore*
Codex Corbie:	nothing indicated
Codex Senlis:	All. *Qui posuit;* All. *Quoniam Deus magnus*
Liber usualis:	All. *Cognoverunt discipuli;* All. *Ego sum.*

For the Sundays after Pentecost, the early sources (including most of the musical manuscripts of the tenth, eleventh, and twelfth centuries) usually omit the Alleluia from the Masses, and give a separate list under such titles as *Alleluiae de circulo anni* or *Alleluiae per singulas Dominicas.* From this list the singer would be free to choose an "alleluia quale volueris," whichever Alleluia he preferred, for that day.

The *Sanctorale* shows an even more striking lack of fixity. Properly speaking, there are only two feasts of Saints which have an unquestionably invariable Alleluia, namely, St. Stephen (*Video caelos; Sext.* 12) and St. John (*Hic est discipulus; Sext.* 14). In addition there are a few feasts which may be regarded as having an invariable Alleluia, although some of the *Sextuplex* Mss (usually Rheinau or Mont-Blandin) fail to indicate an Alleluia. These are: St. Silvester (*Inveni David,* today for St. Basil; *Sext.* 16); St. Prisca (*Diffusa est,* today for St. Lucy; *Sext.* 23); St. Fabian (*Sancti tui; Sext.* 24); St. Vincent (*Beatus vir qui timet,* today for the Common of a Confessor not a Bishop; *Sext.* 27); and Dedication (*Adorabo; Sext.* 100).[11]

It will be noticed that, except for the Dedication, all these feasts fall within the Advent-Epiphany season, the same period which also shows invariable Alleluias for the *Temporale.* Obviously the Alleluias of this period had an authoritative character absent in the other periods, even in Paschal Time, which was the earliest period to acquire an Alleluia. Perhaps we have here an indication of Gregory's activity. The striking

[11] For a table showing the variation of the Alleluias in the *Sanctorale,* see *Sextuplex,* p. cxi.

contrast between the fixity of the Alleluias in the Advent-Epiphany seasons and their variability during the others could be explained by assuming that he extended the use of the Alleluia—or, possibly, of an Alleluia with a specific verse—only to the first part of the liturgical year. As for the variability in Paschal Time, a plausible explanation would be that, in deference to the older tradition, he did not introduce any changes in this period. This would mean that in Paschal Time the Alleluia continued to be sung as a pure melisma and did not acquire a verse until a later time. Naturally, all these considerations refer only to the textual aspect of the Alleluias. We shall see, however, that musical considerations lead to similar conclusions [see pp. 391f].

About half a dozen Alleluias occur in the older sources more or less regularly with two verses. This is particularly true of the Easter Alleluia, which nearly always has the verses *Pascha nostrum* and *Epulemur in azymis*.[12] Other Alleluias with two verses are:

Alleluia ℣. *Laetatus sum;* ℣. *Stantes erant* (Second Sunday of Advent)
Alleluia ℣. *Angelus Domini;* ℣. *Respondens autem* (Easter Monday)
Alleluia ℣. *Venite exsultemus;* ℣. *Preoccupemus* (Sundays after Pentecost)
Alleluia ℣. *Tu es Petrus;* ℣. *Beatus es Simon* (Peter and Paul).

A concomitant of the extraordinary variability of liturgical assignment in the Alleluias is the extensive use of adaptation, that is, of the same melody for different texts. True enough, examples of this method are not missing in other categories, for example, in the Tracts, the Graduals, the Offertories. What distinguishes the Alleluias is not only that adaptations are much more numerous but especially that they occur within the earliest segment of the liturgical year, while in the other chants they are found only for feasts of a later date.[13] The largest group of adaptations is the one that includes the Alleluia *Dominus dixit* from the Midnight Mass of the Nativity:

A. Temporale

Ostende nobis [320]	First Sunday of Advent
Dominus dixit [394]	The Nativity, Midnight Mass
Dominus regnavit, exsultet, [490]	Third Sunday after Epiphany
Haec dies [805]	Saturday in Holy Week
Dominus in Sina [848]	Ascension
Confiteantur [G 411]	First Sunday after Pentecost
	(now St. Peter's Chair, Votive Mass)

12 See the facsimiles following p. 122. The (non-musical) *Gradual* of Compiègne adds a third verse, *Non in fermento.*
13 Trinity is the earliest; see p. 69.

B. Old Sanctorale

Specie tua [1218]	St. Agnes and others; now Mass for a Virgin Martyr
Diffusa est gratia [1323]	St. Lucy
Nimis honorati [1720]	SS. Simon and Jude

C. Modern Feasts

Dominus salvavit [G 464]	St. John Damascene
Mittat vobis [1289]	Nuptial Mass

Hardly less popular was the melody of the Alleluia *Dies sanctificatus* from the Third Mass of the Nativity:

A. Temporale

Dies sanctificatus [409]	The Nativity, Mass of the Day
Vidimus stellam [460]	Epiphany

B. Old Sanctorale

Video caelos [416]	St. Stephen
Hic est discipulus [422]	St. John, Apostle
Inveni David [1489]	St. Silvester (now St. Basil)
Sancti tui [1336]	SS. Fabian and Sebastian
Tu es Petrus [1520]	SS. Peter and Paul

C. Late-Medieval Sanctorale

Tu puer [1501]	St. John the Baptist
Magnus sanctus [1346]	Conversion of St. Paul
Hic est sacerdos [1184]	Mass of a Confessor Bishop

Yet another example of multiple adaptation is the following:

Excita Domine [336]	Third Sunday of Advent
Ascendit Deus [848]	Ascension
Emitte Spiritum [879]	Pentecost
Laudate Deum [486]	Second Sunday after Epiphany
Qui posuit fines [1286]	Mass to Beg for Peace; originally Vigil of Ascension etc.
Benedicite Domino [1664]	Mass for the Guardian Angels; originally?

In most cases the adaptation of the original melody to a new verse is rather strict, the difference being mainly in the omission or addition of notes caused by the varying number of syllables. Occasionally variations of the textual structure necessitated the omission of complete passages, an example in point being *Hic est sacerdos* [1184], which is a considerably shortened adaptation of *Dies sanctificatus* [409]. There are also some Alleluias which combine a borrowed *Alleluia* with a new melody for the verse, e.g.:

Virgo Dei genitrix [1684]   and   *Surrexit Dominus de sepulcro* [790]
Redemptionem [822]   and   *Dies sanctificatus* [409]
Ostende mihi [1377]   and   *In te Domine* [1008]

A long, though not complete list of *contrafacta* is given in Wagner's vol. III, pp. 400ff. It shows that more than seventy of the Alleluias in present-day use, that is, about one-third of the total number, are adaptations. Many more cases can undoubtedly be found in the late-medieval sources, which contain numerous Alleluias that had only local or temporary significance and were not adopted by the modern collections.

If adaptation plays a prominent role in the Alleluias, centonization is conspicuously absent. Like the Offertories, perhaps even more so, the Alleluia melodies are individual compositions rather than representatives of a type. Here the change of emphasis—adumbrated in the Offertories—from the group to the individual, from bondage to liberty, is fully completed. This is not to say that common traits indicative of a unified style are entirely absent, but these enter into the picture to about the same degree as they do in the sonatas of Beethoven. What binds the Alleluias together are mainly aspects of form and structural detail, the same aspects that also provide the common ground for the works of the nineteenth-century master.

As to its form, the Alleluia consists essentially of two sections: the first formed by the word *Alleluia* (A) and a subsequent melisma called *jubilus* (j); the second, by the verse (V). Except for a few special occasions, e.g., on Holy Saturday, the *Alleluia* is repeated after the verse, so that a ternary form results:

$$A + j \quad V \quad A + j^{14}$$

Although the verses, with their full texts, present a strong contrast to the *Alleluia* sections, both sections are unified to a degree not encountered in any other chant of the respond-plus-verse (or antiphon-plus-verse) type by the use of common material. With the exception of perhaps no more than ten melodies,[15] all the verses close with a restatement of the *jubilus,* so that the normal form of an Alleluia is:

$$A + j \quad V + j \quad A + j$$

Actually the musical relationships between the verse and the *Alleluia* are considerably more diversified and extensive than this general scheme suggests. In the great majority of the cases it is not only the *jubilus,* but the complete *Alleluia* section $(A + j)$, that recurs at the end of the verse.

14 For more details concerning the actual performance, see p. 197.

15 In all the subsequent explanations duplications arising from adaptation are disregarded, so that "ten Alleluias" means "ten different melodies," which may occur with any number of different texts.

Moreover, there are a certain number of Alleluias in which the *Alleluia* (sometimes the *Alleluia* with the *jubilus*) is quoted not only at the end but also at the beginning of the verse. Finally, in a few cases the borrowing goes so far that the entire verse consists almost entirely of material taken from the *Alleluia*. In the following tabulation the various "repeat types" are schematically indicated by an equation showing the relationship between the verse and the *Alleluia*. The total number of examples (different melodies) for each type is also given and, for the purpose of fuller illustration, the individual examples found in the Alleluias of mode 7.[16]

1. V = ... A + j:
   Total number *c.* 60.
   Mode 7: *Domine exaudi* [1049]; *In die resurrectionis* [809]; *Levita Laurentius* [1595]; *Post dies octo* [810]

2. V = ... j:
   Total number *c.* 25.
   Mode 7: *Adorabo* [1251]; *Domine refugium* [1034]; *Magnus Dominus* [1014]; *Pascha nostrum* [779]; *Te decet* [1022]

3. V = A ... A + j:
   Total number *c.* 15.
   Mode 7: *Deus qui* [1000]; *Exsultate Deo* [1026]; *Jubilate Deo* [1294]; *Multifarie* [441]; *Quinque prudentes* [1339]

4. V = A ... j:
   Total number *c.* 6.
   Mode 7: *Confitebuntur* [1147]; *De profundis* [1076].

The subsequent repeat structures occur only rarely. Therefore each of them is illustrated by all the examples that occur in any mode.

5. V = A + j ... A + j:
   Christus resurgens [827]; *Dispersit* [1480]; *Loquebantur* [888]; *Loquebar* [1369]; *Exivi a patre* [831]; *Haec est vera* [1508]

6. V = ... A + j A + j:
   Ego sum [818]; *Angelus Domini* [786]

7. V = A + j A + j:
   Surrexit Dominus vere [794]; *O quam pulchra* [1223]; *Spiritus ejus* [902]

Remarks concerning the various types:

1. This form, characterized by the restatement of the entire first section at the end of the verse, is by far the most frequent of all. It is relatively rare in the Alleluias of mode 7, but occurs very frequently in those of the first mode.

---

[16] See *Wagner III*, 413f. Also the study in F. Gennrich, *Formenlehre des mittelalterlichen Liedes* (1932), pp. 107ff: "Die *versus alleluiatici*."

2. In some of the examples of this form, in which only the *jubilus* is repeated at the end of the verse, the melisma is slightly shortened; e.g., in *Adorabo* and *Pascha nostrum;* whereas in *Te decet* the verse closes with an expanded melisma. In some cases the melodic motion immediately preceding is similar to, and evidently borrowed from, the *Alleluia* without, however, amounting to a full restatement of it. Examples in point are *Surrexit Christus* [831], *Sapientia hujus* [1428], and *Timebunt gentes* [1057], all in the first mode. These could also be included under no. 1.

3. In this group, as well as in the subsequent ones, the verse opens as well as closes with the *Alleluia* melody or a section thereof. The quotation at the beginning of the verse is often subject to modification, while that at the end is usually more exact.

4. In these Alleluias the verse is inserted between the *Alleluia* and the *jubilus,* a procedure strikingly similar to the *motets entés* ("grafted" motets) of the thirteenth century. The verse of the Alleluia *Quoniam Deus* [1042] starts with the *Alleluia* melody without, however, employing it at the end (V = A . . .). As far as I know, there is no other example of this kind.

5.–7. All these Alleluias have verses in which the entire *Alleluia* section (A + j) recurs twice, either at the beginning and at the end (no. 5); or twice in succession at the end (no. 6); or, finally, in such a way that the entire verse melody consists of nothing but two statements of the *Alleluia* section (no. 7).[17]

To sum up: in more than ninety per cent (*c.* 115 out of 125) of the Alleluias the verse contains material borrowed from the *Alleluia* section. Nowhere in the entire repertory of chant is there a parallel to such a degree of thematic unification between the verse and the enframing section, whether antiphon or respond. The closest approximation to the repeat structure of the Alleluias exists in the Offertories. However, the Alleluias go much farther in this direction, not only numerically, but also in the establishment of a number of well-defined repeat structures.

There are hardly more than ten Alleluias in which the verse has no musical relationship to the *Alleluia* section. Small though this group is, it is of no little importance because it includes the Alleluias of all three Masses for the Nativity (*Dominus dixit* [394], *Dominus regnavit* [405], and *Dies sanctificatus* [409]). Four others belong to a later layer of the *Temporale;* namely, *Veni Domine* [354] from the Fourth Sunday of Advent; *Venite exsultemus* [1038] from the Fourteenth Sunday after Pentecost;

---

[17] In group 5 the initial A and/or j is usually modified by amplification, contraction, or variation. In the Alleluias *Haec est vera* and *Exivi* the sections marked . . . contain additional quotations from A or j. Particularly the latter is noteworthy for its extended use of motives. In *Magnus Dominus* [1014] the *jubilus* occurs twice in the verse, in *Haec est virgo* [1222], three times.

and *Quoniam Deus* [1042] from the Fifteenth; and *Beatus vir* [1205] from the Third Sunday after Epiphany (now used for the Mass of a Confessor not a Bishop [1205]). Finally there are a few of doubtful authenticity, such as *Ostende mihi* [1377] from the Feast of the Apparition of Our Lady at Lourdes, *Qui ad justitiam* [1466] from the Feast for S. Robert Bellarmine, and *Quasi rosa* [1669] from the Feast of S. Teresa of the Infant Jesus.

The presence, in this group, of such unquestionably old Alleluias as those for Christmas brings up the problem of chronology. One is tempted to speculate that these melodies represent an early tradition in which the Alleluias were composed in a style not too dissimilar from that of other chants, such as Responsories or Graduals, and that the various repeat types are the result of later tendencies in the direction of clear organization, contemporary or perhaps even posterior to those which produced similar results in the Offertories. It will be better to postpone the discussion of this question until we have studied other important aspects of the Alleluias, that is, the form of their melismas and the general characteristics of their style.

The repetitive[18] character of the Alleluias is evident not only in their over-all forms but also in their melismas, the *jubilus* as well as the inner melismas that appear in many Alleluias somewhere near the middle of the verse. For the sake of greater clarity it is advisable to treat these two categories separately, although both of them show the same characteristics.[19]

By far the most frequent form found in the *jubili* is a a b, that is, the same "bar-form" which also occurs in many melismas of the Offertory verses (pp. 368f). Occasionally the repeat of the initial formula is slightly modified, either at the beginning (a 'a b) or at the end (a a' b). In some cases the repeat structure starts shortly before the *jubilus,* with the last two or three syllables of the preceding *Alleluia.* These cases are indicated below by a remark such as "-luia + j." Following is a typical example and a fairly complete list (from *L*).

FIGURE 115

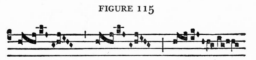

From Alleluia *Tu es sacerdos*

18 Notice the difference between the meaning of "repetitive" and "reiterative" [see p. 262].

19 Much of the subsequent material has been taken from the detailed study in *Wagner III,* 408ff.

a a b: *Non vos relinquam* [856]; *Timebunt gentes* [1056]; *Amavit eum* [1191]; *Sancti . . . florebunt* [1150]; *Tu es sacerdos* [1183]; *Defecit caro* [1479; "-luia + j"]; *Haec est vera* [1508]; *Corpora sanctorum* [1164; "-luia + j"]

a′a b: *In die resurrectionis* [809]; *Surrexit Christus et* [831]; *In exitu* [1068]; *Jubilate Deo* [1294]

a a′ b: *Veni Domine* [354]; *Post partum* [1265]; *Justi epulentur* [1168]

Less frequent is the simple repeat form a a. It occurs mostly with a variant for the repeat, a a′. Sometimes the variant consists of the addition of four or five notes, and such cases could also be considered as examples of the a a b form, with a very short b. An example in point is *Dulce lignum* [1456] which, in fact, is given by Wagner as an example of the bar-form type:

a a′: *Laudate pueri* [428]; *Dicite in gentibus* [801]; *Spiritus est* [901]; *Beatus vir qui suffert* [1202]; *Quinque prudentes* [1339; "-leluia + j"]; *Dulce lignum* [1456]

Of particular interest are a few examples having the form a a b b c, because this shows a certain similarity to the form of the sequence, and may possibly have something to do with its development:

a a b b c: *Oportebat* [822]; *Magnus Dominus* [1014; a a b b′?]; *Beatus vir . . . Martinus* [1747; "Alleluia + j"]

FIGURE 116

From Alleluia *Oportebat*

Finally, there are some *jubili* showing yet other repeat forms, e.g.:

Post dies octo [810; "-luia + j"]: a a a′
Exivi a Patre [831; "-leluia + j," starting with d-e-f-g]: a b a c
De profundis [1076]: a a b c c′
Venite ad me [973]: a a′ b c c′
Tota pulchra [1318]: a b a c a
Verumtamen existimo [1428]: a b a′

Turning now to the inner melismas that occur in many verses, we find the same or similar repeat forms, e.g.:

a a b: *Pascha nostrum* [779] on "(immo)la(tus)"; *Christus resurgens* [827] on "mors"; *In die resurrectionis* [809] on "praece(dam)"; *Juravit Dominus* [1187] on "(se)cundum ordinem" (a a'?); *Confitebuntur* [1147] on "etenim" (a a'?); *Adorabo* [1251] on "et confitebor"; *Loquebar* [1369] on "in conspectu regum"; *Levita Laurentius* [1595] on "operatus"

mors

From Alleluia *Christus resurgens*

a a: *Eripe me* [1018] on "et ab insurgen(tibus)";[20] *Concussum est* [1656] on "terra" (reduced from the "operatus" melisma of *Levita Laurentius*)

a a b b': *Justus ut palma* [1207] on "sicut cedrus"; *Vos estis* [1548] on "sedeatis"

Other forms:

Veni Domine [354] on "facinora": a a' a' b b'
Venite ad me [973] on "qui laboratis": a b b a
Justus germinabit [1192] on "et florebit": a b a c

We reproduce here the melisma from *Justus ut palma,* one of the longest to be found in the Alleluias.

sicut ce-   drus

From Alleluia *Justus ut palma*

From the above explanations it appears that by far the most frequent repeat form is a a b. Our list includes over twenty examples of it. It will be remembered that this form occurs with equal frequency in the Offertories [see pp. 368f].

After having examined the numerous and varied realizations of the principle of repetition, we shall turn to a general consideration of the style of the Alleluias. Although more than any other chant the Alleluias have a

20 Here, as elsewhere, it may be more proper to consider the melisma as extending over the final syllables ("-tibus"), in which case it would adopt the form a a b.

definite emotional association, that is, an expression of joy, their music is not always as exuberant as such a character would seem to warrant. Not a few of them are conspicuous because of their small range, a fact to which we have called attention in our discussion of the chants with a limited ambitus [see p. 146]. Thus, *Dies sanctificatus* [409], an Alleluia of the second mode, moves within the range between the *subtonium* and the upper fifth (d:c-a), except for the passage "venite" in which the A is touched once. The same range is employed in *Regnavit Dominus* [855] of the first mode, except for the single c′ in the melisma on "Deus." Even more limited is the range of *Repleti fructu* [1545] and *Eripe me* [1018], both of which move essentially within the range of a fifth, from the *subtonium* to the upper fourth (d:c-g), except for a single a in the former and a single A in the latter. Equally limited are some Alleluias of the eighth mode; e.g., *Confitemini Domino* [759] (g:f-d′, except for a single e at the very beginning; the *subtonium* f occurs only twice), *Crastina die* [361] (g:g-d′), and *Ego dilecto* [1691] (g:g-c′, except for a single d′ on "Alleluia" and a single d on "conversio").

In contrast to such cautiously moving melodies there are a number of Alleluias which not only employ the full range of their modes but are conspicuous for the occurrence of fairly extended scale formations, usually in descending motion. A number of examples are shown in Fig. 119.[21] Such

FIGURE 119

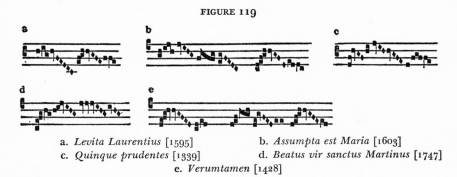

a. *Levita Laurentius* [1595]   b. *Assumpta est Maria* [1603]
c. *Quinque prudentes* [1339]   d. *Beatus vir sanctus Martinus* [1747]
e. *Verumtamen* [1428]

sweeping scalar patterns, consisting of one or more extended *climacus* neumes *(virga sub-tripunctis, sub-quadripunctis)* are as characteristic of the Alleluias as are the reiterative *bistropha* and *tristropha* of the Graduals. They are, without doubt, indicative of a rather late period, and it is no mere coincidence that they occur exclusively in Alleluias for the *Sanctorale*. In fact, only one of the Alleluias of St. Gall *359*, *Deus judex* [982] shows a somewhat similar pattern, which probably means that the stylistic peculiarity under consideration represents an innovation not

21 See also *Haec est virgo* [1222]; *Beatus quem* [1479]; *Stabat sancta Maria* [1633ᵛ]; *Sancte Michael* [1655]; *Vos estis* [1548].

earlier than the tenth century. In this connection it is interesting to notice
that in the twelfth and thirteenth centuries descending-scale formations
became even more extended, often embracing an octave or more. They
occur in late monophonic compositions, e.g., Perotinus' *Beata viscera* (*c.*
1200), as well as in the upper parts of twelfth-century organa, e.g., the
Viderunt Hemanuel from the School of St. Martial or a *Benedicamus
Domino* from the School of Notre Dame, and appear in thirteenth-century
theory under the name of *conjuncturae* or *currentes*.[22]

As for the earlier Alleluias—mainly those that are assigned to the old
Temporale and, in consequence, included in the *Sextuplex* Mss—Wagner
has suggested a chronological distinction on the basis of their structural
features.[23] According to him, the earliest Alleluia melodies are those lacking the repeat of the *jubilus* at the end of the verse, while those showing
this repeat or other traits indicative of a feeling for symmetry (melismas
of the a a b- type) are products of a later period. In support of this theory
he points out that the small group of Alleluias without restatement of the
jubilus includes all three Alleluias from the Nativity, *Dominus dixit,
Dominus regnavit,* and *Dies sanctificatus*,[24] and that most of the Alleluias
of this type are in the second or in the eighth mode, that is, the same modes
that are exclusively used in the Tracts. There can hardly be any question
that Wagner's view is essentially correct. Systematic repeat of musical
phrases in one and the same chant is a method entirely unknown in the
old repertory, a fact all the more remarkable since transfer of musical
phrases from one chant to another is a basic principle of the older types
of chant, the Tracts, Responsories, and Graduals. Since the overwhelming
majority of Alleluias show repeat structures of one kind or another, we
are forced to conclude that these melodies are of a fairly late date, probably
not earlier than the eighth or ninth century—a conclusion which, of course,
is in agreement with other evidence, such as the great variability of assignment that sets the Alleluias apart from practically all other types of chant.
The only defect of this theory is that the Alleluia *Pascha nostrum* of Easter
Sunday, the earliest feast on which the Alleluia was sung, does not belong
to the early group, for it repeats the *jubilus* at the end of the verse, includes
an a a b melisma on "immolatus," and is in the seventh mode. The
conclusion is inevitable that its melody is not only far from being the
original one sung when the Easter Alleluia was introduced but also quite
different from the one that was used when, presumably under Gregory, it

22 See *HAM*, no. 17 (*Beata viscera*); Apel, *Notation of Polyphonic Music* pp. 211
(*Viderunt*), 247 (*Benedicamus*), 241 (*conjuncturae*). See also the late *Sanctus* melodies in
the thirteenth-century Codex Wolfenbüttel *677* (*W₁*); facsimile edition by J. H. Baxter,
An Old St. Andrews Music Book (1931), pp. 169ff.

23 *Wagner III*, 398.

24 See above, p. 385.

was provided with a verse. In other words, the Alleluia *Pascha nostrum* presents almost incontestable proof refuting the long-cherished idea that chronological data of liturgical or literary provenance are also valid for the melodies.

The same reasoning also invalidates or, at least, weakens the theory, advanced by Wagner and adopted by Stäblein,[25] that the new style made its appearance shortly after 600, in the Alleluia *Adorabo* [1251] from the Feast of the Dedication of a Church (originally *Dedicatio S. Mariae,* introduced by Pope Boniface IV in 608). This Alleluia may indeed be regarded as representing the transition between the old and the new style, because it lacks the repeat of the *jubilus* at the end of the verse but, on the other hand, shows a beautifully designed a a b melisma on the words "et confitebor." However, to maintain that the transition took place at about 600, simply because the feast was introduced at this time, is a conclusion that involves a highly questionable surmise.

Be this as it may, there can be no doubt that the Alleluias include a small number of melodies that show unmistakable indications of having been composed at an earlier time than the rest. It seems to me that such stylistic characteristics as small range and absence of repetitive melismas provide a better basis for a chronological distinction than the structural aspect involved in the repetition of the *jubilus* at the end of the verse. This view is confirmed in a most significant manner by a consideration of that small group of "invariable" Alleluias to which we have called attention at the beginning of this chapter, and which consists essentially of the Alleluias assigned to the first season of the liturgical year, from Advent to the last Sunday after Epiphany. The following table shows the characteristic traits of the eleven different melodies used for the Alleluias shown on p. 379 (*Jubilus I* refers to the close of the *Alleluia, Jubilus II* to that of the verse):

	RANGE	JUBILUS I	JUBILUS II	REPEAT MELISMA
Ostende nobis [320]	sixth	short	long, diff.	no
Laetatus sum [329]	octave	long	same	no
Excita Domine [336]	sixth	moderate	same	no
Veni Domine [354]	eleventh	long	long, diff.	yes
Dominus regnavit [405]	sixth	short	short, diff.	no
Dies sanctificatus [409]	sixth	short	short, diff.	no
Jubilate Deo [479]	octave	moderate	same ending	no
Confitemini [759]	fifth	short	same	no
Pascha nostrum [779]	tenth	long	same ending	yes
Laudate pueri [805]	seventh	moderate	same	no
Veni Sancte Spiritus [880]	seventh	long	same	yes

25 See *Wagner III,* 401; *MGG,* I, 343.

It appears that there is no uniform practice as far as the treatment of the two *jubili* is concerned. There is, however, a very remarkable uniformity in the two other traits: nearly all the melodies move in a small range and have no repetitive melismas. The most striking exception is *Veni Domine,* but actually this confirms the rule since it belongs to the Fourth Sunday of Advent, which is a later addition to the *Temporale.* As for *Pascha nostrum* from Easter Sunday, we have already commented upon its relatively late style, and it is not surprising to find a similarly late style in an Alleluia (*Veni Sancte Spiritus*) for Pentecost, a feast which is known to have been modelled after Easter. Aside from these special cases, the invariable Alleluias are noteworthy for their close adherence to a musical style which bears the unmistakable earmarks of an earlier period than that to which the majority of the Alleluia melodies belong. As we have seen, there is good reason to assume that liturgically and textually the Alleluias in question go back to the time of Gregory. We would not subscribe to the conclusion that their melodies are equally old, but there can be no doubt that they were composed at an earlier time than the others. I would be inclined to assign them to the eighth century. Sometime later, perhaps in the early ninth century, the old melody for *Pascha nostrum* may have been replaced by (or remodelled into) one of a more exuberant character, and this melody—perhaps together with those of *Veni Domine* and *Adorabo*—became the point of departure for the numerous late Alleluias.

THE ANTIPHONS

The general meaning of the term "Antiphon" is that of a short text sung at the Office Hours before and after a Psalm or a Canticle, originally also between the verses, as a refrain. It represents an addition to the antiphonal (i.e., double-chorus) method of singing, from which it derived its name. Properly speaking, the term includes also the Antiphons of the Mass—that is, the Introit, the Communion, and possibly the Offertory—but each of these constitutes a separate category and has been previously considered, so that we are here concerned only with the Antiphons of the Office.

The Office Antiphons differ strikingly from the chants considered in the preceding chapters by their shortness and simplicity. Essentially, often completely, syllabic and ranging in length from half a line to an average of two or three lines, they form a stylistic group all their own. As if in recompense for their moderate appearance, they far exceed any other type of chant in their great number. The medieval books contain several thousands of Antiphons, and even today there are more than 1300 in general use. Reflecting the elementary principles of Gregorian art in a thousand different ways, they form a microcosm which, with its multitude of organisms, is almost unlimited in aspects and problems. It is entirely out of the question to study them here with the same degree of "completeness" that has at least been attempted in our investigation of the other types of chant—all the more so since, with one exception,[1] they have never been made the subject of a comprehensive investigation.

Numerous Antiphons, perhaps the majority of them, consist of nothing but single notes interspersed with two-note neumes, *clivis* and *podatus*. This style characterizes not only the Antiphons for weekdays [280-316], but also those for Sunday [224-271] and for many high feasts, e.g., for the Nativity [364], Ascension [850], etc. It is only in the Antiphons for the Canticles, the *Magnificat* of Vespers and the *Benedictus* of Lauds, that a tendency toward a slightly more elaborate style, as well as to greater length is noticeable. Here *podatus* and *clivis* groups appear more frequently, interspersed with three- and four-note neumes, as, for instance, in *Cum ortus fuerit* from the Nativity [367]. Occasionally one finds short melismas, as in *Tribus miraculis* [466] from the Epiphany, *Magnum haereditatis* [444] from the Feast of Circumcision, or *Nativitas tua* [1627] from the Nativity of the Virgin Mary, the latter two obviously of a later date. An unusually long melisma occurs in the *Benedictus*-Antiphon *Ardens est* from Lauds of the Thursday after Low Sunday [*A* 466]:[2]

FIGURE 120

Domi-num me- um : quae-ro,

Another subspecies of a more elaborate character are the Invitatory Antiphons (*Invitatoria*), used in connection with the Invitatory Psalm *Venite exultemus* of Matins. An example is *Christus natus* [368], composed throughout in groups of four, five and six notes. A considerable number of *Invitatoria* are available in *LR* (see the Index, p. 461).

Next to the question of style the phrase structure of the Antiphons is of interest. Although the difficulties and uncertainties inherent in the term "Gregorian phrase" are no less here than elsewhere in the chant [see p. 251], it is nevertheless possible to distinguish several types according to the number of phrases contained in the text, ranging from a short type

[1] Gevaert's *La Mélopée antique,* to which we shall often refer.

[2] The complete series of *Benedictus* Antiphons is found in *A* and *AM*. A limited number is given in *L* 1080-1110 ("At Lauds").

with a single phrase to a full type with four phrases.[3] Following are four rather unequivocal examples for each type:

ONE PHRASE:

> *Inclinavit Dominus* [280]; *De profundis* [291]; *Caro mea* [714]; *Omnis spiritus* [1803]

TWO PHRASES:

> *Dixit Dominus* [252]; *Crastina die* [363]; *Laetentur caeli* [387]; *Si vere fratres* [509]

THREE PHRASES:

> *Tu es qui venturus* [1083]; *Magnificat* [286]; *Accipite Spiritum* [877]; *Simeon justus* [1366]

FOUR PHRASES:

> *Ego sum pastor* [820]; *Prudentes virgines* [262⁹]; *Responsum accepit* [1366]; *Ego sum resurrectio* [1804].

In many cases the phrase structure as well as other details of style, e.g., cadential points or recitation passages, are more clearly discernible on the basis of a comparative study, to which we now turn.

A very important step in the investigation of the copious material under consideration was made by F. A. Gevaert, in his *La Mélopée antique dans le chant de l'église latine* (1895), the major part of which, from p. 83 to p. 381, is devoted to a study of the Antiphons.[4] He showed that from the musical point of view the several thousands of Antiphons can be reduced to a small group of *thèmes mélodiques,* standard melodies each of which is employed, with some variations, in a great number of Antiphons. His *Catalogue thématique des antiennes de l'Office Romain* (pp. 225ff) consists of 47 *thèmes,* each of which includes a varying number of Antiphons, from as few as five (*thème* 32) to as many as seventy-five (*thème* 29).

The "thematic" character of the Antiphons was well-known in the Middle Ages. It is clearly indicated in the Tonaries (Regino, Oddo and others), which group the Antiphons not only as to modes but, within each mode, in subdivisions.[5] Ostensibly, these subdivisions are made according to the

---

3 There are not a few Antiphons with more than four phrases, but these do not crystallize into a recognizable type of phrase structure. For more details concerning this and other aspects see H. Hucke, "Musikalische Formen der Officiumsantiphonen" (*KJ, XXXVII,* 7).

4 The title, reflecting the author's preoccupation with the Greek-influence idea, is rather misleading. His attempts to identify the church modes with the Greek scales lead to a rather arbitrary arrangement as well as to unwarranted "reconstructions" of some melodies. Gevaert also made an attempt to establish a chronology of the Antiphons on the basis of their texts, whether psalmodic (*1re époque*), scriptural but non-psalmodic (*2e époque*), or non-scriptural (*3e époque*); see pp. 509f.

5 See pp. 223ff.

terminations (*differentiae*) of the tones used for the Psalms, but because of the intimate relationship between the termination and the beginning of the Antiphon they also, and primarily, represent groups of Antiphons that are melodically related, at least in their beginnings. In fact, Gevaert's catalogue is based on the Tonary of Regino, and its groups sometimes coincide with Regino's divisions; for instance, *thème 1* is practically identical with the *divisio secunda primi toni* of Regino.[6] Usually, however, Gevaert separates Regino's divisions into a number of *thèmes* which, moreover, often cut across the medieval arrangement. This is particularly true of the divisions containing a great number of Antiphons, such as the main division of the first mode [*CS*, II, pp. 4ff, with *c.* 250 Antiphons]. Considerably closer agreement exists between Gevaert's *thèmes* and the divisions in the *Tonarius* of Oddo [*CS*, II, p. 117], who goes much further than Regino in subdividing each mode into thematically unified groups. For instance, in the second mode Regino lists all the Antiphons under one group, since the second psalm tone has only one termination. Oddo, on the other hand, although stating that the *secundus tonus* "is confined to one *differentia*," distinguishes a *primus, secundus, tertius,* and *quartus modus,*[7] each characterized by a different Antiphon *incipit*. His three last *modi* correspond respectively to Gevaert's *thèmes 46, 45,* and *9,* while the *primus modus* includes mainly Antiphons from *thèmes 10* and *11.*

Gevaert's classification, while not entirely satisfactory, is no doubt valid in its main outlines and useful as a basis of further investigations and improvements.[8] Without making any such ambitious attempts, we shall confine ourselves to an examination of the Antiphons of the seventh mode, mainly in order to obtain an insight into the "thematic structure" of the various groups. This is the same mode that has been considered previously from the point of view of its psalm-tone terminations as well as of the Antiphon groups related to these terminations by a common *incipit*.[9] It may be helpful to indicate here once more Gevaert's *thèmes* in the order in which they appear in his catalogue, and with references to the Tonaries of Regino and Oddo (M stands for Regino's main, initial group; I, II, etc. for his *divisio prima, secunda,* etc.)

[6] *CS*, II, 14/15 and 16/17. Regino opens each mode with an unnamed main division, so that his *divisio prima, secunda,* etc., are actually the second, third, etc., division.

[7] *CS*, II, 123b reads *Tertius modus* instead of *Tertius tonus*.

[8] According to a remark by Handschin (*Acta musicologica,* XXIV, 25, fn.) Gevaert's analysis has been "reprise et précisé" in a thesis by H. Hucke (University of Freiburg, 1952). Mr. Hucke informs me that the main contents of his dissertation, *Untersuchungen zum Begriffe 'Antiphon' und zur Melodik der Offiziumsantiphonen* (typescript), are given in an article "Die Entwicklung des christlichen Kultgesangs" (*Römische Quartalschrift für Christliche Altertumskunde,* XLVII [1953], 147), and in the article mentioned in fn. 3.

[9] See Fig. 52, p. 224.

FIGURE 121

Gevaert	Oddo	Regino	Incipit
19	IV	M, I	
19 var.	IV	M, I	
20	VI	IV	
21	III	IV, V, I	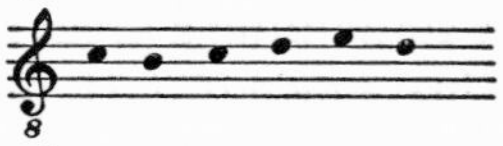
21 var.	IV	M, I	
22	II	II	
23	II	II	
23 var.[10]	I	I	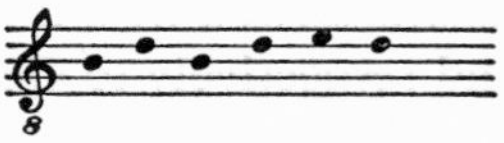
24	II	II	
25	IV	I, III	
26	V	III	
27	IV	M, V	

Following is a table showing a number of examples for each of the twelve *thèmes*.

Thème 19: Magnificat Dominus [286]; *Ecce apparebit* [332]; *Lapides torrentes* [414]; *Videntes stellam* [481]; *In die tribulationis* [642]; *In pace factus est* [729]; *Ascendo ad Patrem* [845; see p. 304]

Thème 19 var.: Ecce apparebit [332]; *Tunc invocabis* [530]; *Viri Galilei* [850]; *Dum praeliaretur* [1659]; *Valerianus in cubiculo* [1756]; *Tunc acceptabis* [A 396]

[10] Gevaert reproduces the Antiphons of *thème 23 var.* with the *incipit* g-d′ b d′, instead of b-d′-b-d′ which they have in all (?) the manuscripts. He bases his reconstruction on the fact that they are included in Regino's "division principale" which, apparently, he assumes was characterized by the beginning g-d′. Actually, they all occur in the *divisio prima*. Whether this or, for that matter, the main division invariably started with g, is difficult to say.

Thème 20: Dixit Dominus Domino [252]; *Alleluia* [256]; *Stella ista* [464]; *Cum angelis* [588]; *Dives ille* [1087]; *Quid me queritis* [1094]

Thème 21: Loquebantur variis [884]; *Confortatus est* [1115]; *Domine ostende* [1450]; *Benedicta filia* [1606]

Thème 21 var.: Alleluia confitemini [228]; *Dixit paterfamilias* [503]; *Accipite Spiritum* [877]; *Exaudisti Domine* [988]; *In caelestibus regnis* [1120]; *Absterget* [1156]; *Benedicta es tu* [1381]

Thème 22: Sit nomen Domini [254]; *Dixi iniquis* [640]; *Angelus Domini* [467]; *Angeli archangeli* [1660]; *Sancti omnes* [*A* 53]; *Fecit Deus* [*A* 162]; *Laetabitur* [*A* 188]

Thème 23: Omnes sitientes [324]; *Si vere fratres* [509]; *Et ecce terraemotus* [782]; etc. [see pp. 400f]

Thème 23 var.: Clamavi [281]; *Exortum est* [412]; *Attendite* [736]; *Tulerunt Dominum* [800]; *Misereor* [1009]; *Orante Sancta Lucia* [1324]

Thème 24: Voce mea [307]; *Liberavit Dominus* [633]; *Proprio Filio* [689]; *Caro mea* [714]; *Me suscepit* [1802]

Thème 25: Redemptionem [412]; *Responsum accepit* [1366]; *Quomodo fiet* [1415]; *Philippe qui videt* [1451]; *Quis es iste* [1536]; *Custodi me* [1888]

Thème 26: Angelus ad pastores [397]; *Facta est cum angelo* [398]; *Pastores venerunt* [468]; *Hosanna filio* [578]; *Simile est* [1109]; *Et venerunt* [1445]; *Puer qui natus* [1505]. Also to this group belongs *Urbs fortitudinis* [332] which, however, because of its b-flat, presents a problem of modal ambiguity [see pp. 177f]

Thème 27: Suscepit Deus [313]; *Veni Domine visitare* [327]; *Sapientia aedificavit* [989]; *Puer Samuel* [960]; *Dirupisti Domine* [1114]; *Domum tuam* [1246]; *Te gloriosus* [1724].

As we have stated, Gevaert's classification is very similar to that of Oddo. In fact, they are identical if we disregard the subdivisions which Gevaert makes in Oddo's group II (*thème 22, 23, 24*) and group IV (*thème 19, 19 var., 21 var., 25, 27*). These subdivisions reflect the different point of view involved in the modern system. Oddo's main concern is, of course, with the psalm-tone terminations, and his six groups are entirely sufficient for this purpose [see Fig. 52, p. 224]. Gevaert's concern is with the Antiphons as such, especially with their thematic relationship established by a common *incipit*. This approach calls not only for subdivisions in the most numerous groups—particularly group IV which, together with V, includes all the Antiphons beginning on g, the final of the mode—but also justifies his view that an *incipit* such as b-d'-b-d'-e'-d' is only a prothetic variant (*thème 23 var.*) of d'-b-d'-e'-d' (*thème 23*), while in Oddo's catalogue they belong to different groups, the former to I, the latter to II.

If we turn from Oddo's (or, for that matter, Gevaert's) classification to the earlier one of Regino, a considerable amount of discrepancy appears. Although both divide the Antiphons of the seventh mode into six groups, only one of these is identical in the two Tonaries, that is, Regino's *divisio secunda* (II; actually his third division) and Oddo's *divisio secunda.* All the others are distributed differently; for instance, Regino's main division (M) includes Antiphons (or, at least, antiphon types) which in Oddo's Tonary belong to groups IV and I. Since Regino's Tonary does not indicate the melodies in a readable form, we can only speculate about the reasons for the differing assignments. Very likely in his day a considerable number of Antiphons had a different *incipit,* perhaps even a completely different melody from the one they acquired in the time of Oddo. For instance, his *diviso tertia* includes eight Antiphons of Gevaert's *thème 26,* with the characteristic ascending fifth, g-d', but also five Antiphons of *thème 25,* with the less striking beginning g-b-d'—a type which Oddo includes in his large group IV, together with themes such as g-b-c'-d', g-c'-b-c'-d', and g-a-c'-d' *(thèmes 19, 19 var., 21 var., 27).* Possibly all the Antiphons of Regino's *divisio tertia* originally had the beginning g-d', for example, *Responsum accepit* [1366] and *Custodi me* [1888], both of which now begin with g-b-d'. With Oddo's Tonary we are on much safer ground, although it goes without saying that his versions also do not always agree with those that became eventually accepted. For instance, a number of Antiphons which in their present form belong to Gevaert's *thème 19* (g-b-c'-d') are given in Oddo's Tonary with the beginning g-a-c'-d', which would put them into Gevaert's *thème 27.* Among these are *Magnificatus est* [364], *De caelo veniet* [1082], and *Cantate Domino [A* 230]. The last two appear in the Codex Lucca with the beginning a-b-c'-d', an *incipit* represented there by about a dozen Antiphons, but which disappeared later.[11]

The foregoing remarks will suffice to indicate the vicissitudes encountered in the field of the Antiphons and the many additional difficulties arising from them. Not only are variants and modifications considerably more frequent here than in other chants but, because of the shortness and simplicity of the melodies, they are also much more decisive and consequential.

We shall now turn to another question arising from the classification of the Antiphons into *thème* groups, that is, to what extent the Antiphons of a given group are related to each other. More specifically, the problem is whether or not they have more thematic material in common than just the standard *incipit,* possibly complete phrases or even complete melodies. There is no simple and unequivocal answer to this question. Once more, the Antiphons present a much more diversified picture than other chants, for which questions of this kind (original melodies, centonization, standard phrases, adaptation) can be answered with a certain degree of conclusiveness. Naturally, the enormous quantity of material involved excludes any

---

11 See *Pal. mus.,* IX, 67f. The major part of the text volume consists of a thematic catalogue of the Antiphons (also the Great Responsories)—a very useful tool of research.

attempt to consider the problem in all its ramifications. We can do no more than present a few of its aspects.

By far the best-known case is that of Gevaert's *thème 29,* including eighty and more Antiphons, nearly all of which employ a complete four-phrase melody with only minor modifications. This group is exceptional, not only because of the large number of adaptations, but also for the melody itself, which stands outside the system of the church modes. It is the same melody, which Regino cites as an example of the *antiphonae nothae,* and which Berno employs in order to demonstrate the principle of transposition.[12] It occurs with three different *incipits,* or rather, with the *incipit* varying in length according to the requirements of the text. Following are three examples, one for each *incipit* (minor differences in the adjustment of the melody are disregarded):

FIGURE 122

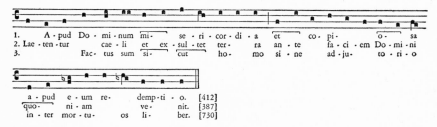

In Regino's Tonary these three subspecies are distinguished as *divisio secunda, tertia,* and *quarta,* in Oddo's Tonary as *divisio secunda, prima,* and *quarta,* in Gevaert's catalogue as *thème 29, 29 variante a,* and *29 variante b.*[13] The first includes *c.* 50 Antiphons, the second, *c.* 25, and the third chiefly the four or five Antiphons which Regino mentions among his *antiphonae nothae.* In all of these Antiphons the full melody is employed with a remarkable degree of stability,[14] variants of some note being confined to one or two examples, for instance, *In odorem* [1233] in which the first phrase closes on a, or *Iste puer* [1496] which employs the same first phrase as well as a different closing phrase. We would like to know why this melody enjoyed such unique popularity, a popularity all the more remarkable because of the highly irregular tonal character of the melody, which caused the theorists so much trouble. Perhaps Wagner is right in assuming that it was of non-liturgical origin.[15]

12 See pp. 175, 162f.

13 See *CS,* II, 26ff; *CS,* II, 126ff; Gevaert, pp. 322ff.

14 See, e.g., *Confundantur* [677]; *Plangent eum* [735]; *Exhortatus est* [649]; *Si quis sitit* [1098]; *Oves meae* [1099], etc. A long list of Antiphons of this type is given in *Wagner III,* 312f.

15 See *Wagner III,* 310.

Brief mention may be made here of another standard melody, similar to the one just considered in its irregular tonality, but represented only by a small number of examples, namely, the Antiphons for which the special psalm tone, *tonus peregrinus,* was devised [see pp. 212f]. In early treatises and manuscripts the melody (Gevaert's *thème 28*) is variously assigned to mode 7 or 4, occasionally even to 1 or 2, sufficient evidence of its tonal irregularity. It is characterized by an initial formula c-d-f-fg-g and a closing formula ga-g-g or ga-a-g. It occurs in its fullest form in *Deus autem,* and in shortened versions in *Martyres Domini* and *Nos qui vivimus:*

FIGURE 123

    De‑us au‑tem no‑ster   in   cae‑   lo om‑ni ‑ a quaecumque   vo‑lu‑ it, fe‑cit.[1]
    Mar‑ty‑res Do‑   mi‑ni, Do‑mi‑num be‑ne‑di‑ci‑te   be‑ne‑di‑ci‑mus   in ae‑ter‑num.[2]
    Nos qui vi‑   vi‑mus   Do‑mi‑no.[3]

                                                        [1][256] [2][1154] [3][AM 132]

The melody of *Martyres Domini* recurs identically in *Angeli Domini* [1660] and *Sancti Domini* [*AM* 1122], that of *Nos qui vivimus* in an Antiphon *In templo Domini* reproduced (from which source?) by Ferretti in his *Esthétique* [p. 326], where the *tonus peregrinus* and its Antiphons are fully discussed.

Very obvious examples of complete adaptation are the so-called Great Antiphons, which are used for the Magnificat during the week preceding the Nativity [340ff]. They all begin with the exclamation "O" (hence the name O-Antiphons) and are sung to the same melody of the second mode, the first half of which consists of a lengthy recitation on d, but closes, rather unexpectedly, with an ascending motion and a six-note melisma, g-a-g a-b♭-a.

After the examination of these special cases we shall return to the Antiphons of the seventh mode, in order to obtain a more balanced view of the extent to which thematic unification prevails in the various groups. The seventh group of our list [p. 397], Gevaert's *thème 23,* includes *circa* thirty Antiphons, seventeen of which employ an entire melody in a process of multiple adaptation similar to the one just observed in the Antiphons of the type *Apud Dominum.* We may call it the group *Si vere fratres,* after its member that belongs to the *Temporale,* the Antiphon from None of Sexagesima Sunday. Most of the other representatives belong to the *Sanctorale,* not a few of them originally to feasts of Virgins, St. Agatha, St. Agnes, and the Virgin Mary. Among these is *Gratias tibi ago* from the Second Vespers of the Feast of St. Agatha, an Antiphon somewhat exceptional because of its fairly extended employment of recitation:

FIGURE 124

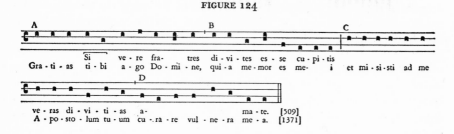

The melody consists of four phrases, A, B, C, and D, closing respectively on d', g, b, and g. In *Si vere fratres* it is shortened into a three-phrase melody by fusing the two last phrases into a single one, and a similar fusion occurs in *Nos autem* [1460]. The complete four-phrase form is employed in the following Antiphons (the final cadence, c'-b-g, may be modified into b-a-g):

Ecce Sacerdos [1176]	*Gratias tibi* [1371]
Non est inventus [1176]	*Domine si adhuc* [1749]
Veni sponsa [1214]	*Vidi supra montem* [1760]
Salve Crux [1307]	*Non meis meritis* [1760]
Annulo suo [1340]	*Si culmen* [A 352]
Ingressa Agnes [1340]	*De sub cuius* [A 928]
Quis es tu [1370]	

In addition to this nucleus of strict *contrafacta*, Gevaert's *thème 23* includes about a dozen Antiphons which utilize only a part of the standard melody or introduce variants of some sort. The main outlines are schematically indicated in the following table:

Mecum enim [1340]	A B D
O magnum pietatis [1459]	A B C X+D
Tu es Petrus [1515]	A B C' D
Dirige Domine [1782]	A B C'' D
Tanto pondere [1325]	A B E F16
Stans Jesus [977]	A B E F
Et ecce terraemotus [782]	
Tu es qui [1083]	
Omnes sitientes [324]	Only the *incipit* (d'-b-d'-e'-d')
Omne quod [1776]	
Mittite in dexteram [A 450]	

The interesting aspect of the entire group is that it represents various

16 Note the cadence of a descending fourth; see p. 266.

degrees of thematic relationship, utilization of the complete melody, shortened and expanded versions, introduction of variants, employment of the
first half (A B) with a different continuation, and finally employment of
the *incipit* only.[17]

On the whole, cases of multiple adaptation such as are represented by
the group *Si vere fratres* let alone the unique case of Gevaert's *thème 29,*
seem to be rare. In most of the groups the various melodies take their cue
from the fixed *incipit,* but continue more or less freely, not, of course, to
the complete exclusion of an occasional borrowing from a common fund.
Thus, the Antiphons of *thème 23 var.* [see Fig. 52, I] have, on the whole
nothing more in common than the *incipit;* but two of them, *Orante sancta
Lucia* [1324] and *Argentum et aurum* [1515] are identical in their complete first phrase and show similarities in their further course. Similarly,
the numerous Antiphons of *thème 19,* related by a common *incipit,* are
otherwise rather independent of each other, although a close examination
may reveal occasional references or reminiscences. It must be borne in
mind that the limited idiom and stylistic simplicity of the Antiphons are
not favorable to the occurrence of material comparable to the standard
phrases of the Tracts, Responsories, etc., but, on the other hand, are
naturally conducive to the emergence, here and there, of formulae showing a more or less similar design. Whether these cases are the result of
premeditation or of inevitable coincidence, is often difficult to decide.

Ferretti has made an attempt to approach the problem of thematic unification in the Antiphons from a different point of view by considering
them as *mélodies-centons,* as centonized chants. He says that "parmi les
chants de l'Office, les plus centonisés sont les Antiennes,"[18] a statement
which seems to be somewhat risky in view of the rather extended amount
of centonization encountered in the Responsories. In support of his view,
Ferretti gives a table of seventeen formulae for the Antiphons of the first
mode, as well as a list of thirty-two melodies composed from these formulae.
Though at first glance this analysis looks quite impressive, it is, upon closer
consideration, hardly substantial enough to serve as convincing evidence.
First, it should be noticed that the material is not taken from a special
incipit-group (*thème*), but is selected from all the Antiphons of the first
mode, more than 330 in number. Of this number, Ferretti's list represents
less than one-tenth, although his remark about "un grand nombre" of
Antiphons consisting of these formulae leads us to expect that there are
more. Moreover, several of the melodies are examples, not of centonization,
but of complete adaptation, e.g.:

17 A great amount of material concerning this question is contained in W. H. Frere's
study of the Antiphons, in *Antiphonale Sarisburiense,* Dissertation, pp. 64ff.
18 *Esthétique,* p. 112.

8. *Subiit ergo* [564] = 10. *Mulieres sedentes* [738]

5. *Omnes qui habebant* [1091] = 6. *Qui non colligit* [556] = 2. *Quod uni* [A 373][19]

3. *Tradetur enim* [1087] = 4. *De quinque panibus* [559] = 9. *Clarifica me* [1101] = 13. *Beati pacifici* [1112] = 15. *Qui ministrat* [1125] = 16. *Euge serve bone* [1195]

14. *In patientia vestra* [1112] = 22. *Lex per Moysen* [A 239] = 23. *Deus a Libano* [A 243].

These cases of identity or near-identity of entire melodies reduce the number of centonized *Antiphons* to twenty-two, a number which, depending upon the point of view, might be lessened yet further. For instance, 5. *Omnes qui* [1091] is only a shortened version of 19. *Qui me misit* [1085] resulting from the omission of the third phrase, and the same relationship exists between 24. *Multiplicabitur* [A 244] and 11. *Hoc genus* [A 547] (second phrase omitted). Nevertheless, these reservations do not invalidate Ferretti's analysis. There still remain a number of Antiphons showing true centonization, that is, various combinations of fixed phrases; e.g. (the figures refer to Ferretti's table of formulae):

3. *Tradetur enim* [1087]	1		6	7	15
1. *Tu autem* [A 361]	1		10b	7	15
25. *Qui verbum* [504]	1		10a	8	14
28. *Corpora sanctorum* [1153]	1		10a	8	17
30. *Quaerite primum* [1040]	2	9	12a	8	17
21. *Levabit Dominus* [A 230]	3		11b	7	15
11. *Hoc genus* [A 547]	3		11a	13	14
17. *Visionem* [550]	4		11b	12a	14
12. *Dixit Dominus paralytico* [A 569]	4		11b	13	14
19. *Qui me misit* [1085]	5		11a	12a	15

It remains for us to consider briefly certain special Antiphons, of a later date generally, which differ from the normal type in their liturgical position as well as in their stylistic characteristics. Most of these are independent chants of considerable extension, and are not (or no longer) connected with a Psalm. To this class belong the Antiphons sung during the Procession of Palm Sunday, some of which (for instance, *Cum appropinquaret Dominus* [584]) are second in length only to the Tracts. The Procession for the Blessing of the Candles on the Feast of the Purification

---

19 In Ferretti's analysis *Quod uni* differs from the two other Antiphons by its closing formula, 14 instead of 15. Actually, the difference between these (also 16) is so slight as to be negligible. It is certainly no greater than the variants that often occur in some of his other formulae.

includes an Antiphon, *Adorna thalamum* [1359], the text of which is the translation of a Byzantine *kontakion, Katakosmeson ton thalamon.* Obviously it was adopted from the Byzantine rites under the Greek Pope Sergius I (687-701), who introduced this Procession ceremony into Rome. The melody shows certain traits that have been interpreted as Byzantine, namely, the successive repetition at the beginning (aa bb c dd ...) and the recurring use of a cadential formula.[20] Another interesting group of "ceremonial Antiphons" are those sung during the Washing of the Feet on Maundy Thursday [660]. The first of these, *Mandatum novum,* has given the name to the entire rite (*Mandatum,* Anglicized Maundy) and ultimately to the liturgical day. The present-day use prescribes nine Antiphons, but the medieval books contain many more; among them one, *Venit ad Petrum,* has recently been recognized as the source for the *Caput* Masses by Dufay, Ockeghem, and Obrecht.[21] Differing from the Antiphons of Palm Sunday, which are entirely self-contained, those of Maundy Thursday are connected with one or two verses, some of them taken from a Psalm (*Ps.*). Another processional Antiphon, *Exsurge Domine* [835], sung at the Procession of Rogation Days, is followed by a psalm verse and the *Gloria Patri,* exactly like an Introit of the Mass. The same form occurs in the Antiphons *Asperges me* [11] and *Vidi aquam* [12] sung at the Aspersion of the Water.

Among the most beautiful creations of the late Middle Ages are the Antiphons in praise of the Virgin Mary, known as Marian Antiphons (*antiphonae B.M.V.,* that is, *Beatae Mariae Virginis*). A great number of such chants were composed during the eleventh, twelfth, and later centuries, but only four of them have survived in present-day usage: *Alma redemptoris mater, Ave regina caelorum, Regina caeli laetare,* and *Salve regina,* the first and possibly the last composed by Hermannus Contractus (1013-54), the other two dating from the twelfth or thirteenth century. In spite of their considerable extension and elaborateness, they were originally used as real Antiphons, with a number of psalm verses and assigned to specific Office Hours; for instance, *Alma redemptoris* was assigned to Sext of the Feast of the Assumption. Beginning with the thirteenth century, they lost their psalmodic connection and received a much more important liturgical position, which they have retained to the present day. Each of them is assigned to one of the four seasons of the year and is sung, during that season, at the end of Office Hours, particularly Lauds and Compline.[22]

20 See the article "Antiphon" (by Stäblein) in *MGG,* I, 542.

21 M. F. Bukofzer, *Studies in Medieval and Renaissance Music* (1950), pp. 217ff.

22 See *L* 273-276. The "Simple Tones" given subsequently probably date from the seventeenth century or later.

THE CHANTS OF THE MASS ORDINARY

The general aspects of the *Ordinarium missae* have been explained in a previous chapter dealing with the structure of the Mass.[1] We may briefly recall that generally the chants of the Ordinary are relatively late accretions to the Gregorian repertory, that they never acquired the authority and fixity of the chants of the Proper, and that the formation of cyclic Mass Ordinaries, each consisting of a *Kyrie, Gloria, Sanctus,* and *Agnus Dei,* with the *Credos* listed separately, is largely a nineteenth-century process of organization.

The development of the chants of the Ordinary of the Mass began, to the best of our knowledge, in the tenth century;[2] it reached its full florescence in the eleventh and twelfth centuries and continued through the fifteenth. During this period a vast body of melodies accrued, of which those reproduced in the modern books represent only a minute fraction. In order to give an idea of the total repertory it may be stated that, according to recent investigations, more than two hundred melodies exist for the *Kyrie,* and about three hundred for the *Agnus* as well as for the *Credo.*[3] Only within the past few years have scholars begun to explore this vast field. The subsequent study, which is based almost exclusively upon the selection given in the *Liber usualis,* is therefore necessarily tentative and incomplete.

THE KYRIE

The Kyrie consists of three acclamations, *Kyrie eleison, Christe eleison,* and *Kyrie eleison,* each of which is sung three times, so that the entire melody consists of nine distinct phrases. Invariably these are organized into a distinct formal structure by the employment of certain principles of repetition. The simplest form consists of only one phrase that is repeated for every acclamation except the last, which may have a varied or even an entirely different melody. Another type has the same melody for the six *Kyrie eleison,* but a different one for the three *Christe eleison* that stand in the middle. Yet other *Kyries* employ three melodies, one for each of the three main groups. Finally, there is a type in which each of the three main groups shows a ternary form, the same melody being used for the first and the third acclamation of the group, a different one for the second. Nearly always the last phrase is varied, usually by the addition of

[1] See pp. 25ff.

[2] The earliest source is a St. Martial Troper (Paris, B. N. *lat. 887*) written in the late tenth century.

[3] For the *Agnus* and *Credo* see the articles in *MGG;* for the *Kyrie,* the publication mentioned in fn. 5.

a final melisma. The following table shows the distribution of the present-day *Kyries* according to these four structural types (*ad lib.* refers to the Chants "ad libitum" [74ff]):

1. aaa aaa aab   Requiem Mass [1807]
2. aaa bbb aaa′   V, XI (= *ad lib.* X), XII, XVI, XVIII
3. aaa bbb ccc′   I, II, IV, VII, VIII, XIII, XIV, XVIIa, XVIIb;[4] *ad lib.* VII, VIII, IX, XI
4. aba cdc efe′   III, VI, IX, X, XV; *ad lib.* I, II, III, IV, V, VI.

The recent publication of a special study based on the entire repertory of more than two hundred *Kyrie* melodies[5] enables us to give a clearer picture of the relative importance of these forms. The first, second, and fourth turn out to be of almost equal frequency, each being represented by about one-fifth of the total, while the third form is twice as frequent than any of the others. No essentially new forms appear in the complete repertory, but modifications or transitional forms of one kind or another are occasionally encountered, for instance, aaa aaa bbb, aaa bcb ded, or aba cdc aca; and two melodies introduce the structural principle of the bar-form, aab ccd efg.[6]

No less interesting is the stylistic aspect of the *Kyrie* melodies. A few of them are written in an extremely simple style which is particularly suit-able for congregational singing. Since originally the *Kyrie* was indeed sung by the congregation, we are perhaps justified in assuming that these melodies are chants of great antiquity. The most primitive of these em-ploy a recitation melody of only two pitches (no. 84: g g g a g; no. 85: g g g g a) which is repeated for all the acclamations except the last. While both of these occur only in a few manuscripts, another of a slightly more developed design (no. 7) was widely disseminated. It employs a short, tetrachordal formula for all the acclamations except the last, which has a rather strikingly different melody with an unexpected termination. Wag-ner, who first called attention to this archaic *Kyrie,* proposed the theory that this termination is designed as a transition to the oldest *Gloria* melody (*Gloria XV;* see Fig. 127), which begins on the same tone on which the *Kyrie* closes:[7]

4 This *Kyrie,* given as an alternate for Mass XVII, could also be considered as falling under the previous form, since c is a variant of a.

5 M. Melnicki, *Das einstimmige Kyrie des lateinischen Mittelalters* (Diss. Erlangen, 1954). Identifications by arabic numbers (e.g., no. 84) refer to the list in this publication (pp. 87ff).

6 See Melnicki, pp. 65, 66, 67.

7 *Wagner III,* 440. Wagner remarks that this melody is very similar to that of the *Kyrie* from the Litany of Holy Saturday [756].

FIGURE 125

Ky - ri - e - le - i - son (3)
Chri - ste e - le - i - son (3)
Ky - ri - e - le - i - son (2) Ky - ri - e- le - i - son. Glo - ri - a in ex - cel - sis ...

Three *Kyries* of the *Liber usualis* show a style of similar simplicity, namely, those of Masses XVI, XV, and XVIII. The last two of these are closely related to each other, being not only in the same mode (the fourth, transposed to the upper fifth) but also employing the same cadential formula, a-a-b (or, occasionally, d'-d'-b) for all the phrases. They may well be variants of one and the same original melody, very much in the character of a litany.

While these *Kyries* stay well within the framework of Gregorian style and may even revert to a very old layer, the majority of the others present an entirely different picture. Not only do they include extended melismas, but these melismas, as well as the melodies in general, show traits not encountered in the Gregorian repertory, but which are similar to those we have found in the late Alleluias: extended range (frequently an octave and more), large leaps, descending-scale formations of four, five, and occasionally six notes, and often an emphasis on the 1-5-8 degrees of the scale. Naturally, some of these details can also be found here and there in the Gregorian repertory, but in the *Kyries* their role changes from incidental occurrence to a basic trait. In their strikingly "Gothic" contours, sweeping motions, quick ascents and descents they indicate a tendency toward assertive expression in clear terms, quite different from the subtly allusive, if not evasive, language of the true Gregorian style. Fig. 126 shows some characteristic formations which, however, will reveal their full significance

FIGURE 126

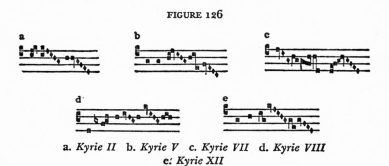

a. *Kyrie II*   b. *Kyrie V*   c. *Kyrie VII*   d. *Kyrie VIII*
e: *Kyrie XII*

only if they are considered within the context of the entire melodies. A formation like that of *Kyrie VII*, in which the interval of the fifth is traversed in straight ascending and descending motion, may safely be said to be non-existent in "Gregorian" chant. The closest approximation to this style occurs in such late Alleluias as *Assumpta est Maria* [1603] or *Beatus vir sanctus Martinus* [1747]; there is practically no doubt that most *Kyries* are equally late, if not even later.[8]

Originally, the *Kyrie* was not a part of the Mass. In Etheria's report from *c.* 390 [see List of Data, p. 40, no. 27] it is mentioned in connection with a litany sung at Vespers, in which a large group of children answers each supplication with *Kyrie eleison*. Later, the Greek words were placed at the beginning of the supplications as an introduction, and this form of the litany survives to the present day in the Procession of Rogation Days [835] and in the archaic Mass of Holy Saturday [756]. In both of these the Greek acclamations are sung to a very simple formula, essentially the same that occurs at the beginning of the old Mass *Kyrie* reproduced on p. 407.

Judging from a letter of Gregory, it would seem that in his day the *Kyrie* of the Mass was still very much like that described by Etheria, consisting of numerous supplications sung by the clerics to which the people responded *Kyrie eleison,* and an equal number of supplications which they answered with *Christe eleison*. On ordinary days, however, the solemn supplications were omitted, and only the *Kyrie* and *Christe* remained, each apparently sung many times.[9] An ad-libitum practice still existed in the late eighth century, as appears from a description in the *Ordo Romanus I:* "After the Antiphon (i.e., the Introit) the *schola* begins the *Kyrie eleison.* The leader of the *schola* watches for the pope to give him a sign if he wishes to change the number of the litany."[10] However, only a few decades later, the *Ordo of St. Amand* clearly prescribes the finite, tripartite form that eventually prevailed: "The pope gives a sign to sing the *Kyrie eleison.* . . . After they have repeated it three times, he gives another nod to say the *Christe eleison.* . . . And after they have completed it nine times in alternation, he makes a sign to stop."[11]

---

[8] In the *Liber usualis* most of the Ordinary chants are dated: x. c. (tenth century), xi. c., etc. Many of these dates are inconclusive, since the chants may well occur in earlier Mss than those that were consulted at Solesmes. More correct dates for the *Kyries* are given in Melnicki's publication. Thus, *Kyrie VIII* should be dated: xii. c., instead of: xv-xvi. c.

[9] *Patr. lat.* 77, p. 956. This is the same letter in which he refutes the complaints about having introduced the Alleluia outside of Paschal Time [p. 376, fn. 3]. As for the *Kyrie* he says: "The *Kyrie eleison* we have never sung, nor do we sing it, as is done by the Greeks. They sing it all together, while here it is sung by the clerics, and the people respond. And in just as many alternations do we sing the *Christe eleison,* which is never sung by the Greeks. In the Masses of ordinary days we omit other things that are usually sung, and sing only *Kyrie eleison* and *Christe eleison,* in order to continue even longer in these words of entreaty."

[10] *Patr. lat.* 78, p. 942.

[11] Duchesne, *Origines*, p. 458. See also Jungmann, *Missarum Solemnia*, I, 412ff; Froger, *Les Chants de la messe*, pp. 14f.

THE GLORIA

The *Gloria in excelsis Deo,* also known as the *hymnus angelicus* or, in distinction from the *Gloria Patri,* as the Greater Doxology, is the second item of the Ordinary of the Mass. Its text, which is of great antiquity (it was used in the Greek Church perhaps as early as the second century) has a structure entirely different from that of the *Kyrie,* consisting of an extended series of short and ever varying sentences. It is very similar to the slightly later text of the *Te Deum* [1832], and both of them are among the few remnants of a once flourishing literary production known as *psalmi idiotici,* that is, new texts fashioned after the general literary style of the Psalms. It begins with the verse "Glory to God in the highest, and on earth peace to men of good will," which, according to Luke (2:14) the angels sang on the night of the birth of Christ—hence the name *hymnus angelicus* —and continues with short expressions of praise to the Lord (*Adoramus te,* etc.), petitions for mercy (three times *miserere nobis*) addressed to the mystic Lamb of God, and a final praise of Christ (*Quoniam tu solus sanctus,* etc.). Like the *Kyrie,* it was originally not a part of the Mass, but was probably sung during one of the Office Hours, perhaps in place of a Psalm.

The psalmodic character of the text is clearly reflected in the music of what may well be the oldest *Gloria* melody that has come down to us, that is, the *Gloria* of Mass XV [56]. The entire melody is nothing but a reiterated psalm tone, skillfully adapted to the phrases of the text which vary considerably as to the number of syllables:

FIGURE 127

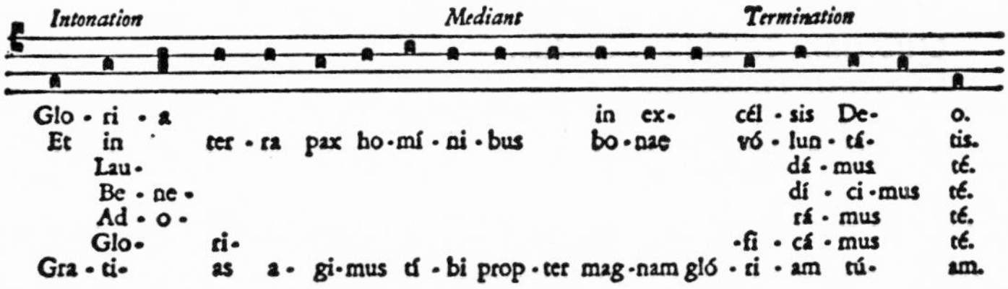

It is not without interest to notice that in this very archaic psalmody the accent of the mediant is always observed (the high note b falls on the accented syllable of *hóminibus, tíbi,* and later *unigéniti, Déi, múndi, Pátris, Spíritu*), while the termination is treated as a cursive, rather than a strictly tonic formula, as appears from the variable placement of the accents. Also noteworthy is the an-hemitonic character of the psalmodic formula.

Even more rudimentary, although not necessarily older, is a melody of the Ambrosian repertory which has been included among the *cantus ad libitum* of the Solesmes *Graduale* [G 89*; *AMM* 604]. Similar to the Gregorian lesson tones, it consists almost entirely of a recitation on a with the final note on g:

    a------------------------------ g
    Gloria in excelsis De- o,
    g------ a------------------- b a-------------------------------- g
    Et in terra pax ho-mi-nibus bonae volunta- tis, etc.

Five syllables of the text—*(ti)bi, (Chris)te, (mun)di, (mun)di,* and *(Chris)te* —are emphasized by an identical melisma of thirteen notes, which presents a strong and somewhat forced contrast to the prevailing style.

None of the other *Gloria* melodies show psalmodic structure as clearly as *Gloria XV.* A fairly close approximation exists in *Gloria VI,* which makes extended use of two basic formulae, one with the outline g-a-b-a-g, the other with the inverted design a-g-f-e-f-g, both sometimes freely modified (sections employing different melodies are indicated by . . .):

g-a-b-a-g	a-g-f-e-f-g
. . . *in excelsis Deo* . . .	*bonae voluntatis.*
Laudamus te.	
Benedicimus te.	
Adoramus te. . . .	
Gratias agimus tibi . . .	*gloriam tuam.*
	. . . *omnipotens.*
	. . . *Jesu Christe.*
Domine Deus	
Agnus Dei	
Filius Patris . . .	*miserere nobis.* . . .
Quoniam tu solus sanctus.	
Tu solus Dominus	
Tu solus Altissimus . . .	*in gloria Dei Patris.*

Other *Gloria* melodies are essentially free and continuously varying in design. Often, however, parallel portions or verses of the text receive similar or identical melodic material. Particularly susceptible of such a repetition technique are the following sections of the text:

(a) *Laudamus te. Benedicimus te. Adoramus te. Glorificamus te.* For these four acclamations we find the schemes a b a b (Gloria III, XIV), a b a′ c (XI), a a′ b a″ (IX), and a a a b (VI).

(b) *Domine . . . omnipotens. Domine . . . Christi. Domine . . . Patris.* Disregarding variants, we find two forms for this tripartite section, a a a (IV, XI, III) or a a b (VI, XII, XIII).

(c) The two *Qui tollis peccata mundi* have the same melody in the Glorias II, III, IV, X, XI, XIII, XIV, XV, and *ad libitum* I, II, III.

Occasionally the two continuations, . . . *miserere nobis* and . . . *suscipe deprecationem nostram,* also have an identical melody, e.g., in *Gloria XI;* but the preferred treatment is to employ different endings for the two verses in question, a *prima* and *seconda volta.*

While the three passages just mentioned are particularly suitable and most frequently selected for melodic unification, other examples of the same or a similar character are to be found in nearly every one of the *Gloria* melodies. *Gloria I* makes repeated use of a standard cadential formula, a-g-a-b-a-g *(bonae voluntatis, Adoramus te,* etc.), thus imparting to the essentially free melody an element of constraint and unification. In *Gloria II* the same effect is achieved by a recurrent motive, a-b♭-c′ c′-b♭-a, not to mention other unifying details. Numerous musical relationships, often of a rather evasive nature, characterize *Gloria VII*. In contrast to such manifestations of a subtle motival technique, *Gloria XI* is interesting for its clearly indicated repeats of five entire phrases, resulting in a form, a a b b c c c d d a a e e f, strikingly similar to, and perhaps suggested by that of the sequence:

a: *Gloria . . . Deo*	b: *Adoramus te. Glorificamus te.*
a: *Et in . . . voluntatis.*	b: *Gratias agimus . . . gloriam tuam.*
c (= a+x): *Domine . . . omnipotens.*	d: *Qui tollis . . . nobis*
c: *Domine . . . Christi*	d: *Qui tollis . . . nostram.*
c: *Domine . . . Patris.*	
a: *Qui sedes . . . Patris*	e: *Tu solus Dominus*	f: *Jesu . . . Amen.*
a: *Quoniam . . . sanctus.*	e: *Tu solus Altissimus.*

The only sections standing outside this scheme are *Laudamus te, Benedicimus te,* and the *miserere nobis* after *Qui sedes.* A somewhat similar structure occurs in *Gloria XIII,* particularly from *Gratias agimus* on.

A rather strange application of the repeat form is found in *Gloria V.* Practically the entire melody consists of nothing but a single phrase which is reiterated eleven times, but with a complete disregard of the textual structure. The phrase itself can be divided into three motives (a, b, c) which can best be seen in connection with the verse *Gratias* (a) *agimus tibi* (b) *propter magnam gloriam tuam* (c). Only in this and three other verses of similar length (*Domine . . . omnipotens,* the second *Qui tollis,* and *Qui sedes*) does the musical phrase coincide with a textual one. Usually the repetition of music cuts right across the textual divisions, so that some verses start with motive b, others consist only of a + b, yet others of c + a. Following is a schematic representation showing the distribution of the melody and its three motives (bracketed sections of the text employ different music):

a	b	c
1. *(Gloria)*	*in excelsis Deo*	2. *Et . . . hominibus (bonae voluntatis).*
3. *Laudamus te.*	4. *Benedicimus te.*	5. *Adoramus te.* 6. *Glorificamus te.*
7. *Gratias*	*agimus tibi*	*propter magnam gloriam tuam.*
8. *Domine*	*Deus Rex caelestis,*	*Deus Pater omnipotens.*
9. *Domine*	*Fili . . . Christe.*	10. *Domine Deus Agnus Dei,*
Filius patris	11. *Qui . . . mundi,*	*miserere nobis.*
12. *Qui tollis*	*peccata mundi,*	*suscipe deprecationem nostram.*
13. *Qui sedes*	*ad dexteram Patris,*	*miserere nobis.*
14. *Quoniam*	*tu solus sanctus.*	
	15. *Tu solus Dominus.*	16. *Tu solus Altissimus,*
Jesu Christe.	17. *Cum Sancto Spiritu,*	*in gloria Dei Patris.*
18. *A-*	*(men.)*	

Only the initial *Gloria,* the words *bonae voluntatis,* and the closing *-men* stand outside this rigid repeat scheme which, for its flagrant violation of the textual structure, is unique in Gregorian chant. No question, this *Gloria* melody belongs to a late period (the *Liber usualis* assigns it, probably correctly, to the twelfth century).

The only *Gloria* melody which can be said to have an entirely free melody is the *ad libitum* I [81]. This is also unique in its musical design, with a range of a twelfth, numerous difficult intervals, and cadential motions normally not encountered in Gregorian chant, that is, the ascending second or the descending fifth (on "caelestis" and "Patris"). Like the above-described *Gloria V* it dates from what is often called the "decadent period;"[12] but such a disapproving adjective, while correct for *Gloria V,* cannot properly be applied to a melody that clearly reveals the impact of novel musical forces, however different they may be from those of the Gregorian tradition.[*]

THE CREDO

Although the text of the *Credo* dates from the fourth century (it was approved by the Council of Nicaea, 325, hence the name Nicean Creed), not until seven centuries later was it introduced into the Roman Mass. Originally an individual confession of faith for those about to be baptized,[13] its use within the Mass is documented for the first time in Con-

---

[12] Ascribed to Pope Leo IX (1048-54); see A. Schubiger, *Die Sängerschule St. Gallens* (1858), no. 59.

[*] For further details see D. Bosse, *Untersuchung einstimmiger Melodien zum "Gloria in excelsis Deo"* (1955?) and the article "Gloria in excelsis Deo" in *MGG.* Both studies reached me after the completion of the manuscript. Acording to Bosse's study there exist 56 melodies.

[13] This function appears clearly from the use of the singular form *Credo* (I believe) instead of the plural form *Credimus* (we believe), which would have been proper in the Mass.

stantinople in the early sixth century,[14] and not long thereafter in Spain (Council of Toledo, 589; see List of Data, no. 46). Two hundred years later we find it in France, but when the German emperor Henry II came to Rome in 1014, he was astonished to find the *Credo* missing in the Mass. It was at his insistence that Pope Benedict VIII finally ordered its introduction, at least for Sundays and on high feasts.[15] To the present day, it is not included in Ferial Masses.

As a result of its late arrival, the *Credo* is not included in the earliest manuscripts containing chants for the Mass Ordinary. Even in the modern publications it is treated as a late-comer and outsider, its melodies being listed separately [64ff] rather than within the Ordinary cycle. Of the numerous melodies that were composed during the late Middle Ages and up to the eighteenth and nineteenth centuries, only four and two *ad libitum* [90ff] have been adopted for present-day use. The oldest of these is the *Credo I,* which occurs in eleventh-century sources but is believed to be derived from much older melodies, possibly of Greek origin.[16] The extended text, similar in its structure to that of the *Gloria,* is set to music in a manner not dissimilar, it seems to me, to that found in the Tracts, there being essentially four standard formulae which recur, in different selections and combinations, with each "verse" of the text. Since the formulae are of a very simple design and, moreover, quite variable, they are not always readily identifiable except through their cadential pitches, which are of the same structural importance here as in the Tracts. Following are the four standard formulae in their essential outline which, as has just been noted, is often modified:

FIGURE 128

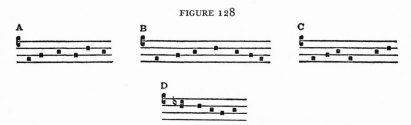

Formula D, closing on g, is the best-defined of all. It is the main formula for the close of the verses. Only once does it appear in the middle of a

---

[14] Theodorus Lector, a sixth-century Greek writer, mentions the Patriarch of Constantinople, Timotheus (511-517), as the one who first ordered the use of the *Credo* in the Mass. Cf. *Patr. gr.* 86, p. 201.

[15] We owe this information to Berno, abbot of Reichenau, who was in the train of the emperor. See his *De quibusdam rebus ad missae officium spectantibus* (*Patr. lat.* 142, pp. 1060f).

[16] Commonly referred to as the "authentic *Credo,*" it has often been studied; see M. Huglo, "Origine de la mélodie du Credo 'authentique' de la Vaticane" (*RG,* XXX, 68). See also the article "Credo" in *MGG.*

verse, namely, at the very beginning, right after the initial *Credo in unum Deum,* on *Patrem omnipotentem.* A plausible explanation for this exceptional case is that originally the first verse closed with *omnipotentem,* and that a second verse began with *Factorem caeli.* In the subsequent representation of the text we have proceeded on this assumption. Formula A, which also closes on g, has a variable function. In some verses it occurs at the beginning, in others at the end, as a substitute for D. Formula C, closing on a, is always employed in a penultimate position, preceding D. B, which closes on e but also may descend to d, usually precedes C and often stands at the beginning of the verse. Outside of this basic material stands the melody for the last verse, *Et vitam venturi saeculi. Amen* as well as that for the opening *Credo in unum Deum.* The latter is famous for having been used by Bach as the theme for the Credo-Fugue in his B-minor Mass:

FIGURE 129

Cre-do in   u - num De - um   *Credo- Fugue*

Following is a schematic representation of the entire *Credo* melody:[17]

1. *Credo . . . omnipotentem:*	X			D		
2. *Factorem . . . invisibilium:*		A	B	D		
3. *Et in unum . . . unigenitum:*			B	C	D	
4. *Et ex Patre . . . saecula:*				C	D	
5. *Deum de Deo . . . vero:*		A	B			A
6. *Genitum . . . facta sunt:*			B	C	D	
7. *Qui propter . . . de caelis:*			B			A
8. *Et incarnatus . . . factus est:*			B	C	D	D
9. *Crucifixus . . . sepultus est:*				C	D	D
10. *Et resurrexit . . . Scripturas:*				C	D	
11. *Et ascendit . . . Patris:*				C	D	
12. *Et iterum . . . erit finis:*		A		C	D	A
13. *Et in Spiritum . . . procedit:*			B		D	A
14. *Qui cum Patre . . . Prophetas:*			B	C	D	A
15. *Et unam . . . Ecclesiam:*			B		D	
16. *Confiteor . . . peccatorum:*			B			A
17. *Et expecto . . . mortuorum:*			B			A
18. *Et vitam . . . Amen.*				free		

17 We feel that our analysis, resulting in a structure similar to that of a Tract, provides a better insight into the formative principles of this interesting melody than the interpretations of Mocquereau (*Pal. mus.,* X, 120) and Wagner (III, 458), who consider it as a psalmodic recitation formula repeated, with numerous variants, for each verse. The very presence, in ℣. 8 and 9, of a "doubled termination" is absolutely impossible in a psalmodic recitation, while it is not at all infrequent in the Tracts or other chants (Responsories) of the centonization type.

Credo II is nothing but a simplified version of the "authentic" *Credo I*. *Credos III* and *IV* are hardly worth our attention, dating, as they do, respectively from the seventeenth and fifteenth centuries. The *ad libitum Credos V* and *VI* are both medieval (twelfth, eleventh century) and have a structure similar to that of a psalmodic recitation repeated for each verse.[18]

THE SANCTUS

The text of the *Sanctus* consists of two sections. The first of these, *Sanctus, Sanctus, Sanctus Dominus Deus Sabaoth. Pleni sunt caeli et terra gloria tua,* is taken from the vision of Isaiah who saw the angels crying unto each other: "Holy, holy, holy is the Lord of hosts: the whole earth is full of his glory" (Is. 6:3). The second, *Benedictus qui venit in nomine Domini. Hosanna in excelsis,* occurs in the Gospel according to St. Matthew (21:9): "Blessed is he that cometh in the name of the Lord: Hosanna in the highest." In the version of the Roman Church the *Hosanna in excelsis* occurs also at the end of the first section.

The *Sanctus* is the only item of the Mass Ordinary whose text is derived from the Old Testament. Isaiah's *Sanctus* survives in the Jewish liturgy in its original language, as the *kadusha,* the threefold "kadosh, kadosh, kadosh." Its Greek counterpart is the *trishagion,* "hagios, hagios, hagios," which was retained in the bilingual *Sanctus* sung during the *Improperia* of Good Friday [705]. The introduction of the *Sanctus* into the Roman Mass is ascribed, not too credibly, to Pope Sixtus I (*c.* 120). The earliest reliable documentation comes from Gaul, where the Council of Vaison (529) ordered the singing of the *Sanctus* in all the Masses, while previously it had been excluded from the "missae matutinales seu quadragesimales," from the morning Masses and those of Lent.[19] Nothing certain is known about its introduction into the Roman liturgy.

The *Sanctus* is sung directly after the Preface, which introduces it with the words: *Cum quibus et nostras voces, ut admitti jubeas, deprecamur, supplici confessione dicentes: Sanctus, Sanctus, Sanctus . . .* (With humble confession we beg you to command that our voices be admitted together with those [of the angels], saying: *Sanctus, Sanctus, Sanctus . . .*[20] Originally, and at least as late as the eighth century, the *Sanctus* was sung by the entire congregation, not by the choir, as became the custom thereafter.

The earliest extant melody for the *Sanctus* is that of Mass XVIII.[21] This

[18] For *Credo VI* see *Nombre,* II, 204; also Gajard and Desroquettes "Le Credo VI" (*RG,* IX, 172).

[19] See List of Data, p. 41, no. 44.

[20] See *Liber,* p. 4.

[21] In *L* 63 this is assigned to the thirteenth century, obviously an entirely misleading dating.

appears not only from its purely syllabic style, the only one suitable for congregational singing, but also from the fact that its beginning is a direct continuation of the closing formula of the Preface;[22] in other words, here the liturgical connection between the Preface and the *Sanctus* is reflected in the music. Moreover, this is the only *Sanctus* melody showing a psalmodic structure. Except for a short introduction, *Sanctus, Sanctus,* and a conclusion, *Hosanna in excelsis,* the melody consists of four statements of a psalmodic recitation formula, with two different endings in alternation. Fig. 130 shows the structure of this very archaic melody, together with the close of the Preface:

FIGURE 130

None of the other melodies show any reminiscence of the psalmodic structure which characterizes *Sanctus XVIII,* with the possible exception of *Sanctus XV* (note the identical cadences for *Dominus Deus Sabaoth, gloria tua,* and *in nomine Domini*). A few melodies are through-composed, mainly nos. VI, IX, XIII, and VIII, the last of which is noteworthy for its repeated use of a short melisma at the end of several phrases, in the manner of a musical rhyme. The great majority of the *Sanctus* melodies employ the tripartite beginning, *Sanctus, Sanctus, Sanctus* or the tripartite close, *Hosanna . . . Benedictus . . . Hosanna . . . ,* as the logical place for a musical repeat, usually in the form A B A. Ternary form at the end of the melody actually occurs in all *Sanctus* melodies except the few that are entirely through-composed. In addition, the beginning is ternary in six melodies; that is, II, III, IV, V, XIV, and XVII. Two others, I and VII, employ an identical short formula for the first and second (not the first and third) *Sanctus,* with a slight modification (A A′ B). In *Sanctus XIV* the two ternary groups, at the beginning and at the end, are musically related, the formula for the first and third *Sanctus* being the same as that for the first and third *excelsis.* Moreover, the formula for the second *Sanctus* is a transposition of that for the first (and third). *Sanctus XVII* is noteworthy for its clear-cut F-major tonality, with constant emphasis on the tonic and dominant, and for a triadic formula for the first and third *Sanctus,* which recurs, in a free inversion, on the second *Sanctus* as well

22 Cf. the Ferial Tone [109], on *Domino Deo nostro.*

as on *Domine Deus*. Moreover, the identical phrase is employed for *gloria tua, Benedictus qui venit,* and *in nomine Domini.* These repeats, together with the ternary form of the *Hosanna—Benedictus—Hosanna* make this *Sanctus* melody the most fully organized of all those in present-day use. According to the indication of the *Liber usualis* it dates from the eleventh century. The following table shows the distribution of the *Sanctus* melodies according to the four structural types we have discussed.

1.	Psalmodic	XVIII
2.	Through-composed	VI, VIII, IX, XIII; *ad lib.* I
3.	Ternary close	X, XI, XII, XV, XVI; *ad lib.* II, III
4.	Ternary beginning and close	I, II, III, IV, V, VII, XIV, XVII

In our discussion of the *Kyrie* melodies we have seen that the four structural types encountered in the small collection of the modern books are sufficient to provide a basis for the formal classification of the entire repertory. Whether the four categories of *Sanctus* melodies have an equally general validity cannot be said at this moment. Nor is it possible to say whether they have any chronological or evolutionary significance, although one cannot help looking at them from such a point of view. It may be noted that there is no *Sanctus* melody having ternary form at the beginning without having it at the end. Assuming that this statement is valid for the entire repertory, one could probably conclude that the former element of structural organization made its appearance after the latter had been established.

Stylistic considerations would seem to support this surmise. Like the *Kyries,* the *Sanctus* melodies can be divided into a small group showing a simple, syllabic style, and a majority written in a fairly elaborate neumatic style which reflects the transition from congregational to professional performance. All the *Sanctus* of our structural category (4) have melodies which suggest a relatively late date; while in those of category (3) we find elaborate as well as simple melodies, the latter in nos. X, XV, and XVI. The through-composed *Sanctus* melodies also include examples of both styles, nos. XIII and *ad lib.* I being syllabic, the others more ornate. At least one of these, *Sanctus IX,* is definitely of a very late date (the *Liber usualis* indicates the fourteenth century), as appears from its modernistic f-major tonality with a surprisingly clear emphasis on the degrees of the triad. Such melodies are of great interest because they may provide the clue for one of the most important phenomena in the development of polyphonic music, that is, the appearance about 1400 of triadic melodies in the compositions of Matheus de Perusio, Ciconia, and, particularly, Dunstable.[23]

[23] See, e.g., Matheus de Perusio's *Pour dieu vous pri* in my publication, *French Secular Music of the Late Fourteenth Century* (1950), no. 18.

THE AGNUS DEI

The last chant of the Mass Ordinary is an acclamation addressed to the mystic "Lamb of God." Its text is derived from the Gospel according to St. John who, seeing Jesus coming unto him, said: "Behold the Lamb of God, which taketh away the sin of the world" (John 1:29). In several respects the *Agnus Dei* resembles the *Kyrie*. Both were used in the Eastern Churches long before they appeared in Rome; both originally formed a part of the litany, the *Kyrie* at its opening and the *Agnus* at its close; and both survived in this archaic function in the litanies of Holy Saturday, Rogation Days and others modelled after these.[24] According to a credible report, the *Agnus Dei* was introduced into the Roman Mass by the Greek Pope Sergius I, who ruled from 687 to 701 [see List of Data, no. 59]. Here it was sung during the ceremony of the breaking of the bread, originally by the entire congregation and the clergy. As early as *c.* 775, however, we find it entrusted to the *schola,* the professional singers.[25]

The *Agnus Dei* resembles the *Kyrie* in the tripartite structure of its text:

> *Agnus Dei, qui tollis peccata mundi: miserere nobis.*
> *Agnus Dei, qui tollis peccata mundi: miserere nobis.*
> *Agnus Dei, qui tollis peccata mundi: dona nobis pacem.*

A "correct" musical setting of this text would call for the use of the same melody three times, except for a different termination to accompany the final words, *dona eis pacem.* This form, a + x, a + x, a + y, however, does not occur among the melodies reproduced in the present-day publications and very likely was never used at all. Not a few *Agnus* employ the same melody for each of the three acclamations (a a a), while others have a different melody for the second or for the third acclamation (a b a; a a b). In some melodies the different conclusions, *miserere nobis* and *dona eis pacem,* are sung to an identical refrain (r). The following table shows the melodies arranged according to structural types:

1.	a	a	a	I, III, V, VI, XVII, XVIII; *ad lib.* I, II
2.	a	b	a	X, XII, XV, XVI
3.	a	a	b	VII (with identical cadence for a and b)
4.	a+r	b+r	a+r	II, IV, VIII, IX, XIII, XIV
5.	a+r	b+r	c+r	XI

24 E.g., in the Litany of Loreto [1857].

25 The *Liber pontificalis* (ed. Duchesne, I, 376), which ascribes the *Agnus* to Pope Sergius, says: "a clero et populo decantetur," while the *Ordo Romanus primus (Patr. lat.* 78, p. 946) has the remark: "archidiaconus . . . respicit in scholam, et annuit eis ut dicant Agnus Dei" (the archdeacon looks toward the *schola* and gives them a sign to sing the *Agnus Dei*).

In two of these *Agnus* melodies there exist melodic relationships beyond those indicated in the table. In *Agnus IX* the three phrases have not only an identical refrain but also an identical beginning, to the words *Agnus Dei,* the only difference being in the music for *qui tollis peccata mundi,* so that the formal scheme becomes a + m + r; a + n + r; a + m + r. In *Agnus X* the first two phrases, although different in the main, have the same melody for *qui tollis peccata mundi,* which thus recurs in each of the three phrases: a + m + r; b + m + s; a + m + r. Finally, *Agnus XVII,* listed above under the simple repeat form (a a a) actually has a different beginning, to the words *Agnus Dei,* for the middle phrase, and one that, in its ascending motion, provides an artistic contrast to the descending formula employed for the first and the third *Agnus Dei.* There is also a slight difference in the beginning of the middle phrase of *Agnus III.*

Stylistically, the *Agnus* melodies, like those for the *Kyrie,* fall into a small group showing an archaic style and a majority written in a later style which, however, is not as "advanced" as that of the late *Kyries.* The simplest, and probably oldest, melody is that of *Agnus XVIII,* which also employs the simple repeat form. It recurs in the Litany [758, 838] as well as in the Mass for the Dead [1815], for which the final *dona eis pacem* is changed into *dona eis requiem aeternam.* Equally simple in style and form is *Agnus II* of the *ad libitum chants* [88], which however, is not an original *Agnus* melody.[26] Tendencies of a later date are evident particularly in *Agnus VI,* noteworthy for its "c-major sixth-chord" (g-c′ c′-g-e) on *mundi.*

THE MASS ORDINARY AS A CYCLE

At the beginning of this section we have said that the formation of fixed cycles of the Mass Ordinary is largely a modern organization. They appear for the first time in Dom Pothier's *Liber gradualis,* which contains sixteen cycles and four *Credo* melodies.[27] Dom Mocquereau (in the *Editio Vaticana, Liber usualis,* etc.) adopted some of Pothier's cycles, changed others, increased the number to eighteen, and added the collection of *ad libitum chants.* The principles that guided Pothier and Mocquereau remained unknown, and it is only recently that the problem of the Mass cycle has been investigated from the historical point of view. The most important study is an article, "Aux origines du Kyriale," by Dom Dominique Catta, which appeared in the *Revue grégorienne* of 1955 (no. 34, p. 175). The results of this highly illuminating investigation are incorporated in the subsequent survey.

26 Mr. Stäblein has kindly informed me that it is a composition by Pothier, modelled after a *Kyrie* trope from St. Gall *546.* We should like to call attention to the interesting discussions, based on a large body of material, in his article "Agnus Dei" in *MGG.*

27 *Editio altera,* 1895, pp. 3*ff (I have been unable to consult the first edition of 1883). Pothier also includes a *Missa regia* by the seventeenth-century composer Henry du Mont.

The earliest sources for the chants of the Mass Ordinary arrange them in separate groups, first all the *Kyries*, then all the *Glorias*, etc. Beginning with the twelfth century, we find occasionally a *Gloria* right after a *Kyrie* or, more frequently, after two or three *Kyries*. Simultaneously there appears the combination of a *Sanctus* and an *Agnus*. However, even these rudimentary groupings are far from being identical in the various manuscripts. Some of these twin groups have been incorporated in the Vatican edition. Thus, the *Kyrie-Gloria* of Masses I, V, IX, and XV occur in one or several manuscripts of the twelfth or later centuries.

Complete cycles of *Kyrie-Gloria-Sanctus-Agnus* occur for the first time in manuscripts of the thirteenth century, for instance, in a Dominican *Gradual* of 1254.[28] This contains one of the few present-day cycles that have medieval (albeit late medieval) authority, that is, Mass IV. Two others of this kind are Masses IX and XI, which occur in manuscripts from the fifteenth or sixteenth century. Naturally, the possibility exists that continued search will show their presence in earlier sources.

Other cycles of the early manuscripts have been partly changed in the Vatican edition. Thus, the above-mentioned Dominican *Gradual* contains Mass XV, but with the present-day *Kyrie XVI,* and Mass IX with *Sanctus II.* We have just seen that this Mass appears in its present-day form in a fifteenth century manuscript.

The most important result of these discoveries is that they invalidate the theory, generally held until recently, that the idea of a Mass Ordinary cycle had its origin in polyphonic Masses, such as the Mass of Tournai (*c.* 1300), the Mass of Machaut (*c.* 1350), or the Mass of Toulouse, also from the fourteenth century.[29] Actually this principle was fully established within the province of monophonic chant at least half a century before it found its first realization in the field of polyphonic music.

In conclusion a few remarks may be added concerning the closing salutation of the Mass, the *Ite missa est.*[30] This is sung to a melody which, in nearly all the Masses, is taken from the *Kyrie* (the only exceptions are the Masses XV, XVI, and XVIII), thus bestowing upon the cycle a noteworthy trait of musical unity. Naturally, the question arises whether this is a medieval or a modern usage. The manuscripts which form the basis of

[28] From the monastery of St.-Jacques in Paris (now in Rome, St. Sabine). Dom Catta remarks that the Dominican, Franciscan, and Premonstratensian Orders played a leading role in the formation of the Mass cycles.

[29] See, e.g., L. Schrade, "The Mass of Toulouse" (*Revue Belge de Musicologie,* VIII [1954], 84); also Schrade, "News on the Chant Cycle of the *Ordinarium Missae*" (*Journal of the American Musicological Society,* VIII [1955], 66).

[30] Meaning: "Go, this is the dismissal." It is a strange fact that the most important liturgical service of the Roman Church was named after the words indicating its conclusion (*missa,* Mass). For Masses in which the *Gloria* is omitted (e.g., during Lent) the *Ite, missa est is* replaced by *Benedicamus Domino.*

Dom Catta's study do not include the *Ite missa est*. According to our present state of knowledge this occurs for the first time in a fourteenth century source, Ms. *94* of the *Bibliothèque municipale* of Toulouse, the same manuscript that contains the recently discovered polyphonic Mass of Toulouse. Its last fascicle contains nine complete cycles of the Ordinary, each for a specific liturgical usage (*in festis duplicibus, semi-duplicibus,* etc.), and each closing with the *Ite missa est* or (in cycles 8 and 9, which lack the *Gloria*) with the *Benedicamus Domino*. In two of these cycles (nos. 2 and 5) the *Ite missa est* is musically identical with the *Kyrie,* and in one (no. 7) the two melodies are similar. In all the others they are different. Six complete cycles contained in Ms. *J.II.9* of the Biblioteca Nazionale in Torino (early fifteenth century) show no melodic relationship between the opening and the closing melody.[31] But further search may well reveal additional examples that would justify the modern practice.

THE HYMNS

In their description of the Last Supper, both Matthew and Mark say: "And when they had sung a hymn, they went out into the mount of Olives" (Matt. 26:30; Mark 14:26). Very likely, the "hymn" mentioned here was not a hymn in the distinctive sense of the word, but a Psalm. In fact, at least as late as *c.* 500 we find the term *hymnus* used in this meaning, while hymns proper, that is, new literary texts in poetic form, were often designated as *carmen*.

We are exceptionally well informed about the early history of hymnody. It seems as though attempts to introduce hymns, whenever they occurred, were considered to be unusual and extraordinary; therefore they were noted by chroniclers who paid little attention to other developments that actually were of much greater importance but which went unnoticed because they followed the normal course of evolution. Remarks by Tertullian and Origen would seem to indicate that hymns existed as early as the first two centuries. The movement received a strong impulse about A.D. 200 among the Gnostics, a Christian-Hellenistic sect in Syria, when Bardesanes (d. 223) and his son Harmonios wrote a Gnostic Psalter, which consisted of versified paraphrases of the Psalms. No doubt this enterprise had a popularizing tendency, similar to that of the French and Dutch Psalters of the sixteenth century. Of particular interest is the fact that the Council of Antioch, held in 269, reproached Bishop Paul of Samosata for having forbidden the singing of hymns. The report shows that at this time not only had hymns gained a foothold among the orthodox Christians but also that they had become a highly controversial matter, subject to approval,

31 See the second article mentioned in fn. 29. I am indebted to Prof. Schrade for additional information concerning the question at hand.

disapproval and re-approval, as was to be the case for many centuries thereafter.

Apparently the Gnostic hymns of Bardesanes were very successful; so much so that the Syrian St. Ephraim (306-73), recognizing the beauty of their words and melodies but insisting that they were "poison offered to healthy people," resolved to combat their heretic tendencies by writing hymns expounding the orthodox doctrine.[1] Ephraim's hymns, which have been preserved both in Syrian and Greek, indicate the beginning of documented Christian hymnody. They also are important in the history of poetry because in them the principle of quantity, which governs the poetry of Greek and Latin antiquity, is largely abandoned, as it was at a considerably later time in medieval Latin poetry.[2]

According to Isidore of Seville, the first writer of Latin hymns was Hilary of Poitiers (d. 367), who, having been banished to the Orient, came to know the Syrian and Greek hymns and upon his return to France wrote a number of Latin hymns, three of which survive. Written in a rather involved and obscure style, they did not become popular and probably were not intended to become so.[3] It fell to Ambrose (d. 397) to take the decisive step by which Latin hymnody left the stage of infancy to enter that of early maturity as well as artistic culmination. Among his successors were Aurelius Prudentius (died after 405), Caelius Sedulius (mid-fifth century), Venantius Fortunatus (died after 600), Paulus Diaconus (d. 799), Theodulphus (d. 821), Hrabanus Maurus (d. 856), and many poets of later centuries.

The Church, however, continued to take a hostile attitude toward this flourishing production. At the very time when Ambrose laid the foundation of Latin hymnody, the Council of Laodicea, which took place from c. 360 to 381, interdicted the singing of hymns. This edict was effective; for many centuries the hymns did not attain a liturgical status in the West-

---

[1] "Ephraim, seeing that the Syrians were charmed by the beauty of the words and the rhythm of the melodies (of Bardesanes and Harmonios) and were thus induced to follow his belief, . . . endeavored to adopt the meters of Harmonios. And to the melodies of his (Harmonios') words, he added other texts which agreed with the ecclesiastical dogma." (Sozomenos, *Historia ecclesiastica*, III, xvi; see *Patr. gr.* 67, p. 1090). Ephraim himself wrote in one of his poems: "He (Bardesanes) created hymns and combined them with music. He composed songs and introduced in them meters, measuring and weighing the words. He offered to healthy people poison dissimulated by beauty . . . He wanted to imitate David . . . and, like David, composed one hundred and fifty songs" (cf. Dom Jeannin, *Mélodies liturgiques syriennes et chaldéennes* [1924], pp. 66, 144).

[2] See pp. 277f. However, the widely-held opinion that in Ephraim's hymns quantity is replaced by quality (natural word accent) is not correct. The prevailing principle of his versification is isosyllabism (same number of syllables in each line). This principle, however, is older than Ephraim and may even antedate Christianity. I am indebted for this information to Prof. Eric Werner of Hebrew Union College, Cincinnati.

[3] See also Gevaert, *Mélopée*, pp. 62ff, with excerpts from Hilary (p. 64).

ern Church—in contrast to the Byzantine liturgy where they soon received and always retained a prominent position. Churchmen of conservative leanings continued to combat the hymn movement, raising more or less the same objections as were voiced in the sixteenth century when the Calvinists condemned the Lutheran hymns as "man-made" and "non-inspired." Others favored them, and through many centuries the battle went on. Thus, in 563 the Council of Braga (Portugal) proscribed them with the words: *extra psalmos . . . nihil poetice compositum in ecclesia psallatur* (aside from the Psalms, no poetry should be sung in the Church), while in 633 the Council of Toledo (Spain) threatened with excommunication those who dared to reject hymns. As far as we know, hymns first gained a secure foothold in some French monasteries of the episcopal see of Arles. Two bishops of Arles, Caesarius (470-542) and Aurelian (546-551), wrote monastic Rules whose *ordo psallendi* includes specific hymns for the Office hours. The decisive impetus leading to the eventual adoption of hymns came from St. Benedict (480-547), founder of the Benedictine order and of the first Benedictine monasteries, in Subiaco and Monte Cassino. It was the Benedictine hymnal that was finally, in the tenth or eleventh century, adopted by the Church of Rome, owing largely to the Benedictine abbey of Cluny which then exercised a great influence.

According to the testimony of Augustine, four hymns can definitely be ascribed to Ambrose, namely, *Aeterne rerum conditor, Deus creator omnium, Jam surgit hora tertia,* and *Veni redemptor gentium.*[4] They are all written in a very simple meter, that is, in stanzas of four lines, and with four iambic feet to each line, e.g.:

> *Veni redémptor géntiúm*
> *Osténde pártum vírginis*
> *Mirétur ómne séculum*
> *Talís decét partús Deúm.*

A great number of hymns, written according to this metrical scheme, are often collectively referred to as "Ambrosian hymns," but modern scholars have shown that hardly more than a dozen of them can credibly be ascribed to St. Ambrose. Prudentius wrote, among others, the hymns *Ales diei nuntius, Lux ergo surgit aurea,* and *Quicumque Christum quaeritis,* all in the Ambrosian versification, while Sedulius contributed *A solus ortus cardine* and *Crudelis Herodes Deum* (originally *Hostis Herodes impie*).

As simple as the Ambrosian scheme, but of a later date, are the trochaic verses. One of the earliest instances is the *Pange lingua* [709] for Good Friday, written in six trochaic tetrameters:

---

[4] Two others, *Illuxit orbi* and *Bis ternas horas,* are mentioned by Cassiodorus; see *Mélopée,* p. 66.

Pánge língua glóriósi
Láureám certáminis.
Ét supér crucis trophaéo
Díc triúmphum nóbilém:
Quáliter Redémptor órbis
Ímmolátus vícerit.

In this type of meter the even-numbered lines are catalectic, i.e., lacking the final weak syllable. A much later example of trochaic verse is the *Stabat mater,* which provides the text for a hymn [1424] as well as for a celebrated sequence [1634^v]. It is written in stanzas of three trochaic tetrameters, the third catalectic:

Stábat máter dólorósa
Júxta crúcem lácrimósa
Dúm pendébat Fíliús.

Although both the *Pange lingua* and the *Stabat mater* employ the same verse, they differ in one interesting aspect, that is, their attitude toward the principle of quantity. The *Pange lingua* is still essentially quantitative, as appears from the third line, which in normal (qualitative) accentuation would be partly iambic: "Et súper crúcis trophaéo." In the *Stabat mater,* however, the last remnants of this method of versification have disappeared.[5] The principle of quantity prevails also in the genuine Ambrosian hymns, although an effort is made to make the accents quantitative and qualitative at the same time. Thus, in *Veni redemptor* all the accents are quantitative, and most of them are also qualitative, the only exceptions being the initial "Vení" (normally, "Véni") and the last line which, in normal accentuation would be a trochaic, not an iambic tetrameter: "Tális décet pártus Déum," in obvious violation of the metrical scheme.

Toward the eighth century, at the time of the "Carolingian renaissance," the elaborate and diversified meters of classical antiquity were discovered and employed by hymn writers. A well-known example, ascribed to Paulus Diaconus (d. 799) is *Ut queant laxis* [1504], the hymn to St. John from which Guido derived his solmization syllables, *ut, re, mi,* etc. It is written in the so-called Sapphic meter:

Út queánt laxís resonáre fíbris
Míra géstorúm   famuli tuórum
Sólve pólluti   labii reátum
Sáncte Johánnes.

Other hymns in the same meter are *Iste confessor* [1177], *Caelitum Joseph* [1438], and *Ecce jam noctis [A* 8]*.

A meter well-known from the odes of Horace (e.g., *Maécenás atavís;*

[5] It should be noticed that in the *Liber* the accents are always placed in their normal position, therefore often in disregard of the versification.

asclepiadean verse) recurs in Hrabanus Maurus' hymn *Sanctorum meritis* [1159], *Festivis resonent* [1537ᵛ], and, somewhat modified, in *Sacris solemniis* [PM 94].

> *Sánctorúm meritis   ínclyta gáudiá*
> *Pángamús, socii,   géstaque fórtiá:*
> *Glíscens fért animús   prómere cántibús*
> *Victorúm genus óptimúm.*

The distich, consisting of two dactylic hexameters, is represented by the *Gloria laus* [588] of Palm Sunday:

> *Glória láus et honór tibi sít Rex Chríste Redémptor*
> *Cui pueríle decús   prómpsit Hosánna piúm.*

Turning now from the literary aspect of the hymns to their music, we find ourselves in a much less fortunate position. The reluctance of the Roman Church to adopt the hymns is reflected in the fact that they are completely absent in the early *Antiphonaries*, e.g., in the Codex Hartker and the Codex Lucca. The first hymns to find official status were a few that are sung during or in connection with the Mass, mainly the *Pange lingua* (with the refrain *Crux fidelis*) [709] which is sung during the Adoration of the Cross on Good Friday, and the *Gloria laus* [588] from the Procession on Palm Sunday. One or both of them occur in such early manuscripts as the *Graduals* of Compiègne, St. Gall *359*, St. Gall *339*, Einsiedeln *121*, and the Codex Montpellier.[6] The Office hymns appear in separate collections, the so-called Hymnaries, first without and later with musical notation, the earliest example of the latter type being the tenth-century Hymnary of Moissac. Such early sources are, of course, notated in staffless neumes. Aside from a single case to be mentioned later [p. 428], it is not until the twelfth or thirteenth centuries that we find hymn melodies which can be read.

On the whole, this situation parallels that encountered in the main repertory of Gregorian chant, with its early, staffless *Graduals* and *Antiphonals* which can only be deciphered with the aid of sources from the eleventh or twelfth centuries. Actually, however, the situation differs in one important respect. While a comparative study of the *Graduals* and *Antiphonals*, whether from the tenth or from the fourteenth century, reveals an essentially fixed repertory of texts and melodies, this is far from being so in the Hymnaries. Not only do they fail to assign the hymns to specific feasts, they also include different selections of hymns and, more often than not, give different melodies for one and the same hymn text.

---

6 Also included among the "hymns" are items such as the *Benedictus es* (*hymnus trium puerorum*, actually a Canticle), the *Gloria in excelsis* (*hymnus angelicus*, actually a *psalmus idioticus*), etc.

Certain hymns of frequent occurrence appear in the *Liber usualis* with ten or more different melodies, and yet other melodies for the same hymn are found in the *Antiphonale romanum* or in the *Antiphonale monasticum* of the Benedictines. Thus, the *Liber usualis* gives thirteen different melodies for the hymn of Compline, *Te lucis ante terminum,* assigning each melody for a different occasion, one for Paschal Time, one for Advent, etc., in a manner similar to that applied to the Ordinary of the Mass. The *Antiphonale monasticum* has seventeen melodies for the same hymn.

No less frequent is the opposite procedure, that is, the use of the same melody for different hymn texts, in other words, adaptation. This method was, of course, greatly facilitated by the fixed poetic structure of the hymns, particularly all those of the "Ambrosian" type, a fact which made it easy to employ a given melody for other hymns written in the same metrical scheme. To give one example for many, the hymns *Jesu redemptor* [365], *Deus tuorum* [419], *Exsultet orbis* [425], and *Salvete flores* [431] all have the same melody.

Easily the most interesting aspect of the hymn melodies is their form. Since the great majority of the hymns have stanzas of four lines, with eight syllables to each line, the melody usually consists of four well-defined phrases of equal length. In most cases these four phrases are different and unrelated, resulting in the form a b c d. There are, however, a number of hymn melodies in which some of the phrases are repeated. The various repetition forms resulting from this procedure are interesting not only in themselves but also because they may well have played a role in the development of the forms of secular monophony of the twelfth and thirteenth centuries, such as the Latin *conductus* or the songs of the troubadours and trouvères.

The most frequent repetition form encountered in the repertory of the hymns is a b c a. Among the hymns included in the *Liber usualis* there are at least eight melodies showing this form. Of particular interest are the forms a a b c and a a b a, characterized by a repetition at the beginning, because they embody a structural principle which can be traced almost through the entire history of music.[7] It is interesting to notice that nearly all the hymns of this group use a somewhat higher range in the third phrase, thus showing an awareness of an aesthetic principle similar in nature to the one realized in the development section of sonata-form. Especially close to sonata-form is the structure a a b a (rounded bar-form), with its "recapitulation" in the final phrase.

The following table shows a number of examples for these and other repetitive forms.[8] An asterisk indicates that the repeated phrase has an essential variant at the end, so that the form would be more correctly represented by a scheme such as a b c a'.

[7] Cf. the article "Barform" in *HDM.*
[8] Cf. Parisot, "Les Hymnes de l'Office Romain" (*TG,* V, 167). The *Antiphonale* of the

1. a b c a: *Deus tuorum* [419]; *Jam lucis* [224]; *Nunc Sancte* [318]; *Nunc Sancte* [569]; *Te lucis* [844]; *Jesu corona* [1211]; *Salvete Christi* [1529]; *Christe redemptor* [AM 238]; *Jam Christe* [AM 338]; *Jesu nostra* [AM 288]

2. a a b c: **Nunc Sancte* [235]; *Iste Confessor* [1178]; *Aeterne rerum conditor* [Wagner II, edition 1905, p. 239]

3. a a b a: *Jam sol* [312]; **Lucis creator* [257]; **Sanctorum meritis* [1157]; **Ales diei* [A 109]

4. a b c b: **Te splendor* [1661]; **Ad regias* [814]; **Jesu dulcis* [452]; *Nunc Sancte* [1256]

5. a b a b: **Immense caeli* [517]; *Lucis creator* [256]; *Fortem virili* [1234]

6. a b b a: **A solis ortus* [400]

7. a b c b a b: *Urbs Jerusalem* [AM 694]

8. a b c d c d (= A B B): *Pange lingua* [709]

In some of these hymns we find a slight variant at the beginning of the repeated phrase, e.g., in *Te lucis* [844] and in *Nunc Sancte* [1256]. This phenomenon leads to another group of hymn melodies, characterized by a musical rhyme. In these there are two or even three phrases which differ for their major part, but close with an identical cadential formula. On the whole, musical rhyme seems to be less frequent than outright repeat of a complete phrase. Following are a few examples:

1. a+r b c d+r: *Te lucis* [367]; *Hostis Herodes* [AM 288]
2. a b+r c d+r: *Creator alme* [324]; *Beata nobis* [876]; *Te lucis* [455]
3. a+r b c+r d+r: *Te lucis* [540]

Finally, some hymns were written and composed in the form of a refrain song, i.e., with an identical text and melody (*R*) sung before and after each stanza: *R S R S ... R.* They were usually sung during processions. The *Liber usualis* contains two such hymns: *Gloria laus* [588] from the Procession of Palm Sunday, and *Pange lingua,* with the refrain *Crux fidelis*[9] [709] from the ceremony of the Adoration of the Cross on Good Friday. The text of *Pange lingua* is by Venantius Fortunatus, who also wrote the refrain hymn *Salve festa dies,* for the procession of Easter Sunday [PM 62]. As stated before, these processional hymns were incorporated in the Roman liturgy long before the Office hymns were admitted. The later medieval books contain several other such hymns, especially for the Litanies.[10]

Vatican edition (1912) has an appendix, *Hymni antiqui*, which may be consulted for additional examples. The *Antiphonale monasticum* presents the hymns often in more authentic versions than the books of the Roman use.

[9] Somewhat inconsistently, the former is named after the refrain, the latter, after the first stanza.

[10] Cf. *Wagner III*, 479ff.

Stylistically the hymns can be divided into three categories:

a. A small number of melodies approach the character of a recitation tone by using the same pitch for the major portion of their phrases. Such simple melodies are used for the Day Hours of ordinary week days and therefore are not included in the *Liber usualis*. An example is the hymn *Nunc sancte* as sung at Terce of Monday in the Benedictine rites [*AM* 93]. The same melody occurs in the *Hymni-antiqui* collection of the Vatican *Antiphonale* employed for the texts *Rector potens* and *Rerum Deus* [Appendix, pp. 4, 5], the former for Sext, the latter for None of week days and simple feasts. Recitation style is also found in the hymn of Prime, *Jam lucis,* as sung on weekdays and simple feasts according to the Benedictine rites [*AM* 1].

b. Quite a number of hymn melodies combine syllabic style with melodic motion in each of the phrases, ascending, descending, or in the contour of a curve. To this category belongs the hymn of Prime, *Jam lucis orto sidere* [224] and that of Compline, *Te lucis ante terminum* [266], as sung on ordinary Sundays. Most of these include a few groups of two or three notes, thus forming a transition to the next category.

c. Here we find melodies of a relatively ornate style, with two- or three-note neumes on a number of syllables, and occasionally with a somewhat more extended "melisma" on the last syllable of a phrase. Hymns of this kind are usually employed on higher feasts, an example in point being the Tone for Solemn Feasts of *Jam lucis orto sidere* [224].

The earliest source for a hymn melody is the *Musica enchiriadis* of the ninth century. It contains, in daseian notation, a melody for *Aeterna Christi munera* which is reproduced in Fig. 131 together with what some scholars believe to be its original form, that is, strictly syllabic and in triple meter:[11]

FIGURE 131

[11] See Gevaert, *Mélopée,* p. 70; also, e.g., G. Reese, *Music in the Middle Ages,* p. 105 (after Dreves, *Aurelianus Ambrosius* [1893], p. 111); H. Besseler, *Musik des Mittelalters und der Renaissance,* p. 47; etc.

This reconstruction is based, first, on the assumption that in the days of Ambrose the hymns were sung in a very simple style, essentially with one note to each syllable; and second, on Augustine's description of an iambic foot as consisting of "a short and a long, of three beats."[12] Both of these premises are of rather doubtful validity, particularly the latter. In spite of its title, Augustine's *De musica* is a treatise, not on music in the proper sense of the word, but on poetic versification according to the classical principle of quantity. In the same table which contains the description of the iambic foot (with the example *părēns;* normal accentuation *párens*), there are examples such as *nātūră* for long-long-short, *cĕlĕrĭtās* for short-short-short-long, and *săcērdōtēs* for short-long-long-long. If we were to apply this principle to the text *Aeterna Christi munera,* its rhythmic structure would have to be as shown in Fig. 132:

FIGURE 132

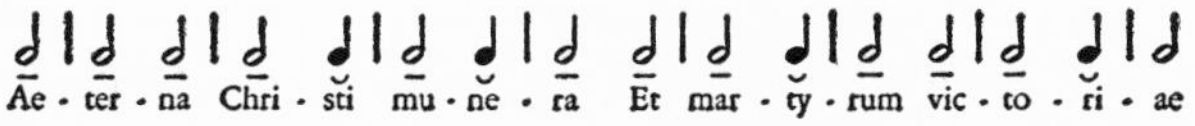

Ae - ter - na Chri - sti mu - ne - ra Et mar - ty - rum vic - to - ri - ae

entirely different from the rhythmic scheme shown in Fig. 131, which is based on the accentual interpretation of the text. It is true that in the genuine Ambrosian hymns the versification is essentially quantitative, but not entirely so. The initial syllables of the lines are often long, for instance, in *Veni redemptor:*

Vēni . . . Ōstende . . . Mīretur . . . Tālis,

not short as would be required in iambic verses. Also inner syllables are occasionally long where they should be short, or *vice versa,* e.g.:

FIGURE 133

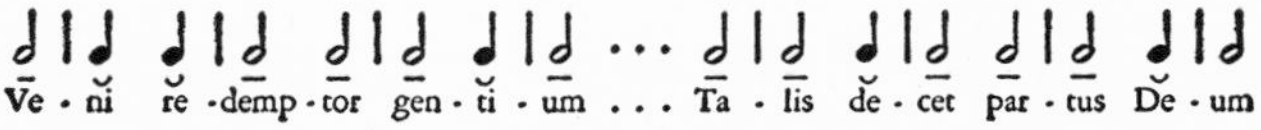

Ve - ni re -demp - tor gen - ti - um . . . Ta - lis de - cet par - tus De - um

It is not impossible that, in spite of these deviations from classical versification, the Ambrosian hymns were originally sung in accordance with their iambic structure, but it is hardly possible to invoke for this surmise the testimony of Augustine, who rigidly adheres to the classical principles of quantity.

THE TROPES

With this and the next section we enter into the consideration of a late efflorescence of the chant, a final and not at all unsuccessful attempt

[12] *De Musica,* II, viii (*Patr. lat.* 32, p. 1108): *brevis et longa, tria temporum.*

to rejuvenate it and to prolong its creative life for another four or five centuries. It is a testimony to the force of the Gregorian tradition that this activity took the form, not of independent creation, but rather of amplification. In fact, the various phenomena to be considered have one thing in common, they are accretions to chants of the old repertory, accretions that may be compared to fresh branches grafted upon old trees. No doubt, the underlying motivation, far from being that of weariness or dissatisfaction, was, on the contrary, a desire to re-affirm the tradition in a new testimony of faith, to re-interpret it in contemporary thought and expression, to add one's own voice to that of a distant past. Viewed in this light, the development, which may have started in the ninth century if not earlier, represents a wholly valid contribution to the repertory of the chant, in fact one that is closer to the "Gregorian" tradition than, for instance, the hymns or the Marian Antiphons. Eventually, however, it began to overstep its boundaries, and to assume undue liberties and excesses which finally led to its downfall. As is well known, all the tropes and nearly all the sequences were abolished by the Council of Trent about 1560.

A standard definition of a trope is that given by L. Gautier, in his basic study, *Les Tropes* (1886): "The trope is the interpolation of a liturgical text." In fact, the addition of a text is the most conspicuous aspect of troping and the one bound to attract the main, if not exclusive, attention of a philologist, such as Gautier. It is, however, not the only nor, in all probability, the original connotation of a trope. Musicologists such as Gastoué, Mocquereau, and Handschin have pointed out that the earliest examples of interpolation or accretion are purely musical, and that this meaning is indicated in the term *tropos* (turn, figure).[1] Although it may be difficult to establish an indisputable proof of priority, there can hardly be any question that not only textual, but also musical interpolations are involved. The entire field of tropes can be divided into three categories: first, the purely musical tropes, which take on the form of a melisma added to a chant; second, the purely textual tropes, characterized by the addition of a text without addition of music, the new words being sung to an already existing melisma; a third category is formed by what may be called the musical-textual tropes, in which a new text appears with new music.

Tropes of one kind or another were affixed to nearly all the types of chant, particularly Introits, Alleluias, Offertories, Responsories, and the various items of the Mass Ordinary, though rarely to the *Credo*. Most of the Alleluia tropes belong to a special type known as sequence, which will

---

[1] See Gastoué, *Cours*, p. 73: "La *séquence*, la *prose* et le *trope* . . . ne consistaient d'abord qu'en longues vocalises;" Mocquereau, *Pal. mus.*, XIII, *Texte*, p. 21: "On commença, semble-t-il, par des neumes sans paroles;" and particularly Handschin, in his chapter on "Trope, Sequence, Conductus" in the *New Oxford History of Music*, II (1954), 128ff. The Roman term for these interpolations was *festivae laudes:* "interserta cantica, quae Romani festivas laudes, Franci tropos appellant" (Paris, B. N. *lat. 2400*, a report ascribed to Adhémar de Chavannes; see Gastoué, *Origines*, p. 119, fn. 4).

be considered separately in the next chapter. As for the tropes proper, we shall begin with those involving the addition of a text, because they are more clearly indicated and more readily discernible than the purely musical tropes.

A. THE TEXTUAL TROPES

The best-known, and possibly the oldest, examples of this kind are the troped *Kyries,* in which the traditional text *Kyrie eleison* is amplified by words that are a laudatory commentary on the word *Kyrie,* e.g., *Cunctipotens dominator coeli et angelorum, terrae, maris, et mortalium* (Almighty ruler of the heavens and the angels, the earth, the sea, and the mortals). A trope of this kind is the *Kyrie fons bonitatis,* ascribed to Tuotilo, a monk of St. Gall who died in 913.[2] Here each of the nine acclamations receives a commentary which is inserted between *Kyrie* (or *Christe*) and *eleison.* The additional text is underlaid to the melisma of the *Kyrie* (*Kyrie II*) which is thereby dissolved into a strictly syllabic melody:

FIGURE 134

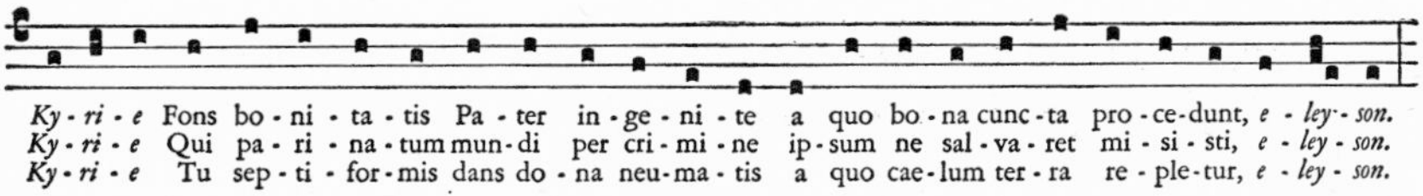

```
Ky - ri - e  Fons bo - ni - ta - tis  Pa - ter  in - ge - ni - te  a  quo bo - na cunc - ta  pro - ce - dunt, e - ley - son.
Ky - ri - e  Qui pa - ri - na - tum mun - di  per cri - mi - ne  ip - sum ne sal - va - ret  mi - si - sti, e - ley - son.
Ky - ri - e  Tu sep - ti - for - mis dans do - na neu - ma - tis  a  quo cae - lum ter - ra  re - ple - tur, e - ley - son.
```

A somewhat different practice is exemplified by the trope *Kyrie Cunctipotens dominator* (sung to the *Kyrie XIV*), which has been frequently reproduced.[3] Here both the troped and the un-troped forms are used; each line is sung twice, first with the troped text in syllabic style, then without it in melismatic style:

Cunctipotens dominator	maris et mortalium.	*Kyrie – – – – – leison.*
Qui de limo formaveras	paradiso posueras.	*Kyrie – – – – – leison.*
Humano semper generi	corde desideranti.	*Kyrie – – – – – leison.*
Tu Christe Domine	missus prodiisti.	*Christe – – – – leison.*
Et crucis patulae	vulnere detersisti.	*Christe – – – – leison.*
Nunc preces populi	clemens audi.	*Christe – – – – leison.*
Spiritus alme	Jordanem transisti.	*Kyrie – – – – – leison.*
Et discipulorum	ut ignis apparens.	*Kyrie – – – – – leison.*
Te corde precamur	implere tui amoris.	*Kyrie – – – – – leison.*

It may be noticed that the medieval sources invariably treat the acclamation as consisting of five syllables: *Ky-ri-e-lei-son* (with the melisma on the middle *e– – –*, not of seven (*Ky-ri-e e-le-i-son*), as is the modern practice.

2 According to Ekkehard IV of St. Gall (*c.* 980-1060). The trope is transcribed from the St. Martial Troper, Bibl. nat. *lat. 3549,* f. 161.

3 *Wagner III,* 504; Reese, *Music in the Middle Ages,* p. 186; O. Ursprung, *Katholische Kirchenmusik,* p. 68; Th. Gérold, *La Musique au moyen âge,* p. 55; *id., Histoire de la musique,* p. 219.

The Beneventan Ms *VI.34,* reproduced in *Pal. mus., XV,* contains fourteen *Kyrie* tropes showing the opposite arrangement of the two forms: each line is sung first without, then with the trope. Fig. 135 shows an example, the *Kyrie Deus genitor alme (Kyrie XVIII):*

FIGURE 135

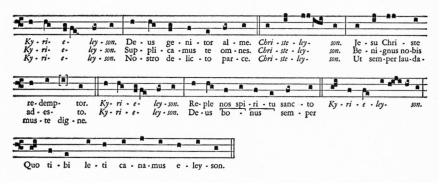

The *Kyrie Cunctipotens (Omnipotens) genitor (Kyrie IV)* found in the same manuscript has a yet fuller form, since each line of troped text closes with the word *eleyson:*

Kyrie – – – – leyson. Cunctipotens genitor . . . creator: *e – – – – leyson.*
Kyrie – – – – leyson. Fons et origo . . . . perennis: *e – – – – leyson.*
Kyrie – – – – leyson. Salvificet pietas . . . . rector: *e – – – – leyson.*

etc.[4]

Most of the *Kyrie* melodies date from the same period (tenth century and later) which saw the rise of the tropes. Moreover, many of them occur in the earliest manuscripts in a troped form, and only later without the trope. These two factors combine to obliterate to a certain extent the process involved, which is usually described as the "underlaying of the new text to a pre-existing melisma." Possibly the *Kyrie* melodies, conspicuous for their consistent use of melismas such as are not elsewhere encountered in the Mass Ordinary, were originally written for the troped texts and received their later form after the elimination of the trope. Whatever the process may have been, the remembrance of the tropes persisted in the names given to the *Kyries* and, eventually, to the complete Mass Ordinaries, e.g., *Kyrie Cunctipotens genitor* or *Missa Cunctipotens genitor* [see *L* 25, etc.].

Incontrovertible examples of textual troping are found in certain responsorial chants, such as Offertories, Alleluias, and Responsories. A most interesting source for troped Offertories and Alleluias is the eleventh-cen-

---

[4] This trope is given in *HAM,* no. 15b (after Schubiger) without the initial acclamations.

tury *Gradual* of St. Yrieix, published in vol. XIII of the *Paléographie musicale*. Here the Offertories appear in their full form, with two or three verses, as in all the sources of the tenth, eleventh, and twelfth centuries. Twenty-five of the Offertories, however, are further amplified by the addition of a *prosula* (indicated in the original *Prosl.* or *Psl.*), that is, a new text appended to the end of a verse, usually the last. In nearly all the cases the new text represents a commentary on the verse, since it starts with the closing words of the verse. For instance, the Offertory *Benedixisti* from the Third Sunday of Advent appears in St. Yrieix (p. 7) as follows:

Off. Benedixisti Domine . . . ℣. Operuisti omnia . . .

℣. Ostende nobis . . . salutare tuum *da nobis.* Remisisti.[5]

Psl. *Da nobis* potentis in celis in terris imperanti virtute tui quod olim nostri refulsit in tenebris.

The music for the *prosula* or, as we would say, for the trope, is identical with the closing passage of the verse, the final melisma being employed for the additional words of the trope. Fig. 136 shows, under (a), the close of the verse *Ostende* and, under (b), the trope:

FIGURE 136

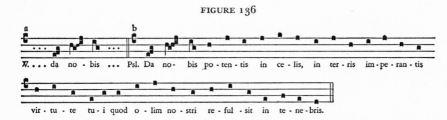

℣. . . . da no - bis . . . Psl. Da no- bis po - ten - tis in ce - lis, in ter - ris im - pe - ran - tis vir - tu - te tu - i quod o - lim no - stri re - ful - sit in te - ne - bris.

Practically all the troped Offertories of St. Yrieix show the same method, that is, the addition of a new text starting with (or closely related to) the final words of a verse (usually the last), with the music taken from the final melisma of the verse.[6]

A similar treatment is found in about a dozen Alleluias. Most of these have two tropes, one for the "Alleluia" and one for the verse. A typical example is the Alleluia *Justus ut palma* [1207], which occurs in St. Yrieix (p. 198) in the following form:[7]

Alleluia. Psl. Oramus te beate baptista Johannes, mundi lucerna ut exores pro hac Domini caterva hic congregata in natale tua devota plebs ut mereamur aula scandere regna.

[5] "Remisisti" is the indication for the repeat of the second half of the respond.

[6] Some Offertories have two *prosulae,* e.g.: Off. Super flumina Babilonis. ℣. 1. In salicibus. ℣. 2. Si oblitus fuero. Pr. Angelico adorando. ℣. 3. Memento Domine. Pr. Hierusalem civitatis magne.

[7] As is customary in modern publications, the original text is given in italics, the trope in roman.

℣. *Justus ut palma florebit et sicut cedrus multiplicabitur.*

Prosula. *Et sicut* liliorum candor in gloria manebis coram Christo, beate,
et sicut pulchritudo rosarum rutilabis magno decore. Quasi arbor in
tellure quae vocitatur nomine *cedrus, multi* florebunt sancti. Sicut sol
ante Dominum refulgentibus in celo. Exultant cum Christo astra si-
dera terraque et maria conlaudantes Deum qui in sede celesti regnant
cum Deo.

As is often the case in tropes, the second *prosula* is skillfully interspersed
between the original text, incorporating some of its words: *Et sicut . . .
cedrus multi-* . . . As for the music, this is taken entirely from the original
chant. The first trope, *Oramus te,* is set to the melody of the "Alleluia" and
the subsequent *jubilus,* while the second, *Et sicut,* employs the melody of
the second half of the verse, from "et sicut" to the close, with the long inner
melisma on "cedrus" and the equally long *jubilus* at the end. Since the
inner melisma has a repeat form, a a b b c,[8] the same form occurs in the
prosula *Et sicut:*

FIGURE 137

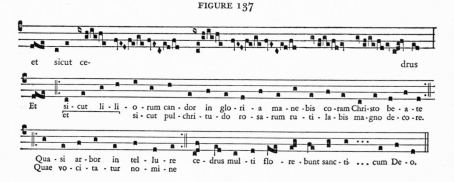

There results a double-versicle structure which is of interest because it
represents the formative principle of a particularly important and well-
known type of Alleluia trope, that is, the sequence.[9]

The method of troping employed in the *Gradual* of St. Yrieix is by no
means the only one. Since, from the musical point of view, the vast repertory of tropes has barely been tapped, it is impossible to make generalizations as to what was done in the different periods or localities. In order to
illustrate the variety of possibilities, a few more examples of Alleluia troping may be given, examples all the more interesting because they show

---

[8] See p. 388.

[9] Aside from its shortness, this *prosula* differs from the real sequences by its being
derived from a (repetitive) melisma of an Alleluia. The sequences show, on the whole, no
musical relationship to the Alleluia melody except for a short quotation of the first four
or five notes. See p. 122 [Plate V] for the Alleluia *Pascha nostrum* with two tropes.

that the sequence was by no means the only kind of Alleluia trope. One of
these, from a twelfth-century codex,[10] shows the Alleluia *Confitemini* of
Holy Saturday combined with a trope, *Jam Domnus optatas,* in a manner
similar to that illustrated by the Kyrie *Cunctipotens dominator* [see p.
431]: the trope is placed at the very beginning and is set to the music of
the "Alleluia" [759], which therefore is sung twice in succession, first with
the troped text in syllabic style, then without it in melismatic style:

FIGURE 138

Jam Dom-nus   o - pta - tas   red - dit   lau - des   pa-scha cum   Chri - sto   ad - est   fa · ve - te   qui

ca - nen - tes   Al- le-   lu-   ia.

Apparently, this arrangement, troped-plus-untroped-melody, was widely
used. Wagner gives an example in which the final melisma "dierum" of the
Offertory *Deus enim firmavit,* ℣. 2 [Ott, 18] is divided into six parts, each
part being sung first to a troping text, then as a melisma. In all these
cases we are probably justified in assuming that a responsorial performance
was involved, the troped part being sung by a soloist, the melismatic repetition as a choral answer.

Yet another method of troping, possibly of a late date, is exemplified
by a troped Alleluia *Justus germinabit* given by Pothier.[11] In this trope
the textual accretion does not form a self-contained entity added at the
beginning or the end of the chant, but consists of small fragments interpolated between the words of the verse. Each interpolation has just the right
number of syllables to take care of the melismas. Referring the reader to
the original melody [1192], we confine ourselves to an indication of the
correlation between the texts of the verse and the trope, an indication
which, in fact, makes it easy to reconstruct the melody for the trope:

Verse: *Justus*   *germi- na-*
Trope: *Justus* Johannes et dilectus, *germen* odoris palmam pudoris
V.:   *bit sicut lili-*   *um* etc.
T.: semper tene-*bit sicut lili-*um candore dealbat*um* etc.

The preceding explanations may suffice to illustrate the purely textual
type of troping. Evidently, this method, characterized by the transformation of a melisma into a syllabic passage, is restricted to ornate chants,

10 *Wagner III,* 505, from a Ms of Graz (Austria).

11 "Alleluia *Justus germinabit* avec Tropes" (*RCG,* V, 169). See also Pothier, "Offertoire
Felix namque es" (*RCG* IX, 17) for the application of the same method to an Offertory.
Furthermore, M.-A. Latil, "Les tropes de la semaine sainte" (*RCG,* XI, 73).

because these are the only ones containing melismas. Thus we find it in Alleluias, Offertories, Responsories, and *Kyrie* melodies.[12] The normal procedure seems to have been, not so much to replace the melisma by the trope, but to add the trope to it, so that the same melody occurs twice, first as a trope and then as a melisma, or the other way around.

B. THE TEXTUAL-MUSICAL TROPES

For the troping of chants lacking sufficiently extended melismas it became necessary to introduce new music together with the new text. This method was used primarily for the Introits and for the simpler chants of the Mass Ordinary, the *Gloria, Sanctus,* and *Agnus Dei*.[13] Before turning to these, we should like to call attention to an interesting procedure forming the transition between categories A and B. It is exemplified by a number of Responsories in the twelfth-century *Antiphonal* of St. Maur-des-Fossés (Paris, Bibl. nat. *lat. 12044*). Here we find troped texts of considerable extension added at the end of Responsories with a modest final melisma, far too short to take care of the entire trope. The solution of this little problem was, as may be expected, to utilize the melisma for the beginning of the trope, and to provide new music for the continuation. An example is the Responsory *Concede nobis* [*PM* 202] which appears in St. Maur-des-Fossés (p. 200ᵛ) in the following form (the strokes in the *prosa* are added in order to clarify the details of its structure; see p. 448, fn. 10).

℞. Concede nobis Domine, . . . ut ad eorum pervenire *mereamur so-cietatem.*

℣. Adjuvent nos eorum merita . . . nobis veniam non deneges peccati. Gloria Patri et Filio et Spiritui Sancto.

Prosa: Perpetua/*mereamur* gaudia/paradysi in aula
        Quam superna majestas/claritate illustrat;

        In qua phalanx/angelica/cum turma gaudet apostolica
        Laureata/et milia/martirum datur palma rosa.

        Veneranda emicat/confessorum caterva
        Candidata viridat/virginalis chorea.

        Salve sancta/tibi proclamat/trinitas
        Quae et vota/nostra sic reddat/placita,

        Illorum ut per merita
        Optatam adipiscemur *societatem.*

[12] Very rarely in Graduals.

[13] Though Introit tropes are very common, I am not aware of any instance of a troped Communion. Its absence (or rarity) is probably explained by liturgical considerations, as is also the case with the *Credo*. As a curiosity, mention may be made of a troped *Credo* in an Office of the thirteenth century; see H. Villetard, *L'Office de Pierre de Corbeil* (1907), p. 172.

The *prosa* is an extended poem in the form of a commentary on the two last words of the respond, *mereamur societatem,* the first of which appears at the beginning, the second at the end of the trope. The music starts with the final melisma of the respond, on "mereamur," which is just long enough to cover the first line of the poem, and is repeated for the second line. For the remaining part of the poem the music is freely invented in such a manner that two successive lines are sung to the same melody. The result is a musical form exactly like a sequence, all the more since the first word, "Perpetua," and the last, "societatem," stand outside of the repeat scheme, obviously in imitation of the single versicle at the beginning as well as at the end of a sequence. Fig. 139 shows portions of the respond and of the trope:

FIGURE 139

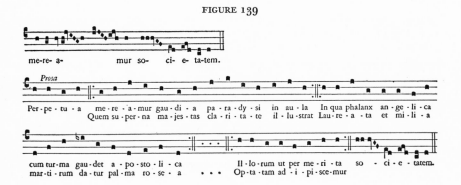

There are at least five other tropes of the same type in the *Antiphonal* of St. Maur-des-Fossés:

p. 145v: ℟. *Inter natos,* melisma "preparavit in heremo"
           Prosa: *Prepara Johannes*

p. 148v: ℟. *Sanctus Domini confessor,* melisma "ante Dominum"
           Prosa: *Angelica condona nobis*

p. 162v: ℟. *Conserva famulos,* melisma "redde beatos"
           Prosa: *Benigne Deus*

p. 163r: ℟. *Beatus martyr Domini,* melisma "promeruit"
           Prosa: *Pro meritis*

p. 214v: ℟. *Clementis Christi gratiam,* melisma "antistitis"
           Prosa: *Adesto Domine*

They illustrate a method of troping which, however limited in time and locale it may have been, shows two traits of special interest: first, the transfer of the sequence form from the Alleluia to the Responsory; and second, a method of borrowing that forms the transition from the textual tropes (which take their entire music from the mother chant) to the textual-musical tropes (which provide new music for the additional text).[14]

As has been pointed out, these occur in the less ornate chants of the Mass Proper and Mass Ordinary, that is, in the Introits, *Gloria, Sanctus,* and *Agnus Dei.* As for the Introits, those of Advent and Nativity in particular were frequently adorned with tropes, none more frequently than *Puer natus est nobis* from the third Mass of the Nativity. The preferred (if not exclusive) method was to interpolate fragments of new text between the original words and, at the same time, new passages of music between those of the traditional chant. Fig. 140 shows the beginning of two Introit tropes from the afore-mentioned Beneventan Codex *VI. 34 (Pal. mus., XV).*

FIGURE 140

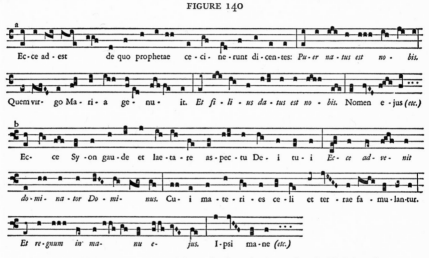

a. Introit *Puer natus* (Nativity) b. Introit *Ecce advenit* (Epiphany)

A comparison of the new and the old sections clearly indicates a tendency toward assimilation and integration. The new music employs the same style (neumatic), the same range and tonality as the traditional chant, and occasionally even borrows a short motive from it. The same intention is evident in other tropes of Italian derivation, for instance three Introit tropes published by A. Latil from an eleventh-century Ms of Montecas-

---

[14] For other "Responsory sequences" see Y. Delaporte, "Un tropo inedito del responsorio *Felix namque*" (*Rass. Greg.*, XII, 225) and the trope *Consors merito,* from the Responsory *O beati viri,* shown in *Wagner III,* 509. The latter, found in the *Antiphonal* of St. Maur-des-Fossés, has the form a bb cc dd e. In distinction to the previously mentioned examples from this source its music is taken entirely from the long final melisma of the Responsory, which has the same repetition form as the *prosa.*

sino.[15] There are, however, tropes indicative of the opposite tendency, that is, to create a contrast of tonality between the troped and the original passages. An interesting example is a *Puer natus* trope from a French Ms (Bibl. nat., *nouv. acquis. 1235*, f. 184'), portions of which are shown in Fig. 141.[16] Wagner comments on this trope by saying that "without doubt,

FIGURE 141

the contrast between the A-tonality of the trope and the G-tonality of the Introit is intentional." Possibly this contrast was enhanced by some sort of *alternatim* performance, with different singers for the trope and for the Introit proper.

The intercalation method of the Introit tropes was also employed for the *Glorias, Sanctus,* and *Agnus.* It will suffice to quote the beginning of a *Gloria* trope (also called *Laudes*) from Benevent *VI. 34* (Pal. mus., XV, 238):

Gloria in excelsis Deo. Et in terra pax hominibus bonae voluntatis. Laus tua Deus resonet coram te Rex. *Laudamus te.* Qui venisti propter nos Rex angelorum Deus. *Benedicimus te.* In sede majestatis tuae. *Adoramus te.* Veneranda Trinitas. *Glorificamus te.* (etc.).

The cultivation of tropes reached a climax in the twelfth century, at the monastery of St. Martial in Limoges. Here the tropes often adopt features of poetry, as in the following *Sanctus* trope in which the inserted passages of text are rhymed:[17]

15 See A. Latil, "I tropi di Natale, di S. Stefano e di S. Giovanni" (*Rass. Greg.*, II, 5). For another Introit trope see: Y. D., "Le Trope *Arbiter aeternus*" (*RG*, XXIV, 140). Tuotilo's famous Introit trope for Christmas, *Hodie cantandus* (*Wagner III*, 511; also in Schering, *Geschichte der Musik in Beispielen*, no. 2) is a fairly extended text, somewhat in the nature of a dialogue, which serves as an introduction to the Introit: "Hodie cantandus est nobis puer. . . . Hic enim est quem praesagus . . . praenotavit sicque praedixit: *Puer natus est . . .*"

16 See *Wagner III*, 511.

17 Paris, B. N. *lat. 3549*, f. 163r.

Sanctus Fons vivus vitae	Qua vivunt Israhelitae
Sanctus Panis adultorum	Fidei mel, lac puerorum
Sanctus Dominus Deus Sabbaoth	
Solamen mentis	Mundum calcare volentis.
Pleni sunt celi et terrae gloria tua.	
Osanna, Vires enerves	Hostiles et tuas serves,
In excelsis.	

The music of this trope (as well as of many others of the School of St. Martial) is interesting because of its rather ornate and melismatic style. The original purpose of the textual accretions was to transform the long melismas of the chant into purely syllabic passages. In fact, the purely textual tropes (i.e., those which do not introduce new music) are all essentially syllabic, although not to the complete exclusion of occasional groups of two or three notes, as for instance in the St. Yrieix trope *Et sicut liliorum* [see p. 434]. In the free tropes (i.e., those which have new text as well as music) restriction to syllabic style was not necessary. Most of these show the tendency to assimilate the musical style of the trope to that of the mother chant. Thus, the Introit tropes are written in the neumatic style characteristic of the Introits, while the tropes of *Gloria* and *Sanctus* melodies imitate the quasi-syllabic style that prevails in the Ordinary of the Mass. These sensible restrictions and artistic considerations were no longer observed in the twelfth-century tropes of St. Martial, many of which are almost as melismatic as an untroped Gradual or Responsory. Following is the beginning of the above-mentioned *Sanctus* trope:

FIGURE 142

Sa-   nctus. Fons   vi-   vus   vi-   tae   *(etc.)*

The melodies for the first and second "Sanctus" are identical with those of *Sanctus XII,* transposed from d to g. However, the subsequent passages of the *Sanctus* text seem to be as freely composed as the troped sections.

Many of the St. Martial tropes are complete poems inserted in a traditional chant, as, for instance, the trope to the Christmas Gradual *Viderunt omnes:*

Viderunt Hemanuel	Patris unigenitum
In ruinam Israel	Et salutem positum
Hominem in tempore	Verbum in principio
Urbis quam fundaverat	Natum in palacio
	omnes fines terrae . . .

This trope, as well as others of a similar kind, occurs in the St. Martial sources as the tenor of a two-voice organum.[18] No less interesting are the numerous *Benedicamus Domino* tropes, extended poems which reveal their ancestry in concluding lines such as *Benedicat chorus celorum Domino* or *Benedicamus socii Domino.*[19] These poetic tropes indicate the increasing emancipation of the tropes from their liturgical bond, and point in the direction of other repertories, particularly that of the conductus.

C. THE MUSICAL TROPES

We finally turn to an examination of the purely musical tropes, that is, of melismas inserted in traditional chants. As was mentioned at the beginning of this chapter, modern musicologists are inclined to consider these as the earliest examples of troping and as indicative of the original meaning of the term; unfortunately, incontrovertible examples of this kind of trope are not too plentiful and not too easy to discover. To prove their existence, we would have to find chants which occur in some sources, preferably the older ones, without a melisma that they show in a later source. Probably examples of this kind exist, but at present the phenomenon of the purely musical tropes has not yet been as fully investigated and as clearly demonstrated as that of the tropes involving a textual accretion.

The most fertile soil for the melismatic tropes seems to have been the Responsories of Matins. In our study of these chants mention has been made of the *neuma triplex* of the Responsory *Descendit de caelis* from the Nativity, three extended melismas that occur at the end of the respond, to the words "fabricae mundi," when the respond is repeated after the verse and the Doxology [see p. 343]. One has only to compare these *neumata* with the corresponding place of the original melody, that is, of the respond as sung at the beginning, in order to realize that we are here in the presence of melismatic insertions that bear all the characteristics of a purely musical trope. Amalarius informs us that originally this triple *neuma* belonged to the Responsory *In medio ecclesiae* for the feast of St. John the Evangelist (now for the Common of a Doctor, *PM* 227; also, with a different verse, *LR* 203), and that "modern" singers transferred it to the Responsory *Descendit.*[20] Nor are these the only Responsories giving evidence of a musical trope: an equally clear example is *Ecce jam coram te* from the Feast of St. Stephen, in which the word "intercedere" has a very modest

18 See Apel, *Notation of Polyphonic Music,* p. 211 (facsimile); *HAM,* no. 27a (transcription).

19 See H. Spanke and H. Anglés, "Die Londoner St. Martial-Conductushandschrift" (*Butlleti de la Biblioteca de Catalunya,* VIII [1928-32], 280).

20 For more details, see *New Oxford History of Music,* II, 142.

melisma in the initial respond, and one enormously enlarged in the final repeat of this respond [*PM* 31f]:

FIGURE 143

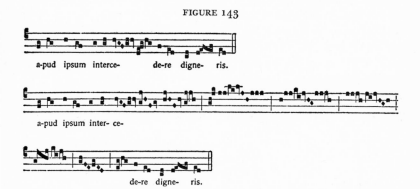

a-pud ipsum interce-   de-re digne-   ris.

a-pud ipsum inter- ce-

de-re digne-   ris.

In our discussion of the Responsories we have called attention to the various examples of "free creation" within melodies that otherwise conform more or less to the standard type. Very likely, all these rather extraneous melismas are tropes, although in most cases the melodies have not been preserved in their "original" form. However, the striking contrast of style that exists between the melismas and the main part of the music marks them rather clearly as later interpolations, in other words, as musical tropes.

THE SEQUENCES

The sequence is usually described as the trope connected with the Alleluia. Although this is a serviceable explanation, it should not be interpreted too rigidly in the sense of a definition. As we have seen in the preceding section, Alleluia tropes exist which are not sequences at all. The sequences are distinguished from these by their special form, and this, therefore, must also be included in the definition. Moreover, to consider the sequence as a subspecies of the trope is a view that, although permissible from the methodological point of view, can hardly be maintained on historical grounds. We have no evidence that the tropes, as a general type, existed before the sequences and that the latter branched off from the former. Certainly, the term *sequentia* (or its early equivalent, *prosa*) is documented at a much earlier time than the term *tropus*. Considering all these facts, we should like to define the sequence as an addition to the Alleluia characterized by a certain repeat structure.[1]

Probably the earliest writer to mention the term "sequence" is Amalarius

[1] Concerning a few sequences which have no repeats see pp. 454f.

who, in his *De ecclesiasticis officiis,* speaks, in connection with the *versus alleluia,* about "haec jubilatio quam cantores sequentiam vocant."[2] Here the term sequence clearly has the meaning of a melisma without text, and this indeed was probably the original form of the sequence, as we shall see. Unfortunately, it is not clear whether Amalarius' *jubilatio-sequentia* is the relatively short *jubilus* traditionally attached to the end of the Alleluia and its verse, or the much more extended melismas that are the source of the sequence. The latter interpretation could perhaps be defended on the ground that the *jubilus* forms an integral part of the Alleluia structure, while the term *sequentia* (things that follow) suggests something in the nature of an extraneous addition. At any rate, there is little doubt that in the earlier part of the ninth century the practice of amplifying the Alleluias by the addition of long melismas existed. Obviously it is to these melismas that the monk of St. Gall, Notker Balbulus (*c.* 840-912) refers in the famous *prooemium* to the collection of his sequences.[3] He says that, when he was a young man, he had to sing *longissimae melodiae,* which he found difficult to remember. A monk from a monastery of Gimedia (Jumièges, near Rouen) came to St. Gall with an *Antiphonary* in which some verses were adapted (?) to the sequences ("aliqui versus ad sequentias erant modulati"). He found them, however, not too satisfactory, and therefore started to write some of his own. Finally, his teacher Iso advised him that it would be best to have only one tone to each syllable of the text.

It is difficult to understand how, on the basis of this report, Notker could have been made to appear as the "inventor of the sequence," as is frequently the case in books on music history. Fully acknowledging the work that was done before him, he described himself as the one who raised the sequence to a higher level of artistic perfection, a claim fully borne out by the great beauty of his poems as well as by the skill with which he adapted them to melodies that probably were not his own.

Notker called his poems "hymns" (the title of his collection is *Liber hymnorum*), but this name was soon superseded, in St. Gall and in Germany generally, by the term *sequentia,* which thus was transferred from the melismatic to the full-text type. In France the latter was called *prosa,* a name which, as we have seen, was later also applied to the textual tropes of Offertories, Responsories, etc. Occasionally we find in French sources the designation *sequentia cum prosa,* a rather unequivocal in-

[2] *De Officiis,* book iii, ch. 16 (*Patr. lat.* 105, p. 1123; ed. Hanssens, II, 304).

[3] Fully reprinted, e.g., in H. Husmann, "Die St. Galler Sequenztradition bei Notker und Ekkehard" (*Acta musicologica,* XXVI, 6; with commentary). Notker's *prooemium,* which Wagner and particularly Bannister (*Anal. hymn.* 53, p. xiii) regarded as of doubtful authenticity and trustworthiness, is now generally accepted as a genuine and highly informative document; see, e.g., Handschin in *New Oxford History,* II, 147f. The question is also thoroughly discussed in W. von den Steinen, *Notker der Dichter* (1948).

dication that we are dealing with melismas (*sequentia*) to which was added a text (*prosa*).[4] In order to simplify the distinction between the forms without and with text, the term sequela has been introduced and generally accepted for the melismatic type, with the term sequence being reserved for those with a full text.[5] We shall see later that an intermediate type existed in which only portions of the melisma were provided with a text.

The place for the sequence (or sequela) was at the end of the Alleluia, following its repetition after the verse: A V A S. The overall structure is therefore the same which we have found in the Offertory tropes from St. Yrieix (p. 433) or in the Responsory tropes from St. Maur-des-Fossés (p. 436) particularly, which are obviously modelled after the sequence. Not a few sequence melodies are named after the verse of the Alleluia to which they were attached, as, *Dominus regnavit, Dominus in Syna, Adducentur, Benedicta sit,* etc. Others, however, carry strange names such as *Puella turbata* (disturbed girl), *Cignea* (swan-like, swan-song?), *Cithara* (cither, lyre), *Duo tres* (two three), or names suggestive of places of origin, such as *Metensis* (Metz), *Bavverisca* (Bavaria?), *Romana, Graeca,* and *Occidentana.* As in the hymns, a given melody was very frequently used for a number of texts, and occasionally the same text occurs with different melodies.[6]

As is well known, the fundamental principle of the sequence is what has been called "progressive repetition," that is, a structure consisting of a succession of paired lines (double-versicles) both of which are sung to the same melody, usually with a single line at the beginning and at the end:

a bb cc dd ee ff g

In order to provide a firm basis for the subsequent discussions, a typical example is reproduced in Fig. 144, the sequence *Psallat ecclesia,* one of the few unquestionably authentic sequences of Notker.[7]

---

[4] The term *prosa,* a late-Latin word derived from *prorsus,* straight, may not have had the same meaning as the modern word prose. At any rate, the *prosa* is definitely a poetic type of Latin literature.

[5] See A. Hughes, *Anglo-French Sequelae* (1934), p. 4. Much better terms for the two types would be *prosa* (with text) and sequence (without text); see H. Husmann, "Sequenz und Prosa" (*Annales musicologiques,* II [1954], 61 ff, esp. p. 63).

[6] An extreme case is the melody *Justus ut palma,* with at least twenty-six different texts; see Hughes, p. 49. See also the list in C.A. Moberg, *Ueber die schwedischen Sequenzen* (1927), I, 151ff which, although not intended to be all-inclusive, provides an insight into the general state of affairs.

[7] According to Notker's own report, it was the first sequence representing the perfection of his attempts: *Hocque modo instructus secunda mox vice dictavi Psallat ecclesia mater illibata* (thus instructed [by his teacher Iso] I wrote soon, as my second [work], *Psallat ecclesia* . . .). For the music see Moberg (fn. 6), II, no. 57; for the full text (Moberg gives only the first line of the double-versicles), *Anal. hymn.* 53, p. 398.

FIGURE 144

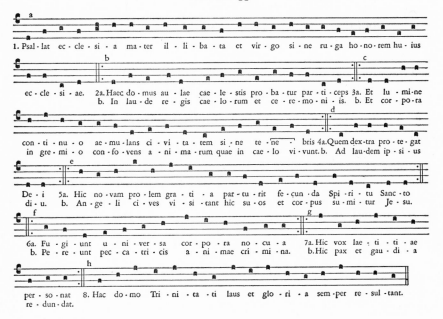

REMARKS:

1. This sequence consists of eight sections, all of which are repeated except for the first and the last. The sections vary greatly in length. Thus, sections d, e, f, and g consist respectively of eight, nineteen, thirteen, and nine notes.

2. In the double-versicles the corresponding lines of text offer many points of interest. Naturally, they agree in number of syllables, a number identical with that of the notes in the section. However, there is much more involved than a mere counting of syllables. There is also a close correspondence between the smaller textual units that occur in the longer lines, for instance, in section e. Usually the correspondence extends even to the individual words, so that a word of three syllables, e.g., "gratia" is matched by another word of three syllables, "visitant," or, at least, by two words together having three syllables, as in "parturit" and "hic suos." In the present sequence there is only one deviation from this principle, that is, at the end of b, where two words of three syllables each, "probatur particeps" have their counterpart in "et ceremoniis." Finally, there is also in many cases a correspondence of accentuation, as at the end of versicle e:

> fe-cún-da   Spí-ri-tu   Sánc-to
> et cór-pus   sú-mi-tur   Jésu.

This principle, however, is not too strictly observed, as appears from such correspondence as "Hic nóvam—Ángeli" and "párturit—hic súos" in the same section, or "univérsa—peccátricis" in section f. In fact, the present sequence is perhaps somewhat exceptional in its fairly complete observance of identical accentuation in corresponding lines. However, there can hardly be a question that the numerous instances of identical accentuation in two corresponding lines, in this and in other sequences, are not merely the result of coincidence.

3. A comparison of our sequence with its purely vocal form, the sequela, shows that Notker, in writing his text, followed the melody not only in its structure-at-large and general outlines, but also in such details as the grouping of neumes. Quite frequently, a word of three syllables appears under a neume of three notes, and a four-syllable word is allocated to a four-note neume. Fig. 145 shows the melodic form of our sequence as given in A. Hughes' *Anglo-French Sequelae*.[8] Although the sequela differs in

FIGURE 145

32. LÆTATUS SUM

[8] P. 51. The sequela is named after the Alleluia *Laetatus sum* from the second Sunday of Advent, from which it is derived. The letter *x* (Gothic for *s, semel,* once) denotes the sections that are sung once, while *d (duplex, denuo)* indicates repetition of the section. The sequela (without text) occurs, among others, in the twelfth-century Troper of Moissac (Paris, B. N. *nouv. acq. lat. 1871*), on fol. 76ᵛ, a facsimile reproduction of which is given in F. Gennrich's *Grundriss einer Formenlehre des mittelalterlichen Liedes* (1932). Here the melody has the title *Regnantem*, after a French sequence, *Regnantem sempiterna* written to the same melody. In both sequelae the music corresponding to section b of the sequence is missing.

some detail from the melody of the sequence, the agreement between neumatic groups and words can be noticed in a number of places, e.g., in section e:

FIGURE 146

Hic novam prolem gratia parturit fecundo Spiritu Sancto

These explanations show that in the writing of sequence texts such as Notker's *Psallat ecclesia* there is much more involved than a mere counting of syllables, much more than a mere transformation of the melisma into a strictly syllabic declamation. There are also involved numerous considerations of detail which actually amount to versification, a versification all the more interesting because it is so much more subtle than that of the hymns.[9]

With this specific sequence-sequela as a point of departure, we may now turn to a consideration of the general aspects of the field. The type of sequence exemplified by *Psallat ecclesia,* usually referred to as the "oldest sequence," prevailed throughout the ninth, tenth, and eleventh centuries. After a transitional stage, designated as the "intermediate sequence," there developed, in the twelfth century, a new type—the "late sequence" of Adam de St. Victor (d. 1192). In strong contrast to the old type, the sequences of Adam and his successors are in a strictly poetic versification. Consisting of a number of stanzas, all in the same meter, their texts are practically indistinguishable from those of hymns; only the musical treatment characterizes them as sequences [pp. 460ff]. The "intermediate" sequences show traits foreshadowing the strict versification of the late sequences.

The old sequences, which deserve our main attention, were cultivated in Germany (St. Gall) as well as in France, not so much perhaps in its northern part where they may have originated (Jumièges), as in monasteries of southern France, at Moissac and particularly at Limoges (St. Martial). Close relationships existed between France and England, and, to a lesser extent, between Germany and Italy, resulting in two rather clearly distinguished repertories, an Anglo-French (perhaps, more properly, Franco-English) and a Germano-Italian.

A distinctive trait of the French and English sequences is that their lines usually close on *-a* (or *-am, -at,* etc.), in assonance with the last syllable of *allelui-a.* A number of them also begin with the word *Alleluia,* thus

9 See G. Reichert, "Strukturprobleme der älteren Sequenz" (*Deutsche Vierteljahrsschrift für Literaturwissenschaft,* XXIII [1949], 227).

revealing a particularly close relationship to the mother chant, for instance:[10]

1. *Alleluia*

2. a. *Laus beata* b. *Qui ab alta*
   vita paxque perfecta, *descendistis ad ima*
3. a. *Visitare nostra.* b. *Dignatus nostram*
   Salus aeterna, *moderare camoenam*
   exaudi fidelia *pietatis gratia.*

etc.

6. *In patriam*
quo nos introducas beatam,
qua nobis cuncta sint serena
et pacatissima
adfatim per saecla.

This is one of the many sequences sung to the melody *Adducentur*, so called because it is derived from the Alleluia *Adducentur* [1217] from the Common of a Virgin Martyr (originally probably from the Feast of St. Agnes). The melody could also be, and, in fact, is sometimes designated as *Veni Domine*, with reference to the Alleluia *Veni Domine* [354] from the Fourth Sunday of Advent, which is practically identical with the Alleluia *Adducentur*, particularly in the Alleluia-plus-*jubilus* section. Following is the beginning of the Alleluia and that of the sequence:[11]

FIGURE 147

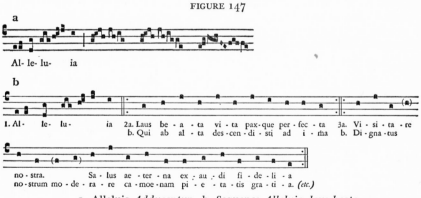

a. Alleluia *Adducentur* b. Sequence *Alleluia, laus beata*

This Alleluia and the derivative sequence may also serve as a point of departure for a question which is of particular interest from the musical

---

[10] *Anal. hymn.* 53, p. 11. This standard collection of *Sequentiae aetatis antiquissimae* (sequences of the earliest epoch) includes twenty-seven sequences beginning with *Alleluia*. All of them show the assonance on -*a*. This is also fully observed in the "Responsory-sequence" *Perpetua mereamur gaudia*, p. 436, in which the assonant subdivisions are indicated by strokes.

[11] For the sequela, see Hughes, p. 21, also the detailed discussion on pp. 77-127.

point of view, that is, the relationship between the two melodies involved. In the present example this relationship is confined to the initial "Alleluia," but possibly extends to the first phrase of the *jubilus* (sequence: "Laus beata . . . perfecta"). After this, however, the sequence melody continues entirely independently from the *jubilus* as well as from the melody for the verse. This is the normal state of affairs. In practically all cases the agreement between the sequence melody and the parent Alleluia (if this can be identified, which is frequently the case) is confined to their beginnings, often not even to the full "Alleluia" but only to its *incipit* of the first five or six notes. Of course, there may be occasional similarities in the further course, but these are hardly ever clear enough to give the impression of deliberate imitation.[12]

Of special interest in the French-English repertory is the existence of a number of examples indicative of an intermediate stage between the sequela and the sequence, the so-called sequelae with *verba* (words).[13] In these a text is underlaid, not to the entire melody, but only to some of its sections. A famous example is the sequela *Fulgens praeclara,* a melody consisting of sixteen sections (all repeated except for the first and the last), but with a text, *Rex in aeternum,* underlaid to only three sections, the fifth, the ninth, and the thirteenth [Hughes, p. 41]. Plate VIII represents this melody as it appears in the manuscript Paris, B. N. *17436.*[14] Hughes' publication contains four other sequelae with *verba, Adest una* with *Ecce*

---

[12] Besseler, in *Musik des Mittelalters und der Renaissance,* p. 84, gives a rather unconvincing reconstruction designed to show that the entire melody of Notker's *Psallat ecclesia* is derived from the Alleluia *Laetatus sum.* Equally unconvincing is a similar reconstruction by Gennrich (*Formenlehre,* p. 97), in which the Alleluia *Levita Laurentius* is literally torn to pieces in order to make it fit the sequence *Alleluia Concelebremus.* A clear case of more extended borrowing is the sequence *Grates nunc omnes,* which not only begins with the *incipit* of the Alleluia *Dominus dixit* (melisma for "Allelu-," reduced to f-g-a a-g a-c'c') but also closes with the last three neumes of the *jubilus* g-c'a b-a a-g); see *Wagner III,* 485. Probably the most extensive borrowing occurs in the sequela *Dulce lignum* (sequences *Salve crux* and others for the Feast of the Holy Cross) which makes uses of the entire "Alleluia" section (including the *jubilus*) of the Alleluia *Dulce lignum;* see Hughes, p. 37.

[13] They are also called *versus ad sequentias* (Bannister, in *Anal. hymn.* 53, p. 37), a term taken from Notker's report, according to which the visiting monk from Jumièges brought with him an *antiphonarium . . ., in quo aliqui versus ad sequentias erant modulati.* Bannister and his collaborator, Cl. Blume, interpreted the term *versus ad sequentias* to refer to the part-text form, for which, consequently, they claimed historical priority over the full-text sequence. This interpretation has been challenged [see Husmann's article (fn. 5), p. 89]. At any rate, our designation "intermediate stage" should be understood as a technical and not necessarily as a chronological designation.

[14] This is the *Gradual* and *Antiphonary* of Compiègne [see List of Sources, p. 53, no. 10) in which an eleventh-century scribe entered melodies on some empty pages. The page shown also contains two purely melismatic sequelae, *Gloriosa* and *Eia recolamus.* The *Fulgens praeclara* with *Rex in aeternum* occurs also on a page from the tenth-century Winchester Troper (Oxford, Bodl. Libr. *775*) which is reproduced in W. H. Frere, *The Winchester Troper* (1894) and in Suñol's *Paléographie grégorienne,* p. 289.

puerpera (p. 22), *Adorabo major* with *Suscipe laus* (p. 23), *Via lux* with
Via lux veritas (p. 73), and *Pretiosa* with *Jam nunc intonant* (p. 65). The
last-named is exceptional in having only one line of text for each of the
verba sections; this, however, is always preceded by a section having the
same music without text. The double-versicle structure is therefore preserved, as shown in the following diagram, where the sections with texts
are represented by italic letters:

a b*b* c*c* d*d* e*e* f*f* g*g* h*h* i*i* k*k* l*l* m

   c: Jam nunc intonant praeconia
   d: Christum Dominum laudantia per saecula
   f: Cujus clara rutilant dona,
       quis aeternae vitae consequimur magna praemia.
   h: Quam beata sanctorum sunt agmina,
   k: Trinitatem sanctam cernentia
       in gloria aeterna.

It should be noticed that all these sequelae with *verba* were, at a later
time, provided with a full text, in the manner of a normal sequence. The
interesting fact is that these texts are not entirely new, but contain the
original *verba* exactly at the place where they occur in the original form.
Thus, the melody *Pretiosa* is found with a sequence *Alleluia Resultet tellus*
which begins as follows:[15]

a. Alleluia

b. Resultet tellus et alta	**b.** In laudem patris superi
caelorum machina	regentis aethera,
c. Cui angelorum chori	**c.** Ipsi etiam et nostra
concordes canunt odas	*jam nunc intonant praeconia*
in poli regia.	voce sonora.

etc.

In fact, a number of sequences exist to this melody (as well as to the others
mentioned above); all of them incorporate the same *verba* at the same
places. Obviously we have here examples of successive troping: first the
addition, to the sequela, of words at separate places; then the filling in of
the "empty" spaces by a continuous text, the full sequence.

Turning now to the purely musical aspects of the French sequences (or,
for that matter, sequelae), we may first consider their form. The great
majority of them adhere strictly to the basic scheme of a series of double-
versicles, preceded and concluded by a single versicle: a bb cc . . . gg h. In
a few cases the repeat is varied, either by an inner amplification, as in
Adducentur, or by a final extension as in *Benedicta sit:*

---

15 *Anal. hymn.* 53, p. 198.

Adducentur (Hughes, p. 21): a bb cc' dd' dd' ee' f
Benedicta (Hughes, p. 28):   a bb cc dd ee' ff g

Slightly greater deviations from the norm occur in *Justus ut palma* (p. 48), which closes with a double-versicle; *Hic est sonus* (p. 44) with the form a bb cc' dd e ff; *Pura Deum* (p. 67), which has two single versicles between the double-versicles; and *Cignea* (p. 31), unique because of its repeated use of a short refrain after some of the double-versicles. Three melodies, *Excita Domine* (p. 40), *Exsultate Deo* (p. 41), and *Ostende minor* (p. 61) stand apart from the rest because they completely lack double-versicles. On the other hand, there are a few melodies which restate the music of one section in another. One of these is the above-mentioned *Adducentur*, which employs identical music (dd') for two consecutive sections, so that the same phrase is sung four times in succession. In others we find identical music at separate places, e.g.:

Pura Deum (p. 67): a bb cc' d ee' d ee' ff g
Chorus (p. 29):   a bb cc dd ee cc ff gg hh i

Finally, it may be noticed that a number of phrases are repetitive in themselves, employing the forms p p q or p p q q r which are known to us from the melismas of the Alleluias and of the Offertory verses. The former scheme occurs in phrase d of *Pura Deum* and in phrases d and f of *Chorus*, the latter in the fifth and sixth sections of *Lyra* (p. 53).

In order to provide an insight into the rather complex structure and multiple melodic relationships encountered in some of the more "developed" sequences, there is reproduced in Fig. 148 the sequence *Ad celebres* for the Feast of St. Michael. It originated in France, probably in the tenth century, but was widely used also in England, Italy, Germany, and Sweden.[16] Textually this consists of ten versicles, all paired except for the first, and varying greatly in length. The assonance on -*a* is observed for the full versicles as well as for their major subdivisions (indicated by a small stroke on the staff). The text does not start with *Alleluia* (which, however, appears at the end), but possibly this is symbolically represented by the succession of the vowels of the first verse: *Ad celebres . . . cuncta = a e u a.* Turning to the music, we find interesting relationships between the various sections. Sections 3 and 4 employ exactly the same melody, as do also 5 and 6, except for an extension at the beginning of 6. Moreover, the melody for 3 (and 4) is nothing but an expanded version of that for 2, so that essentially the same melody appears six times in succession. Verse 8

16 Reproduced from Moberg, II, no. 31. Some minor differences in the repeated sections have been disregarded, a procedure all the more justifiable (or excusable) in view of the numerous variants in the different sources. For the complete text see *Anal. hymn.* 53, p. 306, for the melody, *Mater sequentiarum*, Hughes, p. 56.

is very long, and is sung to a bar-form melody. The same form is employed for the next verse, 9, which borrows its conclusion from the preceding melody. The last verse is shown with a continuous melody, but this also consists of two closely related halves. These various relationships and structural details are indicated in the following schematic representation of *Ad celebres:*

$$a\ b^6\ c^4\ d^2\ e^2 \qquad\qquad f^2 \qquad\qquad gg'$$
$$e = ppqr \qquad f = ssr$$

FIGURE 148

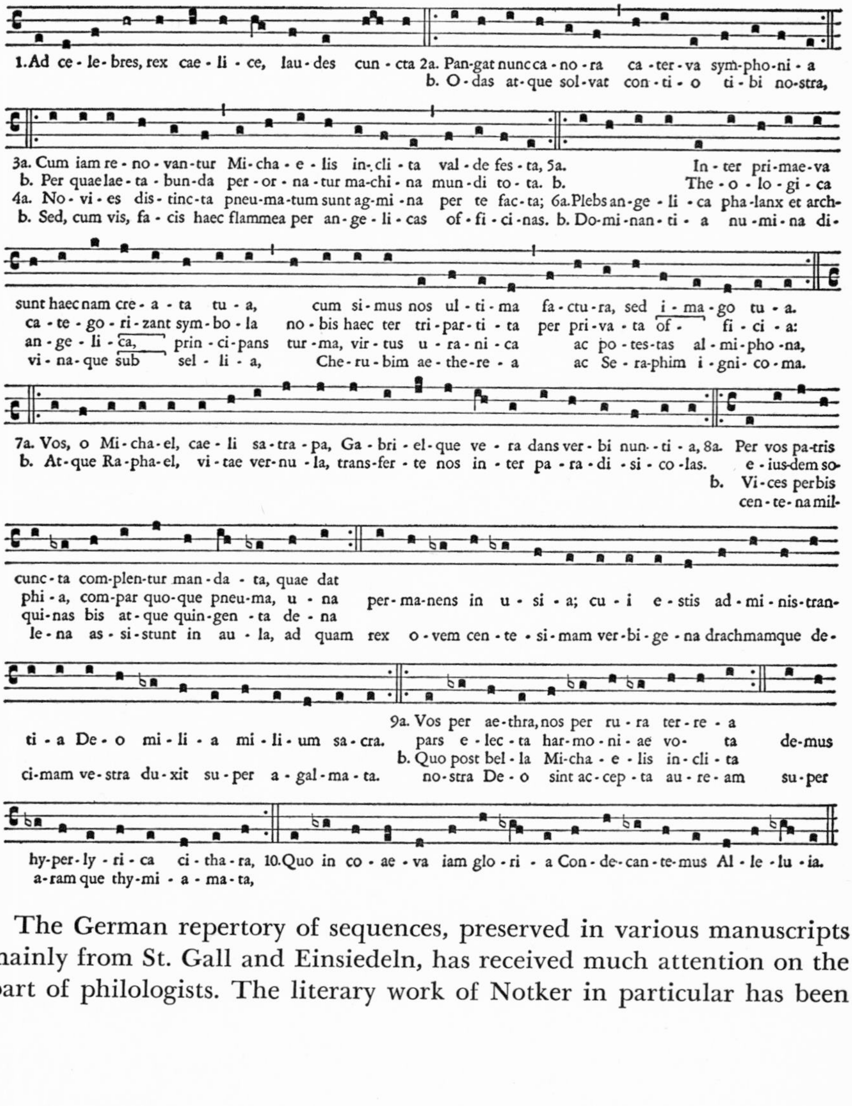

1.Ad ce - le - bres, rex cae - li - ce, lau - des cun - cta 2a. Pan-gat nunc ca - no - ra ca - ter - va sym-pho - ni - a
   b. O - das at - que sol - vat con - ti - o ti - bi no - stra,

3a. Cum iam re - no - van-tur Mi - cha - e - lis in - cli - ta val - de fes - ta, 5a.   In - ter pri - mae - va
  b. Per quae lae - ta - bun - da per - or - na - tur ma-chi - na mun - di to - ta. b.   The - o - lo - gi - ca
4a. No - vi - es dis - tinc - ta pneu-ma-tum sunt ag - mi - na per te fac - ta; 6a. Plebs an - ge - li - ca pha-lanx et arch-
  b. Sed, cum vis, fa - cis haec flammea per an - ge - li - cas of - fi - ci - nas. b. Do-mi-nan - ti - a nu - mi - na di-

sunt haec nam cre - a - ta tu - a,   cum si - mus nos ul - ti - ma fa - ctu - ra, sed i - ma - go tu - a.
ca - te - go - ri-zant sym - bo - la   no - bis haec ter tri - par - ti - ta per pri - va - ta of - fi - ci - a:
an - ge - li - ca,   prin - ci-pans   tur - ma, vir - tus u - ra - ni - ca ac po - tes-tas al - mi-pho - na,
vi - na - que sub   sel - li - a,   Che - ru - bim ae - the - re - a ac Se - ra-phim i - gni - co - ma.

7a. Vos, o Mi - cha - el, cae - li sa-tra - pa, Ga - bri - el - que ve - ra dans ver - bi nun - ti - a, 8a. Per vos pa-tris
  b. At - que Ra - pha - el, vi - tae ver - nu - la, trans-fer - te nos in - ter pa - ra - di - si - co - las.   e - ius-dem so-
                                                               b. Vi - ces per bis
                                                                cen - te - na mil-

cunc - ta com-plen-tur man - da - ta, quae dat
phi - a, com-par quo-que pneu-ma, u - na   per - ma-nens in u - si - a; cu - i e - stis ad - mi - nis-tran-
qui - nas bis at - que quin-gen - ta de - na
le - na as - si-stunt in au - la, ad quam rex o - vem cen - te - si-mam ver-bi - ge - na drachmamque de-

                                            9a. Vos per ae-thra, nos per ru - ra ter - re - a
ti - a De - o mi - li - a mi - li - um sa - cra.   pars e - lec - ta har-mo - ni - ae vo - ta   de-mus
                                           b. Quo post bel - la Mi-cha - e - lis in - cli - ta
ci-mam ve - stra du - xit su - per a - gal - ma - ta.   no-stra De - o sint ac-cep - ta au - re - am   su - per

hy-per - ly - ri - ca   ci - tha - ra, 10.Quo in co - ae - va iam glo - ri - a Con - de-can - te-mus Al - le - lu - ia.
a - ram que thy-mi - a - ma - ta,

The German repertory of sequences, preserved in various manuscripts mainly from St. Gall and Einsiedeln, has received much attention on the part of philologists. The literary work of Notker in particular has been repeatedly studied, most recently in the definitive work of W. von den Steinen, *Notker der Dichter* (1948). The music of the German sequences, on the other hand, is not very well known. To the present day, musicologists must draw upon one of the earliest publications in the field of music history, that is, A. Schubiger's *Die Sängerschule St. Gallens* (1858), which contains the melodies for *c.* fifty sequences. Two more recent publications, the *Variae preces* (Solesmes, 1901) and C. A. Moberg's *Ueber die schwedischen Sequenzen* (2 vols., 1927) contain a few additional examples from the early German repertory or, particularly in Moberg, better versions of those published by Schubiger.

Several characteristic traits of the French sequences are conspicuously absent in the German repertory. We have seen that the French sequences retain a close relationship to their parent chant by the consistent use of the assonance on *-a* (*-am, -at,* etc.) and also, in not a few cases, by starting out with the word *Alleluia.* Neither of these characteristics is found in the German sequences which, it seems, from the beginning acquired a greater independence than was the case in France. Another difference between the French and the German repertories is the absence, in the latter, of the *sequela* with *verba,* that form which represents the transition between the purely melismatic and the fully textual type. Some German collections of the pure *sequela* type exist, and the earliest of these, found in St. Gall *484,* has been considered as representing or including the *longissimae melodiae* which Notker mentions in his report.[17] However, recent investigations have shown rather conclusively that this collection was made at a later time with reference to the fully textual sequences, the texts being omitted for practical considerations.[18]

As for the music, it is important to notice that here the division French *versus* German is not as strict as it is in the literary field. Not a few melodies have come down to us with a "French" as well as with a "German" text, e.g., *Cithara* with the following:[19]

FRENCH:

1. *Rex omnipotens die hodierna*
2. a. *Mundo triumphali redempto potentia*
   b. *Victor ascendit caelos, unde descenderat.*
3. a. *Nam quadraginta, postquam surrexerat,*
   b. *Diebus sacris confirmans pectora*

etc.

[17] See, e.g., *Wagner I,* 223.

[18] Bannister, in *Anal. hymn.* 53, p. xxii, points out that the melodies show liquescent neumes at places where they would be required by the text. Husmann [see fn. 3] supports this view with other arguments.

[19] See Hughes, p. 32. *Sancti Spiritus* is given in *Variae Preces,* p. 160; the text for *Rex omnipotens* and *Sancti Spiritus* in *Anal. hymn.* 53, pp. 111 and 118.

GERMAN:

1.   *Sancti spiritus assit nobis gratia,*
2. a. *Quae corda nostra sibi faciat habitaculum*
   b. *Expulsis inde cunctis vitiis spiritalibus.*
3. a. *Spiritus alme, illustrator hominum,*
   b. *Horridas nostrae mentis purga tenebras.*

etc.

If we consider the sequences of Schubiger's collection from the point of view of form, we find a picture similar to that observed in the Anglo-French repertory, that is, the normal form along with deviations and modifications, but with a considerably greater emphasis on the latter. The normal form, characterized by a succession of musically different versicles, all double except for the first and the last, is found in hardly more than ten sequences. One of these is *Psallat ecclesia* (no. 31) which has been used as our introductory example [p. 444]. Others are *Laude dignum* (no. 1), *Laus tibi Christe* (no. 6), *Cantemus cuncti* (no. 9), *Haec est sancta* (no. 15), etc. This form can be represented by the scheme a b^2 c^2 ... k, where symbols such as b^2 stand for double-versicles.

The most obvious deviations from this form are represented by the sequences lacking the single verse at the beginning, at the end, or at both:

a^2 b^2 c^2 ... k: *Laus tibi Christe* (no. 38)

a b^2 c^2 ... k^2: *Sacerdotem Christi* (no. 33); *Grates honos* (no. 46); *Rex regum* (no. 47); *Veni Spiritus aeternorum* (no. 48); *Victimae paschali laudes* (no. 60)

a^2 b^2 c^2 ... k^2: *Natus ante saecula* (no. 5); *Aurea virga* (no. 49).

It should be noticed that nos. 43ff of Schubiger's *Exempla* are compositions of a later period, having been written, among others, by Ekkehard I (d. 978), Hermannus Contractus (d. 1054), Godeschalc (fl. c. 1050), and Wipo (d. c. 1050). *Grates honos* and *Rex regum,* both by Hermannus, also reveal their late date by the enormous extension of their versicles, some of which have as many as ninety syllables, e.g., the section "O flos virgineae—O consanguineae" in *Rex regum.*

Several of the earliest sequences have no double-versicles (a b c ... k): *Laus tibi sit* (no. 17); *En regnator* (no. 18); *Laeta mente* (no. 19); *O quam mira* (no. 22); *O decus mundi* (no. 51), and *Grates nunc omnes* (no. 54). We have already encountered this type among the Anglo-French sequelae. In fact, *Laeta mente* employs the melody of *Exsultate Deo* (Hughes, no. 41), and *O decus mundi* as well as *Grates nunc omnes* are modelled after *Ostende minor* (Hughes, no. 42). Altogether there are perhaps twenty sequences of the non-repetitive type, and the number of distinctly different melodies is, no doubt, even smaller. Although these form only a minute fraction of the total repertory, they have attracted considerable attention because of the possibility that they may represent an earlier stage of development than the repetitive type.[20] Perhaps they were also repetitive, each section being sung first as a melisma, then with the text (or *vice versa* ?), similar to the manner observed in the sequela *Pretiosa* with the fragmentary text *Jam nunc intonant* [p. 450]. All the examples of this type are conspicuous for their shortness, especially *O decus mundi* and *Grates nunc omnes*. By repeating each section they would more readily fall in line with the normal sequences.

Among the latter we find not a few examples showing multiple repetition, either in immediate succession or at different places, similar to the practice noted in some examples of the Anglo-French group. Some examples follow:

> *Johannes Jesu Christo* (no. 2): $\quad$ a b^2 c^2 d^4 d'^2 d^2 e $\quad$ ($\approx$ a b^2 c^2 d^8 e)
> *Carmen suo dilecti* (no. 3): $\quad$ a b^2 b'^2 c^2 d e^2 f $\quad$ ($\approx$ a b^4 c^2 d e^2 f)
> $\quad$ (b starts with "ecclesia")
> *Agni paschales* (no. 12): $\quad$ a b^3 c^2 c'^2 d^2 e^2 f $\quad$ ($\approx$ a b^3 c^4 d^2 e^2 f)
> $\quad$ (c starts with "sacrosancta")
> *Benedicta semper* (no. 24): $\quad$ a b^4 c^2 d^2 c^2 e^2 f^2 g^2 h^2 i
> *Virginis venerandae* (no. 35): $\quad$ a b^3 c^2 b'^2 b''^2 c'^3 $\quad$ ($\approx$ a b^3 c^2 b^4 c^3)
> $\quad$ (b starts with "de numero")

Carmen suo has a single versicle in the middle (d). No other clear example of this occurs in Schubiger's collection.

The most highly repetitive sequence is *Laudes Salvatori* (no. 11). Its complex structure, involving numerous relationships of one kind or another, can be indicated approximately as follows:

> 1. $\quad$ 2. $\quad$ 3. $\qquad$ 4. $\quad$ 5. $\qquad$ 6. $\qquad$ 7. $\quad$ 8. $\quad$ 9. $\qquad$ 10. $\qquad$ 11.
> a $\quad$ b^2 $\quad$ $(cc'dc)^2$ $\quad$ e^2 $\quad$ $(cc''c)^2$ $\quad$ $(ff')^2$ $\quad$ g^2 $\quad$ h^2 $\quad$ $(iii')^2$ $\quad$ $(kk'k)^2$ $\quad$ m^2

> 1. *Laudes Salvatori* . . . $\qquad$ 7. *Post haec mira* . . .
> 2. *Et devotis* . . . $\qquad\qquad$ 8. *Et se crucifigi* . . .
> 3. *Carne gloriam* . . . $\qquad\quad$ 9. *Illuxit dies* . . .
> 4. *Servi subiit* . . . $\qquad\qquad$ 10. *Favent igitur* . . .
> 5. *Sed tamen* . . . $\qquad\qquad$ 11. *Ergo die ista* . . .
> 6. *Putres suscitat* . . .

---

20 Wagner distinguishes the two types as A (repetitive) and B (non-repetitive); cf. *Wagner I*, 225ff. Moberg says, with reference to Wagner's two types: "Die Forscher sind darin einig, die zweite Gattung als älter anzusehen" (*Schwedische Sequenzen*, I, 223). Certainly, this is an overstatement. Scholars disagree on this point as on so many others concerning the early developments of the sequence (see, e.g., *Anal. hymn.* 53, p. xix, fn. 1). H. Spanke has shown that there exists a Byzantine hymn, *Hymnon aineton*, which may well be the model of *Grates nunc omnes* (see "Aus der Vorgeschichte und Frühgeschichte der Sequenz," in *Zeitschrift für deutsches Altertum und deutsche Literatur*, LXXI [1934], 1-39, esp. p. 23). Both poems have a very similar content and identical versification, four lines with respectively 13, 13, 15, and 10 syllables, except for the closing acclamation which has nine syllables in the Greek version (*Doxa theo to en hypsistois*) and only seven in the Latin (*Gloria in excelsis;* perhaps originally *Gloria in excelsis Deo*, with nine syllables?).

Such extremely involved structures clearly anticipate the even more complex forms encountered in the French *lais* of the thirteenth century. As we have remarked, the above schematic representation gives only an approximately correct picture of the thematic relationship between the various passages. In order to provide a more concrete impression, two complete sections, the third and the sixth, are reproduced in Fig. 149. The reader

FIGURE 149

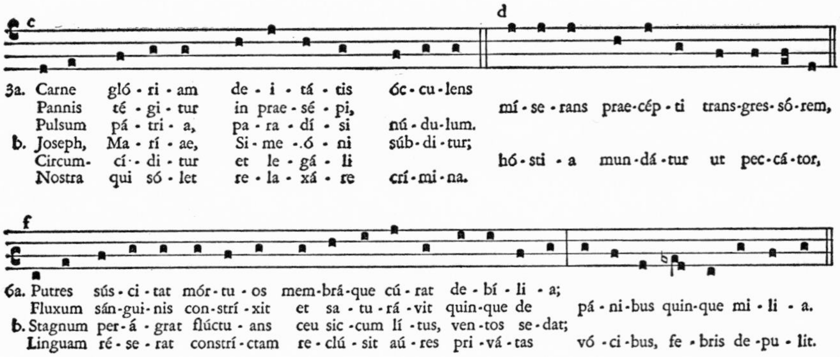

3a. Carne   gló · ri · am   de · i · tá · tis   óc · cu · lens
    Pannis   té · gi · tur   in prae · sé · pi,   mí · se · rans prae · cép · ti trans-gres· só · rem,
    Pulsum   pá · tri · a,   pa · ra · dí · si   nú · du · lum.
b. Joseph, Ma · rí · ae,   Si · me ·.ó · ni   súb · di · tur;
    Circum· cí · di · tur   et le · gá · li   hó · sti · a   mun·dá ·tur   ut pec·cá·tor,
    Nostra   qui só · let   re · la · xá · re   crí · mi · na.

6a. Putres   sús · ci · tat mór· tu · os   mem·brá·que cú · rat de · bí · li · a;
    Fluxum   sán·gui·nis con·strí·xit   et sa · tu · rá·vit quin·que de   pá · ni·bus quin·que mi · li · a.
b. Stagnum per· á · grat flúctu · ans ceu sic ·cum lí · tus, ven·tos se·dat;
    Linguam ré · se · rat constrí·ctam re · clú · sit aú · res pri · vá·tas   vó · ci·bus, fe · bris de ·pu · lit.

will notice readily how perfectly in both versicles the principles of versification are observed, that is, parallelism not only of entire verses but also of individual words, and often of accentuation.

The repeat structure exemplified by the sixth versicle, $(rr')^2$ or r r′ r r′—in other words, the alternation of a melody and its variant—occurs quite a few times in the German sequences, e.g., in:

r	r′	r	r′
Christe hunc diem (no. 21):			
Christe Jesu . . .	*Terras, Deus* . . .	*Officiis* . . .	*Sedqui mirum* . . .
Congaudent angelorum (no. 27):			
Qua gloria . . .	*Quae Domino* . . .	*Quam splendidi* . . .	*Quae omnium* . . .
Stirpe Maria (no. 28):			
Patris tui . . .	*Et Ezechiae* . . .	*Patris Josiae* . . .	*Summi etiam* . . .
Laus tibi (no. 37; same melody as *Christe hunc diem*):			
Qui hodie . . .	*Quos impius* . . .	*Mater gemit* . . .	*Mucro furit* . . .
Sancti Spiritus (no. 23):			
Tu qui omnium . . .	*Tui numinis* . . .	*Ipse hodie* . . .	*Donans munere* . . .
Sancti Baptistae (no. 25):			
Tu qui praeparas . . .	*Ne quid devium* . . .	*Te deposcimus* . . .	*Et facinora* . . .

In *Congaudent angelorum* the variant results from an inner extension, in *Sancti Spiritus* and *Sancti Baptistae* from an extension at the end.

Finally, a number of verses show bar-form, so that the entire double-versicle has the structure ppq ppq, which we have already encountered in several of the Anglo-French sequelae. Examples occur in *Festa Christi* (no. 8) on "Hinc ira—O Christe" and "Anno hominis—Ecce spiritus;" in *Benedicta semper* (no. 24) on "Non tres—Trinus in;" and in *Patre summe* (no. 26) on "Postremo victis—Ibi Neronis."

Multiple repeats of one kind or another are not the only structural peculiarity of the German sequences. Not a few of them show instances of what may be considered the opposite procedure, that is, deviations from exact repetition, caused by the fact that the second of two parallel verses is slightly longer (sometimes shorter) than the first. One of the methods employed in such a case is what may be called "extension by anticipation," which may be illustrated by the two examples in Fig. 150, (a) from *Summi triumphum* (no. 20), (b) from *Christus hunc diem* (no. 21):

FIGURE 150

In other cases the extension is made at the end, either by the addition of a closing passage or by providing a short *prima volta* and a longer *seconda volta*. Fig. 151 shows an example of each kind, the first from *Sancti Baptistae* (no. 25), the second from *Laudes Deo concinat* (no. 14). The former procedure leads to a versicle in strict bar-form, which, however, differs from the previously mentioned cases in that it is not restated.

FIGURE 151

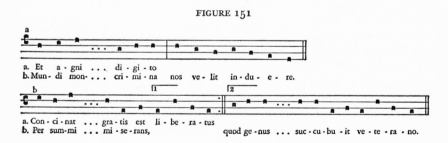

Laudes Deo concinat, from which the last example is taken, is the very first sequence Notker wrote, as he tells us in his *Prooemium,* and the one for which his teacher Iso suggested corrections. The somewhat irregular versicle just quoted occurs at the very beginning, right after the introductory versicle *Laudes Deo.* The latter is unusual for its shortness and for having a short melisma, ac'd'c'bg, on "De(o)," which is practically the only melisma in the entire repertory of early German sequences. The versicle after "Concinat . . . veterano," "Misit huc . . . patriae," is also highly unusual, if not unique because of the ternary form, c d c, of its melody:

c: *Misit huc natum suum in terras*
d: *ut sua dextra jacentes caeno levaret polo*
c: *restitueretque patriae.*

After this the sequence continues in normal double-versicles, but with some restatement of earlier material and with an unusually short final versicle, "Canamus":

a b_1 b_2 c d c e^2 f^2 g^2 $(d'\ e')^2$ f^2 g.

Certainly it is interesting and perhaps relevant to compare the rather irregular form of Notker's first attempt with the entirely regular sequence *Psallat ecclesia,* given at the beginning of our study, which represents the perfection of his method.

Before turning to the sequences of the intermediate and of the late period, we may say a word about the attempts made by many scholars to trace the "pre-history" of the sequence. Where did this form, so unique in its literary as well as its musical aspect, originate? A number of scholars have come out in favor of a theory of Byzantine origin. Perhaps the first to suggest such a connection was Wilhelm Christ, who interpreted the term "sequence" as the Latin translation of Greek *akoluthia,* a designation used by some Greek writers of the twelfth (?) century, though apparently with a different meaning.[21] More promising is the attempt made by Wilhelm Meyer to trace the sequence back to the *kontakion,* the most important form of Byzantine hymnody in the sixth century.[22] Considered as a whole, a *kontakion* is something entirely different from a sequence, since it consists of a great number of stanzas (*troparion*), from eighteen to thirty, of identical structure and melody, preceded by an introductory stanza (*prooemium*) in different versification and with different music, so that, aside from the *prooemium,* the over-all form is that of a strophic hymn rather than of a sequence. There exist, however, *kontakia* in which the individual stanza (i.e., the *troparion*) shows a versification in paired lines similar to that of the sequence. The best-known example is the famous *Akathistos* hymn, *Angelos protostates,* written by the patriarch Sergius about 626, the first *troparion* of which can be diagrammed as follows:[23]

21 See *Wagner I,* 223. The normal meaning of *akoluthia* seems to be sequence in the general sense of "order," specifically the order of the Office Hours as opposed to that of the Mass, which was called *leiturgia* [see *HDM,* s.v. "Akoluthia"].

22 W. Meyer, *Gesammelte Abhandlungen,* II, 76ff. Later he withdrew his theory; see *ibid.,* p. 99.

23 See the detailed description in E. Wellesz, *Byzantine Music and Hymnography,* pp. 163ff.

a b b c c d d e e f f g g h.

The parallel lines, b b, etc., correspond to each other not only in the number of syllables—10 for b, 13 for c, 16 for d, etc.—but also often in the length of the words and the placement of the accent, e.g.:

> d: Chaíre, hýpsos dysanábaton anthropínois logismoís
> d: Chaíre, báthos dystheóreton kai angélon   ophthalmoís,

or:

> f: Chaíre, astér   emphaínou ton hélion
> f: Chaíre, gastér enthéou   sarkóseos,

exactly in the same manner as they do in the sequences. Such similarity, or rather, identity of principles of versification cannot possibly be the result of coincidence. True enough, the progressive repeat is by no means a characteristic trait of the *kontakia* in general, neither in the *prooemium* nor in the *troparia*. It has been found, up to now, only in five or six of the Byzantine hymns.[24] It would therefore be wrong to say that the sequence is derived from the *kontakion* as such. Obviously the impetus came from one specific *kontakion* of the type just described, possibly from the *Akathistos* hymn which enjoyed special fame and which shows the progressive repeat more fully than the others.[25]

In turning from the textual to the musical aspect, we face a more difficult problem. The transfer of the poetic form from the East to the West does not necessarily imply a transfer of the music. The *Akathistos* hymn or some other of the same type may have reached the West through Byzantine singers, or in written form as a purely literary document. Even the former assumption would account only for one melody, not for the entire repertory of melodies which, no doubt, is a Western creation. The main difficulty is to account for the association of the Byzantine literary form and the *longissimae melodiae* of Notker's report. Did these have a repeat form, similar to that of so many Alleluia melismas, and did Notker—or somebody before him—notice the structural similarity between the form of the music and the form of the Byzantine poetry? Or was the musical repeat a modification caused by the parallelism of the text? Here we come close to the field of pure speculation. We prefer to stop at its border and to turn our attention to the later development of the sequence.

In the eleventh century the principles of versification that characterize the early sequence underwent a modification in the direction of greater

---

24 See the article by Spanke (fn. 20), p. 30.

25 Was Notker the central figure in this transfer? As an amusing aside we quote: "Notker kannte nicht griechisch" (Handschin, in *Zeitschrift für Musikwissenschaft*, XVII [1934], 250); "Notker . . . savait certainement le grec" (Huglo, in *RG*, XXVIII, 119, fn. 2). We wish to refer the reader to H. Husmann's interesting study, "Sequenz und Prosa" (see fn. 5), which appeared after our manuscript had been completed.

regularity. One of the first, and certainly the most famous example indicative of this change, is Wipo's Easter sequence, *Victimae paschali laudes* which betrays new tendencies in the occasional use of regular alternation of accented and unaccented syllables, in the more nearly equal length of the lines, and in the use of rhyme. For example:

3. a. *Dic nóbis María*   b. *Angélicos téstes*
  quid vidísti in vía   *sudárium et véstes*
4. a. *Sepúlcrum Chrísti vivéntis* b. *Surréxit Chrístus, spes méa*
  et glóriam vídi resurgéntis *praecédat súos in Galiléam.*

Another transitional sequence is the Christmas sequence *Laetabundus exsultet* [*VP* 70], which enjoyed a unique popularity in the later Middle Ages. Here not only the single versicle at the end, but also that at the beginning is lost, so that the entire text consists of double-versicles of nearly equal length and often in regular versification and rhyme; e.g.:

3. a. *Sícut sídus rádium* b. *Néque sídus rádio*
  prófert vírgo fílium *néque máter fílio*
  pári fórma   *fit corrúpta*
5. a. *Ísa-i-as cécinit*   b. *Sí non súis vátibus*
  Sýnagóga méminit *crédat vél gentílibus*
  númquam támen désinit *Sibyllínis vérsibus*
  ésse caéca.   *haéc praedícta.*

In contrast to *Victimae, Laetabundus* also indicates a change of musical style in its strict f-major tonality, in the cadential emphasis on the triadic pitches, f, a, and c', and in the melody which, by comparison with the older ones, sounds flat and commonplace. A more positive trait is the ex-

FIGURE 152

5a. I - sa - i - as ce - ci - nit Sy - na - go - ga me - mi - nit Numquam ta - men de - si - nit Es - se cae - ca

ploitation of different ranges in the various versicles, such as from f to d' in the first, from c to b-flat in the third, and from e to f' in the fifth. Although such contrasts are not entirely absent in the old sequences, particularly the French, they assume much greater importance in the later ones.

The final stage of the development was reached in the twelfth century, under Adam de St. Victor (d. 1192).[26] An extremely skillful, fluent, and elegant poet, he wrote over fifty sequences, in which the trend toward regu-

[26] Complete edition of his sequences in E. Misset and P. Aubry, *Les Proses d'Adam de Saint Victor* (1900). References are to this edition. A number of late sequences are reproduced in *VP* and in the Appendix of *AR* (e.g., pp. 176*, 187*, 190*, 200*).

larity is carried to a point where it borders on schematization. Each of his sequences consists of a number of strictly versified and rhymed stanzas; for these he employs a limited number of poetic forms, of which the following is by far the most frequent:

A.	*In natale Salvatoris*	8 (syllables in trochees)
	angelorum nostra choris	8
	succinat conditio;	7
	Armonia diversorum	8
	sed in uno redactorum	8
	dulcis est connexio.	7

Occasionally this scheme is enlarged to a similar one of eight lines:

B.	*Consequenter es mutatus*	8
	presulatu sublimatus,	8
	novus homo reparatus	8
	felici commercio;	7
	Ex adverso ascendisti	8
	et te murum objecisti,	8
	caput tuum obtulisti	8
	Christi sacrificio.	7

A fairly frequent modification of A is the following:

C.	*Quid de monte lapis cesus*	8
	sine manu, nisi Jesus	8
	qui, de regum linea	7
	sine carnis opere,	7
	de carne puerpere	7
	processit virginea?	7

Several other schemes are employed, but these need not concern us. Some of Adam's sequences consist entirely of stanzas of type A, e.g., *Jubilemus Salvatori qui spem dedit* (Misset-Aubry, no. 10; see p. 181), *Postquam hostem* (no. 19), or *Qui procedis* (no. 21). *Virgo mater Salvatoris* (no. 9) consists entirely of stanzas of type B, and *Salve dies* (no. 14) or *Sexta passus feria* (no. 15) show the consistent use of other poetic meters. Considered from the textual point of view, such sequences are indistinguishable from strophic hymns. Usually, however, two, three, or more different meters are employed in a sequence, particularly the above-mentioned types A, B, and C. Thus, *Gaude Syon et laetare* (no. 4) has six stanzas A, followed by two stanzas B, and by a final A; *Gaude Roma* (no. 26) has six A, one C, two B and two final stanzas in yet other meters; in *In natale Salvatoris* (no. 1) all the stanzas are A except for the ninth; in *Heri mundus exultavit* (no. 2) we find the types A and B together with several other metrical schemes, etc.

As for the musical treatment, the normal procedure is to provide a melody for the first half of a stanza and to repeat it for the second half. Thus the melody will cover two lines in a four-line stanza, three in a six-line stanza, etc. A perfectly regular example is *Jubilemus Salvatori qui spem dedit* (no. 10; see p. 246). Even the non-symmetrical scheme C is usually treated as a repeat structure by combining two separate notes of an eight-syllable line into a two-note neume for the corresponding seven-syllable line, as in the following example from *Splendor Patris* (no. 5):

FIGURE 153

a. Si cri - stal - lus est hu - me - cta at - que so - li sit ob - jec - ta scin - til - lat i - gni - cu - lum;
b. Nec cri - stal- lus   rum-pi - tur nec in par - tu sol- vi- tur pu -do - ris si - gna - cu - lum.

In not a few cases, however, the double-versicle structure results, not from the division of one stanza but from the combination of two, a melody being provided for an entire stanza and repeated with the next which, in this case, will necessarily be in the same meter. Examples of this procedure occur in many sequences: for instance, in *In natale Salvatoris* (no. 1), stanzas 3-4, 5-6, 7-8; in *Heri mundus* (no. 2), stanzas 3-4; in *Splendor Patris* (no. 5), stanzas 10-11; etc.[27]

Nearly all the sequences of Adam consist exclusively of double-versicles. Thus, the first two can be represented as follows:

$$In\ natale: \quad a^2\ b^2\ c^2\ d^2\ e^2\ f^2\ g^2\ h^2\ i^2$$
$$Heri\ mundus: a^2\ b^2\ c^2\ d^2\ e^2\ f^2\ g^2\ h^2\ i^2\ k^2\ l^2$$

The older form with a single verse at the beginning and/or the end occurs only in a few sequences. *Ecce dies* (no. 12) has a single verse at the beginning; *Laus erumpat* (no. 37), at the end; and *Lux jocunda* (no. 20), in both places (the first double-versicle starts with "Letis cedant"). In *Salve mater* (no. 36) the third versicle, "Porta clausa," is single, but is paired by the sixth versicle, "Palmam prefers":

$$a^2\ b^2\ c\ d^2\ e^2\ c\ f^2\ g^2\ h^2\ i^2$$

As for the individual melodies, a, b, c, etc., the reader is referred to the detailed analysis given by Aubry on pp. 115ff of his edition. Because of the strict versification of the text, each melody (Aubry: *timbre*) falls into a number of short periods (Aubry: *membre*), each of which corresponds to

[27] Occasionally the situation is ambivalent, as appears from the fact that Aubry's numbering of stanzas repeatedly differs from Misset's. Cf. *In natale:* IX (Misset) = 9-10 (Aubry); *Heri mundus:* XI, XII (Misset) = 11-12, 13-14 (Aubry); etc.

a line of the stanza. Thus a melody will consist of two to six periods, occasionally even more. Usually the periods are all different, but a few examples of repeat forms occur, for instance, p p q (no. 21, 6), p p q r (no. 9, 3), or p q p r (no. 25, 7).

Under the heading "Les Timbres," Aubry gives an extended catalogue of the phrases found in Adam's sequences. Of particular interest are those that recur in several compositions, as, for instance, the *timbres 11, 12,* and *13,* each of which are found in the same four sequences, *Splendor Patris* (no. 5), *Genofeve sollempnitas* (no. 8), *Laudemus omnes* (no. 35), and *Superne matris* (no. 44). In fact, all these start out identically, but continue later with more or less different material. A particularly large group of thematically related sequences is the following:[28]

2. *Heri mundus*	a b c	d e	f g	h i i k	
18. *Laudes crucis*	a b c	d e	f g p h i i′ k	
19. *Postquam hostem*	a b c	d e		i	k
20. *Lux jocunda*	a c_1 c_2 d e	f	h i i′ k	
23. *Profitentes*	a b c	d e	f g	k′ q	
27. *Corde, voce*	a c	d e	f+ g	h i	k
30. *Letabundi*	a b c	d e	f g p h i i′ k″ *k*	
37. *Laus erumpat*	a b c s d e t f g		k *u*	

As may be seen from this table, three sequences, *Heri mundus, Laudes crucis,* and *Letabundi,* are almost identical. Taking the first of these as the starting point, *Laudes crucis* is enlarged by one phrase (p), and *Letabundi* by this as well as by a final phrase (*k*, not repeated). The other sequences are reductions of *Heri mundus,* some of them with introduction of new material, especially in *Laus erumpat* (s, t, u). Naturally, in every case the recurrent use of a melody is predicated upon identical, or nearly identical verse schemes in the text. One might compare Adam's method with the centonization practice of the Tracts, Responsories, etc., were it not for the fundamental difference of material, technique, and underlying mentality.

Adam's sequences became the fountain-head of an enormous production which lasted throughout the thirteenth, fourteenth, and fifteenth centuries and resulted in a repertory of well over three thousand sequences, all fashioned after the same pattern. The Council of Trent (1545-63) abolished all sequences except four: *Victimae paschali laudes* (by Wipo) for Easter; *Veni sancte Spiritus* (variously ascribed to Pope Innocent III, d. 1216, and to Stephen Langton, archbishop of Canterbury, d. 1228) for Pen-

---

[28] The indications for repeat are omitted; all phrases are repeated except those represented by italics *(k, u)*. In *Lux jocunda* the long phrase c (normally used for an entire stanza and repeated for the next) is divided into halves, c_1 and c_2, each of which is used (with repeat) for a single stanza. In *Corde vota* the phrases f and g are combined into one, f+g, which is used for one stanza and repeated for the next.

tecost; *Lauda Sion* (by St. Thomas Aquinas, d. 1274) for Corpus Christi, and
Dies irae (attributed to Thomas a Celano, d. *c.* 1250) for the Mass for the
Dead. In 1727 a fifth sequence was adopted for liturgical use, *Stabat Mater*
for the Feast of the Seven Dolours (the text variously ascribed to Jacopone
da Todi, d. 1306; St. Bonaventura, d. 1274; and others). Of these, *Victimae
paschali laudes* [780] is the only remnant of the older type. *Lauda Sion*
[945] employs the same melody as Adam's *Laudes crucis,* except for the
versicle 17-18, "Sumunt boni—Mors est malis" (corresponding to the section p of our schematic representation), which has a melody related to
the *timbres 65, 66* of Aubry's catalogue. *Dies irae* [1810], equally famous
for its dramatic text and its somber melody, is composed in a form which
may be designated as a tripled sequence or sequence with a triple *cursus.*
It consists of eighteen three-line stanzas—each with its own rhyme—and
a conclusion in a somewhat different verse scheme. The first six stanzas
are composed as a sequence, a a b b c c, and this entire melody is employed
again for the two subsequent groups of six stanzas. The over-all form is as
follows:

Stanzas 1 to 6 (*Dies irae . . .*):	a a b b c c
Stanzas 7 to 12 (*Quid sum miser . . .*):	a a b b c c
Stanzas 13 to 18 (*Qui Mariam . . .*):	a a b b c c
Conclusion (*Lacrimosa . . .*):	free

CHAPTER FOUR

Ambrosian Chant

by ROY JESSON

A MBROSIAN CHANT derives its name from Ambrose, who was Bishop of Milan from 374 until his death in 397. It is a complete repertory of music for the Mass and Canonical Hours of the Milanese liturgy, the texts and forms of which differ in many respects from the Gregorian and represent an independent though related liturgical development. Unlike other regional uses, such as the Gallican and Mozarabic, the Ambrosian was never successfully suppressed in favor of the Gregorian, but has continued in use in the diocese of Milan until the present day.

The prestige conferred upon Milan and its diocese by Ambrose, the spiritual father and teacher of Augustine, no doubt contributed much to the ability of the Milanese liturgy to maintain its independence. But deriving from the late date (twelfth century) of the earliest musical manuscript is the obvious fact that Ambrose's connection with the liturgical melodies found there is likely to be entirely nominal. Apart from the writing of hymns and the introduction of antiphonal psalm-singing we know nothing of Ambrose's activities in the field of liturgical music. Medieval sources, however, credit him with the liturgical organization of the Mass, the introduction of the Vigils, and the arrangement of the Offices in Milan,[1] and various references to liturgical matters in his writings bear this out.

It is not to be supposed that the survival of the Ambrosian forms went unchallenged. Many attempts were made to enforce conformity with Gregorian practice, especially by Charlemagne soon after 800, and by Popes Nicholas II and Gregory VII in the eleventh century.[2] By the twelfth cen-

---

[1] See the article "Ambrosius" (Stäblein) in *MGG*.

[2] The Milanese chronicler Landolphus (*c.* 1000) records an interesting legend of Charlemagne's attempt. A trial was arranged to ascertain the will of God by seeing which of the two Sacramentaries, Ambrosian or Gregorian, would open first of its own accord on the altar. Both opened simultaneously. See A. Kienle, "Ueber ambrosianische Liturgie und ambrosianischen Gesang" (*Studien und Mittheilungen aus dem Benedictiner-und dem Cistercienser-Orden*, V [1884], 347).

tury, however, papal recognition was secured in the bulls of Eugenius III (1145) and Anastasius IV (1153), approving the Ambrosian rite.[3] As late as 1440 the papal legate attempted unsuccessfully to introduce Roman forms;[4] support for the Milanese use came once again in 1497 in a Papal bull of Alexander VI.[5] During the sixteenth century St. Charles Borromeo defended the Ambrosian rite against the Spanish occupiers of the city; his fame and honor are second only to that of Ambrose in the Milanese hierarchy.

Ambrosian chant, like Gregorian, underwent much alteration and "improvement" during the Renaissance period, when many of the melodies were pruned and otherwise mutilated. St. Charles Borromeo carried out a number of liturgical reforms intended to restore the authentic use, and a Missal (containing no music) was published in 1594. A short handbook, *La regola del canto Ambrosiano,* written by C. Perego at this time and published in 1622, contains only explanations of the solmisation system and of the traditional church modes and psalm tones, proving that at this time the Ambrosian style was much infiltrated by Gregorian ideas and methods, at least in the simpler daily tones and psalm-singing.

While the traditional commatic melodies seem to have continued in regular use, the full restoration of the medieval tradition has been the achievement of nineteenth- and twentieth-century scholars, outstanding among whom were Dom Cagin of Solesmes, and Dom P. Gregory Suñol, working in Milan.

The extant sources of Ambrosian liturgy and chant date only from the later Middle Ages. A comprehensive list of the liturgical manuscripts is given by Leclerq.[6] For the music itself there is no parallel to the quantity and variety of manuscripts that resulted from the wide dissemination of Gregorian chant. The most important sources are the following:

1. London, Brit. Mus., *add. 34209* (12th century)
2. Oxford, Bodleian, *lat. liturg. a 4* (14th century)
3. Muggiasca (Milan), another copy of 2 (14th century)

The London manuscript has been published in *Pal. mus.,* V (facsimile) and VI (transcription). It contains only the *pars hiemalis* (winter half of the year). Fortunately, the *pars aestivalis* (summer) is preserved in the two other sources.[7]

---

[3] *Messale Ambrosiano,* Latin-Italian edition, 1936, p. [17].

[4] E. Soullier, "Causeries sur le Plain-chant: St. Ambrose" (*Études Religieuses, Philosophiques, Historiques et Littéraires,* XLIX [1890], 273).

[5] Kienle (fn. 2), p. 348.

[6] Article "Milan" in *Dictionnaire d'Archéologie Chrétienne et de liturgie,* ed. Cabrol, XI, 1082ff.

[7] For a complete list of sources see M. Huglo, *Fonti e paleografia del canto ambrosiano* (1956).

All of the Ambrosian manuscripts include both Mass and Office, in an arrangement similar to that of the *Liber usualis*. In 1935 and 1939 their main contents were published in two separate volumes, the *Antiphonale missarum juxta ritum Sanctae Ecclesiae Mediolanensis* [*AMM*] and the *Liber vesperalis juxta . . . Mediolanensis* [*LVM*], the former containing the music for the Mass, the latter that of Vespers. The chants for the other Offices (Matins, etc.) have not been published.

THE LITURGICAL YEAR

The Ambrosian manuscripts reflect the division of the Milanese liturgical year into two parts, winter and summer. The *pars hiemalis* is associated with the Cathedral itself (*ecclesia hiemalis,* or *basilica major*), and begins on the third Sunday of October (the Feast of the Dedication of the Church). The *pars aestiva,* which is associated with the second church nearby (*ecclesia aestiva,* or *basilica minor*), begins at Easter (Vespers of Holy Saturday). Ceremonial processions accompany the change-over from one church to the other; the baptistery provides a third focal point for the processions and stations which are a characteristic feature of the Ambrosian rite. The rubrics *in choro, in baptisterio, in aliud,* and others are found throughout the manuscripts indicating such stations and processions; they are frequently included in the Office of Vespers.

The chief points in which the Ambrosian *Temporale* differs from the Roman may be listed here.

1. There are six Sundays in Advent instead of four (Advent thus corresponds more closely to Lent in duration).
2. The week days after the Sixth Sunday of Advent are called *De exceptato* [*sic*]. This is a feast of the Blessed Virgin; its name is variously interpreted as a corruption of *expectato* (expectation, of the birth of Christ), of *exceptum* (excepted from the rule), or *acceptato* (received, in the womb of the Virgin).
3. The Sunday after Epiphany is called *Christophoria,* or *Reditus Christi ex Aegypto.*
4. Milan has no Ash Wednesday; Lent begins on the Sunday after Quinquagesima (*In Capite Quadragesimae*). Before St. Charles Borromeo it began a day later, on the Monday.
5. The Saturday before Palm Sunday is *Sabbato in Traditione Symboli;* on that day the catechumens are instructed in the Creed (*Symbolum*).
6. The days of Holy Week are called *Feriae in Authentica* up to Good Friday, which is known as *Feria VI in Parasceve.*
7. During Easter Week there are two Masses daily (a usage found also in the Gallican liturgy). The first (*Pro Baptizatis*) is in the *ecclesia*

hiemalis and the second (*De Solemnitate*) is in the *ecclesia aestiva.* The days after Easter are called *Feriae in Albis,* after the white robes of the newly baptized; these are put off on the following Sunday (*Dominica in Albis depositis*).

8. Pentecost is preceded by three Rogation Days (*In Litaniis Minoribus*) and like Easter has two Masses (*Pro Baptizatis* and *De Solemnitate Pentecostes*).

9. The Sundays after Pentecost are named as follows:
   Dominicae I-XV post Pentecostem
   Dominicae I-V post Decollationem (Beheading of St. John Baptist, August 29)
   Dominicae I-II Octobris
   Dominica III Octobris, In Dedicatione Ecclesiae Majoris
   Dominicae I-III post Dedicationem

Only a small number of chants are provided for the Sundays after Pentecost. The Masses draw on a *Commune Dominicale* [*AMM* 277] according to a rotating schedule [*AMM* 324]. This practice, similar to that of the Roman Mass Ordinary, may conserve something in the nature of the earlier Christian liturgy before the practice of proper items for each day had developed. The chants for Vespers are nearly all borrowed from the earlier part of the year [*LVM* 383, 389ff].

The Ambrosian *Sanctorale* naturally honors many local saints, and omits a number of those included in the Roman use.

THE LITURGICAL DAY

Elaborate tables showing the complex and variable structure of the Ambrosian Offices are given by Dom Cagin;[8] in many of their details there are similarities to other early Western liturgies, notably the Gallican. Matins and Lauds appear together in the manuscripts under *Ad Matutinam.* The chief musical items of these Offices are Psalms, Antiphons, Responsories, Canticles, and Hymns. The Psalms of Matins are Psalms 1 to 108. Divided into three Nocturns, each containing from three to five psalms, they are sung through once every two weeks (excluding Sundays). In the Gregorian Matins the cycle of Psalms is completed each week. After the Lesser Hours, which do not contain any important musical items, the rest of the psalter (Psalms 109-150 with some omissions) is sung through each week at Vespers. Five Vesper Psalms with Antiphons are assigned to each day of the week, though proper Psalms are sometimes substituted on the greater feasts. In addition to the *Magnificat,* Vespers also includes an *Antiphona in choro,* a *Responsorium in choro,* a *Responsorium in bap-*

[8] *Pal. mus.,* VI, Introduction.

tisterio, and four verses of a proper Psalm, with *Gloria.* Two other chants serve invariably to open and close the Office: the *Lucernarium*[9] and the *Completorium.* The simpler forms of Vespers end with one or two *Completoria;* the most elaborate forms include four. The *Liber Vesperalis* contains only twelve *Lucernaria* and five *Completoria* (some also in a simple version), which are repeated as required. An interesting feature of the Vespers of Sundays and feast-days is the provision of two *Psallendae,* each consisting of a short verse with *Gloria.* Such *Psallendae* occur in the Ambrosian use wherever a procession is intended: in this case, to and from the baptistery. Another peculiarity is the employment at various points throughout the Offices of a threefold (occasionally twelvefold) *Kyrie eleison,* for which simple syllabic tones are provided. The use of the Greek prayer in the Offices is of Eastern origin, but was widespread in the West long before the *Kyrie* became part of the Gregorian Mass.

The following table shows the structure of Vespers on Sundays and high feasts, a structure hardly less elaborate than that of the Mass:

CHIEF MUSICAL ITEMS OF VESPERS OF SUNDAYS

ORDINARY	PROPER
Lucernarium	
	Antiphona in choro
Hymnus	
	Responsorium in choro
5 Psalms with Antiphons (Kyrie)	
	Magnificat with Antiphon (Kyrie)
	Psallenda I
	Responsorium in baptisterio
	4 Psalm verses with Antiphon and Gloria
Completorium I	
Completorium II (Kyrie)	
	Psallenda II
Completorium I	
Completorium II	

The Ambrosian Mass differs in a number of respects from the Gregorian. It includes no *Kyrie* as a separate chant and no *Agnus Dei,* so that the Ordinary is reduced to three items. The Proper, on the other hand, includes seven chants. It starts with the *Ingressa,* the counterpart of the Roman Introit. The early use of three readings or lessons [see pp. 24f] is

---

9 The *Lucernarium* is a respond, the text of which has invariably some reference to the creation and giving of light. In the Gallican and Mozarabic rites the *Lucernarium* became almost an independent brief Office before Vespers, which itself has been called *Lucernalis gratiarum actio.* In Gallican manuscripts the whole of Vespers was called *Lucernarium.* See Kienle (fn. 2), p. 359.

retained, and each of these is followed by a lesson chant: the Prophecy by the *Psalmellus,* which is the equivalent of the Roman Gradual; the Epistle by the *Hallelujah* (called *Post Epistolam*); and the Gospel by the *Post Evangelium.* In Lent and on some other feasts of a penitential character the *Hallelujah* is replaced by the *Cantus,* which corresponds to the Tract of the Roman Mass. The *Offertorium* and the *Confractorium (frangere,* to break) follow, the latter sung during the breaking of the bread and having no counterpart in the Roman use. The Mass closes with the *Transitorium,* sung at the Communion. The *Gloria* is also called *Laus Missae,* while the *Credo* is known as *Symbolum* [*AMM* 611]. The following table shows the musical items of the Ambrosian Mass in relation to those of the Gregorian.

CHIEF MUSICAL ITEMS OF AMBROSIAN AND GREGORIAN MASS

AMBROSIAN		GREGORIAN	
ORDINARY	PROPER	ORDINARY	PROPER
	Ingressa		Introit
......		Kyrie	
Gloria (Laus)		Gloria	
	Psalmellus		Gradual
	Post Epistolam		
	Hallelujah, Cantus		Alleluia, Tract
	Post Evangelium		......
Symbolum		Credo	
	Offertorium		Offertory
Sanctus		Sanctus	
......		Agnus Dei	
	Confractorium		......
	Transitorium		Communion
......		Ite missa est	

THE PSALM TONES

For the Office Psalms the Ambrosian use retains its own characteristic psalm tones. The Roman forms appear to have been used in Milan for a time,[10] but medieval theorists refer to the fact that the Ambrosian tones included no mediation at the middle of each verse;[11] this usage has been restored together with the rest of the medieval system, as far as possible, in the *Liber Vesperalis.* The Ambrosian psalm tones thus consist of an intonation, a recitation-note or tenor, and a final inflection, or termination. There

[10] See Perego's *La regola* . . . (1622), where the psalm tones in use at Milan in the sixteenth century are shown. In this form they are quoted by Nisard under "Ambrosien (Chant)" in *Dictionnaire liturgique et théorique du plainchant,* ed. Ortigue, 1854, on the assumption that they represent the authentic Ambrosian use.

[11] M. Gerbert, *De Cantu et musica sacra,* I, 254, quoting Radulph de Rivo (of Tongers).

is a great deal of difference in detail between the Gregorian and Ambrosian tones, especially in the general system of the tones and their assignment; in this the Ambrosian use permits considerably more flexibility.

Briefly, the selection of an appropriate psalm tone begins with the consideration of the final note of the Antiphon which "enframes" the Psalm. This note determines the family (*familia*) or *series* of tones which may be drawn upon. There are four *series,* one each for Antiphons ending on *d, e, f,* and *g* (or *a, b c',* and *d'* in transposition). Next must be chosen the tenor, or reciting-tone, which must correspond to the note which "dominates" in the Antiphon;[12] for this purpose each *series* has several possible tenors. Finally a choice of terminations called *clausulae* is provided for each tenor, in order to achieve a smooth link with the beginning of the Antiphon when it is repeated.[13] As an example we may take the first *series* of tones, which is used with all Antiphons ending on d (or a in transposition). In this *series* there are four possible tenors: *a, g, f, e* (*e', d', c', b* in transposition). Each has its own intonation, sometimes with one or two variants. Thus, for the tenor *g* the intonations are *c-e-g, d-e-g,* or *e-f-g.* With each of these tenors a wide selection of *clausulae* ending on various notes is associated. Their number is far in excess of that of the Roman psalm tones, as appears from the fact that 46 *clausulae* exist for *Series I* alone [*LVM* 825]. Their distribution may be seen from the following table:

CLAUSULAE OF PSALM TONE SERIES I

Clausulae ending on:	a	g	f	e	d	c	Total
Tenor on a	4	6	2	–	3	–	15
g	–	3	5	1	4	–	13
f	–	2	1	3	7	1	14
e	–	–	–	1	2	1	4

Each of the remaining three *series* has likewise several possible tenors, each with one or two intonations and with a great number of alternative *clausulae.*

The various points mentioned may be illustrated by the three examples shown in Fig. 154. Each of the three Antiphons ends on d (*Series I*), but the psalm tones have different tenors, which correspond to the dominant pitch of each Antiphon. As can be seen from the second example, the choice of the "dominant" note of the Antiphon seems at times rather arbitrary. Nevertheless, the underlying principle is of great interest, representing as it does, an attempt to weld Antiphon and psalm tone into even closer "tonal unity" than is the case in the Roman system.

[12] "Illa enim veluti tenor sumitur nota quae in Antiphona quasi centrum fuit melodias et magis dominata est ac praevaluit." [*LVM* 819].

[13] *LVM* 825-838.

FIGURE 154

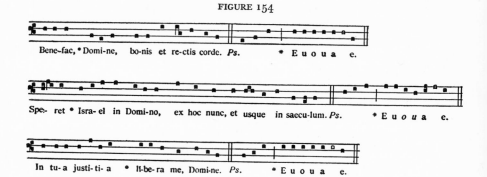

It is quite possible that the flexibility and variability of the Ambrosian psalm tone system is characteristic of a rather irregular practice common to all the western liturgies before the Gregorian system was devised to conform with the theory of the eight church modes. Such a modal basis is clearly not to be found in the Ambrosian tones, though the four *series* may be considered to correspond with the four "maneriae." At any rate, the fixed relation between final and tenor, which is the chief characteristic of the Gregorian system, does not exist.

THE OFFICE CHANTS

The simplest of these are the Psalm Antiphons, of which Fig. 154 shows three examples. Slightly more elaborate are the *Psallendae,* which, from the point of view of style, could perhaps be compared to the Roman *Magnificat* Antiphons. They are connected with the *Gloria Patri* sung to a number of tones organized along the same lines as the psalm tones [*LVM* 840]. Somewhat similar in style are the *Antiphonae in choro* which, however, are not connected with a Psalm or a verse. All these are proper chants and therefore exist in substantial numbers.

Also proper are the *Responsoria* which, in the Ambrosian rite, are sung not only at Matins but also at Vespers. Most Sundays have two, a *Responsorium in Choro* and a *Responsorium in Baptisterio.* Many of them carry designations such as *cum Pueris* or *cum Infantibus* (with a choir of boys), *a Subdiaconis* (by the sub-deacons), *a Diacono, a Notario,* etc. On the Wednesdays of the first five weeks of Lent and on Good Friday three additional *Responsoria* are sung after the Magnificat. All these *Responsoria* consist of a respond and a verse, after which part of the respond is repeated: R V R′. Among those sung *cum infantibus* are some of the longest chants of the Ambrosian repertory, provided with melismas which have no parallel in the Gregorian repertory. The place for these melismas is the repeat of the respond. An example is the Responsory *Ecce completa sunt* from

Epiphany [*LVM* 148], from which the two pertinent sections are shown in Fig. 155.

FIGURE 155

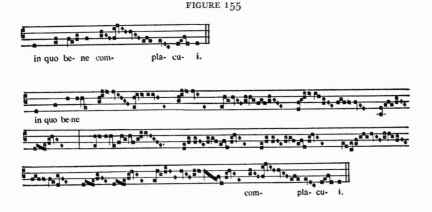

Even longer are the melismas for some of the Responsories of Matins; e.g., *Aspiciens a longe, Sperent in te, Laetetur cor, Tollite portas* from the Third, Fourth, Fifth, and Sixth Sunday of Advent, or *Congratulamini* and *Contremuerunt*, both from the Nativity.[14] *Aspiciens a longe* has two such melismas, entitled *melodiae primae* and *melodiae secundae*, written after the chant with an indication of the syllable, "In po――― pulo," on which they are to be sung. Obviously these are *ad libitum* additions, in other words, tropes, the first probably to be used for the initial respond, the second, for its repetition after the verse. Each of them consists of a number of well-defined phrases, identified in the original manuscript by numerals, I, II, III, etc., most of which recur in irregular repeat schemes, as can be seen in Fig. 156. Needless to say, these *melodiae* are of the greatest interest in connection with the problem of the tropes and sequences.[15]

Both the opening and closing items of Vespers, *Lucernarium* and *Completorium*, are Ordinary and therefore exist only in small numbers. *Lucernarium* (lighting of the lamps) originally was the old name for Vespers. Most of the Ambrosian *Lucernaria* include a reference to "light," e.g., *Quoniam tu illuminas*, or *Paravi lucernam*. The *Liber vesperalis* contains about a dozen *Lucernaria*, three of which are strictly Ordinary: *Quoniam tu illuminas* [*LVM* 1] for Sundays; *Dominus illuminatio* [*LVM* 13] for week days, and *Quoniam tu illuminas* with a simple melody [*LVM* 40] for Saturdays. In addition there are a few Proper chants for high feasts;

14 See *Pal. mus.*, V and VI.

15 See the chapter "Trope, Sequence, and Conductus" (by Handschin) in *The New Oxford History of Music*, II, 128ff, where the Ambrosian *melodiae* are considered as "prototypes" of the tropes and sequences. Cf. p. 508 of the present book concerning this question.

FIGURE 156

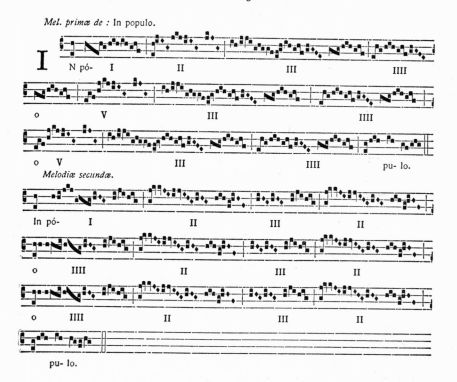

Mel. primæ de : In populo.

Melodiæ secundæ.

pu- lo.

for instance, *Paravi lucernam* for the Nativity, *Apud te Domine* for Epiphany, and *In lumine* for Holy Innocents. All these consist of a main section (antiphon?) and a verse, sung according to the scheme A V A' A. Exceptional is *Dirigatur oratio mea* [*LVM* 208], not only because it is the only one with two verses but also because it is prescribed for a week day, the first Friday in Lent. The style of the *Lucernaria* varies from the most elaborate (*In lumine*) to a simple recitation (*Dominus illuminatio* for week days).

Even more limited in number are the *Completoria*. The four for Sunday, *Regnum tuum, Benedictus es* (both sung to essentially the same melody), *Quoniam tu illuminas,* and *Benedictus es (simplex)* [*LVM* 10, 11], are used throughout the year, except for three occasions, St. Stephen, *Feria IV in Albis,* and *Natale unius Apostoli,* when the first is replaced by *Sancti tui.* As so often in Ambrosian chant, one is struck by the absence of a logical principle underlying this organization. The two *Benedictus es* are followed by a triple *Kyrie eleison.*

THE ORDINARY CHANTS OF THE MASS

Only a small number of chants exist for the three items of the Ordinary, and they are not grouped in any way which would correspond to the Ordinary cycles of the Roman use. There are four settings of the *Gloria* (*Festivus, Simplex, Solemnior,* and *Dominicalis*), one melody for the *Credo,* and four settings of the *Sanctus* (*Festivus, Ferialis, Ad libitum, In Solemnioribus ad libitum*).

The simplest of the Ordinary chants is the *Credo* [*AMM* 611]. It consists of little more than an inflected recitation, which is repeated for all the "verses" of the text (except the beginning and the close) exactly as in a Psalm. The recitation consists of an intonation (f), a tenor (g) and two terminations, the second employed occasionally to mark off some of the main divisions of the text. Only the beginning, *Credo in unum Deum,* and the close, *Et vitam venturi saeculi. Amen,* stand outside this scheme:

Credo in unum Deum.

```
  f     g------------------- f g a g  (g)    a b♭ g a g
        Patrem om-            nipotentem,
  fa-   ctorem cae-           li et terrae,
  vi-   sibilium omnium et in- visibilium.
        etc.
        De- um de Deo . . . Deum verum            de Deo vero.
        Ge- nitum, . . . per quem om-   nia facta sunt.
        etc.
              g a f   g-------------
  Et    expecto resurrectionem       mortuorum.
              Et vitam venturi seculi. Amen.
```

As for the *Gloria* melodies [*AMM* 604ff], the *tonus simplex* is in a very rudimentary style, similar to that of the *Credo*. The *tonus festivus* is an elaboration of the *tonus simplex,* differing mainly by the use of short melismas at the end of certain phrases. It is also transposed down a fourth, to allow for the wider range. The *tonus dominicalis* is a "free" melody, in a mixed syllabic-neumatic style, moving in a small range (c to g). There are a few internal repeats of musical phrases, but the over-all form is irregular.[16] This is also true of the *tonus solemnior,* which however is in an elaborate melismatic style.

It comes as a surprise to find a three-fold *Kyrie* attached to the *Gloria,* sung immediately after the *Amen* as a conclusion of the same chant. It is set invariably to the same music, which is shown in Fig. 157.

[16] This melody is similar to the Gregorian *Gloria Dominicalis* (Mass XI; *L* 46]. The two versions are compared by Pothier (*Les Mélodies grégoriennes,* pp. 253ff) and Ott (*Rass. Greg.,* VI, 398). For the *tonus simplex,* see p. 409.

FIGURE 157

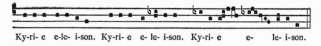

Ky-ri- e e-le- i-son. Ky-ri- e e- le- i-son. Ky-ri- e   e-   le- i-son.

This is the only music provided for the *Kyrie* text in the main body of the Mass, though even simpler tones are provided for its use as a respond after prayers [*AMM* 618], during processions before Mass [*AMM* 629], and as part of the Litany of the Saints [*AMM* 633, 635]. The *Kyrie* is used throughout the Ambrosian Office as a brief respond, in the manner of the words *Alleluia* or *Amen,* being repeated sometimes as many as twelve times together. The form *Christe eleison* apparently is not used.

Of the two chief *Sanctus* melodies, the *tonus festivus* [*AMM* 614] is a transposed neumatic elaboration of the *tonus ferialis,* as can be seen in Fig. 158 (both melodies are shown at the same pitch for the sake of comparison). The method of ornamentation found here is very typical of the Ambrosian style.

FIGURE 158

San - ctus, San - ctus, San - ctus Do - mi - nus De - us Sa - ba - oth, Ple - ni sunt *etc.*

a. *tonus festivus*   b. *tonus ferialis*

The two "ad libitum" melodies for the *Sanctus* are adaptations of other chants; one of them (super *Ecce apertum*) is taken from part of the *Offertorium* for the third Mass of the Nativity [*AMM* 44] in which the words *Sanctus, Sanctus, Sanctus* occur, though in a different context (the text is from various chapters of the Apocalypse).

THE PROPER CHANTS OF THE MASS

The eight items of the Ambrosian Mass Proper can be conveniently arranged in two groups of four each: (a) *Ingressa, Post Evangelium, Confractorium, Transitorium;* (b) *Psalmellus, Hallelujah, Cantus,* and *Offertorium.* The chants of the first group all consist of one section only, which may be considered as an Antiphon, although the dichotomy antiphonal— responsorial is hardly more than a convenient terminology in Ambrosian chant. Those of the second group consist normally of two or more sections, a respond and a verse or, in the case of the *Cantus* (Tract), a number of verses.

The *Ingressa* is the counterpart of the Roman Introit. However, it lacks the psalm verse and the *Gloria Patri* which make the Introit the most complete example of antiphonal psalmody in the Gregorian Mass; only an Antiphon of moderate length remains. The difference corresponds to a change in liturgical function; the *Ingressa* is sung during the censing of the altar at the beginning of the Mass rather than during the processional entry of the celebrant. The only *Ingressa* with a verse is *Requiem aeternam* [*AMM* 589], but this is adapted from the Roman use.

The Ambrosian Mass Antiphons are remarkable for their lack of adherence to a norm. In each category there are examples of all styles, from the simplest syllabic chants to highly ornate melodies, though neumatic chants outnumber the rest. Similarly, there are many variations in the matter of length and range, the latter varying from a fourth to a twelfth. Although the majority of the Mass Antiphons are through-composed, among them are not a few examples of repeat forms, sometimes of considerable complexity. Some examples from the various categories will illustrate these points.

An example of the simplest style is the Post Evangelium *Bene annunciavi* [*AMM* 461] shown in Fig. 159. It has the form aa'b.

FIGURE 159

Be-ne annunci- a- vi   justí-ti- am tu- am, Do- mi-ne,   in Eccle- si- a magna.   Hal-le-lu- jah.

Slightly more developed is the Transitorium *Maria Virgo* [*AMM* 56]. It consists of two identical phrases. This chant, from the *Dominica post Nativitatem Domini,* also occurs as a processional Antiphon for the Feast of Purification [*AMM* 86], an interesting case of borrowing (which way?) from another liturgical category.

FIGURE 160

Ma-ri- a Virgo,   semper laeta- re, quae tantam gra- ti- am me-ru- í-sti,

cae-li   et terrae Cre- a-to- rem de tu- o u-te-ro   ge- ne-ra- re.

As an example of wider range and more interesting intervallic movement a passage from the Post Evangelium *Ipse tamquam* [*AMM* 23] from the Sixth Sunday of Advent may be quoted (Fig. 161).

FIGURE 161

e tha-la- mo   su-   o,   exulta-   vit ut gi-   gas   ad curren- dam vi-   am

Among the most elaborate Antiphons is the Ingressa *Vos qui transituri* from the Feast of Dedication [*AMM* 331]. It is noteworthy for its extremely high range, from g to c″ (final on d′), the like of which occurs only once the Gregorian repertory [see Fig. 62, p. 249]. Its final melisma is shown in Fig. 162.

FIGURE 162

De-   o   ve- stro.

Finally, one of the most unusual Mass Antiphons (possibly of Greek origin) should be quoted: the Transitorium *Te laudamus* [*AMM* 81], remarkable for the similarity of its text to the *Te Deum,* and its music to a psalmody (m stands for a ten-note melisma, c′-d′ d′-c′-b-a g-a-g-f):

g-b	d′ d′ b c′	d′ d′ e′ d′ c′ c′	m	a c′ c′ b c′ d′ a b	a g (f-g) g
	Te laudamus	*Domine omnipo-*	*tens*	*qui sedes super Cherubim*	*et Se- ra- phim*
Quem	*benedicunt*	*Angeli Archange-*	*li*	*et laudant Prophetae et*	*A-po-sto- li*
	Te laudamus	*Domine oran-*	*do*	*qui venisti peccata*	*solven- do*
Te	*deprecamur*	*magnum Redempto-*	*rem*	*quem Pater misit ovium*	*pasto- rem*
	Tu es Christus	*Dominus Salva-*	*tor*	*qui de Maria Virgine*	*es na- tus*
Hunc	*sacrosanctum*	*Calicem sumen-*	*tes*	*ab omni culpa libera*	*nos sem- per.*

It is clearly impossible to reduce the variety of these chants to any kind of system. Their texts also come from widely different sources, and liturgical scholars have commented on many surprising features.[17]

The responsorial chants have survived in varying degrees of completeness. The subsequent table shows the various forms which are found among the *Psalmelli* and *Offertoria* as a result of the supression of most (in many cases all) of the psalm verses, and the modification (or omission) of the repeat of the respond.

FORMS OF RESPONSORIAL MASS CHANTS

	R	RV	RVR′	RV$_1$R′V$_2$R′
Psalmellus[18]	2	75	13	—
Offertorium	63	7	30	3

In the chants of the second type (RV) the omission of the repeat of the

17 See especially Cagin, in *Pal. mus.,* VI, Preface; also the articles "Milan" and "Ambrosienne (Liturgie)" in *Dictionnaire d'Archéologie* . . .

18 The Psalmellus *Benedictus Dominus* [*AMM* 66] has two verses, and *Foderunt* [177], from the Mass of Good Friday, has six; no repeat of the respond is indicated.

respond often causes a lack of tonal balance, since the finals of the verses, and sometimes their general tonality and range, are frequently different from those of the respond.

A special feature of the *Offertoria* is the survival, in many cases, of the verse; three examples exist with two verses: *Haec dicit Dominus* [*AMM* 143] for the Fifth Sunday in Lent; *Angelus Domini* [210] for Easter Sunday; and *Exaudita est* [512] for the Feast of St. Lawrence. These are comparable in their melodic richness to the Gregorian Offertory verses published by Ott, though there are few traces of material common to both repertories. The *Offertoria* also contain several examples of the repetition of phrases, text as well as music, as do the Gregorian Offertories.

A striking difference exists between the *Cantus* and their liturgical counterparts in the Roman Mass, the Tracts. Most of them have only one verse, none more than three. Nor is their use limited to the period of Lent. They replace the *Hallelujah* also during the week *de Exceptato* before the Nativity. They show little, if any traces of the centonization technique which is of such basic importance in the Tracts.

The Ambrosian *Hallelujahs* are particularly interesting. Similar to the Gregorian Alleluia, they consist of three sections, hallelujah, verse, and hallelujah, the hallelujah including a long *jubilus* called *melodiae* in the Ambrosian manuscripts. In difference from the Gregorian type, however, the final hallelujah is never an exact repeat of that at the beginning. It is either considerably modified and extended or practically a new melody. Hence the two sections are distinguished as *primae melodiae* and *secundae melodiae*.

The Ambrosian Mass repertory includes seventy-two *Hallelujahs,* but these have only ten different *melodiae* (more properly, pairs of *melodiae*). Six of these occur only once, each in connection with an individual verse. The remaining four, however, are employed as a kind of "Ordinary," being used in combination with a number of different verses. One of them (I; *AMM* 38) recurs in forty-two *Hallelujahs,* the second (II) in fifteen, the third (III) in five, and the fourth (IV) in four.

As for the verses and their melodies, it must first be noted that adaptation plays an even more prominent role here than in the Gregorian Alleluias. Thus, in the forty-two *Hallelujahs* of the *melodiae* group I we find that twenty-two employ one and the same melody for their verses, while two other melodies are used each for six verses, etc. In group II all the fifteen *Hallelujahs* have not only the same *melodiae,* but also the same melody for the verses. Likewise the *Hallelujahs* of groups III and IV have their verses sung to only one melody, which however, undergoes some variation.[19]

19 For more details, also concerning the centonization practice in the Ambrosian Alleluias, see R. Jesson, *Ambrosian Chant: The Music of the Mass* (Dissertation, Indiana University, 1955), pp. 77ff.

MODALITY

The system of the eight church modes is not applicable to the Ambrosian melodies. In fact, neither the medieval sources nor the present-day books classify the melodies in any way. The only attempt in this direction is made in connection with the psalm tones and their Antiphons, which are grouped into four *series* according to the finals d, e, f, and g or their transposed equivalents, a, b, c′ and d′ [see p. 471]. The addition of four upper finals is very significant because it indicates a most characteristic trait of Ambrosian chant, that is, the exploitation of a much higher range than that in which the Gregorian melodies move.

As for the over-all repertory of chants, no valid distinction can be made between plagal and authentic forms. It is, however, possible to classify the melodies according to their finals with some validity. A representative number of chants (some four hundred) are classified in the following table.

Finals:	d	e	f	g	a	b	c′
Ingressae	24	16	11	33	7	1	5
Transitoria	19	13	6	47	2	2	4
Psalmelli	20	7	16	35	23	–	3
Offertoria	23	15	3	46	8	1	7
	86	51	36	161	40	4	19

It is interesting to note that the chants on d or a (*protus*) and on g (*tetrardus*) easily outnumber the rest; in general this is true of the whole repertory. Possibly the *protus* and *tetrardus* were favored because they avoid the tritonal ambiguity of the *deuterus* and *tritus* and the concomitant problem of the b-flat. Certainly this problem cannot be answered from the Ambrosian manuscripts. The unequivocal fact is that the British Museum Codex does not contain a single authentic indication of b-flat on any of its pages (the other manuscripts are too late to be of value regarding early traditions). Yet it is hardly possible to believe that the Milanese singers of the twelfth century were not expected to introduce the flat as a matter of course to modify the exposed tritonal progressions and tritone leaps which otherwise occur very frequently. We shall probably never fully resolve this problem, but it may be pertinent to recall that Guido himself was clearly familiar with Ambrosian music, and would have been most likely to comment on "hard" progressions if they characterized its style, instead of making his flattering reference "more perdulcis Ambrosii."[20]

[20] See p. 483.

CONCLUDING REMARKS

A general conspectus of the Ambrosian melodies suggests the following generalizations regarding their style.

a. The Ambrosian repertory is equally as varied as the Gregorian, and includes psalmodic and commatic, highly organized and free chants.

b. Syllabic, neumatic, and melismatic styles are about equally represented, but there is very little uniformity of style within each category of chant. In general, however, the most ornate style is found in the responsorial chants with solo verses.

c. Ambrosian melodies show a marked preference for progression by step. This results primarily from the extended use of *climacus* neumes, which are much more frequent than in Gregorian chant, particularly in their extended form with four or five descending pitches. Very often several such neumes occur in succession, forming sequential patterns. Also noteworthy is the relatively frequent occurrence of the "inverted *climacus*," with four or five pitches in ascending order, formations which are extremely rare in Gregorian chant. Fig. 163 shows some characteristic formations, all from pp. 230-233 of *AMM*.[21]

FIGURE 163

Examples of progressions outlining a seventh or a triad are not missing, as a glance at the same four pages (which were chosen at random) will show.

d. Selective quotation has done much to spread the false idea that Ambrosian chant is characteristically prolix and rather shapeless or improvisatory in character. This is quickly disproved by a study of the repertory. Shorter melodies easily outnumber the longer ones, and of the latter only a few can be critized for their apparent lack of shape or direction. Many of the longer melismatic chants employ various

---

[21] This difference was recognized in the eleventh century, as appears from the following passage in Aribo's *De Musica* (c. 1070): "All leaps are praiseworthy, but they appear more excellent to us than to the Lombards. These prefer the "closer" (conjunct) we the "open" (disjunct) melodies (*Omnes saltatrices laudabiles, sed tamen nobis generosiores videntur quam longobardis. Ille enim spissiori, nos rariori cantu delectamur; GS, II, 212b; J. Smits van Waesberghe, Aribonis De musica [1951], p. 55*).

devices to achieve some degree of unity. Internal repetition of complete phrases or melismas is frequently found, as is also musical rhyme between the ends of phrases and sections. Particularly characteristic of the most elaborate chants is the repetition of short motives within the melismas, as in the following:

FIGURE 164

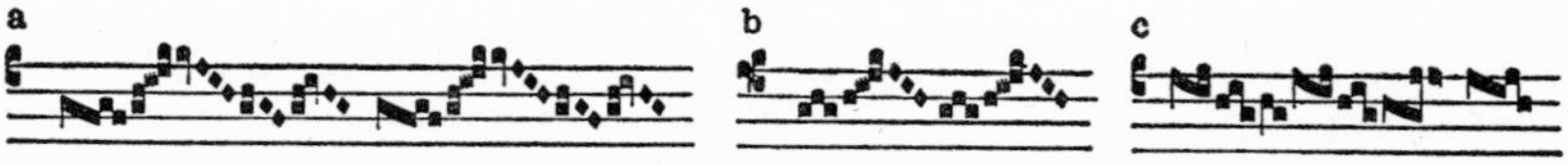

a. Psalmellus *Cor mundum*   b. Psalmellus *Domine audivi*
c. Offertorium *Erit hic vobis*

The main feature which distinguishes the Ambrosian repertory as a whole is clearly freedom from strict rule and system. The chant has never been obliged to codify its procedures in conformity with Roman dictates. As for the relationship between the Milanese and the Roman repertory, Karl Ott was one of the first to point out that they have a number of chants in common and that invariably the Ambrosian version is much more elaborate than the Roman.[22] He assumed that the Ambrosian versions are the earlier ones, and that the Gregorian melodies were derived from them by a process of simplification and methodical organization. On the whole, this view prevails to the present day.[23] However, recent theories of the evolution of Gregorian chant itself may well lead to a complete reconsideration of the problem. Where parallels are found, it is not necessarily accurate to regard the Ambrosian melodies as "primitive" versions of their Gregorian counterparts. They may well represent a later stage characterized by a tendency toward amplification and ornamentation, and paralleling the period of troping in Gregorian chant.

In view of the general tendency of modern scholars to regard the Ambrosian melodies as deficient in form, order, balance, etc., it is interesting to note that the opposite opinion was held by an eminent medieval authority, Guido of Arezzo. In a paragraph of Chapter XV of his *Micrologus* he says that the composer of melodies should employ diverse neumes, much in the same way as the poet combines various feet. However, such variety should not be lacking in correspondence, symmetry, and "dissimilar similarity"—and for such an ideal style of composition he refers to Ambrosian melodies as models:

[22] Carl Ott, "L'antiphona ambrosiana in rapporto al canto gregoriano," etc., in *Rass. Greg.*, V-IX (1906 to 1909).

[23] See, e.g., H. Anglès in *The New Oxford History of Music*, II, 61 (quoting from Wellesz).

Rationabilis vero discretio est, si ita fit neumarum et distinctionum moderata varietas, ut tamen neumae neumis et distinctiones distinctionibus quadam semper similitudini sibi consonanter respondeant, id est, ut sit similitudo dissimilis, more perdulcis Ambrosii.[24]

(Diversity is reasonable if the variety of neumes and members is moderated in such a way that neumes correspond to neumes, and members to members, in a certain similarity, in other words, so that there is a dissimilar similarity, in the manner of the "most sweet" Ambrosius.)

Whether the Ambrosian melodies to which Guido referred were the same as those that are preserved in manuscripts written at least a hundred years later, we cannot say. Possibly they were less overgrown and exuberant. But it cannot be denied that even in its ultimate, and perhaps partly degenerate, form Ambrosian chant is anything but formless or chaotic. In fact, it is especially in its most luxuriant products that it reveals a remarkable feeling for form and order.

[24] *GS*, II, 16b; J. Smits van Waesberghe, *Guidonis Aretini Micrologus* (1955), p. 172.

CHAPTER FIVE

The Old-Roman Chant

by ROBERT J. SNOW

R ECENT studies in Gregorian chant and the consequent re-evaluation of the role traditionally assigned to St. Gregory have intensified the interest of scholars in the unusual chant repertory of a small number of manuscripts of Roman origin. These date from 1071 to before 1250 and are the only musical manuscripts known to have been written and notated at Rome before the mid-thirteenth century. Although they are liturgically similar to the Gregorian, they differ from them radically in regard to their musical content. Unfortunately, none of these manuscripts has as yet been published, and they have been studied by only a few specialists whose opinions as to the origin and date of this tradition and its relation to the Gregorian repertory are in disagreement. As has been outlined in a previous chapter of this book [pp. 77ff], the Old-Roman repertory has been considered as post-Gregorian (tenth to eleventh centuries: Mocquereau, also Ferretti, Brou, Handschin?), as pre-Gregorian (sixth century: Andover, also Bannister, Frere, Besseler, Ursprung, Gastoué), and as properly Gregorian (Stäblein). Dom M. Huglo has approached the problem from the liturgico-historical aspect, and has been able to identify some fifteen non-musical manuscripts which testify to the existence of the Old-Roman tradition between the eighth and the thirteenth centuries. They indicate that during this period it was the official chant of all Rome, and that it was also used in parts of Central Italy and perhaps even in the British Isles before the Norman invasion.

Nothing more specific can be stated on the basis of documentary evidence. Only by a detailed analysis and comparative study of both traditions can we hope to obtain further information concerning their relationship. The present study—which is nothing more than an introductory survey—was undertaken as a first step in this direction. It is hoped that it will stimulate a greater interest in the whole problem and lead to further studies.

THE SOURCES FOR THE MASS CHANTS

Three of the five preserved Old-Roman chant manuscripts are *Graduals.*
The earliest of these, usually cited as *Phillipps 16069,* was written in 1071
for use at the church of St. Cecilia in Trastevere. In the eighteenth cen-
tury, when its text was published by Domenico Giorgi in Vol. IV of his
De liturgia Romani Pontificis, it was owned by Antonio Cardinal Gentili.
It was acquired by Sir Thomas Phillipps in 1861 and then by William H.
Robinson, a London antiquarian, in 1946; at present it is in the possession
of Martin Bodmer of Le Grand Cologny, Cologny-Genève, Switzerland.
Unfortunately, it has not been available for this study.[1]

Originally this *Gradual* contained all the chants of the liturgical year
according to the Old-Roman tradition, but approximately the last thirty
folios, containing the sanctoral cycle for July through November and the
Sundays after Pentecost, have now been lost. Because of the small number
of Alleluias proper to the Old-Roman tradition, some thirty Gregorian
Alleluias have been added throughout the manuscript in order to provide
a greater variety. Many of the principal feasts are provided with a troped
Kyrie and *Gloria* and a sequence, most of which occur in a number of
Gregorian sources, particularly those from Southern Italy.

The second oldest *Gradual,* Rome, *Vaticanum latinum 5319,* was written *c.* 1100. It was intended for use at one of the basilicas, perhaps the
Lateran, since the chants for the Easter Week Vespers proper to the basili-
can liturgy and the feast of the Dedication of the Lateran (*Dedicatio S.
Salvatoris,* Nov. 9) were included in it. At the end of the manuscript there
are several votive Masses, about thirty processional Antiphons for various
occasions and some troped *Kyries,* sequences and Gregorian Alleluias. The
notation and decoration of the manuscript are very similar to those of the
first.[2]

The third *Gradual,* Rome, *Vaticanum Basilicanum F. 22,* dates from
the first half of the thirteenth century. Here the temporal and sanctoral
cycles are separated, and the Offertory verses have all disappeared. It has
no Gregorian Alleluias nor any sequences or tropes.

Liturgically, these manuscripts are essentially the same as those of the
Gregorian tradition. They are characterized by a certain conservatism in

[1] For a complete paleographic and liturgical description of this manuscript see J.
Hourlier and M. Huglo, "Un important témoin du chant vieux-romain: Le Graduel de
Sainte Cécile du Transtévère" (*RG,* XXXI, 26-37). Three facsimiles from the manuscript
occur in *Catalogue No. 83 of Rare Books and Manuscripts offered for Sale by William
Robinson, Ltd.* (London, 1953), pp. 59-62.

[2] Plate VII of this book shows a page from this manuscript. Cf. H. M. Bannister,
Monumenti Vaticani . . ., p. 136, no. 397, and Tavola 81a. Also *Pal. mus.,* II, 4, fn. 1, and
Plate 28.

both their temporal and sanctoral cycles and conform more closely to the eighth and ninth century Gregorian manuscripts than they do to the Gregorian sources contemporary with them. Two feasts of the temporal cycle which are conspicuous by their absence are the Vigil of the Ascension and what in the Gregorian tradition is the Seventh Sunday after Pentecost, with the Introit *Omnes gentes*. This Introit is completely foreign to the Old-Roman tradition, which thus has but twenty-two formularies for the Sundays after Pentecost [see pp. 70f].

There are also considerable differences in the way in which the two traditions deal with the originally aliturgical Sundays following the Ember Days of Advent, Lent and Pentecost Week. The Sunday following the Ember Days of Advent apparently remained aliturgical, even into the thirteenth century at Rome. At least, neither *5319* nor *F. 22* provide any indication for a Mass formulary for this Sunday. Both manuscripts give a formulary for the Sunday after the Lenten Ember Days, and *5319* also gives one for that after the Ember Days of Pentecost Week, but all of these differ from the various ones found in the Gregorian sources. Neither manuscript includes the Feast of the Most Holy Trinity, which is found in nearly all the Gregorian sources dating later than the middle of the ninth century.

The only feast which seems to have been added to the sanctoral cycle after *c.* 800 is that of All Saints. Both manuscripts provide formularies for the Feast and its Vigil, but are not in agreement as to choice of borrowed material, except for the Introit *Gaudeamus* and the Offertory *Laetamini,* both for the Feast itself.

Generally the two traditions have the same Mass formularies, but a number of deviations occur. Thus the Feast of St. Lucia has the Communion *Diffusa est* in the Gregorian sources, while the Old-Roman manuscripts give *Simile est;* on Ember Friday of Advent the Gregorian Offertory *Deus tu convertens* is replaced by *Ad te Domine;* and the Gregorian assignment of the Introits *In excelso throno* and *Omnis terra* to the First and Second Sundays after Epiphany is reversed in the Old-Roman. Altogether about forty such divergencies occur (disregarding the Alleluias).

In a number of cases the texts show minor variations. Usually these result from the presence of an additional phrase in the Old-Roman, sometimes from a different word order in an otherwise identical text. It is such differences of text and of assignment that make it possible to identify Old-Roman manuscripts without musical notation.

Melodically, the Old-Roman chant differs decidedly from the Gregorian and constitutes a distinctive corpus of liturgical music. Nevertheless it has many features of a general nature in common with Gregorian chant. The forms of the various types (Introits, etc.) are essentially identical with the Gregorian. The melodies are composed in (or perhaps more correctly, were at some time subjected to) the same modal system as is used in the Gregorian tradition, and more often than not there is modal agreement between textually identical chants. The psalmodic formulae (psalm tones, tones for the Responsories, Introits, etc.) are practically identical. The free melodies, although usually different, nevertheless often have similar contours or identical melodic skeletons.

The differences between the two traditions result from the specific stylistic characteristics proper to each, from the specific forms assumed by the freely composed melodies (Introits, Communions, etc.) or the standard formulae (Tracts, Graduals, etc.), and from the different manner in which centonization is practiced. All of this can be seen from the subsequent discussion and examples of the various classes of the Old-Roman chant.

THE INTROITS

The Introits of the Old-Roman tradition, 149 in number, are identical in form with the Gregorian and do not significantly differ from them in regard to text. In performance they retained the early practice involving the use of the *versus ad repetendum,* which appears in even the latest of the sources, the thirteenth-century *Gradual, F. 22.* This is another indication of the conservative nature of the tradition since the *versus* had, in general, disappeared from the Gregorian manuscripts by the late eleventh century. The antiphons are more ornate than the Gregorian in their neumatic passages and more barren in their syllabic sections. Many of them have all the characteristics of freely-composed music, but a considerable number have features which indicate that they were derived from psalmodic formulae. In such antiphons as these the various phrases open with a short intonation, continue with simple recitation, and close with a rather extended cadence. This type of design occurs most often in melodies of the third and fourth modes, many of which employ phrases similar to those which open *Timete Dominum* and *Reminiscere:*

FIGURE 165

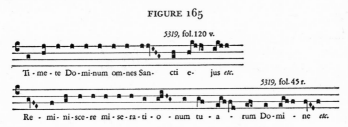

It is interesting to notice that modes 3 and 4, which make extensive use of psalmodic phrases, are also the ones most frequently used in the entire group, as appears from the following chart:

	OLD-ROMAN	GREG.			OLD-ROMAN	GREG.
Mode 1:	19	28	Mode 5:		12	10
2:	14	19	6:		14	11
3:	29	29	7:		6	18
4:	43	19	8:		12	14

As for the specific melodic relationship of the Old-Roman Introit antiphons to the Gregorian, a comparison of the two repertories reveals that modal agreement exists in ninety instances, in most of which some degree of melodic similarity is also present. The degree of melodic similarity, however, of such modally identical chants varies considerably. In a few cases it is very great, as in *Dominus dixit* from the Midnight Mass of the Nativity [cf. *L* 392]:

FIGURE 166

Here the melodic outline, general musical structure and three of the four cadence notes are the same in both versions. In addition to this there is exact identity at the beginning and only a slight difference at "e(go)," which, in fact, disappears if the reading of *F. 22,* which replaces the c-f-g-f of *5319* with d-f-g-f, is used.

In the majority of cases, however, the similarity is not so great and consists of only a general melodic resemblance, such as is to be found between the two versions of *Resurrexi* (Easter Sunday; cf. *L* 778):

FIGURE 167

Here the basic melodic outline is preserved in each phrase, but the melodies themselves sometimes differ, as do the cadential notes. Instances of complete absence of melodic similarity, however, are rare.[3]

The tones to which the Introit verses are sung are indicated in the manuscripts by the notation of the proper intonation and termination at the

3 *Resurrexi* has been published in *Pal. mus.,* II, 8, and in Ursprung, *Die Katholische Kirchenmusik* (1931), p. 20. See also *Ad te levavi* in Andoyer, "Le Chant romain antégrégorien" (*RCG,* XX, 69); *Puer natus* and *Rorate* in *MGG,* art. "Choral" (col. 1273).

conclusion of the antiphons. The mediant and re-intonation formulae can be found only in very rare instances when, for one reason or another, an entire psalm-verse was notated. Consequently, it is impossible to reconstruct some of the formulae completely; others can be reconstructed only tentatively, since often it is the exceptional verses which have been fully notated and these are of but limited value in determining the general practice. The evidence available, however, indicates that the Old-Roman tones were basically the same as the Gregorian but more simple melodically, particularly in their mediant and re-intonation formulae. The terminations seem to have been adapted to the texts according to the tonic rather than the cursive principle. Following are the intonations, tenors, and terminations of modes 1 and 2 [cf. *L* 14]:

FIGURE 168

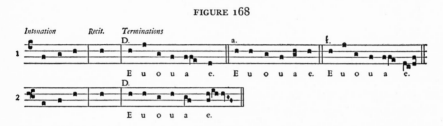

It may be noticed that *5319* and *F*. 22 frequently indicate different terminations when more than one is available.

THE COMMUNIONS

The Communion antiphons of the Old-Roman tradition, of which there are also 149, are, for the most part, textually identical with those of the Gregorian tradition. Sometimes, however, there are slight differences which usually result from the presence of an additional phrase in the Old-Roman or from the use of a different word order in an otherwise identical text. Their original manner of performance was retained and the Psalm to be used is indicated in the majority of cases. Stylistically they are similar to the Introits but have a tendency to use the extremes of the Introit style: if syllabic, they are often excessively so; if neumatic, they sometimes approach the melismatic style, just as do the Gregorian Communions.

Modally they are much more evenly distributed than the Introits, the favored modes being those on G, in which about thirty per cent of them are written. In almost a dozen instances *5319* and *F*. 22 disagree as to the mode. In such cases the two manuscripts will usually notate the larger portion of the antiphon at the same pitch level but will disagree as to the level of the closing phrase, with the result that an antiphon will perhaps seem to be in the sixth mode in one source and in the eighth in the other.

This is a particularly interesting situation since exactly the same kind of confusion is also found in the early Gregorian sources.

There is approximately the same degree of modal correspondence between the Communions of the two repertories as between their Introits, and melodic similarity is also present in about the same degree. Fig. 169 shows the beginning of *Confundantur* [cf. *L* 1220]:

FIGURE 169

This Communion antiphon differs textually from its Gregorian counterpart not only because of the presence of an additional phrase ("fiat cor meum immaculatum," after "mandatis tuis"), but also in the word order of the second phrase: "ego autem exercebor in mandatis tuis," as against the Gregorian "ego autem in mandatis tuis exercebor." Nevertheless, the individual words have the same (or closely related) musical lines, which simply change their position together with the reversed order of "in mandatis tuis" and "exercebor."

The situation of the Communion tones is a rather confused one. As in the Gregorian tradition, the same tones are used for both the Introits and Communions, but more terminations are added and in several cases the use of certain Gregorian formulae is even indicated. The reasons for the use of the additional terminations are not clear and, as in the case of the Introits, *5319* and *F.* 22 often disagree in their assignment of terminations when more than one is available, making it impossible to ascertain specifically what, if anything, prompted the use of one rather than another.

THE OFFERTORIES

The ninety-five Old-Roman Offertories exhibit a greater degree of textual divergency from their Gregorian counterparts than is to be found in the other classes of Mass chants. The verses, in particular, often differ either in their arrangement or in the manner in which portions of the text are repeated. Additional phrases and slight variations in word order can also be found, but not too frequently.

A striking trait of the Offertories is their use of two widely different types of musical material. One of these is a psalmodic formula noteworthy for its employment of a reiterated *torculus* instead of a single recitation note. It can be found in both the antiphons and the verses, and is often used in conjunction with freely composed material. In some cases, however, it alone serves for a whole verse, being repeated as many times as the text might demand. An instance of this occurs in *Confitebuntur caeli*, where verse 1 consists entirely of repetitions of this formula, while the antiphon and verse 2 use it for all but three of their phrases:

FIGURE 170

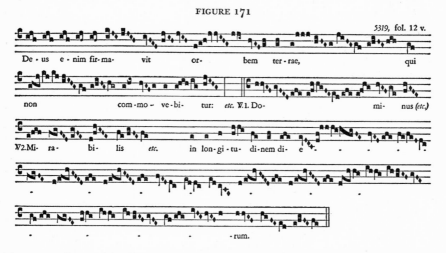

The other type of unusual material consists of long melismas, some including over 150 notes, which occur mostly in the verses. In their use of a wide range and of internal repeats they show general characteristics similar to those of their Gregorian counterparts. One of the longest occurs at the close of *Deus enim firmavit*, sections of which are shown in Fig. 171.

FIGURE 171

A comparison with the Gregorian form [Ott 16] shows that melodic similarity is present in the antiphon from "orbem" on, the point at which the Old-Roman version abandons its peculiar psalmodic-type material. The verses are also melodically similar (perhaps a little more so than is the average) except at melismas, where great divergency occurs. Thus, the Old-Roman melisma at the opening of verse 1 has the general outline c'-f-c', while the corresponding Gregorian melisma rises from d to c'. While the Gregorian version abounds in typically bold formations, the Old-Roman has much smoother contours, particularly at the end of verse 1 ("et praecinxit se virtutem") and in the final melisma.

In general the Old-Roman and the Gregorian Offertories show a high degree of modal identity as well as considerable melodic similarity in their antiphons. In the verses, however, similarity is much less frequent. They pose some very interesting questions, regarding their structure as well as their relationship to the Gregorian tradition, and deserve to be studied in the greatest detail.[4]

THE GRADUALS[5]

The Old-Roman Graduals exhibit the same type of textual and formal relationship with their Gregorian counterparts as do the other classes of previously discussed chants. They also show the same close musical similarity and are confined, as are the Gregorian, almost exclusively to modes 1, 2, 3, 5 and 7. Likewise, they are based almost entirely on standard formulae or, in the case of mode 2, are adapted to a single standard melody. Since the various formulae and the standard melody are themselves very similar to those used in the Gregorian Graduals, the Old-Roman Graduals, as a group, are closely related to the Gregorian. The Old-Roman formulae, however, are more limited in number; from this fact and the fact that centonization is sometimes practiced differently a number of variations between specific chants result.

The favored mode, by far, is the fifth, which contains 44 of the 112 Graduals of the Old-Roman repertory. An examination of the final formulae of their verses immediately reveals the more limited nature of the Old-Roman material. While the Gregorian Graduals of mode 5 have at least two standard formulae for the close of the verse [F_{10} and F_{11} in the tabulation, pp. 346f], the Old-Roman tradition has only one (with one exception), perhaps an indication that earlier the verses were all sung to a single psalmodic formula such as is used in the corresponding Office chants, the Responsories. The responds of the Graduals use a greater variety of cadential formulae (one of which is that of the verse), but here, too, their number is smaller than in the Gregorian repertory.

In order to illustrate the divergency of the centonization method it may suffice to say that in the Gregorian tradition *Misit Dominus* opens with the same formula as *Timebunt gentes* (F_b), while the Old-Roman *Misit Dominus* shares its initial formula—a variant of F_c—with *Justorum animae* and *Probasti*. Other divergencies arise from the fact that sections, which in the Gregorian form are freely composed, sometimes employ standard formulae in the Old-Roman version.

Fig. 172 shows the verse of *Timebunt gentes*. A comparison with the

---

4 Other published Offertories include: *Ad te Domine levavi* (respond only) in Stäblein, "Ambrosianisch-Gregorianisch" (*Kongress-Bericht*, Basel, 1949, p. 188); *Repleti* (beginning of ℣. 2 only) in Stäblein, "Zur Frühgeschichte des römischen Chorals" (*ACI*, p. 272).

5 For a general survey of the Old-Roman Graduals see H. Hucke, "Gregorianischer Gesang in altrömischer und fränkischer Ueberlieferung" (*AfMW*, XII, 74-87).

Gregorian version [*L* 489] shows that the numerous *pressus* formations, so typical of the Gregorian Graduals, are all replaced by smoothly moving *climacus* groups.

FIGURE 172

A situation similar to that existing in the fifth mode Graduals occurs also in the Graduals of the other authentic modes. In mode 3, for example, centonization is also practiced, and only one cadential formula is used for both the responds and verses of all eleven of the Graduals occurring in this mode. An unusual feature of the third mode Gregorian Graduals, the use of the same non-cadential formulae in both respond and verse, appears also in the Old-Roman, but the exact choice of formulae for any specific chant does not always correspond in the two traditions.

The so-called *Justus ut palma* type of Gregorian Graduals have their counterpart in twenty-eight Old-Roman Graduals which are all likewise adapted to a second mode standard melody closely approximating the Gregorian. The Gregorian appellation, however, cannot be used here since the Gradual *Justus ut palma* does not occur in the Old-Roman tradition. This standard melody is treated in the same manner as in the Gregorian and differs from it only in its specific melodic outline. It has several possible opening phrases and is expanded or contracted to fit a text just as in the Gregorian, its most frequent form being that which is used for *In omnem terram*, shown in Fig. 173 [see *L* 1486 for the Gregorian version].

FIGURE 173

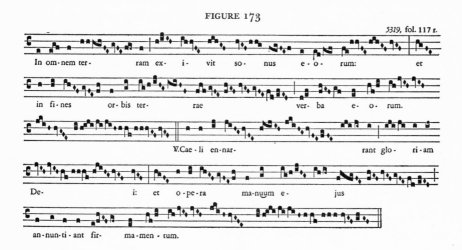

The only Old-Roman Gradual which has the characteristics of free composition is the single fourth mode Gradual *Domine praevenisti*. More in the syllabic-neumatic style of an Introit or Communion, it lacks the final melismas in both respond and verse and seems to date from an entirely different period than do the other Graduals. Perhaps it originally belonged to another class of chants and only later was pressed into service as a Gradual.[6]

THE TRACTS

The Old-Roman manuscripts contain twenty of the twenty-one Tracts found in the earliest Gregorian sources [see p. 313], consistently omitting *Eripe me* of Good Friday and using instead *Qui habitat* from the first Sunday of Lent. Only sixteen of these, however, are proper to the Old-Roman tradition, the other four being borrowed from the Gregorian repertory. These are the four Tracts from Holy Saturday, *Attende caelum, Cantemus Domino, Sicut cervus,* and *Vinea facta est,* which probably replaced the original Old-Roman items in the tenth century.[7]

As for modal assignment, the Old-Roman Tracts correspond exactly and individually to the Gregorian: eleven are in the eighth mode, and five in the second (the former group lacks the Tracts of Holy Saturday, the latter *Eripe me*). In each group extensive use is made of a limited number of standard formulae very similar to those of the Gregorian versions, and combined in much the same way to construct a verse.

The characteristic verse form of the Tracts of mode 8 consists of four phrases (designated here I, II, III, IV), rather than the three usually found in the Gregorian versions [see the tabulation, p. 319]. Their cadential structure is very similar to the Gregorian, g f g g. Phrase I is the least stable of all. It is often constructed out of a number of shorter melodic germs which serve as a sort of building material, together with free material. For phrase II four different but closely related formulae are available. All have the same cadential phrase (closing on f), but differ somewhat in the preceding part. Only one formula exists for phrase III, while in phrase

6 Other published Old-Roman Graduals include: *A summo caelo* in *Pal. mus.,* II, 6, and in Ursprung (fn. 3), p. 20; *Ex Sion species* in Andoyer (fn. 3), p. 107; *Tollite portas, Juravit, Exaltabo te, Exsurge Domine, Exiit sermo* and *Ecce Sacerdos* (reponds only; also the verses of several others) in Hucke (fn. 5), pp. 76ff.

7 Fortunately, the texts of two of these items have been preserved in a non-notated Old-Roman Missal of the eleventh century, and for one of these, *Vinea enim Domini,* the melody has been found in two Gregorian Mss of the twelfth century, where it occurs in addition to the usual Gregorian Tracts. In contrast to these (as well as to the Old-Roman Tracts) it has a responsorial form, each verse closing with the (choral) refrain: *domus Israel.* See M. Huglo, "Notes historiques à propos du second Décret sur la Vigile Pascale" (*RG,* XXXI, 130ff), and "Le Chant 'vieux-romain'" (*Sacris erudiri,* VI, 100 and fn. 4).

IV there is a choice between four formulae, one of which is restricted to the final verse.

Nineteen of the thirty-seven verses of the eighth-mode Tracts employ the full four-phrase structure. Sixteen have a reduced form such as I-II-IV or I-IV, and two have an amplified form involving the repetition of phrases.

Following is a schematic representation of the Tract *Jubilate Deo,* which consists of a three verses of the full four-phrase construction (the figures 1, 2, etc. indicate the shorter motives employed in the initial phrase):

<pre>
       1   2   IIa   III   IVa
℣. 1: Jubilate Deo, omnis terra: servite Domino in laetitia.

      3   4   IIa   III
℣. 2: Intrate in conspectu eius in exsultatione: scitote quod Dominus
      IVa
      ipse est Deus.

      free   IIc   III
℣. 3: Ipse fecit nos, et non ipsi nos: nos autem populus ejus,
      IV final
      et oves pascuae ejus.
</pre>

In the corresponding Gregorian Tract, *Jubilate Domino* [513] the second of these verses is divided into two verses, which therefore consist only of two phrases each [see the tabulation, p. 319]. Fig. 174 shows the first verse of the Old-Roman version, which may be compared with the Gregorian.

FIGURE 174

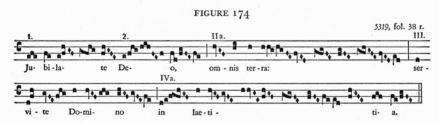

The five second-mode Tracts exhibit closer structural relationship with their Gregorian counterparts than do the eighth-mode Tracts. In both traditions the verse consists normally of four sections which cadence on d, c, f, and d. This structure is used in twenty-six of the forty-one verses of the second-mode Tracts, while most of the remaining verses, characterized by extremely long texts, repeat the music of sections I, II, or III. For example, the most frequently used structure for verses requiring six phrases is I-II-I-II-III-IV.

As for the musical material available for each section, much the same situation exists here as in the eighth mode. Section I uses smaller melodic

units and a limited amount of free material, while for section II three complete standard phrases are available. Only one formula is used in section
III, but there is a choice of four in section IV. As in the case of the Gregorian standard phrases, the various formulae are fixed, particularly at their
end, and may occasionally vary considerably in the preceding portion.

An unusual feature is to be noticed in the use of the formulae for section
IV. One of these (designated here as IVa) serves invariably for the close of
the final verse; but in three Tracts, *De necessitatibus, Domine audivi,* and
Domine exaudi, it also occurs at the close of all the other verses. It is certainly no mere coincidence that these Tracts are the ones which the earliest
sources, both Gregorian and Old-Roman, consistently designate as Graduals [see p. 184].

Fig. 175 shows the first verse of *Domine exaudi.* Section I consists of two
melodic units (1, 2), the first of which opens all five Tracts of the second
mode. A comparison with the Gregorian version [*L* 614] reveals consider-

FIGURE 175

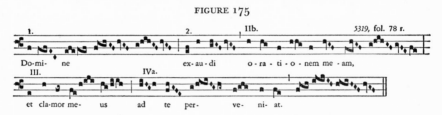

able melodic similarity, particularly at the beginning. The counterpart of
IVa, the closing formula of all the Old-Roman verses, is D_n, which in the
Gregorian Tract is used only for the three last verses. Here we have another
example showing the different manner in which centonization is practiced. On the whole, the Old-Roman method is considerably more systematic and uniform than is the Gregorian.

THE ALLELUIAS[8]

The Alleluias of the Old-Roman tradition are the most intriguing group
of this repertory, both in themselves and in their relationship with the
Gregorian tradition. They have essentially the same form as the Gregorian,
but in a number of cases they employ an *alleluia secundus,* that is an extended version of the opening *jubilus* to be used after the verse, a practice
which is of basic importance in the Ambrosian tradition. Of special interest is the fact that they are also sung in the Vespers of Easter Week and that
a number of them have verses in Greek.

Close agreement of liturgical assignment exists in those instances in
which the Gregorian sources show agreement among themselves, that is
for the feasts shown on p. 379. The main exception are the three Sundays

8 Cf. *MGG,* art. "Alleluia" (Stäblein) for another discussion of the Old-Roman
Alleluias, the findings of which are somewhat different from those presented here.

after Epiphany. For *Feria II post Pascha,* the Old-Roman has the Greek version of *Dominus regnavit,* Ὁ Κύριος ἐβασίλευσεν. No agreement exists in the remainder of the Temporale, and only a few instances of it occur in the Sanctorale.

The Old-Roman repertory has fifty-four Mass Alleluias, seven of which have two verses. Eight Alleluias have proper melodies used only once. The others fall into seven groups, each of which is characterized by an identical Alleluia section (hereafter referred to as *jubilus*) and often also by musical relationship between their verse melodies. Particularly frequent are three *jubili,* one on D, one on E, and on one G, which are used respectively for thirteen, thirteen, and ten Alleluias.[9] As for the verses associated with a given *jubilus,* some of them have identical melodies, and thus represent cases of complete adaptation. In others the melody is divided into phrases, some of which may be restated or omitted, depending upon the requirements of the text. The following two tables provide an insight into the "centonization" technique of the Old-Roman Alleluia verses.

D-jubilus (used for thirteen Alleluias with fourteen verses):

Phrases:	1 – 2 – 3 – 4	five verses
	1 – 2 – 4	one verse
	1 – 2 – 3 – 1 – 2 – 4	six verses
	essentially free	two verses

E-jubilus (used for thirteen Alleluias with sixteen verses):

Phrases:	1 – 2 – 3 – 4	eight verses
	1′ (shortened) – 2 – 3 – 4	two verses
	1″ (variant) – 2 – 3 – 4	three verses
	1 – 2 – 4	two verses
	1 – 2 – free – 4	one verse

Fig. 176 shows the Alleluia *Excita Domine* of the latter group [see L 336 for the Gregorian version]. The melody starts with the standard *jubilus*

FIGURE 176

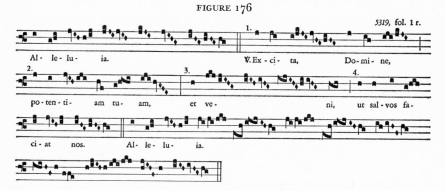

5319, fol. 1 r.

Al - le - lu - ia.   ℣. Ex - ci - ta,   Do - mi - ne,   po - ten - ti - am tu - am,   et ve -   ni,   ut sal - vos fa -   ci - at   nos.   Al - le - lu - ia.

---

[9] The Gregorian equivalents for these three Old-Roman *jubili* are those of *Dies sanctificatus, Excita,* and *Ostende.*

on E, and closes with an *Alleluia secundus,* an internally expanded version of the opening section. The verse consists of four phrases ending on g, c, f, and e.

As was mentioned previously, the Alleluia occurs also in the Old-Roman Vespers of Easter Week, a most interesting service mentioned in several of the early *Ordines Romani.*[10] Like the Mass Alleluias they employ a limited number of *jubilus* melodies for many more verses. The *jubili* (seven in number) are adopted from the Mass Alleluias, while most of the verses are proper to Vespers. With a single exception, all the nineteen Vesper Alleluias have two or three verses, with a total of forty-five verses. Twelve of these are borrowed from the Mass liturgy. The remaining thirty-three verses occur only in Vespers, and these show a radically different musical style. They are all based on the same material consisting of two psalmodic formulae, one ending on a, the other on g. The G-formula is used for the final phrase, the A-formula for all the preceding phrases, as in the following example:

FIGURE 177

Here, as in many other verses of the Vespers Alleluias, a *primicerius* (principal cantor)—in other words, a soloist—sings the A-phrases and an intonation for the final G-phrase, which is then sung, in a responsorial manner, by the *schola.* Some verses, on the other hand, employ the normal performance practice in which the verse is sung straight through, probably by a soloist. In these the final phrase begins with the same intonation and recitation as the A-phrases, but always closes with the elaborate termination of the G-phrase (beginning at *dicam* in the above example).

Another interesting feature of the Old-Roman Alleluias is the fact that they include seven with verses in Greek (written in an extremely corrupt form with Latin letters).[11] The most interesting question raised by their presence is, of course, whether their music might have been derived from Eastern chants. A negative answer can be given in regard to four of them

---

[10] The sections which describe these services have been published, with commentary, by Gastoué in *Les Origines du chant romain,* pp. 286ff. These Vespers were of a complex stational character and were usually celebrated in three different places of the church, with processions from one to the next.

[11] They have been studied by Dom Ugo Gaisser, in "Brani greci nella liturgia latina" (*Rass. Greg.,* I, 126). Unfortunately, the article is not entirely reliable.

which occur only in the Paschal Vespers and which use the psalmodic material common to nearly all the Vesper Alleluias. The remaining three, however, are freely composed and have distinctive musical characteristics which set them apart from all the other Alleluia chants. Two of them, Ἐπὶ σοῖ, Κύριε, ἤλπισα (*In te, Domine, speravi*) and Ὅτι Θεὸς μέγας (*Quoniam Deus magnus*), employ unique material for both their *jubili* and their verses. The third, Ὁ Κύριος ἐβασίλευσεν (*Dominus regnavit*), uses the standard D-mode *jubilus* of the Latin Alleluias, but has entirely different music for its verse.[12] The possibility that these three Alleluias might be based on Greek models, therefore, exists. Whether they actually are or not, I cannot say at the present.[13]

THE SOURCES OF THE OFFICE CHANTS

Two notated Old-Roman *Antiphonaries* have been preserved. The older of these is to be found in London, at the British Museum, where it bears the number *Mus. Add. 29,988*. Dating from *c.* 1150, its notation indicates that it was written in the area lying between Central Italy and Beneventum. The manuscript lacks the series of Gospel Antiphons for the Benedictus and Magnificat for the Sundays after Pentecost which are to be found in the Gregorian *Antiphonaries*, this absence being a feature which Amalarius mentioned as characteristic of the usage in Rome.[14] It includes such specifically Roman elements as the Paschal Vespers, which are also to be found in the *Gradual 5319*, and the double office of Matins on Christmas. At the end is added a series of Invitatories and the Office for the Dead.[15]

The other *Antiphonary*, dating from *c.* 1175, is the manuscript Rome, Vat. Basilic. *B. 79*. Also characterized by all the liturgical features of the above, this source was written for use at St. Peter's and is particularly important from the liturgical point of view since it contains copious rubrics which reveal many interesting details concerning the celebration of the Old-Roman Office.[16]

Although the Old-Roman Office is essentially the same in its general

[12] Published in Gaisser (fn. 11), p. 127, and E. Wellesz, *Eastern Elements in Western Chant*, p. 35. In both publications it is compared with the wrong Gregorian counterpart.

[13] Other published Old-Roman Alleluias include: *Magnus Sanctus Paulus* in Andoyer (fn. 3), p. 108; *Dies sanctificatus* and *Pascha nostrum* (beginning) in *MGG*, art. "Alleluia;" *Dies sanctificatus* also in Dom L. Brou, "L'Alleluia greco-latin *Dies sanctificatus* de la messe du jour de Noël" (*RG*, XXIV, 86).

[14] *De ordine antiphonarii*, cap. LXVIII (ed. Hanssen, III, 99).

[15] Cf. *The Musical Notation of the Middle Ages* (1890), Plate no. 12. (The author considered this manuscript to be of Spanish origin.)

[16] Cf. *Pal. mus.*, II, p. 4, fn. 1. The liturgical texts and rubrics of this manuscript have been published by Tommasi, under the title of *Responsorialia et antiphonaria Romanae Ecclesiae* (1686), pp. i-ccxv (reprinted in his *Opera omnia*, IV, pp. 1-170).

outline as the non-monastic Office of the Gregorian tradition (i.e. it is composed of the usual eight Office Hours using the same classes of chant, etc.), a comparative study of the liturgical aspects of the Old-Roman and Gregorian *Antiphonaries* is a much more difficult task than is such a study of the *Graduals* of the two traditions. The reason for this is that in ninth- and tenth-century Gaul the Gregorian *Antiphonary* was subjected to such a number of revisions and received so many additions that it is nearly impossible to determine its primitive format. Nevertheless, a comparative study of the music of the two traditions reveals the presence of the same sort of musical relationship here as is to be found in the Mass chants.

THE RESPONSORIES

One of the first things that is noticed in an examination of the Old-Roman *Antiphonaries* is the poverty of their repertory in comparison with that of contemporary Gregorian manuscripts. *B. 79* contains only 570 Responsories and *29,988* has even less, just 534, while Gregorian *Antiphonaries* of about the same date, such as that of Worcester, usually contain approximately 1,000. The actual number of different Responsories to be found in the two Old-Roman sources, however, is 636 since each manuscript contains a considerable number of them which are not to be found in the other. Of this total twelve are borrowings from the Gregorian repertory, while two more exhibit stylistic features which differ greatly from the general Old-Roman style and suggest that they, too, may have been borrowed from some other tradition or that perhaps they date from a much later period than the remaining 622 responsories, all of which are in the characteristic Old-Roman style.[17]

The form of the Old-Roman Responsories is, in most cases, the same as that of the Gregorian. That is, they usually consist of a respond, a verse (occasionally two or even three), and a repetition of a closing portion of the respond, the point at which this repeat begins being indicated in the sources either by a rubric at the conclusion of the verse or in the respond itself. On certain greater feasts, however, such as Christmas, Easter, Ascension and Pentecost, *B. 79* indicates (not only by giving the first words of the beginning of the respond at the end of the verse but also by the special rubric *Responsoria reincipiuntur*) that the entire respond is to be repeated after the verse. This was the usual method of performance in Rome in the

[17] The actual number of the Old-Roman Responsories is further reduced owing to the fact that nearly forty of them are nothing more than Mass chants (usually Communion antiphons), which have been transformed into Responsories through the addition of verses sung to one of the eight Old-Roman Responsory tones. The possibility that the borrowing was the other way around cannot be entirely excluded, but is much less probable.

eighth century and earlier while the custom of repeating but a part of the respond was first introduced into the Gregorian tradition in the early ninth century.[18] The use of the partial repeat was apparently introduced into Rome as a result of the influence of the Gregorian practice, probably in the tenth century, and imposed upon responds which were not originally written for this type of performance. This can be seen from the fact that their musical structure frequently fails to lend itself easily to a partial repeat and that consequently the two Old-Roman *Antiphonaries* are often in disagreement as to how much of the respond is to be repeated after the verse. These facts suggest that the majority of the Old-Roman Responsories must then date from before the introduction of the partial-repeat practice. Had they been composed after the introduction of this practice, they undoubtedly would have been designed so as to permit a musically logical partial repeat and the great disagreement between the sources as to where the repeats are to begin would not exist.

The Old-Roman Responsories heavily favor the modes on G, with almost half of the total being written in the seventh or eighth modes, as can be seen from the following chart:

Mode 1:	65	Mode 2:	86
3:	33	4:	82
5:	31	6:	28
7:	122	8:	175

Neumatic in their general style, they exhibit many similarities with the Old-Roman Introits and Communions, with which they actually share a number of short melodic formulae, particularly cadence patterns. As in the Gregorian Responsories, centonization is practiced extensively and free composition plays but a small role. The formulae are often very similar to their Gregorian counterparts. The beginning of *Hodie nobis,* shown in Fig. 178, may be compared with the Gregorian version [*L* 376].

FIGURE 178

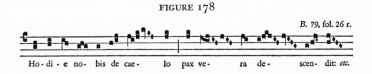

B. 79, fol. 26 r.

Ho-di-e no-bis de cae-lo pax ve-ra de-scen-dit: *etc.*

The verses of the Responsories are sung to a set of eight standard tones, one for each mode. Freely composed verses, such as are found in the later strata of the Gregorian tradition, do not occur in the Old-Roman. The tones are adapted to the verse texts according to both the cursive and the

18 See p. 513 for a discussion of the Roman versus the Frankish practice of repeating the respond which, according to Amalarius, constituted one of the main differences between the two traditions.

tonic principle, but the former prevails. In the Gregorian tradition the cursive principle is used exclusively.[19]

THE ANTIPHONS

The musical material used by the Antiphons of the Old-Roman tradition is closely related to that used by the Gregorian Antiphons, and most of the forty-seven themes catalogued by Gevaert have Old-Roman counterparts. The two traditions frequently disagree, however, in their choice of themes for specific texts, the same texts being set to equivalent themes in both traditions only about sixty per cent of the time. Free composition plays an even smaller role here than in the Gregorian.

The following Antiphons, which are characteristic Old-Roman versions of Gevaert's themes 11, 45, and 23, illustrate the general Old-Roman Antiphon style and the degree of relationship to be found between equivalent themes of the two traditions. (See L 331, 357, and 1176, respectively, for the Gregorian versions.)

FIGURE 179

The psalm tones used with the Antiphons are, in many cases, identical with the Gregorian formulae in their intonations and terminations. Differences do exist, but they are of no great importance.[20]

The *Antiphonaries* also contain a number of Invitatory Antiphons and several tones for their Psalm. In *B. 79* these tones were originally all included in an appendix at the end of the manuscript but unfortunately this is now incomplete; it is thus impossible to reconstruct the entire group of Invitatory tones. As nearly as can be determined, however, nine tones were used, and these exhibited the same general similarity to their Gregorian counterparts as have all the other classes of psalm tones.

[19] Other published Responsories include: *In monte Oliveti* in Andoyer [fn. 3], p. 69; *Lavi pedes* in *Pal. mus.*, xiv, 289.

[20] Other published Antiphons include *Zelus domus tuae, Ecce sacerdos magnus* and *Similabo eum,* in Andoyer [fn. 3], p. 70.

Hymns are almost completely lacking in the Old-Roman *Antiphonaries,* as is to be expected, since they did not form a part of the traditional Old-Roman Office and were only gradually introduced as a result of the influence of the Benedictine Office. Only one occurs in the main body of *B. 79, Te lucis ante terminum,* for Compline, an Office Hour of Benedictine origin, while one more, *Nunc Sancte nobis Spiritus,* for Terce, is to be found, along with several items from the Ordinary of the Mass, on a folio added at the end of the manuscript.

THE PROBLEM OF CHRONOLOGY

From this survey of the Old-Roman chant and from the comparisons of the given examples with their Gregorian counterparts, the close musical relationship existing between the two traditions is immediately evident. This relationship could be explained by the supposition that both repertories were based on a third, common source, but the large number of similarities and parallel situations existing in regard to small details suggest that a more probable explanation would be that one was directly inspired by the other. Whether or not the latter supposition ultimately proves to be the correct one, there arises the question as to the relative dates of origin of the two traditions. As was stated earlier, this can be determined only from purely musical evidence since all extrinsic testimony as to the relative dates of origin of the two traditions is inconclusive and demonstrates no more than that the Old-Roman tradition can be traced as far back in time as can the Gregorian.

When compared with the Gregorian, nearly every aspect of the Old-Roman chant suggests that it is the earlier of the two. The more limited number of formulae used in centonized chants, the greater use of standard melodies and the very limited number of Alleluia *jubili* all indicate that the Old-Roman repertory is musically less developed than the Gregorian and must date from a period in which free composition and variety played an even smaller role than they did at the time of the formation of the original nucleus of the Franco-Roman repertory. It is hardly conceivable that the much more highly diversified Gregorian repertory could have been followed by the thematically more limited Old-Roman unless a practical consideration, such as a notational one, made such diversity impractical and a simplification necessary. This is not the case, however, since a fairly adequate notational system was developed at the very time such a simplification would have taken place, thus obviating any practical reasons for a simplification. (It is, in fact, very possible that the development of neumatic notation shortly after the appearance of the Gregorian repertory was no mere coincidence but rather the result of a pressing need for a means by which to preserve a newer and more varied body of chant, such a need not having been so great when a less diversified repertory was in use.)

Another aspect of the Old-Roman chant which indicates that it must date from a period earlier than that of the Gregorian is the manner and frequency of its use of a psalmodic-type phrase structure, particularly in the Introit and Communion antiphons. Here, long and excessively syllabic phrases with but very little melodic movement often terminate in florid cadences which suddenly seem to interrupt what was hardly more than a declamation of the text with extraneous and unexplained musical material. Such passages as these are nothing other than examples of the first stage of the evolutionary development leading from a psalm-tone to free composition. Here only the termination of the formula is freely developed and elaborated and the resulting musical phrases are unbalanced. In the Gregorian counterparts of such passages, however, all the elements of the formula—intonation and recitation tone, as well as termination—are musically developed and well balanced in relationship to one another and the resulting phrase is an example of free composition which, nevertheless, preserves the outline of a psalm-tone. All of this can be clearly seen in *Timete Dominum* [Fig. 165] and in its Gregorian counterpart.

The almost complete absence of the repetitive type of melodic structure so typical of the Gregorian Alleluias of the ninth and tenth centuries also suggests that the Old-Roman chant dates from a period preceding the use of this principle. Such a principle of melodic construction would undoubtedly have played a large role in the Old-Roman chant if it had been codified at a time when the principle was in use. (Its presence in the Offertory verses, consequently, suggests that these date from a much later period than the remainder of the repertory and that perhaps they were even influenced by the Gregorian Offertory verses.)

Finally, many features of a general nature indicate that the Old-Roman chant is of an earlier date than the Gregorian. Its formulae are less well balanced than those of the Gregorian and are often monotonous as a result of the use of an almost continual stepwise motion, the various members of a chant are sometimes awkwardly connected, and cadential patterns, especially in the Introits, Offertories, Communions and Responsories are more verbose, as it were, and frequently lack the precise and definitive character of those of the Gregorian tradition. In comparison with Gregorian chant, the Old-Roman clearly gives the impression of being an earlier, tentative version of the same body of traditional liturgical chant.

From these several facts it can be safely concluded that the Old-Roman chant is definitely of an earlier date than the Gregorian tradition. This is not to say that the eleventh-century form in which it has come down to us is exactly the same form which it had in the eighth century or earlier. Undoubtedly it underwent certain minor changes and developments but in essence it remained the same, as can be seen from its retention of its archaic features. Consequently, the Old-Roman chant must be considered as the earliest of the preserved repertories of occidental liturgical music and the probable immediate source for much of the original nucleus of the Franco-Roman or "Gregorian" repertory of the late eighth century.

Conclusion: Prolegomena to a History of Gregorian Style

I N CONCLUSION, and as a summary of our studies we propose to return once more to the "central" problem of the chant, that is, the
question concerning its origin and development. In an earlier chapter we
have outlined a theory according to which the final formation of the chant
repertory took place in the Frankish empire during the time of the Carolingian rulers, Pepin, Charlemagne, and Louis, between *c.* 750 and 850.
Whether this theory will turn out to prove valid, remains to be seen. We
believe it will, and in the present chapter we shall try to give a more detailed picture of the development as it appears to us from the point of
view of stylistic analysis. In the course of our study we have repeatedly
mentioned certain details of style or form that have chronological significance; it is these traits that we shall try to combine into a coherent picture.

Before turning to this task it is important to point out certain notions
which until now have been more or less generally accepted, but which, in
our opinion, must be discarded. One of these is the attempt to establish a
chronology of musical evolution on the basis of liturgical or other non-
musical data. The fallacy of this approach has been discussed at an earlier
occasion [see pp. 56f]. Another notion of highly questionable validity is the
idea that some of the most ornate chants, such as Graduals or Tracts, possibly even Alleluias, may well be of an earlier date than many of the simple
syllabic or neumatic chants. Wagner, in particular, has repeatedly emphasized that possibly "the ornate, and more or less highly developed type of
chant is older than the simple chant," although with the reservation that
"in the fourth and fifth centuries the degree of richness may not have been
the same as that of the Gregorian [meaning: sixth-century] solo chants."[1]
In contrast to this opinion (which was also held by Gastoué, Morin, and
others), Gevaert made the categorical statement that: "Le chant syllabique
est antérieur au chant mélismatique."[2] In weighing the *pro* and *con* of this
controversy it is important to distinguish between two entirely different
issues involved, one concerning the state of affairs in the third or fourth
century, the other concerned with the preserved repertory of the melodies.
It is entirely possible that fairly ornate chants were used at a very remote

[1] *Wagner I*, 31.
[2] *Mélopée*, p. xxvii.

time, simultaneously with, or even earlier than simple chants. It would, however, be mere wishful thinking to assume that any of these ornate chants could have survived in even approximately the same form for six or seven centuries, and thus become incorporated in the collection of the earliest notated manuscripts. If we consider the extant repertory from the evolutionary point of view, we can only say that, generally speaking, its oldest nucleus is represented by the most rudimentary types, and that the ornate chants are of a much more recent date.

In this connection we must comment briefly upon another fallacy concerning the early history of Christian music, that is, the relationship between the standard repertory of "Gregorian" chant and that of the Milanese or "Ambrosian" chant. Probably because Ambrose lived two hundred years before Gregory, one often finds statements to the effect that the Ambrosian melodies are even earlier than the Gregorian.[3] Since many of the Ambrosian melodies are extremely ornate and melismatic, they have frequently been considered as evidence of the notion that the chant of the earliest Middle Ages was of a highly embellished character. Needless to say, the idea that the Ambrosian melodies (as we have them) go back to the period of c. 400 is even more fallacious than the assumption that the Gregorian melodies (as we have them) date from c. 600. Once more, we do not mean to deny the possibility that highly ornate melodies may have existed at the time of St. Ambrose, for instance, those "seemingly endless" Alleluia jubilations which are mentioned by Augustine. We only profess our complete ignorance as to what these melodies were like and whether they had any relationship to those that we find either in the Ambrosian or Gregorian repertory. Probably they were forgotten fifty years later. Or are we seriously to believe that during two centuries of the most cruel devastation that Italy ever suffered—under the Huns, Goths, Vandals—music, the most intangible and evasive medium of artistic expression, remained miraculously unaffected? The true relationship between Gregorian and Ambrosian chant can be established only on the basis of stylistic criteria. In the chapter on "Ambrosian Chant" which Mr. Jesson has con-

---

[3] See, e.g., New Oxford History of Music, II (1954), p. 61, where Anglés mentions Wellesz, Wagner, Thibaut, and the editors of the Paléographie musicale in connection with the theory "that the Ambrosian melodies represent the oldest form of Plainchant." Ibid., p. 131, Handschin speaks, somewhat more cautiously, of Ambrosian chant as "probably the oldest type of ecclesiastical chant preserved in the West." B. Stäblein, in his various articles in MGG ("Alleluia," "Choral," etc.) always takes the greater antiquity of the Ambrosian melodies for granted. In the article on "Frühchristliche Musik" Stäblein (following a suggestion by Handschin) reproduces a Milanese Responsory, Deus virtutum converte nos, as an example of music from the time of Augustine (sic), because Augustine tells us that his friend Licentius was so charmed by a new melody for Deus virtutum converte nos that he sang it the whole day. I doubt whether Licentius' melody had even the remotest resemblance to the Milanese Responsory, which clearly shows the ear-marks of the ninth or tenth century.

tributed to this book he pointed out that "it is not necessarily accurate to regard the Ambrosian melodies as 'primitive' versions of their Gregorian counterparts: they may well represent a later stage characterized by a tendency toward amplification and ornamentation, and paralleling the period of troping in Gregorian chant" [see p. 482]. I wholly concur with this view, and would not hesitate to assign to the Ambrosian repertory an even later date than the Gregorian, perhaps of the tenth or eleventh century—naturally once more with the exception of certain elementary types of chant.[4] Comparative studies of Gregorian and Ambrosian melodies therefore lose some of the importance that was formerly attached to them. On the other hand, a detailed comparison of the Gregorian and the Old-Roman repertories may well turn out to be one of the most valuable tools of research in our field.

With these general premises in our mind, we can now turn to our proper task, that is, to reconstruct a picture of the formative processes which led to the final stage of Gregorian chant, as it appears in the earliest manuscripts. That this picture can be expected to be only approximately correct hardly needs to be stated. Without question it will be modified by later research. Nevertheless I hope that it will provide at least a basis for such modifications and corrections.

The earliest layer of the Gregorian repertory is represented by the psalmodic recitations. That the general principle of psalm singing—recitation tenor with initial, medial and final inflections—is of Jewish origin, has become evident through Idelsohn's studies of the chants of Jewish tribes in Yemen and Babylonia [see p. 34]. More recently, however, E. Werner has shown that also for each of the eight psalm tones there exists a close parallel in the repertory of synagogal chants.[5] The lesson tones and the *tonus peregrinus* are likewise a heritage from pre-Christian days. The archaic *Gloria XV*, noteworthy for its psalmodic structure [see p. 409], and the *Te Deum* employ a melodic formula which recurs almost literally in a Yemenite *Sh'ma* (the oldest chant of Hebrew liturgy) and in a Yemenite cantillation of the Thora. All these melodies consist essentially of simple recitation formulae that could easily be memorized and which were indeed orally preserved with but minor modifications.

Next in simplicity to the various recitation tones are the Antiphons. Liturgically they are documented as far back as the fourth century [see p. 187]. Gevaert, in his *La Mélopée antique*, outlined a chronology of the Antiphons on the basis of their texts (pp. 159ff). Those sung to the word Alleluia and to psalm texts he assigned to a period anterior to *c.* 500, those with other scriptural texts to the period from *c.* 530 to 600, those with

---

4 I have recently been informed by Monsignor H. Anglés that liturgists working in Rome have come to the same conclusion.

5 See "The Common Ground in the Chant of Church and Synagogue" [*ACI*, 134].

texts taken from the Acts of the Martyrs or from the life of Roman Saints
to the seventh century. He supported this textual division by a consideration of the musical material (pp. 172ff), pointing out that the majority of
his *thèmes* (34 out of 47) occur with texts from each of the three categories
and that those with psalmodic texts are usually characterized by greater
conciseness and simplicity of contour. More recently the problem was re-
sumed by W. Lipphardt in an article entitled "Gregor der Grosse und sein
Anteil am römischen Antiphonar" [*ACI,* 248], in which he assigned certain groups of Antiphons to Gregory, primarily those with texts from the
Prophecies and the Gospels. According to Gevaert these date from the
period from 530 to 600, that is, shortly before Gregory. From the point of
view of general chronology the difference is, of course, very slight and
practically negligible. If we accept Lipphardt's theory, we would come
to the conclusion that some thirty melodic themes are pre-Gregorian, and
that perhaps a dozen were added under Gregory. Apparently no additions
were made thereafter, because Gevaert points out that the Antiphons of
his third period (that is, those with non-scriptural texts) are all adapted
to melodies that occur already among the two earlier groups. Needless to
say, this is only a very rough sketch, but the resulting picture is plausible
enough to appear acceptable. It would mean that during the fifth and
sixth centuries there were added to the old repertory of psalmodic formula
some forty melodies of a distinctly new type, each of which could be, and
was adapted to a great number of different texts. I would not subscribe
to the idea that each Antiphon was sung at the time of Gregory exactly
as it appears in the earliest musical manuscripts, but the general contours
may very well have been the same as those that were finally recorded in
the Codex Hartker and the later *Antiphonaries.*

Turning now to the ornate types of chant we come to that part of the
Gregorian repertory which, if our theory proves tenable, received its final
form at a datable time, between *c.* 750 and 850. The term "final form" is,
of course, of great importance in this sentence. Nobody in his right mind
would suggest that all the hundreds of elaborate chants—Tracts, Responsories, Graduals, Offertories, Alleluias, etc.—were newly created during
these one hundred years. Most of them probably existed in a much simpler
form before they were transformed into their final, ornate form. Perhaps
Gevaert was the first to point out that many of the more complex chants are
nothing but ornamented versions of simple Antiphons or psalm recitations.[6]
Wagner has pointed out that the melody for the verses of the Graduals of
the *Justus ut palma* type is "nichts als die glänzende, melismatische Um-
hüllung einer ganz alten Psalmformel," which is similar to the second-
mode formula of the *Commemoratio brevis.* A thorough study of the

---

[6] See his *Les Origines du chant liturgique de l'église latine,* 1890 (German transl. by
Riemann, *Der Ursprung des Römischen Kirchengesanges,* p. 11).

chants from the point of view of "decoloration" may well shed much light upon the question concerning their more primitive forms, particularly if it is extended to include the Old-Roman versions.[7]

More than in any other type of chant such a primitive form is discernible in the Tracts. Their extensive use of standard formulae and of largely fixed cadential points suggests that originally they consisted of much simpler psalmodic recitations, probably one and the same for all the Tracts of a given mode. Although the skeleton melody shown in Fig. 91 [p. 324] is probably too simple to be considered as the "original form" of the Tracts (in this case of mode 2), it is not impossible that the application of the method of decoloration just mentioned may lead to what may reasonably be considered as the prototype of the Tracts. As for their final form, we may assume that this was the result of an embellishing process to which they were subjected in Franco-Germanic lands during the eighth century. Of some interest in this connection is the designation, found in a treatise, *Liber de divinis officiis,* of the Tract *Eripe me* as "nuperrime compilatum" —quite recently put together [*Patr. lat.* 101, 1209]. Since the text of this Tract is taken entirely from one and the same Psalm (Ps. 139, without ℣. 11-13), this remark can only refer to the "musical compilation," in other words, to the putting together of standard phrases. Since this Tract is exceptional for its almost formalistic adherence to the basic scheme of cadential points [see p. 325], it may well be the latest of the entire group of medieval Tracts of the second mode. Unfortunately, the date of the *Liber de divinis officiis* is somewhat uncertain. Formerly ascribed to Amalarius or even to Alcuin, it is now believed to have been written later, perhaps about 900.[8] But even if we assume that some of its contents go back to an earlier period, it is safe to assume that the "nuperrima compilatio"—i.e., the composition of the Tract *Eripe me*—cannot have taken place before 800.

Among the Graduals those of the type *Justus ut palma* have repeatedly been acknowledged as representing the oldest recognizable layer in this field, if only for the reason that they include the four Graduals for the Saturday in Ember Week of Advent, that for the Midnight Mass of the Nativity, and those for Easter and Easter Week [see pp. 357f]. They closely resemble the Tracts in their rigid employment of standard formulae, for-

---

[7] I had originally included in this book a chapter on "The Skeleton Melodies," but discarded it because it threatened to become the size of a little book. See, however, p. 324.

[8] Cf. Hanssens' edition of *Amalarius,* I, pp. 52ff. In *Patr. lat.* 101, 1173ff the *Liber* is published among the doubtful works of Alcuin, while later on it was ascribed to Amalarius [see, e.g., Gastoué, *Origines,* p. 248, fn. 3]. As was mentioned previously [p. 494], the Tract *Eripe me* does not occur in the Old-Roman sources, which have retained the two original Tracts for Good Friday, *Domine audivi* and *Qui habitat* [cf. *Sextuplex,* p. lix].

mulae which, no doubt, were much simpler originally than they were ultimately to become. The fact that the melodies for both respond and verse
employ *a* as the tonic and final is probably another indication of an early
stage, prior to the establishment of the eight-modes system for which Alcuin's *Musica* (*c.* 800) provides the earliest evidence. Considered as a whole,
the Graduals are remarkable for their extensive use of a reiterative style,
which is evident particularly in those of the third and of the fifth mode,
and which marks them as a product of a relatively early period. Particularly
interesting is the fact that this reiterative style, with its numerous *pressus*
formations, is not found in the Old-Roman counterparts of the Gregorian
Graduals [see p. 493]. It may well be a remainder of the old Gallican chant,
which the Frankish singers were so reluctant to abandon. On the other
hand, a Gradual such as *Dilexisti justitiam* [*L* 1216], striking for the triadic
outline (c-g-c-e-g-c′-g) of its initial phrase, clearly belongs to a much later
stratum, contemporary with the Offertories and Alleluias.[9]

In our discussion of the Offertories we have noticed that their verses
especially form a veritable mine of bold formations not encountered any-
where else in the repertory of the chant [see p. 364]. We are very fortunate
in possessing information that permits us to date these verses with a fair
degree of accuracy. It is found in Aurelianus' *Musica disciplina,* ch. XVIII,
entitled *Deuterologium tonorum,* in which he enumerates "quot varie-
tates unusquisque contineat tonus,"—how many varieties each *tonus* contains.[10] From the context it becomes perfectly clear that he enumerates
what we would call the "various tones of each mode," that is, the different
recitation formulae (with their *differentiae*) for the verses of the Introits,
Responsories, Antiphons (psalm tones), etc. The important point is that
each modal category includes one tone for the Offertories, for instance:

> *De authentu proto.* Sane authentus protus septemdecim in sese continet varie-
> tates, videlicet introituum tres, offertoriarum unam, communiorum duas, respon-
> soriorum sex, antiphonarum quinque, quae simul iunctae septemdecim faciunt.

We must conclude that at the time of the *Musica disciplina,* that is
about 850, the verses of the Offertories were still sung to a set of eight
standard Offertory tones similar in character to those for the Introits and
Responsories. If, on the other hand, we turn to Regino's Tonary written
about fifty years later, we find that the Offertories are completely absent,
as they are also in the later tonaries (all of which, it will be remembered,
are catalogues of chants whose verses are sung to a standard melody). Obviously about 900 the Offertory tones had already been replaced by free

---

[9] In a recent article, "Die gregorionische Gradualeweise des 2. Tons und ihre ambrosianischen Parallelen" (*AMW,* XIII [1956], 285) H. Hucke discussed the chronology of
the Graduals from a different point of view and with different results.

[10] *GS,* I, 53ff.

melodies similar to, or perhaps identical with those that occur in the musical manuscripts of the tenth and subsequent centuries. Thus the Offertory verses, which represent what we have called the "Beethoven-period" in the evolution of the chant [see p. 375], can safely be assigned to the second half of the ninth century, perhaps, in their final form, even to the early tenth century. They give the impression of having been created at a definite place (Metz?) at the instigation of a monk whose musical daring may well be compared with that of Beethoven.

A very intriguing problem is presented by the Responsories. Evolutionary processes are clearly noticeable in them, perhaps more so than in the other types of chant, but it is not easy to combine them into a convincing general picture. Of particular interest is the information we have concerning the difference between the Roman and the Frankish method of performing the Responsories. In his *Prologus antiphonarii* Amalarius says: ". . . we sing our Responsories differently from the Romans. These start the respond from the beginning after the verse, while we, having finished the verse, rejoin the respond in the middle (*a latere eius*), as if combining two bodies into a single one."[11] In our study of the Responsories we have seen that a considerable number of them show musical evidence of the partial repeat, by employing the termination formula of the responsorial tone not only at the end of the verse, but also within the respond, immediately before the beginning of the repeated section.[12] On the basis of Amalarius' remark one may be tempted to consider these Responsories as representing an old repertory of Gallican chant, the others as later importations from Rome. Only a thorough study of the entire body of "Gregorian" and Old-Roman Responsories can show whether this surmise has any claim to validity.

The verses of the Responsories are remarkable—and unique in the Gregorian tradition—for their highly variable treatment: while many of them are sung to a standard set of eight tones, many others are sung to partly or entirely free melodies [see pp. 239f]. Perhaps this state of affairs indicates a trend similar to the one which we found in the verses of the Offertories,

---

11 Ed. Hanssens, I, 362. In his *Liber de ordine antiphonarii* (Hanssens, III, 55) Amalarius gives a full description of the Roman method of performance, and from this it appears that a partial repeat was also used in Rome, though at a different place, namely, after the Doxology. The Roman method, as described by Amalarius, can be indicated as follows (*pr.* = *praecentor*, i.e., soloist; *su* = *succentores,* a small group of singers):

R (*pr.*)–R (*su.*)–V (*pr.*)–R (*su.*)–D (*pr.*)–R′ (*su.*)–R (*pr.*)–R (*su.*)

Whether such an extremely repetitious scheme was normally used in Rome, or perhaps only for certain high feasts (Amalarius describes it in connection with the feast of St. John and its Responsory *In medio ecclesiae*), is uncertain. Nor are matters much helped by Amalarius' remark that the use of the Doxology in the Responsories was a relatively novel practice, introduced by "modern popes" (ed. Hanssens, III, 21).

12 See p. 334.

but carried out only on a relatively small scale. That the responsorial tones —along with the Introit tones, etc.—existed about 800 (if not earlier) can hardly be doubted. As for the free verses, it is obvious that the majority of them date from "decadent days" (as Frere put it), in other words, from the tenth, eleventh, or later centuries. However, the possibility that at least some of the free verse melodies are of a considerably earlier date cannot be excluded. This appears from an interesting passage in Aurelianus' *Musica disciplina* of *c.* 850, in which he speaks about "the custom of old singers, particularly those living in France, who did not follow *omnem toni authoritatem* but, modifying the *sonoritas tonorum*—because of the difficulty presented by the *multitudo syllabarum*—changed the verses of the Responsories into something quite different." As an example he cites the ℞. *Gaude Maria*, ℣. *Gabrielem Archangelum*, which indeed has a verse with a great number of syllables, set to a free melody noteworthy for its exceptionally high range, including the c″ on "erubescat."[13]

In our study of the Introits we have noticed that not a few of them show a design in the character of a recitative, in difference to others which employ a freely moving melody. Possibly the former represent an early stage of antiphonal psalmody, in which both the psalm verses and the antiphon were sung to a recitation tone [see pp. 307f].

The chants of the Mass Ordinary are generally of a very late date. A few of them, however, may well revert to the earliest period of Christian worship or even to the chant of the Synagogue. To this group belong particularly the archaic *Kyrie* mentioned on p. 406, the *Gloria XV* [p. 409], the *Credo I* [p. 413], and the *Sanctus XVIII* [pp. 415f].

Finally we come to the Alleluias. That the great majority of these are late in comparison with the Tracts, Responsories, and Graduals, becomes abundantly clear on the basis of stylistic criteria such as repeat melismas [see Fig. 115ff; pp. 386ff], extended scale formations [Fig. 119, p. 389], thematic relationships between the *Alleluia* and the verse [pp. 383ff], etc. As has been pointed out in our study of the Alleluias, there is reason to assume that the extended use of *climacus* formations (descending scale patterns) is an innovation not earlier than the tenth century [see p. 389]. We have also pointed out that there exists a relatively small group of Alleluias, characterized by small range, absence of repeat melismas, and assignment to the first season of the liturgical year, which obviously is of an earlier date, perhaps the eight century [see p. 391]. Since in the chapter

---

13 *GS*, I, 50a. Aurelianus adds (with the reservation: "I have learned from a report"— *sicuti relatu didici*) that the author of this Responsory was a blind singer of Rome, named Victor, whose sight was miraculously restored after he had sung it before the altar of *S. Maria Rotunda* (the old Roman *Pantheon*), to melodies which he had learned from singers and memorized. Had these melodies anything in common with those that have been recorded? As was pointed out previously [p. 501], no free verses exist in the Old-Roman repertory.

on the Alleluias we have dealt in detail with the aspect of their evolution and chronology, we can refrain from further comments.

Our late dating of many of the Alleluias brings up the question of the sequences. Sequences are mentioned for the first time by Amalarius in his *De ecclesiasticis officiis* of the early ninth century [see p. 442]. Their main development started in the late ninth century with Notker Balbulus (*c.* 840-912). Since the sequences are troped additions to the Alleluias, one would come to the conclusion that the latter are necessarily of an earlier date, in contradiction to what has been suggested above. However, a closer examination shows that this contradiction is apparent rather than real. In the first place, no conflict exists in the case of sequences related to such "early" Alleluias as those of the Nativity and of Easter, which, we may well assume, existed before *c.* 800 in approximately the same form as we have them today. As for the others, a real difficulty would arise only if an early sequence (for instance, one by Notker) made extended use of an Alleluia melody which, because of its stylistic traits, would have to be assigned to the tenth century or an even later period. I am not aware of any such case. The great majority of sequences, if at all related to an Alleluia, employ only its beginning. It is entirely conceivable that this beginning was taken over from an older form, and we may even speculate that in some cases the entire sequence may have been derived from such an older form to which it was more fully related than to the final form in which the Alleluia has survived.[14]

14 Attention may be called to a number of stylistic details which have been mentioned in the course of our explanations and which may have a bearing upon the problems of chronology: introduction of the low G and F [p. 248]; intervals larger than a fifth [p. 253]; octave formations [p. 257]; ascending cadences [p. 265]; extended *climacus* formations [pp. 389f]; repeat structures [pp. 369f, 390]; perfect score of melismatic accent [p. 287].

Index

MODERN authors of books or articles are indexed only if they are mentioned with some specific information or opinion. Chants are indexed only if they receive individual treatment in the text. Whole chapters or sections are indicated by inclusive page references (e.g., 100-20). A footnote reference is indicated by n following the page number. F following a page reference means that the subject is also represented by, or included in, a Figure (not necessarily on the same page). T following a page reference means that the subject is also represented by, or included in, a Table (not necessarily on the same page).

a (Romanus letter) 117 T
Absolutions 206
absonia 164
accent: original neumes 108f; textual, tonic, etc. 275-97
accentus: acutus 76; neume 108f; type of chant 288
action-chants 28, 189
acutus 76, 109 F
Ad celebres (sequ.) 452 F
Adam de St. Victor 447, 460
adaptation 69, 268; in Resp. 334f; Grad. 345, 350; All. 381ff; Ant. 399, 400; hymns 426
Adducentur (All. with sequ.) 448 F
Adhémar de Chavannes 116 n, 430 n
Adjutor meus (Grad.) 138, 167, 352 n
Adoration of the Cross 31
Adorna thalamum (Ant.) 404
Advent 7; Ember Days 28f; Short Resp. 245; Ambr. 467
Aeterna Christi munera (hymn) 428 F
affinalis: see co-final
Agathon (pope) 46 n, 49
Agnus Dei 25 T, 42 (no. 59), 418-19
Akathistos (hymn) 458
akoluthia 458
akroteleutia 187 n
Albinus: see Alcuin
Albis, Dom. in 11 n
Alcuin: *Musica* 54; *Liber de officiis* 511 n; Trinity 8 n, 274; on modes 134
Alexander VI (pope) 466
Alia musica 55, 221, 358
All Saints 486
Alleluia 25, 40f (nos. 30, 37, 45, 47), 375-92; omitted, doubled 28; variable 65; texts 90; in St. Gall *339* 92; modal distrib. 137 T; range 146; two ɣ. 185; octave formations 257; cadences 265; adaptations 268f; melism. accent 284 T; with tropes 433ff; source of sequ. 442ff; Old-Rom. 496ff. Individual All. are listed under their verses

Alleluia Laus beata (sequ.) 448 F
Alleluia Resultet tellus (sequ.) 450
Alma redemptoris mater (Ant.) 23, 404
Amalarius: his works 54; on Gregory 48; Corbie, Metz 79; Roman, Frankish 80; *Domine exaudi* 184; *neuma triplex* 343, 441; *Vir erat* 367 n; sequ. 442f; *Liber de officiis* 511 n; Resp. 513
ambitus 133, 135 T; see range
Ambrose, St. 40 (no. 28); 186
Ambrosian chant 5, 465-83; chron. 508f
Ambrosian hymns 423
Ambrosian modes 134
Anastasius IV (pope) 466
ancus 104 F
Andoyer, F. 77
Andrews, F. S. 141 n
Andrieu, F. 46 n, 52 n
Angelus Domini (All.) 303
Angelus Domini (Off.) 258 F
Anglés, H. 441 n
annalis cantus 41f (no. 35, etc.), 47, 74, 77
Annunciation 60, 73 T
Anonymus de la Fage 152
anticircumflexus 109 F
Antioch 40 (no. 21), 43, 186; Council of, 39 (no. 14), 421
Antiphon 19, 20, 40 (no. 27), 392-404; mentioned by Etheria 45; B. V. M. 18, 23, 404; texts 96 T; modal distrib. 137 T; for *tonus peregrinus* 213; conn. with Ps. 217ff; tonic accent 294ff; Ambr. 472; Old-Rom. 502; chron. 509f
Antiphonal, Antiphonary 15, 54, 56 T; Old-Rom. 499. See also Manuscripts
antiphonal: data 38ff; psalmody 185-96; perform. 196-98
Antiphonale missarum 54; *A. m. Mediolanensis* 106, 467
Antiphonale missarum sextuplex: see Bibliography
antiphonarius cento: see *cento antiphonarius*

517

783.5
Ap6

Date D